THINK
COMMUNICATION

ISA N. ENGLEBERG
Prince George's Community College

DIANNA R. WYNN
Nash Community College

D1366865

Allyn & Bacon

Boston Columbus Indianapolis New York San Francisco Upper Saddle River Amsterdam
Cape Town Dubai London Madrid Milan Munich Paris Montreal Toronto Delhi Mexico City
Sao Paulo Sydney Hong Kong Seoul Singapore Taipei Tokyo

Editor-in-Chief, Communication: Karon Bowers
Editorial Assistant: Stephanie Chaisson
Development Manager: David B. Kear
Development Editor: Lai T. Moy
Associate Development Editor: Angela Pickard
Marketing Manager: Blair Tuckman
Media Producer: Megan Higginbotham
Project Manager: Barbara Mack
Project Coordination, Text Design, Photo Research, and Electronic Page Makeup: Pre-Press PMG
Operations Specialist: Mary Ann Gloriande
Art Director, Cover: Nancy Wells
Cover Designer: Anne DeMarinis
Cover Photos: First row, left to right: www.photos.com/Jupiter Images; www.photos.com/Jupiter Images; © Stone/Getty Images; BananaStock/Jupiter Images. Second row, left to right: Brand X Pictures/Jupiter Images; www.photos.com/Jupiter Images; www.photos.com/Jupiter Images; Stockxpert/Jupiter Images. Third row, left to right: www.photos.com/Jupiter Images; www.photos.com/Jupiter Images; www.photos.com/Jupiter Images; Jupiter Images Royalty Free. Fourth row, left to right: www.photos.com/Jupiter Images; Stockxpert/Jupiter Images; www.photos.com/Jupiter Images; Comstock/Jupiter Images
Printer and Binder: Webcrafters, Inc.
Cover Printer: Lehigh-Phoenix/Hagerstown

Copyright © 2011 Pearson Education, Inc.

Library of Congress Cataloging-in-Publication Data

Engleberg, Isa N.
    Think communication / Isa N. Engleberg, Dianna R. Wynn. — 1st ed.
        p. cm.
    Includes bibliographical references and index.
    ISBN-13: 978-0-205-76649-9
    ISBN-10: 0-205-76649-8
    1. Interpersonal communication. 2. Communication. I. Wynn, Dianna. II. Title.
HM1166.E545 2011
302—dc22

                                                            2009053021

10 9 8 7 6 5 4 3 2   WC 13 12 11 10

Allyn & Bacon
is an imprint of

www.pearsonhighered.com

ISBN-13: 978-0-205-76649-9
ISBN-10:   0-205-76649-8

brief CONTENTS

Communication in Action
p. 208 How to become an effective group leader

Thank You, Ladies and Gentlemen
pp. 238–324 The most important things you need to know about presentations

on the cover:

THINK COMMUNICATION
ENGLEBERG ▪ WYNN 2011

Communication in Action
How to become an effective group leader

Thank You, Ladies and Gentlemen
The most important things you need to know about presentations

CAN YOU REPEAT THAT?
The not-so tricky "trick" to effective listening

Uncoupling
Why relationships break up when communication breaks down

Can You Repeat That?
p. 72 The not-so tricky trick to effective listening

Uncoupling
p. 156 Why relationships break up when communication breaks down

detailed CONTENTS

four THINK **PRESENTATIONAL COMMUNICATION**

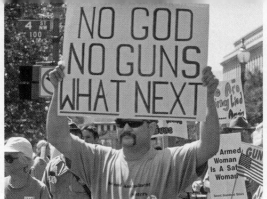

For more advice and design guidelines on how to prepare effective and memorable presentation aids, see "Effective Presentation Aids" at www.thethinkspot.com.

acknowledgments

Although the title page of *Think Communication* puts our names front and center, this project would never have seen the light of day without the talent, dedication, and creativity of our publishing team. We are particularly grateful to the group of production editors, graphic designers, photo editors, copy editors, and behind-the-scenes technicians who transformed a manuscript into an engaging, cutting-edge textbook: at Pre-Press PMG, Melissa Sacco, Senior Project Manager; Amy Musto, Art and Design Director; Brian Molloy, Senior Designer; and Catherine Schnurr, Senior Image Researcher; and at Pearson, Barbara Mack, Project Manager.

We extend very special thanks to Karon Bowers, the dynamic Editor-in-Chief at Pearson/Allyn & Bacon who invited us to take on the challenge of creating *Think Communication*, and David Kear, Development Manager, for his guidance, problem-solving ability, and flexibility. Only we will truly know how much credit goes to Lai T. Moy, our Development Editor, whose patience and professionalism helped us find superior solutions when the challenge of writing this textbook seemed insurmountable.

We also thank Associate Development Editor Angela Pickard and Editorial Assistant Stephanie Chaisson for helping us expertly shepherd this textbook and its ancillaries from manuscript through bound book. We are grateful to Media Producer Megan Higginbotham for all her work and creativity on the ThinkSpot Website, and were it not for Marketing Manager Blair Tuckman and her team, this book would have neither caught the eyes of the faculty who will adopt it nor the attention of the students who will use it to become more effective and ethical communicators.

We are particularly indebted to the students and faculty members who have shared their opinions and provided valuable suggestions and insights about our teaching and our textbooks. They are the measure of all things.

ABOUT THE
authors

ISA ENGLEBERG, professor *emerita* at Prince George's Community College in Maryland, is a past president of the National Communication Association. In addition to writing five college textbooks in communication studies and publishing more than three dozen articles in academic journals, she earned the Outstanding Community College Educator Award from the National Communication Association and the President's Medal from Prince George's Community College for outstanding teaching, scholarship, and service. Her professional career spans appointments at all levels of higher education as well as teaching abroad.

DIANNA WYNN is a professor at Nash Community College in North Carolina. Previously she taught at Midland College in Texas and Prince George's Community College in Maryland, where she was chosen by students as the Outstanding Teacher of the Year. She has co-authored two communication textbooks and written articles in academic journals. In addition to teaching, she has many years of experience as a trial consultant, assisting attorneys in developing effective courtroom communication strategies.

1 HUMAN

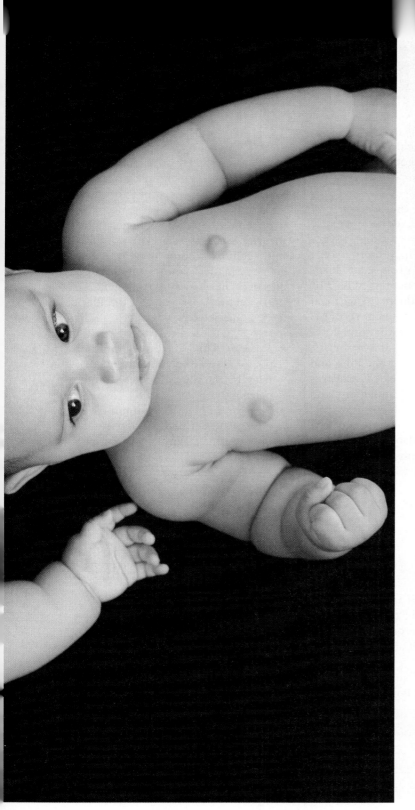

The instant you were born, you began communicating. You squirmed, cried, and even screamed when you were hungry or hurt. You smiled and gurgled when you were happy and content. And as you fussed and cooed, you also began learning how to speak and listen. From a very early age, you faced hundreds of communication challenges—and still do. Communication occupies more of your waking time than anything else you do.[1]

Communication occupies more of your waking time than anything else you do.

You communicate every day: when you greet your friends, participate in a class discussion, interact with co-workers, or shake hands with a new acquaintance. You also live in a competitive world where effective speaking allows you and your message to stand out from the rest of the crowd. Your ability to communicate, regardless of whether you're interacting with one person, a small group, or a large audience, will determine how well you inform, persuade, delight, inspire, and comfort other people.

Most of the time, you communicate well, but what about when you're in the middle of a heated argument, when you can't think of what to say to a troubled friend, or when an important presentation falls short? In such situations, you need more than common sense. Like most complex processes, effective communication requires knowledge, skills, and motivation.

COMMUNICATION

communication IN YOUR LIFE

Communication is the process of using verbal and nonverbal messages to generate meaning within and across various contexts, cultures, and channels.[2] The key phrase in this definition is *generate meaning*. You generate meaning when you speak, write, act, and create visual images, as well as when you listen, read, and react to messages. Although you communicate all the time, you can always learn how to do it better. In fact, your personal, academic, and professional success throughout your lifetime will depend on how well you learn to communicate.[3] Personal relationships are richer and more rewarding when both parties communicate effectively. Colleagues who express respect for one another and argue constructively are more likely to enjoy productive interactions. Work group members who get along with one another are more likely to achieve their goals. And if you are a good speaker, you are more likely to be selected for leadership roles.

According to the *Chronicle of Higher Education*, college faculty members identify speaking, listening, problem solving, interpersonal skills, working in groups, and leading groups as essential skills for every college graduate.[4] A national survey of 1,000 human resource managers concluded that oral communication skills are the *most* critical factor for obtaining jobs and advancing in a career.[5] Executives with Fortune 500 companies claim that the college graduates they employ need better communication skills as well as a demonstrated ability to work in teams and with people from diverse backgrounds.[6]

To become an effective communicator, you need to do more than learn a set of "fool-proof" rules or the "tricks of the trade." You also need to learn how to apply communication theories, strategies, and skills to multiple communication contexts. To gauge whether you communicate effectively in a variety of communication situations, ask yourself the following questions:

- *Personal.* Do I have meaningful personal relationships with close friends, family members, and partners?
- *Professional.* Do I communicate effectively within and on behalf of a business, organization, or work team?
  - *Educational.* Do I demonstrate what I have learned in collegiate, corporate, and other training settings?
  - *Intercultural.* Do I understand, respect, and adapt to people from diverse backgrounds?
  - *Intellectual.* Do I analyze and evaluate the meaning of multiple and complex messages in an ever-changing world?
  - *Societal.* Do I critically analyze and appropriately respond to public and mediated messages?
  - *Ethical.* Do I apply ethical standards to personal and public communication in a variety of situations?

Know Thy Self

Do You Have the Right Stuff for the Job?

The National Association of Colleges and Employers (NACE) asked employers to rate the skills they seek in the college graduates they hire.[7] In your opinion, which of the following skills are most important to employers? Rank them in order of preference, with 1 being the most prized skill, 2 being the next most prized skill, and so on. Then, ask yourself: To what extent do I have these skills?

Now compare your rankings to the NACE study results. Numbers indicate rankings, with 1 going to the most important skill, 2 to the next most important, and so on.

Employee Skills	Rank Order	Your Skill
a. Analytical skills		___ Strong ___ Moderate ___ Weak
b. Computer skills		___ Strong ___ Moderate ___ Weak
c. Interpersonal skills		___ Strong ___ Moderate ___ Weak
d. Leadership skills		___ Strong ___ Moderate ___ Weak
e. Oral communication skills		___ Strong ___ Moderate ___ Weak
f. Proficiency in field of study		___ Strong ___ Moderate ___ Weak
g. Teamwork skills		___ Strong ___ Moderate ___ Weak
h. Written communication skills		___ Strong ___ Moderate ___ Weak

Desired skills in college graduates: a (4); b (8); c (2); d (5); e (1); f (7); g (3); h (6)

Communication The process of using verbal and nonverbal messages to generate meaning within and across various contexts, cultures, and channels

COMMUNICATION
principles

the definition of *communication* describes communication as a *process*, rather than an *activity* or *thing*. A **process** is a set of constantly changing actions, elements, and functions that bring about a result. For example, the digestive process includes ever-changing, interacting body functions that change food into life-giving nutrients. Communication pioneer David Berlo described a process as something that is constantly moving and in which the elements interact with one another.[8] Thus, the characteristics of other communicators can affect your purpose; your choice of message content can affect your style of speaking; and your personal values can determine how you adapt to the context in which you communicate. Unlike a physical process that may follow an established pathway or a predictable set of steps, communication is a psychological and behavioral process that asks you to make multiple, interdependent decisions about how you will use verbal and nonverbal messages to generate meaning.

Consider, for example, what happens when you look at photos of friends and family members at a wedding or party. How do you interpret a photo of a guest holding up a broken wineglass? Although the person in the photo is captured in a moment of communication, the picture tells you very little about the background, complexity, and outcome of the communication situation. Why is the glass broken?

What about the context of the situation might tell you more? What can you learn from examining the person's facial expression and posture?

In scientific disciplines such as physics, chemistry, or biology, you learn "laws" that explain predictable outcomes under the *same* conditions. For example, you learn that if you raise the temperature of water to 212 degrees Fahrenheit under standard conditions at sea level, it will boil.

In communication studies, we do not have such strict "laws" because we cannot predict communication outcomes with such certainty. At best, we can explain how communication works in general under *similar* conditions. Rather than following strict laws, we apply accepted truths or principles about the nature of human communication.

When you communicate effectively, you make strategic decisions about your *self* and how to connect with *others*. You communicate for a *purpose* in a specific *context*, both of which affect the *content*, *structure*, and *expression* of your message.

Whenever all seven key elements and their guiding principles apply to a specific communication concept discussed in this book (for example, ethical speaking in Chapter 12), we alert you with the icon you see at the top of this page.

Process A set of constantly changing actions, elements, and functions that bring about a result

The **7** Key Elements and Guiding Principles of Effective Communication

SELF
Know thy SELF
1

OTHERS
Connect with OTHERS
2

PURPOSE
Determine your PURPOSE
3

CONTEXT
Adapt to CONTEXT
4

CONTENT
Select appropriate CONTENT
5

STRUCTURE
STRUCTURE your message
6

EXPRESSION
Practice skillful EXPRESSION
7

1 Know Thy Self

The first step to effective communication is to *know thy self*. Communication is personal: Each of us communicates in our own unique way. Your genetic code is one-of-a-kind among the billions of genetic codes on earth. Your communication abilities and instincts are also one-of-a-kind. Therefore, make sure you understand how *your* characteristics and attitudes affect the way you communicate.

SELF: Why Are *You* a One-of-a-Kind Communicator?

- How do *your* characteristics, traits, skills, needs, attitudes, values, and self-concept influence your communication goals and style?
- How well do you suspend your personal needs and attitudes when you listen to others?
- What is your ethical responsibility as a communicator?

2 Connect with Others

Regardless of whether you are talking to one person or a large audience, always consider and *connect with others*.

OTHERS: How Well Do You Connect?

- With whom are you communicating? How do their characteristics, traits, skills, needs, attitudes, and beliefs affect the way they listen and respond?
- How can you better understand, respect, and adapt to others when you communicate with them?
- How well do you listen when interacting with others?

Communication is relational; that is, the nature of your relationship with others affects what, when, where, why, and how you communicate. An invitation such as "Let's grab a drink after work" can mean one thing coming from your best friend, but it can mean something entirely different coming from your manager or a colleague who's been trying to date you. The nature of your relationship with another person will affect your choice of specific communication strategies and skills.

The cultural diversity of others plays a critical role in communication. We use the term **culture** to describe "a learned set of shared interpretations about beliefs, values, norms, and social practices which affect the behaviors of a relatively large group of people."[9] Given this definition, a rancher from Texas and an advertising executive from New York can have different cultural perspectives about how to greet an acquaintance, as can a Nigerian, an Indonesian, and a Navajo tribal member. Consider also what happens when you share a message with or respond to someone whose race, age, gender, religious beliefs, political attitudes, or educational level differs from yours.

3 Determine Your Purpose

When you communicate with another person or a group of people, you usually have a reason for interacting with them. That reason, or goal, can be as weighty as proposing marriage, securing a lucrative business contract, or resolving a world

---

Culture A learned set of shared interpretations about beliefs, values, norms, and social practices which affect the behaviors of a relatively large group of people

---

communication&culture

DOES EVERYONE COMMUNICATE THE SAME WAY?

Do the differences between people outweigh what they have in common? How do these differences affect the way we communicate with one another? Carefully consider the following questions and answer *yes* or *no*.

Yes No
- ☐ ☐ 1. Is the U.S. culture the most individualistic (independent, self-centered, me-first) culture in the world?
- ☐ ☐ 2. Are Asian American students smarter than African American and Latino American students?
- ☐ ☐ 3. Do women talk more than men?
- ☐ ☐ 4. Are racial classifications based on significant genetic differences?

Now think about how you responded to each of these questions. Why did you respond this way? After reading through the rest of the book, return to this survey and think about whether you would change any of your answers. If so, why? If not, why not?

"What do you mean we don't communicate? I sent you e-mail on Monday."

In the classroom

"Why are you here?" (Meaning: I can help you achieve your goals if I know why you have enrolled in this course.)

On the job

"Why are you here?" (Meaning: We need to determine how your department will contribute to and benefit from this meeting.)

At a funeral

"Why are you here?" (Meaning: I didn't think you knew Gloria very well.)

At the doctor's office

"Why are you here?" (Meaning: Tell me how you're feeling.)

At a political rally

"Why are you here?" (Meaning: What issues are most important to you?)

At home

"Why are you here?" (Meaning: You're late for school and need to get going.)

crisis, or as simple as asking for the time. *Determining your purpose—what you and others are trying to accomplish by communicating—is essential when deciding what, when, and how to communicate.

Even when you're not fully conscious of your intentions, your communication is purposeful. When you

PURPOSE: What's the Point?

• What do you want others to know, think, believe, feel, or do as a result of communicating with them?
• How might others misunderstand or misinterpret your purpose?
• Can you correctly identify the purpose of other communicators?

say, "Hi, how ya doin'?" as you pass a friend in the hallway, or unconsciously nod as someone talks to you, or touch the arm of a colleague who has received bad news, you are maintaining and strengthening your friendships and working relationships. Even when you have no intention of communicating, someone else may perceive that you have sent a purposeful message. For example, if Fred overhears you talking about a good film you have seen, have you communicated with Fred? If you see your boss frowning, should you assume she wants you to know she is unhappy, worried, or angry? Thus, in a very general sense, some communication occurs whether you intend it or not.

4 Adapt to the Context

All communication occurs within a **context**, the circumstances and setting in which communication takes place. Although this definition may appear simple—after all, communication must occur somewhere—context is anything but simple. Consider, for example, how various contexts (as shown above) affect the implied meaning of the question: "Why are you here?"

There are four types of interrelated communication contexts: psychosocial, logistical, interactional, and mediated.

Context The circumstances and setting in which communication takes place

Psychosocial Context Psychosocial context refers to the psychological and cultural environment in which you live and communicate. For example, consider your relationship with other communicators, their personality traits, and the extent to which they share cultural attitudes, beliefs, values, and behaviors. Look at variables such as age, gender, race, ethnicity, religion, sexual orientation, levels of ability, and socioeconomic class.

The psychosocial context also includes *your* emotional history, personal experiences, and cultural background. Thus, if you have a history of conflict with a work colleague, your feelings, experience, and culture may influence your response to a suggestion made by that colleague.

Logistical Context Logistical context refers to the physical characteristics of a particular communication situation and focuses on a specific time, place, setting, and occasion. Are you talking to your friend privately or in a busy hallway? Are you speaking informally to colleagues in a staff meeting, or welcoming guests to an important celebration? Is there a time limit for your oral report? Can your PowerPoint slides be seen in the back row?

Interactional Context Interactional context refers to the type of interaction, that is, whether communication occurs one-to-one, in groups, or between a presenter and an audience. There are three major types of interactional contexts: interpersonal, group, and presentational.

Psychosocial Context

Logistical Context

Interactional Context

CONTEXT: Does Context Really Matter?
- What role are you assuming in this setting or situation?
- How do you behave in different psychological and interactional contexts?
- How well do you adapt to the logistics and occasion of the place where you will communicate?

Interpersonal communication occurs when a limited number of people, usually two, interact for the purpose of sharing information, accomplishing a specific goal, or maintaining a relationship. Chapters 7, 8, and 9 focus on the fundamentals of interpersonal communication and strategies for effective communication in personal and professional relationships.

Group communication refers to the interaction of three or more interdependent people who interact for the purpose of achieving a common goal. A group is more than a collection of individuals who talk to one another; it is a complex system in which members depend upon one another. Family members and friends, work groups, neighborhood

associations, self-help groups, social clubs, and athletic teams engage in group communication. Chapters 10 and 11 focus on understanding how groups work and discuss strategies for effective group participation, leadership, decision making, and problem solving.

Presentational communication occurs between speakers and their audience members.[10] Presentational communication comes in many forms, from formal commencement addresses, campaign speeches, and conference lectures to informal class reports, staff briefings, and training sessions. You will make many presentations in your lifetime—at school, at work, at family and social gatherings, or at community events. Chapters 12 through 16

Psychosocial context The overall psychological and cultural environment in which you live and communicate

Logistical context The physical characteristics of a particular communication situation; focuses on a specific time, place, setting, and occasion

Interactional context The type of communication interaction; whether communication occurs one-to-one, in groups, or between a presenter and an audience

Interpersonal communication Interaction between a limited number of people, usually two, for the purpose of sharing information, accomplishing a goal, or maintaining a relationship

Group communication The interaction of three or more interdependent people working to achieve a common goal

Presentational communication A form of communication that occurs when speakers generate meaning with audience members, who are usually present at the delivery of a presentation

Mediated Context

cannot see or hear how audience members react as they look and listen. All mass communication is mediated, but not all mediated communication—text messages, letters, greeting cards—is for the masses.

5 Select Appropriate Content

Although both animals and humans can send and receive messages, human beings are "unique in [their] ability to communicate or convey an open-ended volume of

explain how to apply the key elements of effective communication to ensure the successful preparation and delivery of presentations.

Mediated Context When you communicate in a **mediated context**, "something" exists between communicators. That "something" is usually some type of technology. Personal forms of mediated com-

munication include phone calls and e-mail messages. Other forms that occur between a person and a large, often unknown audience are classified as **mass communication**. Radio, television, film, and Websites are forms of mass communication, as are newspapers, magazines, and books.

Usually, the person who shares a message using mass communication

Mediated context Any form of communication in which something (usually technological) exists between communicators; telephone, e-mail

Mass communication A form of mediated communication between a person and a large, often unknown audience; radio, television, film, Websites, newspapers, magazines, and books

Media Richness Theory

THINK ABOUT THEORY

Media Richness Theory examines how the qualities of different media affect communication. The theory also helps explain why your physical presence makes a significant difference in how well you communicate. Let's say you have a message you want to share with a group of people. You can share that message in several ways: face to face, on the telephone, through e-mail or text messages, by sending a personal letter, or by posting a notice.

Face-to-face communication (be it in a conversation, group meeting,

or presentation) is the richest communication medium because you can (1) see and respond instantly to others, (2) use nonverbal communication (body movement, vocal tone, facial expression) to clarify and reinforce messages, (3) use a natural speaking style, and (4) convey your personal feelings and emotions. In contrast, text-based communication channels such as e-mail are quite the opposite. Readers only have printed words and illustrations to interpret someone's meaning. In short, face-to-

face communication engages more of our senses and sensibilities than any other form of communication.[11]

Media Richness Theory
Examines how the qualities of different media affect communication

concepts."[12] Put another way, our language is symbolic; we have the distinct ability to generate meaning by combining letters and/or sounds. We can invent new words, say sentences that have never been said before, and communicate creative ideas. Most animals only have a limited number of messages they can send and comprehend.

A symbol is something that represents something else. In language, a **symbol** is an *arbitrary* collection of sounds or letters that in certain combinations stand for a concept, but do not have a direct

relationship to the things they represent.

Symbols are *not* the things they represent. There is absolutely nothing in the letters *C*, *A*, and *T* that looks, smells, sounds, or feels like a cat. And even though dictionaries may define *cat* as a carnivorous mammal domesticated as a catcher of rodents and as a pet, you would be hard pressed to imagine what a cat looks, smells, sounds, or feels like if you had never seen one. Moreover, whether you like or dislike cats has no connection to the letters (*C*, *A*, and *T*) used to represent them.

Since there is no tangible relationship between a symbol, the thing it represents, and how you may feel about it, there is always the potential for misunderstanding. For example, what does it mean to you if someone says that it's cold outside? If you live in the far north, "cold" can mean more than 40 degrees below zero. If you live at sea level near the equator, "cold" can mean 40 degrees above zero.

6 Structure Your Message

Once you address the challenges of developing an appropriate and purposeful message, you face the additional challenge of *structuring your message* in a way that others will understand.

The word *structure* refers to "the way in which parts are arranged or put together to form a whole."[13] You would not build a house without knowing something about who will live in it, the location and

setting, and the materials needed to assemble it. House construction involves putting all of these elements together into a well-designed, durable structure. The same is true in communication. **Structure** involves organizing appropriate message content into a coherent and purposeful order.

7 Practice Skillful Expression

When two children argue on a playground, one child may yell, "Take it back!" while the other might shriek, "I will not!" Whether you say something you regret or mistakenly hit the "Send" button on your e-mail before you're ready, you can't undo communication. At best, you can attempt to clarify what you've said or try to repair unintended consequences. You can sincerely apologize to someone about something you've said, but you can't literally "take it back." Therefore, because communication is irreversible, the final step to communicating effectively is to *express* your message skillfully and thoughtfully. Effective communicators carefully choose how they will express their intended messages.

Symbol An *arbitrary* collection of sounds or letters that in certain combinations stand for a concept, but do not have a direct relationship to the things they represent

Structure The organization of message content into a coherent and purposeful message

What forms of expression are represented in this photo? How many different communication channels are being used?

EXPRESSION: Talk, Touch, or Twitter?

- Which channels are most appropriate given your purpose, the other communicators, the context, and the message of your content?
- What skills and techniques will improve your ability to express your message?
- How effectively do you express and listen to verbal and nonverbal messages?

Communication **channels** are the various physical and electronic media through which we express messages. You can transmit messages using one or more of your sensory channels: sight, sound, touch, taste, and smell.

Although we use sight and sound most frequently when we speak and listen to others, do not dismiss the power of the other three senses. Perfumes and colognes are designed to communicate attractiveness or mask offensive odors. A carefully prepared dinner or an expensive restaurant meal to which you have been specially invited can communicate a great deal about how the other person feels about you. A warm hug or a rough shove can exhibit intense emotions.

However, the communication channels you use today extend well beyond a face-to-face environment and into the far reaches of cyberspace. The personal computer is also an interpersonal computer. Technology enables you to enlist a variety of electronic media: telephones, television, personal computers, portable electronic communication devices, and the World Wide Web. Whether you're engaged in an online chat or participating in a videoconference, the media you choose and use affect the nature and outcome of your communication.

The seven **guiding principles** of effective communication just described apply to all types of communication, regardless of whether you are talking to a friend, delivering a speech to a large audience, planning a business meeting, or participating in a videoconference. No matter how well you structure the content of your message, you won't achieve your purpose if you do not think carefully about the other factors involved in the communication process. If you offend your listeners or use words they don't understand, you won't achieve your purpose. If you dress perfectly for a job interview but fail to speak clearly and persuasively, you may lose out on a career opportunity. If you hug someone who dislikes being touched, you've chosen the wrong communication channel.

Channels The various physical and electronic media through which we express messages

Guiding principles Communication guidelines focused on *self*, *others*, *purpose*, *context*, *content*, *structure*, and *expression* that help you select and apply effective communication strategies and skills to specific communication situations

Is Twittering the *Next* New Frontier?

While online social networking sites such as Facebook and MySpace are among the most popular ways of communicating with those near and far, Twitter has grabbed the spotlight. "Twitter is an online service that is part blog, part social networking site, part cell phone/IM tool, designed to let users answer the question 'What are you doing?'... by using 140 characters in each 'tweet.'"[14] Twitterers may post what they had for breakfast or share their opinions about life, love, and longevity to a network of "followers"— that can amount up to the hundreds, thousands, or even hundreds of thousands. Like an actual, real-time conversation, followers can instantly post a response and, because a log of these tweets is kept online, everyone can join the conversation long after the original twitterer has gone offline.

Although Twitter started out as a fun, cool way to let others in on the events of your daily life, it has now become a valuable channel for up-to-the-minute citizen reporting and public expression, as in 2009, when Iranian citizens took to the streets to protest the reelection of President Mahmoud Ahmadinejad. During this incident, the U.S. State Department asked Twitter to delay scheduled maintenance to avoid disrupting communications among protesters. An Iranian-

American activist noted that because Iran was restricting the movement of foreign reporters, "the predominant information is coming from Twitter." News agencies "are relying on Iranians and others who are Twittering to get this information out to the mainstream media. A lot of people are coining what is happening in Iran as a Twitter revolution."[15]

Twitter has "fundamentally change[d] the rules of engagement. It add[s] a second layer of discussion and [brings] a wider audience into what would [otherwise be] a private exchange."[16] For all its versatility and popularity, Twitter has its critics. Probably the biggest complaint about Twitter is that many tweets are inconsequential or "empty." Who cares that you bought a new pair of shoes or that you're tired? Do we really need to know that you're twittering during a boring biology class? A second criticism is that it wastes a lot of time. Darren Rowse, a popular blogger, puts this complaint in perspective by writing, "Twitter is a waste of time, unless you use it in a way that isn't." He claims that twittering is no less a waste of time than blogging, attending conferences, social messaging, or talking on the phone. "I would argue," he concludes "that there's never been a type of communication invented that can't be used in a way that is a waste of time."[17]

Although the company does not release the number of active accounts on Twitter, the Nielsen.com blog ranked Twitter as the fastest-growing site in online services in February 2009 with a monthly growth of 1,382 percent![18] As is the case with most new technology, Twitter's growth cannot continue at this rate. Eventually Twitter will join the ranks of e-mail, blogs, Facebook, and MySpace as another useful—but not unique—communication channel in cyberspace.

When government police and militia shot at peaceful protestors in Iran, the tragic death of 26-year-old Neda Soltani was captured on a bystander's cell phone and sent to media sites around the world.

COMMUNICATION models

When we discuss the nature of communication, we often use **communication models**. Communication scholars Rob Anderson and Veronica Ross write that "a model of communication—or any other process, object, or event—is a way of simplifying the complex interactions of elements in order to clarify relevant relationships, and perhaps to help predict outcomes."[19] Communication models:

- identify the basic components in the communication process,
- show how the various components relate to and interact with one another, and

- help explain why a communicative act succeeds or fails.

Communication models
Illustrations that simplify and present the basic elements and interaction patterns in the communication process

Linear Communication Model

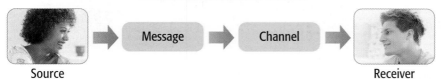

Source → Message → Channel → Receiver

Interactive Communication Model

Source · Channel · Message · Feedback · Channel · Source
Receiver · Receiver

⚡ Noise

The **7** Key Elements and Guiding Principles of Effective Communication

Early Communication Models

The earliest type of communication model, a **linear communication model**, functions in only one direction: a source creates a message and sends it through a channel to reach a receiver. Linear models identify several important components but do not address the interactive nature of human communication.

Communication theorists next devised **interactive communication models,** which include the concepts of noise and feedback to show that communication is not an unobstructed or one-way street. When feedback is added, each communicator becomes both the source *and* receiver of messages. When noise is added, every component becomes susceptible to disruption.

Feedback **Feedback** is any verbal or nonverbal response you can see or hear from others. A person giving feedback may smile or frown, ask questions or challenge your ideas, listen intently or tune out. If you accurately interpret feedback, you can assess how well your message is being received and whether it is likely to achieve your purpose.

A president of a New York marketing and design company told us how much she relies on feedback: "You *know* when they are with you." Expert communicators are sensitive to listener reactions. They use feedback—whether positive or nega-

tive—to evaluate whether and how well they are achieving their purpose, and then they adjust their message accordingly.

Noise Interactive communication models also recognize obstacles that can prevent a message from reaching its receivers as intended; in communication studies, this is referred to as **noise**. Noise can be external or internal. **External noise** consists of physical elements in the environment that interfere with effective communication. Noise is often an audible problem: a police siren outside the window, a soft speaking voice, or a difficult-to-understand accent. However, noise is not limited to just the sounds you hear. An uncomfortably warm room, an unpleasant odor, or even bright and distracting wall colorings can interfere with your ability to be an attentive and effective communicator.

While external noise can be any distracting element in your environment, internal noise is a mental distraction within yourself. **Internal noise** consists of thoughts, feelings, and attitudes that interfere with your ability to communicate and understand a message as it was intended. A listener preoccupied with personal thoughts can miss or misinterpret a message. As a speaker, you may be distracted and worried about how you look during a presentation instead of focusing your attention on your audience. Or, you

may be thinking about your upcoming vacation rather than listening to a co-worker's instructions. Such preoccupations can inhibit your ability to speak and listen effectively.

Encoding and Decoding In most of the early models, communicators have two important functions: they serve as both the source and receiver of messages. The communication **source** is a person or group of people who create a message intended to produce a particular response. Your message has no meaning until it arrives at a **receiver**, another person or group of people who interpret and evaluate your message. These two actions, sending and receiving, are called *encoding* and *decoding*.

Linear communication model The earliest type of communication model that functions in only one direction: a source creates a message and sends it through a channel to reach a receiver

Interactive communication model A model that includes the concepts of noise and feedback to show that communication is not an unobstructed or one-way street

Feedback Any verbal or nonverbal response you can see or hear from others

Noise Internal or external obstacles that can prevent a message from reaching its receivers as intended

External noise Physical elements in the environment that interfere with effective communication

Internal noise Thoughts, feelings, and attitudes that interfere with your ability to communicate and understand a message as it was intended

Source A person or group of people who create a message intended to produce a particular response

Receiver Another person or group of people who interpret and evaluate your message

communication models 13

How Noisy Can It Get?

Noise can affect *every* aspect of the communication process, threatening or preventing you from achieving the intended outcome of your message. For each type of noise described below, add a second example.

- *Noise and Self*: Personal problems and anxieties: (1) Because Katya was worried about her grade, she had trouble concentrating during her class presentation.

  (2) _____.

- *Noise and Others*: Failure to analyze the characteristics, culture, and opinions of others: (1) When you asked Gerald to work on Saturday morning, you forgot that he goes to synagogue that day.

  (2) _____.

- *Noise and Purpose*: Unclear thinking: (1) When no one donated $25 to buy Jill's present, Jack realized he was asking for too much money.

  (2) _____.

- *Noise and Context*: Distraction within and outside a room: (1) When police and fire trucks came screaming down the street, everyone stopped talking and listening.

  (2) _____.

- *Noise and Content*: Invalid research, unclear explanations, or inappropriately chosen words: (1) When Lex began swearing about the group's lack of progress, members decided they would rather stop working than listen to Lex and his foul language.

  (2) _____.

- *Noise and Structure*: A poorly organized message: (1) Telling stories can be a great way to entertain others unless you ramble on and on without making a point or coming to some sort of conclusion.

  (2) _____.

- *Noise and Expression*: A weak voice, defensive posture, or poor graphics: (1) Wanda made a poor impression when she kept twirling her hair and taking her glasses on and off during her presentation.

  (2) _____.

When you communicate with others, you *encode* your ideas: you transform them into verbal and nonverbal messages, or "codes." Thus, **encoding** is the decision-making process by which you create and send **messages** that generate meaning.

Decoding converts a "code" or message sent by someone else into a form you can understand and use. Decoding is the decision-making process you use to interpret, evaluate, and respond to the meaning of verbal and nonverbal messages. Certainly, your own unique characteristics and attitudes influence the decoding process.

Transactional Communication Models

Communication is more complex than the processes depicted in linear or interactive models. In reality, communication is a *simul-taneous* transaction in which we continuously exchange verbal and nonverbal messages, and share meanings. Transactional communication is also fluid, not a "thing" that happens. **Transactional communication models** recognize that we send and receive messages at the same time within specific contexts. Even when we listen to someone, our nonverbal reactions send messages to the speaker.

In an ideal communication transaction, you have a clear purpose in mind. You have adapted your message to others and the context. Your message contains appropriate and well-structured content as it is expressed through one or more channels with a minimum of interfering noise. Effective communicators accept the fact that they may never create or deliver a perfect message, but they never stop trying to reach that ideal.

Encoding Decision-making process by which you create and send messages that generate meaning
Messages Verbal and nonverbal content that generates meaning
Decoding Converts a "code" or message sent by someone else into a form you can understand and use
Transactional communication model Illustrations that show how we send and receive messages at the same time within specific contexts

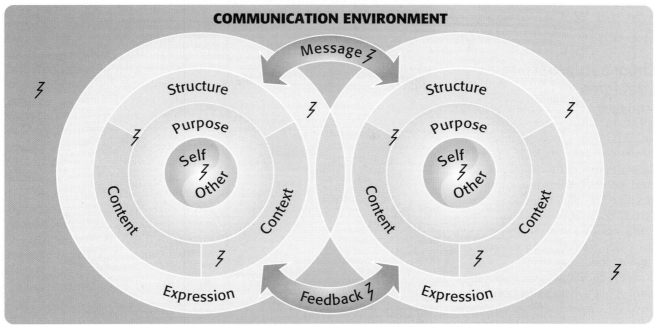

ƻ = Noise

COMMUNICATION
theories,
strategies, AND
skills

most of us would laugh if someone tried to become a champion tennis player, a professional airline pilot, or a gourmet chef just by reading a book. Likewise, no textbook or classroom lecture alone can teach you to become a more effective communicator. The best way to study communication is to apply an understanding of communication theories to appropriate strategies and skills. Communication theories, strategies, and skills are inseparable. Mastering isolated skills will not help you resolve a conflict, lead a discussion, or plan a presentation. Understanding the relationship among theories, strategies, and skills will.

Learn About Theories

Theories are statements that explain how the world works. They try to describe, explain, and predict events and behavior. "Theories are nets to catch what we call 'the world,': to rationalize, to explain, and to master it."[20]

Communication theories have emerged from extensive observation, empirical research, and rigorous scholarship. They help you understand *what* is happening when you communicate and *why* communication is sometimes effective and sometimes ineffective.

However, learning about theories in isolation will not make you a more effective communicator. Theories do not necessarily tell you what to do or what to say. Nevertheless, without theories, we

> **Theories** Statements that explain how the world works; describe, explain, and predict events and behavior

"Theories are nets to catch what we call 'the world': to rationalize, to explain, and to master it."

Karl R. Popper

would have difficulty understanding why or how a particular strategy works or how strategies and skills interact.

Choose Appropriate Strategies

Strategies are the specific plans of action you select to help you communicate. The word *strategy* comes from the Greek word *strategia* and refers to the office of a military general. Like great generals, effective communicators marshal their "forces" to achieve a specific purpose: to comfort a friend, resolve a conflict, lead a group discussion, or deliver an informative presentation.

However, learning about strategies is not enough. Effective strategies are based on theories. If you don't understand theory, you won't know why strategies work in one situation and fail in another. Strategies based on theory help you understand when, where, why, and how to use a particular strategy most effectively.

Develop Effective Skills

Communication **skills** refer to your ability to accomplish communication goals through interactions with others. Communication skills are the tools or techniques you use to collaborate with a colleague, prepare a meeting agenda, and speak loudly enough to be heard by a large audience. Throughout this book, you will read about and practice many communication skills: how to be more assertive, how to think critically, how to resolve conflicts, how to speak clearly, how to organize a message, and how to explain complex concepts or persuade others.

Like strategies, skills are most effective when grounded in theory. Without theories, you may not understand when and why to use a particular strategy or skill to its best advantage. For example, in the hope of improving group morale, you decide to forgo using a well-structured, problem-solving agenda at a critical meeting when, in fact, group morale is low because your approach to

problem solving is disorganized and wastes their time. However, if you are familiar with the theory of reflective thinking, you will know that using a standard agenda helps a group to follow a series of practical steps to solve problems. In our eagerness to communicate effectively, we may grab ready-made, easy-to-use "tricks of the trade" that are inappropriate or ineffective. Enlisting skills without an understanding of theories and strategies can make communication inefficient and ineffective as well as a frustrating experience for everyone.

Skilled speakers and listeners have made effective communication into an enduring habit. As Stephen Covey notes on the next page, a habit has three components: knowl-

---

Strategies Specific plans of action that help you achieve your communication goal
Skills Your acquired ability to accomplish communication goals during an interaction with others

Adapt to others

Improve your personal relationships

COMMUNICATION SKILLS

Prepare and deliver a presentation

Improve your professional relationships

Collaborate with colleagues

edge, skills, and desire. Knowledge plays a role similar to theories and strategies: it describes *what* to do and *why* to do it. Skills represent *how* to do it. And desire is the motivation to communicate effectively and ethically: you *want* to do it. Effective and ethical communication relies as much on your attitude (*want* to do it) as it does on your knowledge and skills.

Learning to communicate is a complex challenge that requires a great deal more than simple rules and superficial imitation. Highly successful communicators internalize the knowledge, skills, and motivation they need to communicate effectively and ethically.

Habits Something you do so frequently and for so long that you've stopped thinking about why, when, how, and whether you do it; something that becomes second nature and requires knowledge, skills, and desire

MAKE EFFECTIVE COMMUNICATION AN ENDURING HABIT[21]

Knowledge (what to do, why to do it)

EFFECTIVE HABITS

Skills (how to do it)

Desire (want to do it)

STEPHEN COVEY is the author of *The 7 Habits of Highly Effective People*, one of the most popular self-help/business books ever published. Covey presents a principle-centered approach for solving personal and professional problems. He claims that effective people transform these principles into enduring habits. We believe the same is true about the principles of communication. Effective communicators transform communication principles into enduring **habits**, things you do so frequently and for so long that you've stopped thinking about why, when, how, and whether you do them. In the following excerpts from *The 7 Habits of Highly Effective People*, Covey uses a communication example to demonstrate this transformation.

"For our purposes, we will define a habit as the intersection of *knowledge, skill*, and *desire*. Knowledge is the theoretical paradigm, the *what to do* and the *why*. Skills represent *how* to do it. And desire is the motivation, the *want to do*. In order to make something a habit in our lives, we have to have all three. . . .

I may be ineffective in my interactions with my work associates, my spouse, or my children because I constantly tell them what I think, but I never really listen to them. Unless I search out correct principles of human interaction, I may not even *know* I need to listen.

Even if I do know that in order to interact effectively with others I really need to listen to them, I may not have the skill. I may not know *how* to really listen deeply to another human being.

But knowing I need to listen and knowing how to listen is not enough. Unless I *want* to listen, unless I have the desire, it won't be a habit in my life. Creating a habit requires work in all three dimensions."

COMMUNICATING
ethically

how would you feel if you learned that:

- a corporate executive hid lavish, personal expenditures while laying off employees?
- a teacher gave higher grades to students he liked and lower grades to students who annoyed him?
- a close friend shared your most intimate secrets with people you don't know or don't like?
- a politician used racial slurs in private to describe a disgruntled group of constituents?

Most of these behaviors are not illegal. They are, however, unethical.

Theories answer *why* (Why does communication work this way?); strategies answer *what* (What should work in this communication situation?); and skills answer *how* (How should I express myself?). An effective communicator also must be able to answer the *whether* questions. That is, whether you should communicate as planned: Is it right? Is it fair? Is it deceptive?[22]

Ethical issues arise whenever we communicate because communication has consequences. What we say and do can help or hurt others. Sadly, the theories, strategies, and skills in this textbook can and have been used for less-than-ethical purposes. Unscrupulous speakers have misled trusting citizens and consumers. Bigots have used hate speech to oppress and discriminate against those who are "different." Self-centered people have destroyed the reputations of their rivals by spreading cruel rumors among friends and colleagues.

Ethics requires an understanding of whether communication behaviors meet agreed-upon standards of right and wrong.[23] The National Communication Association (NCA) provides a Credo for Ethical Communication. In Latin, the word *credo* means "I believe." Thus, the NCA Ethics Credo is a set of belief statements about what it means to be an ethical communicator.

> **Ethics** Agreed-upon standards of right and wrong

ethicalcommunication

The National Communication Association Credo for Ethical Communication[24]

Questions of right and wrong arise whenever people communicate. Ethical communication is fundamental to responsible thinking, decision making, and the development of relationships and communities within and across contexts, cultures, channels, and media. Moreover, ethical communication enhances human worth and dignity by fostering truthfulness, fairness, responsibility, personal integrity, and respect for self and others. We believe that unethical communication threatens the well-being of individuals and the society in which we live. Therefore we, the members of the National Communication Association, endorse and are committed to practicing the following principles of ethical communication:

- We advocate truthfulness, accuracy, honesty, and reason as essential to the integrity of communication.
- We endorse freedom of expression, diversity of perspective, and tolerance of dissent to achieve the informed and responsible decision making fundamental to a civil society.
- We strive to understand and respect other communicators be-

fore evaluating and responding to their messages.
- We promote access to communication resources and opportunities as necessary to fulfill human potential and contribute to the well-being of families, communities, and society.
- We promote communication climates of caring and mutual understanding that respect the unique needs and characteristics of individual communicators.
- We condemn communication that degrades individuals and humanity through distortion, intimidation, coercion, and violence, and through the expression of intolerance and hatred.
- We are committed to the courageous expression of personal conviction in pursuit of fairness and justice.
- We advocate sharing information, opinions, and feelings when facing significant choices while also respecting privacy and confidentiality.
- We accept responsibility for the short- and long-term consequences of our own communication and expect the same of others.

Communication ASSESSMENT

Are you an Effective Communicator?

How can you become a more effective communicator? Use the 5-point scale below to rate the following competencies in terms of their importance. Circle only one number for each item.

Item	Extremely Important	Very Important	Somewhat Important	Not Very Important	Not at All Important
1. Reduce your speaking anxiety	5	4	3	2	1
2. Influence the attitudes and behavior of others	5	4	3	2	1
3. Use humor appropriately	5	4	3	2	1
4. Listen effectively to others	5	4	3	2	1
5. Develop good interpersonal relationships	5	4	3	2	1
6. Hold an interesting conversation	5	4	3	2	1
7. Use your voice effectively	5	4	3	2	1
8. Resolve interpersonal conflicts	5	4	3	2	1
9. Use gesture, movement, and eye contact effectively	5	4	3	2	1
10. Interview for a job	5	4	3	2	1
11. Adapt to people from different cultures	5	4	3	2	1
12. Lead a group or work team	5	4	3	2	1
13. Present visual aids and slides effectively	5	4	3	2	1
14. Tell stories skillfully	5	4	3	2	1
15. Chair or conduct a meeting	5	4	3	2	1
16. Gain audience or listener attention and interest	5	4	3	2	1
17. Prepare and deliver an effective presentation	5	4	3	2	1
18. Explain complex ideas to others	5	4	3	2	1
19. Inspire or motivate others	5	4	3	2	1
20. Assert your ideas and opinions	5	4	3	2	1
21. Participate effectively in a group discussion	5	4	3	2	1
22. Organize the content of a presentation	5	4	3	2	1
23. Begin and end a presentation	5	4	3	2	1
24. Use appropriate and effective words	5	4	3	2	1
25. Develop strong, valid arguments	5	4	3	2	1
26. Interact in business and professional settings	5	4	3	2	1
27. Support and comfort others	5	4	3	2	1

Review your ratings: Circle the item number next to the five skills that, in your opinion, are most important and essential for effective communication. Why did you select these items?

Summary

What is communication, and how does it affect your everyday life?

- Communication is the process of using verbal and nonverbal messages to generate meaning within and across various contexts, cultures, and channels.
- Effective communication helps you meet personal, professional, educational, intercultural, intellectual, societal, and ethical goals.
- Effective communicators accept responsibility for the outcomes of their choices.

What do you need to know to become a more effective communicator?

- Effective communicators make critical decisions about the seven guiding principles of human communication represented by the key elements *self*, *others*, *purpose*, *context*, *content*, *structure*, and *expression*.
- The four types of communication context are psychosocial, logistical, interactional, and mediated.
- The three interactional contexts are interpersonal, group, and presentational communication.

How do communication models help you address communication challenges?

- Unlike linear and interactional communication models, the transactional model depicts communication as a *simultaneous* transaction in which we continuously exchange verbal and nonverbal messages and share meanings.
- In a communication transaction, communicators encode and decode messages at the same time.
- The components of a transactional communication model include all seven elements of effective communication as well as message, feedback, and noise.

How do theories help you choose effective communication strategies and skills?

- Your choices of communication strategies and skills are most effective when they are grounded in theory. Without theory, you may not understand when and why to use a particular strategy or skill to its best advantage.

Why is ethical decision making essential for effective communication?

- Questions of right and wrong arise whenever you communicate. Ethical communication is fundamental to responsible thinking, decision making, and the development of relationships and communication within and across contexts, cultures, and channels.
- The National Communication Association Credo for Ethical Communication endorses nine principles of ethical communication for all communicators.

the **THINK**SPOT
www.thethinkspot.com

TEST *yourknowledge*

1. The textbook defines *communication* as the process of using verbal and nonverbal messages to generate meaning within and across various contexts, cultures, and channels. Which term in this definition refers to the various physical and electronic media through which we express messages?
   a. messages
   b. meaning
   c. contexts
   d. cultures
   e. channels

2. Which of the following skills received the *lowest* ranking in the study of skills employers seek in college graduates?
   a. computer skills
   b. written communication skills
   c. oral communication skills
   d. leadership
   e. proficiency in field of study

3. Which communication principle seeks an answer to the following question: How well do you suspend *your* personal needs and attitudes when you listen?
   a. Know Thy Self
   b. Connect with Others
   c. Determine Your Purpose
   d. Adapt to the Context
   e. Structure Your Message

4. Which communication principle seeks an answer to the following question: How can I adapt to the psychological circumstances and physical setting of the communication situation?
   a. Know Thy Self
   b. Select Appropriate Content
   c. Connect with Others
   d. Adapt to the Context
   e. Structure Your Message

5. The logistical context of communication refers to
   a. the cultural environment in which you live.
   b. your emotional history, personal experiences, and cultural background.
   c. the time, place, setting, and occasion in which you will interact with others.
   d. whether communication occurs one-to-one, in groups, or between a speaker and an audience.
   e. interpersonal, group, and presentational communication.

6. Linear models of communication
   a. include the concepts of noise and feedback.
   b. function in only one direction: a source creates a message and sends it through a channel to reach a receiver.
   c. recognize that we send and receive messages simultaneously.
   d. illustrate the interrelationships among the key elements of human communication.
   e. all of the above

7. The encoding process can be described as
   a. the way you feel about others.
   b. the process of minimizing internal noise.
   c. effective listening.
   d. converting a "code" sent by someone else into a meaningful message.
   e. the decision-making process you use to create messages that generate meaning.

8. Stephen Covey defines a habit as the intersection of
   a. theories, strategies, and skills.
   b. theories, methods, and tools.
   c. knowledge, cognition, and intellectual skills.
   d. knowledge, skill, and desire.
   e. preparation, practice, and performance.

9. Theories answer *why*; strategies answer *what*; skills answer *how*; and ethics answers *questions* of _____.
   a. who
   b. where
   c. when
   d. whether
   e. all of the above

10. Which principle in the NCA Credo for Ethical Communication is violated if a close friend shares your most intimate secrets with people you don't know or don't like?
    a. We advocate truthfulness, accuracy, honesty, and reason as essential to the integrity of communication.
    b. We strive to understand and respect other communicators before evaluating and responding to their messages.
    c. We promote access to communication resources and opportunities as necessary to fulfill human potential.
    d. We advocate sharing information, opinions, and feelings when facing significant choices while also respecting privacy and confidentiality.
    e. We are committed to the courageous expression of personal conviction in pursuit of fairness and justice.

Answers: 1-e; 2-a; 3-a; 4-d; 5-c; 6-b; 7-e; 8-d; 9-d; 10-d

THINK COMMUNICATION

This article from *Communication Currents* has been edited and shortened with permission from the National Communication Association.

Communication
Knowledge for Communicating Well *Currents*

N C A
A Publication of the National Communication Association

Volume 3, Issue 4 - August 2008

Why Communication?

Many people think they know a lot about communication because they do it every day using multiple channels—face-to-face and phone conversations, email and texting. There is, however, much more to the discipline of communication than many people realize. In 2007, *Communication Currents*, an online publication of the National Communication Association, invited five communication scholars to answer frequently asked questions about communication and its impact on everyday life. What follows is a compilation of responses by Dr. Kevin Barge to three of these questions.

What distinguishes Communication from other areas of study? What makes the Communication discipline unique?

Kevin Barge: Psychology is interested in the inner motors—those traits, personality characteristics, and cognitive processing styles that drive people to communicate. Psychology is concerned about what's *inside* people and what causes communication. Sociology, on the other hand, is concerned about what's *outside* people in terms of the social norms and social structures that drive people to communicate. The discipline of Communication is different. Rather than being driven by personality characteristics and social structures, communication is the process that creates our identity and personality. Communication constructs our societies, our relationships, and our norms. What makes Communication distinct is we focus on messages.

In Communication studies we look at how the messages in our talk and conversations create the social context in which we live. For example, you have read or heard discussions about corporate cultures. Where do corporate cultures come from? Corporate cultures evolve from the way people talk about their organization, the way they construct and determine what values are important, what rituals are important, what standards for performance are important, and what it means to be a member of the organization. Communication is not something that's secondary to psychology and sociology. If I can be so bold, we're the game. We're the ones who look at how personalities, individuals, groups, organizations, and societies create verbal and nonverbal messages that generate meaning.

> Do you agree with the writer's claim that *psychology* focuses on what *causes* communication, *sociology* focuses on what *drives* people to communicate, and *communication studies* focuses on how messages *generate* meaning?

What are the common misperceptions people have about communicating and how do those lead to mistakes when they communicate?

Kevin Barge: Most people think that communication is about getting your point across clearly. Regardless of the context, regardless of whom you're talking to, regardless of the situation, all you need to do is be clear when you communicate. I think this is a significant misperception because there are times when being ambiguous can be very effective. For example, think about organizations that issue PR statements during a crisis. They want to be as clear as possible about what they're doing. They may also want to be a little ambiguous to give themselves some wiggle room in case they have to adjust their strategy and messages. I think the misperception—that we need to be clear—is a dominant way of thinking about communication. Communication involves much more than transferring information from one person to another.

We need to think about communication differently and change perceptions about the nature of communication. Communication is about creating relationships: creating romantic relationships; creating relationships in a group or team; creating relationships in the workplace, say between an employee and his or her boss; creating a relationship between a speaker and an audience; or creating relationships among nations and cultures.

Think about how the way you talk and behave creates relationships. A simple example is what happens when students call me Dr. Barge. What relationship have we created? In this relationship, we create a relationship based on a hierarchy. I'm a professor with a Ph.D.; you may be in a subordinate position. My professional role and position creates a formal relationship. What changes if you call me Kevin? Now it's an informal relationship; we're peers. So even the small things we do with words create different kinds of relationships and different ways of interacting.

The misperception that clear communication is good communication needs to be changed. We need to abandon the notion that communication is about transferring information from one person to another. Only when we change perceptions to one that focuses the process of creating relationships can we become more effective communicators.

What are the three most important things people need to know about communicating in an organizational setting?

Kevin Barge: There are three things that I believe are very important to communicating in organizations. First, we must be aware of and sensitive to the context. If you don't understand the context of a situation, you can misinterpret what something means. For example, what does it mean if a CEO earns a thousand times more money than the lowest-paid employee in an organization? To an outside watchdog group, this disparity could be interpreted as corporate greed. To financial analysts on Wall Street, it could signify good management. So you have to understand the context if you're going to understand the meaning of communication.

The second thing I would suggest is thinking about communicating in organizations as a process that creates relationships. There's that old saying, "sticks and stones may break my bones but words will never harm me." It is a terrible, terrible axiom because the words we do use can harm people because they create different relationships. So how you talk does matter.

The third thing I would say is that we need to be more curious about what people mean when they communicate. Many times we act on false assumptions. We need to ask questions such as, "what do you mean by that?" and "where do you think this is going to take us?" We need to sort out what other people mean because we come from different kinds of experiences and different backgrounds. We need to be curious and interested enough to uncover and understand what people mean by the words they use.

ABOUT THE AUTHOR

Dr. Kevin Barge is a professor of Communication at Texas A&M University, College Station, Texas. His major research interests center on developing a communication approach to management and leadership.

2 UNDERSTANDING

O n June 25, 2009, the world learned that the man deemed one of the "greatest entertainers of our time" had died. Thousands upon thousands of shocked fans from New York to Tokyo swarmed the Web to Tweet, Facebook, and Google—crashing Twitter's servers and slowing the Internet down to a snail's pace. Almost everyone who had ever heard him sing, watched him dance, or seen his picture wanted to know: Was the King of Pop really gone?

As his death had such a profound effect on so many people across the globe, we are compelled to ask, "Who was Michael Jackson?" According to *Newsweek's* David Gates, "He was a music legend and a legendary oddball . . . He was the king of pop . . . and he's the last we're ever likely to have."[1] For many of us, when we think of Michael Jackson, we see an artistic genius. We see a little 5-year-old superstar who started singing and dancing his heart out with his older brothers in the Jackson Five; we see the 18-time, Grammy Award-winning solo artist he would eventually become. But in the 1990s, when Jackson's career and personal life began its sad decline, we saw a darker, more elusive side to this former child star. Rumors of his "sleepovers" with young children at his Neverland ranch led to allegations of child abuse.

> For all communication begins with *you*. Who you are and how you think determines how you interact with others and how others interact with you.

YOUR SELF

Vitiligo, an autoimmune disease that destroys the skin coloring pigment known as *melanin*, turned his skin from brown to white.[2] Quite literally, Jackson was changing before our eyes: his naturally curly hair became straighter; his nose became sharper and more synthetic-looking. Eventually, his physical and emotional issues would lead to prescription drug dependence. And yet, "whatever his life felt like from inside, from outside it was manifestly a work of genius, whether you want to call it a triumph or a freak show."[3]

When trying to answer the question, "Who was Michael Jackson?", British blogger *hysperia* writes that he was "a man who couldn't be known and who, most likely, could not know himself . . . who was Michael Jackson? We can never answer that question, finally, about anyone."[4] While reflecting upon Michael Jackson and his life, we should also acknowledge the importance of knowing our own *self*. For all communication begins with *you*. Who you are and how you think determines how you interact with others and how others interact with you.

who ARE YOU?

Your **self-concept** represents the sum total of beliefs you have about yourself. It answers two simple questions: "Who are you?" and "What makes you *you*?" Not only are you defined by characteristics such as your age, nationality, race, religion, and gender (as in "I am a 30-year-old, African American, Catholic female"), your life experiences, attitudes, and personality traits influence your opinion of your self.

Your self-concept changes as you change; you are always *becoming*. A physically awkward child may eventually grow into a confident and graceful dancer. A college student with poor grammar may eventually become a celebrated author. An "ugly duckling" teenager may eventually mature into a beautiful "swan."

Sources of Self-Concept

Where does your self-concept come from? You certainly aren't born with one. Infants only begin to recognize themselves in a mirror between 18 and 24 months of age. Only then do they begin to express the concept of "me."[5] Although many factors influence how you develop a self-concept, the following are among the most significant: self-awareness, the influence of others, past experiences, and cultural perspectives.

Self-Awareness **Self-awareness** is an understanding of your core identity.[6] It requires a realistic assessment of your traits, thoughts, and feelings. In his best-selling book, *Emotional Intelligence*, Daniel Goleman identifies self-awareness as the first and most fundamental emotional competency: the keystone of emotional intelligence.[7] He writes,

"the ability to monitor feelings from moment to moment is crucial to psychological insight and self-understanding. An inability to notice our true feelings leaves us at their mercy. People with greater certainty about their feelings are better pilots of their lives, having a surer sense of how they really feel about personal decisions from whom to marry to what job to take."[8]

Awareness of your thoughts and feelings is referred to as **self-monitoring**. Effective self-monitoring helps you realize, "This is anger I'm feeling." It gives you the opportunity to modify or control anger, rather than allowing it to hijack your mind and body. Self-monitoring also helps you differentiate emotional responses: love versus lust, disappointment versus depression, anxiety versus excitement. By becoming aware of your thoughts and feelings, you can avoid mistaking lust for everlasting love, avoid letting minor problems trigger depression, and avoid mistaking fear for anger. People who are *high self-*

> "People with greater certainty about their feelings are better pilots of their lives, having a surer sense of how they really feel about personal decisions from whom to marry to what job to take." —Daniel Goleman

Self-concept The sum total of beliefs you have about yourself
Self-awareness An understanding of your core identity that requires a realistic assessment of your traits, thoughts, and feelings,
Self-monitoring A sensitivity to your own behavior and others' reactions as well as the ability to modify how you present yourself

THE INFLUENCE OF OTHERS

Significant others are people whose opinions you value, such as family members, friends, co-workers, and mentors. What do such people tell you about yourself? Equally important, how do they act around you?

Reference groups are groups with whom you identify. Think about a high school clique to which you may have belonged (popular, smart, artistic, geeky, athletic). How did that membership affect your self-concept and interaction with others? How do your current group memberships (work team, church group, civic association, professional organization, social or campus club) affect the way you see yourself?

Roles are adopted patterns of behaviors associated with an expected function in a specific context or relationship. Thus, your behavior often changes when you shift to a different role. For example, how does your public role (student, teacher, mechanic, nurse, manager, police officer) affect your view of yourself? How do your private roles (child, parent, spouse, lover, best friend) shape your self-concept? Not surprisingly, you learn how to behave in a role largely by modeling others in that role. For example, for better or worse, you learn the parenting role from your parents.

Rewards are recognitions received at school, on the job, or in a community for good work (academic honor, employee-of-the-month award, job promotion, community service prize). Praise and words of encouragement from others affect your self-concept. Consider how you might feel about yourself if you never received positive feedback.

circumstances. Who would you be if you could not remember your parents or childhood playmates, your successes and failures, the places you lived, the schools you attended, the books you read, and the teams you played for?[10]

It is not surprising that you (and everyone else) have a tendency to distort memories. You tend to remember the past as if it were a drama in which you were the leading player.[11] When asked about high school, many people describe it as "terrible" or "wonderful," when they really mean it *seemed* terrible or wonderful *to them*. When we tell stories about the past, we put ourselves at the center of action rather than as bit players or observers.

Cultural Background Culture plays a significant role in determining who you are and how you understand your self. Intercultural communication scholar Min-Sun Kim explains that cultures have "different ways of being, and different ways of knowing, feeling, and acting."[12] For example, Western cultures emphasize the value of independence and self-sufficiency, whereas East Asian cultures emphasize the value of group memberships.

monitors constantly watch other people, what they do, and how they respond to the behavior of others. They are also self-aware, like to "look good," and usually adapt well to differing social situations. On the other hand, *low self-monitors* are often oblivious to how others see them and may "march to their own, different drum."[9]

The Influence of Others Although self-awareness may be the keystone of emotional intelligence, the influence of other people is a more powerful determinant of your self-

concept. Such influences include significant others, the groups to which you belong, the roles you assume, and the rewards you receive from others.

Past Experiences Without past experiences and personal memories, you would have little basis for a coherent self-concept. For example, vivid memories of traumatic events—the death of a loved one, the September 11 attacks, a serious automobile accident, life-threatening combat—can affect how you interpret and react to current events and personal

Significant others People whose opinions you value such as family members, friends, co-workers, and mentors
Reference groups Groups with whom you identify that influence your self-concept
Role A set of behaviors associated with an expected function in a specific context or relationship
Rewards Recognitions received at school, on the job, or in a community for good work

Self-Concept Continuum
RATE YOURSELF

Attractive	⟵⟶	Unattractive
Respected	⟵⟶	Not respected
Successful	⟵⟶	Unsuccessful
Confident	⟵⟶	Anxious
Good	⟵⟶	Bad
Intelligent	⟵⟶	Unintelligent
Humorous	⟵⟶	Humorless

Who would you be if you could not remember your parents or childhood playmates, your successes and failures, the places you lived, the schools you attended, the books you read, and the teams you played for?

The "self" generally is not perceived outside its relationship to the "other." Chapter 3, Understanding Others, focuses on how the characteristics and cultures of others affect how we communicate.

Assess Your Self

Self-appraisals are evaluations of your self-concept in terms of your abilities, attitudes, and behaviors. "Of all the judgments we pass in life, none is as important as the ones we pass on ourselves."[13]

"I'm not popular" or "I'm an excellent basketball player" are examples of self-appraisals. It is not surprising that when your appraisals are positive, you are more likely to succeed. Positive beliefs about your abilities can make you more persuasive when asking for a promotion or when dealing with rejection. At the same time, your mind may try to protect you from potentially hurtful or threatening feedback from others. These ego-defense mechanisms can mislead you into forming a distorted self-image:[14] "What's the big deal about being late to a meeting? She's just obsessed with time and took it out on me. It's no big deal."

Understandably, examining and understanding your self-concept is difficult because we tend to view ourselves favorably—often more favorably than we deserve. In his book *The Varnished Truth: Truth Telling*

Self-appraisals Evaluations of your self-concept in terms of your abilities, attitudes, and behaviors

and Deceiving in Ordinary Life, David Nyberg writes: "Human self-deception is one of the most impressive software programs ever devised."[15] Most of us seem to be "wired" to fool ourselves about ourselves, often deceiving ourselves about things we want to be true (but aren't).[16]

To minimize this kind of self-deception, you should enlist two forms of self-appraisals—actual performance and social comparison.

Actual Performance Your actual performance or behavior is the most influential source of self-appraisals.[17] If you repeatedly succeed at something, you are likely to evaluate your performance in that area positively. For example, if you were an "A"

Creating Our Selves Online

communication in ACTION

Researchers disagree on whether online communication harms or promotes the development of a self-concept. Some suggest that the limitless number of cyberspace communities with constantly changing contexts, significant others, and reference groups make it difficult for anyone to develop a stable self-identity.[18] Others argue that virtual communities provide opportunities to experiment with identities. For example, shy teenagers may feel more confident and comfortable communicating online than in face-to-face interactions. As they "try on" different selves online, positive feedback from virtual others can help them develop a stronger self-concept and a healthier self-esteem.[19]

The "evolution" of avatars has moved the notion of online identities into a new dimension. First appearing in video games during the 1990s, avatars have now been adopted by online communicators. An **avatar** is a user-created two- or three-dimensional human being who represents your self online. Avatars range from fantastical and bizarre to quite reasonable likenesses of the user. Second Life is just one example of a virtual world in which avatars live, behave, and socialize.

In Second Life, you can create and customize your own digital, three-dimensional body, adding unique clothing, hair, and fashion accessories found in resident-owned shops. Hundreds of universities, school systems, and businesses around the world use Second Life for group-based instruction and conducting meetings.[20]

Unfortunately, the absence of *real*, face-to-face interactions makes it easier to distort aspects of your self, as well as to fabricate a false identity. Many people have been betrayed or seriously hurt by such deceptions—as in the tragic case of Megan Meier, who committed suicide after falling victim to the cruel torment of and rejection by a boy named Josh Evans, someone she'd met on MySpace. It turned out that Josh was actually a fictitious character created by Lori Drew, the mother of a former friend of Megan's. Drew, who created this false identity as a way of humiliating and punishing Megan for supposedly spreading rumors about Drew's daughter, was indicted on misdemeanor charges in November 2008, prompting a public outcry for legislation to prohibit harassment over the Internet. In July 2009, a federal judge threw out Drew's conviction and acquitted her of all charges.[21]

Avatar A two- or three-dimensional human figure you create and use to represent yourself online

What would or does your avatar look like?

How We Make Ourselves Look Good

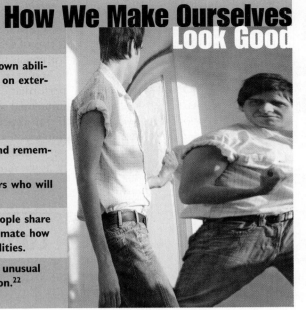

- ➤ attribute successes to our own abilities and blame our failures on external factors.

- ➤ view evidence depicting us unfavorably as flawed.

- ➤ forget negative feedback and remember positive feedback.

- ➤ compare ourselves to others who will make us look good.

- ➤ overestimate how many people share our opinions and underestimate how many people share our abilities.

- ➤ believe our good traits are unusual while our faults are common.[22]

prepared, or less capable than your classmates. On the other hand, if everyone does poorly on the test, comparing yourself with your classmates may make you feel better about yourself because it means you did just as well as everyone else. We also compare ourselves with others in terms of appearance and physical ability. When people compare themselves with fashion models, alluring movie stars, and professional athletes, however, they have chosen an almost impossible ideal.

> **Social comparison** The process of evaluating yourself in relation to the others in your reference groups

student in high school, you probably expect to be a good student in college. Thus, you may be disappointed or distressed if you receive a low grade and, as a result, doubt your academic and intellectual abilities.

Social Comparison According to social psychologist Leon Festinger, **social comparison** is the process of evaluating yourself in relation to the others in your reference groups.[23] The notion of "keeping up with the Joneses" is an example of our need to compare favorably with others. If you are the only one in the class who receives a failing grade on a test, you may conclude that you are less intelligent, less

Fashion models are a poor choice for social comparison.

building SELF-ESTEEM

now that you know something about your self-concept, how do you *feel* about yourself? Are you satisfied, discouraged, delighted, optimistic, surprised, or troubled? **Self-esteem** represents your judgments about your self. Nathaniel Branden puts it this way: "Self-esteem is the reputation we acquire with ourselves."[24] Not surprisingly, your personal beliefs, behavior, and performance influence your level of self-esteem.

> **Self-esteem** Your positive and negative judgments about your self

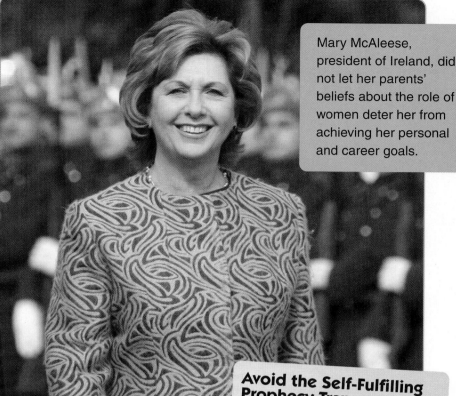

Mary McAleese, president of Ireland, did not let her parents' beliefs about the role of women deter her from achieving her personal and career goals.

Studies consistently find that people with high self-esteem are significantly happier than people with low self-esteem. They are also less likely to be depressed. One especially compelling study surveyed more than 13,000 college students. High self-esteem emerged as the strongest factor in overall life satisfaction.[25]

If your self-esteem isn't very high, you can take steps to improve it by self-monitoring and learning new ways of communicating with others. There are several specific strategies you can try as well. Keep in mind that engaging in these practices requires persistence and effort.

Beware of Self-Fulfilling Prophecies

A prophecy is a prediction. A **self-fulfilling prophecy** is "an impression formation process in which an initial impression elicits behavior . . . that conforms to the impression."[26] More simply, it is a prediction you make that you cause to happen or become true. For example, if young girls are told that boys do better in mathematics, they may believe it and stop trying to succeed. As a result, they won't do as well in math as boys, just as predicted.

In one study, researchers administered a math test to different groups of women. Before taking the test, one group of women was told that men and women do math equally well. Another group was told that there is a genetic difference in math ability that explains why women are not as good at math as men. The women in the first group got nearly twice as many right answers as those in the second group. The researchers concluded that people tend to accept genetic explanations as powerful and permanent, which can lead to self-fulfilling prophecies.[27]

In her commencement address at Mount Holyoke College in 2009, the President of Ireland, Mary McAleese, said: "When I was in my mid-teens, I announced at home that I had decided to become a lawyer. The first words I heard in response were, 'You can't because you are a woman.'"[28] President McAleese did not let these words and her parents' beliefs become a self-fulfilling prophecy.

Avoid the Self-Fulfilling Prophecy Trap

To minimize the chances of falling into the self-fulfilling prophecy trap, ask yourself the following questions:

- What prediction am I making about the behavior of others?
- Why am I making this prediction? Is it justified?
- Am I doing anything to elicit the predicted response?
- What other behaviors could help avoid fulfilling my prophecy?

High self-esteem will not solve all your personal problems, nor will it automatically improve your ability to communicate effectively and ethically. Educators have learned this lesson, much to the detriment of students. For example, some well-meaning school systems have tried to raise the self-esteem of disadvantaged and failing students by passing

Self-fulfilling prophecy An impression formation process in which an initial impression elicits behavior that conforms to the impression

STRATEGIES TO IMPROVE YOUR SELF-ESTEEM[29]

them to the next grade. Unfortunately, such efforts have had no positive effects and demonstrated that inflating self-esteem by itself could actually decrease grades.[30]

Researchers once assumed that people acted violently toward others because they suffered from low self-esteem; rather, the opposite seems to be true. Violent people often act the way they do because they suffer from *high*, but unrealistic, self-esteem. Violent criminals often describe themselves as superior to others. Even playground bullies regard themselves as superior to other children. Low self-esteem is found among the victims of bullies, but not among bullies themselves. In fact, most violent groups generally have belief systems that emphasize their superi-

STRATEGY

Practice self-acceptance
☑ **Self-acceptance** means recognizing, accepting, and "owning" your thoughts, feelings, and behavior. You may not like your actions, but be willing to accept them as part of who you are. No one is perfect.

Practice self-responsibility
☑ **Self-responsibility** means taking responsibility for your own happiness and for achieving your goals. If you assume responsibility for what you do, you are more likely to be happy and satisfied.

Practice assertiveness
☑ Stand up for yourself in appropriate ways to satisfy your needs and pursue your goals. Don't become obsessed with getting approval from others.

Practice personal integrity
☑ **Personal integrity** means behaving in ways that are consistent with your values and beliefs. Do more than think about what you should do and actually do "the right thing."

Practice positive self-talk
☑ **Self-talk** represents the silent statements you make to yourself about yourself. Replace negative, self-defeating statements with more positive and productive statements.

EXCEPTION

But not as an excuse
☒ Self-acceptance is not an excuse for bad behavior. If a boss shouts at employees and justifies it by saying, "I'm a very emotional man. If you can't take it, quit," he has taken the concept of self-acceptance to extremes.

But don't try to control everything
☒ Resist the urge to control everything so you don't end up feeling overburdened, frustrated, and angry with others. Ask for and accept help when you need it.

But respect the needs of others
☒ Be assertive, not aggressive, when you pursue your goals. Don't stand in the way of others when you stand up for yourself.

But understand and respect others
☒ "The right thing" for you may not be "the right thing" for someone else. Make sure your actions do not offend or hurt others.

But listen to others, too
☒ Listening to yourself should never substitute for or prevent you from listening to others.

ority over others.[31] Someone with an overinflated sense of self-esteem may be a braggart, bully, or tyrant rather than a person with a healthy self-concept. Someone with lower self-esteem but a secure and confident sense of self can be a model of humility and goodness.

Self-acceptance A willingness to recognize, accept, and "own" your thoughts, feelings, and behavior, but not as an excuse for inappropriate behavior

Self-responsibility Being accountable for your own happiness and fulfillment of goals without trying to control everything and everyone

Personal integrity The practice of behaving in ways that are consistent with your values and beliefs while also understanding and respecting others

Self-talk The silent statements you make to yourself about yourself

---

STOP & THINK — Practice Positive Self-Talk

Read the example of negative self-talk and its corresponding example of positive self-talk below. Then provide two examples of negative self-talk and corresponding examples of positive self-talk.

Negative Self-Talk

Example: *I won't be able to work as quickly as the other group members.*

Your example: _____

_____

Your example: _____

_____

Positive Self-Talk

Example: *I'll do my best and ask for help if I need it.*

Your example: _____

_____

Your example: _____

_____

The school bully's overinflated self-esteem demonstrates his sense of superiority over Calvin.

Know Thy Self

Assess Your Self-Esteem

The statements below describe different ways of thinking about yourself. Read them carefully and choose the phrase that indicates how much you agree with each statement.[32]

strongly disagree (SD) disagree (D) agree (A) strongly agree (SA)

Scoring: Score items 1, 2, 6, 8, and 10 in a positive direction (i.e., strongly agree = 4, agree = 3, and so on) and items 3, 4, 5, 7, and 9 in a negative direction (i.e., strongly agree = 1, agree = 2, and so forth). The highest possible score is 40 points; the lowest possible score is 10 points. Higher scores indicate higher self-esteem. Please note that there are no good or bad scores; rather, the scale measures how you perceive your level of self-esteem.

_____ 1. I feel that I'm a person of worth, at least on an equal plane with others.

_____ 2. On the whole, I am satisfied with myself.

_____ 3. I wish I could have more respect for myself.

_____ 4. I certainly feel useless at times.

_____ 5. At times I think I am no good at all.

_____ 6. I feel that I have a number of good qualities.

_____ 7. All in all, I am inclined to feel that I am a failure.

_____ 8. I am able to do things as well as most other people.

_____ 9. I feel that I do not have much to be proud of.

_____ 10. I take a positive attitude toward myself.

the power of PERCEPTION

Why does one person experience great satisfaction in a job whereas another person in the same job dreads it? Why do you find a speech inspiring whereas another person finds it offensive? The answer to these questions lies in one word: *perception*. Imagine that you and a colleague are chatting after a meeting. You say, "That was a good session. We got through all the issues and ended early." Your friend responds with "Are you kidding? Didn't you notice that Lynn rushed us through the agenda to avoid any serious discussion or disagreement?" What happened here? You both attended the same meeting, but each of you perceived the experience quite differently.

From a communication point of view, we define **perception** as the process through which you select, organize, and interpret sensory stimuli in the world around you. The accuracy of your perceptions determines how well you interpret and evaluate experiences and the people you encounter. At the same time, once you reach a conclusion, it's often difficult to change your perception.

Generally, we trust our perceptions and treat them as accurate and reliable. We say things such as, "Seeing is believing," "I call it as I see it," or "I saw it with my own eyes." However, as Figure 2.1 shows, we can't always rely on what we see. Police officers know very well that three witnesses to a traffic accident may provide three different descriptions of the cars involved, the estimated speed they were traveling, and the physical characteristics of the drivers. In fact, eyewitness testimony, although

Perception The process we use to select, organize, and interpret sensory stimuli

Figure 2.1 Old Woman or Young Woman?

What you see depends on how your eyes select graphic details, how you organize that information, and how you interpret the results.

persuasive, is often one of the least reliable forms of courtroom evidence.

Even though you run the risk of drawing incorrect conclusions, you would be lost in a confusing world without your perceptions. Not only does perception help you make sense out of other people's behavior, it helps you decide what you will say or do. Suppose you notice that your boss keeps track of employees who arrive late and leave early, and that she rarely grants these employees the special privileges given to those who put in full workdays. These perceptions tell you that it is a good idea to arrive early and stay late if you want a positive evaluation or a future promotion.

There are three components to perception: selection, organization, and interpretation.

Selection

You use your senses (sight, sound, taste, smell, and touch) to notice and choose from the many stimuli around you. Your needs, wants, interests, moods, and memories largely determine which stimuli you will select. For example, when your eyes and ears detect something familiar

or potentially interesting as you flip through television channels, you stop. Or you may be daydreaming in class, but when your professor says, "The following chapters will be covered on the next test," you find yourself paying full attention again.

The optical illusion in Figure 2.2 illustrates the **figure–ground principle** of perception: we focus on certain features (the figure) while deemphasizing less relevant background stimuli (the ground).[33] Thus, while walking down the street, if you notice someone standing against a building, that's what you would see first: a person standing against a building, not a building with a person-shaped hole in it.[34] In communication, you see your friend smile and hear her tell you everything is okay. However, you focus your attention on her red and swollen eyes, suspect she has been crying, and conclude that she is upset. Her smile and verbal assurances are relegated to the background. Ultimately, what you select to focus on will affect how you organize and interpret the events around you *and* how well you communicate in those situations.

Figure 2.2 Reversible Images

Do you see a vase or two people facing each other in the figure? Depending on which elements of the figure you select, you will perceive different images.

Organization

Suppose you see a middle-aged woman wearing a suit walking across campus. You conclude she is a professor. You also observe a young man entering a classroom wearing a school sweatshirt and carrying a backpack that appears to be loaded with textbooks. You assume he is a student. You took the information, or stimuli, you observed and categorized it into "professor" and "student." What these two scenarios demonstrate is how *context* influences the way you organize information. For example, you could conclude that a woman in a suit on campus is a professor, but in a different context, you might conclude that she is a business executive. You may conclude that a young man wearing a school sweatshirt and carrying books on campus is a student, but backstage in a theater, you may decide that he is an actor or stagehand.

Figure–ground principle A perception principle that explains why we focus on certain features—the figure—while deemphasizing less relevant stimuli—the ground

Is this woman a college student? an instructor? a store clerk? an attorney? a business executive?

WEST IS WEST AND EAST IS EAST

The mental process of perception is the same across cultures. Everyone selects, organizes, and interprets stimuli. However, your culture influences *what* you notice, *how* you organize that information, and *how* you interpret information and situations. Psychologist Richard Nisbett argues that each culture can "literally experience the world in very different ways."[35] Look, for example, at the three objects depicted on your right. Which two objects would you pair together?

People from Western cultures are more likely to put the chicken and cow together because they are both animals. East Asians, however, are more likely to pair the cow and the grass because cows eat grass. According to Nesbitt, East Asians perceive the world in terms of relationships whereas Westerners are inclined to see objects that can be grouped into categories. As Chapter 3, Understanding Others, explains, many cultures—and East Asian cultures in particular—are more sensitive to the context in which communication takes place. As Rudyard Kipling wrote in *The Ballad of East and West*, "Oh, East is East, and West is West, and never the twain shall meet."

You sort and arrange the sensory stimuli you select into useful categories based on your knowledge and past experiences with similar stimuli. Four principles influence how you organize or categorize information: the **proximity principle**, the **similarity principle**, the **closure principle**, and the **simplicity principle**.[36]

The Proximity Principle The closer objects, events, or people are to one another, the more likely you will perceive them as belonging together.[37] You go to a restaurant to eat lunch alone, and another person whom you do not know gets in line behind you. The host asks, "Two for lunch?" When you don't want to be perceived as associated with an individual, you may move away from that person to create greater physical distance.

The Similarity Principle Similar elements or people are more likely to be perceived as part of a group. When two individuals share one characteristic or trait, you may conclude that they also have other things in common. For example, you meet a person from Texas and assume that she enjoys country music because other Texans you know listen to that kind of music. Unfortunately, the similarity principle can lead to stereotyping and inaccurate conclusions. Your new acquaintance may dislike country music but love jazz.

Figure 2.3   How Many Triangles Do You See?

Some people see as many as 11 triangles in this drawing. However, given that a triangle is a figure with three attached sides, there are no triangles. If you saw triangles, you mentally filled in or "closed" the image's elements.

The Closure Principle We often fill in missing elements to form a more complete impression of an object, person, or event. Look, for example, at Figure 2.3.

Proximity principle A perception principle that explains why the closer objects, events, or people are to one another, the more they are perceived as belonging together

Similarity principle A perception principle that explains why similar items or people are more likely to be perceived as a group

Closure principle A perception principle that explains why we often fill in missing elements in order to form a more complete impression of an object, person, or event

Simplicity principle A perception principle that explains why we tend to organize information in a way that provides the simplest interpretation of objects, people, or experiences

In what ways does this photo illustrate how we select and organize stimuli to reach conclusions about their meaning?

- *Relational involvement.* This is really important to your friend.

These same factors may also lead to inaccurate perceptions. For example, suppose your best friend's ex-husband is hired to work in your department. You believe that he treated your friend badly and now you will have to endure his inconsiderate attitude and carelessness at work. However, everyone else—supervisors, co-workers, and customers—seems pleased with him. Clearly, your previous experience may create an unfair or erroneous perception of his work.

Perception Checking

Psychologists Richard Block and Harold Yuker point out that "perception often is a poor representation of reality. Yet it is important to recognize that a person's behavior is controlled less by what is actually true, than what the person believes is true. Perceptions may be more important than reality in determining behavior!"[40]

The Simplicity Principle We tend to organize information in a way that provides the simplest interpretation. For example, on a cloudy day, you look out the window and see that the sidewalk is wet, and think that it must have rained. This is a reasonable and simple conclusion. However, there may be other explanations for the wet sidewalk, like automatic sprinklers or a leak in a water pipe, but you chose the simplest one first.

Interpretation

A number of factors influence your interpretation of experiences. Suppose a friend asks you to volunteer your time over the weekend to help build a house for Habitat for Humanity. The following factors may affect your interpretation and reaction to your friend's request:

- *Past experiences.* After volunteering at a soup kitchen last year, you felt really good about yourself.
- *Knowledge.* You spent a summer working as a house painter and believe that you have something useful to contribute.

- *Expectations.* It sounds like fun, and you might meet some interesting people.
- *Attitudes.* You believe that volunteering in the community is important.

ethicalcommunication

The Golden Rule Does Not Always Apply

The Golden Rule, "Do to others what you would have them do to you," comes from the New Testament (Matthew 7:12).[38] However, what you would do is not necessarily what another person wants you to do. In his *Maxims for Revolutionists*, playwright George Bernard Shaw wrote, "The golden rule is that there are no golden rules.... Do not do unto others as you would that they should do unto you. Their tastes may not be the same."[39] Thus, if you wish to follow the Golden Rule, consider these two cautions:

- Consider how another person may perceive the situation differently than you do.
- Look for solutions that would be appropriate and fair from someone else's point of view or culture.

You can improve the accuracy of your perceptions by pausing to check the basis for your conclusions. **Perception checking** involves noticing and analyzing how you select, organize, and interpret sensory stimuli, whether you consider alternative interpretations, and whether you try to verify your perceptions with others.[41]

The 7 Key Elements and Guiding Principles of Effective Communication

Perception checking
A method for testing the accuracy of perceptual interpretations

PERCEPTION CHECKING GUIDELINES

1 **Know thy** *self*
How do factors such as personal biases, your level of self-awareness, past experiences, your cultural background, or the influence of others affect your perceptions?

2 **Connect with** *others*
Do you perceive a situation the same way others do? If not, how can you adapt to their perceptions?

3 **Determine your** *purpose*
How does the way you select, organize, interpret information, and reach conclusions affect your reasons for communicating?

4 **Adapt to the** *context*
How does the psychosocial, logistical, and interactional communication context affect your perceptions and the perceptions of others?

5 **Select appropriate** *content*
How do your perceptions affect the content you choose for a message?

6 **Structure your message**
How do your perceptions affect the way you organize ideas and information in a message? Could others interpret your meaning differently based on the way you organize the content?

7 **Practice skillful** *expression*
How do your perceptions affect the way you express your message and choose communication channels?

communicating
WITH CONFIDENCE

your self-concept and level of self-confidence directly affect how successfully you communicate.[42] Most of us see ourselves as bright and hardworking. At the same time, all of us have occasional doubts and insecurities. If you lack confidence, you are less likely to share what you know or voice your opinions. But when you feel good about yourself, you can engage in a conversation with ease, defend your ideas in a group, and give successful presentations.

Most people experience some anxiety when they are in an important communication situation. In fact, that "keyed-up" feeling is a positive and normal reaction, and demonstrates that you care about what you have to say.

Communication Apprehension

The anxiety you may experience when speaking to others is referred to by many names: *speech anxiety*, *stage fright*, and *communication apprehension*. **Communication apprehension** is "an individual's level of fear or anxiety associated with either real or anticipated communication with another

Communication apprehension
An individual's level of fear or anxiety associated with either real or anticipated communication with another person or persons

person or persons."[43] It occurs in a variety of communication contexts, such as group discussions, meetings, interpersonal conversations, public speaking, and job interviews.

Communication apprehension is not just "in your head;" it is a type of stress that manifests in real physiological responses. Physical reactions such as sweaty palms, perspiring, a fast pulse, shallow breathing, cold extremities, flushed skin, nausea, trembling hands, quivering legs, or "butterflies" in the stomach are the body's response to the release of hormones such as adrenaline.[44]

National surveys have discovered that fear of snakes and fear of speaking in public are the top two common fears among North Americans, way ahead of fear of heights, anxieties about financial problems, and even fear of death. Fortunately, you can learn how to reduce your anxieties and transform that energy into effective communication.

Strategies for Becoming a Confident Communicator

Despite your worst fears, most people are kind and willing to forgive and forget a mistake. No one expects you to be perfect. Also, remember that in most cases, your anxiety is invisible. We can't see your pounding heart, upset stomach, cold hands, or worried thoughts. Most of us think we display more anxiety than listeners report noticing. However, the fact that your anxiety is often invisible to others does not make it feel any less real to you. Fortunately, there are a number of strategies to reduce your anxiety and help you become a more confident communicator.

Prepare Although you may not be able to predict unexpected situations or anticipate the nature of everyday conversations, you can prepare for many of the communication situations you encounter. For instance, you can prepare for a job interview or performance appraisal, a staff meeting or professional seminar, and a public speech or presentation. Thorough preparation changes the unfamiliar into something familiar. With good preparation, you will know a great deal about the ideas you wish to discuss, the others who will be involved, the context of the situation, the content and structure of your message, and how you will express your message.

Relax, Re-think, Re-vision By learning to relax your body, you can reduce your level of communication apprehension. However, a relaxed body is only half the battle; you also need to change the way you think about communication.[45] When you have confident thoughts ("I know I can persuade this group to join the Animal Rescue League"), you begin to feel more confident. Three strategies can help you rethink your attitudes, visualize your message, and relax your body.

Communication Apprehension

THINK ABOUT THEORY

Since the early 1970s, the study of communication apprehension has been a major research focus in the communication discipline. Leading researcher James C. McCroskey explains that "it permeates every facet of an individual's life," including major decisions such as career and housing choices, as well as affects the quality of our communication behavior in a variety of interpersonal, small group, social, educational, work, and public settings.[46]

In the beginning, when McCroskey began studying communication apprehension, he believed that it was a "learned trait, one that is conditioned through reinforcements of the child's communication behavior."[47] More recently, he has argued that a person's environment or situation has only a small effect on that person's level of anxiety. He now believes that communication apprehension is a relatively permanent personality trait, "an expression of principally inborn neurobiological functioning."[48]

Communication apprehension, concludes McCroskey, is "probably the most important factor in causing ineffective communication. . . . For those of us who experience [communication apprehension] to the point that it interferes with our daily lives or stands in our way of personal or professional success, we need not accept this as something we have to endure. . . . Communication apprehension can be reduced by a variety of methods and has already [been] so reduced for literally thousands of individuals."[49] The remainder of this chapter provides a deeper understanding of communication apprehension and a variety of methods for reducing its effects.

Sources of COMMUNICATION APPREHENSION

The process of managing communication apprehension begins with recognizing why you feel anxious when speaking to an individual, group, or audience. Although everyone has personal reasons for nervousness, researchers have identified some of the key fears that underlie communication apprehension.[50]

Many researchers claim that the fear of a negative evaluation is the number-one cause of communication anxiety.[51] When you focus your thoughts on the possibility of failure, you are more likely to fail. Try to shift your focus to the positive feedback you see from others—a nod, a smile, or an alert look. When you sense that a listener likes you and your message, you may gain the extra confidence you need.

Most people fear the unknown. Performing an unfamiliar or unexpected role can transform a usually confident person into a tangle of nerves. If you are attending an event as an audience member and suddenly are called on to introduce a guest to the audience, you can become very unsettled. Similarly, most people feel stressed when interviewing for a job in an office they've never been to and with a person they hardly know. If you've been promoted to a leadership position and are now "the boss," you may feel less comfortable communicating with the colleagues you now supervise.

"Three strikes and you're out" works in baseball, and "What goes up must come down" makes sense in physics, but the rules of communication are not hard and fast and should not be treated as though they are enforceable laws. For example, novice speakers sometimes over-rehearse to the point of sounding robotic for fear of saying "uh" or "um" in a presentation. Good communicators learn not to "sweat the small stuff" and that, sometimes, "rules" should be bent or broken.

FEAR of Failure

FEAR of Breaking the Rules

FEAR of the Unknown

Do you get nervous when interacting with people who have more status or power, education or experience, fame or popularity? Fear of others can be heightened when talking to a powerful person, an influential group, or a large audience. Usually, this fear is based on an exaggerated feeling of being different from or inferior to others. If you don't know much about the people around you, you are more likely to feel apprehensive. Learning more about your listeners or even your classmates can decrease your anxiety. You may have more in common with them than you realize.

FEAR of Others

FEAR of the Spotlight

Although a little attention may be flattering, being the center of attention makes many people nervous. Psychologist Peter Desberg puts it this way: If you were performing as part of a choir, you'd probably feel much calmer than if you were singing a solo.[52] The more self-focused you are, the more nervous you become. This is especially true when giving a presentation to an audience. Try to stay focused on your purpose and message, rather than allowing yourself to be distracted by the spotlight.

- **Cognitive restructuring** is a method for reducing anxiety by replacing negative, irrational thoughts with more realistic, positive self-talk. The next time you feel anxious, tell yourself any one of these positive statements: "My message is important" and "I am a well-prepared, skilled communicator." Or, "I know more about this than the audience does" and "I've done this before, so I'm not going to be as nervous as I've been in the past."
- **Visualization** is a powerful method for building confidence, and it allows you to imagine what it would be like to communicate successfully. Find a quiet place, relax, and imagine yourself walking

Cognitive restructuring A method of reducing communication apprehension by replacing negative thoughts with more positive ones

Visualization A method of reducing communication apprehension by imagining what it would be like to communicate successfully

into the room with confidence and energy. Think about the smiles you'll receive as you talk, the heads nodding in agreement, and the look of interest in the eyes of your listeners. By visualizing yourself communicating effectively, you are mentally practicing the skills you need to succeed while also building a positive self-image.

• **Systematic desensitization** is a relaxation and visualization technique developed by psychologist Joseph Wolpe to reduce the anxiety associated with stressful situations.[53] You start with deep muscle relaxation. In this relaxed state, you then deliberately imagine yourself in a variety of communication contexts ranging from very comfortable to highly stressful. By working to remain relaxed while visualizing various situations, you will gradually associate communication with relaxation rather than nervousness.

Focus One of the best ways to build confidence is to concentrate on your message. Anxiety only draws your attention away from your message and directs it to your fears. When you focus on getting your message across, you don't have time to think about how you might look or sound. This strategy can reduce your level of anxiety and improve your communication.

Practice The best way to become good at something is to practice, regardless of whether it's cooking, serving a tennis ball, or communicating. You can practice wording a request or expressing an emotion to another person, answering questions in an interview, stating your position at a meeting, or making a presentation to an audience.

In addition to enhancing your confidence, practice stimulates your brain in positive ways. As Daniel Goleman notes in *Social Intelligence*, "Simulating an act is, in the brain, the same as performing it."[54] Practicing communication mentally and physically is as important as practicing the piano or a gymnastics routine. Skilled pianists and medal-winning gymnasts spend hours practicing, so at the very least, communicators should practice what they intend to say to others before they say it.

Even rock stars like Sting practice meditation and other relaxation techniques to transform nervousness and anxiety into calmness and confidence.

Systematic desensitization A method of reducing communication apprehension through deep muscle relaxation and visualization

Know Thy Self

Work toward Calm through Systematic Desensitization

The following hierarchy of anxiety-producing communication situations[55] range from least likely to most likely to produce stress. Assess for yourself which of these situations produce the most anxiety; then, as you visualize each context, try to remain calm and relaxed.

1. You are talking to your best friend in person.

2. You are being introduced to a new acquaintance by your best friend.

3. You have to talk to a small group of people, all of whom you know well.

4. You are at a social gathering where you don't know anyone but are expected to meet and talk to others.

5. You are talking to someone in a supervisory role about a problem at work or school.

6. You are going to ask someone to go to a party with you.

7. You are going on a job interview.

8. You have been asked to give a presentation in front of a large group of people.

9. You are to appear on a television show with other panelists to talk about a topic you know well.

10. You are to appear on a television show and debate another person.

Communication ASSESSMENT

Personal Report of Communication Apprehension

The Personal Report of Communication Apprehension (PRCA)[56] is composed of 24 statements concerning feelings about communication with other people. Indicate the degree to which each statement applies to you by marking whether you (1) strongly agree, (2) agree, (3) are undecided, (4) disagree, or (5) strongly disagree. Work quickly; record your first impression.

_____ 1. I dislike participating in group discussions.

_____ 2. Generally, I am comfortable while participating in group discussions.

_____ 3. I am tense and nervous while participating in group discussions.

_____ 4. I like to get involved in group discussions.

_____ 5. Engaging in a group discussion with new people makes me tense and nervous.

_____ 6. I am calm and relaxed while participating in a group discussion.

_____ 7. Generally, I am nervous when I have to participate in a meeting.

_____ 8. Usually, I am calm and relaxed while participating in a meeting.

_____ 9. I am very calm and relaxed when I am called upon to express an opinion at a meeting.

_____ 10. I am afraid to express myself at meetings.

_____ 11. Communicating at meetings usually makes me feel uncomfortable.

_____ 12. I am very relaxed when answering questions at a meeting.

_____ 13. While participating in a conversation with a new acquaintance, I feel very nervous.

_____ 14. I have no fear of speaking up in conversations.

_____ 15. Ordinarily, I am very tense and nervous in conversations.

_____ 16. Ordinarily, I am very calm and relaxed in conversations.

_____ 17. While conversing with a new acquaintance, I feel very relaxed.

_____ 18. I'm afraid to speak up in conversations.

_____ 19. I have no fear of giving a speech.

_____ 20. Certain parts of my body feel very tense and rigid while I am giving a speech.

_____ 21. I feel relaxed while giving a speech.

_____ 22. My thoughts become confused and jumbled when I am giving a speech.

_____ 23. I face the prospect of giving a speech with confidence.

_____ 24. While giving a speech, I get so nervous I forget facts I really know.

Scoring: As you score each subcategory, begin with a score of 18 points. Then add or subtract from 18 based on the following instructions:

Subscores	Scoring Formula
Group discussions	18 + scores for items 2, 4, and 6; – scores for items 1, 3, and 5
Meetings	18 + scores for items 8, 9, and 12; – scores for items 7, 10, and 11
Interpersonal conversations	18 + scores for items 14, 16, and 17; – scores for items 13, 15, and 18
Public speaking	18 + scores for items 19, 21, and 23; – scores for items 20, 22, and 24

To obtain your total score for the PRCA, add your four subscores together. Your score should range between 24 points and 120 points.

Norms for PRCA

	Mean	Standard Deviation
Total score	65.5	15.3
Group	15.4	4.8
Meetings	16.4	4.8
Interpersonal	14.5	4.2
Public speaking	19.3	5.1

Summary

How do *your* characteristics, perceptions, and confidence affect the way you communicate?

- Your self-concept is largely determined by your level of self-awareness, the influence of other people, past experiences, and your cultural perspectives.
- People-based factors (significant others, references groups, your roles, and the rewards you receive from others) are powerful determinants of your self-concept.
- Beware of self-fulfilling prophecies, which are predictions that directly or indirectly cause themselves to become true.
- You can minimize self-deception and trust your view of your self by objectively assessing your own behavior and by comparing yourself to others.

What communication strategies and skills can improve your self-esteem?

- You can improve your self-esteem by practicing self-acceptance, self-responsibility, self-assertiveness, personal integrity, and self-talk.
- Practice converting negative self-talk about yourself into positive self-talk.

How do your perceptions affect the way you select, organize, and interpret the world around you?

- Perception is the process through which you select, organize, and interpret sensory stimuli in the world around you.
- Your needs, interests, moods, wants, and memories largely determine which stimuli you will select.
- Four principles that influence how you organize information are the proximity, similarity, closure, and simplicity principles.
- Your past experiences, knowledge, expectations, attitudes, and relationships affect how you interpret and react to people and events.
- When you engage in perception checking, apply all seven guiding principles of communication to the situation.

How do you become a more confident communicator?

- *Communication apprehension* refers to an individual's level of fear or anxiety associated with real or anticipated communication with another person or persons.
- Sources of communication apprehension include fear of failure, fear of the unknown, fear of the spotlight, fear of others, and fear of breaking the supposed rules.
- Strategies for reducing your level of communication apprehension include (a) preparation, (b) physical relaxation, (c) cognitive restructuring, (d) visualization, (e) systematic desensitization, (f) focus, and (g) practice.

TEST your knowledge

1 Most infants begin to recognize themselves in a mirror _____ months of age.
   a. by 6
   b. between 6 and 12
   c. between 12 and 18
   d. between 18 and 24
   e. after 24

2 If your parents or teachers tell you that you'll never become a doctor because you're not a good science student, you may not pursue this career goal. Which aspect of self-concept may be responsible for your decision?
   a. self-awareness
   b. self-monitoring
   c. self-assertiveness
   d. self-fulfilling prophecy
   e. self-disclosure

3 Which of the following techniques for improving self-esteem can help you stop blaming others for your failures?
   a. self-talk
   b. personal integrity
   c. self-assertiveness
   d. self-responsibility
   e. self-acceptance

4 Which answer is an example of someone who tells you to accept her disruptive behavior because it is just who she is?
   a. She rarely stands up for herself in appropriate ways.
   b. She always reacts in a way that is consistent with her values and beliefs.
   c. She engages in negative rather than positive self-talk.
   d. She suffers from high but unrealistic self-esteem.
   e. She justifies her actions by saying that's just her leadership style.

5 Your textbook uses the example of eyewitness testimony to illustrate
   a. the power of self-concept.
   b. the inaccuracies in human perception.
   c. the role of selection in the perception process.
   d. the role of organization in the perception process.
   e. the role of interpretation in the perception process.

6 When a mother sees blood on her daughter's sleeve, she assumes that her daughter has been badly hurt in an accident. This is an example of
   a. the proximity principle.
   b. the similarity principle.
   c. the closure principle.
   d. the simplicity principle.
   e. the complexity principle.

7 Which guiding principle helps you check your perceptions?
   a. Know Thy Self
   b. Connect with Others
   c. Determine Your Purpose
   d. Select Appropriate Content
   e. all of the above

8 Why doesn't the Golden Rule always work?
   a. Because you have to get to know your neighbor very well before you can "love thy neighbor as thyself."
   b. Because "turning the other cheek" may not help you understand another person's motives.
   c. Because sacrificing yourself for the sake of others may help the other person, but be very detrimental to you.
   d. "Honoring thy father and mother" all of the time may prevent you from realizing your own potential.
   e. Because if you "do to others as you would have them do unto you," you may discover that the other person may not want the same things you do.

9 Which communication scholar has done the most research on communication apprehension?
   a. Hermann Rorschach
   b. Daniel Goleman
   c. James McCroskey
   d. Min-Sun Kim
   e. Leon Festinger

10 Which strategy for reducing your level of communication apprehension involves replacing negative, irrational thoughts with more realistic, positive self-talk?
   a. Be prepared.
   b. Use cognitive restructuring.
   c. Imagine what it would be like to experience an entire communication act successfully.
   d. Use systematic desensitization.
   e. Focus on your message and practice that message.

Answers: 1-d; 2-d; 3-d; 4-e; 5-b; 6-d; 7-e; 8-e; 9-c; 10-b;

3 ADAPTING TO

Not that many years ago, a white American businessman could predict the gender, race, average age, and even religion of his neighbors, friends, and colleagues: They would look like him, speak like him, and share many of the same attitudes, beliefs, and values. Hospital nurses could also predict the gender, predominant race, and average age of their colleagues and the doctors with whom they worked. Today, corporations and hospitals are now global communities in which a 35-year-old woman from India might be a CEO, a surgeon, or a hospital's chief of staff.

The "other" we thought we knew now defies our expectations.

Not that many years ago, an African American could be denied a room or a table at a "white" hotel or restaurant and be ordered to sit at the back of the bus with the rest of the "coloreds." Interracial couples who married could be jailed for "mixing races." Same-sex couples would need to hide—and in

OTHERS

some cases, still do—the fact that they are more than "just friends" in order to be welcomed by their families and to avoid verbal and physical harassment. But, in 2009, the son of an African immigrant and a white American woman became the forty-fourth president of the United States. And just as the laws and attitudes against interracial marriage took many years to change,[1] the laws and attitudes about same-sex marriages are also slowly changing. Gay couples are openly and legally married in states such as Massachusetts, Connecticut, and Iowa. The "other" we thought we knew now defies our expectations.

As such, many people have had to unlearn what they "know" and feel about people of different genders, races, ages, religions, and cultures. Now, more than ever, in order for us to communicate effectively, we must learn to understand, respect, and adapt to the many others we encounter every day.

the many faces
OF OTHERS

learning to communicate effectively in our diverse world requires an understanding of how the characteristics, cultural attitudes, beliefs, and values of others affect the ways in which *they* speak, listen, and behave, as well as how and why *you* respond the way you do.

The increasing diversity of the U.S. population affects us in many ways—socially, economically, artistically, and spiritually.[2] According to the 2000 census, between 1990 and 2000, more than 13 million people immigrated to the United States, the largest influx within a ten-year span in the country's history.

The census shows that, in 2000, three-quarters of the people in the United States were white. By 2006, the percentage of whites had decreased to 56.6 percent.[3] By the middle of this century, whites will become one of the many minority groups living in America.[4] In short, a "majority culture" will no longer exist in the United States.

Defining Culture

When some people hear the phrase *cultural diversity*, they think about skin color and immigrants. Words such as *nationality*, *race*, and *ethnicity* are often used synonymously with the term *culture*. However, culture comprises much more than a country of origin, skin color, or ancestral heritage. In Chapter 1, we defined *culture* as "a learned set of shared interpretations about beliefs, values, and norms which affect the behaviors of a relatively large group of people."[5]

Within most cultures, there are also groups of people—members of **co-cultures**—who coexist within the mainstream society yet remain connected to one another through their cultural heritage.[6] In the United States, Native American tribes are co-cultures, as are African Americans, Hispanic/Latino Americans, Asian Americans, Arab Americans, Irish Americans, and members of large and small religious groups. Given our broad definition of culture, a Nebraska rancher and a Boston professor can have very different cultural perspectives, as would a native Egyptian, Brazilian, Indonesian, and Chippewa tribal member.

> **Co-cultures** A group of people who coexist within the mainstream society yet remain connected to one another through their cultural heritage

What Do *You* Believe Is Culturally "Normal"?

Respond to each of the following seven items by putting a checkmark in the column that best describes the behavior.

Behaviors	Very Common	Common	Neutral	Uncommon	Very Uncommon
1. A man wearing a skirt in public					
2. A woman breast-feeding her child in public					
3. Talking with someone who does not look you in the eye					
4. A woman refusing to shake hands with a man					
5. A family taking a communal bath					
6. A man who stands so close you can smell his breath					
7. People who will not eat the food in your home					

Review your ratings. All seven behaviors are customary *and* normal in another culture or country. What are some of *your* "normal" behaviors, and why might others consider them unusual or strange?[7]

barriers to UNDERSTANDING OTHERS

learning to communicate effectively in the global village that characterizes life in the twenty-first century can be a significant challenge. Yet learning about people from other cultures alone will not make you a more effective and ethical communicator; you must also learn to avoid five obstacles that can inhibit your understanding of others: ethnocentrism, stereotyping, prejudice, discrimination, and racism.

Ethnocentrism

Ethnocentrism is a belief that your culture is superior to others. It is a

BARRIERS
to Understanding Others

Ethnocentrism
Stereotyping
Prejudice
Discrimination
Racism

mistaken idea that your culture is a superior culture with special rights and privileges that are or should be denied to others.

Ethnocentric communicators offend others when they imply that they come from a superior culture with superior values. As an ethical and culturally sensitive communicator, you should examine your own ethnocentric beliefs. You can begin by investigating how your culture and your culture-based perspectives may differ from others. Then, at the end of this chapter, complete the GENE (Generalized Ethnocentrism) Scale to assess your level of ethnocentrism.

Ethnocentrism A belief that your culture is superior to others

Stereotyping

Stereotypes are generalizations about a group of people that over-simplify their characteristics. When we stereotype others, we rely on exaggerated beliefs to make judgments about a group of people. Unfortunately, stereotyping usually attributes negative traits to an entire group when, in reality, only a few people in the group may possess those traits. A study of college students found that, even in the mid-1990s, African Americans were stereotyped as lazy and loud, and Jews were described as shrewd and intelligent.[8] Comments such as "Athletes are poor students," "Old people are boring," and "His-panics never arrive on time" are stereotypical statements.

In addition to negative stereo-types, we may hold positive ones. Comments such as "Women are more compassionate than men," and "Gays dress with style" make positive but all-inclusive generaliza-tions. Although positive stereotypes may not seem harmful, they can lead to unfair judgments. Believing that all Asian students are good in science may overlook someone's in-terest or talent in the arts.

Prejudice

Stereotypes lead to **prejudices**: positive or negative attitudes about an individual or cultural group based on little or no direct experi-ence with that person or group. The word *prejudice* has two parts: *pre*, meaning "before," and *judice*, as in *judge*. When you believe or ex-press a prejudice, you are making a judgment about someone before you get to know that person and see whether your opinions and feelings are justified. Although prejudices can be positive—"He must be bril-liant if he went to Yale"—most prej-udices are negative. Statements such as "I don't want a disabled per-son working on our group project" or "Older employees use more sick leave" are examples of prejudice based on stereotypes about people with disabilities and older adults.

Discrimination

Discrimination describes how we act out and express prejudice. When we discriminate, we exclude groups of people from opportunities granted to others: employment, promotion, housing, political expression, equal rights, and access to educational, recreational, and social institutions.

Stereotypes Generalizations about a group of people that oversimplify their characteristics
Prejudices Positive or negative attitudes about an individual or cultural group based on little or no direct experience with that person or group
Discrimination Behavior that acts out and expresses prejudice

---

How Does Language Shape Stereotypes?

communication in ACTION

Intercultural communication scholars Stella Ting-Toomey and Leeva C. Chung contend that the nature of our language shapes many of our stereotypes. Paired words, for example, encourage either/or thinking: *straight* or *gay, us* or *them, fe-male* or *male, black* or *white, rich* or *poor, old* or *young, red state* or *blue state*. Such either/or perceptions lead us to inter-pret the social world as either good or bad, normal or abnormal, and right or wrong. When you think in either/or terms, you may overlook the fact that a person may not be old *or* young, but somewhere in between, or that there are blue voters in red states and red voters in blue states.[9]

Highlighting a cultural detail about someone while sharing an anecdote can also contribute to stereotyping. Such details are usually superfluous, and rather than strengthening a point, pro-mote a biased view, as in the following example:

> Corrine: You know I have such a bad sense of direction, but I must look like I know where I'm going, because people are always coming up to me to ask for directions. One day, for example, I was wandering through downtown Portland and this young—
> (Corrine pauses at this point to lean in to her friend, raise her hand up to par-tially cover her mouth, and whisper)
> Corrine: *black* guy came up to me to ask for directions to Powell's Books.

Clearly, the point of Corrine's story is to describe how, despite her poor sense of direction, people nevertheless ap-proach her for directions. So, why mention the race of the man who ap-proached her? And why announce his race in such hushed tones? Corrine's ex-traneous details and the manner in which she expresses those details perpetuate stereotypes. Pay careful attention to your word choice—what you say, why you say it, and the way you say it.

The Characteristics of PREJUDICE[10]

- Biased beliefs about group members that are not based on direct experience and firsthand knowledge
- Irrational feelings of dislike and even hatred for certain groups
- A readiness to behave in negative and unjust ways toward members of the group

Sadly, discrimination comes in many forms: discrimination against racial, ethnic, religious, and gender groups; discrimination based on sexual orientation, disability, age, and physical appearance; and discrimination against people from different social classes and political ideologies.

Racism

Racism emerges from ethnocentrism, stereotyping, prejudice, and discrimination. Racist people assume that a person with a certain inherited characteristic (usually something superficial such as skin color) also has negative characteristics and abilities. Racists also believe in the superiority of their own race above all others.

Racism usually leads to the abuse of power. When racists acquire power, they try to control, dominate, restrain, mistreat, and harm people of other races without fear of consequences. In its cruelest form, racism results in the torture, humiliation, and extermination of others—the abuse of black slaves in the Americas by white slave owners; the brutality of the Nazis against Jews and other ethnic minorities in Europe; the genocide in Rwanda in which hundreds of thousands of Tutsi people were murdered by Hutu militia groups and gangs.

Extreme racism can and has led to a rise of hate crimes and hate groups. For example, on June 10, 2009, an 88-year-old gunman stepped through the doors of the U.S. Holocaust Memorial Museum in Washington, D.C., and fatally shot a black security guard. The gunman, James W. von Brunn, was a white supremacist who hosted a racist, anti-Semitic Website and wrote a book titled *Kill the Best Gentiles*, alleging a Jewish "conspiracy to destroy the white gene pool."[11] That was followed by the shooting death of a 23-year-old Army private, William Andrew Long, outside a recruiting office in Arkansas. The shooter, a Muslim convert, claimed the killing was a justified reaction to the U.S. military presence in the Middle East.

The gunmen in these cases were described as loners, but their virulent hatred of blacks, Jews, immigrants, Muslims, and homosexuals reflects the views of many hate groups. "Hate group membership," writes Judith Warner, of *The New York Times*, "has been expanding steadily over the course of the past decade—fueled largely by anti-immigrant sentiment. But after President Barack Obama's election, it spiked. The day after the election, the computer servers of two

> **Racism** The assumption that people with certain inherited characteristics (such as skin color) have negative characteristics and abilities that are inferior to those from other races

Black and White Viewpoints[12]

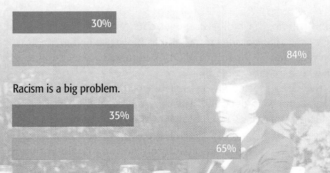

I'd rather have the federal government provide more services, even if it cost more in taxes.

39%

63%

Discrimination is a major reason for the economic and social problems of blacks.

30%

84%

Racism is a big problem.

35%

65%

The average African American is just as well off as the average white person, in terms of income.

44%

0%

% of white respondents   % of black respondents

Acknowledge Unconscious Biases

The National Communication Association's *Credo for Ethical Communication* includes the following principle: We condemn communication that degrades individuals and humanity through distortion, intimidation, coercion, and violence, and through the expression of intolerance and hatred.[13] Practicing this principle, however, is more difficult than it seems. Despite claims of "I'm not prejudiced," most of us have positive and negative attitudes about cultural groups based on little or no direct experience with that group.

Two Harvard researchers, Mahzarin Banaji and Brian Nosek, have developed an implicit association test you can take for free on Harvard's Website at http://implicit.harvard.edu. The results indicate that the majority of Americans, including people of color and other minorities, show a variety of biases they believe they do not have. Banaji and Nosek recommend that when it comes to prejudice, it is less important how biased you are and more important how willing you are to confront your unconscious thoughts about others. When you acknowledge your unconscious biases, you can take steps to confront them.[14]

Two bullet holes in a glass door of the United States Holocaust Memorial Museum mark the hate-crime shooting that left a security officer dead and the gunman wounded.

major white supremacist groups crashed, because their traffic went through the roof."[15]

As disturbing as these incidents may be, columnist Charles Blow asks us an important, related question: Why do we passively condone or avoid objecting to such hatred when we see or hear it first hand?[16] What would you do?

Race A socially constructed concept that is the outcome of ancient population shifts that left their mark in human genes

STOP & THINK | Is There Such a Thing as Race?

According to many anthropologists, biologists, geneticists, and ethicists, race is "a social construct, not a scientific classification," and a "biologically meaningless" concept.[17] They emphasize that 99.9 percent of DNA sequences are common to all humans.[18] Extensive research indicates that pure races never existed and that all humans belong to the same species, *Homo sapiens*, which originated in Africa.

Before the human genome was decoded, most systems of race classification were based on characteristics such as skin color, which often resulted in a cruel agenda that claimed one race's alleged superiority over others. The genetic definition of race has no such agenda and has absolutely nothing to do with any physical or behavioral characteristics.[19]

So what does all of this mean? Is there such a thing as race? The word *race* certainly has meaning and is very real to all of us. Those who believe that one race (depending on their ethnicity or background) is better than another have an erroneous, misguided, or biased view of race. As we see it, **race** should be viewed as both a socially constructed concept *and* understood as the outcome of ancient population shifts that left their mark in our genes. When race is viewed in social and genetic contexts, it becomes a very neutral and natural human characteristic.

How has human genome research and biological studies affected beliefs about race?

UNDERSTANDING
cultural diversity

each one of us has an ethnicity, gender, age, religious belief (including atheism), socioeconomic position, sexual orientation, and abilities. We also live in or have come from a certain region or country. For example:

- A sixth-generation, female, Lutheran schoolteacher whose family still lives in the same Midwestern town
- A 55-year-old Jewish male scientist living in New York whose family emigrated from Russia
- An Islamic, African American female working as a researcher for the federal government in Washington, D.C.
- A 30-year-old executive whose parents are Cuban refugees living in Miami

All of these characteristics contribute to our **social identity**: our self-concept as derived from the social categories to which we see ourselves belonging.[20] However, although we may identify ourselves as Irish, Korean, Ethiopian, or Sioux, many of us have lost touch with our family history and culture.

Understanding *Your* Culture

Culture affects your life in both obvious and subtle ways. Thus, the first step in understanding others is to understand your own culture. You derive a significant part of your social identity from the cultural groups to which you belong as well as the groups to which you do *not* belong: "I know who I am and that I am *not* you." This is a thoroughly natural feeling. However, on the basis of these characteristics, we often divide our world into distinct and very opposite social groups (men

and women, rich and poor, Christian and non-Christian, black and white, young and old, American and foreign) in a way that sets us in opposition to others. A more constructive approach is to explore your own social identity and compare it to people with different kinds of identity. Just as you learn about yourself by interacting with others, you also learn about the culture of your social group by interacting with *other* groups.

For example, many white people in the United States don't think of their behavior as characteristic of a culture. Because whiteness is a historical norm in the United States, it is difficult to classify it as a culture. Yet as Rita Hardiman wrote,

> Like fish, whose environment is water, we are surrounded by

Whiteness and it is easy to think that what we experience is reality rather than recognizing it as the particular culture of a particular group. And like fish who are not aware of water until they are out of it, White people sometimes become aware of their culture only when they get to know, or interact with, the cultures of people of color.[21]

Understanding *Other* Cultures

If you believe you can live a life in which you avoid people from other

---

Social identity Our self-concept as derived from the social categories to which we see ourselves belonging

In the film *Gran Torino*, we see how former Ford factory worker and Korean War vet Walt Kowalski's (Clint Eastwood) prejudice against his next-door Hmong neighbors evolves into friendship.

cultures, you are fooling yourself. Many remote towns have been transformed by influxes of migrant workers (Mexican laborers in Garden City, Kansas), immigrant populations (Hmong communities in Manitowoc County, Wisconsin), and religious groups (Orthodox Jews in Postville, Iowa).

Religion is also a very important aspect of a culture, but what some people forget is that in many countries, and for many groups, the religion *is* the culture, such as Buddhism in Tibet and Islam in Iran. Occasionally, when religious groups attempt to practice their culture in a secular country, they encounter intolerance. In France, for example, religious attire, including headscarves for Muslim girls, skullcaps for Jewish boys, and crosses for Christian children, have been banned from public high schools.[22] Regardless of your individual religious beliefs, "you must remember that people feel strongly about their religion, and that differences between religious beliefs and practices do matter."[23] After all, we live in a pluralistic society; the more knowledge we gain about the people around us, the more we learn to respect others and the better we will be able to communicate with each other. Even on a practical level, your willingness and ability to work in a diverse environment will likely increase your chances of career advancement.

Religious literacy The ability to understand and use the religious terms, symbols, images, beliefs, practices, scripture, heroes, themes, and stories employed in American public life

Know Thy Self

Questions of Faith

According to Stephen Prothero, many of us are illiterate about our own and others' religions. He defines **religious literacy** as "the ability to understand and use the religious terms, symbols, images, beliefs, practices, scripture, heroes, themes, and stories that are employed in American public life."[24] Test your knowledge about a few of the world's major religions by selecting "True," "False," or "I Don't Know" (?) for each of the items below:[25]

T   F   ?   1.   Muslims believe in Islam and the Islamic way of life.

T   F   ?   2.   Judaism is an older religion than Buddhism.

T   F   ?   3.   Islam is a monotheistic religion (belief in one God) just like Christianity and Judaism.

T   F   ?   4.   A Christian Scientist believes that disease is a delusion of the carnal mind that can be cured by prayer.

T   F   ?   5.   Jews fast during Yom Kippur; Muslims fast during Ramadan.

T   F   ?   6.   Jesus Christ was Jewish.

T   F   ?   7.   Roman Catholics throughout the world outnumber all other Christians combined.

T   F   ?   8.   Sunni Muslims compose about 90 percent of all adherents to Islam.

T   F   ?   9.   Hindus believe in the idea of reincarnation.

T   F   ?   10.   The Ten Commandments form the basis of Jewish religious laws.

T   F   ?   11.   Mormonism is a Christian faith founded in the United States.

T   F   ?   12.   The Protestant reformer, Martin Luther, labeled the beliefs of Muslims, Jews, and Roman Catholics as false.

T   F   ?   13.   One-third of the world's population is Christian.

T   F   ?   14.   One-fifth of the world's population is Muslim.

T   F   ?   15.   Hinduism is the oldest of the world's major religions, dating back more than 3,000 years.

Answers: All of the statements are true.

the dimensions
OF CULTURE

We owe a great deal to social psychologist Geert H. Hofstede and anthropologist Edward T. Hall for identifying several important dimensions of culture. Hofstede's groundbreaking research on cultural characteristics has transformed our understanding of others. He defines **intercultural dimension** as "an aspect of a culture that can be measured relative to other cultures."[26] His work on cultural variability identifies several dimensions that characterize cultural groups. Here we look at three of those dimensions—individualism/collectivism, power distance, and masculine/feminine values—because they have received more research attention and support than the others. Edward Hall adds a fourth and fifth dimension: high-context/low-context cultures and monochronic/polychronic time.

5 DIMENSIONS OF CULTURE

1 **Individualism/Collectivism**

2 **Power Distance**

3 **Masculine/Feminine Values**

4 **High/Low Context**

5 **Monochronic/Polychronic Time**

Individualism/ Collectivism

Individualism/collectivism may be the most important factor distinguishing one culture from another.[27] According to Hofstede and many contemporary researchers, while most North Americans traditionally value **individualism**, 70 percent of the world's population values interdependence or **collectivism**.[28] For instance, once children have completed high school or higher education in the United States, many parents encourage them to strike out on their own—to pursue a career and find their own place to live. In China, however, parents encourage their children to stay at home and work until they marry, and once they do, to work for the benefit of the immediate *and* extended family. Figure 3.1 ranks the top countries in each category.[29]

Despite the fact that the United States ranks highest in terms of individualism, not all Americans are individualistic. In fact, many African Americans, Asian Americans, and co-cultures in Hispanic/Latino communities have the characteristics of collectivist societies. Thus, the focus on individual achievement and personal rewards in the United States can make interaction with people from collectivist cultures and co-cultures quite difficult. The U.S. communicator's style and behavior may be viewed as arrogant, antago-nistic, power-hungry, ruthless, and impatient. Yet, interestingly, as poor nations gain wealth, they begin to shift toward greater individualism.[30]

Power Distance

Is it easy to make a personal appointment with the president of your college or university? Can you walk into your boss's office, or do you have to navigate your way through an army of secretaries and administrative assistants? Does our society truly believe in the sentiments expressed in the U.S. Declaration of Independence that all

---

Intercultural dimension An aspect of a culture that can be measured relative to other cultures
Individualism A cultural belief that independence is worth pursuing, that personal achievement should be rewarded, and that individual uniqueness is an important value
Collectivism A cultural belief that emphasizes the views, needs, and goals of the group rather than focusing on the individual

the dimensions of culture **53**

Individualistic Values[31]	Collectivist Values[32]
"I" is important.	"We" is important.
Independence is worth pursuing.	The needs, beliefs, and goals of the "in-group" (e.g., family, community members) are emphasized above those of the individual.
Personal achievement should be rewarded.	Achievements that benefit and foster cooperation in the group should be rewarded.
Individual uniqueness is valued.	Individual uniqueness is not considered important.

MOST INDIVIDUALISTIC COUNTRIES

1. United States
2. Australia
3. Great Britain
*4/5. Canada and
       The Netherlands

MOST COLLECTIVIST COUNTRIES

1. Guatemala
2. Ecuador
3. Panama
4. Venezuela
5. Colombia   * Tied rankings.

Figure 3.1 Individualism and Collectivism

people are created equal? These are the questions addressed in Hofstede's power distance dimension. **Power distance** refers to the physical and psychological distance between those who have power and those who do not in relationships, institutions, and organizations. It also represents "the extent to which the less powerful person in society accepts inequality in power and considers it normal."[33]

In cultures with **high power distance**, individuals accept differences in power as normal, that all people are *not* created equal. In such cultures, the privileged have much more power and use it to guide or control the lives of people with less power. In a high-power-distance culture, you accept and do not challenge authority. Parents have total control over their children. Husbands may have total control over their wives. And government officials, corporate officers, and religious authorities may dictate rules of behavior and have the power to ensure compliance.

In cultures with **low power distance**, power distinctions are minimized: supervisors work with subordinates, professors work with students, elected officials work with constituents. Figure 3.2 ranks the top countries in each category of this dimension. Despite the fact that the United States claims to be the greatest democracy on earth and an equal opportunity society, it is sixteenth on the list after low-power-distance countries such as Finland, Switzerland, Great Britain, Germany, Costa Rica, Australia, The Netherlands, and Canada.[34]

Power distance has enormous implications for communicators. For example, in Australia (a low-power-distance country), students and professors are often on a first-name basis, and lively class discussions are the norm. However, in Malaysia (a high-power-distance country), students show up and are seated *before* class begins; almost no

> **Power distance** The physical and psychological distance between those in a culture who have power and those who do not have power
>
> **High power distance** Cultures in which individuals accept differences in power as normal and allow the privileged to use their power to guide or control the lives of people with less power
>
> **Low power distance** A cultural belief in which power distinctions are minimized

Figure 3.2 Power Distance

HIGHEST POWER-DISTANCE COUNTRIES

1. Malaysia
*2/3. Guatemala
*2/3. Panama
 4. Philippines
*5/6. Mexico and Venezuela

LOWEST POWER-DISTANCE COUNTRIES

1. Austria
2. Israel
3. Denmark
4. New Zealand
5. Ireland   * Tied rankings.

one comes late. Students are polite and appreciative but rarely challenge a professor's claims. In a high-power-distance culture, you do not openly disagree with teachers, elders, bosses, law enforcement officials, or government agents.

If you compare Figures 3.1 and 3.2, you will notice a strong correlation between collectivism and high power distance, and between individualism and low power distance. If you are individualistic and strongly encouraged to express your own opinion, you are more willing to challenge authority. If, on the other hand, your culture is collectivist and your personal opinion is subordinate to the welfare of others, you are less likely to challenge the collective authority of your family, your employer, or your government.

Masculine/Feminine Values

Hofstede uses the terms *masculine* and *feminine* to describe whether masculine or feminine traits are valued by a culture. The terms are used to describe a societal perspective, rather than individuals.

In **masculine societies**, men are supposed to be assertive, tough, and focused on material success, whereas women are supposed to be more modest, tender, and concerned with the quality of life. In **feminine societies**, gender roles overlap: Both men and women are supposed to be modest, tender, and concerned with the quality of life.[35] Figure 3.3 highlights the countries that differ in terms of masculine/feminine values.[36]

Hofstede ranks the United States as fifteenth in terms of masculine values, but less masculine than Australia, New Zealand, and Greece. In masculine societies, personal success, competition, assertiveness, and strength are admired. Unselfishness and nurturing may be seen as weaknesses or "women's work." Although women have come a long way from the rigid roles of past centuries, they have miles to

go before they achieve genuine equality in masculine cultures.

High/Low Context

In Chapter 1, we defined *context* as the psycho-social, logistical, and interactional environment in which communication occurs. Anthropologist Edward T. Hall sees context as the information that surrounds an event, inextricably bound up with the meaning of the event. He claims that a message's context—in and of itself—may hold more meaning than the actual words in a message.[37] Like Hofstede's dimensions, we can place cultures on a continuum from high context to low context.

In a **high-context culture**, very little meaning is expressed through words. Gestures, silence, and facial expressions, as well as the relationships among communicators, have meaning. In high-context cultures,

How could the cultural dimensions discussed in this chapter affect negotiations among world leaders such as Chinese President Hu Jintao, German Chancellor Angela Merkel, and Indian Prime Minister Manmohan Singh?

meaning can be conveyed through status (age, gender, education, family background, title, and affiliations) and through an individual's informal network of friends and associates.

COUNTRIES WITH THE HIGHEST MASCULINE VALUES

1. Japan
*2/3. Austria
*2/3. Venezuela
*4/5. Italy and Switzerland

COUNTRIES WITH THE HIGHEST FEMININE VALUES

1. Sweden
2. Norway
3. The Netherlands
4. Denmark
*5/6. Costa Rica and Yugoslavia (now the republics of Serbia and Montenegro)

* Tied rankings

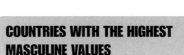

Figure 3.3 Masculine and Feminine Values

Masculine societies Societies in which men are supposed to be assertive, tough, and focused on material success, whereas women are supposed to be more modest, tender, and concerned with the quality of life
Feminine societies Societies in which gender roles overlap: both men and women are supposed to be modest, tender, and concerned with the quality of life
High-context culture A cultural dimension in which very little meaning is expressed through words; gestures, silence, and facial expressions, as well as the relationships among communicators, have meaning

In a **low-context culture**, meaning is expressed primarily through language. As members of a low-context culture, people in North America tend to speak more, speak more loudly, and speak more rapidly than a person from a high-context culture. We "speak up," "spell it out," "just say no," and "speak our mind." Figure 3.4 contrasts the characteristics of high- and low-context cultures.[38]

High-context communication usually occurs in collectivist cultures in which members share similar attitudes, beliefs, and values. As a result, spoken communication can be indirect, implied, or vague because everyone *gets* the meaning by understanding the context, the person's nonverbal behavior, and the significance of the communicator's status.

Shirley van der Veur, a former Peace Corps volunteer and now a professor in a North American university, relates the following story: A scholar from Kenya was invited to dinner at an American colleague's home. Even though he ate ravenously, not leaving a morsel of food on his plate, the American hosts were not convinced that he liked his dinner because he had not *said* so. In Kenya, if his hosts saw him appreciatively eating his meal, they would know that he was enjoying it

without necessarily needing him to express his pleasure verbally.[39]

Monochronic/Polychronic Time

In northern Europe and North America, time is a very valuable commodity. As a result, we fill our time with multiple commitments and live a fast-paced life. However, the pace of life in India, Kenya, and Argentina, as well as life in the South in the United States, for example, is driven less by a need to "get things done" than by a sense of participation in events that create their own rhythm.[40]

Anthropologist Edward T. Hall classifies time as a form of communication and claims that cultures treat time in one of two ways: as monochronic or polychronic.[41] In **monochronic time**, or M-time, events are scheduled as separate items—one thing at a time. M-time people like to concentrate on one job before moving to another and may become irritated when someone in a meeting brings up a personal topic unrelated to the purpose of the meeting.

In **polychronic time**, or P-time, schedules are not as important and are frequently broken. People in polychronic cultures are not slaves to time and are easily distracted and tolerant of interruptions. P-time people

are frequently late for appointments or may not show up at all.[42] If you are a P-time person, you probably find it stimulating to think about several different problems at the same time, and feel comfortable holding two or three conversations simultaneously.

Hall maintains that these two time orientations are incompatible. When monochronic and polychronic people interact, the results can be frustrating. Hall notes that monochronic North Americans become distressed by how polychronic people treat appointments. Being on time in some countries simply doesn't mean the same thing as it

---

Low-context culture A cultural dimension in which meaning is expressed primarily through language; people tend to speak more, speak more loudly, and speak more rapidly than a person from a high-context culture

Monochronic time A cultural dimension in which events are scheduled as separate items—one thing at a time

Polychronic time A cultural dimension in which schedules are not important and are frequently broken; people are not slaves to time and are easily distracted and tolerant of interruptions

---

HIGH-CONTEXT CULTURES

Examples

Chinese
Japanese
South Korean
Native American
African American
Mexican American and Latino

Characteristics

Implicit meaning

Nonverbal communication

Reserved reactions

Strong in-group bonds

High level of commitment

Time open and flexible

LOW-CONTEXT CULTURES

Characteristics

Explicit meaning

Verbal communication

Reactions on the surface

Flexible group memberships

Low level of commitment

Time highly organized

Examples

German
Swiss
White American
Scandinavian
Canadian

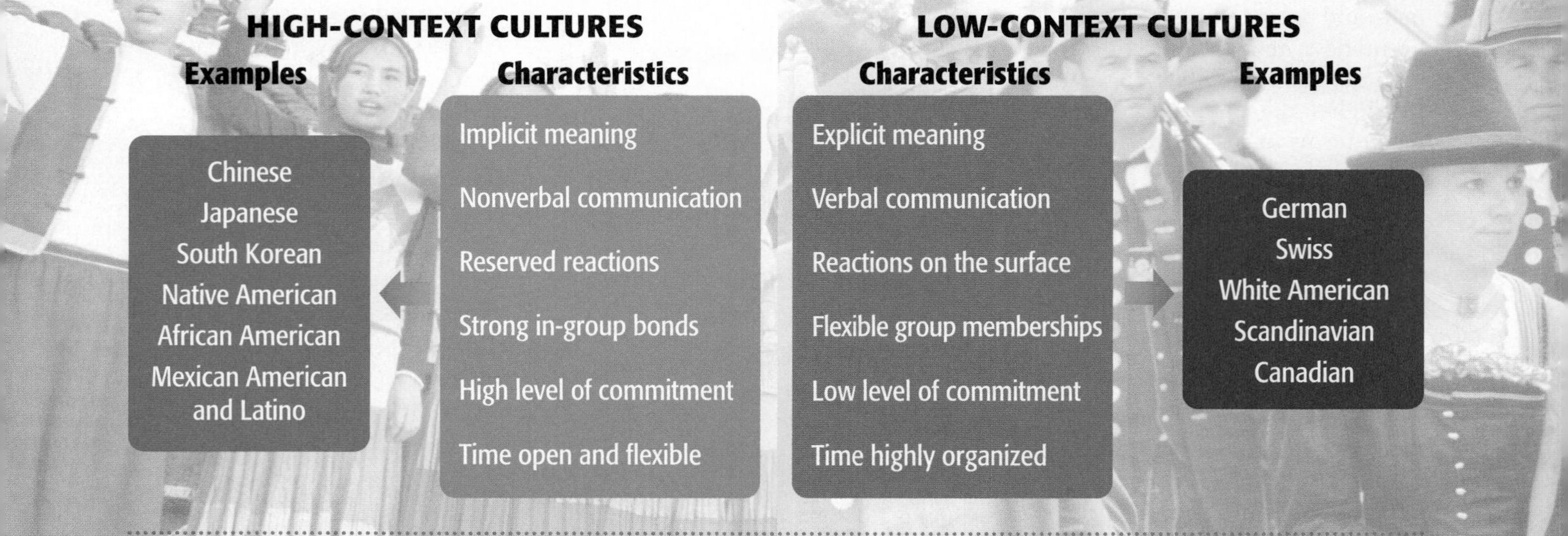

Figure 3.4 Characteristics and Examples of High- and Low-Context Cultures

Why Don't We Hear Others' "Voices"?

Muted group theory observes that powerful, wealthy groups at the top of a society determine who will communicate and be listened to. For this reason, women, the poor, and people of color have trouble participating and being heard.[43] The following three assumptions in muted group theory explain how women's voices are subdued or silenced in many cultures:

1. Women perceive the world differently than men because of traditional divisions of labor. Examples: Homemaker versus breadwinner, nurse versus doctor.

2. Women's freedom of expression is limited by men's dominance in relationships and institutions. Examples: Women in the United States only gained the right to vote in 1920. The "glass ceiling" prevents women from achieving professional advancement.

3. Women must transform their thinking and behavior to participate fully in society. Examples: Women have become politically active and even militant to make sure that sexual harassment, date and marital rape, and spousal abuse are seen as serious crimes against women rather than practices that may be excused or tolerated.

Although muted group theory focuses on women, its assumptions apply to many cultures. People of color, recent immigrants, the disabled, and the poor are also muted.

does in the United States. For P-time people, schedules and commitments, particularly plans for the future, are not firm, and even important plans may change right up to the last minute.[44]

If you are an M-time person, you can try to modify and relax your obsession with time and scheduling. If you are a P-time person, you can do your best to respect and adapt to a monochronic person's need for careful scheduling and promptness. Figure 3.5 depicts several differences between monochronic and polychronic perspectives and cultures.

MONOCHRONIC CULTURES		POLYCHRONIC CULTURES	
Examples	**Characteristics**	**Characteristics**	**Examples**
German Austrian Swiss White American	Do one thing at a time Concentrate on the job Take time commitments (deadlines, schedules) seriously Adhere to plans Emphasize promptness Engage in short-term relationships	Do many things at once Are easily distracted Take time commitments less seriously Often change plans Base promptness on the importance of a relationship Build lifetime relationships	Latin American Arab African African American

Figure 3.5 Monochronic and Polychronic Time: Characteristics and Cultures

intercultural
COMMUNICATION
STRATEGIES

as a way of understanding the perspectives of others, intercultural communication trainers often urge their trainees to "see the world through other people's eyes."

The fundamental purpose of understanding others—seeing the world as others see it—is to minimize miscommunication and prejudice. Thus, learning about and adapting to the many "others" you encounter every day may require changes in longstanding habits of thought and action.

Be Mindful

Mindfulness is both a very old and a very new concept. The ancient concept can be traced back to the first millennium B.C. to the foothills of the Himalayas, when it is believed that Buddha attained enlightenment through mindfulness.[45] **Mindfulness** means being fully aware of the present moment without making hasty judgments. Mindful communicators understand what they experience *inside themselves*

(body, mind, heart, spirit) and pay full attention to what is happening *around them* (people, the natural world, surroundings, events).[46]

Before explaining mindfulness in more detail, let's take a look at its opposite: mind*less*ness. **Mindlessness** occurs when we allow rigid categories and false distinctions to become habits of thought and behavior.[47] For example, you approach a sales counter and say "Excuse me" to the salesperson. Why did you say that? Are you apologizing for interrupting someone who should have been paying more attention to you in the first place? All of us engage in some mindless behavior without any serious consequences. But when mindlessness occurs in a sensitive situation, the results can be detrimental to a relationship or damaging to an important project. For example, after the 9/11 tragedy, many patriotic Muslim Americans suffered stereotyping, prejudice, and discrimination as a result of a larger ignorance about the Islamic faith and culture. If

you are mindless, you are trapped in an inflexible, biased world in which your religion is always right and good; people from other cultures are inferior and untrustworthy; boys will always be boys and girls will always be girls; and change is a terrible and scary thing.[48]

Mind*ful*ness, therefore, requires paying attention to how you and another person communicate. It asks you to observe what is happening as it happens, without forming opinions or taking sides as you learn more about someone else.[49] When you are mindful, you recognize stereotypical thinking and prejudices, and try to overcome them. Mindfulness gives you the freedom and motivation to understand, respect, and adapt to others.

Be Receptive to New Information Mindful communicators learn more about others and their cultures by being open to new information. Too often, we dismiss another person's belief or behavior as irrational or bizarre when more information about that belief or behavior would help us understand it. Once you learn why observant Muslims and Jews won't eat pork products or why Hindus won't eat the meat of sacred cows even under famine conditions, you may become more mindful and tolerant of their customs.

Respect Others' Perspectives In addition to being open to new information, mindful communicators are open to other points of view. Psychologist Richard Nisbett credits a graduate student from China with helping him understand such differences. After he and the student tried to work together and communicate successfully with each other, his Chinese student said, "You know,

Mindful communicators understand what they experience *inside themselves* (body, mind, heart, spirit) and pay full attention to what is happening *around them* (people, the natural world, surroundings, events).

Mindfulness The ability to be fully aware of the present moment without making hasty judgments
Mindlessness Occurs when people allow rigid categories and false distinctions to become habits of thought and behavior

Western

- Focuses on discovering the basic and predictable nature of objects and events
- Tries to control objects, events, and environments
- Puts things in discrete categories
- Uses formal logical rules
- Insists on the correctness of one belief vs. another

East Asian

- Focuses on the interacting, unpredictable relationships among events
- Doubts that objects, events, and environments are controllable
- Describes relationships and connections, not categories
- Accepts contractions and dissimilar beliefs

Western and Asian Ways of Thinking

the difference between you and me is that I know the world is a circle, and you think it's a line. The Chinese believe in constant change, but with things always moving back to some prior state . . . Westerners live in a simpler world . . . and they think they can control events because they know the rules that govern the behavior of objects."[50]

When you cling to one way of seeing a person or interpreting an event, you have stopped being mindful. Every idea, person, or object can be many things, depending on the perspective from which it is viewed. A cow is steak to a rancher, a sacred creature to a Hindu, a collection of genes and proteins to a biologist, and a mistreated animal to members of PETA (People for the Ethical Treatment of Animals).[51]

Adapt to Others

You probably feel most comfortable when you "fit in" with the people around you. To fit in, you may modify the way you talk to family members, friends, colleagues, authority figures, and strangers. For example, two people may be from different areas of the country, one from Maine and the other from Alabama. When they go "home," their dialects, vocabulary, sentence structure, rate of speech, and even volume change to accommodate their home

communication&culture

WHY DON'T HUNGRY HINDUS EAT SACRED COWS?

Among India's Hindus, cows are a sacred symbol of life. There is no greater sacrilege for a Hindu than killing a cow. At first, this belief may seem irrational, particularly in light of India's food shortage and poverty. If you have visited or seen pictures of India, you've seen cows wandering city streets and sidewalks, highways and railroad tracks, gardens and agricultural fields. You've also seen pictures of extreme poverty and hunger.

In his book, *Cows, Pigs, Wars, and Witches: The Riddles of Culture*, Marvin Harris offers a justification for Hindus' treatment of cows.[52] Cows give birth to oxen, which are the principal source for plowing fields. Unfortunately, there are too few oxen for India's 60 million farms. Without oxen to plow fields, farmers cannot farm, food shortages result, and people go hungry. If you kill a cow, you eliminate your source of oxen. During the worst famines, killing a cow only provides temporary relief. Once a cow is killed, there will be no more oxen to plow the field in future years. The long-term effect may be a much more devastating famine. Harris offers this conclusion:

What I am saying is that cow love is an active element in a complex, finely articulated material and cultural order. Cow love mobilizes the latent capacity of human beings to persevere in a low-energy ecosystem in which there is little room for waste or indolence.[53]

In light of Harris's anthropological explanation, you can begin to understand and respect why hungry peasants in India refuse to eat the cows that surround them.

culture. Yet, in professional settings, their speech may be more formal in style and substance.

Howard Giles explores these adaptive tendencies in **Communication Accommodation Theory**,[54] which states that in every communication situation, we compare ourselves with speakers from other groups. If we believe that another group has more power or has desirable characteristics, we tend to "accommodate" our conversations to the accepted speech behaviors and norms of that group. According to Communication Accommodation Theory:

1. *Communication similarities and differences exist in all conversations.* Regardless of whether you talk to an international student or your grandmother, you will encounter differences.
2. *The manner in which we perceive the communication of others will determine how we evaluate our interaction with others.* Effective communicators avoid stereotyping by carefully listening to others and attentively observing what they do.
3. *Language and behavior convey information about social status and group membership.* Usually, the person or group with more status and power establishes the "accepted" type of talk and behavior. For example, if you are being interviewed for a job by someone who behaves formally, you are likely to behave the same way.
4. *Accommodation varies in its degree of appropriateness, and norms guide the accommodation process.* When a situation is awkward, you will try to accommodate the behavior of the group in that situation. Thus, if you interact with a culture that respects its elders, you may hesitate questioning the views of an older person or senior official. And when you learn that a particular behavior is *inappropriate*, you will not go along with the group in that situation. For example, if you and your colleagues are on a deadline at work and they decide to leave the office before they complete the project, you may not leave with them.

Actively Engage Others

Direct, face-to-face interaction with people from culturally diverse backgrounds benefits everyone. You and others may transform long-held negative beliefs about each other's cultures into positive opinions. If you succeed in minimizing your level of anxiety and uncertainty when encountering others, you may discover new worlds with fascinating people who can enrich your life. The fact is, regardless of culture, nationality, gender, religion, age, and ability, all of us share the traits unique to the amazing human condition.[55]

> **Communication Accommodation Theory** When people believe that another group has more power or has desirable characteristics, they tend to accommodate their conversations to the accepted speech behaviors and norms of that group

COMMUNICATION TRAITS WE ALL SHARE[56]

We **SMILE** when happy.

We **WAVE** as a greeting.

We **LAUGH** when amused.

We **BLUSH** when embarrassed.

We **CRY** when sad or in pain.

We **FROWN** when concerned or ill at ease.

We adopt a **FETAL POSITION** when dejected, cold, or in a hopeless situation.

We **SHRUG** to express "I don't know."

We **SLUMP** when dejected or tired.

We **STAND STRAIGHT** when alert or confident.

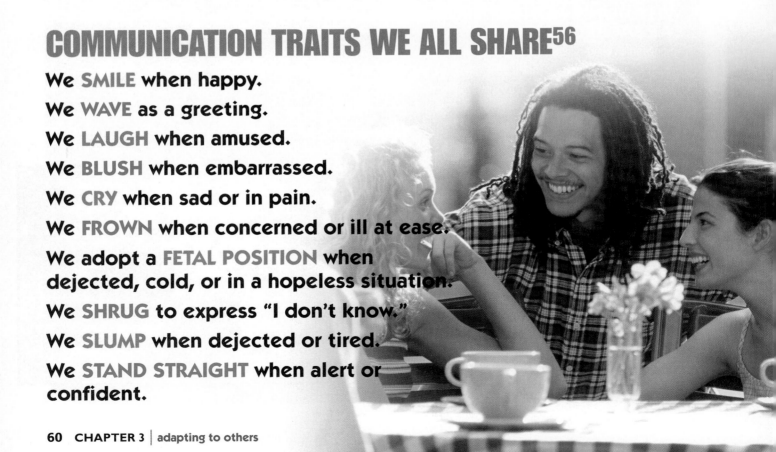

Communication ASSESSMENT

The Generalized Ethnocentrism (GENE) Scale[57]

Read the following statements concerning your feelings about your and others' cultures. In the space provided, indicate how each statement applies to you by marking whether you (5) strongly agree, (4) agree, (3) are undecided, (2) disagree, or (1) strongly disagree. There are no right or wrong answers. Some of the statements may seem very similar to another. Remember, everyone experiences some degree of ethnocentrism. Be honest. Work quickly and record your first response.

_____ 1. Most other cultures are backward compared with my culture.

_____ 2. My culture should be the role model for other cultures.

_____ 3. People from other cultures act strangely when they come to my culture.

_____ 4. Lifestyles in other cultures are just as valid as those in my culture.

_____ 5. Other cultures should try to be more like my culture.

_____ 6. I'm not interested in the values and customs of other cultures.

_____ 7. People in my culture could learn a lot from people in other cultures.

_____ 8. Most people from other cultures just don't know what's good for them.

_____ 9. I respect the values and customs of other cultures.

_____ 10. Other cultures are smart to look up to our culture.

_____ 11. Most people would be happier if they lived like people in my culture.

_____ 12. I have many friends from different cultures.

_____ 13. People in my culture have just about the best lifestyles anywhere.

_____ 14. Lifestyles in other cultures are not as valid as those in my culture.

_____ 15. I am very interested in the values and customs of other cultures.

_____ 16. I apply my values when judging people who are different.

_____ 17. I see people who are similar to me as virtuous/good.

_____ 18. I do not cooperate with people who are different.

_____ 19. Most people in my culture just don't know what is good for them.

_____ 20. I do not trust people who are different.

_____ 21. I dislike interacting with the values and customs of other cultures.

_____ 22. I have little respect for the values and customs of other cultures.

To determine your ethnocentrism score, complete the following four steps:

1. Add your responses to items 4, 7, and 9.
2. Add your responses to items 1, 2, 5, 8, 10, 11, 13, 14, 18, 20, 21, and 22.
3. Subtract the sum from step 1 from 18 (i.e., 18 minus step 1 sum).
4. Add results from step 2 and step 3. This is your generalized ethnocentrism score. Higher scores indicate higher ethnocentrism. Scores more than 55 points are considered high ethnocentrism.

Summary

How has the "changing face" of the United States affected your daily interactions?

- Effective communicators learn how to understand, respect, and adapt to cultural diversity.
- By mid-century, there will be no majority white culture in the United States.
- Culture is a learned set of shared interpretations about beliefs, values, and norms which affect the behaviors of a relatively large group of people.
- Co-cultures exist within the mainstream of society yet remain connected to one another through their cultural heritage.

What are the causes and effects of ethnocentrism, stereotyping, prejudice, discrimination, and racism?

- Ethnocentrism is a belief that your culture is superior to others, whereas stereotypes are generalizations about a group of people that oversimplify their characteristics.
- Stereotypes lead to prejudices, which are positive or negative attitudes about an individual or cultural group based on little or no direct experience.
- Prejudice leads to discrimination, the exclusion of groups of people from opportunities granted to others.
- In the extreme, prejudice and discrimination lead to racism, which justifies dominating and mistreating people of other races with little or no fear of negative consequences.

Why is understanding cultural diversity so important?

- When we view race as a socially constructed concept, it becomes a very neutral and natural human characteristic.
- Members of the white culture in the United States enjoy many race-based privileges, such as high incomes as well as corporate and political leadership positions.
- Many people are not literate about others' religions or about their own religion.

What dimensions of culture affect how well you understand your own culture and how well you communicate with others?

- The individualism/collectivism cultural dimension contrasts independence and personal achievement with interdependence and group values.
- The power distance cultural dimension examines the physical and psychological distance between those with power and those without power.
- The masculine/feminine cultural dimension contrasts an assertive and tough perspective with a more modest and tender perspective, concerned about the quality of life.
- The high/low context cultural dimension focuses on whether meaning is expressed in words or through nonverbal communication and the nature of personal relationships.
- The monochronic/polychronic time cultural dimension contrasts cultures that value time and concentrate on one job at a time and cultures that are not slaves to time and are easily distracted by interruptions.

What communication strategies can help you understand, respect, and adapt to the many "others" you encounter in everyday life?

- Effective communicators are mindful, that is, they are receptive to new information and are responsive to and respectful of other perspectives.
- Communication Accommodation Theory provides principles to help you understand, respect, and successfully adapt to others without stereotyping.
- Find ways to interact and actively engage people who are different than you are.

1 In 2000, 75 percent of the people in the U.S. were white. By 2006, _____ percent were white.
a. 38.8
b. 42.2
c. 56.6
d. 67.7
e. 84.4

2 Jack sincerely believes that most people would be better off if their government and country were more like the United States. Which barrier to understanding others does Jack exemplify?
a. ethnocentrism
b. stereotyping
c. prejudice
d. discrimination
e. racism

3 When the courts examined a supermarket's hiring record, they found that the company never hired non-white applicants for the better-paying job of working cash registers. Which barrier to understanding others does this example exemplify?
a. ethnocentrism
b. stereotyping
c. prejudice
d. discrimination
e. racism

4 When James W. von Brunn fatally shot a black security guard at the U.S. Holocaust Memorial Museum in Washington, D.C., his actions were described as the consequences of _____.
a. ethnocentrism
b. stereotyping
c. prejudice
d. discrimination
e. racism

5 A study in the 1990s found that many college students described African Americans as lazy and loud, and Jews as shrewd and intelligent. Which barrier to understanding others is demonstrated in this study?
a. ethnocentrism
b. stereotyping
c. prejudice
d. discrimination
e. racism

6 At the beginning of the 2008 presidential campaign, some U.S. voters said that they just couldn't vote for an African American as president of the United States. These voters were demonstrating _____.
a. ethnocentrism
b. stereotyping
c. prejudice
d. discrimination
e. racism

7 Which of the following countries exhibits the most individualism?
a. Australia
b. Indonesia
c. Taiwan
d. Peru
e. Pakistan

8 There is a strong correlation between collectivist cultures and cultures in which there is _____.
a. individualism
b. high power distance
c. low power distance
d. high-context communication
e. monochronic time

9 Which behavior is characteristic of a society with feminine values?
a. Men are assertive, tough, and focused on success, whereas women are more modest and tender.
b. Men's and women's gender roles overlap.
c. Women assume most homemaking and child-rearing responsibilities.
d. Men assume most homemaking and child-rearing responsibilities.
e. Women are assertive, tough, and focused on success, whereas men are more modest and tender.

10 Which behavior is characteristic if you are being mindful when communicating with people from other cultures?
a. You pay attention to how you and another person are communicating.
b. You recognize your personal prejudices and try to overcome them.
c. You engage in perception checking and self-talk.
d. You are receptive to new ideas and respect other people's perspectives.
e. You do all of the above.

Answers: 1-c; 2-a; 3-d; 4-e; 5-b; 6-c; 7-a; 8-b; 9-b; 10-e

THINK COMMUNICATION

This article from *Communication Currents* has been slightly edited and shortened with permission from the National Communication Association.

Communication
Knowledge for Communicating Well
Currents

NCA
A Publication of the National Communication Association

Volume 3, Issue 1 - February 2008

Culture and Deception: Moral Transgression or Social Necessity?

Review the differences between individualistic and collectivist cultures in Chapter 3, pp. 53–54.

Lies, dishonesty, trickery, fraud, duplicity, betrayal—these words are often entangled together in the proverbial web of deceit. But does lying receive an unnecessary bad rap? Recent cross-cultural research suggests that deceptive communication can actually serve more functional purposes than our society generally wishes to acknowledge.

People choose to lie for a variety of reasons. Motives for not telling the truth typically fall into two categories: lies to benefit the self and lies to benefit the other. People will often tell lies in pursuit of personal gain, to escape punishment, or to make themselves appear better than their characteristics actually deserve. At other times, people will lie to protect another's image, to avoid hurting the other, or to avoid unwanted relational trauma. It is no secret that lies have indeed spared many a person from unnecessary distress and possible harm.

Cultural identity reflects the values endorsed by a culture. Your cultural identity is the lens through which you think and behave.

While people may have their own motives for avoiding the truth, the pervasive influence of culture is less often recognized as a key factor affecting one's ultimate decision to tell the truth. Results of a recent cross-cultural study conducted by researchers of the University of Hawai'i revealed that a person's motivation to deceive is clearly influenced by his or her cultural self-identity. They also found that one's cultural identity greatly influenced whether or not a message was perceived to be deceptive.

Employing samples from Hong Kong, Hawai'i and mainland U.S., the study revealed that people who strongly valued their own independence and individuality over the social relationships in which they are embedded reported having a lower overall motivation to deceive. By contrast, people who possessed cultural self-identities which emphasize placing group needs over the individual reported having a greater overall motivation to avoid telling the truth.

Remember that the majority of the world's cultures are collectivist in nature.

An interesting twist, however, is that when people were presented with a scenario in which deception would serve to benefit them personally, those who valued their independence were more willing to use deception than in cases where deception would benefit someone else. People who valued social relationships over individuality, however, reported a greater willingness to use deception to benefit others rather than for self-serving purposes.

How does one go about explaining these particular findings? Western as well as European cultures have long been noted to cultivate members who value their individuality and prefer more explicit and direct styles of communicating in order to emphasize their uniqueness. In this case, being a moral and ethical human being would require avoiding any type of communication that would jeopardize one's own personal integrity. Lying is a form of communication that could possibly compromise that integrity.

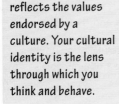

Review the differences between high-context and low-context cultures in Chapter 3, pp. 55–56.

By comparison, East Asian cultures have been well-known for endorsing more indirect styles of communication in order to protect the image of the other and promote trouble-free relationships. In this regard, deceptive communication has and continues to serve as a useful tool in the maintenance and preservation of significant social relationships.

It should not come as a surprise then that when people of varying cultural backgrounds were asked to rate the deceptiveness of different types of deceptive responses, highly independent people rated messages that departed from the truth as highly deceptive, while highly interdependent people viewed the exact same deceptive responses as not deceptive. For example, when asked to comment on a coworker's repulsive style of dress, those high in independent cultural orientation rated the "When is lunch?" evasive response as highly deceptive, whereas those high in interdependent orientation rated the same response as not at all deceptive.

Just as cultures differ in their regard for the value of the individual versus the group, cultural influences are likely to impress upon the meaning of morality. Cultures in which the needs of the group take precedence over the individual tend to regard morality strictly as a social phenomenon that takes into account the needs and expectations of group members. Being a moral human being in the collective sense requires protecting the image and welfare of others in the group. If avoiding the truth will serve to achieve this end, then telling a lie would be the most moral choice. In light of this fact, it is not surprising that those with high regard for social relationships would be more inclined to avoid the truth to escape potential conflict with others.

Costly misunderstandings can arise from an interaction in which the truth was told when a less than true response was expected, or vice versa. A poignant illustration is one in which Americans and Japanese conduct business together. A Japanese businessperson who is highly *interdependent* in cultural orientation, asks his American colleague who is highly *independent* in cultural orientation to comment on his less than average performance on a presentation. The American, being a person of integrity, might respond with an honest "It was really disorganized. What happened?" despite the Japanese colleague's expectation of a more socially acceptable and less face-threatening response. This can potentially lead to strained relations between the two which can, in turn, have detrimental effects on the business.

Alternatively, if the American businessperson were to ask his Japanese colleague to comment on her less than average performance on a presentation, the Japanese counterpart might respond with what she regards as a less face-threatening response: "Well, you tried your best and that's what really counts." However, the American colleague expecting an honest and candid evaluation, now doubts that her Japanese colleague can be trusted to give an honest evaluation. Cross-cultural misunderstandings of this nature are commonplace. Damages to significant social relationships as a result of these misunderstandings can run the gamut from trivial to severe.

In the final analysis, the various motivations for and perceptions that people hold about deception are greatly influenced by dominant cultural values. From greater awareness comes greater cultural sensitivity; from greater sensitivity comes a greater ability to adapt one's communication styles to the other. The result is more effective intercultural interactions and more satisfying intercultural relationships.

What would you think if someone responded this way to you? Would you feel hurt, or would you appreciate the person's honest assessment?

How would you rate this response to the way a person is dressed? Are *deception* and *evasion* the same?

How would you feel if someone responded this way to you? Would you distrust the other person, or would you just assume the person is trying to be nice by not wanting to hurt your feelings?

Name five collectivist cultures that focus more on the needs and expectations of group members than on the needs of individuals.

ABOUT THE AUTHORS

Karadeen Y. Kam is Instructor of Speech at Honolulu Community College. **Min-Sun Kim** and **William F. Sharkey** are Professors in the Department of Speech at the University of Hawaii at Manoa. **Theodore M. Singelis** is Professor in the Department of Psychology at California State University, Chico. This essay is based on Kim, M. S., Kam, K. Y., Sharkey, W. F., & Singelis, T. M. (2008). "Deception: Moral transgression or social necessity? Cultural-relativity of deception motivations and perceptions of deceptive communication." *Journal of International and Intercultural Communication,* 1, 23–50. The *Journal of International and Intercultural Communication* and *Communication Currents* are publications of the National Communication Association.

4 LISTENING AND

Y ou're walking down the street with a friend, when she sees a man she knows. Your friend waves at him and pulls you over to meet him. You extend your hand or smile in an inviting manner while your friend introduces the two of you, saying each of your names clearly. After a couple of minutes, you realize that you cannot recall the other person's name. You don't want to seem dumb by asking for his name again, especially because he's been saying your name several times during the conversation. Two weeks later, you bump into him at a local coffee shop. He greets you by name. You cannot return the honor. Why is it that so many people have difficulty recalling a new acquaintance's name even a few minutes after hearing it—let alone two weeks later?

> **People feel flattered, important, and special when you remember their name.**
>
> —Don Gabor.

In *How to Start a Conversation and Make Friends*, Don Gabor notes that "people feel flattered, important, and special when you remember their name."[1] So why do so many of us forget it? Gabor claims that it is because we're not *listening* effectively. We're too busy thinking about ourselves, what we're going to say, whether we will make a good impression, and how other people will react to us. Add to that the physical distractions around us and it's no wonder we can't remember a person's

CRITICAL THINKING

name. To remedy this problem, he suggests using a five-step strategy: (1) Focus on the moment of introduction; (2) don't think about what to say—listen for the name; (3) repeat the name aloud when you hear it; (4) think of someone you know or someone famous with the same name; and (5) use the name during and at the end of the conversation.[2]

Remembering someone's name—as well as the many more complex messages you hear every day—requires two communication skills: effective listening *and* critical thinking. These skills are two sides of a single coin, twin competencies that rely on and reflect one another. After all, if no one listens to you, why communicate? And if you have not given serious thought to your message, why *should* anyone listen?

THE NATURE OF listening

the International Listening Association defines **listening** as "the process of receiving, constructing meaning from, and responding to a spoken and/or nonverbal message."[3] This definition describes what effective listeners *do*; however, it does not explain *how* the listening process works. Listening—just like speaking, reading, and writing—is a complex process that goes beyond "you speak, I listen." Because many people do not appreciate this complexity, listening may appear to be easy and natural. In fact, just the opposite is true. Although most of us can *hear*, we often fail to *listen* to what others say. Hearing only requires physical ability; listening requires complex thinking ability.

Listening is our number-one communication activity. A study of college students found that listening occupies more than half of their communicating time.[4] Although percentages vary from study to study, Figure 4.1 shows how most of us divide up our daily communicating time.

In the business world, many executives devote more than 60 percent of their workdays to listening to others.[5] Listening is often cited as the communication skill most lacking in new employees.[6] A study of hundreds of businesses by researchers at Loyola University in Chicago concludes that listening is a manager's most important skill.[7] In his book, *In Search of Excellence*, Tom Peters claims, "Excellent companies are not only better at service, quality, and reliability . . . they are also better listeners."[8]

How Well Do You Listen?

We often take listening for granted and think we're better listeners than we really are.[9] For instance, immediately after listening to a short talk, most of us cannot accurately report 50 percent of what was said. Without training, we listen at about 25 percent efficiency.[10] And, of that 25 percent, most of what we remember is distorted or inaccurate.[11]

A study of Fortune 500 company training managers concludes that "ineffective listening leads to ineffective performance or low productivity." These same problems also appear in studies of sales professionals, educators, health practitioners, lawyers, and religious leaders.[12] Similarly, poor listening by the person who cuts your hair can result in a month of "bad hair days."

Effective listening is hard work. Researchers note that active listeners register an increase in blood pressure, a higher pulse rate, and even more perspiration.[13] Active listeners try to understand what a speaker is saying, the emotions behind the content, and the conclusion the speaker is making without stating it openly.[14] Effective listening also requires the kind of preparation and concentration required of attorneys trying a case and psychologists counseling a client. Effective listening can be an exhausting experience, but willingness to work at it will make you a better listener.

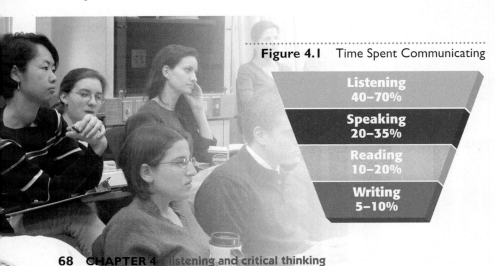

Figure 4.1   Time Spent Communicating

Listening
40–70%

Speaking
20–35%

Reading
10–20%

Writing
5–10%

Listening The process of receiving, constructing meaning from, and responding to a spoken and/or nonverbal message

Listening and Working Memory

Early listening research focused on **short-term memory**, the content you remember immediately after listening to a series of numbers, words, sentences, or paragraphs. Psychologist Samuel Wood and colleagues note that "short-term memory has a very limited capacity—about seven (plus or minus two) different items or bits of information at one time. This is just enough for phone numbers and ordinary zip codes."[15] We use something much more complex than short-term memory to engage in effective listening.

Working Memory Theory recognizes that listening involves more than the ability to tap your short-term memory. Effective listening engages your **working memory**, which is "the memory subsystem we use when we try to understand information, remember it, or use it to solve a problem or communicate with someone."[16] Listening researcher Laura Janusik describes working memory as "a dual-task system involving processing and storage functions. The processing function is synonymous with attention, and the storage function is synonymous with memory. Attention is allocated, and resources not used for attention are available for storage."[17] Your working memory does more than store what you've heard; it allows you to shift what you've heard and understood "from and into long-term memory" as a way to create new meanings.[18]

Communicators with a greater working memory capacity can better understand what other people mean, can analyze complex issues and discussion threads as they de-velop, are able to track relevant and irrelevant interactions, and are skilled at developing appropriate responses. Engaging your working memory is a complex process in which you must both listen and be able to respond, on the spot, to ideas and views you haven't anticipated.

Short-term memory The limited capacity to remember content immediately after listening to a series of numbers, words, sentences, or paragraphs

Working Memory Theory Explains the dual-task system of working memory (rather than short-term memory) that involves information processing and storage functions as well as creating new meanings

Working memory The memory subsystem you use when trying to understand information, remember it, or use it to solve a problem or communicate with someone; working memory allows you to shift message content from and into long-term memory

Types of Listening

Different situations require different types of listening. For example, if you are listening to a political debate, you may engage analytical listening skills. However, if you are watching a funny movie, you put aside analytical listening to enjoy the entertainment. It is not surprising that there are several types of listening, each of which calls upon a combination of unique listening skills.[19]

Discriminative Listening Discriminative listening is the ability to accurately distinguish auditory and/or visual stimuli. It also describes the amount of attention you give to nonverbal stimuli such as a smile, a groan, or the shrug of a shoulder. Thus, if you do not listen discriminatively, you may miss the vocal cues that distinguish a particular word and its meaning. If you are distracted or there is competing noise in a room, you may not hear the differences between similar

Discriminative listening The ability to accurately distinguish auditory and/or visual stimuli

TYPES OF LISTENING

	Definition	Listening Question
Discriminative listening	The physical ability to accurately distinguish auditory and/or visual stimuli	Do I hear and see accurately?
Comprehensive listening	The ability to accurately understand the meaning of another person's spoken and nonverbal messages	What does the speaker mean?
Empathic listening	The ability to understand and identify with a person's situation or feelings	How does the speaker feel?
Analytical listening	The ability to evaluate another person's message objectively	What is my opinion of this message?
Appreciative listening	The ability to take pleasure in *how* someone thinks, performs, and speaks	Do I like, value, or enjoy what I am hearing?

words (Did she say she *hit* the ball or *hid* the ball?) or the vocal inflection that changes the meaning of a word (When he said he'd *love* to do it, was he serious or sarcastic?). Furthermore, if you cannot hear the difference between an on-key or off-key note, you may not be able to listen *appreciatively* to a singer. If you cannot hear or recognize the distress in a person's voice, you may not be able to listen *empathically*.

Comprehensive Listening You use **comprehensive listening** to understand the meaning of spoken and nonverbal messages, as when someone presents a report at a meeting, describes the advantages of buying a new car, or speaks on behalf of a public interest group at a hearing.

If you don't understand someone's meaning, you can't be expected to respond appropriately. To make sure you comprehend what's being said, use the following strategies:[20]

- *Have a questioning plan.* Make sure you know what you want to accomplish by listening as well as the questions you need answered.
- *Keep the questions simple.* Ask one question at a time and make sure it's applicable.

- *Ask nonthreatening questions.* Avoid highly evaluative questions such as those that begin with "Why didn't you . . . ?" or "How could you . . . ?" Judgmental questions can alienate the other person, as well as anyone who overhears the question.
- *Ask permission.* If a topic is sensitive, explain why you are asking the question and ask permission before continuing. "You say you're worried about Tom's recent behavior. Would you mind telling me . . ."

- *Avoid manipulative questions.* Tricking someone into giving you the answer you want can destroy trust. There's a big difference between "What speed was the car going

Comprehensive listening The ability to accurately understand the meaning of spoken and nonverbal messages
Golden listening rule Listen to others as you would have them listen to you

ethicalcommunication

Apply the Golden Listening Rule

The **golden listening rule** is easy to remember: *Listen to others as you would have them listen to you.* Unfortunately, this rule can be difficult to follow. It asks you to suspend your own needs and opinions to listen to someone else's.[21]

The golden listening rule is not so much a "rule" as it is an ethical listening practice. It reflects a principle in the National Communication Association's Ethics Credo: "We strive to understand and respect other communicators before evaluating and responding to their message."[22] When you follow the golden listening rule, you communicate your interest, patience, and open-mindedness.

when you drove past the school?" and "How fast was the car going when you sped past the school?"

- *Wait for the answer.* After you ask a good question, give the other person time to think and then wait for the answer.

Empathic Listening Even if you understand every word a person says, you can miss the anger, enthusiasm, or frustration in a speaker's voice if you do not listen for feelings. **Empathic listening** asks you to understand and identify with another persons feelings or experiences without judging whether the message is good or bad, right or wrong.[23] Empathic listeners' facial expressions often reflect the other person's emotions. You may smile and nod or show concern and sadness to communicate emotional support and interest. In *The Lost Art of Listening*, Michael Nichols notes, "When we're with someone who's . . . a good listener, we perk up and come alive. . . . [Listening] involves learning how to suspend our own emotional agenda and then realizing the rewards of genuine empathy."[24]

Moreover, if you listen with genuine empathy, you will listen more effectively and retain more information.

> **"[Listening] involves learning how to suspend our own emotional agenda and then realizing the rewards of genuine empathy."**
> —MICHAEL NICHOLS

Analytical Listening When you engage in **analytical listening**, you make judgments based on your evaluation of another person's message. Is the speaker right or wrong, logical or illogical? Should I accept or reject the speaker's ideas and suggestions? Analytical listeners are open-minded. They put aside any biases or prejudices about the speaker or message when they analyze what they hear in order to arrive at a rational conclusion or decision.

Appreciative Listening **Appreciative listening** describes someone who listens in order to enjoy and value another person's ability to use humor, tell stories, argue persuasively, demonstrate understanding, or even sing a song. When someone's words, stories, or sense of humor delight us, we listen appreciatively. Appreciative listening is very personal. While listening to a singer, you and a friend may use discriminative listening and recognize that the singer hit a couple of wrong notes. As appreciative listeners, however, one of you may think the melody is lovely, while the other thinks it's dull.

Empathic listening The ability to understand and identify with another person's feelings or experiences
Analytical listening The ability to evaluate another person's message objectively
Appreciative listening The ability to value and enjoy another person's message

---

Personal Listening Styles

communication in ACTION

Effective listeners know how and when to use discriminative, comprehensive, empathic, analytical, and appreciative listening. Effective listeners also understand that most of us have a preferred listening style. Identifying your own listening style as well as the listening styles of others makes a big difference in how well you communicate.[25] As you read the descriptions of these four listening style preferences, ask yourself whether you recognize the way you listen to others as well as the ways in which other people listen to you.

Listening Style	Positive Listening Characteristics	Negative Listening Characteristics
Action-oriented	Focus on what will be done, what actions will happen, when and who will do them. Interested in results, objectives, and performance; appreciate clear, structured messages.	Impatient; critical of people who don't reach a conclusion or propose an action. More concerned with control than the well-being of others.
Time-oriented	Focus on the clock. Time and listening are organized into neat segments. Interested in short answers.	Annoying to action-, people-, and content-oriented listeners; tend to be impulsive decision-makers because they don't take enough time to think.
People-oriented	Focus on feelings, emotions, and showing concern for others; responds with "we" statements. Interested in understanding others rather than criticizing them.	Blind to faults in others; may be perceived as meddling. Generally not as skilled at assessing the strength of an argument or the credibility of an expert.
Content-oriented	Focus on what is being said rather than who is saying it; not very concerned about feelings. Interested in facts, evidence, logic, and complex ideas.	Tend to ignore the ideas and needs of others; reject information because it does not meet their tests for evidence and truth.

listening
strategies
AND SKILLS

at this point, you should know *why* good listening is essential for effective and ethical communication and *want* to listen. Now it's time to learn *how*. In this section, we present a group of listening strategies and skills that can improve your listening ability and help you develop effective listening habits. When and how you use these strategies depends, in part, on whether you are the speaker or the listener (or both) and whether you are speaking to one person or a large group of people.

Use Your Extra Thought Speed

Most people talk at about 125 to 150 words per minute. But most of us can *think* at three to four times that rate.[26] Thus, we have about 400 extra words of spare thinking time during every minute a person talks to us.

Thought speed is the speed (words per minute) at which most people can think compared with the speed at which they can speak. Poor listeners use their extra thought speed to daydream, engage in side conversations, take unnecessary notes, or plan how to confront a speaker. Conscientious listeners use their extra thought speed to enhance comprehensive, empathic, and analytical listening.

Listen to Feedback

One of the most important and challenging communication skills is listening to and providing appropriate feedback to others during a conversation, meeting, or presentation. Feedback, the verbal and nonverbal responses others communicate as they listen, tells you how your listeners react—negatively or positively—to you and your message.

How to Use Your
THOUGHT SPEED

- Identify and summarize key ideas and opinions
- Pay extra attention to the meaning of nonverbal behavior
- Analyze the strengths and weaknesses of arguments
- Assess the relevance of a speaker's message

All listeners react in some way. They may smile or frown, or nod "yes" or "no." They may break into spontaneous applause or not applaud at all. They may sit forward at full attention or sit back and look bored. Analyzing your listeners' feedback helps determine how you and your message affect others. As you speak, look and listen to the ways in which people react to you. Do they look interested or uninterested, pleased or displeased? If you can't see or hear reactions, ask for feedback. You can stop in the middle of a conversation, meeting, or presentation to ask whether others understand you. This feedback helps you adapt to your listeners and tells your listeners that you are interested in their reactions. It also helps others focus their attention and listen more effectively to your message.

Listen to Nonverbal Behavior

Very often, another person's meaning is expressed through nonverbal behavior (see Chapter 6). For example, a change in vocal tone or volume may be another way of saying, "Listen up! This is very important." A person's sustained eye contact may mean, "I'm talking to you!" Facial expressions can reveal whether a person is experiencing joy, skepticism, or fear. Research indicates that next to the words you say, your face is the primary source of information about you and the meaning of your message.[27]

Even gestures express emotions that words cannot convey. For example, at the moment during a trial when an attorney makes his final argument to the jury that his client should be acquitted, one juror, almost imperceptibly, moves her head back and forth, signifying "no." When the attorney states that his client had no idea that a crime had been committed, another juror raises one eyebrow with a look that says,

> ... next to the words you say, your face is the primary source of information about you and the meaning of your message.

"Okay, you've done your best to defend your client, but you and I know he's guilty as sin." In the end, the jury finds the defendant guilty as charged.

Thought speed The speed (words per minute) at which most people can think compared to the speed at which they can speak

If the participants in Sacha Baron Cohen's mockumentary *Borat* had been better listeners and critical thinkers, fewer would have been fooled and embarrassed.

Listen Before You Leap

Ralph Nichols, often called the "father of listening research," counsels listeners to make sure they understand a speaker's message *before* reacting, either positively or negatively. This strategy requires taking time to bring your emotions under control. You may comprehend a speaker perfectly, but be infuriated or offended by what you hear. If an insensitive speaker refers to women in the room as "chicks" or a minority group as "you people," you may need to count to 20 to collect your thoughts and refocus your attention on comprehensive listening. If a speaker tells an offensive joke, you may react with both anger at the speaker and disappointment with those who laughed. Try to understand the effects of offensive comments and emotion-laden words without losing your composure or concentration. According to Nichols, "We must always withhold evaluation until our comprehension is complete."[28]

> ## "We must always withhold evaluation until our comprehension is complete."
> —Ralph Nichols

When you listen before you leap, you are using your extra thought speed to decide how to react to controversial, prejudiced, or offensive comments. Listening before you leap gives you time to adjust your reaction and therefore to clarify and correct a statement rather than offend, disrupt, or infuriate others.

Minimize Distractions

Have you ever attended a lecture where the room was too hot, the seats were uncomfortable, or people in the hallway were talking loudly? Distractions such as loud and annoying noises, poor seating arrangements, foul odors, frequent interruptions, and unattractive décor can make listening very difficult.[29] Other forms of distraction include a speaker's delivery that is too soft, fast, slow, or

Know Thy Self

Do You Have Irritating Listening Habits?

Speaking to an impatient, rude, or irritating listener is frustrating and discouraging. Consider the following list of irritating listening habits and ask yourself, "Have I ever talked to someone who listened to me this way?" Then add a few more irritating listening habits to the list.[30]

1. Interrupting you while you're speaking.
2. Not looking at you when you're speaking.
3. Showing interest in something else.
4. Finishing your thoughts for you.
5. Not responding to requests you make.
6. Saying, "Yes, but" when you state a fact or opinion.
7. Topping your story with one of theirs.
8. Asking too many questions while and after you speak.
9. *Another irritating listening habit:* _____
10. *Another irritating listening habit:* _____

monotone; an accent that is unfamiliar; or mannerisms and appearance that appear unusual or unconventional.

You can help people listen better by taking action to overcome distractions. For example, when a distraction is physical, you are well within your rights as a listener or speaker to shut a door, open a window, or turn on more lights. In large groups, you may need to ask permission to improve the group's surroundings. Depending on the circumstances and setting, you can also take direct action to reduce behavioral distractions. If someone is talking or fidgeting while the speaker is addressing the audience, ask that person to stop. After all, if someone is distracting you, he or she is probably distracting others. If someone is speaking too quietly, kindly ask the presenter to speak more loudly.

Paraphrase

Paraphrasing (also called *reflective listening*) is the ability to restate what people say in a way that indicates you understand them. When you paraphrase, you go beyond the words you hear to understand the feelings and underlying meanings that accompany the words. Too often, we jump to conclusions and incorrectly assume we know what a speaker means and feels. Paraphrasing is a listening check that asks, "Am I right? Is this what you mean?" It requires finding *new* words to describe what you hear, rather than repeating what a person says. In addition to rephrasing another person's message, a paraphrase usually includes a request for confirmation.

Effective paraphrasing requires *mindful* listening. Paraphrasing says, "I want to hear what you have to say, and I want to understand what you mean." If you paraphrase accurately, the other person will appreciate your understanding and support. And if you don't quite get the paraphrase right, your feedback provides another opportunity for the speaker to explain.[32]

FUNCTIONS OF PARAPHRASING

- To ensure comprehension before evaluation
- To reassure others that you want to understand them
- To clear up confusion and ask for clarification
- To summarize lengthy comments
- To help others uncover thoughts and feelings
- To provide a safe and supportive communication climate
- To help others reach their own conclusions[31]

Effective paraphrasing requires *mindful* listening. Paraphrasing says, "I want to hear what you have to say, and I want to understand what you mean."

Paraphrasing Restating what people say in a way that indicates you understand them

STOP & THINK   Paraphrase This

Read the following three statements and write a response that paraphrases their meaning, as demonstrated in the following example:

Group member: "I get really annoyed when André yells at one of us during our meetings."

Paraphrase: *"You sound as though you become very upset with André when he shouts at you or other group members. Is that what's bothering you?"*

1. **Friend:** I have the worst luck with computers. Every single one I've ever owned had problems. Just when the warranty runs out, something goes wrong. The computer I have now has crashed twice, and I lost all of my documents. Maybe I'm doing something wrong. Why me? I must be cursed or something.

   Paraphrase: _____

2. **Colleague:** I dislike saying *no* to anyone who asks for help, but then I have to rush or stay up late to get my own work done. I want to help, but I also want to do my own job—and do it well.

   Paraphrase: _____

3. **Classmate:** How on earth am I going to get an A on this exam if I can't even find time to read the textbook?

   Paraphrase: _____

SPECIAL listening challenges

effective listening requires more than learning a set of skills. You also must learn how to adapt to a variety of special listening challenges, such as understanding the effects of gender and culture on listening, learning how to "take notes" effectively, and listening accurately to your self.

Gender and Cultural Differences

Adapting to the diverse listening skills, types, and levels of others can be a challenging task, particularly when gender and cultural differ-ences are taken into account. Keep in mind that there are many excep-tions to the research summaries we present about listening differences. As you read, you may say, "But I know women who don't listen this way." The existence of exceptions does not mean the general claim is false. Diversity research provides useful insights that help explain common differences in listening behavior.

Gender Differences The listening behaviors of women and men often differ. In general, men are more likely to listen to the content of what is said, whereas women focus on the relationship between the speaker and listener. Males tend to hear the facts, whereas females are more aware of the mood of the communication. In other words, men generally focus on compre-hensive and analytical listening, whereas women are more likely to be empathic and appreciative listeners.

Cultural Differences In Chapter 3, Adapting to Others, we introduced the concept of high- and low-context cultures. In high-context countries such as Japan, China, and Korea, and in African American, Native American, and Arab cultures, very little meaning is expressed

---

How Men and Women Listen to Each Other

communication in ACTION

Many women complain that their male partners and colleagues don't listen to them. Interestingly, men sometimes make the same complaint about women. Linguist Deborah Tannen ex-plains that the accusation "You're not listening" often means, "You don't un-derstand what I said" or "I'm not get-ting the response I want."[33]

Tannen offers an explanation for why it may *seem* that men don't listen. Quite simply, many men don't *show* they are listening, whereas women do. In gen-eral, women provide more feedback when listening: They provide listening responses, like *mhm*, *uh-huh*, and *yeah*. And women respond more positively and enthusiastically by nodding and laughing. To a man (who expects a lis-tener to be quiet and attentive), a woman giving off a stream of feedback and support will seem to be "talking" too much for a listener. To a woman

(who expects a listener to be active and show interest, attention, and sup-port), a man who listens silently will seem to have checked out of the con-versation. The bottom line is this: Women may get the impression that men don't listen when, in fact, they are listening. Unfortunately, there are men who really don't want to listen because they be-lieve it puts them in a subordinate position to women.[34]

Researchers also note that men often tune out things they can't solve, or wonder why they should even listen if there isn't a problem to solve. Women may become more in-volved and connected to the speaker and see lis-tening as something im-portant to do for the other person.[35] Although men use talk to establish sta-tus, women are more likely to use lis-tening to empower others. Unfortu-nately, people who listen much more than they talk are often viewed as sub-ordinate and subservient, rather than powerful.[36]

through words. Much more attention is given to nonverbal cues as well as the relationships among the communicators. As a result, listeners from high-context cultures "listen" for meanings in your behavior and in who you are, rather than the words you say. However, most listeners from Germany, Switzerland, Scandinavia, and the United States focus on words. They expect speakers to be direct. When high-context speakers talk to low-context listeners—and vice versa—misunderstanding, offense, and even conflict may result. In many Asian cultures, the amount of time spent talking and the value placed on talking are very different than they are in the United States, Latin America, and the Middle East. As the Buddhist expression says, "There is a truth the words cannot reach."

Taking Notes

Given that most of us only listen at 25 percent efficiency, why not take notes and write down important facts and big ideas? Research has found that notetakers recall messages in more detail than non-notetakers.[37] Taking notes makes a great deal of sense, but only if it is done skillfully.

If you are like most listeners, only one-fourth of what is said may end up in your notes. Even if you copy every word you hear, your notes will not include the nonverbal cues that often tell you more about what a person means and feels. And if you spend all your time taking notes, when will you put aside your pen and ask or answer an important question?

Ralph Nichols summarizes the dilemma of balancing notetaking and listening when he concludes that "there is some evidence to indicate that the volume of notes taken and their value to the taker are inversely related."[38] This does not mean you should stop taking notes, but you should learn how to take *useful* notes—the key to which is adaptability.

Effective listeners adjust their notetaking to the content, style, and organizational pattern of a speaker. So, if someone tells stories to make a point, jot down a brief reminder of the story and its point. If someone provides a list of tips, dos and don'ts, or recommendations, include those lists in your notes. If someone asks and answers a series of questions, your notes should reflect that pattern. If someone discusses a new concept or complex idea, try to paraphrase the meaning in your notes or jot down questions you want to ask. Good listeners are flexible and adaptable notetakers.

Listening to Your Self

As important as it is to listen to others, it is just as important to listen to yourself. Poor self-listening is often the cause of communication breakdowns. Rebecca Shafir, author of *The Zen of Listening* notes, "If we could hear our words through the ears of our listeners, we would be appalled at the overgeneralizations, the inaccuracies, and the insensitive, negative comments we make about ourselves and others."[39] Three self-listening questions can help you become more aware of your internal thought processes: (1) Have I listened appropriately and well? (2) What are the likely consequences of saying what I *want* to say? and (3) What *should* I say to ensure that I am understood?

communication&culture

THE ART OF HIGH-CONTEXT LISTENING

High-context communicators listen beyond a person's words to interpret meaning by paying close attention to nonverbal cues. Interestingly, the Chinese symbol for "to listen" includes characters for eyes, ears, and heart.

For the Chinese, "it is impossible to listen . . . without using the eyes because you need to look for nonverbal communication." The Chinese also listen with their ears because they speak a tonal language in which intonation determines meaning. They claim that "you listen with your heart because . . . [you must sense the] emotional undertones expressed by the speaker." In Korean, the word *nunchi* means that you communicate through your eyes. "Koreans believe that the environment supplies most of the information that we seek, so there is little need to speak."[40]

Chinese symbol for listening

CRITICAL
thinking

When you listen effectively, you do much more than hear and recognize the words in a message. Regardless of whether you are listening comprehensively, analytically, empathically, or appreciatively, you should always think critically about what you hear. **Critical thinking** is the thought process you use to analyze what you read, see, or hear to arrive at a justified conclusion or decision. It is a conscious process that, when effective, can result in a conclusion, decision, opinion, or behavior.[41] It can also result in a more meaningful conversation, group discussion, or presentation. Good critical thinkers know how to develop and defend a position on an issue, ask probing questions, be open-minded, and draw reasonable conclusions.[42] Critical thinking puts your mind to work on complex communication problems—from applying for a job promotion to solving a family crisis, from making an effective classroom presentation to critiquing a politician's campaign commercial. The best and brightest communicators also tend to be excellent critical thinkers.[43]

The rest of this chapter focuses on critical thinking strategies and skills to help you analyze the claims, facts, inferences, arguments, and thinking errors you encounter every day.

Think Critically About Claims

A **claim** is a statement that identifies your belief or position on a particular issue or topic. For example, claims answer the question: What am I trying to explain or prove? There are several types of claims, as shown below. You might claim that something is true or false, probable or improbable, good or bad, or reasonable or unreasonable.

> **Critical thinking** The process you use to analyze what you read, see, or hear to arrive at a justified conclusion or decision
> **Claim** A statement that identifies your belief or position on a particular issue or topic

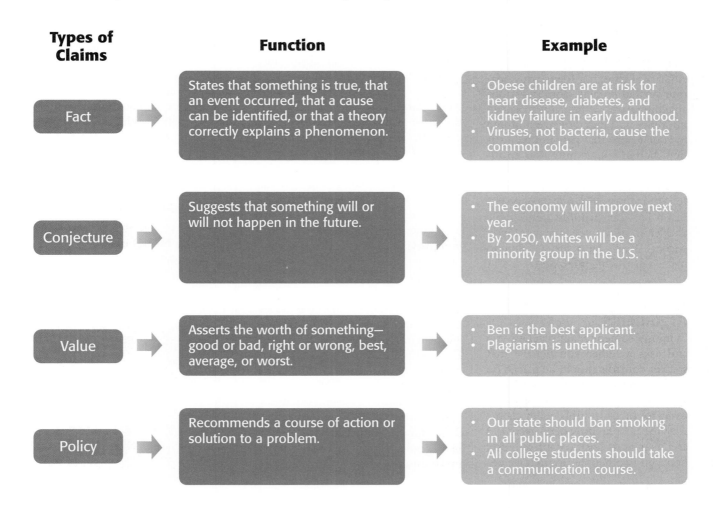

Types of Claims	Function	Example
Fact	States that something is true, that an event occurred, that a cause can be identified, or that a theory correctly explains a phenomenon.	• Obese children are at risk for heart disease, diabetes, and kidney failure in early adulthood. • Viruses, not bacteria, cause the common cold.
Conjecture	Suggests that something will or will not happen in the future.	• The economy will improve next year. • By 2050, whites will be a minority group in the U.S.
Value	Asserts the worth of something—good or bad, right or wrong, best, average, or worst.	• Ben is the best applicant. • Plagiarism is unethical.
Policy	Recommends a course of action or solution to a problem.	• Our state should ban smoking in all public places. • All college students should take a communication course.

Critical thinking puts your mind to work on complex communication problems.... The best and brightest communicators also tend to be excellent critical thinkers.

Think Critically About Facts and Inference

In addition to understanding the different types of claims, critical thinkers know how to separate claims of fact (a statement that can be proved true or false) from inferences. An **inference** is a conclusion based on claims of fact. For example, "Julia has been late to the last three project meetings" is a claim of fact. You can document the truth of this statement. However, the statement "Julia does not care about our team's project" is an inference.

Critical thinking helps you separate verifiable facts from questionable inferences. When you accept an inference as a fact, you are jumping to conclusions that may not be justified. When you assume that an inference is true, you may be led down a path that leads to a poor decision. Julia's tardiness might instead be the result of car trouble, unreliable childcare, or the needs of an elderly parent. More facts are needed to make a justifiable inference.

Think Critically About Arguments

Suppose someone approaches you and asks whether you believe that stricter controls should be placed on the sale and possession of handguns. Do you know how to argue effectively for or against this policy claim?

Some people think of an *argument* as a dispute or hostile confrontation between two people. Rather, we de-fine an **argument** as a claim supported by evidence for or against a claim. For example, "The Latino/Latina Heritage Club should be given more funds next year" is simply a claim of policy because no reasons for this pronouncement are provided. To turn this claim into an argument, we would say, "The Latino/Latina Heritage Club should be given more funds next year because it has doubled in size; without an increase in funding, it cannot provide its members the same number or quality of programs."

To help understand the structure of an argument, we turn to the **Toulmin Model of an Argument**, which was developed by Stephen Toulmin, a British philosopher. This framework for developing and analyzing arguments includes the following six components: data, claim, warrant, backing, reservation, and qualifier.[44]

Data, Claim, and Warrant The data, claim, and warrant make up the three primary elements of an argument. The first component, the claim, is simply a conclusion or a position you advocate. For example, the statement "My group will do well on our class project" is a claim of conjecture. **Data**, the second component, constitute the evidence you provide to support your claim: "During the first meeting, all group members said they would work hard on the project."

The third component of the model is the **warrant**, which explains how and why the data support the claim. For example, "In the past, when everyone in the group worked hard together, our projects always turned out successfully." A warrant can mean "justification for an action or belief" as in, "Given that plastic bags cannot biodegrade, using recyclable bags makes more sense." Thus, a warrant justifies your claim based on evidence. It authorizes or confirms the validity of a conclusion and gives you the right to make your claim.

In their book *The Well-Crafted Argument*, Fred White and Simone Billings write that "Compelling warrants are just as vital to the force of an argument as are compelling data" because they reinforce validity and trustworthiness of both the data and claim.[45] Here's an example of an unwarranted argument:

> Girlfriend to boyfriend: You only saw me walking to my car with your friend Joe and jumped to the conclusion that we were seeing each other behind your back. That's ridiculous and totally unfair!

In this argument, the evidence (she is walking to her car with Joe) is insufficient to make the claim (she's seeing Joe without her boy-friend's knowledge), because the warrant is unreasonable (if a woman is seen talking to a man, she must be romantically or sexually interested in him).[46]

Backing, Reservation, and Qualifier In addition to the three *primary* elements of an argument, there are three other components of the Toulmin Model: backing, reservation,

---

Inference A conclusion based on claims of fact
Argument A claim supported by evidence or reasons for accepting it
Toulmin Model of an Argument Stephen Toulmin's framework for developing and analyzing arguments that includes the following components: claim, data, warrant, backing, reservation, and qualifier
Data The component of the Toulmin Model that provides evidence to support a claim
Warrant A component of the Toulmin Model that explains how and why the evidence supports a claim

Know Thy Self

Can You Tell a Fact from an Inference?[47]

Read the story carefully and assume that all the information presented is accurate and true, while understanding that the story has ambiguous parts purposely designed to lead you astray. Next, read the statements about the story and for each, select one of the following options:

T: The statement is definitely true on the basis of the information presented.

F: The statement is definitely false.

?: The statement may be true or false, but it is unclear from the information available.

Answer each statement in order, and do not go back to change previous answers. Once you have completed and scored the quiz, take time to analyze the answers you selected and why.

STORY: A businessman had just turned off the lights in the store when a man appeared and demanded money. The owner opened the cash register. The contents of the cash register were scooped up and the man sped away. A member of the police force was notified promptly.

Statements about the Story:

T	F	?	1. A man appeared after the owner had turned off his store lights.
T	F	?	2. The robber was a man.
T	F	?	3. The man who appeared did not demand money.
T	F	?	4. The man who opened the cash register was the owner.
T	F	?	5. The store owner scooped up the contents of the cash register and ran away.
T	F	?	6. Someone opened the cash register.
T	F	?	7. After the man who demanded the money scooped up the contents of the cash register, he ran away.
T	F	?	8. While the cash register contained money, the story does not state how much.
T	F	?	9. The robber demanded money of the owner.
T	F	?	10. A businessperson turned off the lights when a man appeared in the store.
T	F	?	11. It was broad daylight when the man appeared.
T	F	?	12. The man who appeared opened the cash register.
T	F	?	13. No one demanded money.
T	F	?	14. The story concerns a series of events in which only three persons are referred to: the owner of the store, a man who demanded money, and a member of the police force.
T	F	?	15. The following events occurred: someone demanded money, a cash register was opened, its contents were scooped up, and a man dashed out of the store.

Answers: (1) ?, (2) ?, (3) F, (4) ?, (5) ?, (6) T, (7) ?, (8) ?, (9) ?, (10) ?, (11) ?, (12) ?, (13) F, (14) ?, (15) ?.

and qualifier. **Backing** provides support for the argument's warrant, as in "The group that worked hardest last time received the best grade." However, not all claims are true all the time. The **reservation** recognizes exceptions to an argument or concedes that a claim may not be true under certain circumstances: "Even though group members say they will work hard, the group won't do well if members miss meetings or make mistakes." The final component is the **qualifier**, which states the degree to which a claim appears to be true. Qualifiers are usually words or phrases such as *likely*, *possibly*, *certainly*, *unlikely*, or *probably*. A claim with a qualifier might state, "Our group will probably do well on the class project."

Applying the Toulmin Model of Argument

Toulmin's model depicts a complete argument. In everyday communication, however, we rarely express all six components. We're more likely to say, "I'm sure we'll get an A on this project because we're all working so hard." This claim and evidence, however, has built-in assumptions about the warrant, backing, reservations, and qualifier.

In some situations, your arguments will be more powerful and persuasive if you include all six components. In other cases, you may need nothing more than a claim to secure agreement. Yet, even if you don't express every component, the Toulmin Model provides a way to diagram and evaluate arguments. Understanding the model lets you know what critical-thinking questions to ask.

- *Claim.* What type of claim is being made?
- *Data.* What data supports this claim?
- *Warrant.* How does the data lead to the claim?
- *Backing.* How strong and valid are the warrant and evidence?
- *Reservation.* Under what circumstances might the claim not be warranted or true?
- *Qualifier.* With how much certainty can the claim be made (e.g., *possibly*, *unlikely*, *probably*)?

If you encounter an unsupported claim, ask for supporting evidence or data. If the warrant is questionable, ask for backing. If a situation alters the certainty of a claim, suggest a more reasonable position. When developing your own arguments, the Toulmin Model can help you test the strength of your ideas. Thinking critically about someone else's argument helps you decide whether to accept an idea, reject it, or ask for more information.

Backing The component of the Toulmin model that provides support for an argument's warrant

Reservation The component of the Toulmin model that recognizes exceptions to an argument or concedes that a claim may not be true under certain circumstances

Qualifier The component of the Toulmin model that states the degree to which a claim appears to be true, e.g. *likely, possibly, certainly, unlikely,* or *probably*

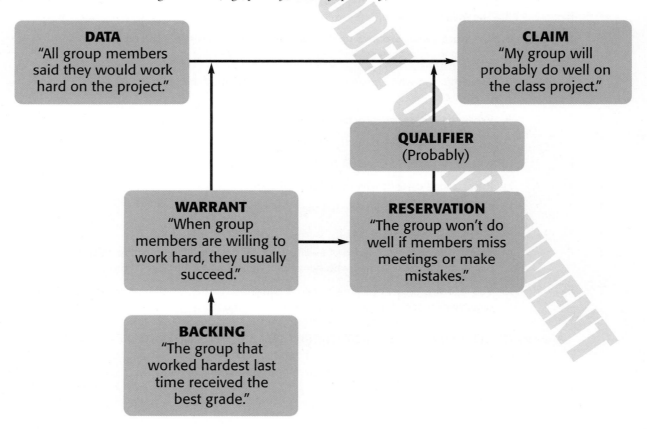

fallacies of ARGUMENT

if you listen effectively and think critically about the content of conversations and quarrels, group discussions and meetings, speeches and presentations, media reports and books, you will encounter valid and invalid claims. One way to recognize invalid arguments is to look for fallacies. A **fallacy** is an error in thinking that has the potential to mislead or deceive others. Fallacies can be intentional or unintentional. However, when an unethical communicator misuses evidence or reasoning, or when a well-meaning person misinterprets evidence or draws erroneous conclusions, the result is still the same—inaccuracy and deception.

After you've learned to identify a variety of fallacies, don't be surprised if you begin noticing them everywhere—in television commercials, in political campaigns, on talk radio, and in everyday conversations. What, for example, is fallacious about advertisers' claims that "No other aspirin is more effective for pain than ours" and "Buy America's best-selling pickup truck"? Are fallacies involved when a political candidate talks about an opponent's past as an antiwar protester or drunk driver?

Attacking the Person

The fallacy of **attacking the person** also has a Latin name—*ad hominem*—which means "against the man." An *ad hominem* argument makes irrelevant attacks against a person rather than against the content of a person's message. Responding to the claim "Property taxes should be increased" with "What would you know? You don't own a home!" attacks the person rather than the argument. Name-calling, labeling, and attacking a person rather than the substance of an argument are unethical, *ad hominem*

fallacies. Political campaign ads are notorious for attacking candidates in personal ways rather than addressing important public issues.

Appeal to Authority

Expert opinion is often used to support arguments. However, when the supposed expert has no relevant experience on the issues being discussed, the fallacy of **appeal to authority** occurs. For example, "I'm not a doctor, but I play one on TV, and I recommend that you use Nick's Cough Syrup." Unless the actor has expert credentials on medical issues, the argument is fallacious. You often see television and magazine advertisements in which celebrities praise the medicines they use, the companies that insure them, the financial institutions that manage their money, and the beauty products that make them look young and attractive.

Because Oprah Winfrey is viewed as an authority, the titles she's chosen for her Book Club have turned obscure authors into popular ones.

Appeal to Popularity

An **appeal to popularity** claims that an action is acceptable or excusable because many people are doing it. "Most of your neighbors have agreed

to support the rezoning proposal" is an appeal to popularity. Just because a lot of people hold a particular belief or engage in an action does not make it right. If most of your friends overindulge on alcohol, should you? If lots of people tell you that penicillin can cure your common cold, should you ask your physician for a prescription? Instead, it may mean that a lot of people are wrong. Unfortunately, appeals to popularity have been used to justify discrimination, unscrupulous financial schemes, and dangerous behavior.

Appeal to Tradition

Claiming that a certain course of action should be followed because it was done that way in the past is an **appeal to tradition**. "We must have our annual company picnic in August because that's when we always schedule it" appeals to tradition. Just because a course of action was followed for a time does not mean it is the best option.

Fallacy An error in thinking that leads to false or invalid claims

Attacking the person A fallacy of reasoning in which irrelevant attacks are made against a person rather than the substance of an argument

Appeal to authority A fallacy of reasoning in which the opinion of someone who has no relevant experience is used to support an argument

Appeal to popularity A fallacy of reasoning that claims an action is acceptable because many people do it

Appeal to tradition A fallacy of reasoning that claims a certain course of action should be followed because that is the way it has been done in the past

Most superstitions are faulty cause fallacies.

Faulty Cause

"We are losing sales because our sales team is not working hard enough." This statement may overlook other causes for low sales, such as a price increase that made the product less affordable or a competitor's superior product. The **faulty cause** fallacy occurs when you claim that a particular situation or event is the cause of another event before ruling out other possible causes. Will you catch a cold if you don't bundle up when you go outside? Will you have bad luck if you break a mirror? If you answer yes to either of these questions, you are not thinking critically. *Viruses* cause colds, although a chill can weaken your immune system. Be-

liefs about breaking a mirror or walking under a ladder or allowing a black cat to cross your path are nothing more than superstitions.

Hasty Generalizations

All it takes to commit a **hasty generalization** fallacy is to jump to a conclusion based on too little evidence or too few experiences. The fallacy argues that if it is true for some, it must be true for all. "Don't go to that restaurant. I went once and the service was awful" is a hasty generalization. One negative experience does not mean that other visits to the restaurant would not be enjoyable.

Faulty cause A fallacy of reasoning that claims a particular event is the cause of another event without ruling out other possible causes

Hasty generalization A fallacy of reasoning in which a conclusion is based on too little evidence or too few experiences

---

STOP & THINK | Do Emotions Matter in Critical Thinking?

Sometimes, our emotions trigger a response that defies rational thinking. In such cases, our instincts may be more reliable than a conclusion based on detailed analysis. Antonio Damasio, a neurologist, maintains that emotions play a crucial role in critical thinking. In his studies of patients with damage to the emotional centers of their brains, Damasio found that a lack of feelings actually impaired rational decision-making.[48]

Emotions, gut feelings, instincts, hunches, and practical wisdom can help you make good decisions. They help you understand how decisions affect others and provide a way of assessing value when considering competing options.

Although you should pay attention to your emotions, they can also act as a barrier to critical thinking and decision-making. Your intuitions and hunches are not always correct. For this reason, emotions must be balanced with critical thinking. Think about these popular sayings: "Opposites attract" and "Absence makes the heart grow fonder." Are these statements true? As much as your personal experiences or conventional wisdom may confirm both of these maxims, social science research suggests that both are usually wrong.

Communication ASSESSMENT

Student Listening Inventory[49]

Use the following numbers to indicate how often you, as a student, engage in the following listening behaviors. The "speaker" can refer to the instructor or a student.

1 = almost never   2 = not often   3 = sometimes   4 = more often than not   5 = almost always

Scoring: Add up your scores to assess how well you think you listen.

Listening Behavior

1. When someone is speaking to me, I purposely block out distractions such as side conversations and personal problems. _____

2. I ask questions when I don't understand something a speaker has said. _____

3. When a speaker uses words I don't know, I jot them down and look them up later. _____

4. I assess a speaker's credibility while listening. _____

5. I paraphrase and/or summarize a speaker's main ideas in my head as I listen. _____

6. I concentrate on a speaker's main ideas rather than the specific details. _____

7. I try to understand people who speak directly and indirectly as well. _____

8. Before reaching a conclusion, I try to confirm fully with the speaker my understanding of the message. _____

9. I fully concentrate when a speaker is explaining a complex idea. _____

10. When listening, I devote my full attention to a speaker's message. _____

11. I apply what I know about cultural differences when listening to someone from another culture. _____

12. I watch a speaker's facial expressions and body language for meaning. _____

13. I give positive nonverbal feedback to speakers—nods, eye contact, vocalized agreement. _____

14. When listening to a speaker, I establish eye contact and stop doing other nonrelated tasks. _____

15. I avoid tuning out speakers when I disagree with or dislike their message. _____

16. When I have an emotional response to a speaker or the message, I try to set aside my feelings and continue listening to the message. _____

17. I try to match my nonverbal responses to my verbal responses. _____

18. When someone begins speaking, I focus my attention on the message. _____

19. I try to understand how past experiences influence the ways in which I interpret a message. _____

20. I attempt to eliminate outside interruptions and distractions. _____

21. When I listen, I look at the speaker, maintain some eye contact, and focus on the message. _____

22. I avoid tuning out messages that are complex, complicated, and challenging. _____

23. I try to understand the other person's point of view when it is different from mine. _____

24. I try to be nonjudgmental and noncritical when I listen. _____

25. As appropriate, I self-disclose similar personal information as the other person shares with me. _____

Score	Interpretation
0–62	You perceive yourself to be a poor listener.
63–86	You perceive yourself to be an adequate listener.
87–111	You perceive yourself to be a good listener.
112–125	You perceive yourself to be an outstanding listener.

Summary

Why is listening so critical for effective communication?

- We spend most of our communicating time engaged in listening.
- Most people cannot accurately recall 50 percent of what they hear after listening to a short talk. Without training, we listen at about 25 percent efficiency.
- Five types of listening—discriminative, comprehensive, empathic, analytical, and appreciative—call for unique listening skills.
- The golden listening rule is easy to remember but often difficult to follow: Listen to others as you would have them listen to you.

What listening strategies and skills can help you communicate more effectively with others?

- Conscientious listeners use their extra thought speed to enhance listening.
- Effective communicators skillfully listen to feedback and nonverbal behavior, while also making sure that they withhold evaluation until their comprehension is complete.
- Effective listeners are proactive in avoiding and minimizing distractions to themselves and others.
- Effective paraphrasing requires an ability to restate what others say in a way that indicates you understand their meaning.

What unique challenges do you face as a listener?

- Adjusting to diverse listening styles, particularly those involving differences in gender and culture, is a challenging task that requires an understanding, respect, and adaptation to others.
- Adaptability and flexibility is the key to listening and taking useful notes.
- Listening to and analyzing your own thought processes enables you to choose useful and appropriate responses in listening situations.

How do effective listening and critical thinking help you arrive at justified conclusions and decisions?

- Critical thinking is the kind of thinking you use to analyze what you read, see, or hear to arrive at a justified conclusion or decision.

- Critical thinking requires an understanding of the nature and types of claims including claims of fact, conjecture, value, and policy.
- Critical thinkers understand and can separate verifiable facts from unsubstantiated inferences.
- An argument is a claim supported by evidence or reasons for accepting it. Toulmin's model of an argument includes a claim, data, and warrant, as well as backing, reservation, and qualifier for some arguments.

How does critical thinking help you recognize and respond to invalid arguments?

- Effective communicators can identify and avoid using fallacies such as attacking the person, appeal to authority, appeal to popularity, appeal to tradition, faulty cause, and hasty generalizations.
- In addition to thinking critically, emotional responses in the form of gut feelings, instincts, hunches, and practical wisdom can help you make good decisions.

TEST your*knowledge*

1 In general, we spend 40–70 percent of our communicating time engaged in _____.
a. writing
b. speaking
c. reading
d. listening
e. reading and writing

2 Immediately after listening to a short talk or lecture, most people cannot accurately report _____ percent of what was said.
a. 10
b. 30
c. 40
d. 50
e. 70

3 *Discriminative listening* refers to
a. how accurately you understand the meaning of another person's message.
b. your ability to distinguish auditory and/or visual stimuli in a listening situation.
c. how you act out ethnocentrism and stereotyping of others.
d. your ability to evaluate the validity of a message.
e. how well you focus on understanding and identifying with a person's situation, feeling, or motives.

4 Which of the following listening strategies involves using your extra thought speed productively?
a. Identify the key ideas in a message.
b. Pay attention to the meaning of a speaker's nonverbal behavior.
c. Analyze the strengths and weaknesses of arguments.
d. Assess the relevance and ethics of a speaker's comments.
e. all of the above

5 Read the following statement and a listener's paraphrase that follows. What characteristic of paraphrasing has the listener failed to take into account?
Grace: My whole family—parents, sisters, and Aunt Ruth—bug me about it, and sometimes I can tell they're very angry with me and how I'm overdrawn at the bank.
Listener: In other words, your family is angry because you're overdrawn at the bank; am I right?
a. The listener is not mindful.
b. The listener is not using new words to express Grace's message.
c. The listener has not heard Grace's words correctly.
d. The listener has not asked for confirmation.
e. all of the above

6 In general, men are more likely to listen comprehensively and analytically, whereas women are more likely to listen _____.
a. only comprehensively
b. empathically
c. empathically and appreciatively
d. appreciatively and comprehensively
e. only emotionally

7 "The economy will improve next year" is an example of which type of argumentative claim?
a. fact
b. conjecture
c. value
d. policy
e. emotion

8 Consider the following argument:
John is coughing with a lot of chest congestion. He's also been throwing up and has had a temperature of 102 degrees for several days. Given that all of these symptoms are signs of the flu, he probably has the flu.
In terms of Toulmin's model of an argument, which statement is the claim?
a. John is coughing with a lot of chest congestion.
b. He's also been throwing up.
c. [He] has had a temperature of 102 degrees for several days.
d. [A]ll of these symptoms are signs of the flu.
e. [H]e probably has the flu.

9 What fallacy is committed in this statement: "John went outside in the cold without his hat or gloves. No wonder he has a cold."
a. attacking the person
b. appeal to authority
c. appeal to popularity
d. appeal to tradition
e. faulty cause

10 What fallacy is committed in this statement: "Congestion and nausea! Oh, my God. John must have the swine flu!"
a. hasty generalization
b. appeal to authority
c. attacking the person
d. appeal to tradition
e. faulty cause

Answers: 1-d; 2-d; 3-b; 4-e; 5-b; 6-c; 7-b; 8-e; 9-e; 10-a

5 VERBAL

There is no denying the power of language, but it also comes with potential hazards. Once the words are out of your mouth, you cannot take them back. For example, when President Bill Clinton categorically claimed, "I've had no sexual relations with that woman, Miss Lewinski," his words came back to haunt him during the 1998 impeachment hearings. When Chef Gordon Ramsey of the reality cooking show *Hell's Kitchen* derisively told contestant and sous chef Joseph, "I know you're a little bit stupid," Chef Ramsey found himself challenged to a parking-lot brawl.

> **The difference between the almost right word and the right word is really a large matter—'tis the difference between the lightning bug and the lightning.**
>
> **— Mark Twain**

A survey of college students enrolled in basic communication courses in 2007 ranked "Choosing appropriate and

COMMUNICATION

effective words" as one of the top ten speaking skills. When asked to explain their reasons for choosing this item, students replied with the following comments: "I'm afraid that right in the middle of speaking, I'll have trouble finding the words I need." "Sometimes, when someone asks me a question at work, I fumble with the answer—not because I don't know the answer but because I can't find the right words to explain what I know." "When someone disagrees with me, I can't seem to explain my position. I can't find the right words."[1]

Well-chosen words lie at the heart of electrifying, memorable presentations and at the core of meaningful and long-lasting interpersonal relationships. The right words explain, teach, support, comfort, persuade, inspire, and delight. As Mark Twain wrote, "The difference between the almost right word and the right word is really a large matter—'tis the difference between the lightning bug and the lightning."[2]

HUMAN language

humans do not share the remarkable sensory skills of many animals. You cannot track a faint scent through a forest trail or camouflage your skin color to hide from a predator. Many mammals do a much better job of interpreting body movement than you do.[3] Yet you can do something that no animal can: You can speak.

Even though animals use sophisticated communication systems, they do not use a language as complex and powerful as the one you are reading right now. In fact, the ability to learn words and to combine, invent, and give meaning to new words makes humans different from animals.[4]

Researchers estimate that the first humans to speak language as we know it lived in East Africa about 150,000 years ago.[5] In a 100,000-year-old skull, anthropologists found a modern-shaped hyoid bone, which fits right at the top of the windpipe and resembles part of the apparatus we need to speak. Fully modern language probably evolved only 50,000 years ago.[6] Thus, the ability to speak is relatively modern, particularly given that our earliest known ancestors lived about 3.3 million years ago in what is now Ethiopia.[7]

Our early ancestors also walked upright rather than hunched over like apes. Standing up on their own two feet made it possible for humans to use their hands to carry things, make tools, and gesture in complicated ways. Equally important, it contributed to physiological changes in the larynx, lungs, throat, and vocal cavity that enabled them to talk. As a result, we are the only species specialized for speech and complex language development.

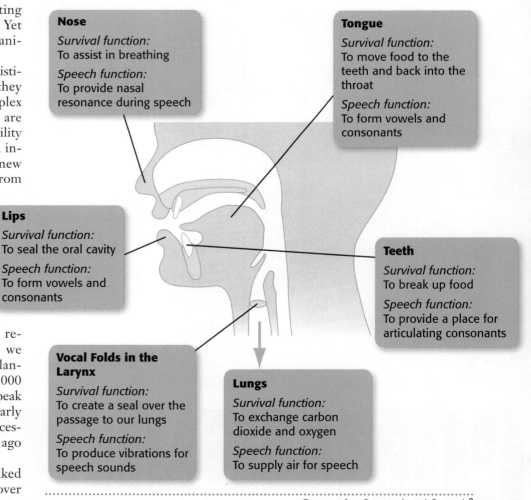

Nose

Survival function:
To assist in breathing

Speech function:
To provide nasal resonance during speech

Tongue

Survival function:
To move food to the teeth and back into the throat

Speech function:
To form vowels and consonants

Lips

Survival function:
To seal the oral cavity

Speech function:
To form vowels and consonants

Teeth

Survival function:
To break up food

Speech function:
To provide a place for articulating consonants

Vocal Folds in the Larynx

Survival function:
To create a seal over the passage to our lungs

Speech function:
To produce vibrations for speech sounds

Lungs

Survival function:
To exchange carbon dioxide and oxygen

Speech function:
To supply air for speech

Organs for Survival and Speech[8]

Human **language** is a system of arbitrary signs and symbols used to communicate thoughts and feelings. Every language spoken on this planet is a *system:* an interrelated collection of words and rules used to construct and express messages that generate meaning. In addition to the meanings of words, all languages impose a grammar that arranges words in a meaningful way. "The went store he to" makes no sense until you re-arrange the words: "He went to the store." And although "Him go to store" may be understandable, it breaks several grammatical rules.

A *Wall Street Journal* article warns that you risk "derailing your career" when you use language incorrectly. Evidence for this claim took the form of personal stories:

A recruiter refused to recommend a financial manager for a chief financial officer position in another company because he often said "me and so-and-so," followed by the wrong verb form.

The president of a publishing company rejects sales and editorial candidates because they exhibit grammatically incorrect speech. The president complained that such behavior "reflects a low level of professionalism."[9]

Linguists Victoria Fromkin and Robert Rodman note that "whatever else people do when they come together—whether they play, fight, make love, or make automobiles—they talk. We live in a world of language."[10] Well-chosen words lie at the heart of effective communication, regardless of whether you are chatting with a friend, leading a group, addressing an audience, or writing a novel.

Moreover, humans communicate nonverbally (see Chapter 6) as well as verbally. This chapter focuses on **verbal communication**—the ways in which we use the words in a language to generate meaning. Verbal communication can be expressed face-to-face, fax-to-fax, cell-phone-to-cell-phone, or e-mail-to-e-mail.[11]

> **"Whatever else people do when they come together—whether they play, fight, make love, or make automobiles—they talk. We live in a world of language."**
> —Victoria Fromkin and Robert Rodman, linguists

Language A system of arbitrary signs and symbols used to communicate thoughts and feelings
Verbal communication The ways in which we use the words in a language to generate meaning

LANGUAGE AND meaning

Words do not have meanings; people have meanings for words.

When you don't know the meaning of a word, you may look it up in a dictionary. Depending on the word, however, you can find several definitions. In fact, no two people share exactly the same meaning of the same word. Words do not have meanings; people have meanings for words.[12]

Signs and Symbols

As noted earlier, all languages are human inventions composed of signs and symbols: The words we speak or write, and the system that underlies

The Many Meanings of LOVE

Consider the many ways in which people define the word *love*.

Romantic **love**

Love for family and friends

Love for hobby or sport

Love of country

their use, have all been made up by people.[13] A **sign** stands for or represents something specific and often looks like the thing it represents. Thus, it has a visual relationship to that thing. For example, the graphic depictions of jagged lightning and dark clouds on a weather map are signs of a storm. Images are also used as international traffic signs to help drivers navigate the roads in countries where they may not speak the language.

Unlike signs, **symbols** do *not* have a direct relationship to the things they represent. Instead, they are an *arbitrary* collection of sounds that in certain combinations stand for concepts. Nothing in the compilation of letters that make up the word *lightning* looks or sounds like lightning. The letters making up the word *cloud* are neither white and puffy nor dark and gloomy. You cannot be struck by the word *lightning* or get wet from the word *rain*.

When you see or hear a word, you apply your knowledge, experience, and feelings to decide what the word means. For example, if someone talks about a steak dinner, you may have very different reac-

Common Signs

Rain

Rain and Lightning

Partly Cloudy

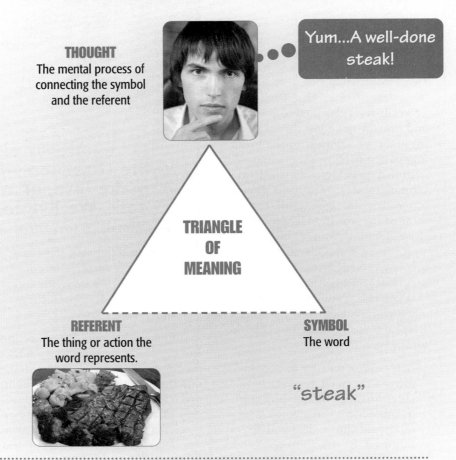

THOUGHT
The mental process of connecting the symbol and the referent

Yum...A well-done steak!

TRIANGLE OF MEANING

REFERENT
The thing or action the word represents.

SYMBOL
The word

"steak"

Ogden and Richards's Triangle of Meaning[14]

tions to the word *steak* depending on whether you are a rancher, a gourmet chef, a vegetarian, or an animal-rights activist.

Language scholars C. K. Ogden and I. A. Richards provide a classic explanation of this phenomenon. They use a triangle to explain the three elements of language: the thinking person, the symbol (or sign) used to represent something, and the actual thing, idea, or feeling being referenced.[15] The Ogden and Richards triangle does not have a solid base because the symbol and the referent are *not* directly related. The symbol must be mentally processed before it has meaning.

Denotative and Connotative Meaning

One of the great myths about language is that every word has an exact meaning. The truth is just the opposite: Just as no two communi-

cators or communication contexts are exactly alike, no two word meanings can ever be the same.[16]

Two linguistic concepts—denotation and connotation—help explain the elusive nature of word meanings. **Denotation** refers to the specific and objective-dictionary-based meaning of a word. For example, most of us would agree that a *snake* is a scaly, legless, sometimes venomous reptile

---

Sign Stands for or represents something specific and may look like the thing it represents

Symbol An *arbitrary* collection of sounds and letters that stand for a concept but do not have a direct relationship with the things they represent

Denotation Refers to the specific and objective dictionary-based meaning of a word

STOP & THINK | What's in a Name?

Our ability "to name" is uniquely human. It has been considered a holy privilege as well as a magical gift. In Judaism and Christianity, the first honor God confers on Adam, even before the creation of Eve, is that of naming the animals.[17]

Many of our first names also have interesting histories as well as special meanings. For example, the English name *Dianna* is probably derived from an old Indo-European root meaning "heavenly" and "divine" and is related to Diana, the Roman goddess of the moon, hunting, forests, and childbirth. The name *John* comes from the Greek name meaning "gracious." This name owes its popularity to John the Baptist and the apostle John in the *New Testament*. All cultures have their own naming traditions. Consider, for example, the story of a Nigerian student named Ifeyinwa:

> In Africa, back in the days when my grandparents were alive, names meant many things and people named their children from events or circumstances.

When my father was about six years old, his mother gave birth to twin babies. They did not survive because they were put in a special clay pot and left in the fields until they died. That was the tradition of the land then. It was taboo for a woman to give birth to more than one child at a time. My father named me after this ordeal. My name Ifeyinwa means "child is supreme" and "precious." He knows a child is a precious gift from God and each child is unique in his or her own special ways. I have always loved my name but even more after learning its meaning. I wish to live up to my father's expectations of me and the meaning of my name.[18]

Now consider *your* name. Why did your parents choose this name? Does their choice say something about your family's history or your culture? How has your name affected your life?

---

with a long, cylindrical body. Plumbers have their own version of a *snake*—a flexible metal wire or coil used to clean out pipes. Each of these "snakes" have denotative meanings.

Connotation refers to the emotional response or personal thoughts connected to the meaning of a word. Semanticist S. I. Hayakawa refers to connotation as "the aura of feeling, pleasant or unpleasant, that

> **Connotation** The emotional responses and personal thoughts connected to the meaning of a word

the serpent   the plumbing tool

> **"CONNOTATION is the aura of feeling, pleasant or unpleasant, that surrounds practically all words."**
> **— S. I. Hayakawa, semanticist**

surrounds practically all words."[19] Connotation, rather than denotation, is more likely to influence your response to words. For example, just the thought of a snake is enough to make some people who have a fear of snakes tremble. Others may immediately think of the snake in the Garden of Eden, who lured Adam and Eve to eat forbidden fruit. Yet a serpentologist—a scientist who studies snakes—would try to convince you that snakes are among the most intriguing and magnificent of animals.

For most people, a word's connotation has much more significance than its denotation. For African Americans, the word *plantation* has negative connotations. Whereas you may tell someone that a *cop* pulled you over and gave you an undeserved ticket, a *police officer* may have helped you with a flat tire. What seems like a neutral word to you can have strong connotations to others.

General and Specific Language

The choice of a general or more specific word can have an enormous impact on meaning. Some words are very **concrete**; they refer to things you perceive with your senses—things you can smell, taste, touch, see, or hear. The words *table*, *Paris*, *giraffe*, and *red rose* are concrete because, unlike *furniture*, *city*, *animal*, and *flower*, they narrow the number of possible meanings and decrease the likelihood of misinterpretation.

An **abstract word** refers to an idea or concept that usually cannot be observed or touched and often requires interpretation. The word *animal* is more abstract than *giraffe* because there are a huge number of different kinds of animals. Moreover, you can see a giraffe in your mind, but what does an animal look like? A crayfish and a giraffe are both animals. Similarly, words such as *fairness*, *freedom*, and *evil* can have an almost endless number of different meanings and don't specifically refer to something we can see, hear, smell, taste, or touch. The more abstract your language is, the more likely it is that your listeners may interpret your meaning other than the way you intended.[20]

Language has three general levels of meaning that range from highly abstract to very concrete.[21] **Superordinate terms** group objects and ideas together very generally, such as *vehicle*, *animal*, or *location*. **Basic terms** exemplify a superordinate term, such as *car*, *van*, *truck*; *cat*, *chicken*, *mouse*; or *New England*, *Deep South*, *Appalachia*. **Subordinate terms** offer the most concrete and specialized descriptions. The vehicle parked outside is not just a *car*. It is a 1988 red Mercedes sports car convertible. The cat purring on your lap is not just a cat; it is a blue-eyed Siamese cat named Gatsby.

Concrete word Words that refer to specific things that *can* be perceived by our senses
Abstract word Words that refer to an idea or concept that *cannot* be observed or touched
Superordinate terms Words that group objects and ideas very generally, such as *vehicle* or *animal*
Basic terms Words that come to mind when you see an object, such as *car* or *cat*
Subordinate terms The most concrete words that provide specific descriptions

THREE LEVELS OF MEANING

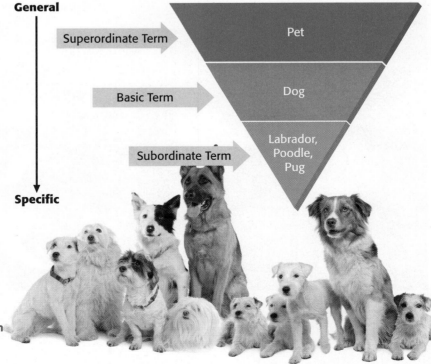

General

Superordinate Term → Pet

Basic Term → Dog

Subordinate Term → Labrador, Poodle, Pug

Specific

LANGUAGE AND
culture

there are approximately 5,000 to 6,000 languages spoken in the world, all of them with different vocabularies and rules of grammar.[22] Have you ever tried to talk to or understand someone who speaks very little English? The experience can be frustrating, comical, enlightening, or even disastrous.

In one of Tony Hillerman's mystery novels, a Navaho tribal police officer explains to an FBI agent who cannot come up with anything better than the word *rocks* to describe a murder scene, "It's said the Inuits up on the Arctic Circle have nine words for snow. I guess, living in our stony world, we're that way with our rocks."[23] The words in a language often reflect what is important to the people in a specific culture. If there are hundreds of words used to describe camels in Arabic languages and snow in Eskimo languages, there are hundreds of English words to describe the many kinds of vehicles driven in the United States, as well as the extraordinary number of names for coffee drinks served at a local Starbucks. In many countries, there are significant regional differences in vocabulary. For example, a sandwich on a large roll with a variety of meats and cheeses on it may be called a *grinder*, a *hero*, a *sub*, a *hoagie*, or a *po'boy*, depending on the region of the country.[24]

"Tall skim mocha no whip, please."

Whorf Hypothesis A theory claiming that language influences how we see, experience, and interpret the world around us

The Whorf Hypothesis

THINK ABOUT THEORY

One of the most significant and controversial language theories attempts to explain why people from different cultures speak and interpret messages differently from one another. Linguist Edward Sapir and his student Benjamin Whorf spent decades studying the relationship between language, culture, and thought. Whorf's most controversial theory contends that the structure of a language *determines* how we see, experience, and interpret the world around us. For example, if you don't have a word for *red*, will you be able to see red or separate it from other colors you do recognize?

In English, we understand the grammatical differences between "I saw the girl," "I see the girl," and "I will see the girl." Whorf observed that the Hopi Indians of Arizona make no past, present, and future tense distinctions in their language. Therefore, he concluded, they must perceive the world very differently. He also noted that the Hopi have a single word, *masa'ytaka,* for everything that flies, from insects to airplanes. Does that mean the Hopi cannot think about tomorrow and cannot see the differences between an airplane and a fly? Originally, many linguists believed that the answer was *yes.* Now linguists understand that the Hopi *do* think about tomorrow, even if they may lack a word for it. While language does not determine everything we think, it does influence the way we perceive others and the world around us.[25]

Like many controversial theories, the Whorf hypothesis (also referred to as the Sapir-Whorf Hypothesis) has been accepted, rejected, resurrected, and amended—several times. Today, most linguists accept a more moderate version of the **Whorf Hypothesis**: Language *reflects* cultural models of the world, which in turn influence how the speakers of a language come to think, act, and behave.[26] For example, in English, terms that end with *man,* such as *chairman*, *fireman,* and *policeman,* may lead us to view certain roles and jobs as only appropriate for men. Substituting words such as *chairperson, firefighter,* and *police officer* may change perceptions about who can work in these careers.

Pronouns

As we noted in Chapter 3, individualism-collectivism is the single most important dimension of cultural difference and the most important factor for distinguishing one culture from another. Individualistic cultures have an "I" orientation; collectivist cultures have a "we" orientation. Interestingly, "English is the only language that capitalizes the pronoun *I* in writing. English does not, however, capitalize the written form of the pronoun *you*."[27] By contrast, people of the Athabaskan-speaking community in Alaska speak and think in a collective plural voice. The word for *people*, *dene*, is used as a kind of *we*, and is the subject for almost every sentence requiring a personal pronoun.[28]

When speaking to others, pay attention to the individualistic or collectivist tendencies in the way they use languages. Although frequent use of the words *I* and *you* may be appropriate for a group of ambitious corporate executives in the United States, the word *we* might be more appropriate for African Americans or people from Central and South America, who are less individualistic.

Verbal Directness

Most people living in the United States have a very low-context, direct way of speaking. In the eyes of other cultures, we get to the point with blunt, straight talk. When we say no, we mean no! Many other cultures view this direct use of language as a disregard for others that can lead to embarrassment and injured feelings.[29] At a news conference, President George W. Bush acknowledged that his all-American speaking style may have been too direct when dealing with the leaders of other nations. "'I explained to the prime minister [Tony Blair of Great Britain] that the policy of my government is the removal of Saddam.' Catching himself, Bush added: 'Maybe I should be a little less direct and be a little more nuanced, and say we support regime change.'"[30]

Most North Americans learn to say yes or no when expressing their opinions; however, a Japanese person may say yes to a suggestion or business proposal because it is what you want to hear; in fact, their real response may actually be no.

LANGUAGE AND gender

most languages reflect a gender bias. These differences can be minor or major depending on the language and context in which communication takes place.[31] In English, we struggle with the words *he* and *she*. For many years, the pronoun *he* was used to refer to an unspecified individual. Older English textbooks used sentences such as: *Every speaker should pay attention to his words*. Other languages have more gender-related challenges. French, for example, has separate third-person plurals: masculine and feminine versions of *they*.

Japanese distinguishes gender in both the first and second person; they use a different version of *you* for men and women. The language of Finland may have the best solution. All pronouns are gender neutral; there is only one word for *he* and *she*.[32]

Although some languages, such as Finnish, make very few distinctions between men and women, English favors men over women. Most gender-related word pairings begin with the male term: male and female, boys and girls, husband and wife, Jack and Jill, Romeo and

Gender-Neutral Terms for Jobs and Professions

Gender-Biased Terms	Gender-Neutral Terms
Stewardess	Flight attendant
Fireman	Firefighter
Female soldier	Soldier
Chairman	Chairperson
Male nurse	Nurse

Use gender-neutral terms to describe jobs and professions. In the theater and film industries, for example, the word *actor* is replacing actress for female performers.

How do you talk about a couple when using their first names? Is it Dick and Jane, or Jane and Dick? Adam and Eve, or Eve and Adam?

Juliet, Mr. and Mrs.[33] If you doubt this preference, think about the married couples you know. Would you address a letter to Mrs. and Mr. Smith? How do you talk about a couple when using their first names? Is it Dick and Jane, or Jane and Dick? Adam and Eve, or Eve and Adam?

Unfortunately, because of the male bias in English and in American society, female terms tend to take on demeaning connotations. The connotations of the second word in the following pairings are negative or outdated for women: *wizard/witch*, *governor/governess*, *master/mistress*. Women are also compared with animals: *bitch*, *cow*, *shrew*, *old crow*, *vixen*, *dog*.[34] One study lists more than 500 English

slang terms for *prostitute*, but only 65 for the men who are their willing clients.[35]

Robin Lakoff, one of the first linguists to write about gender differences, in *Language and Woman's Place*, contends that women tend to use language that expresses uncer-

STRATEGIES FOR AVOIDING GENDER BIAS WITH PRONOUNS

- **Use plural forms.** Instead of saying, "Every speaker should pay attention to his words," consider, "All speakers should pay attention to their words."
- **Avoid using any pronoun.** Instead of using a pronoun at all, consider, "Good speakers pay careful attention to language."
- **Use variations on the phrase "he or she" as well as "his and hers."** Instead of saying, "Every speaker should pay attention to his or her words," consider, "Every speaker should pay attention to her or his words."

tainty, lack of confidence, and excessive deference or politeness.[36] For example, women tend to use questions tagged onto sentences (*tag questions*) to gain approval, such as "don't you agree?" and "haven't you?" They also tend to avoid direct requests, using super-polite forms such as "Could you please close the door?" or "Would you mind closing the door?" Women's speech is also observed as more tentative, using such hedges or "fillers" as *like*, *you know*, *well*, and *kind of*.

We would be guilty of stereotyping if we didn't note the exceptions to such tendencies. Certainly, many men speak tentatively and cooperatively, and many women speak directly and assertively. When the communication goal is significant and personally important, *both* men and women use highly powerful language.

> **When the communication goal is significant and personally important, *both* men and women use highly powerful language.**

communication&culture

DO WOMEN TALK MORE THAN MEN?

One of the great language myths is that women talk more than men. This belief is neither new nor confined to the United States.[37] Most research studies, however, portray a different picture. A recent study of 400 college students found that the number of words uttered by males and females were virtually the same. An analysis of 63 studies of gender differences in talkativeness found that men actually "yakked slightly more than women, especially when interacting with spouses or strangers and when the topic was non-personal." Women talked more with classmates, with parents and children, and in situations where the topic of conversation required disclosure of feelings.[38]

In work settings, men do most of the talking. Even when women hold influential positions, they often find it hard to contribute to a discussion as much as men do. This pattern is also evident in educational settings (from kindergarten through university), where males usually dominate classroom talk. Sadly, when women talk as much as men do, they may be perceived as talking "too much."[39]

To the question "Do women talk more than men?" linguist Janet Holmes concludes, "It depends." It depends on the social context, the kind of talk, the confidence of the speaker, the social roles, and the speaker's expertise. Generally, men are more likely to dominate conversation in formal, public contexts where talk is highly valued and associated with status and power. Women, on the other hand, are likely to contribute more in private, informal interactions; when talk functions to maintain relationships and in situations where women feel socially confident.[40]

LANGUAGE AND
context

What kind of language would you use in a college classroom, at a family member's funeral, at a critical job interview, at a political or pep rally, at home with your parents, or at a party with your friends? There would be subtle and not-so-subtle differences in your choice of words and grammar. We naturally change our language based on our relationships with other communicators, their psychological traits and preferences, and the extent to which they share our cultural attitudes, beliefs, values, and behaviors.

The phrase *code switching* is a common strategy for adapting to the many contexts in which we communicate. If you can speak more than one language, you already code switch as you move from one language to another. Here we use the term **code switching** in a broader sense: to describe how we modify our verbal and nonverbal communication in different contexts.

Effective communicators learn to adapt their language to the communication context. Although a swear word would never pass your lips at a job interview, during a church service, or in a formal public speech, you may curse in the company of close friends and like-minded colleagues. In his book *Word on the Street*, linguist John McWhorter notes that many middle-class African Americans typically speak both Black English (the language they would speak at home) and Standard English (the language they would speak among white people), switching constantly between the two, often in the same sentence.[41] For example, a Black English speaker may use double negatives ("He don't know nothing") and delete *to be* verbs ("She fine") within statements made in Standard English. McWhorter also notes that African Americans usually code switch between Standard and Black English when the topic or tone is informal, lighthearted, or intimate. As a result, African Americans are competent in two sophisticated dialects of English.[42]

How does context affect what is considered appropriate language in each of these situations?

> **Code switching**
> Modifying how we use verbal and nonverbal communication in different contexts

OVERCOMING COMMON
language barriers

despite our best efforts to understand the complex relationship between language and meaning, misunderstandings are inevitable. Three common language barriers to effective communication are bypassing, exclusionary language, and offensive language.

Bypassing

When two people have different meanings for the same word or phrase, they risk bypassing each other. **Bypassing** is a form of miscommunication that occurs when people "miss each other with their meanings."[43] If you have ever found yourself saying, "But, that's not what I meant," you have experienced bypassing.

Note the problem created in the following example of bypassing: A high school graphic design teacher wrote a letter to Randy Cohen, the official "ethicist" for *The New York Times Magazine*. The teacher explained that students were assigned the task of creating a guitar using

Photoshop. A few asked if they could use an online tutorial. The teacher said *yes*, assuming and quite sure they'd merely consult it for help. Three students handed in identical work because they'd carefully followed the tutorial to the letter. The teacher wanted to give each student a C on the assignment because the other students created their work from scratch. Thus his question: Should he give them the C, or is he bound by having given them the okay to use the tutorial?

The ethicist wrote back, saying, "There's something not quite right about penalizing these students for doing what you explicitly permitted them to do. It's a teacher's obligation to be clear about what is and what is not acceptable."[44] The students clearly believed they had permission to use the tutorial to create the guitar graphic, whereas the teacher assumed they would only consult the tutorial for help.

William Haney, an organizational communication scholar, maintains

that effective "communicators who habitually look for meanings in the people using words, rather than in the words themselves, are much less prone to bypass or be bypassed."[45] Remember that it's not what words mean to you, but what speakers mean when they use words.

> ## Remember that it's not what words mean to you, but what speakers mean when they use words.

Bypassing A form of misunderstanding that occurs when people miss each other with their meanings
Euphemism Mild, indirect, or vague word that substitutes for a harsh, blunt, or offensive one

---

Tiptoeing Around Words

communication in ACTION

When you use a **euphemism**, you substitute a mild, indirect, or vague term for a harsh, blunt, or offensive one.[46] Rather than say someone has died, we may say he or she has "passed away." In Victorian England, the word *limb* was used for *leg,* a word that had sexual connotations. Even a chair leg wasn't referred to as such because it

might spark thoughts of sexuality. In U.S. restaurants, we usually ask for directions to the restroom rather than the toilet.[47] Some euphemisms also substitute letters in a word to make it less offensive. You frequently hear people say "jeeze" instead of "Jesus," "darn" instead of "damn," and "heck" rather than "hell."

Euphemisms, however, can be used to mask the truth. The Pentagon referred to the information-seeking techniques Americans used on Iraqis in Abu Ghraib as *interrogation*, whereas many critics described these techniques (food and sleep deprivation, waterboarding, stress positioning, hooding, and attacking with dogs) as *torture*.[48]

- ✓ **Age.** Instead of *little old lady*, use *older woman* or just *woman*.
- ✓ **Politics.** Political words are rife with positive and negative connotations. Take care with words like *radical, left wing,* and *right wing*; avoid using qualifiers such as *crazy* with liberal or conservative.
- ✓ **Religion.** Avoid using *extremists* or *fanatics* for religiously devout people.
- ✓ **Health and Abilities.** Rather than use terms such as *cripple* or *head case*, use instead *physically disabled* and *person with an emotional illness*. Never use the word *retarded* to refer to mental ability.
- ✓ **Sexual Orientation.** Never assume that the sexual orientation of others is the same as your own. *Homo* or *fairy* is unacceptable; use instead *gay* or *lesbian*.
- ✓ **Race and Ethnicity.** Avoid using stereotypical terms and descriptions based on a person's race, ethnicity, or region, such as *hick*. Use the names people prefer to describe their racial or ethnic affiliations, such as *black, African American, Latino/a, Hispanic,* and *Asian*. Rather than say that "white, female supervisor manages a large staff" or "that Polish guy down the block owns several repair shops," say instead, "that supervisor manages a large staff" or "that guy down the block owns several repair shops."

Exclusionary Language

Exclusionary language uses words that reinforce stereotypes, belittle other people, or exclude others from understanding an in-group's message. Exclusionary language widens the social gap by separating the world into *we* (to refer to people like you) and *they* or *those people* (to refer to people who are different). Such terms can offend others. You don't have to be excessive in your zeal to be "politically correct," using *underachieve* for *fail*, or *vertically challenged* for *short*, for example, but you should avoid alienating others by using language that includes, rather than excludes, them. Specifically, avoid mentioning anything about age, political stance, religion, health and abilities, sexual orientation, and race and ethnicity unless these characteristics are relevant to the discussion.

In addition to stereotyping others, exclusionary language can prevent others from participating or joining a discussion that relies on specialized jargon. **Jargon** is the specialized or technical language of a profession or homogenous group. English professor William Lutz points out that we all use jargon as "verbal shorthand that allows members to communicate with each other clearly, efficiently, and quickly."[50] In some settings and on some occasions, such as at a meeting of psychiatrists, attorneys, information technology professionals, or educators, the ability to use jargon properly is a sign of group membership, and it speeds communication among members.

Some speakers use jargon to impress others with their specialized knowledge. For example, a skilled statistician may bewilder an audience by using unfamiliar terms to describe cutting-edge methodologies for establishing causality. In other situations, people use jargon when they have nothing to say; they just string together a bunch of nonsense and hope no one notices their lack of content.[51] Such tactics fail to inform others, and often result in misunderstandings and resentment.

Offensive Language and Swearing

During the first half of the twentieth century, many words were considered inappropriate, particularly those that referred to private body parts and functions. Women went to the *powder room* and men to the *lavatory*.

> **Exclusionary language** Uses words that reinforce stereotypes, belittle other people, or exclude others from understanding an in-group's message
> **Jargon** The specialized or technical language of a profession or homogenous group

ethicalcommunication

Sticks and Stones May Break Your Bones, but Words Can Hurt Forever

Movie director Spike Lee rejects being labeled as a "black" filmmaker. "I want to be known as a talented young filmmaker. That should be first. But the reality today is that no matter how successful you are, you're black first."

Two problems occur when you label someone or accept a label you hear or see. First, you reduce an entire person into a label: black filmmaker, dumb blonde, female doctor, or rich uncle. Second, the label can affect your perceptions or relationship with that person. For example, if you label a person as inconsiderate, you may make excuses for an act of kindness: "I wonder what prompted her to do that?" When you label someone as near perfect, you may go to great lengths to justify or explain less-than-perfect behavior: "Nicole is still the best player on the softball team; she's just having an off year." Labels also influence how we interpret the same behavior:

- I'm energetic; you're overexcited; he's out of control.
- I'm laid-back; you're untidy; she's a slob.
- I'm smart; you're intelligent; Chris is brilliant!

Even the word *pregnant* was once considered improper. Instead, a woman was "in a family way" or "with child." In 1952, Lucille Ball became the first pregnant woman to appear on a television show. The scripts called her an "expectant mother," never using the word *pregnant*. All of the *I Love Lucy* scripts were reviewed by a priest, a rabbi, and a minister to make certain they were in good taste.[52] And until quite recently, swear words were literally unheard of on radio and television. Today you may hear dozens of swear words on cable television shows, and you might easily witness steamy sexual scenes that would have given the *I Love Lucy* censors heart attacks. And then there's the Internet, where swearing and pornography are only a few clicks away.

Researchers who study the evolution of language report that swearing or cursing is a human universal. According to Natalie Angier, science writer for the *New York Times*, "Every language, dialect or patois ever studied, living or dead, spoken by millions or by a small tribe, turns out to have its share of forbidden speech."[53]

How would you define swearing? Is it bad language, embarrassing language, profane language? **Swearing** refers to using words that are taboo or disapproved of in a culture that should *not* be interpreted literally and can be used to express strong emotions and attitudes."[54] When we use swear words, we rarely wish that someone would literally "go to hell" or be "damned." Rather, we are using the words as a coping mechanism to express a strong emotion or to release stress.[55] In some cases, swearing may be signs of a neurological disorder, such as the small percent of people with Tourette's syndrome, who cannot control their tendency to swear.[56]

There are good reasons to stop swearing or, at least, to control where, when, and with whom you use such language. For example, swearing frequently offends others.

> "Every language, dialect or patois ever studied, living or dead, spoken by millions or by a small tribe, turns out to have its share of forbidden speech."
> — NATALIE ANGIER

One study reported that 91 percent of respondents ranked foul language as "the most ill-mannered type of workplace behavior."[57] People who do *not* swear are seen as more intelligent (because they can find more accurate and appropriate words) and more pleasant (because they don't offend anyone). They are also perceived as effective communicators who have greater control over their emotions.

If swearing is a problematic habit of speech, you can take steps to break it. Like any habit—biting your nails, overeating, or abusing alcohol—you must *want* to stop doing it. When you feel like swearing, use a euphemism such as *darn* or *good grief*. Rather than say, "Who the @%*$ cares?" say, "Who cares?" Look for better, more interesting words to describe what you hear rather than jumping to a conclusion that accuses.

Cursing and using sexually explicit language was once taboo on television and not considered "ladylike." Although some women now believe swearing is "liberating," it remains a stigma in many contexts—for both women *and* men.

Swearing Using words that are taboo or disapproved of in a culture, but that should *not* be interpreted literally and can be used to express strong emotions and attitudes

improving
YOUR WAY WITH WORDS

In the previous section, we emphasized what *not* to do if you want to be understood and respected by others. Here we take a more positive approach by examining five ways in which you can use language to express messages clearly and appropriately: Expand your vocabulary; use oral language; use active language; use *I* and *you* pronouns wisely; and know your grammar.

Expand Your Vocabulary

How many words do you know? By the age of five, you probably knew about 10,000 words, which means that you learned about ten words a day. Children have an inborn ability for learning languages that diminishes at around age 12 or 13. Although children can learn a second or third language with relative ease, adults struggle to become fluent in a second language.[58]

By the time you are an adult, your vocabulary has expanded to include tens of thousands of words. Not surprisingly, finding the "right" word is a lot easier if you have many words from which to choose. When your only ice cream choices are vanilla or chocolate, you miss the delights of caramel butter pecan, mocha fudge swirl, and even simple strawberry. When you search for words in the English language, you have more than a million choices.

As you learn more words, make sure you understand their meaning and usage. For example, you should be able to make distinctions in meaning among the words in the following groups:[59]

- Absurd, silly, dumb, ridiculous, ludicrous, idiotic
- Pretty, attractive, gorgeous, elegant, lovely, cute, beautiful

Remember, the difference between the almost-right word and the right word is a very large matter. You may not mind being called "silly," but may have serious objections to being called "idiotic." Improving your vocabulary will be a lifelong task—and one that will be made much easier if you are an avid reader.

Use Oral Language

Usually, there is a big difference between the words we use for written documents and the words we use orally in conversations, group discussions, and presentations. In his book *How to Win Any Argument*, Robert Mayer writes: "The words you'll craft for a listener's ears are not the same as the words you'll choose for a reader's eyes. Readers can slow their pace to reread, to absorb, and to understand—luxuries listeners don't have."[60] Say what you mean by speaking the way you talk, not the way you write.

Use Active Language

Effective communicators use active language: vivid, expressive verbs, rather than passive forms of the verb *to be* (*be, am, is, are, was, being, been*). Consider the difference between "Cheating is a violation of the college's plagiarism rules," and "Cheating violates the college's plagiarism rules." The second sentence is stronger because it draws attention to the subject—cheating as a plagiarizing act—making it *active*, and eliminating the passive verb *to be*.

Voice refers to whether the subject of a sentence performs or receives the action of the verb. If the subject performs the action, you are using

Crafting Language for the Ear

Oral Style	This	Not This
Shorter, familiar words	Large	Substantial
Shorter, simple sentences	He came back.	He returned from his point of departure.
Contractions	I'm not going and that's that.	I am not going and that is that.
Informal, colloquial expressions	Give it a try.	You should attempt it first.
Incomplete sentences	Old wood, best to burn; old wine best to drink	Old wood burns the best, and old wine is best to drink.

an **active voice**. If the subject receives the action, you are using a **passive voice**. A strong, active voice makes your message more engaging, whereas a passive voice takes the focus away from the subject of your sentence. "The *Iliad* was read by the student" is passive. "The student read the *Iliad*" is active. Because an active voice requires fewer words, it also keeps your sentences short and direct. Simply state who is doing what, not what was done by whom.

Say what you mean by speaking the way you talk, not the way you write.

Less committed and confident speakers often have trouble using the active voice because they worry about sounding too direct. Look at the differences in these sentences:

Active verb: Sign this petition.

Passive verb: The petition should by signed by all of you.

The more passive the sentence, the less powerful the message.

Use *I* and *You* Language Wisely

The kinds of pronouns you use can affect the quality and meaning of your verbal communication. Understanding the nature and power of these pronouns can help you improve your way with words.

When you use the word *I*, you take responsibility for your own feelings and actions: *I* feel great. *I* am a good student. *I* am not pleased with the team's work on this project. Some people avoid using the word *I* because they think they're showing off, being selfish, or bragging. Other people use the word *I* too much and appear self-centered or oblivious to those around them.

Unfortunately, some people avoid *I* language when it is most important. Instead, they shift responsibil-

ity from themselves to others by using the word *you*. *You* language can be used to express judgments about others. When the judgments are positive—"You did a great job" or "You look marvelous!"—there's rarely a problem. When *you* is used to accuse, blame, or criticize, however, it can arouse defensiveness, anger, and even revenge. Consider the following statements: "You make me angry." "You embarrass me." "You drive too fast." Sometimes, the word *you* is implied, as in "What a stupid thing to do."

When you use *you* language, you are saying that another person makes you feel a certain way rather than accepting that you control how you feel. *You* language often expresses your frustration rather than the behavior of another person. To take personal responsibility and decrease the probability of defensive reactions, try to use *I* language when your impulse tells you to use *you*.

The Three Components of *I* Language

1. **Identify your feelings.**

2. **Describe the other person's behavior.**

3. **Explain the potential consequences.**

The following examples demonstrate how the three components of *I* language can help you express yourself by describing someone's behavior and explaining how it affects you. Also note that the *you* statements are short. The *I* statements are longer because they offer more information to explain the speaker's feelings.

You versus I

You **Statement**

You embarrassed me last night.

I **Statement**

I was really embarrassed last night when you interrupted me in front of my boss and contradicted what I said. I'm afraid she'll think I don't know what I'm doing.

You **Statement**

What a stupid thing to do!

I **Statement**

When you turn on the gas grill and let it run, I'm terrified that it will blow up in your face when you light it.

Active voice The subject of a sentence performs the action, as in *Bill read the book*

Passive voice When the subject of a sentence receives the action, as in *The book was read by Bill*

Gobbling Gobbledygook

Semanticist Stuart Chase defines **gobbledygook** (the sound of which is supposed to imitate the nonsense gobbling of a turkey) as "using two or three or ten words in place of one, or using a five-syllable word where a single syllable would suffice." He gives us this example: The word *now* has been replaced by the five-word, 17 letter phrase "at this point in time."[61]

In his book, *Say What You Mean,* Rudolf Flesch contends that long words are a curse, a special language that comes between a speaker and listener.[62]

To demonstrate the value of clear, plain language, John Strylowski, of the U.S. Department of the Interior and a frequent speaker at plain language seminars, offers several recommendations:

- Never write a sentence with more than 40 words.
- Treat only one subject per sentence.
- Don't include information just because you know it. Think about what the reader needs.
- Use shorter words and phrases such as "now" rather than "at the present time."[63]

If you doubt the need for plain language, try to decipher the gobbledygook captured to the right from former Secretary of Defense Donald Rumsfeld.

REPORTS THAT SAY SOMETHING HASN'T HAPPENED ARE ALWAYS INTERESTING TO ME, BECAUSE AS WE KNOW, THERE ARE KNOWN KNOWNS; THERE ARE THINGS WE KNOW WE KNOW. WE ALSO KNOW THERE ARE KNOWN UNKNOWNS; THAT IS TO SAY, WE KNOW THERE ARE SOME THINGS WE DO NOT KNOW. BUT ALSO UNKNOWN UNKNOWNS— THE ONES WE DON'T KNOW WE DON'T KNOW.[64]

Use Grammatical Language

In his book *If You Can Talk, You Can Write*, Joel Saltzman notes that when you're talking, you rarely worry about grammar or let it stand in the way of getting your point across. You probably never say to yourself, "Because I don't know if I should use *who* or *whom*, I won't even ask the question." According to Saltzman, when you're talking, 98 percent of the time, your grammar is fine and not an issue. For the 2 percent of time your grammar is a problem, many of your listeners won't even notice your mistakes.[65]

We are not saying that grammar isn't important. However, worrying about it all the time may make it impossible for you to write or speak. If you have questions about grammar, consult a good writing handbook.[66] Although most listeners miss or forgive a few grammatical errors, consistent grammatical problems can distract listeners and seriously harm your credibility. Your ability to use grammar correctly makes a public statement about your education, social class, and even intelligence.

Gobbledygook Several words used in place of one, or multiple-syllable words used where a single syllable word would suffice

Communication ASSESSMENT

Writing Apprehension Test (WAT)[67]

Writing apprehension is the fear or anxiety associated with writing situations and topic-specific writing assignments. The following statements about writing attempt to measure how you feel about the process of putting your ideas and opinions on paper. Indicate the degree to which each statement applies to you by marking whether you (1) strongly agree, (2) agree, (3) are uncertain about, (4) disagree, or (5) strongly disagree with the statement. Although some of these statements may seem repetitious, take your time and try to be as honest as possible.

_____ 1.   I avoid writing.

_____ 2.   I have no fear of my writing being evaluated.

_____ 3.   I look forward to writing down my ideas.

_____ 4.   My mind seems to go blank when I start to work on a composition.

_____ 5.   Expressing ideas through writing seems to be a waste of time.

_____ 6.   I would enjoy submitting my writing to magazines for evaluation and publication.

_____ 7.   I like to write my ideas down.

_____ 8.   I feel confident in my ability to express my ideas clearly in writing.

_____ 9.   I like to have my friends read what I have written.

_____ 10. I'm nervous about writing.

_____ 11. People seem to enjoy what I write.

_____ 12. I enjoy writing.

_____ 13. I never seem to be able to write down my ideas clearly.

_____ 14. Writing is a lot of fun.

_____ 15. I like seeing my thoughts on paper.

_____ 16. Discussing my writing with others is an enjoyable experience.

_____ 17. It's easy for me to write good compositions.

_____ 18. I don't think I write as well as other people write.

_____ 19. I don't like my compositions to be evaluated.

_____ 20. I'm not good at writing.

> **Writing apprehension** The fear or anxiety associated with writing situations and topic-specific writing assignments

Scoring: To determine your score on the WAT, complete the following steps:

1. Add the scores for items 1, 4, 5, 10, 13, 18, 19, and 20.
2. Add the scores for items 2, 3, 6, 7, 8, 9, 11, 12, 14, 15, 16, and 17.
3. Complete the following formula:

   WAT = 48 − total from step 1 + total from step 2
   Your score should be between 20 and 100 points. If your score is less than 20 or more than 100 points, you have made a mistake in computing the score. The higher your score, the more apprehension you feel about writing.

Score	Level of Apprehension	Description
20–45	Low	Enjoys writing; seeks writing opportunities
46–75	Average	Some writing creates apprehension; other writing does not
76–100	High	Troubled by many kinds of writing; avoids writing in most situations

What makes human language a unique form of communication?

- The ability to learn words and to combine, invent, and give meaning make humans different from animals.
- Language is a system of arbitrary signs and symbols used to communicate with others.

How do the characteristics of language affect the way you interpret meaning?

- Whereas signs often look like the thing they represent, symbols are arbitrary collections of sounds that in certain combinations stand for concepts.
- Words have both denotative and connotative meaning, and also differ in terms of whether they are concrete or abstract.

How do language and culture interact with and affect one another?

- The Whorf hypothesis claims that the nature of your language reflects your culture's view of the world.
- Individualistic cultures have an "I" orientation, whereas collectivist cultures have a "we" orientation.
- People living in low-context cultures rely on words to convey meaning. In high-context, collectivist cultures, people rely on nonverbal behavior and the relationship between communicators to generate meaning.

How do gender differences influence the way we use language?

- Most languages have a gender bias that privileges men more than women.
- In general, men talk more than women even though many people believe the opposite.
- Avoid gender bias by avoiding male and female pronouns when possible.

How does context affect your language choices?

- Code switching refers to modifying verbal and nonverbal communication when interacting with people from other cultures.

How do bypassing, exclusionary language, and offensive language inhibit effective communication?

- Communicators who look for meaning in words rather than in the people using words are more likely to bypass and be bypassed.
- Exclusionary language uses words that reinforce stereotypes, belittle other people, or exclude others from understanding an in-group's message.
- People who rarely swear or use offensive language are seen as more intelligent, more pleasant, and more skilled at controlling their emotions.

What strategies and skills can improve your way with words?

- You can improve your way with words by expanding your vocabulary, using oral language when you speak, speaking in an active voice, using the pronouns *I* and *you* wisely, and avoiding gobbledygook.
- An excessive number of grammatical errors in your speech can derail a career or create a negative personal impression.

the THINKSPOT
www.thethinkspot.com

TEST your*knowledge*

1 Approximately how many languages are spoken on planet Earth today?
   a. 50–60
   b. 500–600
   c. 5,000–6,000
   d. 50,000–60,000
   e. 500,000–600,000

2 _____ are an arbitrary collection of sounds that in certain combinations stand for concepts.
   a. Signs
   b. Symbols
   c. Denotations
   d. Connotations
   e. Vocalized grunts

3 Which of the following words would be classified as a superordinate term?
   a. liquid
   b. water
   c. rain
   d. ocean
   e. Caribbean Sea

4 According to the more modern version of the Whorf Hypothesis,
   a. people without a word for "airplane" cannot see airplanes.
   b. primitive people, even with training, cannot understand modern technology.
   c. language reflects cultural models and influences how people think and act.
   d. people without a word for "tomorrow" or "future" cannot plan.
   e. all of the above are true.

5 The only language that capitalizes the first person singular pronoun is
   a. English.
   b. Finnish.
   c. French.
   d. Hopi.
   e. Korean.

6 Which of the following demonstrates the male bias in the English language?
   a. Grammar books advised using the pronoun "he" to describe both men and women.
   b. Words such as *stewardess* instead of *flight attendant* and *mankind* instead of *human beings* demonstrate gender bias.
   c. Gender word pairings such as *Mr. and Mrs., men and women,* and *husband and wife* demonstrate gender bias.
   d. Word pairings such as *wizard and witch* as well as *master and mistress* demonstrate gender bias in English.
   e. All of the above demonstrate the male bias in English.

7 Which cultural group uses code switching?
   a. African Americans
   b. Hispanic Americans
   c. Asian Americans
   d. Native Americans
   e. All cultural groups may use code switching.

8 All of the following are examples of exclusionary language except:
   a. The man who served us at lunch was very professional.
   b. A little old lady tipped the young man.
   c. Even though she's a cancer victim, she has a very positive attitude.
   d. What do you expect from such a right-wing nut?
   e. Oriental women are quiet and polite.

9 Which of the following strategies can help you control cursing?
   a. When you feel like swearing, bite your tongue until it hurts.
   b. Ask a friend to hold her nose if she hears you swearing.
   c. Do not participate in an argument or a heated exchange with others.
   d. Describe what you see or hear rather than swearing about what happens.
   e. Swear in another language so no one understands what you are saying.

10 Effective oral language
   a. uses shorter, familiar words.
   b. uses shorter, simpler sentences.
   c. uses an informal speaking style.
   d. uses colloquial expressions.
   e. uses all of the above.

Answers: 1-c; 2-b; 3-a; 4-c; 5-a; 6-e; 7-e; 8-a; 9-d; 10-e

THINK COMMUNICATION

This article from *Communication Currents* has been slightly edited with permission from the National Communication Association.

Communication Currents
Knowledge for Communicating Well

NCA
A Publication of the National Communication Association

Volume 4, Issue 2 - April 2009

Language Convergence; Meaning Divergence

We've probably all begun a conversation with, "But I thought we said" or "I thought we agreed." It usually occurs after people leave a conversation thinking that they have reached agreement. Later, they are surprised by the other person's interpretation of the interaction. This example illustrates a new theory of communication called *language convergence/meaning divergence*. The theory emerged during a study attempting to identify the difference between how people define flirting and sexual harassment.

We began our study hoping to discover how people differentiate flirting from sexual harassment in the workplace. We were not so much interested in the legal definitions, as we were interested in the practical definitions people use to distinguish between the two concepts. To accomplish this, we interviewed 14 men and 14 women in a variety of occupations. We asked them for their definitions of each term and for examples of each that they had either seen or experienced. We also specifically asked them what distinguishes flirting from sexual harassment. What we found surprised us.

To understand the findings of our study, it is first necessary to understand the difference between language and meaning. Language is quite simply the words that we use. People who speak a common language typically use the same words. Meaning, on the other hand, constitutes the underlying definition of a given word. Words are necessarily a shortcut for meanings. Conversations would be exhausting if we had to define each word. Unfortunately, language as a conversational shortcut can also create the illusion of a shared meaning—in other words, it makes people think they agree when they really don't.

We discovered that people use the same words but with different meanings. For example, the study participants all used the word *flirting*, but with different meanings. Sometimes meanings were radically different; sometimes the meanings were subtly different. To illustrate, we provide radically different examples of flirting from two women who participated in the study.

Susan: "You know, the men were always just making inappropriate comments to the girls. Um, we had one manager in particular who all this happened with. His sales name was Cloud. Huge um, I don't know maybe a 350 pound, you know, black guy. He was a very, he was an intimidating kind of guy and definitely used that to his power. Um, you know and there was an incident where we were all out at a, it wasn't at work but it was a work function, work sponsored it kind of thing. And he, um, you know came up and grabbed my butt and said,

> Identify some of the *connotations* people associate with the word *flirting*.

> How *do you define flirting?* Is it a way to let someone know you're interested in them romantically or sexually? Is it a way to interact with someone in a playful manner? Is it a threat to a relationship if you flirt with someone else?

> How do you feel about Cloud's remarks to Susan? What would you do, if anything, if someone you worked with behaved this way?

What does the phrase *sexual harassment* mean to you? In your opinion, is this an example of sexual harassment?

How would you define the concept of *othering*? Can you think of examples in which you have experienced or engaged in *othering*?

'Have you ever had chocolate love?' I said, 'No.' He goes, 'Well do you want some?' kind of thing."

The interviewer asked Susan three times if this was really an example of flirting. Didn't she mean it was sexual harassment? This woman momentarily contemplated this possibility, but then confirmed that she did not consider it to be sexual harassment because it was normal behavior in her workplace. For this woman, normal behavior could not be sexual harassment.

Now contrast Susan's story with Elaine's story . . . Elaine described a situation in which she felt that the main character on the television show *Blue's Clues*, was flirting with the children in the audience when he said, "Oh, I'm going to play, that game with the ball and you know, uh, you shoot it through something, and there's a net on it. What do you call that? Oh, right, basketball. You are so smart." For Elaine, flirting is nonsexual, playful banter.

Although both of these women use the word *flirting*, their examples make it clear that their meanings for this term are radically different. Examples like these seem to represent very different understandings of a common language. To describe this phenomenon, we propose a communication theory of language convergence/meaning divergence (LC/MD). Simply put, the theory suggests that people often reach agreement on language to describe or define a particular situation, concept, or plan of action, but the meanings they assign are different. These differences may be so great that it is difficult to imagine that the parties had participated in the same communication or used the same words.

So how do people respond when they use a shared language with different meanings? First, sharing a common language but with different meanings can create the illusion of shared meaning. People think they agree when they really don't. When this illusion of agreeing on meaning begins to fracture, people's natural tendency is to wonder what is wrong

Is the woman's statement about what is *normal* another example of the authors' *language convergence; meaning divergence* theory? Could the authors have misinterpreted the woman's meaning when she used this word?

with the other person. They might categorize the other person as crazy, not very bright, or morally questionable. This tendency is called *othering*. Othering is problematic because instead of trying to understand the other person so we can solve a problem or resolve a conflict, we assume that the other person *is* the problem.

LC/MD emphasizes an important misconception that is common in our understanding of communication. Generally, explanations of communication suggest that if we improve the clarity or precision of our communication, we will better understand each other. This study suggests that not only do we need to provide clear language, but we also need to check underlying meanings in order to increase the odds that similar understanding will occur.

This theory helps explain why men and women often evaluate sexual behavior in the workplace in significantly different ways. LC/MD would also be useful for exploring intercultural communication in which reaching language convergence is often challenging enough, but reaching meaning convergence is particularly difficult. Finally, LC/MD might be useful in understanding those conflicts we have with others, such as a friend or a spouse. By asking questions more often like "what do you mean by that?" perhaps we can begin fewer conversations with "But I thought we said. . ."

ABOUT THE AUTHORS

Michael W. Kramer is Professor and **Debbie S. Dougherty** is Associate Professor of Communication at the University of Missouri, Columbia, Missouri. This essay is based on Dougherty, D. S., Kramer, M. W., Hamlett, S. R., & Kurth, T. (2009). "Language convergence and meaning divergence: An examination of language and meaning for social-sexual behaviors in organizations." *Communication Monographs*, 76, 20–46. *Communication Monographs* and *Communication Currents* are publications of the National Communication Association.

How, if at all, does this explanation of *language convergence/meaning divergence theory* differ from Haney's definition of bypassing, discussed on p. 97 of Chapter 5?

Relate this statement to Kevin Barge's claim that "Communication involves much more than transferring information from one person to another" in his article "Why Communication?" on p. 22.

6 NONVERBAL

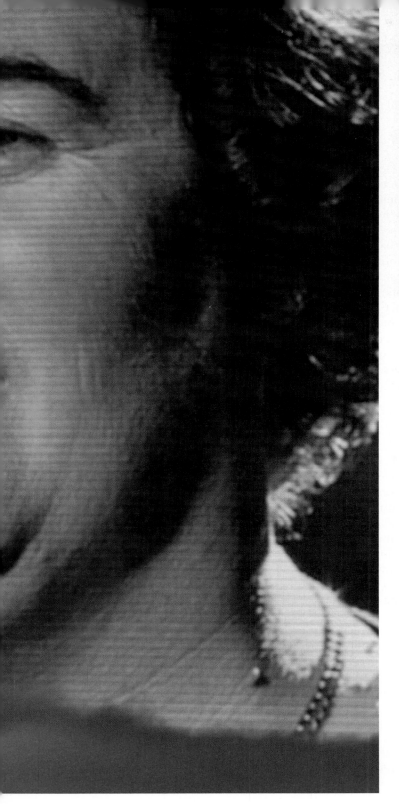

n April 2009, the world met Susan Boyle, the unfashionable, unmarried, unemployed, 47-year-old church volunteer from Scotland who sang her way to instant fame on the television show, *Britain's Got Talent*. When she walked onto the stage, the judges' faces registered skepticism. Camera pans of the audience revealed looks of disdain and disbelief. After Ms. Boyle announced that she would sing "I Dreamed a Dream," a song from the musical *Les Miserables*, the judges smirked and the audience snickered. When the music started, the judges sat back, and braced themselves for what judge Simon Cowell would later describe as "something extraordinary."

> **Actions really *do* speak louder than words.**

And then Susan Boyle began to sing. The judges' skeptical gazes turned into expressions of delight; these coupled with their hands held in eager applause and anticipation, said it all. Everyone rose in a standing ovation, and the rest of Ms. Boyle's story is entertainment history.

Ms. Boyle's story teaches us that actions really *do* speak louder than words. What can a hug from a friend, a raised eyebrow from a co-worker, tears from a child, or the applause of an audience tell you? The answer to this question depends on many factors—the communicators, their purpose, the context, content, and structure of a message, *and* how our nonverbal behavior communicates as much or more than the words we say.

COMMUNICATION

COMMUNICATING
without words

nonverbal communication refers to message components other than words that generate meaning. In fact, 60 to 70 percent, or about two-thirds, of the meaning we generate may be conveyed through nonverbal behaviors.[1] Whereas verbal communication relies on words, nonverbal communication is more multidimensional, relying on such things as physical appearance, body movement, facial expressions, touch, vocal characteristics, and the communication context.

Everyone uses nonverbal communication. When you are aware of your own nonverbal behavior and are sensitive to others' unspoken messages, you are more likely to experience academic and occupational success, better social relationships (and, consequently, less loneliness, shyness, depression, and mental illness), more satisfying marriages, and less stress, anxiety, and hypertension.[2]

Goals of Nonverbal Communication

Because nonverbal communication allows you to send and receive messages through all five of your senses, you have more information to draw upon when generating or interpreting a message. You can achieve many communication goals through nonverbal behavior, ranging from creating a positive impression to detecting deception.

Create an Impression As soon as you walk into a room, your physical appearance, clothing, posture, and facial expression create an impression. When attorneys prepare witnesses to testify in court, they advise them about how to dress and how to look and sound confident, knowing that jurors begin forming opinions of witnesses before they utter a word. Whether it's a first date, a job inter-

view, or a meeting with a new client, nonverbal messages create strong impressions.

Express Emotions We rely on nonverbal communication to express the emotional components of a message. For example, if Jason says, "I'm angry," he simply labels an emotion, but his nonverbal behavior—vocal intensity, facial expression, and body movement—tell you how to interpret his anger. Expressing emotions by smiling, laughing, frowning, crying, grimacing, and even walking away from an encounter can make words unnecessary.

Define Relationships The nature of a relationship is often expressed nonverbally. For example, the closeness and duration of a hug can reveal the level of intimacy between friends. A group member may take a central position at the head of a conference table to establish leadership.

Establish Power and Influence Do you know people who are powerful and persuasive? What kind of nonverbal characteristics do they display? Powerful people often take up more space by having a bigger office or desk. They often touch others more than they are touched. They look at others less unless they want to stare someone down. By using a powerful voice and confident posture, they command attention and influence.

Interpret Verbal Messages Nonverbal communication provides us with a message about a message,

---

Nonverbal communication
Message components other than words that generate meaning

The Nature of NONVERBAL COMMUNICATION

MORE CONVINCING
Nonverbal communication is more believable because it seems spontaneous and revealing. Caution: Perceptions can deceive. Think of the times you've heard, "He *seemed* so honest when I met him," or "She behaved as though she really cared."

HIGHLY CONTEXTUAL
The meaning of nonverbal messages depends on a situation's psychosocial, logistical, and interactional context. Caution: Depending on the context, a laugh can be interpreted as amusement, approval, contempt, scorn, or embarrassment.

CONTINUOUS
Whereas verbal communication may stop and go, nonverbal communication usually continues uninterrupted. Caution: People will interpret your opinions and feelings even when you are not talking.

LESS STRUCTURED
Unlike verbal communication, nonverbal communication has few agreed-upon rules. Caution: Nonverbal behavior can communicate multiple and ambiguous meanings, and can be difficult to interpret.

LEARNED INFORMALLY
You learn to communicate nonverbally by watching others and interpreting feedback about your nonverbal behavior. Caution: Failure to learn appropriate nonverbal behavior can embarrass you and result in misunderstanding and confusion.

Can You Detect a Lie?

Most of us aren't very good at detecting a lie. According to Judee Burgoon, a noted researcher in human deception, most people's ability to detect deception accurately is equivalent to the flip of a coin: about 50/50.[3] Paul Ekman, another leading researcher in deception and nonverbal communication, points out that accurately identifying that someone is lying is further complicated by the fact that there is no single facial expression or body movement that serves as a reliable sign of deceit.[4]

Yet, many liars do give themselves away by displaying **leakage cues,** unintentional nonverbal behaviors that may reveal deceptive communication. These cues, which fall into three categories, are what you need to look for when trying to detect a lie.

1. *Displays of nervousness*: More blinking, higher pitch, vocal tension, less gesturing, more fidgety movements, longer pauses, fewer facial changes

2. *Signs of negative emotions*: Reduced eye contact, fewer pleasant facial expressions, agitated vocal tone

3. *Incompetent communication*: More speech errors, physical rigidity, hesitations, exaggerated movements, lack of spontaneity[5]

Keep in mind that leakage cues are not the same for everyone. For example, rather than reduce or eliminate eye contact, a skillful liar may look you in the eye. In addition, some nonverbal behaviors are better lie detectors than others. For instance, since facial muscles are generally easier to control than other muscles in the body, facial expressions can be managed and therefore won't necessarily reveal a liar. However, vocal pitch is less controllable, so any noticeable changes may well give a liar away.

Mark Knapp, another prominent researcher in lying and deception, acknowledges that a small minority of people are highly skilled lie detectors. These human "lie detectors" pay close attention to what nonverbal communication tells them; they look for discrepancies between verbal and nonverbal behavior.[6] So pay attention to what people say, not just how they act. For example, researchers have noted that people telling the truth tend to add 20 to 30 percent more external detail to their stories and explanations than do those who are lying.[7]

> **"He that has eyes to see and ears to hear may convince himself that no mortal can keep a secret. If his lips are silent, he chatters with his fingertips; betrayal oozes out of him at every pore."**
>
> **SIGMUND FREUD**

poker players have mastered this skill. However, most of us are amateurs. Our "innocent" smile may seem false, our gestures may look awkward, our voice may sound shaky, and our persistent toe-tapping or knee-jiggling may broadcast our anxiety.

According to Sigmund Freud, "He that has eyes to see and ears to hear may convince himself that no mortal can keep a secret. If his lips are silent, he chatters with frozen fingertips; betrayal oozes out of him at every pore."[8]

or a **metamessage**, by offering important clues about how to interpret its verbal aspects. For example, you may doubt a person who says he's feeling fine after a fall because he winces when he walks. If someone says she's glad to see you, but is looking over your shoulder to see who else is in the room, you may distrust her sincerity.

Deceive Others and Detect Deception Have you ever tried to hide your feelings from others—whether it's denying wrongdoing or keeping a secret? Of course you have. Great

Leakage cues Unintentional nonverbal behavior that may reveal deceptive intentions

Metamessage A message about a message

linking verbal
AND NONVERBAL COMMUNICATION

Verbal communication and nonverbal communication often rely on each other to generate and interpret the meaning of a message. When you verbally congratulate someone, you may smile, shake hands, or hug that person. When you verbally express anger, you may also frown, stand farther away, clench your fists, or use a harsh voice. Even in an online message, you may type a section in capital letters for emphasis or add a happy face to show your feelings.

Psychologist Paul Ekman notes that most nonverbal behaviors repeat, complement, accent, regulate, substitute for, and/or contradict verbal messages.[9]

Repeat

Repetitive nonverbal behaviors visually repeat a verbal message. For example, when a waiter asks if anyone is interested in dessert, Elaine nods as she says, "Yes." She then points at a selection on the dessert tray and says, "I want the cheesecake." Ralph says he would like the same, so Elaine holds up two fingers and says, "Make it two slices, then." Nodding, pointing, and holding up two fingers repeats some of Elaine's words nonverbally.

Complement

Complementary nonverbal behaviors are consistent with the verbal message. During a job interview, your words state that you are a confident professional, but what you say will be more believable if nonverbal elements such as posture, facial expressions, and vocal quality send the same message. Even the meaning of a simple *hello* can be strengthened if your facial expression and tone of voice communicate genuine interest and pleasure in greeting someone.

Accent

Accenting nonverbal behaviors emphasize important elements in a message by highlighting its focus or emotional content. Saying the words "I'm angry" may fail to make the point, so you may couple this message with louder volume, forceful gestures, and piercing eye contact. Stressing a word or phrase in a sentence also focuses meaning.

Regulate

We use **regulating nonverbal behaviors** to manage the flow of a conversation. Nonverbal cues tell us when to start and stop talking, whose turn it is to speak, how to interrupt other speakers, and how to encourage others to talk more. If you lean forward and open your mouth as if to speak, you are signaling that you want a turn in the conversation. In a classroom or large meeting, you may raise your hand when you want to speak. When your friend nods her head as you speak, you may interpret her nod as a sign to continue what you're saying.

Substitute

Nonverbal behavior can take the place of verbal language. This is called using **substituting nonverbal behaviors**. When we wave hello or goodbye, the meaning is usually clear even in the absence of words. Without saying anything, a mother may send a message to a misbehaving child by pursing her lips, narrowing her eyes, and moving a single finger to signal "stop."

Contradict

Contradictory nonverbal behaviors conflict with the meaning of spoken words. Upon receiving a birthday gift from a co-worker, Sherry says, "It's lovely. Thank you."

However, her forced smile, flat vocal expression, and lack of eye contact suggest that Sherry does not appreciate the gift. This is a classic example of a **mixed message**: a contradiction between verbal and nonverbal meanings. When nonverbal behavior contradicts spoken words, messages are confusing and difficult to interpret. In addition to the fact that nonverbal channels carry more information than verbal ones, we usually rely on the nonverbal elements of communication to determine the true meaning of a message.

Repetitive nonverbal behavior Nonverbal behavior that visually repeats a verbal message

Complementary nonverbal behavior Nonverbal behavior that is consistent with the verbal message being expressed at the same time

Accenting nonverbal behavior Nonverbal behavior that emphasizes important elements in a message by highlighting its focus or emotional content

Regulating nonverbal behavior Nonverbal behavior that manages the flow of a conversation

Substituting nonverbal behavior Nonverbal behavior that replaces verbal language; for example, waving hello instead of saying "hello"

Contradictory nonverbal behavior Nonverbal behavior that conflicts with the meaning of spoken words

Mixed message A contradiction between verbal and nonverbal meanings

Expectancy Violation Theory

The following two scenarios are very similar, but may solicit significantly different reactions.

Scenario 1. You have stopped at a local convenience store for a cup of coffee on your way to work, and you notice a poorly dressed man looking at you as you walk into the store. You've never seen him before. While you are preparing your coffee, he approaches and stands right next to you, smiling. As he reaches for a cup, his hand brushes against your arm. You turn to leave. Now he is standing directly behind you to pay for the coffee—and smiles again. As you leave, he follows you out the door.

Scenario 2. You have stopped at the office snack bar to get a cup of coffee, and you notice a well-dressed man looking at you. He's a valued friend and colleague you've worked with for many years. While you are preparing your coffee, he approaches and stands right next to you, smiling. As he reaches for a cup, his hand brushes against your arm. You turn to leave. Now he is standing directly behind you to pay for the coffee—and smiles again. As you leave, he follows you out the door.

Both scenarios are similar. Yet, in the first case, you may react with suspicion and disapproval, whereas in the second case you may feel more relaxed and positive. According to **Expectancy Violation Theory**, your expectations about nonverbal behavior have a significant effect on how you interact with others and how you interpret the meaning of nonverbal messages. When you enter an elevator, you probably conform to nonverbal expectations: You turn around and face front, avoid eye contact with others, avoid movement, refrain from talk-ing or touching others, and stare at the numbers as they go up or down. But how would you react if someone entered a cramped elevator with three unruly dogs and lit a cigar? You'd probably disapprove or object, because this is not the kind of behavior you'd expect in a confined public space.

At least three characteristics influence how you react to the nonverbal behavior of another person.[10] Think of the previous two scenarios as you consider these characteristics.

1. *Communicator Characteristics.* Similarities and differences in personal characteristics, such as age, gender, ethnicity, and physical appearance, as well as personality and reputation

2. *Relational Characteristics.* Level of familiarity, past experiences, relative status, and type of relationship with others, such as close friend, romantic partner, business associate, service provider, or stranger

3. *Contextual Characteristics.* Physical, social, psychological, cultural, and professional settings and occasions, such as football games, stores, religious services, classrooms, or business meetings

Clearly, the first scenario highlights differences in communicator, relational, and contextual characteristics, whereas the second scenario highlights similarities. In the first scenario, the man violates a number of nonverbal expectations: Don't stare, follow, or touch strangers. In the second scenario, the man is "allowed" to violate the same nonverbal expectations because you know him well.

Violations of nonverbal expectations may be positive or negative. Generally, a positive reaction occurs when the violation comes from someone you know, like, or admire. Likewise, a negative reaction may result when the violation comes from someone you don't know or don't like.

Expectancy Violation Theory
Your expectations about nonverbal behavior significantly affect your interactions with others and the way you interpret nonverbal messages

types OF NONVERBAL COMMUNICATION

nonverbal communication is undeniably complex. To interpret nonverbal meaning accurately, you must pay attention to many nonverbal dimensions. Effective communicators consider the totality of their own and others' nonverbal behavior.

Physical Appearance

When you first meet someone, you automatically analyze a person's physical appearance to form an impression. Although it seems unfair to judge a person's personality and character based on physical characteristics such as attractiveness, clothing, and hairstyles, these factors strongly influence how we interact with others.

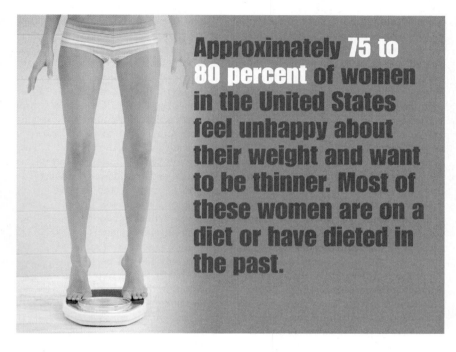

Approximately **75 to 80 percent** of women in the United States feel unhappy about their weight and want to be thinner. Most of these women are on a diet or have dieted in the past.

Types of NONVERBAL CUES

Physical Appearance

Body Movement and Gestures

Touch

Facial Expressions

Eye Behavior

Vocal Expressiveness

Silence

Space and Distance

Time

Environment

Attractiveness For better or worse, attractive people are perceived as kinder, more interesting, more sociable, more successful, and sexier than those considered less attractive. One study found that good-looking people tend to make more money and get promoted more often than those with average looks.[11] In their quest to be more attractive, many people try to alter their physical appearance. Approximately 75 to 80 percent of women in the United States feel unhappy about their weight and want to be thinner. Most of these women are on a diet or have dieted in the past.[12]

Some people alter the color of their skin by tanning or with cosmetics. Hair color and style can easily be changed, and plastic surgery and chemical enhancements allow people to alter their facial structure and body shape.

Certainly the images of attractive men and women on television and in popular magazines and film influence how we see others. Most of us were not born with movie-star features and never will meet those standards of "beauty." Yet, there is no question that physical attraction plays a significant role in selecting romantic partners, getting and succeeding in a job, persuading others, and maintaining high self-esteem.

Clothing and Accessories Your clothing and accessories send messages about your economic status, education, trustworthiness, social position, level of sophistication, and moral character. For example, a person wearing a stylish suit and carrying an expensive leather briefcase suggests a higher income, a college education, and more status within a company than a person wearing a uniform and carrying a mop. Accessories such as a college ring, a wedding band, or a religious necklace reveal a great deal about another person.

However, judging others based on their clothing can lead to inaccurate

Can Tattooing and Body Piercing Hurt Your Image?

In many cultures, both past and present, people have pierced and tattooed their bodies. These markings often commemorated a rite of passage such as puberty, marriage, or a successful hunt. However, in most Western cultures, tattoos have traditionally been associated with people of lower social status, gangs, "bikers," and lower-ranked military personnel.

Just a short time ago, a pierced nose, tongue, eyebrow, lip, navel, or other body part was virtually unheard of in mainstream society; however, that has changed. Today, tattooing and body piercing have become a popular trend, especially among adolescents and young adults. A 2006 study published by the American Academy of Dermatology reports that 36 percent of 18- to 29-year olds have a tattoo. A Harris survey in 2008 reports similar numbers.[13] David Brooks, political and cultural commentator for the *New York Times,* observes that "a cadre of fashion-forward types thought they were doing something to separate themselves from the vanilla middle class but are now discovering

that the signs etched into their skins are absolutely mainstream."[14]

Yet, despite their popularity, tattoos and body piercings continue to create unintended impressions that may not serve you well. According to *USA Today* writer Oren Dorell, "Cities and school districts across the country are forcing their employees to cover up tattoos if they want to keep their jobs."[15] Many young job-seekers have learned this as well, as they find themselves having to conceal tattoos and remove body piercings for job interviews.[16] While public perception may change as a younger generation of tattooed and pierced people rise to leadership positions in their companies and communities, recognize that these markings can distract from and misrepresent your intended impression.

assumptions. For example, what type of clothing does a millionaire wear? In their book, *The Millionaire Next Door: The Surprising Secrets of America's Wealthy*, marketing researchers Thomas Stanley and William Danko reveal that the vast majority of millionaires do not wear expensive suits, shoes, or watches. "It is easier to purchase products that denote superiority than to actually be superior in economic achievement."[17]

Hair Hair is something of an obsession in the United States. In *Reading People*, jury consultant Jo-Ellan Dimitrius and attorney Mark Mazzarella use hair as a predictor of people's self-image and lifestyle. They claim that your hairstyle can reveal

"how you feel about aging, how extravagant or practical you are, how much importance you attach to impressing others, your socioeconomic background, your overall emotional maturity, and sometimes even the part of the country where you were raised or now live."[18] If you doubt their claim, think about the ways in which very long hair on men communicated antiwar rebellion and hippie lifestyles in the late 1960s and early 1970s.

However, be careful when drawing conclusions about others based on their hairstyle. A man who wears short hair may be an ultraconservative or a rebel, an athlete or a cancer patient, a police officer or a fashion model. A short and chic haircut on

a woman can signify an artistic, creative, and expressive nature, or may indicate a more practical nature.

Body Movement and Gestures

Jamal points to his watch to let the chairperson know that the meeting time is running short. Karen gives a thumbs-up gesture to signal that her friend's speech went well. Robin stands at attention as the American flag is raised. How you sit, stand, position the body, or move your hands generates nonverbal messages. Even your posture can convey moods and emotions. Slouching back in your chair may be perceived as lack of interest or dislike, whereas sitting upright and leaning forward communicates interest and is a sign of active listening.

Gestures are body movements that communicate an idea or emotion. They can emphasize or stress parts of a message, reveal discomfort with a situation, or convey a message without the use of words. The hands and arms are used most frequently for gesturing, although head and foot movements are also considered types of gestures.[19]

Many people have difficulty expressing their thoughts without using gestures. Why else would we gesture when speaking to someone on the phone? Gesturing can also ease the mental effort required when communication is difficult. For example, we tend to gesture more

MANY PEOPLE HAVE DIFFICULTY EXPRESSING THEIR THOUGHTS WITHOUT USING GESTURES.

when using a language that is less familiar or when describing a picture that a listener cannot see. Paul Ekman and Wallace Friesen classify hand movements as emblems, illustrators, and adaptors.[20]

Touch

Touch is one of the most potent forms of physical expression. It not only has the power to send strong messages, but it also affects your overall well-being. Being deprived of touch can have a negative effect on your physical and psychological health.[21] For example we know that

babies need human touch to survive and develop. When new parents and hospital nurses engage in more touching behavior, infant death rates decrease.

We use touch to express a wide range of emotions. An encouraging pat on the shoulder from a co-worker or a lover's embrace can convey encouragement, appreciation, affection, empathy, or sexual interest. Playful touches tend to lighten the mood without expressing a high degree of emotion. A light non-threatening punch in the arm between friends or covering another's eyes and asking, "Guess who?" is a playful touch.

> **Gesture** A body movement that communicates an idea or emotion

TYPES OF GESTURES

TYPE OF GESTURE	CHARACTERISTICS	EXAMPLES
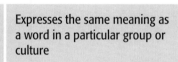  **EMBLEM**	Expresses the same meaning as a word in a particular group or culture	• Forming a V with your index and middle finger as a sign of victory or peace • Raising your hand in class to indicate, "I want to speak" • Placing your index finger over your lips to mean "be quiet" • Making a circle with thumb and index finger to indicate "OK" • Extending the middle finger to offend someone or declare "up yours"
 **ILLUSTRATOR**	Used with a verbal message that would lack meaning without the words	• Holding your hands two feet apart and saying, "The fish I caught was this big" • Counting out the steps of a procedure with your hand while orally describing each step • Snapping your fingers while saying, "It happened just like that," to indicate that an event occurred quickly
 **ADAPTOR**	Habitual gestures that help manage and express emotions	• Clenching or pounding your fists in anger • Chewing your nails because you are worried or anxious • Drumming your fingers on a table because you are impatient • Wringing your hands because you are distressed • Playing with your hair or an object to relieve stress or impatience

IS THE OK SIGN ALWAYS OK?

Keep in mind that the examples of emblems, illustrators, and adaptors introduced in this chapter are gestures commonly used in the United States and have very specific meanings. Therefore, before interacting with people from other countries and of other cultures, think before you gesture. For example, the sign that means "OK" to most Americans (forming a circle with the thumb and index finger) is actually considered an obscene gesture to Brazilians, and signifies money to the Japanese.[22] When describing the height of a person, we may hold an arm out, palm down, and say, "My friend is this tall." In some South American cultures, this same gesture is fine for describing a dog, but would not be used for describing a person. To designate a person's height, a South American would hold her arm out with her palm sideways. Even putting your hands in your pockets can offend others, as a professor friend of ours learned when he spent a year teaching in Indonesia.

Touch is also used to express control or dominance. In some instances, only a minor level of control is needed, such as when we tap someone on the shoulder to get her or his attention. In other cases, touch sends very clear messages about status or dominance. Research shows that individuals with more power and status are more likely to touch someone of lesser status, but subordinates rarely initiate touch with a person of higher status.[23]

Some people are more comfortable with touch than others. **Touch approachers** tend to be comfortable with touch and often

Know Thy Self

Are You Touchy?[24]

How touchy are you? Indicate the degree to which each of the statements below applies to you using the following rating scale: (5) strongly agree, (4) agree, (3) undecided or neutral, (2) disagree, or (1) strongly disagree.

_____ 1. I don't mind if I am hugged as a sign of friendship.

_____ 2. I enjoy touching others.

_____ 3. I seldom put my arms around others.

_____ 4. When I see people hugging, it bothers me.

_____ 5. People should not be uncomfortable about being touched.

_____ 6. I really like being touched by others.

_____ 7. I wish I were free to show my emotions by touching others.

_____ 8. I do not like touching other people.

_____ 9. I do not like being touched by others.

_____ 10. I find it enjoyable to be touched by others.

_____ 11. I dislike having to hug others.

_____ 12. Hugging and touching should be outlawed.

_____ 13. Touching others is a very important part of my personality.

_____ 14. Being touched by others makes me uncomfortable.

Scoring:

1. Add up the responses you put next to the following items: 1, 2, 5, 6, 7, 10, and 13. Your Step 1 score = _____.

2. Add up the responses you put next to the following items: 3, 4, 8, 9, 11, 12, and 14. Your Step 2 score = _____.

3. Complete the following formula: 42 + total of step 1 − total of step 2 = _____

Your score should be between 14 and 70 points. A score of more than 53 points suggests that you are a touch approacher. A score of less than 31 points indicates that you tend to avoid touch.

initiate touch with others. A touch approacher is more likely to initiate a hug or a kiss when greeting a friend. Some touch approachers even touch or hug people they don't know very well. At the extreme end of the continuum are touch approachers who touch too much and violate nonverbal expectations.

Touch avoiders are less comfortable initiating or being touched. They are also more conscious of when, how, and by whom they are touched. Extreme touch avoiders avoid any physical contact even with loved ones. Most of us are somewhere in the middle of the continuum. Obviously, misunderstandings can result when touch approachers and avoiders meet. Approachers may view avoiders as cold and unfriendly, and avoiders may perceive approachers as invasive and rude.

Not surprisingly, norms for touch depend on the context. For example, violating touch norms in the workplace can result in misunderstandings or allegations of sexual harassment. Norms for touch also vary according to gender and culture. Most North American men avoid same-sex touch except for the hugging and high-fiving we see on sports teams.

Facial Expression

Your face is composed of complex muscles capable of displaying well over a thousand different expressions. Facial expressions let you know if others are interested in, agree with, or understand what you have said. Generally, women tend to be more facially expressive and smile more often than men. But although men are more likely to limit the amount of emotion they reveal, everyone relies on a person's facial expressions to comprehend the full meaning of a message.

We learn to manage facial expressions in order to convey or conceal an emotion and to adapt our facial expressions to particular situations. The most common techniques for adapting facial expressions are masking, neutralization, intensification, and deintensification.[25]

Making Faces Online When you communicate face-to-face, you can listen to how words are said and observe nonverbal behavior. However, we increasingly rely on technology to communicate. For example, we use e-mail to communicate with co-workers and friends. Virtual work groups may use technologies that don't allow members to hear each other or to see the facial expressions, head nods, gestures, or posture of others. In order to add emotional flavor to text-based communication, some people use **emoticons,** typographical characters that convey nonverbal expressions.

In theory, emoticons serve as substitutes for nonverbal behavior.

Touch approachers People who tend to be comfortable with touch and often initiate touch with others

Touch avoiders People who tend to be uncomfortable initiating touch or being touched

Emoticons Typographical characters that are used to convey nonverbal expressions

---

Techniques for Adapting Facial Expressions

TECHNIQUE	CHARACTERISTICS	EXAMPLES
Masking	Conceals true emotions by displaying expressions considered more appropriate in a particular situation	• Smiling and congratulating a colleague for getting a promotion you wanted • Looking stern when reprimanding a toddler who has dumped a bowl of spaghetti on his head
Neutralization	Eliminates all displays of emotions	• Avoiding any display of emotion when serving as a juror during a trial • Displaying a "poker face" during a card game
Intensification	Exaggerates expressions to meet other people's needs or to express strong feelings	• Hugging someone a few more seconds than usual to communicate how much you care • Pouting dramatically when you do not get your way
Deintensification	Reduces or downplays emotional displays to accommodate others	• Looking mildly disapproving when a committee member rudely interrupts another speaker during a meeting • Subduing smiles of happiness after defeating a highly competitive friend in a tennis match

Facial Expressions in CYBERSPACE

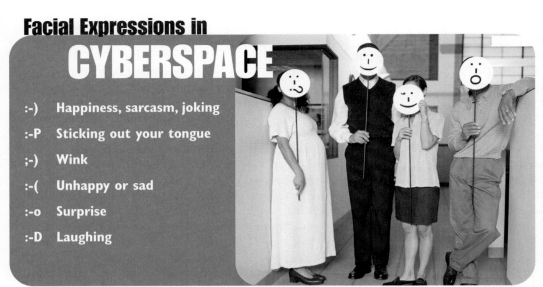

:-)   Happiness, sarcasm, joking

:-P   Sticking out your tongue

;-)   Wink

:-(Unhappy or sad

:-o   Surprise

:-D   Laughing

However, research suggests that emoticons have become less and less useful as nonverbal cues and have little or no effect on the interpretation of a typed message. We are more likely to rely on the words or abbreviations such as BTW (by the way) or LOL (laugh out loud) rather than the emoticons when interpreting the meaning of a written message. Apparently this is because emoticons are "now overused, and the impact that [they are] supposed to have diminished, either culturally/historically, or as an individual user is first entertained, and later bored, with the cuteness of them all."[26]

Eye Behavior

Your eyes may be the most revealing and complex of all your facial features.

Our eyes can signify social position, express both positive and negative emotion, and indicate a willingness to relate.[27] When we try to understand what someone else is saying, most of us will look at a speaker more than 80 percent of the time. A group member who wants to be viewed as a leader may choose a seat at the head of the table to gain more visual attention. We tend to increase gaze in response to positive emotions such as surprise and avert our eyes in response to negative experiences like disgust or horror. We use eye contact to get a server's attention in a restaurant and avert our eyes when we don't want the instructor to call on us.

As with all nonverbal behavior, norms for eye contact vary according to gender and culture. Women tend to engage in more eye contact when listening than men. In North America, lack of eye contact is frequently perceived as rudeness, indifference, nervousness, or dishonesty. However, this is not true across all cultures. For example, "direct eye contact is a taboo or an insult in many Asian cultures. Cambodians consider direct eye contact an invasion of one's privacy."[28]

Vocal Expressiveness

How you *say* a word significantly influences its meaning. Your vocal quality also affects how others see

What Do We Know About EYE BEHAVIOR?

Researchers have arrived at several conclusions about eye behavior.[29] Rate each of the following behaviors as *generally* true or false. Keep in mind that factors such as personality, gender, culture, and context influence our eye behavior.

True/False

_____ 1. We look at people and things we like.

_____ 2. We avoid looking at people and things we do not like.

_____ 3. We look more at another person when seeking approval or wanting to be liked.

_____ 4. When we avert our gaze from someone, it's an intentional act.

_____ 5. Deception can rarely be detected by looking solely at another person's eye behavior.

_____ 6. Our pupils dilate when we look at someone or something that is appealing or interesting to us.

_____ 7. Our pupils constrict when we look at someone or something that is not appealing or interesting to us.

_____ 8. Women often look longer at their conversational partner than will men.

Scoring your answers: All of the statements are true.

you. For example, it can be difficult to listen to a person with a very high-pitched or monotone voice.

Some of the most important vocal characteristics are volume, pitch, and word stress. **Volume** refers to the loudness of the voice. Whispering can indicate that the information is confidential; yelling suggests urgency or anger. **Pitch** refers to how high or low your voice sounds. In the United States, Americans seem to prefer low-pitched voices. Men and women with deeper voices are seen as more authoritative and effective. Men with a naturally high pitch may be labeled effeminate or weak, and women with very high pitches may be labeled as childish, silly, or anxious.

In Chapter 14, Language and Delivery, we take a closer look at these and other vocal characteristics and see how they contribute to the success of a presentation.

When volume and pitch are combined, they can be used to vary the stress you give to a word or phrase. **Word stress** refers to the "degree of prominence given to a syllable within a word or words within a phrase or sentence."[29] Notice the differences in meaning as you stress the italicized words in the following sentences:

Is *that* the report you want me to read?

Is that the report you want *me* to read?

Is that the report you want me to *read*?

Although the same words are used in all three sentences, the meaning of each question is quite different.

Silence

The well-known phrase "silence is golden" may be based on a Swiss saying, "*Sprechen ist silbern; Swchweigen ist golden,*" which means "speech is silver; silence is golden." This metaphor contrasts the value of speech and silence. Although

Silence is also speech. (African proverb)

A loud voice shows an empty head. (Finnish proverb)

Those who know, do not speak. Those who speak, do not know. Lao Tzu, *Tao Te Ching* (Chinese book of wisdom written in the fifth century B.C.)

speech is important, silence may be even more significant in certain contexts.

Understanding the value of silence is important because we use silence to communicate many things: to establish interpersonal distance, to put our thoughts together, to show respect for another person, or to modify others' behaviors.[31]

Volume The loudness level of your voice

Pitch How high or low your voice sounds in terms of notes on a musical scale

Word stress The degree of prominence given to a syllable within a word or words within a phrase or sentence

---

ethicalcommunication

The Dark Side of Nonverbal Behavior

Just as a smile or a pat on the back can communicate, so too can an angry shove or a slap. Unfortunately, some people use violent nonverbal communication to express negative emotions or exert power over others. Each year, approximately 1.5 million women and more than 800,000 men are victims of violence from an intimate partner such as a husband, wife, boyfriend, girlfriend, or date.[33] Although female victims are more likely to need medical attention, research reveals that women hit men as often as men hit women.[33] Violence also occurs in the workplace between co-workers and by frustrated customers. Fifteen percent of homicides in the workplace are committed by co-workers.[34]

Physical intimidation and violence includes acts such as hitting, restraining, and shoving, as well as behavior that stops short of physical contact, such as throwing things, pounding on a desk, or destroying property. Intimidating nonverbal communication can also take more subtle forms, such as physically blocking another's path, moving aggressively and too close, or creating a threatening presence. The use of unjustified physical aggression violates the National Communication Association's Credo for Ethical Communication, which specifically condemns communication that is intimidating, coercive, or violent.[35]

> **Fifteen percent of homicides in the workplace are committed by co-workers.**

Space and Distance

The ways in which we claim, use, and interpret space and distance are significant dimensions of nonverbal communication.

In nonverbal terms, **territoriality** is the sense of personal ownership attached to a particular space. For instance, most classroom students sit in the same place every day. If you have ever walked into a classroom to find another person in *your* seat, you may have felt that your territory had been violated. Ownership of territory is often designated by objects acting as **markers** of territory. Placing a coat on a chair or books on a table can send a clear message that a seat is taken or saved.

Anthropologist Edward T. Hall uses the term **proxemics** to refer to the study of spatial relationships and how the distance between people communicates information about their relationship. Hall maintains that we have our own personal portable "air bubble" that we carry around with us. This personal space is culturally determined. For example, the Japanese, who are accustomed to crowding, need less space around them, whereas "wide open spaces" North Americans need more space around them to feel comfortable.[36]

Hall contends that most Americans interact within four spatial zones or distances: intimate, personal, social, and public.[37]

Not surprisingly, we reduce the distance between ourselves and others as our relationships become more personal. Intimate distance is usually associated with love, comfort, protection, and increased physical contact. In most situations, you encounter a mixture of distances. You may feel comfortable using an intimate or personal distance with a good friend at work, but use social distance with other colleagues.

Time

In Chapter 3, we discussed the cultural dimension known as mono-

Hall's FOUR Spatial Zones

Intimate (0–18 inches)

Personal (18 inches–4 feet)

Social (4–12 feet)

Public (12+ feet)

chronic-polychronic time. We noted that people with these two time orientations may not be compatible. Monochronic people want things to run on schedule because time is valuable. They become frustrated by polychronic people who are not slaves to time and tolerate interruptions in a schedule.

Although researchers have studied how people make use of and respond to time, making rules about it proves difficult. For example, it's unforgivable to be late for an interview, but okay to be late for a party. And what, according to some research, do U.S. students see as the most disruptive thing in a classroom? The answer:

Students walking in after the class has begun.[38] As you pay attention and observe others' nonverbal behavior, try to learn what their attitudes are about time and punctuality and com-

---

Territoriality The sense of personal ownership attached to a particular space
Marker The placement of an object to establish nonverbal "ownership" of an area or space
Proxemics The study of spatial relationships and how the distance between people communicates information about their relationship

pare it to yours. Understanding differences in time orientation can help you accommodate others and communicate more effectively.

Environment

Do you behave the same way in the classroom as you do at work?

Context, or the environment, does more than influence nonverbal communication; it is a part of nonverbal communication. In other words, context alone can communicate a message. For example, an office with stacks of unorganized papers crowding the room, a stale smell, uncomfortable chairs, and ugly orange walls may create a negative impression of the occupant, but it may also affect how comfortably you interact in that space. Environmental elements such as furniture arrangement, lighting, color, temperature, and smell communicate.

Most environments are designed with a purpose in mind. An expensive restaurant's dining room may separate tables at some distance to offer diners privacy. The restaurant's atmosphere may be comfortable, quiet, and only subject to the mouth-watering aroma of good food. How does this differ from the environmental features at your local fast-food restaurant?

improving
NONVERBAL SKILLS

most people learn to communicate nonverbally by imitating others and by paying attention to and adapting to feedback. Thus, when someone responds positively to a particular nonverbal behavior, you tend to keep using it. If you receive negative reactions, you may choose a more effective behavior next time. Training and practice can help you develop more effective nonverbal communication skills.

Be Other-Oriented

Other-oriented people are effective self-monitors and sensitive to others. They give serious, undivided attention to, feel genuine concern for, and focus on the needs of other communicators. For example, during a casual phone conversation, note whether your friend's tone of voice communicates more than the words you hear. During face-to-face encounters, observe and "listen" to the nonverbal messages; that is, *look* while you listen. The more of your five senses you use, the more nonverbal cues you will notice.

As you make your own observations, ask yourself some of these questions:

- Does their nonverbal behavior repeat, complement, accent, regulate, or substitute for what they say, or does it contradict their verbal messages?
- Are their gestures emblems, illustrators, or adaptors?
- Do facial expressions mask, neutralize, intensify, or deintensify their thoughts and feelings?
- Do they maintain or avoid eye contact?
- Do they display leakage cues that may reveal a lie or deceptive communication?

LOOK LIKE YOU ARE LISTENING

If you have difficulty interpreting the meaning of nonverbal behavior, ask for help. Describe the message as you understand it. For example, if someone tells you about a tragic event while smiling, you might say, "George, you don't seem very upset by this. Maybe your smile is just a sign of nervousness?" If you are having trouble setting up a meeting with someone and sense a problem, ask the person, "You seem to be avoiding me—or is it just my imagination?" In Chapter 7, Listening and Critical Thinking, we discuss several techniques for ensuring that you understand the meaning of verbal and nonverbal messages.

Not only should you look *while* you listen, but you should also look like you *are* listening. Nodding your head, leaning forward, and engaging in direct eye contact are just some of the nonverbal cues that indicate to

---

Other-orientation Giving serious attention to, feeling concern for, and showing interest in other communicators

How Immediate Are Your Teachers?

Several studies find positive links between immediacy and learning. Teachers who are immediate generate more interest and enthusiasm about the subject matter.[39] Some of the nonverbal characteristics of high immediacy include

- consistent and direct eye contact
- smiling
- appropriate and natural body movement
- vocal variety
- maintaining closer physical distance[40]

Think of some of the teachers you've had throughout your lifetime. Were they all effective and memorable? Which teachers left the most indelible impressions? How would you describe their nonverbal behaviors? Were their bodies glued to their desk or lectern, or did they come from behind that barrier, gesture openly, and move closer to you and the other students? Did they smile and look at you directly, use an expressive voice, and listen actively? Did you like them more and learn more from them?[41]

Similarly, we tend to feel more comfortable and want to approach people who seem warm and friendly. **Immediacy** is the degree to which a person seems approachable or likable. Imagine approaching a customer service counter where you see two workers, both available to help you. One of the workers leans away from the counter, does not make eye contact with you, and is frowning. The other worker looks directly at you and smiles. The principle of immediate communication suggests that you will walk up to the worker who appears friendly.

A variety of nonverbal behaviors can promote immediacy.[42] Neat, clean, and pleasant-smelling people are, understandably, more approachable than those who are dirty, sloppy, and smelly. The degree to which you are perceived as likable and approachable may be the difference between a smile and a frown, leaning toward rather than away from another person, direct eye contact versus looking away, a relaxed rather than a rigid body posture, or animated instead of neutral vocal tones. When you use nonverbal immediacy behaviors, other people are more likely to want to communicate with you, and those interactions will be warmer and friendlier for everyone involved.

others that you are paying attention and interested. Furthermore, your nonverbal feedback lets another communicator sense your response to a message. For example, if your nonverbal behaviors suggest you don't understand or that you disagree with what is being said, the other person may try to clarify information or present a better argument.

Use Immediacy Strategies

Generally, we avoid individuals who appear cold, unfriendly, or hostile.

> **Immediacy** The degree to which a person seems approachable or likable

Communication ASSESSMENT

Read the items on Brian Spitzberg's **Conversational Skills Rating Scale**.[43] Check the items that describe verbal communication and those that describe nonverbal communication in a face-to-face conversation. When you are finished, add up the number of items you checked as verbal and nonverbal. What percent of communication behaviors did you label as nonverbal? To what extent do you use these nonverbal communication behaviors skillfully when you're talking to someone else?

Conversational Skills Rating Scale

Verbal or Nonverbal	Communication Behavior
___ Verbal ___ Nonverbal	1. Speaking rate (neither too slow nor too fast)
___ Verbal ___ Nonverbal	2. Speaking fluency (pauses, silences, frequent "uhs")
___ Verbal ___ Nonverbal	3. Vocal confidence (neither too tense/nervous nor overly confident-sounding)
___ Verbal ___ Nonverbal	4. Articulation (clarity of individual sounds and words)
___ Verbal ___ Nonverbal	5. Vocal variety (neither overly monotone nor dramatic voice)
___ Verbal ___ Nonverbal	6. Volume (neither too loud nor too soft)
___ Verbal ___ Nonverbal	7. Posture (neither too closed/formal nor too open/informal)
___ Verbal ___ Nonverbal	8. Lean toward partner (neither too forward nor too far back)
___ Verbal ___ Nonverbal	9. Shaking or nervous twitches (aren't noticeable or distracting)
___ Verbal ___ Nonverbal	10. Unmotivated movements (tapping feet, fingers, hair-twirling)
___ Verbal ___ Nonverbal	11. Facial expressiveness (neither neutral/blank nor exaggerated)
___ Verbal ___ Nonverbal	12. Nodding of head in response to partner statements
___ Verbal ___ Nonverbal	13. Use of gestures to emphasize what is being said
___ Verbal ___ Nonverbal	14. Use of humor and/or stories
___ Verbal ___ Nonverbal	15. Smiling and/or laughing
___ Verbal ___ Nonverbal	16. Use of eye contact
___ Verbal ___ Nonverbal	17. Asking questions
___ Verbal ___ Nonverbal	18. Speaking about partner (involvement of partner as a topic of conversation)
___ Verbal ___ Nonverbal	19. Speaking about self (neither too much nor too little)
___ Verbal ___ Nonverbal	20. Encouragements or agreements (encouragement of partner to talk)
___ Verbal ___ Nonverbal	21. Personal opinion expression (neither too passive nor too aggressive)
___ Verbal ___ Nonverbal	22. Initiation of new topics
___ Verbal ___ Nonverbal	23. Maintenance of topics and follow-up comments
___ Verbal ___ Nonverbal	24. Interruption of partner speaking turns
___ Verbal ___ Nonverbal	25. Use of time speaking relative to partner

Summary

What is nonverbal communication, and how does it affect your everyday life?

- Nonverbal communication refers to message components other than words you use to generate and respond to meaning.

- Nonverbal communication accounts for between 60 to 70 percent of the meaning generated in a face-to-face message.

- In everyday life, you use nonverbal communication to express emotions, define relationships, establish power and influence, interpret verbal messages, deceive, and detect deception.

How do verbal and nonverbal communication interact to create meaning?

- Nonverbal communication differs from verbal communication in that it is more convincing, highly contextual, learned informally, less structured, and continuous.

- Nonverbal behavior can repeat, complement, accent, regulate, substitute, and/or contradict verbal messages.

- Expectancy Violation Theory demonstrates how your expectations about nonverbal behavior significantly affect how you interact with others and how you interpret the meaning of nonverbal messages.

What types of nonverbal communication should you pay attention to when interacting with others?

- Nonverbal communication has many dimensions, including physical appearance, body movement and gestures, touch, facial expressions, eye behavior, vocal expressiveness, silence, space and distance, time, and environment.

- Physical appearance includes nonverbal elements such as attractiveness, the presence or absence of tattoos and body piercing, clothing and accessories, and hair styles.

- Hand movement can be classified as emblems, illustrators, and adaptors.

- Facial expressions can function to mask, neutralize, intensify, or deintensify an emotion.

- *Proxemics* refers to the study of how the distance between people communicates information about the nature of their relationship.

How can you improve your ability to recognize, use, and adapt to nonverbal communication?

- By observing others', nonverbal behavior and confirming your interpretation of its meaning, you can become more "other"-oriented.

- Nonverbal immediacy strategies such as maintaining eye contact, smiling, using vocal variety and appropriate body movements, and maintaining close physical distance can enhance your interactions with others.

the THINK SPOT
www.thethinkspot.com

TEST your knowledge

1. The textbook defines *nonverbal communication* as message components other than words that generate meaning. Which of the following answers is *not* an example of nonverbal communication?
   a. using :-) in an e-mail to highlight your feelings
   b. reading an old letter from a good friend who was living abroad
   c. putting on perfume or cologne before going to a party
   d. brightening up your apartment with flowers before your parents come over for dinner
   e. sitting in a middle position at the side of a table during a staff meeting

2. Even though Fiona has nothing but good things to say about her boyfriend, her family can tell she's angry at him. Which unique feature of nonverbal communication helps explain this experience?
   a. Nonverbal communication is more convincing.
   b. Nonverbal communication is highly contextual.
   c. Nonverbal communication is learned informally.
   d. Nonverbal communication is less structured.
   e. Nonverbal communication is continuous.

3. Which of the following nonverbal communication goals could Sigmund Freud have been describing when he wrote that "He who has eyes to see and ears to hear may convince himself that no mortal can keep a secret"?
   a. to express emotions
   b. to define relationships
   c. to establish power and influence
   d. to interpret verbal messages
   e. to deceive and detect deception

4. Most people can detect deception accurately about _____ percent of the time.
   a. 25   d. 75
   b. 30   e. 80
   c. 50

5. According to research reported by Mark Knapp, the small minority of people who are *highly* skilled lie detectors look for
   a. higher voice pitch and vocal tension in a speaker.
   b. exaggerated movements and longer pauses.
   c. discrepancies between verbal and nonverbal behavior.
   d. more blinking and less eye contact.
   e. fidgety movements and less gesturing.

6. Which of the following nonverbal hand movements is an example of an illustrator?
   a. Making a circle with your thumb and index finger to indicate "OK."
   b. Holding your thumb and fingers about two inches apart as you describe how much shorter your hair was after your last haircut.
   c. Putting your face in the palms of your hands when you realize that you've forgotten to buy your spouse a Valentine's present.
   d. Raising your hand in class so the instructor will call on you.
   e. Crossing your index and middle fingers as a good-luck signal.

7. If one of your co-workers tells you that she got the promotion that both of you applied for, you may smile at the news even though you feel awful. Which technique for adapting facial expressions are you using?
   a. masking   d. unmasking
   b. neutralizing   e. deintensification
   c. intensification

8. Based on stressing the word indicated in italics, which of the following statements means "I was born in New Jersey, not in New York as you seem to think."
   a. "*I* was born in New Jersey."
   b. "I *was* born in New Jersey."
   c. "I was *born* in New Jersey."
   d. "I was born *in* New Jersey."
   e. "I was born in *New Jersey*."

9. According to anthropologist Edward Hall, how close to a good friend does the average person in the United States stand?
   a. 0 to 6 inches
   b. 6 to 18 inches
   c. 18 inches to 4 feet
   d. 4 feet to 12 feet
   e. more than 12 feet

10. _____ refers to the degree to which you seem approachable and likeable.
    a. Other-oriented
    b. Immediacy
    c. Observant
    d. Confirming
    e. Conversational

Answers: 1-b; 2-a; 3-e; 4-c; 5-c; 6-b; 7-a; 8-e; 9-c; 10-b

7 UNDERSTANDING

What do most films, novels, and television series have in common? They tell stories. Now go one step further: What do these stories have in common? They are stories about interpersonal relationships. For example, are the Harry Potter books and films about wizards and magic, or are they about Harry's relationships with his friends, his foes, his teachers, and his dysfunctional Muggle family?

According to psychologist David Myers, "There are few stronger predictions of happiness than a close, nurturing, equitable, intimate, life-long companionship with one's best friend."[1] In this chapter, we examine the nature of and need for interpersonal relationships, as well as the personal traits you and others bring to every relationship. We also explore how your ability to resolve interpersonal conflicts, manage anger, and communicate assertively affects the quality and happiness of your life.

> " There are few stronger predictions of happiness than a close, nurturing, equitable, intimate, lifelong companionship with one's best friend. "
>
> —David Myers, psychologist

RELATIONSHIPS

the need for INTERPERSONAL RELATIONSHIPS

how many people do you talk with on a typical day? Like most people, you may discuss your plans for the evening with a family member or roommate, ask a classmate about an upcoming exam, discuss your grade with a professor, share gossip with a close friend, talk to colleagues or customers at work, or phone your auto mechanic or doctor's office. All these interactions are examples of how we use interpersonal communication in our relationships.

Interpersonal communication occurs when a limited number of people, usually two, interact and generate meaning through verbal and nonverbal messages. This interaction typically results in sharing information, achieving a goal, or maintaining a relationship. When we use the word **relationship** in this textbook, we are referring to a continuing and meaningful attachment or connection to another person. There are many types of interpersonal relationships—perhaps as many as there are people you know.

In addition to the emotional connec-tion and commitment you have in close **personal relationships** with friends, romantic partners, and fam-ily members, you also have work-based relationships. **Professional relationships** involve connections with people with whom you associ-ate and work to accomplish a goal or perform a task.

As you might expect, some of your relationships fall into both cate-gories. Your best friend may also be a colleague or supervisor at work—making this relationship both a per-sonal and a professional one.

Myers-Briggs Type Indicator

Isabel Briggs Myers and her mother, Katharine Briggs, developed a per-sonality type measure that examines the ways in which we perceive the world around us as well as how we reach conclusions and make deci-sions.[2] Thousands of corporations use the **Myers-Briggs Type Indica-tor** to help employees develop ef-fective on-the-job communication skills.[3] The Myers-Briggs Type Indi-cator also tells us a great deal about how and why we get along with some people and have difficulty in-teracting with others.

According to Myers-Briggs, all of us have preferred ways of think-ing and behaving that can be di-vided into four categories, with two opposite preferences in each cate-gory, as indicated in Figure 7.1.

Thousands of corporations use the Myers-Briggs Type Indicator to help employees develop effective on-the-job communication skills.

> **Interpersonal communication** Interaction between a limited number of people, usually two, for the purpose of sharing information, accomplishing a goal, or maintaining a relationship
>
> **Relationship** A continuing and meaningful attachment or connection to another person
>
> **Personal relationship** A relationship characterized by a high level of emotional connection and commitment
>
> **Professional relationship** A connection with people with whom you associate and work to accomplish a goal or perform a task
>
> **Myers-Briggs Type Indicator** A personality type theory that identifies preferred ways of thinking and behaving with two opposite preferences in each of four personality traits: extrovert–introvert, sensor–intuitive, thinker–feeler, and judger–perceiver

What possible types of relationships are illustrated here?

Schutz's Interpersonal Needs Theory

Psychologist William Schutz's **Fundamental Interpersonal Relationship Orientation (FIRO) Theory** claims that we interact with others in order to satisfy one or all three basic interpersonal needs: the needs for inclusion, control, and affection.[4]

The **inclusion need** represents a desire to belong, to be involved, and to be accepted. When inclusion needs are met, the result is what Schutz calls an *ideal social person*: one who enjoys being with others but is also comfortable being alone.

If, however, your inclusion needs are *not* met, you may engage in undersocial or oversocial behavior. An *undersocial person* feels unworthy or undervalued. Such people often withdraw and become loners. Because they believe that no one values them, they avoid interpersonal relationships. An *oversocial person* also feels unworthy and undervalued but tries to compensate for these feelings by attracting attention and impressing others with what and who they know. They dread being alone and actively seek companionship.

The **control need** refers to whether you feel competent and confident. When control needs are met, the result is what Schutz calls a *democratic person*: someone who has no problems with power and control and who feels just as comfortable giving reasonable orders as they do taking them.

Unmet control needs can result in the emergence of an abdicrat or autocrat. The *abdicrat* wants control but is reluctant to pursue it and therefore is often submissive. The *autocrat* also wants control and tries to take over or dominate others. Autocrats may criticize other people and force decisions on them. Dealing with abdicrats and autocrats is very challenging, but

---

Fundamental Interpersonal Relationship Orientation (FIRO) Theory People interact with others to satisfy their needs for inclusion, control, and affection
Inclusion need The need to belong, to be involved with others, and to be accepted
Control need The need to feel competent and confident

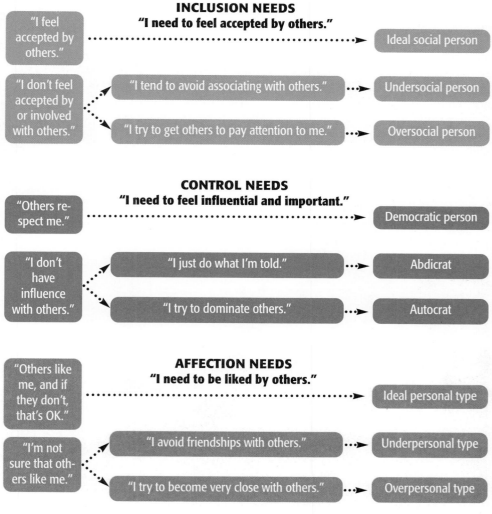

INCLUSION NEEDS
"I need to feel accepted by others."

"I feel accepted by others." ·····> Ideal social person

"I don't feel accepted by or involved with others."
→ "I tend to avoid associating with others." ···> Undersocial person
→ "I try to get others to pay attention to me." ···> Oversocial person

CONTROL NEEDS
"I need to feel influential and important."

"Others respect me." ·····> Democratic person

"I don't have influence with others."
→ "I just do what I'm told." ···> Abdicrat
→ "I try to dominate others." ···> Autocrat

AFFECTION NEEDS
"I need to be liked by others."

"Others like me, and if they don't, that's OK." ·····> Ideal personal type

"I'm not sure that others like me."
→ "I avoid friendships with others." ···> Underpersonal type
→ "I try to become very close with others." ···> Overpersonal type

Schutz's Fundamental Interpersonal Relationship Orientation (FIRO) Theory[5]

continued

possible. If, for example, a quiet person at work shows a desire to take control but doesn't pursue the opportunity, you may ask her to suggest a plan of action or to take on an important responsibility.

The **affection need**[6] refers to our desire to feel liked by others. When we need affection, we seek close friendships, intimate relationships, and expressions of warmth from others. When affection needs are met, the result is what Schutz calls an *ideal personal type:* a person who wants to be liked but who also is secure enough to function in situations where social interaction and affection are not high priorities.

According to Schutz, when affection needs are not met, people may develop underpersonal or overpersonal characteristics. *Underpersonal* *types* believe they are not liked and establish only superficial relationships with others. They rarely share their honest feelings and may appear aloof and uninvolved. *Overpersonal types* try to get close to everyone. They may seek intimate relationships despite the disinterest of others.

Affection need The need to feel liked by others

As you read about the types and their traits, ask yourself which preferences best describe how you communicate.[7]

Extrovert or Introvert Extrovert and introvert are two traits that describe where you focus your attention: outward or inward. **Extroverts** are outgoing; they talk more, and gesture when they speak. They get their energy by being with people and enjoy solving problems in groups. They also have a tendency to dominate conversations without listening to others.

Introverts think before they speak and are rarely as talkative as extroverts. They prefer socializing with one or two close friends rather than spending time with a large group of people. Introverts recharge by being alone and often prefer to work by themselves.

"Extroverts complain that introverts don't speak up at the right time in meetings. Introverts criticize extroverts for talking too much and not listening well."[8] In classrooms, extroverts like to participate in heated discussions whereas introverts hate being put on the spot.

The Myers-Briggs THINKER type: "I like this guy because he's smart, analytical, well organized, and takes a firm, but tough and fair approach to grading."

The Myers-Briggs FEELER type: "I like this teacher because he takes an interest in every student, cares whether we learn or not, and never puts down anyone in class."

Sensor or Intuitive How do you look at the world around you? Do you see the forest (the big picture) or the trees (the details)? **Sensors** focus on details and prefer to concentrate on one task at a time. **Intuitives** look

---

Extrovert An outgoing person who talks more than others and enjoys working in groups

Introvert A person who thinks before speaking, is not very talkative, and prefers to do work alone

Sensor A person who focuses on details and prefers to concentrate on one task at a time

Intuitive A person who looks for connections, overall concepts, and basic assumptions rather than details and procedures

---

In the TV show *Two and a Half Men,* Charlie's carefree approach to adult responsibilities (a Myers-Briggs Perceiver type) challenges the sensibilities of his brother, Alan (a Myers-Briggs Judger type), whose rule-oriented and structured approach to life can sometimes work against him.

The Myers-Briggs INTUITIVE is thinking: "Oceans are the source of life. Without our oceans, the smallest one-cell organisms, all human beings, and the giants animals of land and sea would perish. We live on a planet made by unfathomable oceans."

The Myers-Briggs SENSOR is thinking: "The ocean is huge, wet, salty, and dangerous during storms. I know lots of people who like to go to the ocean for vacations."

for connections and concepts rather than rules and flaws. They come up with big ideas but are bored with details. Sensors focus on regulations, step-by-step explanations, and facts, whereas intuitives focus on outwitting regulations, supplying theoretical explanations, and skipping details. Whereas sensors follow directions, intuitives skip directions and follow their hunches.

Thinker or Feeler Thinker and feeler are two traits that explain how you go about making decisions. **Thinkers** are analytical and task-oriented, and take pride in their ability to make difficult decisions. They want to get the job done, even at the cost of others' feelings. **Feelers** are more people-oriented. They want everyone to get along. Feelers will spend time and effort helping others.

Thinkers may appear unemotional and aggressive, whereas feelers may annoy others by "wasting time" with social chit-chat. Thinkers decide with their head; feelers decide with their heart.

Judger or Perceiver Do you approach the world and its challenges in a structured and organized way? If so, you are most likely a judger. **Judgers** are highly structured people who plan ahead, are very punctual, and become impatient with others who show up late or waste time. **Perceivers** are less rigid than judgers. Because they like open-endedness, being on time is less important than being flexible and adaptable. Perceivers often procrastinate and end up in a frenzy to complete a task on time.

Judgers and perceivers often have difficulty understanding each other. To a judger, a perceiver may appear scatterbrained. To a perceiver, a judger may appear rigid and controlling. In classroom settings, judgers usually plan and finish class assignments well in advance, whereas perceivers may pull all-nighters to get their work done. It's important to note that both types get their work done—the difference is when and how they go about doing it.

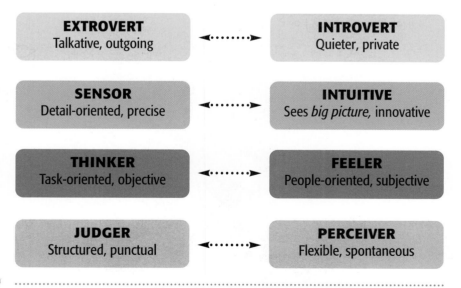

EXTROVERT Talkative, outgoing	◄┈┈┈►	INTROVERT Quieter, private
SENSOR Detail-oriented, precise	◄┈┈┈►	INTUITIVE Sees *big picture,* innovative
THINKER Task-oriented, objective	◄┈┈┈►	FEELER People-oriented, subjective
JUDGER Structured, punctual	◄┈┈┈►	PERCEIVER Flexible, spontaneous

Figure 7.1 Myers-Briggs Type Indicator Preferences

Thinker A person who is analytical and task-oriented
Feeler A people-oriented person who helps others and wants everyone to get along
Judger A highly structured, punctual person who likes to plan ahead
Perceiver An adaptable person who likes open-ended thinking and is less concerned with rules and punctuality

Know Thy Self

What Is Your Personality Type?

Read the pairs of descriptions for each Myers-Briggs personality trait, and put a check mark next to the phrases that *best* describe you. When you have finished, add up the check marks and note the personality traits with the most check marks.

1.   Are you an extrovert or an introvert?

____ I am outgoing, sociable, and expressive.	OR	____ I am reserved and private.
____ I enjoy groups and discussions.	OR	____ I prefer one-to-one interactions.
____ I often talk first, think later.	OR	____ I usually think first, then talk.
____ I think out loud.	OR	____ I think to myself.
____ Other people give me energy.	OR	____ Other people often exhaust me.
_____ **Total** (Extrovert/E)		_____ **Total** (Introvert/I)

2.   Are you a sensor or an intuitive?

____ I focus on details.	OR	____ I focus on the big picture.
____ I am practical and realistic.	OR	____ I am theoretical.
____ I like facts.	OR	____ I get bored with facts and details.
____ I trust experience.	OR	____ I trust inspiration and intuition.
____ I want clear, realistic goals.	OR	____ I want to pursue a vision.
_____ **Total** (Sensor/S)		_____ **Total** (Intuitive/N)

3.   Are you a thinker or a feeler?

____ I am task-oriented.	OR	____ I am people-oriented.
____ I am objective, firm, analytical.	OR	____ I am subjective, humane, appreciative.
____ I value competence, reason, justice.	OR	____ I value relationships and harmony.
____ I am direct and firm-minded.	OR	____ I am tactful and tenderhearted.
____ I think with my head.	OR	____ I think with my heart.
_____ **Total** (Thinker/T)		_____ **Total** (Feeler/F)

4.   Are you a judger or a perceiver?

____ I value organization and structure.	OR	____ I value flexibility and spontaneity.
____ I like having deadlines.	OR	____ I dislike deadlines.
____ I will work now, play later.	OR	____ I will play now, work later.
____ I adjust my schedule to complete work.	OR	____ I do work at the last minute.
____ I plan ahead.	OR	____ I adapt as I go.
_____ **Total** (Judger/J)		_____ **Total** (Perceiver/P)

Summarize your decisions by indicating the letter that best describes your Myers-Briggs personality traits and preferences:

_____	_____	_____	_____
E or I	S or N	T or F	J or P

Each of these characters from the TV series *The Family Guy* displays a distinct personality. How would you assign Myers-Briggs traits to each of them?

initiating
INTERPERSONAL RELATIONSHIPS

all interpersonal relationships begin somewhere. Your best friend's sister or brother may have been an annoyance when you were in elementary school, but she or he may become your prom date in high school. Someone you meet on an airplane may eventually offer you a job.

Is there a "best" way to get a relationship started? Do you just let things happen, or do you make them happen? In order to develop satisfying relationships, you need to make a good impression and carry on an interesting conversations with others.

Impression Management

You know from experience that first impressions count. If you don't make a good impression on a first date, it may be your last with that person. If you don't impress someone at a job interview, you won't be hired. You don't get a second chance to make a first impression.

Once you form an initial impression, your subsequent behavior can reinforce and maintain that im-

Steve Jobs (co-founder and chief executive officer of Apple Inc.) and Bill Gates (co-founder and chairman of Microsoft) have created unique public images. What is your overall impression of each man?

You don't get a second chance to make a first impression.

pression or can weaken and even reverse it. Sociologist Erving Goffman claims that we assume a social identity that others help us to maintain.[9] This perspective is useful in understanding **impression management**, the strategies people use to shape others' impressions of themselves in order to achieve such personal goals as gaining influence, power, sympathy, or approval.[10] These strategies include ingratiation, self-promotion, exemplification, supplication, and intimidation.[11]

Ingratiation (But Not Phony Flattery) *Ingratiation* is a way of complimenting someone with whom you disagree in order to ease tensions and reopen communication channels. But insincere *ingratiation*—giving compliments and doing favors so another person will like or agree with you—has the potential to damage rather than enhance your image. Honest flattery ingratiates you with others; insincere flattery has the opposite effect.

Self-Promotion (But Not Big-Headed Bragging) Announcing "I'm a fast writer" can earn you a place on an important work team that has short-deadline projects and reports. At the same time, over-the-top *self-promotion*—describing your achievements and skills in order to impress others—may create a negative impression that is difficult to change. No one likes a braggart,

so promote yourself honestly and appropriately, and do not make promises you can't keep.

Exemplification (But Not Just in Public) *Exemplification* entails offering yourself as a good example or a model of noteworthy behavior. But make sure you practice what you preach. If you claim it's wrong to pirate CDs but you photocopy entire books rather than buy them, no one will believe your claims about honesty and moral values. Don't declare you're on a strict diet and then get caught with your hand in the cookie jar.

Supplication (But Not Endless Whining) *Supplication* describes a humble request or appeal for help from others. Appropriate supplication causes other people to feel resourceful and valued. When, as a supplicant, you express a need for help, you demonstrate that you are human like everyone else. But don't rely on supplication; if you cry out for help when you don't need it, you will soon be ignored.

> **. . . we assume a social identity that others help us to maintain.**
> **—Erving Goffman, sociologist**

Intimidation (But Not Brutality) In order to be seen as powerful, an intimidating person may demonstrate a willingness and ability to cause personal harm. *Intimidation* strategies use threats to subdue or control others. "If you speak to me that way again, I will file a formal grievance against you." In most communication situations, we do *not*

Impression management The strategies people use to shape others' impressions of themselves in order to achieve personal goals such as gaining influence, power, sympathy, or approval

recommend intimidation. In some instances, however, you may need to establish your authority and willingness to use power. If people take advantage of you, you may need to show them that you won't take it anymore—that *you* won't be intimidated.

Effective Conversations

A **conversation** is an interaction, often informal, in which we exchange speaking and listening roles. On any given day, you may have a conversation with a classmate in the hallway, a co-worker at the next desk, or someone you've just met at a reception or party. Context influences the nature of interactions. For example, you may wait until others aren't around or until a championship game on television is over to have a serious and private conversation with a close friend. The nature of a relationship also influences what you talk about in a conversation. You may discuss highly personal issues with your life partner, but you probably won't share as much with someone you've just met.

Starting a Conversation Introducing yourself and sharing some general personal information is the most obvious way to begin a conversation with someone you do not know: "I'm Allison; my family and I are here on vacation from Nebraska." The other person will usually reciprocate by offering similar information or following up on what

you've shared: "I have cousins in Nebraska and visited them one summer when I was a kid." A second approach to opening a conversation is to ask questions: "Do you know anything about this movie?" "How far a walk is the campus bookstore from here?"

Maintaining a Conversation One of the best ways to keep a conversation going is to ask **open-ended questions** that encourage specific or detailed responses. "What do you think of Dr. Pearson's course and assignments?" invites someone to share an observation or opinion. A **closed-ended question**, "Is this class required for your major?" requires only a short and direct response and can generally be answered with a direct response, such as *yes* or *no*.

When you answer questions during a conversation, give a response that provides the other person with information about your thoughts or experiences. An engaging conversation requires the effort and commitment of two people. Otherwise, the conversation will quickly deteriorate into an awkward silence.

Finally, make sure you balance talking with listening. Successful conversationalists takes turns listening and speaking. We negotiate conversational turn-taking primar-

" ... AND I DON'T APPRECIATE YOU READING THAT PAPER WHEN I'M TRYING TO NAG YOU."

ily through our nonverbal behavior. **Turn-requesting cues** are verbal and nonverbal messages that signal a desire to speak, such as leaning forward, providing direct eye contact, and lifting one hand as if beginning to gesture. **Turn-yielding cues** are verbal and nonverbal messages that signal that you are completing your comments and are preparing to listen, such as slowing down your speaking rate, relaxing your posture or gestures, and leaning slightly away. Good conversationalists are sensitive to turn-taking cues. If someone dominates a conversation and forces you to interrupt to get a turn, you may avoid future interactions. Talking with someone who never seems willing to speak or

Conversation An interaction, often informal, in which people exchange speaking and listening roles

Open-ended question A question that requires or encourages a detailed answer

Closed-ended question A question that requires only a short answer, such as yes or *no*

Turn-requesting cues Verbal and nonverbal messages that signal your desire to speak during a conversation

Turn-yielding cues Verbal and nonverbal messages that signal you are completing your comments and preparing to listen during a conversation

We negotiate conversational turn-taking primarily through our nonverbal behavior.

make a contribution can be equally frustrating and awkward.

Ending a Conversation Ending a conversation abruptly can send a rude message to the other person. It is better to look for a moment in the conversation where an ending seems natural—either when the topic seems fully exhausted, or when someone shifts to the edge of a chair, stands up, looks away, leans away, or picks up personal belongings.[12]

STRATEGIES FOR ENDING A CONVERSATION

End on a positive and courteous note. Refer to comments the other person made to show you listened and are interested.

Make plans to meet again. Extend an invitation for meeting again at a specific date, time, and place.

Make a concluding statement. Describe how the conversation has affected you or how you will use the information you gained.

State the need to leave. When there is no good time to end a conversation or the other person is ignoring your hints, state clearly and directly that you must leave.

Cell Phone Conversations

communication in ACTION

Cell phone etiquette has been the subject of countless newspaper and magazine articles—and for good reason. There is almost nothing as annoying and even embarrassing as being forced to listen in on someone else's cell phone conversation.[13] We're sure you've heard people complain to their spouses and colleagues or have heard boyfriends and girlfriends express their puppy love for one another. Surveys indicate that the majority of cell phone users believe that loud or private calls made in public settings are inappropriate. However, "that same majority indulges in such calls themselves."[14]

To avoid embarrassing yourself, annoying others, or humiliating the person you're talking to, follow a few simple rules when talking on a cell phone in public:[15]

- Do not make or take personal calls during business meetings.
- Maintain a distance from others of at least ten feet when talking on the phone.
- Avoid cell phone conversations in enclosed public spaces such as elevators, waiting rooms, or buses.
- Avoid cell phone conversations in public places where side talk is considered bad manners, such as libraries, muse-

ums, theaters, restaurants, places of worship, and classrooms.
- Avoid loud and distracting ring tones.
- Control the volume of your voice. Don't force everyone around you to listen to your private conversation. Tilt your chin downward so that you're speaking toward the floor. That way, your voice won't carry as far.
- Avoid cell phone conversations when engaging in other tasks such as driving or shopping.
- Take advantage of the phone's many features, such as vibrate mode and voice mail. When you step into your workplace or a classroom, put your cell phone on vibrate and let your calls roll to your voice mail.

RESOLVING
interpersonal conflict

all healthy relationships, no matter how important or well-managed, experience interpersonal conflict. Although conflict is often associated with quarreling, fighting, anger, and hostility, conflict does not have to involve negative emotions. We define **conflict** as the disagreement that occurs in relationships when differences are expressed.

Many people avoid conflict because they do not understand the

Conflict Disagreement that occurs in relationships when differences are expressed

... conflict does not have to involve negative emotions.

differences between destructive and constructive conflict. **Destructive conflict** is the result of behaviors that create hostility or prevent groups from achieving their goal.[16] Constant complaining, personal insults, conflict avoidance, and loud arguments or threats all contribute to destructive conflict.[17] In contrast, **constructive conflict** occurs when you express disagreement in a way that respects others' perspectives and promotes problem solving.

Conflict Styles

When you are involved in a personal conflict, do you jump into the fray or run the other way? Do you marshal your forces and play to win, or do you work with everyone to find a mutually agreeable solution? Psychologists Kenneth Thomas and Ralph Kilmann claim that we use one or two of five conflict styles in most situations: avoidance, accommodation, competition, compro-

mise, and collaboration.[18] These five styles represent the extent to which you focus on achieving personal needs or mutual needs. People who are motivated to fulfill their own needs tend to choose more competitive approaches, whereas collaborative people are more concerned with achieving mutual goals. Figure 7.2 illustrates the relationship of each conflict style to an individual's motives.[19]

Avoidance If you are unable or unwilling to stand up for your own needs or the needs of others, you may rely on the **avoidance conflict style**. People who use this style often change the subject, sidestep a controversial issue, or deny that a conflict exists. Avoiding conflict can be counterproductive because it fails to address a problem and can increase tension in a relationship. Furthermore, ignoring or avoiding conflict does not make it go away.

However, in some circumstances, avoiding conflict is an appropriate approach. Consider avoiding conflict when the issue is not important to you, when you need time to collect your thoughts or control your emotions, when the consequences

of confrontation are too risky, or when the chances of resolution are unlikely.

Accommodation Do you give in to others during a conflict at the expense of meeting your own needs? If so, you use the **accommodating conflict style**. You may believe that giving in to others preserves peace and harmony.

When the issue is very important to the other person but not very important to you, an accommodating conflict style may be appropriate and effective. Accommodation is also appropriate when it is more important to preserve harmony in a relationship than to resolve a particular issue, when you realize you are wrong, or if you have changed your mind.

Competition If you are more concerned with fulfilling your own needs than with meeting the needs of others, you are using a **competitive conflict style**. Quite simply, you want to win because you believe that your ideas are better than anyone else's. When used inappropriately, the competitive style is characterized by hostility, ridicule, and personal attacks against others. Approaching conflict competitively tends to reduce people to winners or losers.

CONSTRUCTIVE CONFLICT

- **Focuses on issues**
- **Respects others**
- **Supportive**
- **Flexible**
- **Cooperative**
- **Committed to conflict management**

DESTRUCTIVE CONFLICT

- **Attacks others**
- **Insults others**
- **Defensive**
- **Inflexible**
- **Competitive**
- **Avoids or aggravates conflict**

Constructive and Destructive Conflict[20]

Destructive conflict The result of behaviors that create hostility or prevent groups from achieving their goal
Constructive conflict Expressing disagreement in a way that respects others' perspectives and promotes problem solving
Avoidance conflict style A conflict style in which people change the subject, sidestep a controversial issue, or deny that a conflict exists
Accommodating conflict style Giving in to others for the purpose of preserving peace and harmony
Competitive conflict style A conflict style in which people are more concerned with fulfilling their own needs than they are with meeting the needs of others

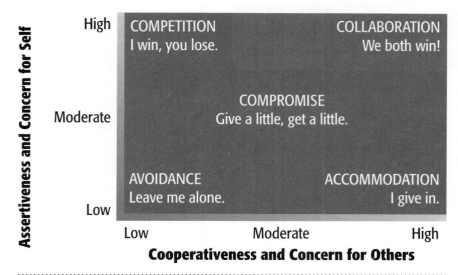

Figure 7.2   Conflict Styles

In certain situations, however, the competitive approach may be the most appropriate style. Approach conflict competitively when you have strong beliefs about an important issue or when immediate action is needed in an urgent situation. The competitive approach is particularly appropriate when the conse-quences of a bad decision may be harmful, unethical, or illegal.

Compromise The **compromising conflict style** is a "middle ground" approach that involves giving up some of your own goals to achieve other goals. Many people believe that compromise is an effective and fair method of resolving problems,

particularly given that each person loses and wins equally. However, if everyone is only partially satisfied with the outcome, no one may be committed to supporting or imple-menting the solution.

The compromise approach should be used when you are unable to reach a unanimous decision or resolve the problem. Consider compromising when other methods of conflict reso-lution are not effective, when you have reached an impasse, or if there is not enough time to explore more creative options.

Collaboration The **collaborative conflict style** searches for new so-lutions that will achieve both your goals and the goals of others. Also referred to as a *problem-solving* or *win–win approach*, the collaborative conflict style avoids arguments about whose ideas are superior. In-stead, the parties collaborate and look for creative solutions that sat-isfy everyone.

There are two potential draw-backs to the collaborative approach. First, collaboration requires a lot of

Ignoring or avoiding conflict does not make it go away.

Compromising conflict style A "middle ground" approach to conflict resolution that involves giving up some of your own goals to achieve other goals

Collaborative conflict style A conflict style in which people search for new solutions that will achieve their personal goals as well as the goals of others

Monologue An interaction in which one person does all or most of the talking

Dialogue A conversation in which two people interact in order to understand, respect, and appropriately adapt to one another

time and energy, and some issues may not be important enough to justify the extra time and effort. Second, in order for collaboration to be successful, everyone—even the avoiders and accommodators—must fully participate in the process.

Collaboration works best when new and creative ideas are encouraged, when both parties must commit to the final decision, and when you have enough time to spend on creative problem solving.

Conflict Resolution Strategies

Effective communicators are flexible and use a variety of approaches to resolve conflict. In this section, we present two conflict resolution strategies: the A-E-I-O-U Model, and the Six-Step Model.

The A-E-I-O-U Model If you want to resolve a conflict, you should try to understand the attitudes, beliefs, and values of those involved in that conflict. The **A-E-I-O-U Model of Conflict Resolution** focuses on communicating personal concerns

The AEIOU Model of Conflict Resolution

Assume the other person means well and wants to resolve the conflict. "I know that both of us want to do a good job and complete this project on time."

Express your feelings. "I'm frustrated when you ask me to spend time working on a less important project."

Identify what you would like to happen. "I want to share the responsibility and the work with you."

Outcomes you expect should be made clear. "If both of us don't make a commitment to working on this full-time, we won't do a good job or get it done on time."

Understanding on a mutual basis is achieved. "Could we divide up the tasks and set deadlines for completion or bring in another person to help us?"

and suggesting alternative actions to resolve a conflict based on the assumption that everyone means well and wants to resolve the conflict.[22]

The Six-Step Model The **Six-Step Model of Conflict Resolution** offers a series of steps to help you move a conflict toward successful resolution. The six steps illustrated below are neither simple nor easy. They do, however, tell you "what to do and what not to do when confronting someone" in a conflict situation.[23]

> **A-E-I-O-U Model of Conflict Resolution** Focuses on sharing personal concerns and suggesting alternative actions to resolve a conflict based on the assumption that everyone means well and wants to resolve the conflict
>
> **Six-Step Model of Conflict Resolution** A series of six steps (preparation, initiation, confrontation, consideration, resolution, reevaluation) that help you move through a conflict toward successful resolution

The Six-Step Model of Conflict Resolution

	Step	Task	Strategies
1	**Preparation**	Identify the problem, needs, issues, and causes of the conflict.	Analyze the conflict by asking yourself: Who is involved; what happened; where, when, and why did the conflict occur; and how did things go wrong?
2	**Initiation**	Invite the other person to talk.	Ask the other person to meet and talk about the problem. Provide some information about the subject. Example: "Can we get together for lunch and talk about the late report?"
3	**Confrontation**	Talk to the other person about the conflict and the need to resolve it.	Express your feelings constructively and describe, specifically, what you see as a solution. Example: "I want you to come to the family reunion with us."
4	**Consideration**	Consider the other person's point of view.	Listen, empathize, paraphrase, and respond with understanding. Example: "I didn't realize your mom was sick when I asked you to stay late."
5	**Resolution**	Come to a mutual understanding and reach an agreement.	Specify an outcome that both parties accept: "Okay. I'll make sure to call you if they make me stay at work later than 6 p.m."
6	**Reevaluation**	Follow up on the solution.	Set a date for seeing whether the solution is working as hoped. Example: "Let's meet for lunch in two weeks to see if this works the way we hope it will."

MANAGING anger

anger is a natural, human emotion. Everyone feels angry at times. In many instances, anger may be fully justified. If a friend lies to you, a co-worker takes credit for your work, or an intimate partner betrays you, **anger**—an emotional response to unmet expectations that ranges from minor irritation to intense rage—is a natural response. The issue is not whether you are angry, but how well you understand and manage your anger. Thus, effective anger management requires that you know how to communicate your angry feelings appropriately while treating others with respect.

Common Anger Myths

Many people have mistaken beliefs about anger that prevent them from dealing with this strong emotion. Acting out your anger is not inevitable, instinctual, or something you need to do.[24] Consider how the three common anger myths described here can inhibit your ability to manage anger effectively.

Three Anger Myths

1. *Anger and aggression are human instincts.* There is *no* scientific evidence to support the claim that humans are innately aggressive. Rather, our survival depends on cooperation, not destructive conflict and aggression.[25]
2. *Anger is always helpful.* Anger can be beneficial when it warns you of danger or prepares your body for a fight-or-flight response. However, anger fueled by hostility to others (as opposed to anger that serves as a warning) is bad for your health, particularly for your heart.[26]
3. *Anger is caused by others.* When you're angry, you may say "She made me angry when she showed up late" or "The boss made me angry when he forgot to give me credit for writing the report." By blaming others for your anger, you don't have to change your own behavior in any way. As a result, you stay angry.[27]

Constructive Anger Management

Shouting may let others know you are angry, but *calmly* stating "I am angry" will let them know how you feel and pave the way for resolving conflict constructively. Furthermore, although you have a right to your feelings, screaming angrily at someone is disruptive and disrespectful, and rarely solves anything. Avoid making personal attacks; these only escalate a conflict. Use "I" statements ("I expected you to . . .") instead of "you" statements ("You messed up when you . . ."). Finally, help others understand why you are angry: "Because the report isn't finished, I'm now in a bind with my supervisor."

Social psychologist Carol Tavris writes that anger "requires an awareness of choice and an embrace of reason. It is knowing when to become angry—'this is wrong, this I will protest'—and when to make peace; when to take action, and when to keep silent; knowing the likely cause of one's anger and not berating the blameless."[31]

Although it is important to express your anger appropriately, it is equally important to respond to someone else's anger constructively.

STOP & THINK | Should You Hold It In or Let It Out?

What's the best way to deal with anger—hold it in or let it out? Some people see anger as a destructive emotion that should be suppressed. However, when you suppress justified anger, it can fester or build while recurring problems go unresolved. Psychotherapist Bill DeFoore compares suppressed anger with a pressure cooker. "We can only suppress or apply pressure against our anger for so long before it erupts. Periodic eruptions can cause all kinds of problems."[28]

Other people believe in fully expressing their anger, regardless of how intense or potentially damaging it is. They also believe that angry outbursts release tension and calm them down. Psychologists explain that venting anger to let off steam "is really worse than useless. Expressing anger does not reduce anger. Instead it functions to make you even angrier."[29] Moreover, people on the receiving end of angry outbursts usually get angry right back—which only makes the problem worse.

Both of these extreme views about anger can be counterproductive. Not only can they damage interpersonal relationships, they may contribute to serious health problems such as heart disease and hypertension.[30]

Acting out your anger is not inevitable, instinctual, or something you need to do.

Anger An emotional response to unmet expectations that ranges from minor irritation to intense rage

Strategies for Responding Effectively to Others' Anger[32]

- *Acknowledge the other person's feelings of anger.* "I understand how angry you are."

- *Identify the issue or behavior that is the source of the anger.* "I don't believe I promised to work both your shifts next weekend, but you seem to think we made this agreement."

- *Assess the intensity of the anger and the importance of the issue.* "I know it's important for you to find someone to cover your shifts so you can attend your friend's wedding."

- *Encourage collaborative approaches to resolving the conflict.* "I can only cover one of your shifts this weekend. Why don't we work together to find someone else who will take the second shift?"

- *Make a positive statement about the relationship.* "I enjoy working with you and hope we can sort this out together."

developing
ASSERTIVENESS

What should you do if your boss wants you to work longer hours, but you want more time with your family? What if your friend wants to go to a party, but you need to stay home and study? How do you balance these competing needs and resolve potential conflicts? We believe the answer lies in how ready, willing, and able you are to be assertive. **Assertiveness** enables you to promote your own needs and rights while also respecting the needs and rights of others.

Passivity and Aggression

Assertiveness is best understood in relation to three alternatives: passivity, aggression, and passive aggressiveness. **Passivity** is characterized by giving in to others at the expense of your own needs in order to avoid conflict and disagreement. For exam-

THE BENEFITS OF ASSERTING YOURSELF[33]

- **Expressing your feelings appropriately**
- **Accepting compliments graciously**
- **Speaking up for your rights when appropriate**
- **Enhancing your self-esteem and self-confidence**
- **Expressing disagreement on important issues**
- **Modifying your own behavior**
- **Asking others to change their inappropriate or offensive behavior.**

ple, Joe's boss asks him to work over the weekend. Joe agrees and says nothing about his plans to attend an important family event. Not surprisingly, passive individuals often feel taken advantage of by others and blame them for their unhappiness. As a result, they fail to take responsibility for their own actions and the consequences of those actions.[34]

Assertiveness Promoting your own needs and rights while also respecting the needs and rights of others
Passivity Giving in to others at the expense of your own needs in order to avoid conflict and disagreement

The opposite of passive behavior is **aggression**, which puts personal needs first, often at the expense of someone else's needs. Aggressive individuals demand compliance from others. Although aggressive behavior can be violent, it is usually displayed in more subtle behavior such as raising your voice, rolling your eyes, or glaring at someone else.[35]

Sometimes people may *seem* passive when, in fact, their intentions are aggressive. Although **passive–aggressive** individuals may *appear* cooperative and willing to accommodate others and their needs, their behavior is a subtle form of aggressive behavior. Passive–aggressives manipulate others to get what they want. For example, when you refuse to do a favor for your brother, he mopes around the house until you finally give in to his request. Initially, while aggressive, passive, and passive–aggressive behavior may seem effective, in the long run, they damage interpersonal and professional relationships.

Assertiveness Skills

Assertiveness can be difficult to learn, particularly if you are passive or aggressive when challenged, or if you primarily rely on an avoiding, accommodating, competing, or compromising conflict style.

Bower and Bower recommend **DESC scripting**, a four-step process for becoming more assertive. DESC is an acronym for Describe, Express, Specify, and Consequences, and can be used in both personal and professional relationships.[36]

Initially, assertive behavior may feel strange or uncomfortable because asserting your rights can open the door to conflict. Practicing as-sertive behavior will ultimately improve your self-esteem, your ability to resolve conflicts, and the quality of your interpersonal relationships.

> Practicing assertive behavior will ultimately improve your self-esteem, your ability to resolve conflicts, and the quality of your interpersonal relationships.

Aggression Putting personal needs first and demanding compliance from others, often at the expense of someone else's needs

Passive–aggressive Communication that only appears to accommodate another person's needs, but actually represents subtle aggressive behavior

DESC scripting A four-step process (describe, express, specify, consequences) that provides a way of addressing another person's objectionable behavior

adapting to
CULTURE AND GENDER

Cultural values can reveal how people feel about conflict and the methods they use to resolve conflict. For example, collectivist cultures place a high value on "face." From a cultural perspective, **face** is the positive image you wish to create or preserve. Cultures that place a great deal of value on "saving face" discourage personal attacks and outcomes in which one person "loses." Figure 7.3 summarizes individualistic and collectivist perspectives about conflict.[37]

Gender roles vary across cultures and as such will add another level of complexity to the way individuals approach and attempt to resolve conflict. According to sociolinguist Deborah Tannen, men and women in the United States, in particular, approach conflict differently.[38] In general, men tend to be competitive arguers, whereas women are more likely to seek consensus. Men tend to view issues as only two-sided: for or against, right or wrong. Women are

Face The positive image you wish to create or preserve when interacting with others

more likely to search out many perspectives on a subject. Men also tend to use a competitive style, whereas women are more likely to compromise or avoid conflict altogether.[39] On the other hand, research aimed at predicting divorce has found that unhappy marriages are often characterized by wives who feel comfortable engaging in conflict and husbands who withdraw from conflict.[40] Gender differences in conflict styles, however, are generalizations. Overall, men and women in the United States are more similar in how they approach conflict than they are different. Both can and do use all five conflict resolution styles. In most instances, the context of the communication and the nature and history of the relationship will be as influential in conflict resolution as any gender differences.

Christine Ohuruogu of Great Britain wins an Olympic gold medal in Beijing, 2008.

A Zulu chief, his council, and tribal members collaborate to resolve conflict and make decisions.

INDIVIDUALISTIC CULTURES

- Conflict is closely related to individual goals.
- Conflict should be dealt with openly and honestly.
- Conflict should result in a specific solution or plan of action.
- Conflict is addressed appropriately in terms of timing and situation.

COLLECTIVIST CULTURES

- Conflict is understood within the context of relationships and the need to preserve "face."
- Conflict resolution requires that "face" issues be mutually managed before a discussion of other issues.
- Conflict resolution is considered successful when both parties are able to save "face" and when both can claim they have "won."
- Conflict resolution requires attention to both verbal and nonverbal communication as well as the nature of the relationship.

Figure 7.3   Cultural Perspectives on Conflict

communication&culture

UNDERSTANDING DIVERSITY AND CONFLICT

Part of knowing how to manage conflict effectively is recognizing and understanding that differences in culture and gender matter, and that they *will* influence how you choose to resolve both personal and professional altercations. For example, an individual's culture can determine the likelihood of whether or not someone will express disagreement. Conformist cultures such as the Japanese, German, Mexican, and Brazilian are less likely to express disagreement than individualistic cultures such as the Swedish and French.[41]

Culture may also dictate *who* should argue. Many cultures give enormous respect to their elders. In these cultures, a young person arguing with an older adult is viewed as disrespectful. Among several Native American and African cultures, older adults are considered wiser and more knowledgeable, and young people are expected to accept the views of elders rather than challenge or rebel against them.

Companies that fail to respect and adapt to cultural differences are likely to have more strikes and lawsuits, lower morale among workers, less productivity, and higher employee turnover.[42] Thus, when attempting to resolve conflict in personal or professional relationships, ignoring cultural differences can only make matters worse.

Communication ASSESSMENT[43]

How Do *You* Respond to Conflict?

The following 20 statements are remarks made by someone facing a conflict situation. Consider each message separately and decide how closely it resembles *your* attitudes and behavior in a conflict situation, even if the language does not exactly represent how you would express yourself. From the following scale, select the rating that best matches your approach to conflict. Choose only one rating for each message.

5 = I always do this   3 = I sometimes do this   I = I never do this
4 = I usually do this   2 = I rarely do this

When I'm involved in a CONFLICT . . .

_____ 1.   I try to change the subject.

_____ 2.   I play down the differences of opinion so the conflict doesn't become too serious.

_____ 3.   I don't hold back, particularly when I have something I really want to say.

_____ 4.   I try to find a trade-off to which everyone can agree.

_____ 5.   I try to look at the conflict objectively rather than taking it personally.

_____ 6.   I avoid contact with the people involved when I know there's a serious conflict brewing.

_____ 7.   I'm willing to change my position to resolve the conflict and let others have what they want.

_____ 8.   I fight hard when an issue is very important to me and others are unlikely to agree.

_____ 9.   I understand that you can't get everything you want when resolving the conflict.

_____ 10.   I try to minimize status differences and defensiveness in order to resolve the conflict.

_____ 11.   I put off or delay dealing with the conflict.

_____ 12.   I rarely disclose much about how I feel during the conflict, particularly if it's negative.

_____ 13.   I like having enough power to control the conflict situation.

_____ 14.   I like to work on hammering out a deal among conflicting parties.

_____ 15.   I believe that all conflicts have potential for positive resolution.

_____ 16.   I give in to the other person's demands in most cases.

_____ 17.   I'd rather keep a friend than win an argument.

_____ 18.   I don't like wasting time in arguments when I know what should be done.

_____ 19.   I'm willing to give in on some issues, but not on others.

_____ 20.   I look for solutions that meet everyone's needs.

Your scores identify the conflict style(s) you use most often. There are, however, no right or wrong responses. The conflict style(s) you use may differ, depending on the issues, the people involved, and the situation's context. The conflict style(s) with the highest scores reflect how you generally respond to a conflict situation.

Conflict Style	Avoid	Accommodate	Compete	Compromise	Collaborate
Item Scores	1 = _____	2 = _____	3 = _____	4 = _____	5 = _____
	6 = _____	7 = _____	8 = _____	9 = _____	10 = _____
	11 = _____	12 = _____	13 = _____	14 = _____	15 = _____
	16 = _____	17 = _____	18 = _____	19 = _____	20 = _____
Total Scores	_____	_____	_____	_____	_____

Summary

Why are personal relationships essential for a happy and rewarding life?

- There are few stronger predictions of happiness than a close, nurturing, equitable, intimate, lifelong companionship with another person.
- William Schutz's Fundamental Interpersonal Relationship Orientation (FIRO) Theory identifies three interpersonal needs that affect the quality of every relationship: the needs for inclusion, control, and affection.
- The Myers-Briggs Type Indicator measures the extent to which we are extroverts or introverts, sensors or intuitives, thinkers or feelers, and judgers or perceivers.

How do you make a positive impression on other people, particularly when you talk to them for the first time?

- Impression management strategies that help you shape your image in positive ways include ingratiation, self-promotion, exemplification, and intimidation.
- A conversation is an interaction, often informal, in which people exchange speaking and listening roles.
- Begin initial conversations by self-disclosing and asking effective questions. Keep conversations going by asking open-ended questions, and appropriately do turn-

taking. End conversations in a positive, complimentary way.
- Use a cell phone appropriately in public to avoid embarrassing yourself, annoying others, or humiliating the person you're talking to.

What communication strategies and skills can help you resolve interpersonal conflicts?

- Conflict is the disagreement that occurs in relationships when differences are expressed.
- Conflict can be constructive or destructive depending on your intentions and how well you communicate.
- Most people use one or two of the following five conflict styles: avoidance, accommodation, competition, compromise, and collaboration.
- Consider using one of the following conflict resolution strategies: the A-E-I-O-U Model and the Six-Step Model.

How well do you understand and manage your own anger and appropriately respond to anger in others?

- Anger is a natural, human emotion that varies in terms of its causes and effects.
- Some common myths about anger are: anger is a human instinct, anger is always helpful, and my anger is caused by others.

- You can express anger appropriately by stating that you are angry without venting or exploding, by avoiding personal attacks, and by identifying the source of your anger.

How does assertiveness advance your own needs and rights while also respecting the needs and rights of others?

- Assertiveness involves promoting your own needs and rights while also respecting the needs and wants of others.
- Whereas passivity is characterized by giving in to others at the expense of your own needs, aggression involves putting your own needs first, often at the expense of someone else's needs.
- Passive–aggression may appear to accommodate others but is a subtle form of aggressive behavior.
- DESC scripting is a four-step process (describe, express, specify, and consequences) for becoming more assertive.

How do cultural and gender differences affect conflict resolution?

- Cultures that value "saving face" discourage personal attacks and outcomes in which one person loses.
- Generally, men and women in the United States are more similar in how they approach conflict than they are different.

TEST your knowledge

1. According to Schutz's FIRO Theory, an _____ is a submissive person who wants and needs control, but is reluctant to pursue it.
   a. autocrat
   b. abdicrat
   c. undersocial type
   d. underpersonal type
   e. ideal personal type

2. The Myers-Briggs Type Indicator measures
   a. the way we perceive the world around us.
   b. how we reach conclusions and make decisions.
   c. our preferred ways of thinking and behaving.
   d. the extent to which we are extroverts or introverts, thinkers or feelers.
   e. all of the above.

3. Read the following description: A person who is a risk-taker and willing to try new options, they often procrastinate and end up in a frenzy to complete a task on time. Which Myers Briggs personality trait does it describe?
   a. extrovert
   b. feeler
   c. perceiver
   d. intuitive
   e. thinker

4. Which impression-management strategy involves flattering and praising someone with whom you disagree in order to ease tensions and reopen communication channels?
   a. supplication
   b. self-promotion
   c. exemplification
   d. ingratiation
   e. intimidation

5. In which of the following conflict styles do people respond by giving in to others at the expense of meeting their own needs?
   a. avoidance
   b. accommodation
   c. competition
   d. compromise
   e. collaboration

6. Littlejohn and Domenici recommend all of the following communication strategies for engaging in a constructive and ethical dialogue to resolve conflict *except:*
   a. Speak to be understood rather than to win.
   b. Simplify complex issues so everyone understands the problem.
   c. Explore ideas and potential solutions in new ways.
   d. Express uncertainty rather than blindly adhere to a single position.
   e. Explain your own views rather than criticizing the other person's opinions or behavior.

7. Which of the steps in the Six-Step Model of Conflict Resolution requires you to listen empathically, use paraphrases, and respond with understanding?
   a. preparation
   b. confrontation
   c. consideration
   d. resolution
   e. reevaluation

8. All of the following answers are myths about anger *except:*
   a. Anger is a human instinct.
   b. Anger is beneficial.
   c. Anger is caused by others.
   d. All of the above answers are myths about anger.
   e. None of the above is a myth about anger.

9. Which of the following behaviors characterizes passive–aggressive behavior?
   a. You advance your own needs and rights while also respecting the needs and rights of others.
   b. You give in to others at the expense of your own needs in order to avoid conflict and disagreement.
   c. You put your personal needs first, often at the expense of someone else.
   d. You appear to go along with others but sabotage their plans behind their backs.
   e. You focus on the most important issues and have no desire to make personal attacks on others.

10. Which of the following perspectives about conflict is most true in collectivist cultures?
    a. Conflict is closely related to achieving individual goals.
    b. Conflict should be dealt with openly and honesty.
    c. Conflict should result in a specific solution or plan of action.
    d. Conflict is addressed appropriately in terms of timing and the situation.
    e. Conflict resolution requires attention to both verbal and nonverbal communication as well as the nature of the relationship.

Answers: 1-b; 2-e; 3-c; 4-d; 5-b; 6-b; 7-c; 8-d; 9-d; 10-e

8 IMPROVING

Why and when do couples break up? In *Uncoupling: How and Why Relationships Come Apart*, sociologist Diane Vaughan notes that a couple's breakup is rarely sudden. "Uncoupling begins with a secret." One of the partners starts to feel uncomfortable in the relationship—and keeps those thoughts, feelings, or actions secret. "The world the two of them have built together no longer 'fits.'"[1] In some cases, the secret is huge and devastating, particularly when the secret goes public, as when Jon Gosselin of *Jon & Kate Plus Ei8ht*—a show about how the two parents of sextuplets and a set of twins are making it as a family—was reported to have been cheating on his wife, Kate Gosselin.

> **" Uncoupling begins with a secret. "**
> **— Diane Vaughan**

The kinds of secrets that Diane Vaughan describes, however, are much less volatile and are rarely about daily life, financial problems, or visits from the in-laws. Typically, they concern one partner's feeling of dissatisfaction, discomfort, unhappiness, or fear about the future of the relationship. For various reasons, the partner leaves these private concerns and feelings unspoken. He

PERSONAL RELATIONSHIPS

or she may be uncertain about their cause, their depth, and their implications, or afraid to share them for fear of hurting the other person or discovering that the other harbors much worse secrets.[2]

If you are reluctant or unwilling to share your honest thoughts and feelings with someone you love, you will have difficulty addressing and resolving many relationship problems.

In this chapter, we examine the complex and contradictory nature of personal relationships as well as strategies for building closer bonds with the people who matter most in your life.

quality
PERSONAL RELATIONSHIPS

your ability to communicate effectively in close personal relationships influences your psychological and physical health, your personal identity and happiness, your social and moral development, your ability to cope with stress and misfortunes, and the quality and meaning of your life.[3]

John Gottman, who studies the value and consequences of close personal relationships and strong marriages, offers several conclusions drawn from his own and others' research:

- People with good friends usually have less stress and live longer.
- Longevity is determined far more by the state of people's closest relationships than by genetics.
- People who have good marriages live longer than those who don't.
- Loners are twice as likely to die from all causes over a five-year period as those who enjoy close friendships.[4]

Do not misinterpret Gottman's conclusions to mean that you should make as many friends as possible and (if not married) get married as soon

> **. . . meaningful and lasting personal relationships do not just happen. *You* make them happen.**

as possible so you can live longer. Gottman's point is that meaningful and lasting personal relationships do not just happen. *You* make them happen; the success of those relationships depends largely on how well you communicate.

Relational Dialectics

How often in your close relationships have you said, "I want *both* this *and* that," even when those desires contradict each other? The following pairs of common folk sayings illustrate several contradictory beliefs about personal relationships:

"Opposites attract" *but* "Birds of a feather flock together."
"To know him is to love him" *but* "Familiarity breeds contempt."

Rather than trying to prove that one of these contradictory proverbs is truer than the other (an "either/or" response), Leslie Baxter and Barbara Montgomery's **Relational Dialectics Theory** takes a "both/and" approach. This theory focuses on interpersonal *dialectics*, the interplay of opposing or contradictory forces in three domains: integration versus separation, stability versus change, and expression versus privacy.[5]

Generally, most of us want to be close to others without having to give

up our separate selves. For example, as you grow up, you may want to remain closely connected to your parents but still live an independent life free from their intrusion. Or, let's say you want to build a life with your partner, but you also want to maintain your own career and bank account. In order to maintain this relationship,

Relational Dialectics Theory
Relationships are characterized by ongoing tensions between contradictory forces

The integration-separation dialectic often surfaces when a child leaves home for college.

you need to successfully negotiate the **integration–separation dialectic**: a desire for *both* connection *and* independence.

Most of us like the security of a stable relationship *and* the novelty and excitement of change. To achieve this *both/and* result, we negotiate the **stability–change dialectic**. For example, a couple may share a stable, relationship and home together, but take separate vacations every other year.

The **expression–privacy dialectic** focuses on your conflicting desire to be open and honest with another person, while also protecting your privacy.[6] Do your best friends, romantic partner, and close family members know every secret you have? Should they? For example, when Jane tells Jack she'd like to rent an apartment in a building closer to where she works, he says he wants to stay in the suburbs. In truth, he doesn't want to move to a building where a former girlfriend lives. The question at the heart of this dialectic is: "Can I balance my need for privacy and the benefits of self-disclosure?"

Although Relational Dialectics Theory does not offer simple guidelines for improving interpersonal communication, it does help explain your experiences in ongoing personal relationships and offer a strong justification for seeking a "both/and" focus.

> **Integration–separation dialectic** The relational tension between wanting both interpersonal dependence and independence
>
> **Stability–change dialectic** The relational tension between wanting both a stable relationship and the novelty and excitement of change
>
> **Expression–privacy dialectic** The relational tension between wanting both openness and privacy

sharing your self
WITH OTHERS

Willingness to share your self with others is essential for developing and improving personal relationships. Whether you are talking about your favorite movies with a new acquaintance or revealing your deepest fears to a loved one, both of you must be willing and able to share personal information and feelings with one another.

Self-disclosure is the process of sharing personal information, opinions, and emotions with others that would not otherwise be known to them. This is not to say you should reveal the most intimate details of your life to everyone you meet. Rather, you must judge whether and when sharing is appropriate by understanding and adapting to the other person's attitudes, beliefs, and values.[7] Deciding what, where, when, how, and with whom to self-disclose is one of the most difficult communication challenges you face in a personal relationship.

The Johari Window Model

Psychologists Joseph Luft and Harrington Ingham provide a useful model for understanding the connections between self-disclosure and feedback.[8] They use the metaphor of a window and by combining their first names (Joe and Harry) call their model the **Johari Window**.[9] The Johari Window looks at two interpersonal communication dimensions: willingness to self-disclose and receptivity to feedback. *Willingness to self-disclose* describes the extent to which you are prepared to disclose personal information and feelings with other people. *Receptivity to feedback* describes your awareness, interpretation, and response to someone else's self-disclosure about you.[10] When these two dimensions are graphed against each other, the result is a figure that resembles a four-paned window. Each pane means something different, and each pane can vary in size as shown on p. 153.

> **Self-disclosure** The process of sharing personal information, opinions, and emotions with others that would not otherwise be known to them
>
> **Johari Window** A model for understanding the connections between willingess to disclose and receptivity to feedback

Social Penetration Theory

Social Penetration Theory, developed by Irwin Altman and Dalmas Taylor, describes the process of relationship bonding in which individuals move from superficial communication to deeper, more intimate communication.[11] According to Altman and Taylor, the process of developing an intimate relationship is similar to peeling an onion. The outer skin of the onion represents superficial and mostly public information about yourself. The inner layers—those closest to the core—represent intimate information.

Social Penetration Theory explains that self-disclosure has three interconnected dimensions: depth, breadth, and frequency.[12] *Deep* self-disclosure is intimate and near the core of the onion; for example, there's a big difference between telling someone "You're OK" and telling someone "I love you." When self-disclosure is *broad*, it covers many topic areas, some very personal, some impersonal. For example, in addition to sharing information about your hobbies and job, you may also share your strong beliefs and values about family and religion. Self-disclosure becomes more *frequent* as the depth and breadth of your relationship expands.

The animated film *Shrek* captures the underlying premise of Social Penetration Theory. As Shrek, the large, lumbering, green ogre, and his hyperactive companion, Donkey, trek through fields and forests, Shrek tries to explain himself to Donkey:

Shrek: For your information, there's a lot more to ogres than people think.

Donkey: Example?

Shrek: Example? Okay. Um. Ogres are like onions.

Donkey: They stink?

Shrek: No.

Donkey: Oh, they make you cry?

Shrek: No.

Donkey: Oh, you leave them out in the sun and they get all brown and start sprouting little white hairs?

Shrek: No! Layers. Onions have layers. Ogres have layers. You get it? We both have layers![13]

Social Penetration Theory contends that as two people get to know each other better, they reveal personal information, feelings, and experiences below the public image layer. Relationships develop when this process is reciprocal—that is, one person's openness leads to another's openness, and so on.

> **Social Penetration Theory** The process of relationship bonding in which individuals move from superficial communication to deeper, more intimate communication

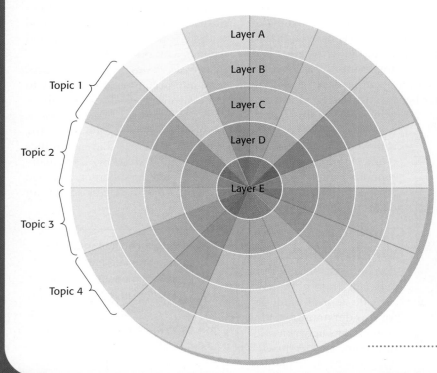

EXAMPLES OF LAYERS

Layer A: Most impersonal layer (music, clothing, food preferences)

Layer B: Impersonal layer (job, politics, education)

Layer C: Middle layer (religious beliefs, social attitudes)

Layer D: Personal layer (personal goals, fears, hopes, secrets)

Layer E: Most personal layer (inner core, self-concept)

EXAMPLES OF TOPICS

Topic 1: Leisure activities

Topic 2: Career

Topic 3: Family

Topic 4: Health

The Social Penetration Process

Four Different Panes

The *open area* of your Johari Window contains information you are willing to share with others as well as information you have learned about yourself by accurately interpreting others' feedback. For example, suppose you wonder whether it's okay to tell an embarrassing but funny personal story to a group of new colleagues. You decide to take the risk. If your listeners laugh and seem to appreciate your sense of humor, you've learned two things: It's safe to share personal stories with this group and that you are, in fact, funny.

The *hidden area* represents your private self, which includes information you know about yourself ("I am attracted to you," "I was once arrested") but that you are not yet willing to share with others. The hidden area contains your secrets. Some people retain a lot of personal information in this area that could enhance their personal relationships and likeability if that information were shared.

The *blind area* contains information others know about you but that you do *not* know about yourself be-

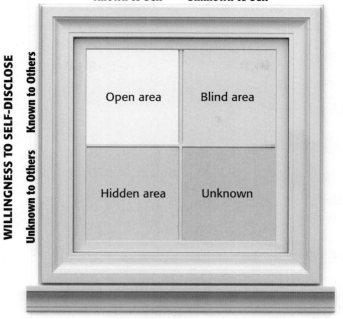

The Johari Window[14]

cause you don't correctly interpret feedback from others. If you don't notice that someone disapproves of your behaviors or wants your praise for a job well done, you may not develop or maintain a close relationship with that person. Many of us are "blind" when we don't see how an annoying habit bothers someone or how a critical remark hurts a person's feelings.

Information unknown to *both* you and others exists in the *unknown*

area. For example, suppose you have always avoided doing any writing at work because you don't think you're a good writer. And yet, when working with a group of colleagues on an interesting project, you end up doing most of the writing. As time passes, you and your co-workers recognize and praise your writing talent. This "discovery" about yourself now moves from your unknown area to your open area.

Varying Size of Panes

Depending on how willing you are to self-disclose and how receptive you are to feedback, each of the four panes in the Johari Window will differ in size. Although this makes a very unusual-looking window, it does a good job of reflecting your level of self-awareness. As a relationship develops, you should disclose more, which enlarges your open area and reduces the amount of information in your hidden area. As you become more receptive to feedback, you reduce your blind area and enlarge your open area.[15] And as your open area expands, your unknown area gets smaller.

expressing
YOUR self APPROPRIATELY

as you get to know your self and others better you may find yourself engaging in more intimate self-disclosure and responding more to feedback. Both of these communication skills help to increase your self-awareness and the overall quality of your personal relationships. While Social Penetration Theory and the Johari Window Model help explain the need for appropriate self-disclosure and receptivity to feedback, this section describes communication strategies and skills that can help you express your self appropriately and thereby strengthen and preserve your relationships with others.

STRATEGIES FOR EFFECTIVE SELF-DISCLOSURE

Strategy	Rationale
Focus on the present, not the past.	Obsessing about past problems may not help or enlighten either person.
Be descriptive, not judgmental.	Criticizing someone's behavior can result in a hostile argument.
Disclose your feelings, not just the facts.	Explaining how you feel about what is happening clarifies and justifies your reactions.
Adapt to the person and context.	Revealing intimate personal information to the wrong person, at the wrong time, in the wrong place benefits no one.
Be sensitive to others' reactions.	Changing or discontinuing self-disclosure is essential if the other person's reaction is extreme (rage, crying, hysteria).
Engage in reciprocal self-disclosure.	Modifying or discontinuing your self-disclosure is appropriate if the other person does not respond in kind.
Gradually move disclosure to a deeper level.	Increasing the breadth, depth, and frequency of your self-disclosure should occur as your level of comfort with the other person increases.

Although it can be painful and risky, when the emotional stakes are high, self-disclosure can benefit a relationship in significant ways.

Effective Self-Disclosure

When you self-disclose, you reveal how you are reacting to a situation while sharing relevant information about yourself and your experiences. Successful self-disclosure is also not a solo activity. If the other person does not self-disclose or respond to your self-disclosures, you may want to rethink the relationship or stop sharing your thoughts and feelings. Although it can be painful and risky, when the emotional stakes are high, self-disclosure can benefit a relationship in significant ways.[16]

Effective Feedback

Effective interpersonal communication relies on giving and receiving feedback from others. No matter where or when you provide feedback, it should not be threatening or demanding. At the same time, remember that there is only so much that you and another person can comprehend and process at one time. Too much personal information can overwhelm a relationship.

Effective Communication Climates

Communication scholar Jack Gibb describes six behaviors that create a supportive climate for communication and six that cause defensiveness.[17] **Defensive behaviors** reflect

---

Defensive behaviors Behaviors that reflect our instinct to protect ourselves when being physically or verbally attacked by someone

---

STRATEGIES FOR GIVING AND ASKING FOR FEEDBACK[18]

- Focus on behavior, not on the person.
- Make it specific, not general or abstract.
- Use "I" rather than "you" statements.
- Focus on what was said and done, not on why it was said and done.
- Focus on immediate behavior, not behavior from the past.
- Share information, perceptions, and feelings, not advice.
- Provide feedback at an appropriate time and place.
- Focus on actions that both of you can change.

DEFENSIVE BEHAVIORS

EVALUATION: Judges another person's behavior. Makes critical statements. "Why did you insult Sharon like that? Explain yourself!" "What you did was terrible."

CONTROL: Imposes your solution on someone else. Seeks control of the situation. "Give me that report and I'll make it better." "Since I'm paying for the vacation, we're going to the resort I like rather than the spa you like."

STRATEGY: Manipulates others. Hides or disguises personal motives. Withholds information. "Frankie's going to Florida over spring break." "Remember when I helped you rearrange your office?"

NEUTRALITY: Appears withdrawn, detached, indifferent. Won't take sides. "You can't win them all." "Life's a gamble." "It doesn't matter to me." "Whatever."

SUPERIORITY: Implies that you and your opinions are better than others. Promotes resentment and jealousy. "Hey—I've done this a million times—let me have it. I'll finish in no time." "Is this the best you could do?"

CERTAINTY: Believes that your opinion is the only correct one. Refuses to consider the ideas and opinions of others. Takes inflexible positions. "I can't see any other way of doing this that makes sense." "There's no point in discussing this any further."

SUPPORTIVE BEHAVIORS

DESCRIPTION: Describes another person's behavior. Makes understanding statements. Uses more *I* and *we* language. "When we heard what you said to Sharon, we were really embarrassed for her." "I'm sorry about that."

PROBLEM ORIENTATION: Seeks a mutually agreeable solution. "Okay. Let's see what we can do to get that report finished to specifications." "Let's talk and figure out how both of us can enjoy our vacation."

SPONTANEITY: Makes straightforward, direct, open, honest, and helpful comments. "I'd like to go to Florida with Frankie over spring break." "Would you help me move some heavy boxes?"

EMPATHY: Accepts and understands another person's feelings. "I can't believe she did that. No wonder you're upset." "It sounds as though you're having a hard time deciding."

EQUALITY: Suggests that everyone can make a useful contribution. "If you don't mind, I'd like to explain how I've handled this before. It may help." "Let's tackle this problem together."

PROVISIONALISM: Offers ideas and accepts suggestions from others. "We have a lot of options here—which one makes the most sense?" "I feel strongly about this, but I would like to hear what you think."

Gibb's Defensive and Supportive Behaviors[19]

our instinct to protect ourselves when we are being physically or verbally attacked by someone. Even though such reactions are natural, they also discourage reciprocal self-disclosure. On the other hand, **supportive behaviors** create an encouraging and caring climate in which self-disclosure and responsiveness to feedback benefit both communicators.

The paired behaviors in Gibb's model are not "good" and "bad" be-haviors. Rather, they represent dialectic tensions. For example, you may behave strategically when you have important and strong personal motives. You may behave with certainty when your expertise is well-recognized and a critical decision must be made. And you may respond neutrally when the issue is of little consequence to you or others. Thus, if you're not sure how to self-disclose or are reluctant to provide feedback, look to Gibb's 12 supportive and defensive behaviors. His categories offer both a strategy and skills set for developing a supportive communication climate that fosters appropriate self-disclosure and feedback.

> **Supportive behaviors** Behaviors that create an encouraging and caring climate in which self-disclosure and responsiveness benefit both communicators

strengthening
PERSONAL RELATIONSHIPS

most people have three types of significant personal relationships in their lives: friend relationships, romantic relationships, and family relationships. Because these three kinds of relationships function in different contexts, we need specialized communication strategies and skills to enhance their quality and longevity.

Friend Relationships

The ancient Roman statesman Cicero wrote, "If you take friendship out of life, you take the sun out of the world." Modern researchers confirm Cicero's outlook: Having friends increases life satisfaction and helps increase your life expectancy.[20]

Although just about everyone has friends, not all friendships are alike. Several factors influence the type of friendship you have with another person. For example, for young children, a friend is simply someone with whom a child shares toys and plays; when these activities are absent, so is the friendship.[21]

In adolescence and young adulthood, we often establish enduring and intimate relationships with best friends. **Intimacy**, the feeling or state of knowing someone deeply, occurs in many forms. For example, in most romantic relationships, intimacy is a physical way of expressing affection, love, and passion. In friend relationships, intimacy takes a different form. It can be emotional (sharing private thoughts and feelings), intellectual (sharing attitudes, beliefs, and interests), and/or collaborative (sharing and achieving a common goal).[22]

Close friends learn that it's okay to share personal thoughts, secrets, hopes, and fears, but whether we do so at this life stage depends on our ability (1) to disclose personal information in a way that maintains the relationship; (2) to recognize that most of these disclosures center on mundane, everyday issues; and (3) to respect that some topics are taboo, such as negative life events and serious relationship issues.[23]

During late adolescence and young adulthood, most of us leave home—to work, to go to college, to marry and raise a family. The dual tasks of developing new friendships while adapting to a new job, new living conditions, or new academic settings can take its toll. Although adolescents and young adults have more opportunities to make friends than any other age group, this stage, more than at any other life stage, proves to be one of their loneliest times.[24]

Romantic Relationships

Researchers confirm that people who need others, and can admit to this, are the lucky ones. And, according to Richard Layard, a British economist who is also a leading scholar in modern happiness research, "People who are in loving relationships with another adult have better hormonal balance and better health, and are of course happier."[25]

How do you let another person know that you like her or him? How do you find out whether that person likes you? The process of romancing another person begins with generating and assessing *liking*, which can be communicated both nonverbally and verbally. In Chapter 6, Nonverbal Communication, we introduced the concept of immediacy. Nonverbal cues such as increased eye contact, touch, standing closer, and leaning forward can signal liking. When it

Intimacy The feeling or state of knowing someone deeply in physical, psychological, emotional, intellectual and/or collaborative ways because that person is significant in your life

age the other person to share personal information while also sharing our own when appropriate; presenting ourselves as positive, interesting, and dynamic; doing favors for or assisting the other person; and seeking and demonstrating similarities in tastes, interests, and attitudes.[26]

Taken one at a time, these strategies may not seem significant or romantic, but when combined, they let the other person see that the relationship is becoming closer and has the potential for future development.

Romantic relationships do not happen by chance, nor do they magically come into being. Rather, you start, develop, maintain, strengthen, and end romantic relationships. Mark

Knapp and Anita Vangelisti describe ten predictable stages in intimate relationships.[27] Their model is heavily oriented toward male–female romantic couples, yet they also account for many child–parent relationships, close work relationships, and same-sex relationships. Knapp and Vangelisti divide relationship stages into two major processes: coming together and coming apart. Figure 8.1 describes the ten interaction stages using the example of a romantic relationship.

comes to expressing liking verbally, most people don't take the direct route. We don't walk up to someone and say, "I like you." Instead, we tend to use subtler strategies, such as inviting the other person to social activities; asking questions to encour-

Jealousy An intense feeling caused by a perceived threat to a relationship

---

STOP & THINK | Beware of Jealousy

Jealousy has the power to damage and end a relationship beyond repair. Although jealousy occurs among friends, it plays a much more significant role in romantic relationships. **Jealousy** is an intense feeling caused by a perceived threat to a relationship—from spending time with other friends to being honored for achievements at work. Highly jealous people may interpret an innocent look or a conversation with another person as signs of sexual unfaithfulness and may also see other people as potential rivals, whether they are or not.

People express jealousy in several ways: through accusations and sarcasm, depression and physical withdrawal, or the "silent treatment." Extremely jealous people are often aggressive, manipulative, or violent. Pathologically jealous individuals are highly sensitive to "every nuance in [their] environment that may hint of unfaithfulness." Jealousy taken to extremes can destroy relationships and lead to stronger feelings of resentment and inferiority.[28]

The following communication strategies can address and reduce your own or someone else's jealousy, particu-

larly when you are highly motivated to maintain the relationship:

- *Integrative communication.* Provide direct but nonaggressive communication about your jealousy in an effort to work things out. In other words, talk about it calmly and compassionately.
- *Compensatory restoration.* Work to improve the relationship or make yourself more desirable. Strategies such as giving a gift, appearing more attractive and affectionate, and being extra-nice can reduce or counteract jealous feelings.
- *Negative affect expression.* Express yourself nonverbally so the jealous person can see how it affects you (e.g., appearing hurt, distressed, or crying).[29]

If someone's jealousy becomes extreme or is based on unfounded beliefs, none of the above strategies may help. When jealous people become cruelly aggressive, manipulative, or violent, professional counseling may be necessary.

186—200

RELATIONSHIP STAGES

5 **Bonding.** The couple makes a public commitment to one another. The couple enjoys a stable relationship.

"I want to be with you always."

4 **Integrating.** Personalities, opinions, and behaviors join together. Individuals become a couple.

"What happens to you happens to me."

3 **Intensifying.** There is more intimate physical contact, more talk, and more self-disclosure.

"I . . . I think I love you."

2 **Experimenting.** The two people look for and learn about similarities and common interests. There is pleasant and casual small talk.

"Oh, so you like to ski . . . so do I."

1 **Initiating.** There is a cautious assessment of the other person and polite communication.

"Hi, how ya doin'?"

Coming Together

Differentiating. Each person becomes distinct and different in character. More use of "I" and "you" than "we" and "our." There is more conflict. **6**

"I don't like big social gatherings."

Circumscribing. There is a decrease in communication. Personal and important topics are no longer discussed. **7**

"Did you have a good time on your trip?"

Stagnating. Communication shuts down. More time and attention is devoted to work and other friends. **8**

"What's there to talk about?"

Avoiding. There is a lack of desire to spend time together. Communication may become antagonistic or unfriendly. **9**

"I may not be around when you call."

Terminating. Psychological and physical barriers are created. Each person is more concerned about self. **10**

"I'm leaving you . . . and don't bother trying to contact me."

Coming Apart

Figure 8.1 The Stages of a Relationship[30]

What Do You Know About Marriage?

It's a volatile time for traditional marriages. Most states have legalized no-fault divorces. An increasing number of states are legalizing same-sex marriages. According to Stephanie Coontz from the Council on Contemporary Families, "marriage isn't what it used to be." She also notes that what most people think they "know" about marriage is wrong.[31] Find out how much you know about marriage by answering the true-or-false questions below:

_____ 1. Women are more eager to marry than men.

_____ 2. Men are threatened by women who are their intellectual and occupational equals, preferring to be with much younger, less accomplished women.

_____ 3. The preferred form of marriage through the ages has been between one man and one woman.

_____ 4. There are more long-term marriages today than in the past.

_____ 5. Born-again Christians are *much* less likely to divorce than non-religious Americans.

_____ 6. The growth in the number of couples living together and even having children without formal marriage ceremonies or licenses reflects a sharp break with centuries-old tradition.

_____ 7. Divorce rates in the 1950s were lower than they are now.

Answers:

1. **False** More men than women report that marriage is an ideal lifestyle.

2. **False** By the end of the 1990s, 39 percent of women aged 35–44 lived with younger men. Today, men are more likely to seek a mate with the same level of education and earning potential.

3. **False** Polygamy—one man and many women—has been the preferred form of marriage throughout most of history.

4. **False** More couples will celebrate their fortieth wedding anniversaries now than at any time in the past. The divorce rate reached its peak more than 25 years ago and has fallen 25 percent since 1981.

5. **False** Whereas 35 percent of born-again Christians have divorced, 37 percent of atheists and agnostics have divorced—and 23 percent of born-again Christians have divorced twice. Among Pentecostals, the divorce rate is more than 40 percent.

6. **False** For the first thousand years of its existence, Christianity held that a marriage was valid if a couple claimed they had exchanged words of consent—even if there were no witnesses and no priest to officiate. Not until 1754 did England require a license for marriage to be valid. In nineteenth century America, one-third of all children were born to couples who were not legally married.

7. **False** Aside from a spike in divorce immediately after World War II, divorce rates in the 1950s were higher than in any previous decade since the Depression. Divorce rates continued to increase through the 1970s but have fallen since 1981. Marriage rates, however, have also fallen significantly in the past 25 years.

Knapp and Vangelisti's model only scratches the surface of each stage in a relationship. Just because your partner doesn't like big social gatherings as much as you does not mean your relationship will come apart. "It is not necessarily 'bad' to terminate a relationship nor is it necessary 'good' to become more intimate with someone. The model is descriptive of what seems to happen—not what should happen."[32]

Family Relationships

There was a time when an ideal nuclear family was viewed as a mother, father, and their biological children. *The New York Times* reports that in 1960, about 45 percent of U.S. families were nuclear families but that by 2001 only 23 percent of families could be described as nuclear families.[33] By 2007, more women (51 percent) were living without a husband than with one.

The U.S. Census Bureau also notes that only about 30 percent of African American women were living with a spouse compared with about 49 percent of Hispanic women, 55 percent of non-Hispanic white women, and more than 60 percent of Asian women.[34] So, what *is* a family? In their book on family communication, Lynn Turner and Richard West define a **family** as "a self-defined group of intimates who create and maintain themselves through their own interactions and their interactions with others."[35] A family may include both involuntary relationships (you don't get to choose your biological parents) and voluntary relationships (you choose your spouse).[36]

In the following sections, we examine two communication variables that affect all types of families: (1) family roles and rules and (2) parenting skills.

Family Roles and Rules When you watch children play "house," they take on roles—mother, father, and children. Even at an early age, children learn that certain patterns of behavior and expectations are characteristic of each family member. Family roles are often linked to family rules. For example, "Dad will deal with the car problem" may be interpreted as a rule, which in turn suggests that dad's role is vehicle caretaker. Family rules are contextual; they vary according to the situation and family culture. In some cultures, a daughter may not date until her parents meet the young man and approve her choice. In other cultures, grandparents are revered as the wisest members of the family, and their advice and approval are sought by all family members.[37]

Family rules serve an important purpose: They allow family members to make sense of family episodes. Rules also help family members understand one another's behavior. Although some family rules may seem unfair or arbitrary, they do help families define and maintain themselves.[38] Some common family rules might include: *Tell the truth*; *Say "please" or "thank you"*; and *Don't talk back to your parents or grandparents*.[39]

Parenting Skills In supportive, healthy families, parents give children love, values, and social skills. Socially skilled children are better at understanding and appropriately reacting to the emotions of others, understand how their behavior impacts others in interpersonal conflict situations, and communicate more effectively.[40]

Not all parents raise such children. One key factor is their parenting style. The three **parenting styles** on p. 161 are stable sets of behaviors that characterize parent–child interactions over a wide range of situations.

In your opinion, which parenting style is most effective? As you might guess, there is no "correct" answer. However, research suggests that **authoritative parenting** is the most flexible and therefore has the potential to be the most effective. Authoritative parenting adapts to the individual characteristics and needs of children by being *both* compassionate *and* firm. Children are given

> **Family** A self-defined group of intimates who create and maintain themselves through their own interactions and their interactions with others
>
> **Parenting style** A stable set of behaviors that characterizes parent-child interactions over a wide range of situations
>
> **Authoritative parenting** Parents are flexible and adapt to the individual characteristics and needs of their children

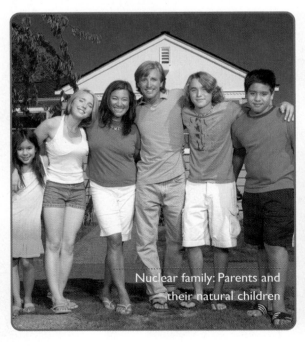

Nuclear family: Parents and their natural children

Step family and adopted family: Her child, his child, and their adopted child

Three Parenting Styles

1. **Authoritative.** Parent is respected, trustworthy, reliable, firm, confident, and flexible.
2. **Coercive/Authoritarian.** Parent is strict, severe, demanding, controlling, and rigid.
3. **Permissive.** Parent is lenient, tolerant, nonjudgmental, indulgent, and accepting.

Single-parent family: A father and his two sons

Authoritative parents prepare children for life rather than regulate and control them.

the freedom to make decisions within a reasonable limit. Authoritative parents prepare children for life rather than regulate and control them.[41] They are more likely to help their children develop effective and ethical communication skills that will enable them to become socially skilled in a wide range of personal interactions.[42]

Coercive/Authoritarian parenting is less flexible. Children are expected to follow a set of rigid rules that may not account for their individual characteristics and needs. Coercive/Authoritarian parents are very strict, may use physical punishment, and may ridicule their children by putting them down or holding power over them. Although this can result in immediate compliance and "good" behavior, these children may never learn to regulate their own behavior from within or take responsibility for their decisions and actions.[43]

Permissive parenting is perhaps too flexible. Permissive parents are often less involved in their children's lives and may overindulge or neglect them. They tolerate their children's impulses (including aggression), encourage children to make decisions without providing limits, and refrain from imposing structure on children's time for such activities as bedtime and television watching. They make few demands for mature behavior and they do not impose consequences for misbehavior. Children raised by highly permissive parents may have difficulty respecting others, coping with frustration, delaying gratification, and following through with their plans.[44]

Coercive/Authoritarian parenting Parents are not flexible and expect their children to follow a set of rules that may not adapt to their characteristics and needs
Permissive parenting Parents are less actively involved in their children's lives and may overindulge or neglect them

Do parents really make a major difference in the way children behave outside the home—and the way they grow up? Developmental psychologist Judith Rich Harris believes that parenting has almost no long-term effects on a child's personality, intelligence, or mental health. Instead, children are most influenced by two other factors: their genes and their peers. Harris uses this example to make her point: Children born of immigrant parents (who speak English poorly) quickly learn to speak Standard English. They learn this from their peers, who have more influence on how they speak and sound.[45]

Same-age peers also show children how to fit in and behave—in the classroom, on the ball field, or at parties.

Children adopt certain behaviors in social settings to win acceptance from their peers, and it's those behaviors outside the home that remain steadfast through adulthood. Blame your peers, Harris says, not your parents.[46]

Do you believe Harris's claims? Or do you give more credit to good parenting? How do you explain what happens when the child of two "good" parents turns out "bad"? Should parents be more concerned about the kind of neighborhood they live in than how they parent? Judith Harris's research raises many questions and has created considerable controversy and debate among psychologists, communication scholars, and family members.[47]

EXPRESSING **emotions** APPROPRIATELY

emotions play a major role in all relationships. An **emotion** is the feeling you have when reacting to a situation, and is often accompanied by physical changes. Emotions are fundamental to effective and ethical communication. They play a significant role in how you develop, maintain, and strengthen interpersonal relationships.

The Basic Emotions

For the most part, everyone experiences basic, primary emotions, but researchers disagree on the number of such emotions. Robert Plutchik's **Psychoevolutionary Emotion Theory** helps explain the development and meaning of emotions.[48] According to this theory, each basic emotion has a range of feelings (from mild to intense).

But what about love? Plutchik explains that some emotions, including love, are combinations of two or more of the basic emotions. Our basic emotions can be mixed—just as primary colors are mixed—to yield other emotions. As shown in the figure below, love is a combination of joy and acceptance. Contempt is a combination of anger and disgust.

Emotion The feeling you have when reacting to a situation, often accompanied by physical changes
Psychoevolutionary Emotional Theory Robert Plutchik's theory that explains the development, meaning, and range of emotions

Plutchik's Primary and Compound Emotions[49]

Communication Strategies	As an Emotionally Intelligent Communicator, You . . .
Intrapersonal Communication Strategies	
Develop Self-Awareness	Monitor and identify your feelings in order to guide your decision making. *Example:* Noticing whether you have raised your voice because you are angry or surprised.
Manage Your Emotions	Restrain or release your emotions when the situation is appropriate. Practice relaxation to recover from emotional distress. *Example:* Deciding whether expressing strong emotions will facilitate or interfere with your goals.
Motivate Yourself	Persevere in the face of disappointments and setbacks. Seek the support of friends, colleagues, and family members to stay motivated, improve your mood, and bolster your confidence. *Example:* Seeking help from a trusted mentor.
Interpersonal Communication Strategies	
Listen to Others	Engage effective listening skills to ensure you understand what another person means. Use effective, empathic listening. *Example:* Paraphrasing what you hear to make sure you understand someone before responding emotionally.
Develop Interpersonal Skills	Use self-disclosure, assertiveness, and appropriate verbal and nonverbal communication. Try to resolve conflicts. *Example:* Deciding whether and how to share your emotions with a close friend.
Help Others Help Themselves	Help others become more aware of their emotions. Help them speak and listen more effectively. *Example:* Providing emotional support to a distressed friend.

Emotionally Intelligent Communication[50]

Emotional Intelligence

Science writer Daniel Goleman defines **emotional intelligence** as "the capacity for recognizing our own feelings and those of others, for motivating ourselves, and for managing emotions well in ourselves and in our relationships."[51] His influential book, *Emotional Intelligence: Why It Can Matter More Than IQ*, is based on the work of two psychologists, Peter Salovey and John Mayer, who coined the term *emotional intelligence* in 1990. You can examine emotional intelligence as a set of communication competencies summarized and described in the chart above.

What happens when people cannot make emotions work for them? Neurologist Antonio Damasio, who studies patients with damage to the emotional center of their brains, reports that these patients make terrible decisions even though their IQ scores stay the same. So even though they test as "smart," they "make disastrous choices in business and their personal lives, and can even obsess endlessly over a decision as simple as when to make an appointment." Their decision-making skills are poor because they have lost access to their emotions. Damasio concludes that feelings are *indispensable* for rational decision making.[52] Consider whether you could answer any of these questions without taking emotions into account: Whom should I marry? What career should I pursue? Should I buy this house?

What should I say to my bereaved colleague?

The Need for Emotional Support

How many times have you felt at a loss for words when someone needed emotional support and comfort? A colleague's home is destroyed in a fire. Your partner fails to get a "sure-thing" job she or he

Emotional intelligence The capacity for recognizing our own feelings and those of others, for motivating ourselves, and for managing emotions well in ourselves and in our relationships

The Ethics of Caring

The NCA Credo for Ethical Communication includes a principle that speaks directly to interpersonal relationships: "We promote communication climates of caring and mutual understanding that respect the unique needs and characteristics of individual communicators."[53] Philosopher and educator Nel Noddings believes we make moral choices based on an ethic of caring. For example, a mother picks up a crying baby, not because of a sense of duty or because she is worried about what others will say if she doesn't, but because she cares about the child. Relationship theorists emphasize that this is not a gender-based ethic. Rather, it is based on a way of thinking that honors two fundamental characteristics of ethical behavior: avoiding harm and providing mutual aid.

Most of us have a basic and universal aversion to harm, both physical and psychological. We also have a basic and universal urge to help others, particularly when they suffer from harm. Interpersonal ethics calls for rational justifications, flexibility, self-control, and self-monitoring in our communication and interactions with others. As ethical communicators, we must accept the difficult challenge of defending our choices and taking responsibility for the consequences of our actions.[54]

In what way does this scene depict an ethic of caring, and how does such behavior promote effective communication?

applied for. What do you say or do? As a concerned and compassionate person, you probably look for ways to comfort your friend, colleague, partner, or family member. Unfortunately, many of us feel inadequate to this task. We worry about saying the wrong thing. We search through racks of greeting cards to find a card that can "say it" better than we can.

As much as we may want to support and comfort a person in distress, many of us lack an understanding of the basic nature of emotional support as well as the communication skills needed to achieve its purpose. Communication scholar Brant Burleson defines **emotional support** as "specific lines of communicative behavior enacted by one party with the intent of helping another cope effectively with emotional distress." The distress can be acute (disappointment over not getting a promotion, anxiety over an upcoming exam) or chronic (grief over the loss of a loved one, lingering depression over poor health) and may be mild or intense in character.[55]

Constructing Supportive Messages

Emotionally supportive communication strategies can help you become a more compassionate, comforting, and effective communicator. These strategies include being clear about your intentions, protecting the other person's self-esteem, and centering your messages on the other person.

Communicate Your Intentions Clearly When someone is in great distress, you may think this person knows you want to be helpful and supportive. You may assume that just "being there" tells the other person that you care. In some cases,

> **Emotional support** Specific communication behaviors enacted by one party with the intent of helping another cope effectively with emotional distress

your assumptions are correct. In other situations, a person in distress needs to know that you *want* to help or provide assistance. Supportive intentions should be clear and sincere. You can enhance the clarity of your supportive messages by stating them directly ("I want to help you") and by making it clear you care ("I'm here for you"). You can also intensify the perceived sincerity of your response by emphasizing your desire to help ("I really want to help however I can"), by reminding the person of the personal history you share ("You know we've always been there for each other"), and by indicating what you feel ("Helping you is important to me; I'd feel terrible if I weren't here to help").[56]

Protect the Other Person's Self-Esteem Make sure that your offer of help does not imply that the other person is incapable of solving the problem or dealing with the situation. Otherwise, you may damage someone's self-esteem. Even with the best of intentions, expressions of sympathy ("Oh, you poor thing") can convey judgments about the person's lack of competence and lack of independence. Try to encourage and praise the other per-

...a person in distress needs to know that you want to help or provide assistance.

son: "I know you can deal with this—as you have many times before," "I can see you're trying very hard to overcome this problem," or "I really respect what you're trying to do here."[57]

Offer Person-Centered Messages Messages that reflect "the degree to which a helper validates [a] distressed person's feelings and encourages him or her to talk about the upsetting event" are **person-centered**.[58] Rather than focusing on helping someone feel better, your goal is helping the person develop a deeper understanding of the problem, and take on the task of solving or coping with it.

You can help someone in distress understand the problem by encouraging her or him to tell an extended,

personal story about the problem or upsetting event. People in need of emotional support may want nothing more than to share the details with a trusted friend.

While these communication strategies express your willingness to help, your supportive feelings, and your personal commitment, take care to avoid counterproductive strategies. For example, do not focus

---

Person-centered message
Reflects the degree to which a supportive helper validates a distressed person's feelings and encourages that person to talk about the upsetting event

---

communication&culture

GENDER DIFFERENCES IN EXPRESSIONS OF EMOTIONAL SUPPORT

When we face a distressing or tragic situation, we may seek or want others to provide emotional support. There are, however, differences in the way men and women behave when trying to express their support. "Although men and women are similar in the type of emotional support they typically want to receive from others . . . they differ quite reliably when it comes to providing emotional support to others."[59]

Research by Brant Burleson and colleagues concludes that, in general, men are less effective at providing "comforting messages (even if they have the ability to do so) because they desire to avoid engaging in behaviors they view as especially

feminine"—that is, behaviors that are inconsistent with their male gender role. In addition, demonstrating "stereotypical feminine behaviors (such as offering comfort) is more threatening to the gender identity of men," particularly when communicating with other men.[60] Despite these conclusions, Burleson and his colleagues caution us against assuming that men cannot or will not provide effective comfort. When men care a great deal about another person and are highly motivated to provide support, they will do so. And when men offer comforting messages highly focused on the individual seeking that emotional support, male recipients do not react negatively. In short, all of us—male or female—seek, accept, and appreciate effective emotional support from others.[61]

> **People in need of emotional support may want nothing more than to share the details with a trusted friend.**

on or share *your* emotional experiences, as in "I know exactly how you feel. Last year, I went through a similar kind of problem. It all started when . . ." Not only does this stop the other person from sharing, but it also shifts the focus to yourself. You should also avoid messages that criticize or negatively evaluate another person, because these can hurt more than help. Do not tell others that their feelings are wrong, inappropriate, immature, or embarrassing.

STRATEGIES FOR
Encouraging Coping through Storytelling[62]

✔ Ask for your friend's version of the situation. ("What happened here? Can you tell me about it?")

✔ Create a supportive environment and provide enough time for the person to talk. ("Take your time. I'm not going anywhere. I want to hear the whole story.")

✔ Ask about the person's feelings, not just the events. ("How did you feel when that happened?" "What was your reaction when she said that?")

✔ Legitimize the expression of feelings. ("Be angry. It's okay." "I certainly understand why you'd feel that way.")

✔ Indicate that you connect with what the other person is saying. ("If that happened to me, I'd be furious too.")

The Comforting Touch

communication in ACTION

As a child, you experienced nonverbal comforting well before you understood and communicated with language. "Not surprisingly, the nonverbal behaviors first used in infancy continue as expressions of emotional support throughout a lifetime. Hugs, touches and pats, hand-holding, focused looks and soothing sounds can be remarkably effective ways of expressing reassurance, love, warmth, and acceptance."[63] In terms of physical health, researchers note that a hospital patient's family and friends help just by visiting, regardless of whether they know what to say.[64] According to another study, a five-second touch can convey specific emotions such as sympathy and sadness.[65] Put another way, "touch can be worth a thousand words."

Touch plays a significant role in comforting others. "Skin-on-skin touch is particularly soothing because it primes oxytocin," a neurotransmitter that causes our body to undergo many healthy changes. Blood pressure lowers and we relax. Our pain threshold increases so that we are less sensitive to discomforts. Even wounds heal more rapidly.[66]

How would you react nonverbally if a close same-sex friend told you that she or he had just ended a serious romantic relationship? College students largely agree on what they would do. In one study, hugging emerged as the number-one response. Other high-ranking responses included being attentive, moving closer to the other person, using certain facial expressions, increasing touch, and making eye contact. Not surprisingly, men and women suggested different nonverbal responses. Men were less likely than women to hug their troubled friend; they were more likely to pat their friend on the arm or shoulder and to suggest going out and doing something to take his mind off the problem. Women were more likely to cry with their friend and to use a variety of comforting touches.[67]

Evacuees of Hurricane Katrina find solace and comfort in the warm embrace of others.

Communication ASSESSMENT

How Emotionally Intelligent Are You?[68]

Daniel Goleman proposes five basic emotional competencies, expressed in the following headings.[69] Use the rating scale listed here to assess your level of competence for each question:

5 = always, 4 = usually, 3 = sometimes, 2 = rarely, and 1 = never.

Know Thy Self

_____ 1. Can you accurately identify the emotions you experience and why you experience them?

_____ 2. Do you have a strong self-concept?

_____ 3 Are you aware of your strengths and limitations?

Control Your Emotions and Impulses

_____ 4. Can you keep disruptive emotions under control?

_____ 5. Do you take responsibility for your emotions and resulting actions?

_____ 6. Are you open-minded and flexible in handling difficult situations?

Persevere

_____ 7. Do you strive to improve or meet high standards of excellence?

_____ 8. Do you persist in the face of obstacles and setbacks?

_____ 9. Can you postpone gratification and regulate your moods?

Empathize

_____ 10. Do you accurately interpret others' feelings and needs?

_____ 11. Do you provide appropriate emotional support to others?

_____ 12. Do you paraphrase appropriately?

Interact Effectively

_____ 13. Do you listen appropriately and effectively?

_____ 14. Do you make a positive social impression?

_____ 15. Do you work effectively with others to achieve shared goals?

Scoring: Add up your ratings. The higher your score, the more "emotionally intelligent" you are. Keep in mind that your ratings are only your _perceptions_ of your feelings and behaviors. For example, despite what you think, you may not interpret others' feelings and needs accurately or persist in the face of obstacles. On the other hand, you may not recognize that you provide appropriate emotional support to others, even though your friends often turn to you when they need an empathetic ear.

Summary

How important is the quality of your personal relationships?

- Good personal relationships positively affect your health, happiness, and success.
- Relational Dialectics Theory explains how the interplay of opposing or contradictory forces affects personal relationships in three domains: integration–separation, stability–change, and expression–privacy.

How does self-disclosure and sensitivity to feedback improve personal relationships?

- Self-disclosure involves sharing personal information, opinions, and emotions with others.
- Social Penetration Theory describes how we move from superficial communication to deeper, more intimate relationships.
- The Johari Window displays the extent to which you are willing to self-disclose and are receptive to feedback from others.

What strategies and skills are appropriate for expressing your thoughts and feelings?

- Effective self-disclosure requires the ability to focus on the present, be descriptive, and reciprocate self-disclosure.

- Effective feedback requires giving and asking for responses about behaviors, perceptions, and feelings.
- Gibb's communication climate behaviors include evaluation/description, control/problem orientation, strategy/spontaneity, neutrality/empathy, superiority/equality and certainty/provisionalism.

How can you strengthen personal relationships with friends, family members, and romantic partners?

- Intimacy is the feeling or state of knowing someone deeply in physical, emotional, intellectual, or collaborative ways.
- Strong friendships increase life satisfaction and life expectancy.
- People in loving relationships have better health and happier lives.
- There are ten common stages in romantic relationships, divided into five coming-together steps and five coming-apart steps.

- Healthy families have both roles and rules as well as distinctive parenting styles.

What is the role of emotions in developing, maintaining, and strengthening close relationships?

- Robert Plutchik's eight primary emotions are: fear, acceptance, anger, disgust, joy, anticipation, sadness, and surprise.
- Emotional intelligence is the capacity to recognize and responsibly manage your own feelings.
- Emotional support represents the way you communicate when trying to help another person cope with emotional distress.
- When comforting another person, make your intentions clear, protect the other person's self-esteem, and center your message on the other person, not on yourself.

the **THINK**SPOT

www.thethinkspot.com

TEST your knowledge

1. In *Uncoupling: How and Why Relationships Come Apart,* sociologist Diane Vaughan notes that a couple's breakup is rarely sudden. It all begins with _____.
   a. jealousy
   b. a financial problem
   c. admitting an act of infidelity
   d. a secret
   e. different attitudes and values

2. Which relational dialectic is involved when you're looking for some excitement in your life while your partner is content to stay home, work on hobbies, and interact with lifelong friends?
   a. fight versus flight
   b. integration versus separation
   c. work versus play
   d. expression versus privacy
   e. stability versus change

3. Social Penetration Theory explains that relationships are closest when communication is:
   a. friendly, frequent, and fair
   b. deep, broad, and frequent
   c. private, patient, and powerful
   d. narrow, shallow, and occasional
   e. open, hidden, and unknown

4. According to the Johari Window Model, the more receptive and adaptive you are to feedback from others, the smaller your _____ window pane is.
   a. open
   b. hidden
   c. blind
   d. known
   e. unknown

5. All of the following behaviors are characteristics of effective self-disclosure *except*:
   a. Focus on the person's past behavior.
   b. Be descriptive, not judgmental.
   c. Disclose your feelings as well as facts.
   d. Adapt to the person and context.
   e. Engage in reciprocal self-disclosure.

6. In terms of Gibb's categories of behavior for creating a positive communication climate, how would you classify the following statement? "Let's figure out a way for both of us to go where we want on our vacation."
   a. description
   b. strategy
   c. empathy
   d. neutrality
   e. problem orientation

7. According to the research in your textbook, which age group often describes their life stage as the loneliest time in their lives?
   a. young children
   b. adolescents and young adults
   c. 30-45 year olds
   d. 45-60 year olds
   e. senior citizens

8. In terms of Knapp and Vangelisti's model of relationship stages, in which stage do the personalities, opinions, and behaviors of two people join together so that they become a couple rather than two separate individuals?
   a. intensification
   b. integration
   c. differentiation
   d. circumscribing
   e. experimenting

9. Which two emotions combine to create the emotion of love?
   a. submission and surprise
   b. anticipation and awe
   c. acceptance and joy
   d. optimism and submission
   e. none of the above

10. Which of the following statements communicates your desire to help and support a person dealing with emotional distress?
    a. I'm here for you.
    b. I really want to help however I can.
    c. Helping you is important to me; I'd feel terrible if I weren't here to help you.
    d. You know we've always been there for each other.
    e. all of the above

Answers: 1-d; 2-e; 3-b; 4-c; 5-a; 6-e; 7-b; 8-b; 9-c; 10-e

test your knowledge   **169**

THINK COMMUNICATION

This article from *Communication Currents* has been slightly edited with permission from the National Communication Association.

Communication Currents
Knowledge for Communicating Well

NCA
A Publication of the National
Communication Association

Volume 4, Issue 2 - June 2009

10 Communication Strategies to Keep Marriages Strong

> Some couples leave phrases like this out of their marriage vows. Why do you think they do this? What realities about married life are these couples acknowledging?

> Where, if at all, would you draw the line on sharing your personal thoughts, feelings, and goals with someone you love?

When couples promise to *love, honor, and cherish* their spouses *until death do us part* they are making a commitment they hope will lead to a strong marriage. Most people want to be in relationships where they care about and are cared for by their spouse, where they intend to persevere through the inevitable ups and downs, and where they have a long-term view of the relationship. One mechanism through which these goals are met is communication. Through the utilization of verbal and nonverbal communication strategies, couples in committed marriages develop a sense of *we-ness* that sustains them through difficulties and over time.

A wealth of research has shown that communication plays an essential role in maintaining committed, satisfying marriages. In our research over almost two decades, we have asked a large number of couples in a variety of ways what things do they do or say to show commitment to their partners. Their responses have led to the identification of ten communication strategies that keep marriages strong.

> Before reading the rest of this essay, which communication strategies and skills do you believe are most important in a successful marriage? See Chapter 8, pp. 156–157, 159.

1. *Make a conscious effort to communicate* – Research has shown that it is not only the big important moments, but also the small day-to-day, seemingly mundane interactions that form and sustain relationships. These day-to-day conversations reinforce marital commitment. It is critical that couples share personal thoughts, feelings, and goals with one another on a regular basis.

2. *Express commitment verbally* – Behaviors in which partners specifically tell one another of their commitment and intention to remain in the relationship reinforce satisfaction with and confidence in the relationship for both partners. Couples express commitment when they say things like: "I am committed to our marriage" and "I am in this for the long haul."

3. *Behave with integrity* – Integrity deals with communicating in an open, honest manner and involves keeping promises, remaining loyal, and being honest and trustworthy. Having integrity builds trust and confidence in partners and the relationship.

4. *Show affection* – Affection is an important aspect of commitment and refers to verbal and physical displays that demonstrate partners' positive feelings toward one another. Spouses telling each other that they care, giving gifts and surprises, and

> According to *Social Penetration Theory*, relationships are closest when communication is deep, broad, and frequent. How should married couples express their commitment to one another in each of these three ways? See Chapter 8, p. 152.

How often do you see married couples *touch* each other in public—hold hands, hug, kiss, stroke an arm, pat a knee? What does touching behavior tell you about a couple's relationship? How, if at all, does touching differ when a couple isn't married or hasn't been dating for a long time?

engaging in physical expressions of affection (hugs, kisses, touch) are examples of behaviors couples engage in to show their affection for each another.

5. *Share companionship* – Companionship refers to the enjoyment couples find in spending time together and including each other in valued activities. The old adage that *couples who play together stay together* is applicable. Mutual liking as well as enjoyment of time spent together is critical to commitment.

Research by Brant Burleson and his colleagues describes the need for *emotional support* as well as the specific ways to construct supportive messages. See pp. 163–166 in Chapter 8.

6. *Give emotional support* – Emotional support deals with being there in difficult times, providing support and encouragement, offering direct assistance and help when needed, building up self esteem and showing interest in one another's well-being. Emotional support strategies provide a safe, nurturing environment in which partners are encouraged to grow and reach their potential.

7. *Show respect* – Doing and saying things to show respect, accepting partners for who they are, and allowing them space and independence when needed are ways spouses communicate consideration for one another. Interacting in respectful ways conveys the message that one's spouse is valued and important.

8. *Create a positive atmosphere* – Behaviors spouses use that create a positive atmosphere include: being courteous to each other, trying not to complain, and speaking well of their partner to others. These behaviors encourage an optimistic tone in the relationship that leads to positive feelings between partners and toward the relationship.

9. *Celebrate the relationship* – Behaviors that celebrate the relationship reinforce the long-term prospects of the relationship by emphasizing important events in the

How can you use Gibb's *defensive and supportive behaviors* to create a positive and supportive climate in a marriage or close personal relationship? See pp. 154–155 in Chapter 8.

past, present, and future. Couples mark relationship milestones and anniversaries, make preparations for special days, and plan the future of the relationship together. When spouses interact in ways that celebrate the relationship they reinforce how important the marriage is to them.

10. *Work through problems* – Conflict inevitably arises in relationships. Actively engaging in strategies to manage and, where possible, resolve conflict prevents problems from becoming issues that undermine commitment and ultimately the relationship. Successful couples listen, hear their partners out fully, express their needs and issues clearly, remember that no one can read their minds, and look at the bigger picture rather than focusing on winning or losing. The critical issue is to focus on the problem rather than to attack.

In conclusion, research has shown that marriages are stronger when couples communicate in ways that deepen and sustain commitment to one another and the relationship. When couples use communication strategies like those above, they tend to have higher levels of relationship commitment and satisfaction and experience greater feelings of love, passion, and trust. They are also more positive about the long-term prospects of their relationships. In short, couples who communicate to maintain their marriages are more likely to be able to *love, honor, and cherish* one another for the long haul.

In addition to these communication strategies, what other methods can help a couple resolve *conflict*? See Chapter 7, pp. 137–140. Which method or methods would you use?

Now that you have read this essay, are there other interpersonal communication strategies important for a successful marriage? If so, what are they? In your opinion, which of the ten communication strategies identified by the authors are the most important?

ABOUT THE AUTHORS

Deborah Ballard-Reisch is Professor and the Kansas Health Foundation Distinguished Chair in Strategic Communication at Wichita State University, Wichita, Kansas. **Daniel J. Weigel** is a faculty member in Cooperative Extension, the Department of Human Development and Family Studies, and the Social Psychology doctoral program at the University of Nevada, Reno, Nevada. *Communication Currents* is a publication of the National Communication Association.

9 PROFESSIONAL

Consider the number of hours many of us spend at work each day. If you work full-time, you probably spend more hours interacting with co-workers, managers, clients, or customers than you do with your family and friends. Whereas your personal relationships focus on private interactions with friends, romantic partners, and family members, your *professional relationships* focus on interactions with others to accomplish a goal or to perform a task in a workplace context. Researchers who study the nature of professional relationships report a host of depressing statistics related to our interactions at work: 55 percent of managers are seen as unfit for their jobs,[1] 60 percent of employees consider dealing with a supervisor the most stressful part of their jobs,[2] and 85 percent of workers who quit their jobs report doing so because they are unhappy with their boss.[3]

> **Your professional relationships are among the most important in your life, and they present unique interpersonal communication challenges.**

Despite these distressing numbers, there is good news: Effective and ethical communication can create a more positive and productive work environment, reduce interpersonal conflicts, and help frustrated employees deal with work-related problems. Your professional relationships are among the most important in your life, and they present unique interpersonal communication challenges. This chapter focuses on communication strategies and skills that can enhance the quality of your professional relationships.

RELATIONSHIPS

the nature of
PROFESSIONAL RELATIONSHIPS

the nature of professional relationships reflects your work responsibilities, the quality of your relationships with colleagues, and the organizational culture in which you work. You also have professional relationships beyond traditional work-place settings. For example, you may have professional interactions with the members of a labor union, an academic association, a community organization, a volunteer group, or a medical office.

Types of Professional Relationships

The quality and success of your professional relationships depend on how well you communicate with your boss or supervisor, your co-workers, and your customers or clients. For example, a corporate attorney may communicate differently when interacting with a paralegal or assistant (superior–subordinate relationship),

when resolving a dispute with a colleague (co-worker relationship), or when counseling a client (customer relationship).

Superior–Subordinate Relationships In **superior–subordinate relationships**, the superior (supervisor) has formal authority over the work and behavior of subordinates (workers).[4] Superiors direct work, authorize projects, describe policies, and assess subordinates' performance. Subordinates provide information about themselves, about co-workers, and about the progress of their work as well as "what needs to be done and how it can be done" to supervisors.[5]

Poor superior–subordinate relationships negatively affect productivity, job satisfaction, and employee retention. Recall some of the statistics presented at the beginning of this chapter. In addition to considering interactions with a supervisor the most stressful part of their jobs, the majority of employees who quit their jobs do so because they are unhappy with their boss.

SUPERVISORY STRATEGIES
for Promoting
Trust and Openness[6]

- Behave in a consistent and predictable manner.
- Be honest and keep your promises.
- Share decision-making control.
- Clearly explain policies, procedures, and decisions.
- Express concern for others' well-being.

85% of workers who quit their jobs report doing so because they are unhappy with their boss.

Can you tell who the supervisor is and who the subordinates are in this photo? What nonverbal cues might help you decide?

Superior–subordinate relationship A type of professional relationship characterized by the formal authority one person has over another person's work and behavior

Difficult Behavior at Work

Supervisors and co-workers who are difficult to work with can negatively affect your ability to do your job and to enjoy what you're doing. They engage in counterproductive behaviors such as chronic lateness, poor performance, derogatory e-mailing, persistent negativity, resisting needed change, shooting down new ideas, complaining constantly, neglecting commitments as well as more serious forms of behavior such as harassment, work sabotage, and even physical abuse.[7]

Dealing with difficult behavior at work is, not surprisingly, difficult. Failure to remedy such behavior, however, perpetuates a work environment that takes its toll on everyone. In his book *Dealing with Difficult People*, Hal Plotkin recommends a six-step approach to providing feedback to such people and to helping them realize their full potential:[8]

1. *Identify specific successes and failures.* Rather than saying, "You're always late," state the exact number of times the person has been late during a defined period of time. Be equally specific when offering praise.

2. *Stop talking and start listening.* Use all types of listening—discriminative, comprehensive, empathic, analytical, and appreciative listening—to make sure you understand the other person's point of view.

3. *Describe the implications of behavior.* Help people understand the consequences of their behavior—in both organizational and personal terms.

4. *Link past accomplishments to needed change.* Point out how the traits that have led them to successes can be applied to areas that need improvement.

5. *Agree on an action plan.* Work *together* to come up with a plan that has specific ideas or steps, clear timetables, and realistic standards for success.

6. *Follow up.* Stay engaged and set up times to meet again. Use follow-up sessions to help the other person deal with problems, provide personal support, and offer praise.

Finally, change how you define the problem. If you refer to *people* as difficult, you are shifting attention from what they *do* to who they *are*. Rather, identify their *behavior* as the problem and then maybe you can do something about it.[9]

If you are a supervisor, your success largely depends on your ability to establish trust with subordinates, convey immediacy and caring, and give useful feedback about the subordinates' work and progress.[10] Although some superior–subordinate relationships are formal and distant, others thrive on informal, friendly, and nonthreatening interaction without sacrificing respect and productivity.

Co-Worker Relationships Interactions with people who have little or no official authority over one another but who must work together to accomplish the goals of an organization are known as **co-worker relationships**. Good relationships with co-workers are the primary source of most job satisfaction.[11]

A co-worker who won't share important information or who has a different work style can derail the performance of others. A colleague who does a poor job or is uncooperative won't be respected. Satisfying relationships with your co-workers make the difference between looking forward to and dreading another day at work.

Satisfying relationships with your co-workers MAKE THE DIFFERENCE between looking forward to and dreading another day at work.

Criteria for a Satisfying Co-Worker Relationship[12]

- **Individual Excellence.** Do both of you perform well in the job?
- **Interdependence.** Do both of you have complementary skills and need one another to do the job?
- **Investment.** Do both of you devote time and resources to helping each other succeed?
- **Information.** Do both of you share information openly?
- **Integration.** Do both of you have compatible values about and styles of work?
- **Integrity.** Do both of you treat each other with respect?

Co-worker relationship A type of professional relationship that involves interacting with people who have little or no official authority over one another but who must work together to accomplish the goals of an organization

Customer Relationships The success of any business or organization depends on effective and ethical communication with customers and clients, particularly in the United States, where the average company loses half its customers within five years.[13] **Customer relationships** involve interactions between someone communicating on behalf of an organization with an individual who is external to the organization. They include the way colleges treat students, the way medical professionals take care of patients, and the way police officers respond to crime victims.

Unfortunately, some employees lack appropriate training or have inaccurate assumptions about customer service. One study checked thousands of applications for grocery store workers and identified several false assumptions about customer service.[14] Almost half the applicants believed that customers should follow company policies to deserve help and should be told when they are wrong. Approximately 10 percent of would-be employees would not help a customer if it wasn't part of their jobs and would not volunteer to assist customers unless they asked for help.

The quality of customer relationships affects the financial health of a business and employee job security. Effective employees understand that, in a typical customer relationship, the customer has several basic communication needs.[17] First, the customer or client needs to feel welcome. Many retail staff members are trained to greet customers the moment they enter a store or business. Second, customers need enough information to make a decision or solve a problem regarding a service or product. Thus, sales and customer service representatives must be product experts who offer information and ask insightful questions. Finally, customers need to be treated with respect, especially because they have the power to take their business elsewhere and to encourage others to do the same.

> **The quality of customer relationships affects the financial health of a business and employee job security.**

Does customer relationship describe the interaction between teachers and students? Or are these relationships more like superior–subordinate or co-worker relationships?

STOP & THINK

Is the Customer Always Right?

Dealing with dissatisfied and angry customers can be difficult and stressful, especially when customers with legitimate complaints behave in inappropriate ways. When a customer is rude or disrespectful, you may become angry. Expressing your anger, however, may only escalate the conflict. The Better Business Bureau points out that even when a customer isn't happy with the solution, an employee who listens and attempts to help will be perceived as cooperative.[15] The following strategies can help calm an unruly customer and promote effective problem solving:[16]

- Don't take a complaint personally.
- Listen attentively and ask questions.
- Try to separate the issues from the emotions. Rude customers may have legitimate complaints and may only be expressing frustration.
- Make statements that show you empathize: "I can understand why you're upset."
- Share information or explain the reasons for a decision, but do not argue with a customer.
- If the company is at fault, acknowledge it and apologize.
- Ask the customer how she or he would like the problem to be resolved.

Customers may not always be right, but they should always be treated with courtesy and respect.

Customer relationship A type of professional relationship that involves interaction between someone communicating on behalf of an organization with an individual who is external to the organization

Organizational Culture Theory The shared symbols, beliefs, values, and norms that affect the behavior of people working in and with an organization

Organizational subculture A group of individuals who engage in behaviors and share values that are different from that of the larger organizational culture

Organizational Culture Theory

Many workplaces are organized in a structured hierarchy that establishes levels of authority and decision-making power. That hierarchy may influence who talks to whom, about what, and in what manner. In large organizations, employees are often expected to convey information and voice concerns to their immediate supervisor. Only when a problem cannot be remedied at that level do employees have the "right" to speak to the next person up the hierarchy.

In general, the more levels within an organization's structure, the more likely it is that information will be distorted as communication goes up or down the "chain of command." The accuracy of information can be reduced by up to 20 percent every time a message passes through a different level.[18]

How would you describe the organizational culture being depicted in this photo of Google employees?

In addition to an organizational structure, every organization has a unique culture that influences member communication. According to Michael Pacanowsky and Nick O'Donnell-Trujillo, **Organizational Culture Theory**[19] describes the ways in which shared symbols, beliefs, values, and norms affect the behavior of people working in and with an organization. For example, one company may expect their employees to wear suits, spend much of their time working silently in their offices, arrive and leave promptly, and get together in small groups to socialize only after hours. Just as cultural beliefs, norms, and traditions change when you travel from one country to another, organizational culture can vary from job to job. Customs in an organizational culture include personal, celebratory, and ritual behaviors (checking e-mail, celebrating birthdays, attending department meetings), social behaviors (politeness, thanking customers, sup-

porting worried colleagues), and communication behaviors (retelling legendary stories, using in-house-only jargon, giving colleagues nicknames).

Organizations also have subcultures. An **organizational subculture** consists of a group of people who engage in behaviors and share values that are, in part, different from that of the larger organizational culture. For example, the marketing department in an organization may develop different customs than the accounting department across the hall. The regional sales office in Texas may have different traditions than the Chicago office.

CLASSIC ORGANIZATIONAL HIERARCHY

BOARD OF DIRECTORS
Makes policy and key decisions

UPPER MANAGEMENT
Senior executives who implement Board policies and decisions

MIDDLE MANAGEMENT
Managers who link upper management to supervisors and their workers

LOWER MANAGEMENT
Supervisors or team leaders who have regular and direct contact with workers

SUPPORT STAFF
Secretaries, administrative assistants, project directors

FRONTLINE WORKERS
People who do the fundamental tasks of the organization

professional
COMMUNICATION CHALLENGES

maria didn't want anyone at work to know that she was dating her co-worker James. Unfortunately, her officemate overheard her talking with James on the phone and told several co-workers about the relationship. Soon there was a buzz in the office. Maria was worried not only that their boss would disapprove, but that her co-workers would mock or harass them.

Ineffective and inappropriate communication in professional settings can result in serious consequences: tension in the workplace, limited advancement opportunities, or even job loss. In this section, we examine some of the difficult communication situations that occur within organizations: office gossip, workplace romances, sexual harassment, working with friends, and quitting or losing a job.

In some workplaces, malicious gossip infects the workplace and creates a climate of hostility and distrust.

Office Rumors and Gossip

Whereas a **rumor** is an unverified story or statement about the facts of a situation, **gossip** is a type of rumor that focuses on the private, personal, or even scandalous affairs of other people. Nicholas DiFonzo of the Rochester Institute of Technology describes gossip as a rumor that is "more social in nature, usually personal and usually derogatory." When spreading "gossip, truth is beside the point. Spreading gossip is about fun."[20]

Most of us listen to rumors because we want to have as much information as everyone else. Typically, we spread gossip because we want to be perceived as "in the know."[21] In one survey of office workers, more than 90 percent of employees admitted to engaging in gossip.[22] The study also found that after learning information about a colleague

STRATEGIES FOR Managing Office Gossip

- ▶ Do not spread malicious rumors. If you don't know whether the information is accurate, don't repeat it.
- ▶ Evaluate the reliability of a rumor or gossip by asking questions and checking facts.
- ▶ When others gossip, change the subject, tell them you prefer not to discuss certain topics, or say that you're too busy to talk at the moment.
- ▶ Consider the potential consequences of divulging confidential information or spreading a rumor.
- ▶ Before self-disclosing to a co-worker, assume that your secret will be told to others.
- ▶ If you believe that gossip has created a serious problem, talk to someone with more power or influence.[23]

that was intended to be secret, 75 percent of employees revealed that secret to at least two other employees that same day.

While rumors and gossip have the potential to be harmful, they can also serve an important social function. Consultant Annette Simmons observes that "a certain amount of small talk—sharing small details of your life—helps people feel closer to co-workers. It is what humanizes the

Rumor An unverified story or statement about the facts of a situation

Gossip A type of rumor that focuses on the private, personal, or even scandalous affairs of other people

An organization can take measures that prevent the *need* for gossip by keeping employees well-informed.

workplace and helps people bond."[24] However, unchecked or malicious gossip can have serious consequences. Private and potentially embarrassing information, even if untrue, can damage your professional credibility. Divulging company secrets can get you fired. Time spent gossiping is time not spent doing your job. In some workplaces, malicious gossip infects the workplace and creates a climate of hostility and distrust.

An organization can take measures that prevent the *need* for gossip by keeping employees well-informed.[25] For example, when a company is purchased by a larger corporation, many employees worry about losing their jobs and spend hours talking about who will stay and who will be asked to leave. If no personnel cutbacks are planned, employees should be told. When cutbacks are anticipated, an organization should inform everyone about how and when those decisions will be made—this way, everyone will have more accurate information. When organizations learn that misinformation is making its way through the rumor mill, they should address and correct it quickly before any more harm is done.

Know Thy Self

How Satisfied Are You with Your Job?

For each of the job-related items on the following list, rate your level of satisfaction with your current or most recent job:

1 = very dissatisfied
2 = somewhat dissatisfied
3 = somewhat satisfied
4 = very satisfied

Add your responses to determine your total score.

16–27 points	Very dissatisfied
28–39 points	Somewhat dissatisfied
40–51 points	Somewhat satisfied
52–64 points	Very satisfied

Review your responses to identify specific areas of dissatisfaction. You may enjoy your co-workers but dislike your boss. You may have a good relationship with your boss but be unhappy with organizational policies. You may enjoy a friendly work environment but believe you are underpaid. Once you have identified the problems, you can then work to improve that area and your overall job satisfaction.

Are you satisfied with . . .

_____ 1. your job responsibilities?
_____ 2. your workload?
_____ 3. your salary or hourly pay relative to your responsibilities and experience?
_____ 4. your level of job security?
_____ 5. how your work is evaluated and rewarded?
_____ 6. the extent to which the organization helps you grow professionally?
_____ 7. the relationship you have with your boss?
_____ 8. how your boss makes decisions?
_____ 9. the extent to which you are treated fairly?
_____ 10. the relationships you have with co-workers?
_____ 11. the overall quality of work by colleagues?
_____ 12. how well co-workers cooperate with one another?
_____ 13. your level of influence in decision making?
_____ 14. how information is shared within the organization?
_____ 15. how the organization handles dissent and disagreement?
_____ 16. the ethics of the organization's practices?

The stars of *Grey's Anatomy* demonstrate how professional relationships can evolve into workplace romances.

Workplace Romances

Approximately one-third of all romantic relationships begin in the workplace.[26] In one study, 93 percent of people surveyed report that they have worked in places where colleagues had a romantic relationship,[27] and more than 60 percent say they have been involved in at least one workplace romance.[28] Although some workplace romances result in long-lasting relationships and marriages, it can be difficult to manage the blurred distinction between private and professional lives.

For example, a public display of affection in the workplace may be viewed as unprofessional and may make other colleagues feel uncomfortable. Co-workers may also suspect that a romantic partner receives preferential treatment. Romantically involved couples may find it difficult to separate issues at work

Approximately 1/3 of all romantic relationships begin in the workplace.

from personal issues that arise after work. And if a romantic relationship ends, the professional relationship may become strained or awkward. Half the romantic relationships begun in the workplace will also end there.[29]

Why do many organizations disapprove of office romance? Many corporate executives believe that office romances almost always end badly and therefore should be banned in the workplace.[30] They are concerned that an office romance may eventually result in a claim of sexual harassment or retaliatory behavior after the relationship ends.[31] They also worry that romantically involved employees will become less productive and that their relationship will affect the morale of coworkers or create a climate of unprofessionalism.[32]

Workplace Sexual Harassment

Workplace romances should not be confused with sexual harassment. Romance in the workplace involves two individuals who agree to a close, personal relationship, whereas **sexual harassment** is characterized by unwelcome sexual advances for sexual favors, inappropriate verbal or physical conduct of a sexual nature, or an intimidating, hostile, or offensive work environment.[33] Sexual harassment is rarely an isolated incident. Usually, it is a pattern of offensive or unwelcome behavior

Sexual harassment Unwelcome sexual advances for sexual favors, inappropriate verbal or physical conduct of a sexual nature, or an intimidating, hostile, or offensive work environment

The Effects of the Office Romance

Wall Street Journal columnist Sue Shellenbarger suggests that if you can answer *yes* to any of the following questions, your employer may be justified in warning, reprimanding, transferring, or even firing you if you are involved in a romantic relationship at work:[34]

- Are you romantically involved with a subordinate or your boss?
- Are both of you assigned to the same team or division?
- Is the relationship negatively affecting your work?
- Will your work be negatively affected if the relationship ends?
- Could others perceive favoritism as a result of the relationship?

Shellenbarger also suggests that if you pursue an office romance, keep in mind that in all likelihood it will eventually end. "If it does end, you have to be mature enough and professional enough to handle seeing the other person every day."[35]

that takes place over a period of time. In many instances, sexual harassment involves a supervisor or colleague using power to demand sexual favors—from coercing a subordinate to perform sexually in order to guarantee her or his job to making sex a prerequisite for securing a promotion, a higher salary, or extra time off. Sexual harassment may also include demeaning or offensive communication, namely in the form of e-mails containing sexually explicit messages and jokes, inappropriate comments made directly to a co-worker, or postings of sexual images in staff rooms.

In some cases, romantic relationships that end badly result in sexual harassment. If, for example, an employee posts embarrassing photographs of an "ex" in the office lunchroom as a way of getting back for a hostile breakup, the person in those photos may feel humiliated, offended, and unable to work productively with colleagues. The distressed employee may also end up with grounds for a sexual harassment suit.

Research reports that many victims of sexual harassment experience "decreased work performance, anxiety, depression, self-blame, anger, feelings of helplessness, fear of further or escalating harassment, and fear of reporting the incident."[36] Although most workers say they would immediately address or report harassment, research reveals that, when confronted with the situation, many people feel uncomfortable and fail to report the behavior.[37]

Most organizations take allegations of sexual harassment very seriously—if for no other reason than to avoid costly lawsuits.

As a result, they establish policies against sexual harassment as well as grievance procedures for reporting such behavior. If you believe you are the victim of sexual harassment, keep in mind that complaints are taken more seriously when brought to the attention of management immediately.[38]

Sexual harassment is rarely an isolated incident.

communication&culture

DIFFERING VIEWS ON SEXUAL HARASSMENT

Identifying sexual harassment is complicated by the fact that men and women often have different perceptions of similar behavior. Thus, telling a sexually explicit joke in the office may be viewed by women as harassment, whereas men may see it as harmless. Both men and women, however, judge overt behavior, such as demands for sexual favors, as harassment. According to the Equal Employment Opportunity Commission (EEOC), approximately 15,000 complaints of sexual harassment are filed every year.[39] Thirteen percent of these are filed by men.[40]

How would you answer this question: Have any of the following incidents happened to you or someone you know in the workplace?

1. Unwanted and deliberate touching, leaning over, cornering, or pinching
2. Unwanted sexually suggestive looks or comments
3. Unwanted letters, telephone calls, or materials of a sexual nature
4. Unwanted pressure for dates
5. Unwanted sexual teasing, jokes, remarks, or questions

Now ask yourself this question: Are any of the above incidents examples of sexual harassment? A large study asked these same questions to more than 8,000 federal government employees; the results indicated that women are more likely than males to view all of these behaviors as sexually harassing. No one should have to tolerate a sexually hostile work environment. All of us should treat our colleagues with respect and refrain from behavior that could be perceived as sexually offensive.[41]

Working with Friends

Many co-worker relationships are personal as well as professional. Mixing personal and professional relationships, however, can be difficult to negotiate: You want your friend to like you, but you also need co-workers, superiors, and subordinates to respect you; you want approval from your friend, but you also must make objective decisions in the workplace; you hope for your friend's professional success, but not at the expense of your own.

In *Organizational Communication*, communication scholar Daniel Modaff and his colleagues recommend that you seek your most important relationships outside the workplace and that, if you do have a personal relationship at work, you should be prepared to manage the consequences.[42] Telling a best friend that he has not met expectations on a work team can be difficult and even impossible if you want to preserve the friendship. At the same time, letting a friend get away with less-than-excellent work can destroy the morale of a group and put your reputation and leadership at risk.

STRAINS[43]

on Friendships

- Equal status in a friendship may be compromised by inequality at work.
- The need to withhold confidential work information may clash with the need for openness in a friendship.
- Collaboration with a friend may be impossible when one friend has more decision-making power at work.
- The friendship may be damaged by negative feedback given at work.
- Public expressions of friendship may need to be minimized in the workplace.

on Professional Relationships

- A friendship may make it difficult to manage unequal levels of power at work.
- It may be difficult to handle sensitive work information with discretion.
- Personal knowledge and feelings about a friend may compromise objectivity at work.
- Friends may be held to a higher performance standard at work.
- Socializing may adversely affect productivity and the quality of performance at work.

Summary of the strains that occur when friendship and work relationships collide.

Leaving a Job

According to the U.S. Department of Labor, the typical American will change *careers* approximately seven times.[44] And according to the Bureau of Labor Statistics, before the age of 32, the average American has had nine jobs and one-third of workers predict they will probably change jobs again within five years.[45] There are many reasons for leaving a job or changing one's career. Whatever your reason, always try to depart on as good terms as possible and handle your resignation or exit with professionalism and courtesy.

Just as you want to make a good first impression when interviewing and beginning a new job, it is equally important to leave a positive impression when departing from or ending a job.

Even when a resignation is the result of dissatisfaction with the job or a poor relationship with a boss or co-workers, leaving on good terms is important. After you resign, a supervisor or human resources manager may request an *exit interview*. Organizations gather information in exit interviews to develop strategies for retaining other employees and to improve the workplace for those who remain. Because you don't know how the information will be used or whether it will be

LEAVING YOUR JOB—Best Practices[46]

- Follow company policies and procedures when resigning.
- Tell your immediate supervisor first.
- Resign in person, but also write a brief resignation letter.
- Give the appropriate advance notice.
- Phrase explanations positively.

... the typical American will change *careers* approximately 7 times.
— U.S. Department of Labor

treated confidentially, remain calm and convey a positive attitude. Focus on issues, not people. An "exit interview is not the time to burn bridges. Most industries are small, and bad behavior is not something you want people remembering about you."[47]

Sometimes, leaving a job is not a decision you make by choice. As a stressful event, job loss ranks right up there with death in the family, divorce, and serious illness. Job loss can have a profound effect on your emotional well-being. Typically, most people experience a resulting cycle of denial, anger, frustration, and eventually adaptation.[48] If your anxiety seems out of control, go back to the section on communication apprehension in Chapter 2. Many of the relaxation strategies we recommend—cognitive restructuring, visualization, and systematic desensitization—can help you build confidence and reduce stress.

CHECKLIST

for Coping with Job Loss[49]

Be Proactive

■ Did you discuss with appropriate parties the details of your unemployment benefits (e.g., severance, health insurance, life insurance)?

■ Did you assess the reasons why you lost your job?

Explore Thy Self

■ Have you asked yourself whether you want to stay in the same field?

■ Is a *career change* in order?

■ Is there a *skill* you need to learn or further develop to become an *indispensable* employee?

Use Your Communication Skills

■ Did you network with family members, friends, and colleagues to connect with potential employers?

■ Did you consult employment agencies, check the classifieds, and surf the Internet for available jobs?

■ Do you know the Dos and Don'ts of effective job interviewing?

Craft a Persuasive Message

■ Does your résumé highlight your marketable skills?

■ Does your résumé reflect your knowledge of the industry's trends?

■ Does your cover letter express how ready, willing, and able you are to give 110 percent to a new position?

What form of interview is depicted in this television interview? How is it similar to or different from a type of workplace interview?

job INTERVIEWS

When you see the phrase "job interview," what comes to mind? Most people think of a job interview as one of the last steps in the job application process. However, interviews do not end once you get a job; you'll encounter several other types in the workplace, including selection interviews, appraisal interviews, information-gathering interviews, disciplinary interviews, and exit interviews. Each type of interview has a unique purpose and process. In the world of work, an **interview** is an interpersonal interaction between two parties in which at least one party has a predetermined purpose and uses questions and answers to share information, solve a problem, or influence the other.[50]

Interview An interpersonal interaction between two parties, at least one of whom has a predetermined and serious purpose, that involves asking and answering questions in order to share information, solve a problem, or influence the other

The saying that you never get a *second* chance to make a *first* impression is especially true for job interviews.

Although a traditional job interview (a form of selection interview) can be a stressful communication situation, a good interview can land you the job of your dreams. Unfortunately, a poor interview can result in a major disappointment and the loss of a promising career opportunity. The saying that you never get a *second* chance to make a *first* impression is especially true for job interviews. In this section, we focus on the communication skills needed to prepare for, participate in, and follow up on a job interview.

Before the Interview

In *What Color Is Your Parachute*, the bestselling guidebook for career changers and job seekers, Richard Bolles tells the story of an interview between an IBM recruiter and a college senior. The recruiter asked the student, "What does IBM stand for?" The student didn't know and thus ended the interview.[51] As with any important communication situation, a successful job interview requires careful preparation. In a survey of the most common job interview mistakes, senior executives identified three major errors, all of which related to poor interview preparation: (1) having little or no knowledge of the company, (2) being unprepared to discuss skills and experiences, and (3) being unprepared to discuss career plans and goals.[52] Thus, before going to an interview, make sure you research the organization, assess your own

Types of Workplace Interviews	Purpose	Process
Selection interview	To evaluate and choose a candidate for a job or promotion	Potential employers assess whether your knowledge, maturity, personality, attitude, communication skills, and work record match the job.
Appraisal interview	To evaluate an employee's job performance	Employers assess an employee's work record, identify training needs, and provide motivation through constructive feedback.
Information-gathering interview	To obtain facts, opinions, data, feelings, attitudes, and reactions	Employer and employee analyze important issues and try to solve identified problems.
Disciplinary interview	To identify, discuss, and/or correct problematic behaviors	Employer assesses why problems are occurring and how, if at all, the employee can change behavior and resolve the problem.
Exit interview	To learn why an employee is leaving and whether problems contributed to that decision	Employer provides closure for the departing employee and identifies ways to improve other employees' satisfaction and retention.

strengths and weaknesses, and practice interviewing.

Research the Organization Learn as much as you can about the organization. You can contact the company or organization directly and request documents they make available to the public, such as brochures, catalogs, newsletters, and annual reports. If you know current or former employees, ask them about the organization.

A company or organization's Website tells you a great deal about the organization's mission, products

and services, and achievements. If the Website includes information about key employees, research the person or persons you will meet at the interview. You also may find news stories about the company or organization on other Websites. The more you know, the easier it is to explain how you can make a positive contribution. Research may also uncover reasons you don't want to work for that organization, ranging from a company's policy on unions or political issues to concerns about health benefits or pension options.

Assess Your Strengths and Weaknesses Identify what you can bring to the job that will promote the organization's goals. Ron, a 32-year-old man with some sales experience, was preparing to interview for a sales director position at a mid-sized company. He found a story on the Internet reporting that the company was considering restructuring its product pricing. Although the job description did not mention needing experience with this task, Ron decided to make a point of saying that his last job involved reevaluating product pricing. Using the information he researched about the organization helped Ron demonstrate why he was the best candidate for the position.

Be prepared to explain your weaknesses as well as your strengths. How will you address unexplained gaps of time on your résumé, several jobs in a short period of time, or the lack of a skill specifically mentioned in the job description? The time to develop an acceptable

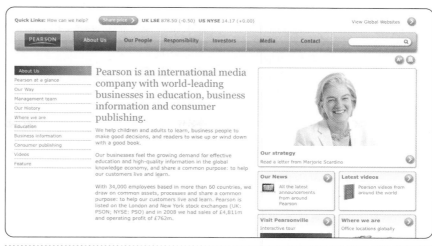

In addition to telling you about an organization's mission, products, services, and achievements, a Website gives you a feel for the company's organizational culture.

answer to such reasonable concerns is not in the middle of an interview. For example, Sharon quit her graphic design job when her first child was born and was a stay-at-home mother for seven years. When she decided to reenter the workplace, she knew she would have to address concerns about being up-to-date in her field. After careful consideration, she developed an answer that focused on refresher courses she had taken during the past two years as well as the volunteer design work she had done for community groups. She also suggested that her design "eye" had matured and grown more sophisticated than it was when she was a younger artist. Whatever your weakness might be, don't assume that the interviewer hasn't noticed it on the application or résumé. Instead, be ready with a thoughtful response.

> **Identify what you can bring to the job that will promote the organization's goal.**

ethicalcommunication

Never Lie During a Job Interview

Approximately 20 to 45 percent of applicants lie on a résumé or in a job interview.[53] Another study reports that 11 percent of applicants do not tell the truth about why they left a previous job and 9 percent lie about their education and responsibilities in previous jobs.[54] Not only is lying to a prospective employer unethical, it can backfire and have serious personal consequences.

Most organizations have become much more rigorous when screening applicants. Private detective Fay Faron explains that many organizations conduct extensive background checks to avoid a lawsuit and ensure the safety of customers.[55] So count on being carefully screened, having your references checked, and being investigated for a criminal background. Furthermore, if your lie is discovered, your application will be rejected or, if you're already hired, you will be fired. A survey conducted by an executive search firm revealed that 95 percent of employers would reject applicants who lied about a college degree and 80 per-

cent would not hire someone who falsified previous job titles.[56]

Your goal is more than getting a job, but getting a job that is right for you.[57] If you have to falsify your credentials or work experience, you are probably not qualified for the job. Moreover, the consequences of lying can be long-lasting. If your lie is discovered, it can ruin your reputation for years to come.

Practice Interviewing During a job interview, you need to make a good impression in a limited amount of time in a fairly stressful communication situation. Engaging in a mock interview will make a difference. Create a list of interview questions you might be asked (see the list of common questions on this page).

Because the interview will probably take place in a meeting room or office, sit at your desk or a table and practice your answers out loud and confidently. After you are comfortable with your responses, ask a few friends or family members to interview you. They can give you feedback on the quality of your answers and may suggest some additional questions to consider.

During the Interview

An interview is a golden opportunity for both you and the interviewer. The interviewer wants to learn more about you, and you have the opportunity to learn about the job and the organization while creating a positive impression. The extent to which you accomplish these goals depends on how well you respond to questions and present yourself.

Most interviews are structured around a series of five standard questions. As we note in Chapter 7, a closed-ended question requires only a short answer, such as *yes* or *no*. An open-ended question requires or encourages a more detailed answer. A **hypothetical question** describes a set of circumstances and asks how you would respond. A **leading question** suggests or implies the desired response. A **probing question** is used to follow up another question and/or response by encouraging clarification and elaboration.

Regardless of the type of question, you must know how to formulate an appropriate response for every question asked of you. Consider, for example, how the following answers to two commonly asked interview questions illustrate the differences between an effective and an inappropriate response.

Question 1: Why did you leave your last job?

Answer: My boss and I just didn't get along. She expected me to do work that was really her responsibility. They didn't pay me enough to do my job and someone else's. When I complained, nobody did anything about it.

Analysis: While honest, this is not a very effective or flattering response. Interviewers often ask questions like these to determine whether you had problems with a former employer and whether you will be just as troublesome in a new job. In this example, the interviewer could conclude that the applicant doesn't work well with others, resists doing required work, may complain a lot, and evaluates work only in terms of a paycheck. A better approach is to focus on why a

---

Common Interview Questions⁵⁸

1. Briefly, tell us about yourself.

2. What do you hope to be doing five years from now?

3. Where do you hope to be in ten years?

4. In terms of this job, what is your greatest strength?

5. What, in your opinion, is your greatest weakness?

6. What motivates you to work hard and do your best?

7. How well do you deal with pressure? Can you give an example?

8. What are the two or three characteristics you look for in a good job?

9. Describe a major problem you encountered on the job. How did you deal with it?

10. What kind of relationship should be established between a supervisor and subordinates?

11. Why did you choose to pursue this particular career?

12. Why did you leave your last job(s)?

13. How can you contribute to our company?

14. How do you evaluate or determine success?

15. Given the fact that we have other applicants, why should we hire you?

Hypothetical question Describes a set of circumstances and asks how you would respond

Leading question Suggests or implies the desired response

Probing question Follows up on another question and/or response by encouraging clarification and elaboration

Standard Interview Questions and Examples[59]:

Closed-ended question — Are you able to work on weekends?

Open-ended question — What do you view as the most significant challenges facing this industry over the next few years?

Hypothetical question — How would you handle an employee who does good work but, even after being warned, continues to arrive late?

Leading question — Do you think the ability to work well in a group is just as important as the ability to perform routine technical tasks?

Probing question — Could you explain what you mean by a "difficult client"?

new job would offer more desirable opportunities and better match your values and goals. A job interview is not the time or place to vent frustrations about a former boss.

Question 2: What, in your opinion, is your greatest job-related weakness?

Answer: My natural tendency is to focus on one thing at a time until it's completed. However, most of my jobs have required me to manage several projects at once. I've had to learn how to juggle a variety of tasks, particularly when things get hec-

> **Never hesitate to ask a question of clarification before giving a response.**

tic. A couple of years ago I started using a project management software system to track projects and help me keep things organized. This has helped me shift attention back and forth among projects without losing track of priorities and deadlines.

Analysis: This answer is effective and strategic. When answering a question about a weakness, figure out how to acknowledge it while simultaneously demonstrating how you learned to deal with or overcome it. As a result, you transform the weakness into an example of your problem-solving abilities. Also, don't exaggerate. When asked about your weakness, don't say, "I work too hard." We all do that. Working hard is usually considered a strength.

In addition to preparing to answer questions, be prepared to ask some questions. Never hesitate to ask a question of clarification before giving a response. Also, before ending an interview, interviewers often ask if you have additional questions. Use this opportunity to learn more about the job, its employees, and the organization.

Making a Good Impression Interviews provide employers with a way of deciding whether you are the right person for a job, not just from your answers, but also from the way you speak and behave during the inter-

Questions TO ASK During an Interview:[60]

- Can you tell me more about the specific, everyday responsibilities of this position?
- What, in your opinion, are the major challenges facing the organization?
- What is the most important characteristic you are looking for in an employee for this position?
- How would you describe the culture of your organization?
- How will success be measured for this position?
- What other people or departments will I be working with?

view. Remember that you are being observed from the moment you arrive until the time you leave the building. In fact, it's not unusual for an interviewer to ask receptionists or secretaries for their impressions of you.

In a survey conducted by Northwestern University, 153 companies were asked why they rejected job applicants.[61] Of the 50 reasons identified, almost half were related to lack of communication skills and failure to create a positive impression. Per-

STRATEGIES for
Enhancing Your First Impression during an Interview

- Arrive a few minutes early.
- Wear appropriate business attire.
- Listen attentively.
- Use correct grammar and appropriate language.
- Smile and be facially expressive.
- Use direct eye contact.
- Use a posture that appears relaxed but not too informal.
- Try to appear calm and confident; avoid fidgeting behavior.
- End the interview on a positive note.

haps the one mistake that people often take for granted is talking too much. If you talk *too* much, you may bore your listeners or may appear insensitive to the time limits of an interview. According to Richard Bolles, when it is your turn to speak or answer a question in an interview, try "not to speak any longer than two minutes at a time if you want to make the best impression."[62] Generally, it's better to leave interviewers hungry for more information about you, rather than to wear them out with more information than they need or want.

After the Interview

Immediately after an interview, send a note thanking the interviewer for her or his time and consideration. The note should briefly refer to issues discussed in the interview and emphasize that you can perform the job and help the organization meet its goals. A brief but well-written letter (not text message) reinforces that you have a professional approach to and enthusiasm for the job.

Although it's natural to wonder how well you did during the interview, you may never learn how the interviewer evaluated you and your responses. An analytical self-evaluation may be more useful (See the Communication Assessment: Evaluating Your Interview Performance).

Keep in mind that you can make an excellent impression during an interview and still not be hired because you may have been one of several out-standing candidates. Regardless of whether you are selected, view each interview as an opportunity to practice your skills. The more practice you have, the more your interviewing skills will improve.

> **"Try not to speak any longer than two minutes at a time if you want to make the best impression."**
> — Richard Bolles

COMMON INTERVIEW Mistakes TO AVOID[63]

- Unprofessional appearance
- Aggressive or arrogant manner
- Poor grammar and vocal expression
- Lack of interest or enthusiasm
- Lack of confidence
- Evasiveness and tendency to make excuses
- Lack of tact

- Immaturity
- Poor manners
- Tendency to criticize past employers
- No direct eye contact
- Weak or limp handshake
- Late to the interview
- Vague responses to questions

STOP & THINK | How Would You Handle Inappropriate Questions?

Federal and state laws prohibit discrimination in hiring. Generally, an interview should not include a discussion of race or ethnicity, gender, marital status, religion, sexual orientation, or disabilities. The best approach to answering inappropriate questions depends on the situation, what information you feel comfortable revealing, and your personal communication style. Now consider the following questions; which, in your mind, are inappropriate during a job interview? Why?

_____ What does your husband or wife do?

_____ Do you plan to have children?

_____ How many more years do you plan to work before retiring?

_____ Which religious holidays will you take off from work?

_____ Do you have any disabilities?

_____ What country are your parents or grandparents from?

Answers: All of the above questions are inappropriate for a job interview.[64]

You have the right to refuse to answer a question you believe is inappropriate, but before you assume it is inappropriate, assess the purpose of the question. Once you've assessed the intent and decide you will respond, be as tactful as possible so as not to embarrass the interviewer, and redirect the interview to a discussion of your qualifications. For example, "Do you have children?" may reflect the interviewer's concern that a busy parent won't work the number of hours necessary to demonstrate a full commitment to the job. An appropriate response might be, "If you're asking whether I can balance a demanding job with family obligations, I have always effectively done so in the past."

Furthermore, don't assume that the interviewer intends to discriminate. For instance, a hiring manager who asks whether you plan to have children may simply want to talk about the company's excellent maternity and childcare benefits or brag about his or her own newborn child. These types of questions are often asked out of simple curiosity or an effort to engage in conversation.

Communication ASSESSMENT

Evaluating Your Job Interview Performance

Use this instrument to evaluate your performance in a past job interview or in a classroom interview assignment, or to help prepare for an upcoming interview. Using criteria based on the seven key elements of communication, rate yourself as an interviewee with the following scores:
E = excellent, G = good, A = average, W = weak, M = missing, or N/A = not applicable.

The **7** Key Elements and Guiding Principles of Effective Communication

Job Interview Competencies	E	G	A	W	M	N/A
Self: I was well-prepared and confident.						
Others: I listened effectively and adapted to the interviewer.						
Purpose: I could explain how hiring me would promote my personal and professional goals as well as the organization's mission.						
Context: I adapted to the logistics and psychosocial climate of the interview.						
Content: I included ideas and information relevant to and needed in the job or assignment; I asked good questions; I knew a great deal about the organization.						
Structure: I organized the content of my answers in a clear and memorable way. I asked questions at appropriate points in the interview.						
Expression: I used verbal and nonverbal behavior appropriately and effectively. I was dressed appropriately and professionally.						
Overall Assessment:						

Additional Assessment Questions:

1. Which questions did I answer best? What made my answers effective?

2. Which questions were the most difficult? Are these questions likely to be asked in future interviews? How could I answer such questions more effectively?

3. Did I miss opportunities to emphasize particular strengths? How might I have incorporated those into my other answers?

4. Are there questions I should have asked before leaving?

5. What could I do differently in my next job interview?

Summary

How can you improve your professional relationships with superiors, subordinates, co-workers, and customers or clients?

- Whereas superiors request work, supervise projects, and assess a subordinate's performance, subordinates provide information about themselves and co-workers as well as information about the progress of work, what needs to be done, and how to do it.

- Satisfying co-worker relationships are characterized by individual excellence, interdependence, investment, information, integration, and integrity.

- Customers have three basic communication needs: to feel welcome, to have enough good information to make a decision, and to be treated with respect.

- When dealing with someone's difficult behavior at work, identify specific successes and failures, listen actively, explain the consequences of the behavior, call upon the person's strengths, and mutually agree and follow up on an action plan.

What communication strategies can help you handle office rumors and gossip, workplace romances, working with friends, and leaving a job?

- Although rumors and gossip serve several positive social functions in an organization, self-serving rumors and malicious gossip can have serious consequences, embarrass others, damage your credibility, waste time, and create a hostile and distrustful work environment.

- Many organizations disapprove of office romances because they can decrease productivity, make other colleagues feel uncomfortable, create suspicions that a romantic partner receives preferential treatment, and eventually end badly.

- Sexual harassment is characterized by unwelcome sexual advances for sexual favors, inappropriate verbal or physical conduct of a sexual nature, or an intimidating, hostile, or offensive work environment.

- Working with a close friend at work can put strains on the friendship (e.g., the need to withhold confidential information, giving a friend negative feedback) and the professional relationship (e.g., socializing decreases productivity, treating all co-workers equally).

- Leaving a job—either voluntarily or involuntarily—requires professional communication strategies and skills that leave a good impression with your former employer and create an equally good impression with your new or potential employer.

How should you prepare for, participate in, and follow up on a job interview?

- Before going to an interview, make sure you research the organization, assess your own strengths and weaknesses, and practice answering probable questions.

- During an interview, you should answer questions directly and concisely while presenting yourself and your skills positively.

- In addition to sending a follow-up note or message to the interviewer after an interview, assess your own performance in terms of the seven key elements of effective communication.

the THINKSPOT
www.thethinkspot.com

TEST your *knowledge*

1 According to a study quoted in your textbook, what percent of workers quit their jobs because they are unhappy with their bosses?
a. 15%
b. 30%
c. 45%
d. 60%
e. 85%

2 In a superior–subordinate relationship at work, effective subordinates provide all of the following types of information to their boss or manager *except*:
a. information about themselves and co-workers.
b. information on the progress of work.
c. information on what needs to be done.
d. information about how to do the work more effectively.
e. Subordinates usually provide all of the above types of information.

3 According to Organizational Culture Theory, the practice of giving colleagues unique nicknames would be an example of a _____ behavior.
a. ritual
b. impersonal
c. communication
d. celebratory
e. personal

4 Whereas a rumor is an unverified story or statement about the facts of a situation, gossip
a. is a type of rumor that focuses on the private and personal interactions of other people.
b. focuses on the scandalous affairs of other people.
c. is more social in nature.
d. is usually more personal and derogatory in nature.
e. All of the above are characteristics of gossip.

5 All of the following answers represent reasons organizations and corporate executives disapprove of office romances *except*:
a. Office romances often result in long-lasting relationships and marriages.
b. Most workplace romances almost always end badly.
c. Office romances may result in a claim of sexual harassment.
d. Office romances may result in retaliatory behavior after the relationship ends.
e. Romantically involved employees may be less productive than other employees.

6 All of the following behaviors constitute examples of sexual harassment *except*:
a. A supervisor demands sexual favors from a subordinate as a guarantee of keeping a job.
b. A supervisor demands sexual favors from a subordinate in order to earn a promotion.
c. A colleague passes around sexually explicit images and jokes via e-mail.
d. A co-worker makes sexually demeaning comments about another co-worker.
e. All of the above are examples of sexual harassment.

7 Which type of interview is conducted for the purpose of evaluating an employee's job performance?
a. selection interview
b. appraisal interview
c. information-gathering interview
d. disciplinary interview
e. exit interview

8 "What are the most significant challenges facing this industry in the current economic climate?" is what type of interview question?
a. closed-ended question
b. leading question
c. probing question
d. open-ended question
e. hypothetical question

9 Which one of the following questions is technically inappropriate and illegal during a job interview?
a. Do you plan to have children?
b. Do you have any physical or mental disabilities?
c. What country are your parents or ancestors from?
d. Which religious holidays will you take off from work?
e. All of the above are inappropriate and illegal questions.

10 Before ending an interview, interviewers often ask if you have additional questions. Which of the following questions would be an appropriate question for this purpose?
a. Do you have any disabilities?
b. Will I be permitted to take off three very important holidays celebrated by my religion?
c. What position does this company take on the abortion issue?
d. How will my success be measured for this position?
e. Will I be working with a culturally diverse group of people?

Answers: 1-e; 2-e; 3-c; 4-e; 5-a; 6-e; 7-b; 8-d; 9-e; 10-d

THINK COMMUNICATION

This article from *Communication Currents* has been slightly edited with permission from the National Communication Association.

Communication
Knowledge for Communicating Well
Currents

N C A
A Publication of the National
Communication Association

Volume 2, Issue 14 - February 2007

How Employees Fight Back Against Workplace Bullying

Research characterizes affected workers as powerless in the face of more powerful bullies. Workers faced with relentless attacks also say they feel unable to protect themselves against or stop bullying. However, a recent study conducted by Dr. Pamela Lutgen-Sandvik, Assistant Professor of Communication at the University of New Mexico, suggests that workers may have more power than they think.

Even though workers say they feel like there is nothing they can do to stop abuse, they take a stand by leaving the workgroup or organization, or they can fight back by gathering peer support and taking collective action, documenting abuse and allying themselves with powerful others, withholding work or information, and directly confronting bullies. In most cases, they use a combination of these tactics.

At first glance, it may appear that leaving is simply running away or giving up. However, the mass departure of workers in the face of bullying is marked by anger, disgust, and a desire to "send a message" to those in power. Amy, who worked in the sports fishing industry, said she wanted her resignation to "send a message to the bully. . . . He crossed *my* personal line in the sand . . . so I quit." She went on to explain . . . "He'd debase [my two best executives], and blame them, and debase them, and blame them, and he chipped away at them, and chipped away at them, until they both found other jobs. . . . It was just *morally wrong.*" Similarly, Steve left his 15-year position as a highly trained specialist in state government giving three days notice in order to "open their eyes." As he explained, "I did everything I could . . . [and] nobody did anything. . . . I spent two days training my replacement . . . and was out of there. Let 'em go down in flames! Maybe this will open their eyes."

Amy and Steve's accounts are not unique. Other stories are filled with tales of quitting, intentions and threats to quit, transfers and requests for transfers, and even helping each other get out—usually with the goal of sending a message or punishing the organization for allowing abuse to continue. Additionally, those left behind make use of the high staff turnover and hold it up to decision makers as proof that there is something very wrong in the organization. If bullying-affected workers have a theme song, it is David Allan Coe's "Take This Job and Shove It." The song title resonates with employees who have been bullied, since many quit specifically to communicate their frustration, disgust, and anger, or to punish the orga-

> *Bullying* in the workplace is very common. Researchers believe that almost 40 percent of American workers have experienced bullying on the job.

> Interestingly, about 40 percent of bullies in the workplace are women, who choose other women as targets more than 70 percent of the time. How would you explain this finding?

How could you use *Gibb's six supportive communication behaviors* (Chapter 8, pp. 154–155) for avoiding or reducing the defensiveness or denial that may accompany a complaint about a bully?

Think of how you could use *Toulmin's Model of an Argument* (Chapter 4, pp. 78, 80) to put all of these tactics into a strong argument that would persuade upper management to take corrective action against a workplace bully.

nization by permanently withdrawing their experience, knowledge, and skills.

Quitting is a visible way to resist, because speaking out is often such risky business. . . . Fighting back against bullies at work, often bullying managers or supervisors, can result in further harm to workers. Those who summon the courage to speak out want change but may receive punishment. They report abuse but might be labeled insubordinate for their efforts. If they go to upper-management, they can be accused of going outside the chain of command, although in most cases, doing so is crucial to ending bullying. . . . Despite the risks, workers fight to change hostile work environments. They fight to end bullying both in groups with their coworkers and individually without support of others. When workers resist collectively, even in the absence of labor unions, organizational decision makers more often take action to stop abuse than in cases where workers fight back individually. Collective resistance usually includes both bullied and non-bullied workers. In fact, when those who are not being bullied speak out alongside those who are, change is more likely to occur. It also appears that collective resistance has fewer downsides for workers. For example, of those who collectively resisted in the study, none were fired, but 20% of those individually resisting were fired. It seems that collective resistance provides a safer and more powerful way for workers to speak out against bullying at their jobs. This does not mean that individual resistance has no effect. In many cases, individuals resist without knowledge that others in their workgroup are also making complaints. In some cases, this buildup of individual reports gets the attention of upper-management.

Whether resisting collectively or individually, two tactics seem ineffective at stopping abuse. These are confronting the bully and withholding labor or information. Confronting the bully probably aggravates rather than improves the situation, and withholding work or information may go unnoticed. On the other hand,

there are tactics that more often lead to upper-management taking corrective action. Organizational change occurs most often when workers use three tactics in combination: (1) informal verbal or formal written complaints to organizational authorities, (2) written documentation of bullying (times, dates, concrete details), and (3) expert opinion (published research on workplace bullying). Although change often takes months to materialize, cases where workers fight back by going up the formal chain of command and working within the organization's grievance system are most often associated with ending abuse.

. . . Documentation—of bullying incidents and the potential costs of bullying for the organization—is an invaluable tool for upper-management. Upper-management needs this information for investigation and to take actions deemed necessary to end abuse. . . . Written documentation is even more convincing when combined with published research that verifies and names such occurrences as *workplace bullying*. Bullying research names the problem and verifies that it is a real, confirmable phenomenon and not simply an overreaction from thin-skinned employees. When targets and witnesses collectively resist, work through the formal problem-solving systems available to them, and provide decision makers with documented evidence of abuse, this combination often moves decision makers to action. Using research and other published material also supports workers' complaints and educates decision makers about the phenomenon of workplace bullying.

ABOUT THE AUTHOR

Pamela Lutgen-Sandvik is Assistant Professor of Communication at University of New Mexico. This essay is based on Lutgen-Sandvik, P. (2006). "Take this job and . . . Quitting and other forms of resistance to workplace bullying." *Communication Monographs, 73,* 406–433. *Communication Monographs* and *Communication Currents* are published by the National Communication Association.

Chapter 2 quotes research from *Scientific American* that claims "low self-esteem is found among the victims of bullies, but not among bullies themselves." To what extent do you believe the same findings hold true for the victims and the bullies at work? How can collective resistance change this equation?

10 WORKING IN

J ames Surowiecki, the author of *The Wisdom of Crowds*, presents one, deceptively simple idea: Large groups of people are smarter than an elite few, no matter how brilliant; they are better at solving problems, fostering innovation, coming to wise decisions, even predicting the future.[1]

To support his claim, Surowiecki tells the story of a finance professor who conducted a study in which he asked 56 students to estimate the number of jelly beans in a jar. When the professor added up and averaged their individual guesses, the group estimate was 971 jelly beans. The correct number was 850. Only one student in the class made a more accurate guess. Surowiecki notes that if you run ten different jelly-bean-counting games, only one or two students will outperform the group, *but* they will not be the same students each time. Thus, the simplest way to get reliably good answers is to ask and average the group answers each time.[2]

> **"Large groups of people are smarter than an elite few, no matter how brilliant."**
>
> James Surowiecki

In this chapter, we look at the nature of groups: how they form and the communication challenges they face as they develop into productive teams.

GROUPS

the challenges
OF WORKING IN GROUPS

everyone works in groups. You work in groups to make decisions, solve problems, share information, and resolve conflicts. You also rely on groups to produce products, provide services, and build friendships. You may be surprised by the long list of groups to which you belong. College students typically list family, friends, study groups, and campus clubs. After graduation, you may be involved in civic organizations, management teams, work groups, and professional associations.

The need for teamwork skills extends well beyond the boundaries of a communication classroom. A comprehensive study commissioned by the Association of American Colleges and Universities asked employers to rank essential learning outcomes for college graduates entering the workplace. In two major categories—*intellectual and practical skills*, and *personal and social responsibility*—the top ranked outcome was "teamwork skills and the ability to collaborate with others in diverse group settings." Recent graduates ranked the same learning outcome as a top priority.[3] As one business executive wrote "I look for people [who] are good team people over anything else. I can teach the technical."[4]

The Nature of Group Communication

In 2009, the Educational Testing Service unveiled the Personal Potential Index, an evaluation instrument professors can use to rate students on their potential for success in graduate school. The instrument includes six critical traits, two of which are *communication skills* and *teamwork*. The teamwork trait specifies skills such as the abilities to work well in group settings, to behave in an open and friendly manner, to support the efforts of others, and to share ideas easily.[5] These abilities characterize the nature of effective **group communication**—the interaction of three or more interdependent people working to achieve a common goal.[6]

> ## "I look for people [who] are good team people over anything else. I can teach the technical."
> ### —business executive

Group Size The phrase "two's company; three's a crowd" recognizes that a conversation between two people is quite different from a three-person discussion. The ideal size for a problem-solving group is five to seven members. To avoid ties in decision making, an odd number of members is usually better than an even number. Groups larger than seven tend to divide into subgroups; talkative members may dominate or drown out quiet members.

Group communication The interaction of three or more interdependent people working to achieve a common goal

Members of a rafting group depend on one another to achieve a common goal—if one side were to paddle out of sync with the other, the chances of tipping over would increase.

Interaction and Interdependence
Next time you're in a group, observe the ways members behave toward one another. A group member raises a controversial issue. In response, everyone starts talking at the same time. Later, the group listens intently to a member explain an important concept or describe a possible solution to a problem. When tensions arise, a funny comment eases the strain. Finally, members exchange good cheer as they conclude their meeting or finalize a course of action. What you have just observed is group *interaction*—a necessity for effective group communication in both face-to-face and virtual meetings.

Group members are also *interdependent*—that is, the actions of an individual group member affect every other member. For example, if a member fails to provide needed background information at an important meeting, the group as a whole will suffer when it attempts to make an important decision or solve a significant problem.

Common Goal Group members come together for a reason: a collective purpose or goal that defines and unifies the group. A classic study by Carl Larson and Frank LaFasto concludes that "in every case, without exception, where an effectively functioning team was identified, it was described . . . as having a clear understanding of its objective."[7] Without a common goal, groups wonder: Why are we meeting? Why should we care or work hard?

Advantages and Disadvantages of Working in Groups

If you're like most people, you have had to sit through some long and boring meetings. You may have lost patience (or your temper) with a group that couldn't accomplish a simple task you could have done better and more quickly by yourself. In the long run, however, the ad-

Without a common goal, groups wonder: why are we meeting? why should we care or work hard?

Working in groups often leads to friendships, enhanced learning, and member satisfaction.

vantages of working in groups usually outweigh the potential disadvantages.

Advantages In *The Wisdom of Teams*, Jon Katzenbach and Douglas Smith note that groups "outperform individuals acting alone . . . especially when performance requires multiple skills, judgments, and experiences."[8] In general, the "approaches and outcomes of cooperating groups are not just better than those of the average group member, but are better than even the group's best problem solver functioning alone." Furthermore, the lone problem solver can't match the diversity of knowledge and perspectives of a group.[9]

Many of us also belong to and work in groups because we can make friends, socialize, and feel part of a successful team. Moreover, working in groups can enhance learning when members share information, stimulate critical thinking, challenge assumptions, and expect high standards of achievement.

Disadvantages Working in groups requires time, energy, and resources. For example, when 3M Corporation researchers computed the hourly wages and overhead costs of workplace meetings, they concluded that meetings cost the company $78.8 million annually.[10] In addition to cost, there is also the potential for conflict.

As much as we may want everyone in a group to cooperate and work hard, the behavior of some members may create problems. They may talk too much, arrive late for meetings, and argue aggressively. However, these same members may also be excellent researchers, effective critical thinkers, and good friends.

Types of Groups

Groups are as different as the people in them and the goals they seek. Yet there are common characteristics that can be used to separate groups into several categories. These categories range from the most personal and informal types of groups to more professional and formal types. You can identify each type of group by noting its purpose (why the group meets) and by its membership (who is in the group).

The first six types of groups described in the figure on the next page serve your personal needs and interests. In Chapter 8, we examined the importance of effective communication with family members, friends, and romantic partners—the people who belong to family and social groups. Self-help, learning, service, and civic groups are groups you join by choice because they offer support and encouragement, help you gain knowledge, and assist others. There are, however, two types of groups—work groups and public groups—that serve the diverse interests of organizations and public audiences. Understanding your role in these types of groups requires more detailed information about their various forms and functions.

Work Groups Labor crews, sales staff, faculty, management groups, and research teams are all **work groups**—groups that assume primary responsibility for making decisions, solving problems, implementing projects, or performing routine duties in an organization. **Committees** (social committees, budget committees, and awards committees) are created by a larger group or by a person in a position of authority to take on specific tasks. **Work teams** are usually given full responsibility and resources for their performance. Unlike committees, work teams are relatively permanent. They don't take time *from* work to meet—they unite *to* work.

Public Groups Panel discussions, symposiums, forums, and governance groups are types of **public groups** that discuss issues in front of or for the benefit of the public. Their meetings usually occur in un-

---

ethicalcommunication

Making *Good* Group Decisions

When you work closely with group members, your communication choices have ethical consequences that extend well beyond your self and your relationship with one or two people. Not only do your choices affect the entire group, but the decisions and actions of that group also have the potential to affect many others. Consider the unethical corporate officers who masked the financial losses and bad mortgages that triggered the 2008 economic crisis or how Bernard Madoff and associates conspired to cheat his once-wealthy investors out of nearly $3 billion. The consequences of these decisions were magnified well beyond the room in which they were made, affecting thousands of investors and employees.

Read the following scenarios and decide whether the behavior described in each is unethical or merely unpopular but justified.

1. A group member assigned to take notes at a meeting changes the wording of recommendations and motions so they reflect her personal preferences.

2. Although company employees are accustomed to lax rules and lush parties at the annual sales meeting, a new company president insists, upon the penalty of fines, demotions, and even firing, that all members attend every work session.

3. Your group worked many months developing a plan that could revolutionize a challenging business practice. The group member assigned to write the plan for others to read puts her name on it as the author and lists the other group members at the end of the report.

4. After you explain your recommendations to a group, members reject your ideas without discussion. You believe that your contributions were purposely ignored, so you share your ideas with your manager and explain why the group's actions are wrong.

5. A group seeking funds to assist disadvantaged families inflates the program's success rate to justify their funding request.

Work group A group that assumes responsibility for making decisions, solving problems, implementing projects, or performing routine duties in an organization
Committee A group created to complete a specific assignment by a larger group or by a person in a position of authority
Work team A group that is usually given full responsibility and resources for its performance
Public group Groups that discuss issues in front of or for the benefit of public audiences

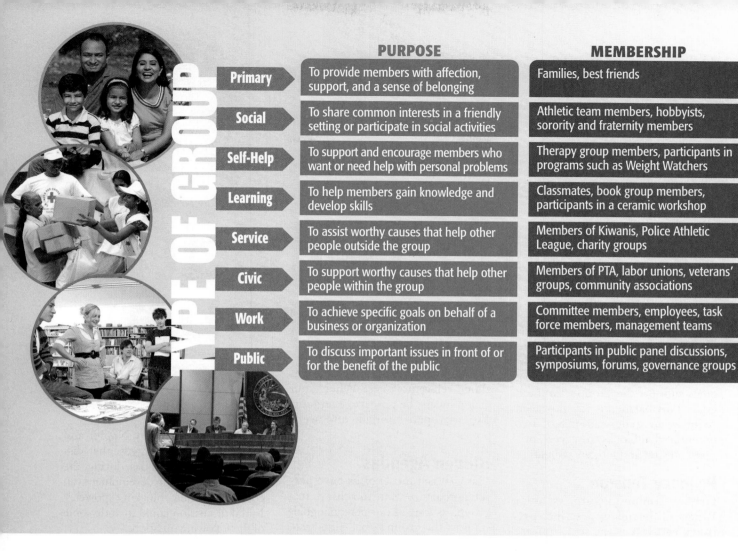

TYPE OF GROUP	PURPOSE	MEMBERSHIP
Primary	To provide members with affection, support, and a sense of belonging	Families, best friends
Social	To share common interests in a friendly setting or participate in social activities	Athletic team members, hobbyists, sorority and fraternity members
Self-Help	To support and encourage members who want or need help with personal problems	Therapy group members, participants in programs such as Weight Watchers
Learning	To help members gain knowledge and develop skills	Classmates, book group members, participants in a ceramic workshop
Service	To assist worthy causes that help other people outside the group	Members of Kiwanis, Police Athletic League, charity groups
Civic	To support worthy causes that help other people within the group	Members of PTA, labor unions, veterans' groups, community associations
Work	To achieve specific goals on behalf of a business or organization	Committee members, employees, task force members, management teams
Public	To discuss important issues in front of or for the benefit of the public	Participants in public panel discussions, symposiums, forums, governance groups

restricted public settings in front of public audiences. During a **panel discussion**, several people interact about a common topic to educate, influence, or entertain an audience. In a **symposium**, group members present short, uninterrupted presentations on different aspects of a topic for the benefit of an audience. Very often, a panel or symposium is followed by a **forum**, which provides an opportunity for audience members to comment or ask questions. A strong moderator is needed in a forum to make sure that all audience members have an equal opportunity to speak and that the meeting is orderly and civil. **Governance groups** (state legislatures, city and county councils, and governing boards of public agencies and educational institutions) make policy decisions in public settings.

Virtual Groups In addition to face-to-face meetings with others, technology has made it possible for you to work in virtual groups. A **virtual group** relies on tools such as e-mail, audio conferencing, video conferencing, and web conferencing to communicate across time, distance, and organizational boundaries. Unfortunately, when some members participate in virtual groups, they mistakenly believe it will be easy. As a result, they underestimate the time needed to prepare, coordinate, and collaborate.[11] Members may also find it easier to "hide" during remote conferences. Although you may not be in the same room or even on the same continent as the other members of a virtual group, you are just as personally responsible for being fully prepared to contribute to the group's work.

Panel discussion Several people interact about a common topic in order to educate, influence, or entertain an audience

Symposium Group members present short, uninterrupted presentations on different aspects of a topic for the benefit of an audience

Forum Audience members comment on or ask questions after a public discussion or presentation

Governance group An elected or appointed group that makes public policy decisions in public settings

Virtual group A group that relies on technology to communicate often across time, distance, and organizational boundaries

When conducting or participating in a virtual team meeting, each member should:

- prepare for the meeting by reading the background material and becoming familiar with the technology

- speak out during the meeting (or respond using the available media)
- listen to and consider others' ideas
- make suggestions and decisions
- follow up on meeting actions[12]

BALANCING individual AND group goals

as groups form and develop, effective members learn how to balance individual and group goals. In the best of groups, your personal goals support the group's common goal. This balancing act, however, requires an understanding of two potential roadblocks to success: primary tension and hidden agendas.

Primary Tension

Group communication scholar Ernest G. Bormann describes **primary tension** as the social unease and inhibitions that accompany the getting-acquainted period in a new group.[13] Because most new group members want to create a good first impression, they tend to be overly polite with one another.

In most groups, primary tension decreases as members feel more comfortable with one another. But if a group is bogged down in primary tension, you can and should intervene by talking about it and discussing how to break the cycle. Urge members to stick to the group's

Characteristics of PRIMARY TENSION

- Members rarely interrupt one another.
- Long, awkward pauses often come between comments.
- Members are soft-spoken and very polite.
- Members avoid expressing strong opinions.

agenda and express their opinions about relevant issues. When your group meets, be positive, energetic, patient, open-minded, and well-prepared.

Hidden Agendas

Many (if not most) of us have personal goals we want to achieve in a group. As long as our personal goals support the group's goal, all is well. A **hidden agenda,** however, occurs when a member's private goals conflict with the group's goals. Hidden agendas represent what people *really* want rather than what they *say* they want. When hidden agendas become more important than a group's public agenda or goal, the result can be group frustration, unresolved conflicts, and failure.

Even when a group recognizes the existence of hidden agendas, some of them cannot and should not be shared because they may create an atmosphere of distrust. For instance, not many people would want to deal with the following revelation during a group discussion: "The reason I don't want to be here is that I don't want to work with Kenneth, who isn't trustworthy or competent." Dealing with hidden agendas means knowing that some of them can and should be confronted, whereas others cannot and should not be shared with the group.

Sociologists Rodney Napier and Matti Gershenfeld suggest that discussing hidden agendas during the early stages of group development can counteract their blocking power.[14] Initial discussion could include some of the following questions:

- What are the group's goals?
- Do any members have any personal concerns or goals that differ from these?
- What outcomes do members expect?

If unrecognized and unresolved, hidden agendas can permeate and infect *all* stages of group development.

> **Dealing with hidden agendas means knowing that some of them can and should be confronted, whereas others cannot and should not be shared.**

Primary tension The social unease and inhibitions that accompany the getting-acquainted period in a new group
Hidden agenda When members' private goals conflict with the group's goals

Tuckman's Group Development Model

Most groups experience recognizable milestones. Like people, groups move through stages as they develop and mature. A "newborn" group behaves differently from an "adult" group that has worked together for a long time. In 1965, Bruce Tuckman, an educational psychologist, identified four stages in the life cycle of groups.[15] Since introducing his **Group Development Model**, more than one hundred theoretical models have described how a group moves through several "passages" during its lifetime.[16] Tuckman's original four stages are, however, considered one of the most comprehensive models relevant to *all* types of groups.[17]

Stage 1: FORMING

During the **forming stage**, group members may be more worried about themselves ("Will I be accepted and liked?") than about the group as a whole. Understandably, members are hesitant to express strong opinions or assert their personal needs during this phase until they know more about how other members think and feel about the task and about one another. Although little gets done during this stage, members need time to become acquainted with one another and define group goals.

Stage 2: STORMING

During the **storming stage**, groups become more argumentative and emotional as they discuss important issues and vie for leadership. Some groups are tempted to suppress this phase in an effort to avoid conflict. However, conflict can help members develop relationships, decide who's in charge and who can be trusted, and clarify the group's common goal.

Stage 3: NORMING

During the **norming stage**, members define roles and establish norms. The group begins to work harmoniously as a cohesive team and makes decisions about the best ways to achieve a common goal. At this point in group development, members feel more comfortable with one another and are willing to disagree and express their opinions.

Stage 4: PERFORMING

During the **performing stage**, members focus their energy on working harmoniously to achieve group goals. Roles and responsibilities change according to group needs. Decisions are reached, problems are solved, and ideas are implemented. When the performing stage is going well, members are highly energized, loyal to one another, and willing to accept every challenge that arises.

Tuckman's group development theory helps explain why and how groups and their members behave at different stages in their development. Imagine how disruptive it would be if, at your group's first meeting, a member demanded acceptance of a particular decision or solution to a problem. Moreover, if members never matured beyond the forming stage, your group would become bogged down in polite conversation and procedural details rather than dealing with its task. Understanding the natural development of a group can help explain, predict, and improve group productivity and member satisfaction.

> ### Like people, groups move through stages as they develop and mature.

Tuckman's Group Development Model Comprehensive four-stage development model (forming, storming, norming, performing) relevant to *all* types of groups

Forming stage A group development stage in which members become acquainted with one another and define group goals

Storming stage A group development stage in which members argue about important issues and vie for leadership

Norming stage A group development stage in which members define roles and establish norms

Performing stage A group development stage in which members focus their energy on working harmoniously to achieve group goals

BALANCING conflict AND cohesion

Conflict is valuable in groups because it forces us to analyze our opinions and decisions. As groups develop and begin discussing important issues, members become more argumentative and emotional. Many groups are tempted to discourage or avoid conflict. When conflict is accepted as normal and beneficial, it helps es-tablish a climate in which members feel free to disagree with one another.[18] At the same time, groups also benefit from **cohesion**—the mutual attraction that holds the members of a group together. Effective groups learn to balance conflict and cohesion as they interact to achieve a common goal.

Secondary Tension

When a group moves from the polite interactions of the forming stage to the storming stage, confident members begin to compete with one another. They openly disagree on substantive issues. It is still too early in the group's existence to predict the outcome of such competition. At this point, a different kind of tension may emerge. **Secondary tension** describes the frustrations and personality conflicts experienced by group members as they compete for social acceptance, status, and achievement.[19] Regardless of the causes, a group cannot hope to achieve its goals if secondary tension is not managed effectively.

> **When conflict is accepted as normal and beneficial, it helps establish a climate in which members feel free to disagree with one another.**

Characteristics of SECONDARY TENSION

- Energy and alertness levels are high.
- The group is noisy and dynamic; members are loud and emphatic.
- Several members may speak at the same time.
- Members sit up, lean forward, and squirm in their seats.

Cohesion The mutual attraction that holds the members of a group together

Secondary tension The frustration and personality conflicts experienced by group members as they compete for social acceptance, status, and achievement

Cohesive group members feel responsible for and take pride in their own work as well as the work of other members.

If you sense that your group cannot resolve its secondary tension, it is time to intervene. One strategy is to joke about the tension. The resulting laughter can ease individual and group stress. Another option is to work outside the group setting and discuss any personal difficulties and anxieties with individual group members.

Most groups experience some primary and secondary tension. In fact, a little bit of tension can motivate a group toward action and increase a group's sensitivity to feedback. As Donald Ellis and Aubrey Fisher point out, "the successful and socially healthy group is not characterized by an absence of social tension, but by successful management of social tension."[20]

Group Cohesion

Group cohesion can be expressed as "All for one and one for all!" Cohesive groups are united and committed to a common goal, have high levels of interaction, and enjoy a supportive communication climate. Their members also share a sense of teamwork and pride in the group, want to conform to group expectations, and are willing to use creative approaches to achieve the group's goals.[21]

Cohesive groups are happier and get more done, and members refer to the group in terms of *we* and *our* instead of *I* and *my*. Members of a cohesive group treat one another with respect, showing concern for their personal needs, and appreciating the value of member diversity.

Cohesive groups create an encouraging climate that rewards praiseworthy contributions. Many groups use celebration dinners, letters of appreciation, certificates, and gifts to reward individual effort and initiative, although even a simple compliment can make a group member feel appreciated. And, rather than take personal and individual credit for success, members of a cohesive group emphasize the group's accomplishments.

BALANCING
conformity AND
nonconformity

during the norming stage of group development, members define their roles and determine how the group will do its work. Effective groups learn to balance a commitment to group customs, rules, and standards (conformity) with a willingness to differ and change (nonconformity).

Group Norms

Communication scholar Patricia Andrews defines **norms** as "sets of expectations held by group members concerning what kinds of behavior or opinions are acceptable or

Norms Sets of expectations held by group members concerning what kinds of behavior or opinions are acceptable or unacceptable

How does this parade of Marine Corps soldiers demonstrate the importance and value of group norms?

How does this photo depict the value of constructive nonconformity?

unacceptable, good or bad, right or wrong, appropriate or inappropriate."[22] Group norms express the values of a group, help the group to function smoothly, define appropriate and inappropriate behavior, and facilitate group success.[23] Norms are the group's rules of behavior; they determine how members dress, speak, listen, and work. For example, one group may discourage interruptions, whereas another group may view interruptions and overlapping conversations as acceptable forms of interaction. Without norms, a group lacks agreed-upon ways to organize and perform a task. Group norms function only to the extent that members conform to them.

Group norms can have positive or negative effects on member behavior and group success. For ex-

ample, if your group's norms place a premium on pleasant and peaceful discussions, members may be reluctant to voice disagreement or share bad news. If group norms permit members to arrive late and leave early, you may not have enough members to do the job. Norms that don't support your group's goals can prevent the group from succeeding. When this is the case, you are perfectly within your rights (in fact, it may be your duty) to engage in nonconforming behavior. **Constructive nonconformity** occurs when a member resists a norm while still working to promote the group goal.

"I know we always have our annual retreat at a golf resort, but many of our new staff members don't play golf and may feel out of place or bored."

Constructive nonconformity contributes to effective group decisions and more creative solutions, because it allows members to voice serious and well-justified objections without fear of personal criticism or

exclusion for taking a different position. In contrast, **destructive nonconformity** occurs when a member resists conformity without regard for the best interests of the group and its goal, such as by showing up late to attract attention or interrupting others to exert power.

When members do not conform to group norms, a group may have to discuss the value of a particular norm and then choose to change, clarify, or continue to accept it. At the very least, nonconforming behavior helps members recognize and understand the norms of the group. For instance, if a member is reprimanded for leaving early, other members learn it is not acceptable to leave before a meeting is adjourned.

Group norms function ONLY to the extent that members conform to them.

Constructive nonconformity
Resisting a group norm while still working to promote a group's common goal

Destructive nonconformity
Resisting a group norm without regard for the best interests of the group and its goal

---

Can You Name Your Norms?

The left-hand column in the following table describes several types of group norms. In the middle column, identify the related group norms in your classroom. In the right column, identify the related group norms in your current or former workplace. Examine all of these norms with a critical eye. Do they help the group achieve its common goal? If not, are you willing to challenge these norms for the good of the group?

Types of Group Norms	Classroom	Workplace
Verbal (e.g., formal, casual, jargon, profanity)		
Nonverbal (e.g., formal or informal attire, seating arrangements, activity level)		
Interactional (e.g., use of first or last names, nicknames, speaking turns, listening behavior, unruly behavior)		
Content (e.g., discussions are serious, work-related, social, intimate, humorous)		
Status (e.g., who makes decisions, who has influence, whether disagreement is allowed)		
Rewards (e.g., how success is determined, how achievement is rewarded)		

BALANCING task AND maintenance roles

every group member brings unique talents, preferences, and perspectives to a group. As a result, group members assume different roles depending on the nature of the group, its membership, and its goal. A **group role** is a pattern of behaviors associated with an expected function within a particular group context. For example, when someone asks, "Who will get the information we need for our next meeting?" all eyes turn to Brian because researching and sharing information are tasks he performs well. If a disagreement between two group members becomes heated, the group may look to Alicia for help because she has a talent for resolving conflicts and mediating differences.

Group Task and Maintenance Roles

Group member roles are divided into two functional categories: task roles and maintenance roles. Group **task roles** focus on behaviors that help manage the task and complete the job. When members assume task roles, they provide useful information, ask important questions, analyze problems, and help the group stay organized. Group **maintenance roles** affect whether group members get along with one another while pursuing a common

> **Group role** A pattern of behavior associated with an expected function within a particular group context
>
> **Task role** A member role that positively affects a group's ability to manage a task and to achieve its common goal
>
> **Maintenance role** A member role that positively affects how group members get along with one another while pursuing a common goal

goal. Members who assume maintenance roles help to create a supportive work climate, resolve conflicts, and encourage members or praise good work.

In addition to assuming roles on your own, analyze the group to determine whether important roles are missing. For example, if members are becoming frustrated because one or two people are doing all the talking, you might suggest that someone serve as a gatekeeper. If the group has trouble tracking its progress, suggest that someone take on the role of recorder–secretary. In highly effective groups, all the task and maintenance roles are available as strategies to mobilize a group toward achieving its common goal.

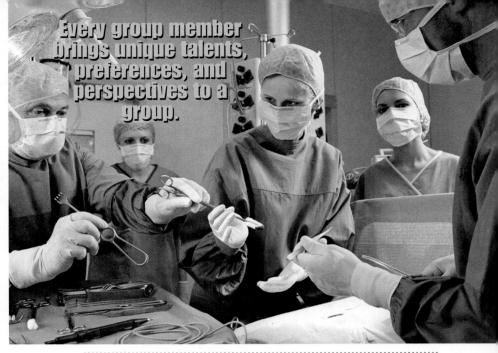

Every group member brings unique talents, preferences, and perspectives to a group.

What task roles are critical to the success of a surgical team? Is there an appropriate place for maintenance roles in this group?

GROUP TASK ROLES[24]

ROLE	DESCRIPTION	EXAMPLE
Initiator/ Contributor	Proposes ideas; provides direction; gets the group started	"Let's begin by considering the client's point of view."
Information Seeker	Asks for relevant information; requests explanations; points out information gaps	"How can we decide on a policy without knowing more about the cost and the legal requirements?"
Information Giver	Researches, organizes, and presents relevant information	"I checked with human resources and they said . . ."
Opinion Seeker	Asks for opinions; tests for agreement and disagreement	"Lyle, what do you think? Will it work?"
Opinion Giver	States personal belief; shares feelings; offers analysis and arguments	"I don't agree that he's guilty. He may be annoying, but that doesn't constitute harassment."
Clarifier/Summarizer	Explains ideas and their consequences; reduces confusion; summarizes	"We've been trying to analyze this problem for two hours. Here's what I think we've agreed upon."
Evaluator/Critic	Assesses the value of ideas and arguments; diagnoses problems	"These figures don't consider monthly operating costs."
Energizer	Motivates members; creates enthusiasm, and, if needed, a sense of urgency	"This is incredible! We've come up with a unique and workable solution to the problem."
Procedural Technician	Helps prepare meetings; makes room arrangements; provides materials and equipment	"Before our next meeting, let me know if you will need a flip chart again."
Recorder/Secretary	Keeps accurate written records of group recommendations and decisions	"Maggie, please repeat the two deadline dates so I can get them into the minutes."

Self-Centered Roles

Sometimes group members assume **self-centered roles** in which they put their own goals ahead of the group's goal and other member needs. Self-centered roles can disrupt the work of a group, adversely affect member relationships, and prevent the group from achieving its common goal.

Three strategies can help you and your group deal with self-centered members: accept, confront, or even exclude the troublesome member. Acceptance is not the same as approval. A group may allow disruptive behavior to continue when it's not detrimental to the group's ultimate success or when the member's positive contributions far outweigh the inconvenience or annoyance of putting up with the negative behavior. For example, a "clown" may be disruptive on occasion but may also be the group's best report writer or a valued harmonizer.

When it becomes impossible to accept or ignore self-centered behavior, the group should take action. For instance, members can confront a member by making it clear that the group will progress despite that person's nonproductive behavior. "Ron, I think we fully understand your strong objections, but ultimately this is a group decision." In a moment of extreme frustration, one member may say what everyone is thinking— "Lisa, please let me finish a sentence!" Although such an outburst may make everyone uncomfortable, it can put a stop to disruptive behavior.

When all else fails, a group may ask disruptive members to leave the group and bar them from meetings; this is a humiliating experience that all but the most stubborn members would prefer to avoid.

Common Self-Centered Roles[25]:

- **Aggressor.** Puts down other members, is sarcastic and critical, takes credit for someone else's work or ideas
- **Blocker.** Stands in the way of progress, presents uncompromising positions, uses delay tactics to derail an idea or proposal
- **Dominator.** Prevents others from participating, interrupts others, tries to manipulate others
- **Recognition Seeker.** Boasts about personal accomplishments, tries to be the center of attention, pouts if not getting enough attention
- **Clown.** Injects inappropriate humor, seems more interested in goofing off than working, distracts the group from its task
- **Deserter.** Withdraws from the group, appears "above it all" and annoyed or bored with the discussion, stops contributing
- **Confessor.** Shares very personal feelings and problems, uses the group for emotional support in ways that inappropriately distract members from the group's task

Self-centered role A role in which members adversely affect a group by putting their own goals ahead of the group's goal and other members' needs

GROUP MAINTENANCE ROLES[26]

ROLE	DESCRIPTION	EXAMPLE
Encourager/Supporter	Praises and encourages group members; listens empathically	"Thanks for taking all that time to find the information we needed."
Harmonizer	Helps resolve conflicts; mediates differences; encourages teamwork and group harmony	"I know we're becoming edgy, but we're almost done. Let's focus on the task, not our annoyances."
Compromiser	Offers suggestions that minimize differences; helps the group reach consensus	"Maybe we can improve the old system rather than adopting a brand-new way of doing it."
Tension Releaser	Uses friendly humor to alleviate tensions, tempers, and stress	"Can Karen and I arm-wrestle to decide who gets the assignment?"
Gatekeeper	Monitors and regulates the flow of communication; encourages productive participation	"I think we've heard from everyone except Michelle, who has strong feelings about this issue."
Standard Monitor	Reminds group of norms and rules; tests ideas against group-established standards	"We all agreed we'd start at 10 A.M. Now we sit around waiting for latecomers until 10:30."
Observer/Interpreter	Monitors and interprets feelings and nonverbal communication; paraphrases member comments	"Maybe we're not really disagreeing. I think we're in agreement that . . ."
Follower	Supports the group and its members; willingly accepts others' ideas and assignments	"That's fine with me. Just tell me when it's due."

Disruptive group behavior comes in all varieties. Do any of the following types describe the way you communicate in groups?[27] For each item, indicate how frequently you behave like the description: (1) usually, (2) often, (3) sometimes, (4) rarely, or (5) never.

_____ 1. *The Put-Downer.* Do you assume that members are wrong until they're proven right? Do you make negative remarks such as "That will never work," "Been there, done it, forget it," or "I don't like it" before the group has had time to discuss the issue in detail?

_____ 2. *The Interrupter.* Do you start talking before others are finished? Do you interrupt because you're impatient or annoyed?

_____ 3. *The Nonverbal Negative Naybobber.* Do you disagree nonverbally in a dramatic or disruptive manner? Do you frown or scowl, shake your head, roll your eyes, squirm in your seat, audibly sigh or groan, or madly scribble notes after someone has said something?

_____ 4. *The Laggard.* Are you late to meetings? Do you ask or demand to be told what happened before you arrived? Are you usually late in completing assigned or agreed-upon tasks?

_____ 5. *The Chronic Talkaholic.* Talkaholics are compulsive communicators who have great difficulty (and often little desire) being quiet in groups. Chronic talkaholics talk so much, they disrupt the group and annoy or anger other members. Do you ever talk when you know it would be much smarter to keep quiet? Do other group members often tell you that you talk too much?[28]

DEVELOPING group leadership

Without leadership, a group may be nothing more than a collection of individuals lacking the coordination and will to achieve a goal. Whereas a leader is a person, **leadership** is the ability to make strategic decisions and use communication to mobilize group members toward achieving a common goal.

Even though just about everyone recognizes the importance of leadership, it is not always easy to practice effectively. One review of leadership studies estimates that leadership incompetence is "as high as 60 to 75 percent—and that our hiring practices are so flawed that more than 50 percent of leaders hired by organizations are doomed to fail."[29]

Leaders who fail to demonstrate effective leadership often lack effective communication skills. In his book on leadership, Antony Bell describes communication as the mortar or glue that connects all leadership competencies. The abilities to think and act, while remaining self-aware and self-disciplined, are critical

building blocks to leadership competency; but it takes communication to bind these blocks together.[30]

Three Approaches to Leadership

Leadership is a quality that defies precise measurement. However, three theories can help you understand your own and others' approaches to leadership: Trait Theory, Styles Theory, and Situational Theory.

Trait Theory Based on the belief that leaders are born, not made, the **Trait Theory of Leadership** identifies specific characteristics associated with leadership. Most of us can come up with a list of desirable leadership traits: intelligence, confidence, enthusiasm, organizational talent, and good listening skills. The weakness of Trait Theory is that it doesn't account for the fact that many effective leaders possess

only a few of these traits. Just because you have most of these traits does not mean that you will be a great leader. At the same time, great

> **Without leadership, a group may be nothing more than a collection of individuals lacking the coordination and will to achieve a goal.**

Leadership The ability to make strategic decisions and use communication to mobilize group members toward achieving a common goal
Trait Theory of Leadership Based on the belief that leaders are born with specific leadership characteristics

leaders have emerged with very few of these traits. For example, Harriet Tubman, an illiterate slave, did little talking but led hundreds of people from bondage in the South to freedom in the North.

Styles Theory The **Styles Theory of Leadership** examines a collection of specific behaviors that constitute three distinct leadership styles: autocratic, democratic, and laissez-faire. **Autocratic leaders** try to control the direction and outcome of a discussion, make many of the group's decisions, give orders, expect followers to obey orders, focus on achieving the group's task, and take credit for successful results. An autocratic style is often appropriate during a serious crisis when there may not be time to discuss issues or consider the wishes of all members. In an emergency, the group may want its leader to take total responsibility. However, too much control can lower group morale and sacrifice long-term productivity.

A **democratic leader** promotes the social equality and task interests of group members. This type of leader shares decision making with the group, helps the group plan a course of action, focuses on the group's morale as well as on the task, and gives the entire group credit for success. In groups with democratic leadership, members are often more satisfied with the group experience, more loyal to the leader, and more productive in the long run.

Laissez-faire is a French phrase that means "to let people do as they choose." A **laissez-faire leader** lets the group take charge of all decisions and actions. Such a leader may be a perfect match for mature and highly productive groups because a laid-back leadership style can generate a climate in which communication is encouraged and rewarded. Unfortunately, some laissez-faire leaders do little or nothing to help a group when it needs decisive leadership.

Three Theoretical APPROACHES to Leadership

1 TRAIT THEORY ▶ You Have It or You Don't.

2 STYLES THEORY ▶ Are Democracies Always Best?

3 SITUATIONAL THEORY ▶ Matching Leaders and Jobs

Situational Leadership Theory Rather than describing traits or styles, **Situational Leadership Theory** seeks an ideal fit between leaders and leadership roles.[31] The situational approach explains how leaders can become more effective by analyzing themselves, their group, and the context.

Situational Theory identifies two leadership styles: task-motivated and relationship-motivated. **Task-motivated leaders** want to get the job done. They gain satisfaction from completing a task even if it results in bad feelings between the leader and group members. As a result, task-motivated leaders are often criticized for being too focused on the job and overlooking group morale. **Relationship-motivated leaders** gain satisfaction from working well with other people even if the cost is failing to complete a task. Not surprisingly, they are sometimes criticized for paying too much attention to how members feel and for tolerating disruptive behavior.

Situational Theory requires you to match your leadership style to the situation in terms of three important dimensions: leader–member relations, task structure, and power. **Leader-member relations** can be positive, neutral, or negative. Are group members friendly and loyal to the leader and the rest of the group? Are they cooperative and supportive? **Task structure** can range from disorganized and

---

Styles Theory of Leadership Examines three distinct leadership styles: autocratic, democratic, and laissez-faire leadership

Autocratic leader Tries to control the group, makes decisions, gives and expects members to follow orders, and takes credit for successful results

Democratic leader Promotes the social equality and task interests of group members

Laissez-faire leader Lets the group take charge of all decisions and actions

Situational Leadership Theory Seeks an ideal fit between leaders and leadership roles

Task-motivated leader A leader who gains satisfaction by completing a task even at the expense of group relationships

Relationship-motivated leader A leader who gains satisfaction from working well with others even if the group's task or goal is neglected

Leader–member relations A situational leadership factor that assesses how well a leader gets along with group members

Task structure A situational leadership factor that assesses how a group organizes or plans a specific task

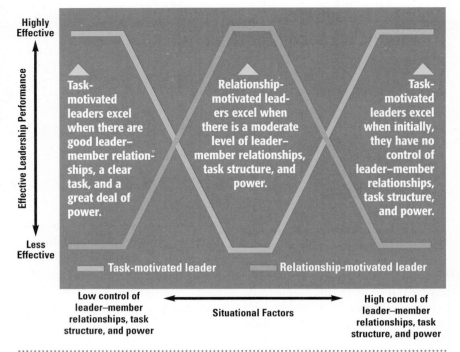

Figure 10.1 shows that task-motivated leaders perform best in extremes, such as when the situation requires high levels of leader control or when it is almost out of control. They excel when there are good or poor leader–member relationships, a clear or unclear task, and a great deal of or no power. Relationship-motivated leaders do well when in the middle ground where there is a mix of conditions, such as a semi-structured task or a group of interested but not eager followers.

chaotic to highly organized and rule-driven. Are the goals and task clear? The third situational factor is the amount of power and control the leader possesses.

Figure 10.1   Relationship between leadership style and situational factors

How to Become a Leader

The path to a leadership position can be as easy as being in the right place at the right time or being the only person willing to take on a difficult job.[32] Although there is no foolproof method, there are ways to improve your chances of becoming a group's leader.

- *Talk early and often (and listen).* The person who speaks first and most often is more likely to emerge as the group's leader.[33] How frequently you talk is even more important than what you say. The quality of your contributions becomes more significant *after* you become a leader.

- *Know more (and share it).* Leaders often are seen as experts. A potential leader can often explain ideas and information more clearly than other

group members, and therefore be perceived as knowing more. While groups need well-informed leaders, they do not need know-it-alls who see their own comments as most important; effective leaders value everyone's contributions.

- *Offer your opinion (and welcome disagreement).* Groups appreciate someone who offers valuable ideas and informed opinions. However, this is not the same as having your ideas accepted without question. If you are unwilling to compromise or listen to alternatives, the group may be unwilling to follow you. Effective leaders welcome constructive disagreement and discourage hostile confrontations.

The strategies for becoming a leader are *not* necessarily the same strategies for successful leadership. After you become a leader, you may find it necessary to listen more than talk, welcome and reward better-informed members, and strongly criticize the opinions of others. Your focus should shift from *becoming* the leader to *serving* the group you lead.

Sarah Palin's political star rose when, as McCain's charismatic vice presidential candidate, she claimed expertise, offered strong opinions, and expressed her ideas in ways that others understood. For some, however, her credibility eroded when she seemed unwilling to listen and engaged in confrontations with opponents and the media.

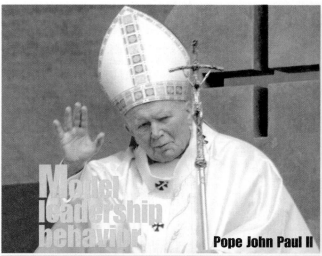
Model leadership behavior

Pope John Paul II

Manage group processes

Nancy Pelosi

Motivate members

Martin Luther King

Make decisions

John F. Kennedy

the 4-M model
OF LEADERSHIP EFFECTIVENESS

thousands of books and articles have been published about leadership. To help you understand contributions made by these many approaches, we offer the **4-M Model of Leadership Effectiveness**,[34] an integrated model of leadership effectiveness that emphasizes specific communication strategies and skills.

Model Leadership Behavior

Model leaders project an image of confidence, competence, and trustworthiness. Yet, no matter how much you may want to be a model leader, only your followers can grant you that honor. Model leaders publicly champion the group and its goals rather than their personal accomplishments and ego needs. They speak and listen effectively, behave consistently and assertively, confront problems head-on, and work to find solutions.

Motivate Members

Motivating others is a critical task for leaders. Effective leaders guide, develop, support, defend, and inspire group members. They develop relationships that meet the personal needs and expectations of followers. Motivational strategies include rewarding deserving members, helping members solve interpersonal problems, and adapting tasks and assignments to member abilities and

4-M Model of Leadership Effectiveness A model that identifies four interdependent leadership functions: Modeling, Motivating, Managing, and Making decisions

expectations. Most important of all, motivating leaders give members the authority to make judgments about doing the group's work.

Manage Group Processes

From the perspective of group survival, managing group processes may be the most important function of leadership.[35] If a group is disorganized, lacks sufficient information to solve problems, or is unable to make important decisions when necessary, the group cannot be effective. Effective leaders are well-organized and fully prepared for all group meetings and work sessions. They adapt to member strengths and weaknesses and help solve task-related and procedural problems. They also know when to monitor and intervene to improve group performance.

Make Decisions

An effective leader is willing and able to make appropriate, timely, and responsible decisions. When you assume or are appointed to a leader-ship role, you should accept the fact that some of your decisions may be unpopular, and some may even turn out to be wrong. But you still have to make them. It's often better for a group leader to make a bad decision than no decision at all, "for if you are seen as chronically indecisive, people won't let you lead them."[36]

In "Building the 21st Century Leader," Carol Tice reviews the evolution of corporate leadership, claiming that today's leaders must be able to do *both*—collaborate with others *and* be decisive. "The desire to reach consensus or get buy-in from all parties has to be curtailed at some point, and the leader has to make a decision."[37]

Several strategies can help a leader make decisions that help a group achieve its goal. First, make sure everyone has and shares the information needed to make a quality decision. If appropriate, discuss your pending decision and solicit feedback from members. Listen to members' opinions, arguments, and suggestions *before* making a decision. When you make a decision, explain your reasons for doing so and communicate your decision to everyone.

Effective leaders intervene and tell members what to do when a group lacks the confidence, willingness, or ability to make decisions. However, when group members are confident, willing, and skilled, a leader can usually turn full responsibility over to the group and focus on helping members implement the group's decision.[38]

> **" ...if you are seen as chronically indecisive, people won't let you lead them."**
> —Harvey Robbins and Michael Finley

communication&culture

DIVERSITY AND LEADERSHIP

In the early studies of leadership, there was an unwritten but additional prerequisite for becoming a leader: Be a man. Despite the achievements of exceptional female leaders, some people still question the ability of women to serve in leadership positions.

A summary of the research on leadership and gender concludes that "women are still less likely to be preselected as leaders, and the same leadership behavior is often evaluated more positively when attributed to a male than a female."[39]

Developing a leadership style is a challenge for most young managers, but particularly for young women. If their behavior is similar to that of male leaders, they are perceived as unfeminine, but if they act "like a lady," they are viewed as weak or ineffective. One professional woman described this dilemma as follows:

I was thrilled when my boss evaluated me as "articulate, hard-working, mature in her judgment, and a skill-ful diplomat." What disturbed me were some of the evaluation comments from those I supervise or work with as colleagues. Although they had a lot of good things to say, a few of them described me as "pushy," "brusque," "impatient," "disregards social niceties," and "hard driving." What am I supposed to do? My boss thinks I'm energetic and creative while other people see the same behavior as pushy and aggressive.

Cultural differences also affect whether members become and succeed as leaders. For example, individualistic Western cultures (United States, Canada, Europe) assume that members are motivated by personal growth and achievement. However, a collectivist member might desire a close relationship with the leader and other group members rather than personal gain or growth. The same member may act out of loyalty to the leader and the group rather than for personal achievement or material gain.[40]

Communication ASSESSMENT

Group Member Participation and Leadership Evaluation

Evaluate the quantity and quality of participation by the members of a group to which you belong or have belonged by circling the number that describes its performance.

1. **Task Functions.** Members provide or ask for information and opinions, initiate discussion, clarify, summarize, evaluate, energize, and so on.

5	4	3	2	1
Excellent		**Average**		**Poor**

2. **Maintenance Functions.** Members serve as encourager, harmonizer, compromiser, tension releaser, gatekeeper, standard monitor, observer, follower, and so on.

5	4	3	2	1
Excellent		**Average**		**Poor**

3. **Group Processes.** Members avoid disruptive behavior, follow the agenda, adapt to group development stages and group norms, and so on.

5	4	3	2	1
Excellent		**Average**		**Poor**

4. **Manage Difficulties.** Members are ready, willing, and able to deal with difficult behavior and overall group problems.

5	4	3	2	1
Excellent		**Average**		**Poor**

5. **Leadership.** One or more members model leadership behavior, motivate others, help manage group processes, and make necessary decisions.

5	4	3	2	1
Excellent		**Average**		**Poor**

6. **Group's Overall Effectiveness.**

5	4	3	2	1
Excellent		**Average**		**Poor**

Summary

What are the pros and cons of working in different types of groups?

- Group communication refers to the interaction of three or more interdependent people working to achieve a common goal.
- In general, the advantages of working in groups far outweigh the disadvantages.
- Groups differ in terms of whether they are meeting personal goals, work goals, or public goals.
- Bruce Tuckman's Group Development stages include forming, storming, norming, and performing.

How can you balance individual and group needs when working in groups?

- During the forming stage of group development, most groups experience primary tension, the social unease and inhibitions that accompany the getting-acquainted period in a new group.
- Hidden agendas occur when a member's private goals conflict with the group's goals.

How can you balance conflict and cohesiveness in groups?

- During the storming stage of group development, groups must resolve secondary tensions and personality conflicts in order to achieve cohesion.
- Cohesive groups share a sense of teamwork and pride in the group.

How can you balance conformity and nonconformity in groups?

- During the norming stage of group development, groups establish norms.
- Whereas constructive nonconformity is appropriate and helps a group achieve its goal, destructive nonconformity has no regard for the best interests of the group and its goal.

How can you balance task and maintenance roles in groups?

- Group task roles help a group achieve its goals. Group maintenance roles affect how group members get along.
- Self-centered roles adversely affect task and social goals.

What are the characteristics of a successful group leader?

- A leader is a person; leadership is the ability to make strategic decisions and use communication to mobilize group members toward achieving a common goal.
- The Trait Theory of Leadership identifies individual leadership characteristics.
- The Styles Theory of Leadership examines autocratic, democratic, and laissez-faire leadership.
- Situational Leadership Theory seeks an ideal fit between a leader's style and the leadership situation.

What communication strategies and skills characterize effective leadership?

- The 4-M Model of Leadership Effectiveness identifies four critical leadership tasks: (1) Model leadership behavior, (2) Motivate members, (3) Manage group processes, and (4) Make decisions.
- People become leaders by talking more, knowing more, and offering their opinions.
- Female and non-majority group members are less likely to be pre-selected as leaders and are often evaluated less positively than are male leaders.

the THINKSPOT
www.thethinkspot.com

TEST your *knowledge*

1 The ideal size for a problem-solving group is —— members.
a. 2–4
b. 3–5
c. 5–7
d. 7–12
e. 12–15

2 Which type of group has a primary purpose of supporting worthy causes that help other people outside the group?
a. social
b. self-help
c. learning
d. service
e. civic

3 Which of the following describes a forum?
a. Several people interact about a common topic in front of an audience.
b. Group members present short, uninterrupted presentations on different aspects of a topic for the benefit of an audience.
c. Audience members comment or ask questions to a speaker or group of speakers.
d. Elected officials and governing boards of public agencies conduct their meetings in public.
e. None of the above is an example of a forum.

4 Which is the correct order for Tuckman's group development stages?
a. forming, storming, norming, performing
b. storming, forming, performing, norming
c. forming, norming, storming, performing
d. norming, forming, performing, storming
e. performing, norming, storming, forming

5 Which of the following answers is the best depiction of secondary tension in groups?
a. The group resolves conflicts and establishes norms.
b. the frustrations and conflicts experienced by group members as they compete for status, acceptance, and achievement
c. the social unease and inhibitions that accompany the getting-acquainted period in a new group
d. the social unease and inhibitions that accompany the process of competing for status, acceptance, and achievement in groups
e. the process during which group decisions are reached, problems are solved, and plans are implemented

6 Which of the following answers represents a group task role?
a. tension releaser
b. compromiser
c. gatekeeper
d. encourager/supporter
e. clarifier/summarizer

7 Which of the following answers represents a self-centered group role?
a. evaluator/critic
b. opinion giver
c. gatekeeper
d. confessor
e. follower

8 Which leadership theory or model can be summarized as "Either You Have It or You Don't"?
a. Trait Theory
b. Styles Theory
c. Situational Theory
d. The 4-M Model of Leadership
e. The Styles and Situational Theories

9 According to Situational Leadership Theory, which style of leadership is most appropriate when a leader has poor leader–member relations, a highly organized task, and little or no power or control?
a. a laissez-faire leader
b. a task-motivated leader
c. a democratic leader
d. a relationship-motivated leader
e. an autocratic leader

10 Which of the following strategies is most likely to help you *become* a leader?
a. Talk early
b. Talk often
c. Know more
d. Offer your opinion
e. all of the above

Answers: 1-c; 2-d; 3-c; 4-a; 5-b; 6-e; 7-d; 8-a; 9-b; 10-e

11 GROUP

The classic 1957 film *12 Angry Men* is a story about decision making and problem solving.[1]

Twelve jurors (all male, mostly middle-aged, white, and generally of middle-class status) must reach a verdict in a seemingly open-and-shut murder trial. The film examines how the jurors' deep-seated prejudices, unreliable judgments, cultural differences, ignorance, and fears taint their decision-making abilities, cause them to ignore the real issues in the case, and potentially lead them to a miscarriage of justice. Fortunately, one brave dissenting juror votes "not guilty" because of his reasonable doubt. Persistently and persuasively, he forces the other men to slowly reconsider and review the shaky case.[2]

In all likelihood, you have been or will be called for jury duty. Like the characters in *12 Angry Men*, you will have to make a decision—guilty or not guilty; liable or not liable; severe or light sentence. The fairness of that decision will rely, in large part, on how well jury members communicate with one another and use rational thinking to reach a just decision. Clearly there is a world of difference between making any decision and making a good decision.[3]

> **There is a world of difference between making any decision and making a good decision.**

DECISION MAKING AND PROBLEM SOLVING

prerequisites for
GROUP DECISION MAKING AND PROBLEM SOLVING

You make hundreds of decisions every day. You decide when to get up in the morning, what to wear, when to leave for class or work, and with whom to spend your leisure time. Many factors influence how you make these decisions—your culture, age, family, education, social status, and religion, as well as your dreams, fears, beliefs, values, interpersonal needs, and personal preferences.[4] Now take five people, put them in a room, and ask them to make a *group* decision. As difficult as it can be to make personal decisions, the challenge is multiplied many times over in groups.

Fortunately and in large part because of the many differences among members, effective groups have the potential to make excellent decisions because more minds are at work on the problem. As we noted in Chap-

ter 10, Working in Groups, groups generally accomplish more and perform better than individuals working alone. So, while the road may be paved with challenges, group decision making and problem solving can be more satisfying, creative, and effective.

Although the terms *decision making* and *problem solving* are often

> As **difficult** as it can be to make personal decisions, the **challenge** is multiplied many times over in groups.

used interchangeably, their meanings differ. **Decision making** refers to the "passing of judgment on an issue under consideration" and "the act of reaching a conclusion or making up one's mind."[5] In a group setting, decision making results in a position, opinion, judgment, or action. For example, hiring committees, juries, and families decide which applicant is best, whether the accused is guilty, and whom they should invite to the wedding, respectively. Peter Drucker put it simply: "A decision is a judgment. It is a choice between alternatives."[6]

Most groups make decisions, but not all groups solve problems. **Problem solving** is a complex *process* in which groups make *multiple* decisions as they analyze a problem and develop a plan for solving the problem or reducing its harmful effects. For instance, if student enrollment has significantly declined, a college faces a serious problem that must be analyzed and dealt with if the institution hopes to survive. Fortunately, there are decision-making and problem-solving strategies that can

Decision making The act of reaching a conclusion; a process in which a group chooses from among alternative decisions

Problem solving A complex process in which groups make multiple decisions as they analyze a problem and develop a plan for solving the problem or reducing its harmful effects.

help a group "make up its mind" and resolve a problem.

However, before a group takes on such challenges, three prerequisites should be in place: a clear goal, quality content, and structured procedures.

Clear Goal

The first and most important task for all groups is to make sure that everyone understands and supports the group's goal. One way is to word the goal as a question. In Chapter 4, we discussed the importance of critical thinking and how identifying claims of fact, conjecture, value, and policy helps you decide whether you should accept, reject, or suspend judgment about an idea, belief, or proposal. Groups face the same challenge when framing a discussion question.

Effective group members ask four key questions to achieve a group's goal: *Questions of fact* investigate the truth, reliability, and cause of something using the best information available. *Questions of conjecture* examine the possibility of something happening in the future using valid facts and expert opinions to reach the most probable conclusion. *Questions of value* consider the worth or significance of something, and *questions of policy* investigate a course of action for implementing a plan.

Group members understand that the differences in each type of question will shape the discussions that ensue. In some group contexts, the questions are dictated by an outside group or authority. For example, a work group may be asked to find time-saving ways to process an order or contact a customer. A research group may be asked to test the durability of a new product.

Quality Content

Well-informed groups are more likely to make good decisions. The amount and accuracy of information

> **"The ability of a group to gather and retain a wide range of information is the single most important determinant of high-quality decision making."**
> — Randy Hirokawa

available to a group are critical factors in predicting its success. Group communication scholar Randy Hirokawa claims that "the ability of a group to gather and retain a wide range of information is the single most important determinant of high-quality decision making."[7]

The key to becoming a well-informed group lies in the ability of members to collect, share, and analyze the information needed to achieve the group's goal. When a group lacks relevant and valid information, effective decision making and problem solving become difficult, even impossible. During an initial meeting, a group should discuss how to become better informed.

Structured Procedures

Groups need clear procedures that specify how they will make decisions and solve problems. Group communication scholar Marshall Scott Poole claims that structured procedures are "the heart of group work [and] the most powerful tools we have to improve the conduct of meetings."[8]

There are, however, many different kinds of procedures, including complex, theory-based problem-solving models designed to tackle the overall problem, as well as decision-making methods designed for interim tasks such as idea generation and solution implementation. The next few sections of this chapter describe how various procedures can and should be used to improve group decision making and problem solving.

STOP & THINK | **Can You Identify the Question Type?**

Each of the following examples represents a question members might address while trying to make a group decision. Identify the type of question (fact, conjecture, value, or policy) asked below.

1. What causes global warming?
2. Are community colleges a better place than a prestigious university to begin higher education?
3. Will company sales increase next quarter?
4. Which candidate should we support for president of the student government association?

Groupthink

In his book, *Group Genius*, Keith Sawyer retells a story about a group of 12 heavy smokers who signed up for a stop-smoking group at a local health clinic. One heavy smoker revealed that he had stopped smoking right after joining the group. His comment infuriated the other 11 members. They ganged up on him so fiercely that at the beginning of the next meeting, he announced that he'd gone back to smoking two packs a day. The entire group cheered. "Keep in mind," writes Sawyer, "that the whole point of the group was to reduce smoking!"[9]

What happened in the stop-smoking group is not unusual. Although conforming to group norms and promoting group cohesiveness benefit groups in many ways, too much of either can result in a phenomenon that Yale University psychologist Irving Janis identified as **groupthink**—the deterioration of group effectiveness as a consequence of in-group pressure.[10] Groupthink stifles the free flow of information, suppresses constructive disagreement, and erects nearly impenetrable barriers to effective decision making and problem solving.

Janis's groupthink theory focuses on patterns of behavior in policy-making fiascoes, such as the failed Bay of Pigs invasion in Cuba, the tragic Challenger space shuttle disaster, and George W. Bush's decision to invade Iraq in 2003, to name a few. Fortunately, there are ways to minimize the potential for groupthink.

Every member should assume the role of critical evaluator and should ask questions, offer reasons for their positions, express disagreement, and evaluate one another's ideas.

Periodically invite an expert to join your meeting and encourage constructive criticism. If nothing else, the group should discuss the potential negative consequences of any decision or action. Finally, before finalizing a decision, give members a second chance to express any lingering doubts.

Effective groups avoid groupthink by spending time and energy working through differences without sacrificing group cohesiveness in pursuit of responsible decisions.

Symptoms of Groupthink[11]

The eight symptoms of groupthink as identified by Irving Janis.

SYMPTOMS	DESCRIPTION	EXPRESSION
Invulnerability	Group is overconfident; willing to take big risks	"We're right. We've done this before and nothing's gone wrong."
Rationalization	Group makes excuses; discounts warnings	"What does he know? He's only been here three weeks."
Morality	Group ignores ethical and moral consequences	"Sometimes the end justifies the means. Only results count."
Stereotyping Outsiders	Believes opponents are too weak or stupid to make trouble	"Let's not worry about them— they can't get their act together."
Self-Censorship	Members doubt their own reservations; are unwilling to disagree	"I guess it's okay if I'm the only one who disagrees."
Pressure on Dissent	Members are pressured to agree	"Why are you holding this up? You'll ruin the project."
Illusion of Unanimity	Group believes that everyone agrees	"Hearing no objections, the motion passes."
Mindguarding	Group shields members from adverse information or opposition	"Tamela wanted to come to this meeting, but I told her that it wasn't necessary."

> **Groupthink** The deterioration of group effectiveness as a consequence of in-group pressure

EFFECTIVE GROUP
decision making

all groups make decisions. Some decisions are simple and easy; others are complex and consequential. Regardless of the issue, effective groups look for the best way to reach a decision, one that considers the group's common goal and the characteristics and preferences of its members.

Decision-Making Methods

Although there are many ways to make decisions, certain methods work best for groups trying to reach a decision consistent with their common goal. Groups can let the majority have its way by voting, reaching consensus, or leaving the final decision to a person in a position of authority. Each approach has its strengths and should be selected to match the needs and purpose of the group and its task.

Voting When a quick decision is needed, there is nothing more efficient and decisive than voting. Sometimes, though, voting may not be the best way to make important decisions. When a group votes, some members win, but others lose.

A **majority vote** requires that more than half the members vote in

When a **group votes**, some members **win**, but others **lose**.

favor of a proposal. However, if a group is making a major decision, there may not be enough support if only 51 percent of the members vote in favor of the project, because the 49 percent who lose may resent working on a project they dislike. To avoid such problems, some groups use a two-thirds vote rather than majority rule. In a **two-thirds vote**, at least twice as many group members vote for a proposal as against it.

Consensus Because voting has built-in disadvantages, many groups rely on consensus to make decisions. **Consensus** is reached when all group members agree to support a group decision. A consensus decision is one "that all members have a part in shaping and that all find at least minimally acceptable

as a means of accomplishing some mutual goals."[12] Consensus does not work for all groups. Imagine how difficult it would be to achieve genuine consensus among pro-life and pro-choice or pro-gun-control and anti-gun-control group members. If your group seeks consensus when

Majority vote The results of a vote in which more than half the members favor a proposal

Two-thirds vote The result of a vote in which at least twice as many group members vote for a proposal as against it

Consensus A process in which all group members agree to support a group's decision

---

VOTING WORKS BEST WHEN . . .

- a group is pressed for time.
- the issue is not highly controversial.
- a group is too large to use any other decision-making method.
- there is no other way to break a deadlock.
- a group's constitution or rules require voting to make decisions.

Guidelines for Achieving Group Consensus

DO THIS:

- Listen carefully to and respect other members' points of view.
- Try to be logical rather than emotional.
- If there is a deadlock, work to find the next best alternative that is acceptable to all.
- Make sure that members not only agree but also will be committed to the final decision.
- Get everyone involved in the discussion.
- Welcome differences of opinion.

DON'T DO THIS:

- Don't be stubborn and argue only for your own position.
- Don't change your mind to avoid conflict or reach a quick decision.
- Don't give in, especially if you have a crucial piece of information to share.
- Don't agree to a decision or solution you can't possibly support.
- Don't use "easy" ways to reach a solution such as flipping a coin, letting the majority rule, or trading one decision for another.

making decisions, follow the above guidelines.

Before choosing consensus as a decision-making method, make sure that group members trust one another and expect honesty, directness, and candor. Avoid rushing to achieve consensus—make sure that everyone's opinion is heard. Finally, be wary of a dominant leader or member who may make true consensus impossible. Sociologists Rodney Napier and Matti Gershenfeld put it this way: "A group that wants to use a consensual approach to decision making must be willing to develop the skills and discipline to take the time necessary to make it work. Without these, the group

becomes highly vulnerable to domination or intimidation by a few and to psychological game playing by individuals unwilling to 'let go.'"[13]

Authority Rule Sometimes a single person or someone outside the group will make the final decision. When **authority rule** is used, groups may be asked to gather information for and recommend decisions to another person or larger group. For example, an association's nominating committee considers potential candidates and recommends a slate of officers to the association. Or a hiring committee screens dozens of job applications and submits a top-three list to the person or persons making the hiring decision.

Authority rule A situation in which the leader or an authority outside the group makes the final decisions for the group

False consensus Occurs when members reluctantly give in to group pressure or an external authority in order to make a decision masquerading as consensus

---

STOP & THINK | Is There Consensus About Consensus?

Many groups fall short of achieving their common goal because they have total faith in the virtues of achieving consensus. As a result, they believe the group *must* reach consensus on *all* decisions. The problem of false consensus haunts every decision-making group. **False consensus** occurs when members reluctantly give in to group pressures or an external authority. Rather than achieving consensus, the group agrees to a decision masquerading as consensus.[14]

In addition, the all-or-nothing approach to consensus "gives each member veto power over the progress of the whole group." In order to avoid this impasse, members may "give up and give in" or seek a flawed compromise.

When this happens, the group will fall short of success as "it mindlessly pursues 100% agreement."[15]

In *The Discipline of Teams*, John Katzenbach and Douglas Smith observe that members who pursue complete consensus often act as though disagreement and conflict are bad for the group. Nothing, they claim, could be further from the reality of effective group performance. "Without disagreement, teams rarely generate the best, most creative solutions to the challenges at hand. They compromise . . . rather than developing a solution that incorporates the best of two or more opposing views. . . . The challenge for teams is to learn from disagreement and find energy in constructive conflict, not get ruined by it."[16]

If, however, a leader or outside authority ignores or reverses group recommendations, members may become demoralized, resentful, and unproductive on future assignments. Even within a group, a strong leader or authority figure may use a group and its members to give the appearance of collaborative decision making. The group thus becomes a "rubber stamp" and surrenders its will to authority rule.

Group scholars Randy Hirokawa and Roger Pace warn that "influential members [can] convince the group to accept invalid facts and assumptions, introduce poor ideas and suggestions, lead the group to misinterpret information presented to them, or lead the group off on tangents and irrelevant discussion."[18] One powerful but misguided member can be responsible for the poor quality of a group's decision.

Decision-Making Styles

In Chapter 7, we described the Myers-Briggs Type Indicator. Two traits—thinking and feeling—focus on how we make decisions. Thinkers, for example, are task-oriented members who prefer to use logic in making decisions. Feelers, on the other hand, are people-oriented members who want everyone to get along, even if it means spending more time on a task or giving in to members to avoid interpersonal problems. Each type of decision making impacts a group's choice of decision-making methods and their outcomes.

In "Decision Making Style: The Development of a New Measure,"

Suzanne Scott and Reginald Bruce describe five decision-making styles, each of which has the potential to improve or impair member interaction and group outcomes.[19]

Rational decision makers carefully weigh information and options before making a decision. They claim, "I've carefully considered all the issues," and make decisions systematically using logical reasoning to justify their final decisions. However, they must be careful not to analyze a problem for so long that they never make a decision. **Intuitive decision makers**, on the other hand, make decisions based on instincts, feelings, or hunches. They tend to say, "It just feels like the right thing to do." They may not always be able to explain the reasons for their decisions, but know that their decisions "feel" right.

Dependent decision makers solicit the advice and opinions of others before making a decision: "If you think it's okay, then I'll do it." They feel uncomfortable making decisions that others disapprove of or oppose. They may even make a decision they aren't happy with just

> One powerful but misguided member can be responsible for the poor quality of a group's decision.

Rational decision maker A person who carefully weighs information and options before making a decision

Intuitive decision maker A person who makes decisions based on instincts, feelings, or hunches

Dependent decision maker A person who solicits the advice and opinions of others before making a decision

to please others. **Avoidant decision makers** feel uncomfortable making decisions. As a result, they may not think about a problem at all or will make a final decision at the very last minute: "I just can't deal with this right now." **Spontaneous decision makers**, however, tend to be impulsive and make quick decisions on the spur of the moment: "Let's do it now and worry about the consequences later." As a result, they often make decisions they later regret.

Now consider what would happen if you had a group where half the members were rational decision makers and the other half were intuitive decision makers. Or, what would happen if the group included *only* dependent or avoidant decision makers? Different decision-making styles can disrupt a group, but having only one type also has its pitfalls. The key is learning to recognize and adapt to different decision-making styles while pursing a common goal.

Avoidant decision maker A person who is uncomfortable making decisions, may not think about a problem at all, or will make a final decision at the last minute

Spontaneous decision maker A person who tends to be impulsive and make a quick decision on the spur of the moment

Know Thy Self

What Is Your Decision-Making Style?[20]

Indicate the degree to which you agree or disagree with each of the statements below by circling the appropriate number on the following scale: (1) strongly disagree, (2) disagree, (3) undecided (neither agree nor disagree), (4) agree, or (5) strongly agree. There are no right or wrong answers; answer as honestly as you can. Think carefully before choosing option 3 (undecided)—it may suggest you cannot make decisions.

1. When I have to make an important decision, I usually seek the opinions of others.	1 2 3 4 5
2. I tend to put off decisions on issues that make me uncomfortable.	1 2 3 4 5
3. I make decisions in a logical and systematic way.	1 2 3 4 5
4. When making a decision, I usually trust feelings or gut instincts.	1 2 3 4 5
5. When making a decision, I generally consider the advantages and disadvantages of many alternatives.	1 2 3 4 5
6. I often avoid making important decisions until I absolutely have to.	1 2 3 4 5
7. I often make impulsive decisions.	1 2 3 4 5
8. When making a decision, I rely upon my instincts.	1 2 3 4 5
9. It is easier for me to make important decisions when I know others approve or support them.	1 2 3 4 5
10. I make decisions very quickly.	1 2 3 4 5

Scoring: To determine your score for each type of decision making, add the total of your responses to specific items as indicated below. Your higher scores identify your preferred decision-making styles.

Answers to items 3 and 5 = ____ (rational decision maker)
Answers to items 4 and 8 = ____ (intuitive decision maker)
Answers to items 1 and 9 = ____ (dependent decision maker)
Answers to items 2 and 6 = ____ (avoidant decision maker)
Answers to items 7 and 10 = ____ (spontaneous decision maker)

EFFECTIVE GROUP
problem solving

althought there are several problem-solving methods, there is no "best" model or magic formula that ensures effective problem solving. However, as groups gain experience and succeed as problem solvers, they learn that some procedures work better than others and some need modification to suit group needs. Here we offer three problem-solving methods: Brainstorming, the Decreasing Options Technique (DOT), and the Standard Agenda.

Brainstorming

In 1953, Alex Osborn introduced the concept of brainstorming in *Applied Imagination*.[21] **Brainstorming**, a fairly simple and widely used method, is used for generating as many ideas as possible in a short period of time. It assumes that postponing the evaluation of ideas improves the quality of participants' input. It also assumes that the quantity of ideas breeds quality, based on the notion that creative ideas will come only after we have gotten the obvious suggestions out.[22] More than 70 percent of businesspeople claim that brainstorming is used in their organizations.[23] Unfor-

Brainstorming Guidelines[24]

Sharpen the Focus	• Start with a clear question or statement of the problem. • Give members a few minutes to think about possible ideas before brainstorming begins.
Display Ideas for All to See	• Assign someone to write down the group's ideas. • Post the ideas where everyone can see them.
Number the Ideas	• Numbering can motivate a group: e.g., "Let's try to get 100 ideas." • Numbering makes it easier to jump back and forth among ideas.
Encourage Creativity	• Announce that wild and crazy ideas are welcome. • Announce that quantity is more important than quality.
Emphasize Input, Prohibit Putdowns	• Keep the ideas coming. • Evaluate ideas only after brainstorming is over.
Build and Jump	• Build on, modify, or combine ideas offered by others to create new ideas.

tunately, many groups fail to use brainstorming effectively.

Brainstorming is a great way to tackle open-ended, unclear, or broad problems. If you're looking for lots of ideas, it is a very useful technique. But if you need a formal plan of action or you have a critical problem to solve that requires a single "right" answer, try another method.

There are several sure-fire ways to derail a productive brainstorming session.[25] If, for example, the boss or a dominant member speaks first and at length, she or he may influence and limit the direction and content of subsequent input and ideas. In an effort to be more democratic, some brainstorming groups require members to speak in turn. This approach prevents a group from building momentum and will probably result in fewer ideas. Finally, members who try to write down all of the group's ideas may end up being so focused on note taking that they rarely contribute

> **Brainstorming** A group technique in which members generate as many ideas as possible in a short period of time

WHEN **NOT** TO BRAINSTORM

• **In a crisis.** If the group needs to make decisions quickly or follow a leader's directions.

• **To repair.** If the group knows what went wrong and how to fix it, organize a repair team.

• **For planning.** If the group knows exactly what it has to do to reach its goal, hold a planning session to map out details.

ideas. It is better to have one person record all the ideas contributed by the group members.

Although many groups use brainstorming, their success depends on the nature of the group and the character of its members. If a group is self-conscious and sensitive to implied criticism, brainstorming can fail. However, if a group is comfortable with such a freewheeling process, brainstorming can enhance creativity and produce numerous ideas and suggestions.

Decreasing Options Technique

The **Decreasing Options Technique (DOT)** helps groups reduce and refine a large number of suggestions and ideas into a manageable set of options.[26] In our work as professional facilitators, we have used this technique to assist small and large groups facing a variety of decision-making tasks, such as creating an ethics credo for a professional association and drafting a vision statement for a college. The DOT method works best when a group must sort through a multitude of ideas and options.

Generate Individual Ideas At the beginning of the DOT process, group members generate ideas or suggestions related to a specific topic. Ideas can be single words or full-sentence suggestions. For

✔ **Generate Ideas**
✔ **Post Ideas**
✔ **Sort Ideas**
✔ **Prioritize Ideas**

example, when creating a professional association's ethics credo, participants contributed words such as *honesty*, *respect*, and *truth*.[27]

Post Ideas for All to See Each idea should be written on a separate sheet of thick paper in large, easy-to-read letters—only one idea per page. These pages are posted on the walls of the group's meeting room for all to see and consider. Postings should be displayed only after all members have finished writing their ideas on separate sheets of paper.

Sort Ideas Not surprisingly, many group members will contribute similar or overlapping ideas. When this happens, sort the ideas and post similar ideas close to one another. For example, when facilitating the development of a college's vision statement, phrases such as *academic excellence*, *quality education*, and *high-*

quality instruction were posted near one another. After everyone is comfortable with how the postings are sorted, give a title to each grouping of ideas. In the vision statement session, for instance, the term *quality education* was used as an umbrella phrase for nearly a dozen similar concepts.

Prioritize Ideas At this point, individual members decide which of the displayed ideas are most important: Which words *best* reflect the vision we have for our college? Which concepts *must* be included in our association's ethics credo?

Decreasing Options Technique (DOT) A technique that helps groups reduce and refine a large number of suggestions and ideas into a manageable set of options

CRITERIA FOR USING THE DOT APPROACH

- when the group is so large that open discussion of individual ideas is unworkable
- when a significant number of competing ideas are generated
- when members want equal opportunities for input
- when dominant members do not exert too much influence
- when there is not enough time to discuss multiple or controversial ideas

Decision Making and Problem Solving in Virtual Groups

The group decision-making and problem-solving methods in this chapter were designed for face-to-face meetings. These methods also work well in virtual groups using commonly available technology. Additionally, specialized computer software, or groupware, can facilitate group collaboration, decision making, and problem solving.

Different types of technology, however, are not equally suited to all types of virtual groups. In *Mastering Virtual Teams*, Deborah Duarte and Nancy Tennant Snyder offer a matrix that rates the effectiveness of different types of technology in relation to the goals of a meeting.[28] In this matrix, *product production* refers to a meeting in which group members work on a collaborative project such as analyzing complex data, developing a design, or drafting a policy. Electronic meeting systems are used in face-to-face settings and range from electronic voting systems to computer-aided systems in which members use a laptop computer to provide input into a central display screen.[29]

Meeting Selection Matrix for Virtual Groups

Type of Technology	Purpose of Meeting			
	Information Sharing	Discussion & Brainstorming	Decision Making	Product Production
Telephone or Computer Audioconference	Effective	Somewhat effective	Somewhat effective	Not effective
E-mail	Effective	Somewhat effective	Not effective	Not effective
Bulletin Board, Restricted Blog	Somewhat effective	Somewhat effective	Not effective	Not effective
Videoconference without shared documents	Effective	Somewhat effective	Effective	Not effective
Videoconference with text and graphics	Effective	Effective	Effective	Effective
Electronic Meeting System with audio, video, and graphics	Effective	Highly effective	Highly effective	Effective
Collaborative Writing with audio and video	Effective	Effective	Somewhat effective	Highly effective

Group experts John Katzenbach and Douglas Smith remind us that "whenever teams gather through groupware to advance, they need to recognize and adjust to key differences between face-to-face and groupware interactions."[30] In short, a virtual group should select the technology that is best suited to its problem-solving method.

Interestingly, virtual groups have the potential to stimulate more ideas and overall productivity with fewer blocking behaviors. Some studies have found that idea generation and consolidation using computers are more productive and satisfying than if done face-to-face.[31] However, computer groups require more time for task completion and group members may become frustrated or bored.

In order to prioritize ideas efficiently, every member receives a limited number of colored sticker dots. They use their stickers to "dot" the most important ideas or options. For example, after giving ten dots to each member of the vision statement group, they were told to "dot" the most important concepts from among the 25 phrases posted on the walls. After everyone has finished walking around the room and posting dots, the most important ideas are usually very apparent. Some ideas will be covered with dots; others will be speckled with only three or four; some will remain blank. After a brief review of the outcome, the group can eliminate some ideas, decide whether marginal ideas should be included, and end up with a limited and manageable number of options to consider and discuss.

Advantages of the DOT Method When a group generates dozens of ideas, valuable meeting time can be consumed by discussing every idea, regardless of its merit or relevance. The DOT method reduces the quantity of ideas to a manageable number.

Although the examples described focus on face-to-face interaction, the DOT strategy also works very well in virtual settings. A virtual group can follow the same steps by using e-mail or networked software designed for interactive group work.

The Standard Agenda

The founding father of problem-solving procedures is a U.S. philosopher and educator named John Dewey. In 1910, Dewey wrote a book titled *How We Think* in which he described a set of practical steps that a rational person should follow when solving a problem.[32] These guidelines have come to be known as Dewey's *reflective thinking process.*

Dewey's ideas have been adapted for group problem solving. The reflective thinking process begins with a focus on the problem itself and then moves to a systematic consideration of possible solutions. We offer one version of this process: the **Standard Agenda** involves clarifying the task at hand, understanding and analyzing the problem, assessing possible solutions, and implementing the decision or plan.[33]

Task Clarification: Make Sure That Everyone Understands the Group's Assignment

The primary purpose of a group's first meeting is to determine what the group wants or needs to accomplish so that everyone is working to achieve a common goal. During this phase, group members should ask questions about their roles and responsibilities in the problem-solving process.

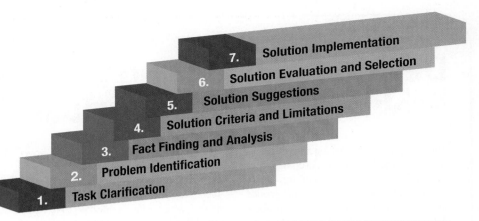

Summary of the seven basic steps in the Standard Agenda.

7. Solution Implementation
6. Solution Evaluation and Selection
5. Solution Suggestions
4. Solution Criteria and Limitations
3. Fact Finding and Analysis
2. Problem Identification
1. Task Clarification

Problem Identification: Avoid Sending the Group in the Wrong Direction

Once a group understands and supports a common goal, members should focus on understanding the problem and developing a set of key questions. Identifying questions of fact, value, conjecture, and/or policy can help focus and direct the group in the right direction.

Fact Finding and Analysis: Ask Questions of Fact and Value

The following questions require research and critical thinking about the facts, causes, and seriousness of a problem, as well as an analysis of the barriers that prevent a solution:

• What are the facts of the situation?
• What additional information or expert opinion do we need?
• How serious or widespread is the problem?
• What are the causes of the problem?
• What prevents or inhibits us from solving the problem?

Although carefully evaluating facts and opinions is critical to effective problem solving, groups must also avoid analysis paralysis. **Analysis paralysis** occurs when groups are so focused on analyzing a problem that they fail to make a decision.[34] "Chances are you've been caught

up in [situations where] good ideas have been presented, but by the time enough people consider and reconsider the situation, it seems more complex, or not as great an idea as you originally thought. Or, in most cases, a conclusion about how to act is never reached."[35]

Rather than spending months arguing about the issue or giving up on finding the correct answer, a group may have to move on and begin its search for solutions.

Solution Criteria and Limitations: Set Standards for an Ideal Resolution

Solution criteria are standards that should be met for an ideal resolution of a problem. A group can establish criteria by asking questions such as "Is the solution reasonable

> **Standard Agenda** A procedure that guides a group through problem solving by using the following steps: clarifying the task, understanding and analyzing the problem, assessing possible solutions, and implementing a decision or plan
> **Analysis paralysis** A situation that occurs when group members are so focused on analyzing a problem that they fail to make a decision

and realistic? Is it affordable? Do we have the staff, resources, and time to implement it?" The development of solution criteria should also include an understanding of solution limitations, which may be financial, institutional, practical, political, and legal in scope.

Solution Suggestions: Consider Multiple Solutions without Judgment

At this point in a group's deliberations, some solutions are probably obvious. Even so, the group should suggest or engage in brainstorming to identify as many solutions as possible without criticizing them. Having spent time analyzing the problem and establishing solution criteria, members should be able to offer numerous solutions.

Solution Evaluation and Selection: Discuss the Pros and Cons of Each Suggestion

During this phase, a group should return to the solution criteria and use them to evaluate the strengths and weaknesses of each suggested solution. This stage of the Standard Agenda may be the most difficult and controversial. Questions of conjecture such as "What will happen if we decide to do X?" arise as the group considers the possible consequences of each suggestion. Discussion may become heated, and disagreements may grow fierce. If, however, the group has been conscientious in analyzing the problem and establishing criteria for solutions, some solutions will be rejected quickly whereas others will swiftly rise to the top of the list.

Solution Implementation: Decide on a Plan of Action

Having made a difficult decision, a group faces one more challenge: How should the decision be implemented? For all the time a group spends trying to solve a problem, it may take even more time organizing the task of implementing the solution. Brilliant solutions can fail if no one takes responsibility or has the authority to implement a group's decision.

communication&culture

MOTIVATING MULTICULTURAL GROUP MEMBERS

In Chapter 3, we described five cultural dimensions, each of which has implications for motivating group members to fully participate in group decision making and problem solving.

- *Individualism–collectivism.* Individualistic members may need praise and seek public recognition for their personal contributions. Collectivistic members may be embarrassed by public praise and prefer being honored as a member of an outstanding group.
- *High power distance–low power distance.* Members from high-power-distance cultures value recognition by a leader and take pride in following instructions accurately and efficiently. Members from low-power-distance cultures prefer compliments from other group members and enjoy working in a collaborative environment.
- *Masculine–feminine.* Members—both male and female—who hold masculine values are motivated by competition, opportunities for leadership, and tasks that require assertive behavior. Members with more feminine values may be extremely effective and supportive of group goals but have difficulty achieving a respected voice or influence in the group. Such members are motivated by taking on group maintenance roles,

such as encourager/ supporter, harmonizer, or compromiser.

- *High context–low context.* Group members from high-context cultures do not need to *hear* someone praise their work—they are highly skilled at detecting admiration and approval because they are more sensitive to nonverbal cues. Members from low-context cultures often complain that they never receive praise or rewards when, in fact, other members respect them and value their contributions. Low-context members need to hear words of praise and receive tangible rewards.
- *Monochronic–polychronic.* Members from monochronic cultures are motivated in groups that concentrate their energies on a specific task and meeting deadlines. Members from polychronic cultures often find the single-mindedness of monochronic members stifling rather than motivating. Giving polychronic members the opportunity to work on multiple tasks with flexible deadlines can motivate them to work more effectively.

EFFECTIVE GROUP
meetings

more than ten million business meetings occur daily in the United States,[36] and studies show that this is how managers spend 30 to 80 percent of their time.[37] Ninety percent report that half the meetings they attend are "either unnecessary or a complete waste of time."[38] How bad is this problem? The National Manage-ment Association reports that "too many meetings" is the second biggest employee complaint, with "too much work" being the first.

Before looking at how to plan and conduct a meeting, we should specify what we mean by the word. A random gathering of people in one place does not constitute a meeting. Rather, a **meeting** is a scheduled gathering of group members for a structured discussion guided by a designated chairperson. The leader designated as a meeting's chairperson has a tremendous amount of influence over and responsibility for its success.

Planning the Meeting

Proper planning largely determines the success or failure of a meeting. In fact, careful planning can prevent at least 20 minutes of wasted time for each hour of a group's meeting.[39] To help make your meeting more efficient and effective, and to decide whether one is even necessary, ask and answer the five W questions: Why are we meeting? Who should attend? When should we meet? Where should we meet? and What materials do we need?

Meeting A scheduled gathering of group members for a structured discussion guided by a designated chairperson

Five Ws to Planning a Meeting

Why Are We Meeting? The most important step in planning a meeting is defining its purpose and setting clear goals. Merely asking what a meeting is about only identifies the topic of discussion: "employer-provided daycare." Asking *why* this topic is being discussed will lead you to the actual purpose: "to determine whether our employer-provided day-care system needs to be expanded." Groups should be able to achieve their purpose by the end of a single meeting. However, if this is not possible, the purpose statement should be revised to focus on a more specific outcome. If many cases, a series of meetings are needed to achieve the group's goal.

Who Should Attend? Most group membership is predetermined. However, if a task requires input only from certain people, you should select only those participants who can make a significant contribution. In addition, invite participants with special expertise, different opinions and approaches, and the power to implement decisions.

When Should We Meet? Seek input and decide on the best day and time for the meeting, as well as when a meeting should begin and end. Schedule the meeting when the most essential and productive participants are free. For a time-consuming and difficult goal, you may discover that more than one meeting will be necessary.

Where Should We Meet? Choose a location that is appropriate for the purpose and size of the meeting. Do your best to find a comfortable setting, making sure that the meeting room is free of distractions such as ringing phones and noisy conversations. An attractive and quiet meeting location will help your group stay motivated and focused on the group's discussion.

What Materials Do We Need? The most important item to prepare and distribute to the group is the meeting's agenda. You may also need to distribute reports or other reading material for review before the meeting. Distribute all materials far enough in advance of the meeting so that everyone has time to prepare. In addition, make sure that supplies and equipment such as pens, paper, or computers and screens are available to participants.

Careful planning can prevent at least 20 minutes of wasted time for each hour of a group's meeting.

Preparing the Agenda

An **agenda** outlines the items to be discussed and the tasks to be accomplished at a meeting. A well-prepared agenda serves many purposes. First and foremost, the agenda is an organizational tool—a road map for the discussion that helps a group focus on its task and goal.

In *Meetings: Do's, Don'ts, and Donuts*, Sharon Lippincott uses a simile to explain why a well-planned agenda is essential for conducting effective meetings:

> Starting a meeting without an agenda is like setting out on a journey over unfamiliar roads with no map and only a general idea of the route to your destination. You may get there, but only after lengthy detours. A good agenda defines the destination of the meeting, draws a map of the most direct route, and provides checkpoints along the way.[40]

Complex III
987 So. Highland Street
Homegrown, USA 01234

"A" is for Apple
Produce Company

(777) 555-4119
cservice@aisforapple.com
www.aisforapple.com

RECYCLING TASK FORCE

Date: November 20th
Time: 1:00–3:00 pm
Place: Conference Room 352

Purpose: To recommend ways to increase the effectiveness of and participation in the company's recycling program.

I.   What is the goal of this meeting? What have we been asked to do?

II. How effective is the company's current recycling effort?

III. Why has the program lacked effectiveness and full participation?

IV. What are the requirements or standards for an ideal program?
  A. Level of participation
  B. Reasonable cost
  C. Physical requirements
  D. Legal requirements

V.   What are the possible ways in which we could improve the recycling program?

VI. What specific methods do we recommend for increasing the recycling program's effectiveness?

VII. How should the recommendations be implemented? Who or what groups should be charged with implementation?

~ America's Oldest Producer of Quality Fruits and Vegetables ~

Sample Meeting Agenda
Sample discussion agenda for a group examining a specific issue: ways to improve a company's recycling program.

Sample Agendas

Complex III
987 So. Highland Street
Homegrown, USA 01234

"A" is for Apple
Produce Company

(777) 555-4119
cservice@aisforapple.com
www.aisforapple.com

AGENDA

Date: September 15th
Time: 12:30–4:45 pm
Place: Presidential Ballroom

I.   Call to order by president

II.   Approval of minutes and agenda

III. Reports by officers and committees

IV.   Unfinished business

V.   New business

VI.   Announcements

VII. Adjournment

~ America's Oldest Producer of Quality Fruits and Vegetables ~

Standard Business Agenda
Basic components of a standard business agenda that follows a traditional format for formal business meetings.

When used properly, an agenda identifies what participants should expect and prepare for in a meeting.

After a meeting, the agenda can be used to assess a meeting's success by determining the extent to which all items were addressed.

Although a group's leader usually prepares and distributes an agenda in advance of the meeting, group input can ensure that the agenda covers topics important to the entire group. The customs of the group and the purpose of the meeting will determine the format of the agenda. For example, if the purpose of the meeting is to solve a problem, the agenda items may be in the form of questions rather than the key-word format of a formal business agenda.

An agenda ... is a road map for the discussion that helps a group focus on its task and goal.

Agenda An outline of items to be discussed and the tasks to be accomplished at a meeting

Information to Include While Taking Minutes

✔ Name of the group

✔ Date and place of the meeting

✔ Names of those attending and absent

✔ Name of the person chairing the meeting

✔ Exact time the meeting was called to order

✔ Exact time the meeting was adjourned

✔ Name of the person preparing the minutes

✔ Summary of the group's discussion and decisions, using agenda items as headings

✔ Specific action items, or tasks that individual members have been assigned to do after the meeting

CLOSE TO HOME   JOHN McPHERSON

© 1994 John McPherson/Dist. by Universal Press Syndicate

8:45, 8:46, 8:47, 8:48, 8:49, 8:50, 8:51......

As soon as Mrs. Felster began to read the minutes of the last meeting, the board members knew she was not going to work out as the new secretary.

Taking Minutes

Most business and professional meetings require or benefit from a record of group progress and decision making. Responsible group leaders assign the important task of taking **minutes**—the written record of a group's discussion and activities—to a recorder, secretary, or a volunteer. The minutes cover discussion issues and decisions for those who attend the meeting, and provide a way to communicate with those who do not attend. Most important, minutes help prevent disagreement about what was said or decided in a meeting and what tasks individual members agreed to or were assigned to do.

Well-prepared minutes are brief and accurate. They are not, however, a word-for-word record of everything that members say. Instead, they summarize arguments, key ideas, actions, and votes. Immediately after a meeting, minutes should be prepared for distribution to group members. The longer the delay, the more difficult it will be for members to remember the details of the meeting and the individual task assignments made at the meeting.

Chairing a Meeting

The responsibilities of planning a meeting, preparing an agenda, and making sure that accurate and useful minutes are recorded belong to the person with the title of *chair*. Effective chairs move a group through an agreed-upon agenda, enforce group rules and regulations, and assign tasks. The person who chairs a meeting may be the group leader, a designated facilitator, or a group member who usually assumes that role.

The 3M Meeting Management Team describes the critical role of the chair as "a delicate balancing act" in which chairpersons must . . . influence the group's thinking—not dictate it. They must encourage participation but discourage domination of the discussion by any single member. They must welcome ideas but also question them, challenge them, and insist on evidence to back them up. They must control the meeting but take care not to overcontrol it.[42]

Minutes The written record of a group's discussion and activities

---

GUIDELINES FOR CHAIRING A MEETING

- **Begin on time. Discourage chronic or inconsiderate late arrivals.**

- **Create a positive climate. Establish ground rules for member behavior.**

- **Delegate someone to take the minutes.**

- **Follow the agenda. Keep the group on track and aware of its progress.**

- **Facilitate the discussion. Ensure that all views are heard. Intervene when members ramble or discuss irrelevant topics. Clarify and summarize ideas and suggestions.**

- **Provide closure and stop on time.[41]**

Communication ASSESSMENT

Group Problem-Solving Competencies

Use this assessment instrument to evaluate how well you or another group member participates in a problem-solving discussion. Rate yourself or another group member on each item by placing a check mark in the appropriate column, using the following scale:

1 = excellent   **2** = satisfactory   **3** = unsatisfactory

Group Problem-Solving Competencies	1	2	3
1. *Clarifies the task.* Helps clarify the group's overall goal as well as member roles and responsibilities.			
2. *Identifies the problem.* Helps the group define the nature of the problem and the group's responsibilities.			
3. *Analyzes the issues.* Identifies and analyzes several of the issues that arise from the problem. Contributes relevant and valid information.			
4. *Establishes solution criteria.* Suggests criteria for assessing the workability, effectiveness, and value of a solution.			
5. *Generates solutions.* Identifies possible solutions that meet the solution criteria.			
6. *Evaluates solutions.* Evaluates the potential solutions.			
7. *Plans solution implementation.* Helps the group develop a workable implementation plan that includes necessary resources.			
8. *Maintains task focus.* Stays on task and follows the agreed-upon agenda. If responsible for taking or distributing minutes, makes sure the minutes are accurate.			
9. *Maintains supportive climate.* Collaborates with and appropriately supports other group members.			
10. *Facilitates interaction.* Communicates appropriately, manages interaction, and encourages others to participate.			

What makes this group effective or ineffective?

_____

How could this group improve its problem-solving strategies and skills?

_____

Summary

What prerequisites help groups make good decisions and solve problems?

- Whereas *decision making* refers to the passing of judgment or making up your mind, *problem solving* is a complex process in which groups make multiple decisions while trying to solve a problem.

- Groups should take steps to prevent groupthink, which results in the deterioration of group effectiveness as a consequence of in-group pressure.

- The first and most important task for all groups is to make sure that all members understand and support the group's common goal. Group members should determine whether they are trying to answer a question of fact, conjecture, value, or policy.

- In addition to being well-informed, groups need clear procedures that specify how they will make decisions and solve problems.

What are the advantages and disadvantages of using various decision-making methods?

- Although voting is the easiest way to make a group decision, some members win while others lose.

- Consensus requires that all members agree to support a decision.

Groups should look for and prevent false consensus.

- Authority rule occurs when a single person or someone outside the group makes the final decision.

- Different decision-making styles—rational, intuitive, dependent, avoidant, and spontaneous—have the potential to improve or impair group decision making.

Which problem-solving procedures should groups use to achieve their goals?

- Brainstorming, a group technique for generating as many ideas as possible in a short period of time, works well when members are comfortable with the rules.

- The Decreasing Options Technique (DOT) helps groups reduce and refine a large number of suggestions or ideas into a manageable set of options.

- The Standard Agenda is based on Dewey's reflective thinking process and divides problem solving into

a series of ordered steps: task clarification, problem identification, fact finding and analysis, solution criteria and limitations, solution suggestions, solution evaluation and selection, and solution implementation.

How should you plan and conduct an effective group meeting?

- Before calling a meeting, make sure you decide or know why the group is meeting, who should attend, when and where the group should meet, and what materials are needed.

- An agenda—the outline of items to be discussed and the tasks to be accomplished at a meeting—should be prepared and delivered to all group members in advance of a meeting.

- The minutes of a meeting are the written record of a group's discussion, actions, and decisions.

- When chairing a meeting, begin and end on time, create a positive climate, delegate someone to take minutes, follow the agenda, and facilitate the discussion.

the THINKSPOT
www.thethinkspot.com

TEST your knowledge

1. Which of the following groups is *primarily* responsible for solving a problem?
   a. a jury
   b. a hiring committee
   c. a department's social committee
   d. a toxic waste disaster team
   e. None of the above is a problem-solving group.

2. Which of the following symptoms of groupthink is expressed by a member who says, "Let's not worry about how the other departments feel about this—they're so dumb they don't even know there's a problem."?
   a. invulnerability
   b. stereotyping others
   c. rationalization
   d. mindguarding
   e. illusion of unanimity

3. All of the following answers are guidelines for achieving consensus *except*:
   a. Use stress-free ways of achieving consensus such as flipping a coin or letting the majority make the decision.
   b. Try to be logical rather than highly emotional.
   c. Welcome differences of opinion.
   d. Listen carefully to and respect other members' points of view even if they are very different from your point of view.
   e. Get everyone involved in the discussion.

4. Which ethical responsibility are you assuming in a group if you treat other group members as equals and give everyone, including those who disagree, the opportunity to respond to an issue?
   a. the research responsibility
   b. the common good responsibility
   c. the social code responsibility
   d. the moral responsibility
   e. the reasoning responsibility

5. Under which circumstances is brainstorming not very useful as a problem-solving method?
   a. if there is a crisis in which the group needs rapid decisions and clear leadership
   b. if you need to correct something and know how to fix the problem
   c. if your group knows its goal and how to achieve it, but needs a planning session to map out details
   d. Brainstorming would *not* be very useful in the above situations.
   e. Brainstorming would be very useful in all of the above situations.

6. Use the Decreasing Options Technique (DOT) when
   a. the group is small and can discuss individual ideas openly.
   b. the group must confront and discuss two competing ideas.
   c. the group wants to prevent a dominant member from sharing ideas.
   d. the group does not want to discuss controversial ideas.
   e. ensuring equal opportunities for input by all members is important.

7. Which of the following answers presents the correct order for the first three steps in the Standard Agenda model of problem solving?
   a. fact finding and analysis, problem identification, solution suggestions
   b. task clarification, problem identification, fact finding and analysis
   c. solution suggestions, solution evaluation and selection, solution implementation
   d. problem identification, fact finding and analysis, solution criteria and limitations
   e. None of the above answers represents the first three steps.

8. If your group is using the Standard Agenda model to discuss a question (What is the best way to reduce domestic violence in our community?), in which agenda steps would you ask the following questions: "What are the causes of domestic violence?" and "How widespread and serious is the problem?"
   a. task clarification
   b. problem identification
   c. fact finding and analysis
   d. solution suggestions
   e. solution evaluation and selection

9. Before calling a meeting, ask all of the following questions *except*:
   a. Why are we meeting?
   b. Who should attend?
   c. When and where should we meet?
   d. What materials do we need?
   e. Who will implement decisions?

10. All of the following responsibilities are essential for chairing an effective meeting except:
    a. Begin on time.
    b. Create a positive communication climate and ground rules for member behavior.
    c. Take the minutes.
    d. Follow the agenda.
    e. Provide closure and stop on time.

Answers: 1-d; 2-b; 3-a; 4-c; 5-d; 6-e; 7-b; 8-c; 9-e; 10-c

THINK COMMUNICATION

This article from *Communication Currents* has been slightly edited with permission from the National Communication Association.

Communication Currents
Knowledge for Communicating Well

NCA
A Publication of the National Communication Association

Volume 4, Issue 2 - April 2009

Why Can't Groups Focus on New Information?

In discussions, groups often fail to adequately use the unique information of their members. Rather, groups focus upon and repeat information that all group members knew, even before the discussion began. That is, group members repeat what they know and every other group member knows, and fail to share new information with others. When this happens, the group cannot take advantage of the diverse informational perspectives available from its members. However, recent research has found that structuring group members into the roles of decision-maker and advisor may increase the focus on unique information.

Imagine a group of three members (member A, member B, and member C) discussing whether to hire a job applicant. Assume all members of the hiring team have read the applicant's resume. This would be shared information. However, from individual interviews with the applicant, each learned information that the other two did not. For example, A may have had knowledge about the applicant's educational history that B and C did not have, and C may have talked to the applicant about a mutual professional interest, but A and B did not. According to research on the discussion of information in groups, members of the hiring team would probably mention and repeat more information about the applicant's resume—the shared information—in their discussion and fail to integrate the unshared information that each member has.

One reason shared information is mentioned more is that all group members have access to it. However, once shared information is mentioned, groups often keep repeating the same shared information.

When unshared information is mentioned, groups often fail to repeat and integrate the unshared information into discussion. Thus, an opportunity

---

The roles of *decision-maker* and *advisor* are not included in the list of positive *group member roles* in Chapter 10, pp. 206–207. After reading this article, do you think these roles should be added, or do the listed roles capture the functions of a decision-maker and advisor? Which roles—if any—entail these functions?

To what extent can the tendency of members to keep repeating the same shared information increase the chance of *groupthink*? See Chapter 11, p. 220.

Whittenbaum (Michigan State University) explains that group members experience *mutual enhancement* when they evaluate one another's contributions and competencies more positively because they are discussing shared rather than unshared information.

Think of the groups to which you now belong or have belonged. Did this tendency to focus on shared information occur? If so, how did it affect group decision making?

to gain a new perspective is lost. Research by Gwen Whittenbaum on *mutual enhancement* has helped shed light on why groups continue to focus on shared information. When shared information is first mentioned, other members can validate this information because they too are aware of it. They might respond by nodding their head or making comments affirming the information, such as "Yes, yes, I know." Group members observe this positive response to the shared information and may be more likely to then repeat that information later in the discussion. However, when unshared information is mentioned, other group members may not be able to respond to the information and cannot validate it. They may not completely trust the information since they are learning about it secondhand from another person. Therefore, members may respond less enthusiastically to unshared information. This can cause the member who mentioned the unique information to not repeat it. In support of mutual enhancement, it has been found that members who mention shared information are more influential and viewed as more competent in the group discussion.

Would the same pattern of information sharing hold true in groups that have differences in status and roles? What if one group member holds the decision-making power for the group? Imagine a group in which a cancer patient is meeting with a medical team to discuss treatment options, a congresswoman is meeting with constituents to get feedback about upcoming legislation that she needs to vote on, or a manager is meeting with subordinates to discuss reducing the budget. In each case there is a group discussion, but

Why, in your opinion, does this perception occur in group discussions? How could an assigned decision-maker or advisor affect this perception?

only one person will ultimately make the decision.

Research by Lyn Van Swol has found that in structured groups with one decision maker and multiple advisors, there is greater focus on unshared information. Moreover, members are more likely to repeat unshared information. For example, several studies have found that decision makers prefer to receive advice from group members who have more unshared information than those with shared information. Decision makers perceive group members with more unshared information as more competent. This is the opposite of studies about unstructured groups. In unstructured groups, members who shared information were more influential and perceived as more competent.

There are several reasons why structured groups may focus more on unshared information. Unstructured groups need to reach a group consensus. Because shared information influences everyone's opinion, it validates everyone's opinion and facilitates reaching consensus. When one person is the decision-maker in a group, consensus is not necessary, so group members may be more open to new information and viewpoints and do not have to worry about the new information upsetting group agreement. Also, when put in the role of advisor, a group member may feel more responsible for providing a unique perspective than when a group member is in an unstructured group and has no assigned role. Decision-makers may also try to pool more unique perspectives from their advisors and may expect advisors to provide new information as part of their role. These expectations may not exist for members of unstructured groups.

In conclusion, if your goal is to encourage your group or team members to share information that is unknown to others, then assigning members the roles of advisor and decision-maker may help.

ABOUT THE AUTHOR

Lyn M. Van Swol is an Assistant Professor of Communication Arts at University of Wisconsin–Madison, Wisconsin. This essay is based on Van Swol, L. M. (2009). "Discussion and perception of information in groups and judge advisor systems." *Communication Monographs* 75, 99–120. *Communication Monographs* and *Communication Currents* are publications of the National Communication Association.

The discussion of *consensus* in Chapter 11, pp. 221–222, explains that when group members reluctantly give in to group pressures, they may achieve a *false consensus*. To what extent— if at all—would Van Swol's recommendation to assign members the roles of advisor and decision-maker help avoid this problem?

12 PLANNING YOUR

"**So**, you know, in case there's anybody who wandered in and doesn't know the back story, my dad always taught me that when there's an elephant in the room, introduce them. If you look at my CAT scans, there are approximately 10 tumors in my liver, and the doctors told me 3–6 months of good health left. That was a month ago, so you can do the math. I have some of the best doctors in the world. So that is what it is. We can't change it, and we just have to decide how we're going to respond to that. We cannot change the cards we are dealt, just how we play the hand. If I don't seem as depressed or morose as I should be, sorry to disappoint you.

[laughter from audience]

And I assure you I am not in denial."

—Randy Pausch

Effective presentations have enormous power. You do not have to be famous or well-known for your eloquence to be a great speaker. What matters is that you have a worthy message you want to share with others.

In September 2007, a year after being diagnosed with incurable pancreatic cancer, Randy Pausch, a computer science professor at Carnegie Mellon University, delivered a speech titled "Last Lecture." It was viewed by millions on the Internet and resulted in a book by the same name, raising both awareness and funding for pancreatic cancer research. A short excerpt from the beginning of his lecture appears to your left.[1]

Pausch goes on to talk about his childhood dreams and what it takes to achieve them. He concluded his lecture with words of wisdom about life and death. Randy Pausch died on July 25, 2008, at the age of 47.[2]

Regardless of whether you make a public speech to millions of people or present an oral report to 20 classmates, presentations are a fact of life. In this chapter and the four that follow, we review the theories, strategies, and critical skills needed to plan and deliver effective presentations.

PRESENTATION

the challenge
OF PRESENTATION SPEAKING

presentation speaking is the process of using verbal and nonverbal messages to generate meaning with audience members, who are usually present at the delivery of a presentation. In addition to sharing a message, an effective presentation lets your knowledge, talents, and opinions stand out. The person who speaks well and knows how to keep an audience interested is more likely to be noticed, believed, respected, and remembered. Two national surveys—one administered to working professionals and the other to public-speaking students from a variety of colleges and universities—asked respondents to identify the *most* important skills for effective presentations. Interestingly, as the chart on the right shows, of the top-ten skills, "keeping your audience interested" ranked number one in both groups.[3]

When preparing a presentation, the elements of *purpose, others, self,* and *context* are interconnected.

In Chapter 1, we introduced seven key elements of human communication: *self, others, purpose, context, content, structure,* and *expression.* These key elements and guiding principles also provide a framework for effective presentation speaking. The remainder of this chapter applies the first four principles to the task of presentation planning.

When preparing a presentation, the elements of *purpose, others, self,*

and *context* are interconnected. As you do your research, you may discover that your purpose will change because of audience expectations or the time limit you've been given. As you organize your content, you may find that you need more presentation aids (or none) to make your point. As you practice your presentation out loud, you may discover

that you are more comfortable using fewer notes or that you will need a lectern.

Presentation speaking The process of using verbal and nonverbal messages to generate meaning with audience members, who are usually present at the delivery of the presentation

---

TOP-RANKED SPEAKING SKILLS[4]

	WORKING PROFESSIONALS	COLLEGE STUDENTS
1	Keeping your audience interested	Keeping your audience interested
2	Beginning and ending your presentation	Organizing your presentation
3	Organizing your presentation	Deciding what to say; choosing a topic or approach to your presentation
4	Selecting ideas and information for your presentation	Using your voice effectively
5	Deciding what to say; choosing a topic or an approach	Selecting ideas and information for your presentation
6	Understanding and adapting to your audience	Determining the purpose of your presentation
7	Determining the purpose of your presentation	Overcoming/reducing nervousness/stage fright
8	Choosing appropriate and effective words	Understanding and adapting to your audience
9	Enhancing your credibility	Beginning and ending your presentation
10	Using your voice effectively	Choosing appropriate and effective words

DETERMINE YOUR purpose AND topic

determining your purpose is the most important decision you have to make as you begin the process of preparing a presentation. Your purpose answers the following question: What do I want my audience to know, think, feel, or do as a result of my presentation? Purpose focuses on *why*: Why am I speaking, and what outcome do I want?

Presentation Goals

Having a clear purpose does not guarantee you will achieve it. But without a purpose, it is difficult to decide what to say, what materials to include, and how to deliver your presentation. Begin your search for a purpose by deciding whether you want to inform, persuade, entertain, inspire, or combine all four goals.

Speaking to Inform An **informative presentation** is designed to instruct, enlighten, explain, describe, clarify, correct, remind, and/or demonstrate. Teachers spend most of their lecture time informing students. Sometimes, an informative presentation explains a complex concept, demonstrates a complicated process, or clears up misunderstandings. Informative presentations take the form of class reports,

committee updates, and formal lectures. (See Chapter 15, Speaking to Inform.)

Speaking to Persuade A **persuasive presentation** is designed to change or influence audience opinions and/or behavior. These changes may be directed toward an idea, a person, an object, or an action.

Advertisements persuade customers to buy products. Political candidates persuade audiences to elect them. Persuasive presentations occur in courtroom trials, religious services, college classrooms, around the dinner table, and in daily conversations. (See Chapter 16, Speaking to Persuade.)

Informative presentation A presentation designed to instruct, enlighten, explain, describe, clarify, correct, remind, and/or demonstrate

Persuasive presentation A presentation designed to change or to influence audience opinions and/or behavior

Entertainment speaking A presentation designed to amuse interest, divert, or "warm up" an audience

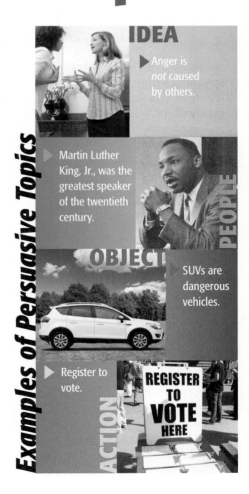

Examples of Persuasive Topics

IDEA
▶ Anger is *not* caused by others.

Martin Luther King, Jr., was the greatest speaker of the twentieth century.

PEOPLE

OBJECT

SUVs are dangerous vehicles.

▶ Register to vote.

ACTION

REGISTER TO VOTE HERE

Speaking to Entertain **Entertainment speaking** amuses, interests, diverts, or "warms up" an audience. Standup comedy is a form of entertainment speaking. After-dinner speakers amuse audiences too full to move or absorb serious ideas and complex information. At a retirement party, friends may "roast" a retiree. Humorous speaking requires more than funny content. It requires comic timing—knowing when and how forcefully to say a line, when to pause, and when to look at the audience for reactions. (For more details on using humor in a presentation, see Chapter 15.)

Humorous speaking requires more than funny content. It requires comic timing . . .

Speaking to Inspire **Inspirational speaking** brings like-minded people together, creates social unity, builds goodwill, or celebrates by arousing audience emotions. Inspirational speaking occurs in special contexts, takes many forms, and can tap a wide range of emotions by appealing to societal and cultural values. It is also more common than you think. Examples include sermons, motivational speeches, toasts at weddings and anniversaries, eulogies to honor the dead and comfort the grieving, commencement addresses, dedications, and tributes, as well as award presentations and acceptances. (For more on inspiring an audience, see Chapter 16.)

Inform, Persuade, Entertain, *and* Inspire Presentations that only inform, persuade, entertain, or inspire are rare. You can make your presentation more compelling by doing all four. A professor's lecture may inform students about intercultural communication theories as well as

persuade students that understanding cultural differences will improve communication in their daily lives and careers. To entertain them, the professor might use humorous examples of cultural misunderstandings, and stories about other cultures that may inspire students to travel abroad.

Choose an Appropriate Topic

Your topic is the subject matter of your presentation. A topic is often a simple word or phrase: *rap music*. Yet two presentations on the same topic can have very different purposes. Look at the differences between these two purpose statements:

> "I want my audience to understand and appreciate rap and hip-hop music."

"I want my audience to boycott recording companies that promote rap music with violent and offensive lyrics."

When looking for a good topic, ask yourself: (1) What interests me and takes up my free time? (2) What do I value? and (3) What's new and interesting on the Web?

What Interests You or Takes Up Your Free Time? If called upon to make a presentation and you find yourself stuck on a topic, consider any hobbies, special expertise, un-

---

Inspirational speaking A presentation that brings like-minded people together, creates social unity, builds goodwill, or celebrates by arousing audience emotions

---

Should You Speak or Write?

Before identifying your presentation's purpose and topic, you should make a more basic decision: Should you speak or should you write? Presentations may be more appropriate than written messages when

- the situation calls for a presentation: a wedding toast
- immediate action is needed: a justification for employee pay cuts
- the topic is controversial: condom distribution in high schools
- the audience may have questions: a news conference
- *you* will make a difference: a fundraiser for cancer research

Now look at the following situations. In your opinion, which form of communication is the best choice for sharing the following messages? Remember to apply the guidelines just listed and put a check mark in the appropriate column. Deciding whether to speak or write is not a minor decision. It influences whether and how well you achieve your communication purpose.[5]

Speak	Write	
———	———	Describe how to assemble a computer system.
———	———	Warn preteens about alcohol abuse.
———	———	Teach someone how to meditate.
———	———	Explain why you are the best applicant for a job.
———	———	Convince a company or interviewer to hire you.
———	———	Share a recipe for lemon poppy-seed pound cake.
———	———	Persuade nonvoting friends to vote.

Presentations that only inform, persuade, entertain, or inspire are rare. You can make your presentation more compelling by doing all four.

usual jobs, backgrounds, or causes you support. If you still have difficulty identifying a topic, think about how you might complete the following sentences:

- I've always wanted to know more about . . .
- If I could make one new law, I would . . .
- I've always wanted to . . .
- I spend a lot of my free time . . .

Or, create a chart in which you list potential topics under broad headings—sports, food, hobbies, places and destinations, famous people,

music, important events, personal goals, community issues, etc.

What Do You Value? Values are beliefs that guide your ideas about what is right or wrong, good or bad, just or unjust, and correct or incorrect. Values also trigger emotions and guide your actions.[6] If you examine the values that are most important to you, you may find a topic

> **Values** Beliefs that guide your ideas about what is right or wrong, good or bad, just or unjust, and correct or incorrect

Know Thy Self

Value + Issue = Topic

The Institute for Global Ethics identified eight universal values: love, truthfulness, fairness, freedom, unity, tolerance, responsibility, and respect for life.[7] Next to each value, we've listed a related issue. Fill in the blank with a presentation topic for this value and issue.

- *Love*. Marital infidelity. Presentation topic: _____
- *Truthfulness*. Plagiarism. Presentation topic: _____
- *Fairness*. Gender biases. Presentation topic: _____
- *Freedom*. Gun control. Presentation topic: _____
- *Unity*. Labor unions. Presentation topic: _____
- *Tolerance*. Hate speech. Presentation topic: _____
- *Responsibility*. Parental accountability. Presentation topic: _____
- *Respect for life*. Human cloning. Presentation topic: _____

that's right and proper for you and your audience.

Be cautious when you search your personal values for a topic; they may not align with those of your audience. For example, you may strongly support gun control, but audience members may consider gun ownership a basic freedom. Also, remember that cultures often differ in what they value. Although most Americans value individualism, other cultures may place greater value on community and group goals.

What's Interesting on the Web? The World Wide Web is a wonderful resource for finding interesting presentation topics. Major search engines have subject directories that suggest numerous topics, within which are dozens of subtopics. For example, the Health and Fitness directory on one site begins with Alternative Medicine and ends with Women's Health. The Disease directory begins with AIDS and ends with Thyroid Disease.

Narrow Your Topic

Make sure that you appropriately narrow or modify your topic to achieve your purpose and adapt to listeners' needs and interests. Narrowing a topic involves selecting the most important and interesting

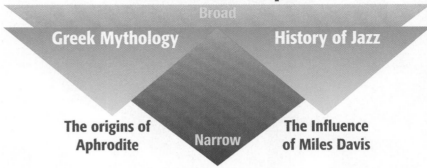

ideas and information for your presentation, rather than telling your audience everything you know about a topic.

Although you may be an expert on your topic, your audience may be hearing about it for the first time. Don't bury them under mounds of information. Ask yourself: If I only have time to tell them one thing about my topic, what would it be? Chances are that conveying a single important idea is enough to achieve your purpose.

Develop a Purpose Statement

When you know *why* you are speaking (your purpose) and *what* you are speaking about (your topic), develop a clear **purpose statement**, a spe-

A purpose statement guides how you research, organize, and present your message.

cific, achievable, and relevant sentence that identifies the purpose and main ideas of your presentation. It is not enough to say, "My purpose is to tell my audience about my job as a phone solicitor." This statement is too general and probably an impossible goal to achieve in a time-limited presentation. Instead, your purpose statement must convey the specific focus of your presentation, such as "I want my audience to recognize two common strategies used by effective phone solicitors to overcome listener objections."

A purpose statement is similar to a writer's thesis statement, which identifies the main idea you want to communicate to your reader. Regardless of whether you are speaking or writing, a purpose statement guides how you research, organize, and present your message.

> **Purpose statement** A specific, achievable, and relevant sentence that identifies the purpose and main ideas of your presentation

Major search engines such as Google offer a rich source of presentation topics.

Characteristics of an Effective Purpose Statement

	YES	NO
SPECIFIC Narrows a topic to content appropriate for the purpose and audience.	I want my audience to understand how to use the government's new food group recommendations as a diet guide.	The benefits of good health.
ACHIEVABLE Purpose can be achieved in the given time limit.	There are two preferred treatments for mental depression.	You should learn all the causes, symptoms, treatments, and preventions of mental depression.
RELEVANT Topic should be related to audience needs and interests.	Next time you witness an accident, you'll know what to do.	Next time you encounter an exotic Australian tree toad, you'll appreciate its morphology.

analyze AND adapt
TO YOUR AUDIENCE

audience analysis refers to your ability to understand, respect, and adapt to audience members before and during a presentation. It involves researching your audience, interpreting those findings, and, as a result, selecting appropriate strategies to achieve your purpose. The examples in your presentation, the words you choose, and even your delivery style should be adapted to your audience's interests and needs.

Know Your Audience

Knowing your audience means asking questions about audience members' values, backgrounds, and needs, and what they may already know about your topic. The answers to these questions will also

> **The examples in your presentation, the words you choose, and even your delivery style should be adapted to your audience's interests and needs.**

help you understand your audience, and help you to decide what to include in your presentation.

Who Are They? Gather as much general **demographic information** (audience characteristics) as you can about the people who will be watching and listening to you. If the audience is composed of a particular group or is meeting for a special reason, gather more specific demographic information as well. (See Figure 12.1.)

Avoid "one-size-fits-all" conclusions about audience members based on visible or obvious characteristics such as age, race, gender, occupation, nationality, or religion. As you know from Chapter 3, Understanding Others, these oversimplified conclusions are stereotypes that can distort your perceptions. In addition, remember that *your* age, nationality, race, gender, educational level, and socioeconomic background may be just as critical in determining how well an audience listens to you.

Why Are They Here? Audiences attend presentations for many reasons. They may need to satisfy a class requirement or have nothing

better to do. They also may attend presentations because they are interested in the speaker, for example, a candidate running for local office or a famous writer giving a public talk.

Audience members who are interested in your topic or who stand to benefit from attending a presentation will be different from those who don't know why they are there or who are required to attend. Each type of audience presents its own unique challenges. A highly interested and well-informed audience demands a compelling, knowledgeable, well-prepared speaker. An audience required or reluctant to attend may be pleasantly surprised

---

Audience analysis The ability to understand, respect, and adapt to audience members before and during a presentation
Demographic information Information about audience characteristics such as age, gender, marital status, race, religion, place of residence, ethnicity, occupation, education, and income

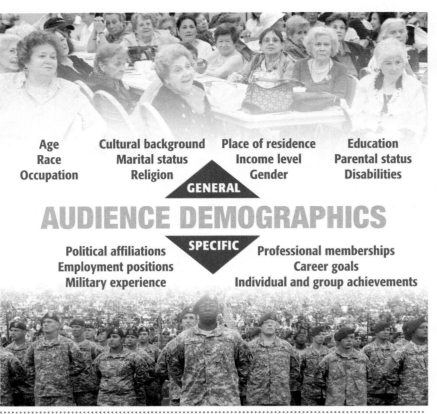

Age   Cultural background   Place of residence   Education
Race   Marital status   Income level   Parental status
Occupation   Religion   Gender   Disabilities

GENERAL

AUDIENCE DEMOGRAPHICS

SPECIFIC

Political affiliations   Professional memberships
Employment positions   Career goals
Military experience   Individual and group achievements

Figure 12.1   What do you know about your audience?

There can be as many opinions in your audience as there are people.

and influenced by a dynamic speaker who gives them a good reason to listen. Entire audiences rarely fit into one type or group. Your audience may include people representing many different reasons for attending.

What Do They Know? Almost nothing is more boring to an audience than hearing a speaker talk about a subject they know well or listening to a speaker talk over their heads. To ensure that your presentation matches your audience's level of understanding about the topic, ask questions to assess their level of knowledge: How much do they know about this topic? How much

Know Thy Self

Do You Honor the Audience's Bill of Rights?

The **7** Key Elements and Guiding Principles of Effective Communication

In his book, *Say It with Presentations*, Gene Zelazny proposes an Audience's Bill of Rights.[8] Here we present a modified version of Zelazny's rights that align with the seven key elements of effective communication. Review each of the audience's rights listed in the left-hand column. In the right-hand column, describe a speaking strategy you would use to ensure this right.

Audience Rights	Speaker Strategies
1. *Self*. The right to receive value for the time you spend attending a presentation.	I would _____
2. *Others*. The right to be spoken to with respect for your experience, intelligence, knowledge, and culture; the right to ask questions and expect answers.	I would _____
3. *Purpose*. The right to know what the speaker wants you to do or think as a result of a presentation.	I would _____
4. *Context*. The right to have a presentation start and stop on time and to know, in advance, how much time it will take.	I would _____
5. *Content*. The right to know the speaker's position, the rationale for that position, and the evidence that supports the position; the right to have complex charts explained.	I would _____
6. *Structure*. The right to know where the speaker is going and how the presentation will progress.	I would _____
7. *Expression*. The right to hear and see a speaker from anywhere in a room; the right to be able to read every word on every visual no matter where you sit.	I would _____

background material should I cover? Will they understand topic-related terms or jargon?

What Are Their Interests? Find out if audience members have interests that match your purpose and topic. Consider two types of interests: self-centered interests and topic-centered interests.

Self-centered interests are aroused when a presentation can result in personal gain. Some audience members are enthralled by a speaker who teaches them how to earn or save money. Others will be riveted by ways to improve their appearance or health. In all these cases, the listener stands to gain something as a result of the presentation and its outcome.

Audiences also have **topic-centered interests**—subjects they enjoy hearing and learning about. Topic-centered interests include hobbies, favorite sports or pastimes, or subjects loaded with intrigue and mystery. However, topic-centered interests tend to be personal. A detailed description of a Civil War battle may captivate Civil War history buffs but bore the other audience members. Whether self-centered or topic-centered, listener interests have a significant effect on how well an audience pays attention to you and your message.[9]

What Are Their Attitudes? When assessing **audience attitudes**, you are asking whether they agree or disagree with you as well as how strongly they agree and disagree. There can be as many opinions in your audience as there are people. Some audience members will already agree with you, others will disagree no matter what you say, and others will be undecided or have no opinion.

Adapt to Your Audience

Everything you learn about your audience tells you something about how to prepare and deliver your presentation. Depending on the amount of audience research and analysis you do, you can adapt your presentation to your audience as you prepare it. In other cases, you may use audience feedback to modify your presentation as you speak.

Modifying Your Purpose to Suit the Audience

Preliminary Purpose. To describe journalism in the 21st century.

Who Are They? They are ten women and four men; some are 18–20 years old; others appear to be in their late 30s, early 40s.

Why Are They Here? They are students in an intro to mass communication course.

What Do They Know? They already know that the face of journalism is changing—that many, if not most, people get their news from online sources; they know that print newspapers are in financial trouble.

What Are Their Interests? Some are more interested in public relations; others want to know about specific types of journalism; many are concerned about future job opportunities.

What Are Their Attitudes? Some think that as long as they are armed with a video phone, Internet access, and can write, anyone can become a journalist.

Revised Purpose. To explain recent trends in journalism—backpack journalism and citizen journalism—and their uncertain potential as career paths.

Pre-presentation Adaptation After researching and analyzing information about your audience's characteristics and attitudes, go back to your purpose statement and apply what you've learned. Answers to the five basic audience questions shown above can help you modify your preliminary purpose into one that better suits your audience.

Self-centered interests
Aroused when a presentation can result in personal gain
Topic-centered interests
Subjects audience members enjoy hearing and learning about
Audience attitudes A measure of whether audience members agree or disagree with a speaker's purpose statement as well as how strongly they agree or disagree

Note the diversity of the audience in this photo. How can this park ranger adapt to her audience?

Mid-presentation Adaptation No matter how well you prepare for an audience, you must prepare for the unexpected. What if audience members seem restless or hostile? How can you adjust? What if you must shorten your 20-minute presentation to 10 minutes to accommodate another speaker?

Adapting to your audience *during* a presentation requires you to do three things at once: deliver your presentation, correctly interpret audience feedback as you speak, and successfully modify your message. Interpreting audience responses requires that you look at your audience members, read their nonverbal signals, and sense their moods. If audience feedback suggests that you're not getting through, don't be afraid to stop and ask comprehension questions such as, "Would you like more detail on this point before I go on to the next one?"

Think about adjusting your presentation in the same way you adjust your conversation with a friend. If your friend looks confused, you might ask what's wrong. If your friend interrupts with a question, you probably will answer it or ask if

you can finish your thought before answering. If your friend tells you that he has a pressing appointment, you are likely to shorten what you have to say. The same adaptations work just as well when speaking to an audience.

Adapt to Cultural Differences

Respecting and adapting to a diverse audience begins with understanding the nature and characteristics of various cultures. Two of the cultural dimensions we examined in Chapter 3, Understanding Others, stand out as especially critical for presentations: power distance and individualism/collectivism.

Power Distance As we indicated in Chapter 3, *power distance* refers to varying levels of equality and status among the members of a culture. In the United States, authority figures may play down status differences. U.S. presidents are often photographed wearing casual clothes, corporate executives may promote an open-door policy, and college freshmen and full professors may interact on a first-name basis.

If most audience members represent a low-power-distance culture, encourage them to challenge authority and make independent decisions. However, if most embrace a high-power-distance perspective *and* if you also command authority and influence, you can tell them exactly what you want them to do—and expect compliance.

Individualism and Collectivism When speaking to individualistic audiences (e.g., listeners from the United States, Great Britain, and Australia), you can appeal to their sense of adventure, their desire to achieve personal goals, and their defense of individual rights. When speaking to a collectivist audience (e.g., listeners from most Asian and Latin-American countries), demonstrate how a particular course of action will benefit their company, family, or community. If you are an individualistic American who feels comfortable drawing attention to your own or your organization's accomplishments, you may find a collectivist audience disturbed by your seeming arrogance and lack of concern for others.

communication&culture

ADAPT TO NONNATIVE SPEAKERS OF ENGLISH

Have you studied a foreign language in school? If so, what happens when you listen to a native speaker of that language? Do you understand every word? Probably not. Such an experience can be difficult and frustrating. Imagine what it must be like for a nonnative speaker of English to understand a presentation in English. The following guidelines are derived from general intercultural research and from observations of international audiences, both at home and abroad.[10]

• *Speak slowly and clearly.* Many nonnative speakers of English need more time because they translate your words into their own language as you speak. But don't shout at them; they are not hearing-impaired.

• *Use visual aids.* Most nonnative speakers of English are better readers than listeners. Use slides or provide handouts for

important information. Give the audience time to read and take notes.

• *Be more formal.* In general, use a more formal style and dress professionally when speaking to international audiences.

• *Adapt to contextual perspectives.* If you are addressing an audience from a high-context culture, be less direct. Let them draw their own conclusions. Give them time to get to know and trust you.

• *Avoid humor and clichés.* Humor rarely translates into another language and can backfire if misunderstood. Avoid clichés—overused expressions familiar to a particular culture. Will a nonnative speaker of English understand "Cool as a cucumber" or "Shop 'til you drop"?

ENHANCE your credibility

Speaker credibility represents the extent to which an audience believes a speaker and the speaker's message. The dictionary defines credibility as the "quality, capability, or power to elicit belief."[11] In other words, the more credible you are in the eyes of your audience, the more likely it is that you will achieve the purpose of your presentation. If your audience rates you as highly credible, they may excuse poor de-

The more credible you are in the eyes of your audience, the more likely it is that you will achieve the purpose of your presentation.

livery. They are so ready to believe you that the presentation doesn't have to be perfect.[12]

Components of Speaker Credibility

Researchers identify three major components of speaker credibility that have a strong impact on the believability of a speaker: character, competence, and charisma.[13] The speaker credibility chart on the next page summarizes the distinct characteristics that personify each of these three components.

Character Of the three components of speaker credibility, **character**—a speaker's perceived

honesty and good will—may be the most important. A speaker of good

Speaker credibility The characteristics of a speaker that determine whether the audience believes the speaker and the message

Character A component of speaker credibility that relates to a speaker's perceived honesty and good will

Rhetoric According to Aristotle, the ability to discover the available means of persuasion appropriate for a particular audience in a particular circumstance

Aristotle's Ethos

THINK ABOUT THEORY

The concept of speaker credibility is more than 2,000 years old. Aristotle's *Rhetoric*, written during the late fourth century B.C., established many of the public-speaking strategies we use today. His definition of **rhetoric** as the ability to discover "in the particular case what are the available means of persuasion"[14] focuses on strategies for selecting the most appropriate persuasive arguments for a particular audience in a particular circumstance. His division of proof into logical arguments (*logos*), emotional arguments (*pathos*), and arguments based on speaker credibility (*ethos*) remains a basic model for teaching the principles of persuasive speaking.

Here we focus on Aristotle's *ethos*, a Greek word meaning *character*. "The character [ethos] of the speaker is a cause of persuasion when the speech is so uttered as to make him worthy of belief. . . . His character [ethos] is the most potent of all the means to persuasion."[15] Aristotle's concept of ethos evolved into what we now call *speaker credibility*.

Aristotle confines his discussion of ethos to what a speaker does *during* a speech because what people think of a speaker *before* a speech is not related to the three modes of persuasion.[16] Later in our discussion of speaker credibility, we examine the

ways in which an audience's previous knowledge and beliefs about a speaker affect speaker credibility. At the same time, we want to emphasize that a speaker's ethos varies with audiences and varies over time. "That is to say, a speaker may have a positive ethos with one set of listeners and a negative ethos with another; a speaker who is highly regarded at one time may be considered a has-been ten years later."[17] For example, when campaigning for public office, Republican candidates usually have higher ethos when speaking to conservative audiences than to liberal audiences.

character is seen as a good person—trustworthy, sincere, and fair. Is your evidence valid, the reservations acknowledged, and the claims warranted? Are you doing what is right and ethical? If an audience doesn't trust you, it won't matter if you are an expert speaker or an electrifying performer.

Competence **Competence** refers to a speaker's perceived expertise and abilities. Proving that you are competent can be as simple as mentioning your credentials and experience. An audience is unlikely to question a recognized brain surgeon, a professional baseball player, or famous fashion designer, as long as they stick to brain surgery, baseball, and fashion, respectively. An auto mechanic, a waitress, a parent of six children, a nurse, and a government employee can all be experts in their own right. Such speakers rely on their life experiences and opinions to demonstrate competence.

But what happens when you are not an expert? How can you demonstrate that you know what you're talking about? The answer lies in one word: *research*. Thorough research arms you with enough up-to-date content to become a well-informed speaker. If you don't have firsthand experience or cannot claim to be an expert, let your audience know how well-prepared you are: "I conducted a phone survey of more than 30 individuals and found . . ." or "After reviewing the top ten textbooks on this subject, I was surprised that only one author addresses . . ."

Charisma Your perceived level of energy, enthusiasm, vigor, and commitment reflects your **charisma**. A speaker with charisma is seen as dynamic, forceful, powerful, assertive, and intense. President Barack Obama is a charismatic speaker who motivates and energizes audiences. John F. Kennedy and Senator Barbara Jordan were and Supreme Court Justice Sonia Sotomayor is as well. Charisma has more to do with how you deliver a presentation than with what you have to say; in that regard, Adolf Hitler was also a charismatic speaker.

Speakers with strong and expressive voices are seen as more charismatic than speakers with hesitant or unexpressive voices. Speakers who gesture naturally and move gracefully are viewed as more charismatic than those who look uncomfortable and awkward in front of an audience. Speakers who look their audiences in the eye are thought of as more charismatic than those who avoid eye contact with members of the audience. Practicing and developing your performance skills enhances your charisma in the same way that preparation helps you to be seen as a competent speaker.

Developing Speaker Credibility

Credibility does not exist in an absolute sense; it is solely based on the attitudes and perceptions of the audience. Thus, even if you are the world's greatest expert on your topic and deliver your presentation with skill, the ultimate decision about your credibility lies with your audience. Credibility is "like the process of getting a grade in school. Only the teacher (or audience) can assign the grade to the student (or speaker), but the student can do all sorts of things—turn in homework, prepare for class, follow the rules—to influence what grade is assigned."[18] So

> **Charisma has more to do with how you deliver a presentation than with what you have to say.**

Competence A component of speaker credibility that relates to the speaker's perceived expertise and abilities

Charisma A component of speaker credibility that relates to the speaker's perceived level of energy, enthusiasm, vigor, and/or commitment

SPEAKER CREDIBILITY

Good Character	Competent	Charismatic
Honest	Experienced	Active
Kind	Well-prepared	Enthusiastic
Friendly	Qualified	Energetic
Fair	Up-to-date	Confident
Respectful	Informed	Stimulating
Caring	Intelligent	Dynamic

What makes Holocaust survivor and Nobel Peace Prize winner Elie Wiesel a credible speaker when speaking out against hatred, racism, and genocide?

what can you do to influence your audience's opinion of you and your presentation? Find out what you have to offer to your audience, prepare an interesting presentation, and show your audience why you're uniquely qualified to deliver it. In other words, do a personal inventory and toot your own horn.

Do a Personal Inventory All of us can do something that sets us apart from most other people. It's just a matter of discovering what that something is. A personal inventory is a way of identifying the unique gifts and talents that contribute to your

Credibility does not exist in an absolute sense; it is solely based on the attitudes and perceptions of the audience.

credibility. Begin your self-inventory by answering three questions: (1) What are my experiences? (2) What are my achievements? and (3) What are my skills and traits?

An experience that seems routine to you may be a new experience for your listeners. You don't have to land on the moon to achieve something important. Consider how you might answer the following questions: Have you lived or worked in another town, city, state, or country? Do you have or have you had an unusual job? What experiences have had a big impact on your life (childbirth, a visit to a foreign country, combat experience)? What can you do that most people cannot (play the cello, write a song or short story, speak Turkish)? What awards or contests have you won (an award for public service, a cooking contest, an athletic championship)?

Toot Your Own Horn A presentation lets you show an audience that your ideas and opinions are based on more than good preparation. They are based on personal experiences, accomplishments, and special skills. There is nothing wrong with using words such as *I* and *my* and *me* if they are appropriate—overuse, however, can sound boastful. For example, at an honors awards ceremony for students, one faculty member talked more about herself than about the student who was being honored: "As chairman of the department and an expert in this field of study, I decided . . ."; "As outgoing president of the association, I was the first person to . . ." By using the awards presentation to spotlight herself, the speaker undermined her credibility.

If you're an expert, find a way to tell the audience: "In my ten years of

leading . . . " or "When my partner and I won the state's debate championship . . . ." In neither case would you be exaggerating or boasting. Rather, you would be explaining how and why you know what you're talking about.

The Ethical Speaker

The words *ethos* and *ethics* come from the Greek word meaning *character*. As we indicated in our discussion of character, the apparent "goodness" of a speaker is important in determining whether an audience believes a speaker. Audiences are also more likely to believe you if they see you as an ethical speaker. *Ethos* and *ethics*, however, are not the same. **Ethos**, or speaker credibility, relies on the perceived character, competence, and charisma of the speaker. The audience determines a speaker's ethos, but a speaker's beliefs about what is right or wrong, moral or immoral, good or bad determine her or his *ethics* (see this illustrated on the next page). Ethics is a set of personal principles of right conduct, a system of moral values.[19] Only you can determine how ethical you are.

The Key Elements of Ethical Speaking Ethical decisions about your presentation should be based on all seven key elements of human communication. Start with considering your *self* and remember that ethical speakers are liked and respected by their audiences because they are honest, fair, caring, informed, and justifiably confident.

The 7 Key Elements and Guiding Principles of Effective Communication

Do not use what you know about the audience, the occasion, the setting, or the time limits to take unfair advantage of the audience or to achieve unethical goals. If you accomplish your purpose, make sure that both you and the audience benefit from it. Always check that

---

Ethos Speaker credibility that relies on the perceived competence, character, and charisma of a speaker

your content and your sources of information are truthful and qualified. Furthermore, if you present an argument, acknowledge both sides—you can do this without resorting to fake emotions as a way of gaining sympathy or inciting an audience with your content.

Avoiding Plagiarism in Your Presentation Any discussion of a speaker's ethics must consider the perils of plagiarism. The word **plagiarism** comes from the Latin, *plagium*, which means "kidnapping." Thus, when you plagiarize, you are stealing or kidnapping something that belongs to someone else. Simply put, if you include a quotation or idea from another source and pretend it's your idea and words, you are plagiarizing. Unfortunately, some speakers believe that plagiarism rules don't apply to them. Others think they can get away with it. Still others plagiarize without knowing they are doing it. Ignorance, however, is no excuse.

In some cases, using certain popular phrases that may not be your own is allowable because everyone is fa-

Plagiarism is not just unethical; it is illegal.

ETHOS
determined by audience

ETHICS
determined by speaker

miliar with them. For instance, anyone who's seen the film *The Wizard of Oz* knows that "There's no place like home," is the magic phrase Dorothy recites to get home to Kansas. Making an allusion to a famous quotation or idea is not plagiarism as long as the phrase or idea

is well-known and is used to inspire or interest audience members.[20]

The Ethical Audience

Ethical audience members listen for ideas and information with open minds. They withhold evaluation until they comprehend what a speaker means. Ethical audiences are active listeners; they listen to understand, to empathize, to analyze, and to appreciate. They think critically about a speaker's message. Unfortunately, some audience members may lack these skills. Even worse, they may not listen because they have decided, even before the presentation begins, that they don't like the message or the speaker.

While the audience has the final say, they also have an ethical responsibility to do unto the speaker as they would have the speaker do unto them. An audience with open, unprejudiced minds is essential for a genuine transaction to occur between speakers and listeners.

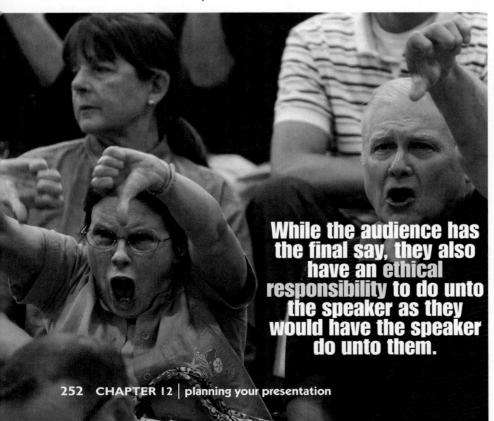

While the audience has the final say, they also have an ethical responsibility to do unto the speaker as they would have the speaker do unto them.

Plagiarism Using or passing off the ideas or writing of another person as your own

Avoid the Perils of Plagiarism

The key to avoiding plagiarism and its consequences is to identify the sources of your information in your presentation. Changing a few words of someone else's work is not enough to avoid plagiarism. If they're not your original ideas, and most of the words are not yours, you are ethically obligated to tell your audience who wrote or said them and where they came from. The bottom line is this: Plagiarism is not just unethical; it is illegal. The following guidelines are criteria for avoiding plagiarism:

- If you include an identifiable phrase or an idea that appears in someone else's work, always acknowledge and document your source orally.

- Do not use someone else's sequence of ideas and organization without acknowledging and citing the similarities in structure.

- Tell an audience exactly when you are citing someone else's exact words or ideas in your presentation.

- Never buy or use someone else's speech or writing and claim it as your own work.

adapt
TO THE CONTEXT

Whether you are preparing a presentation for a public speaking course or formal banquet, a prayer meeting or a retirement party, take time to analyze the context of the situation.

Analyze and Adapt to the Logistics

Logistics refers to the strategic planning and adapting a presentation to the audience size, the physical location, the equipment, and the amount of time you have.[21]

Audience Size Knowing the size of your audience helps you choose appropriate audio and visual aids. For example, if there are hundreds of people in your audience, plan to use a microphone and make sure it's supported by a good sound system. If you expect five hundred people in your audience, projecting images onto a large screen is more effective than using a small chart or demonstrating a detailed procedure.

Facilities Make sure you know as much as you can about where you will be speaking. Will audience members be seated in a theater-style auditorium, around a long conference table, or at round tables scattered throughout a seminar room? If you are in an auditorium that seats eight hundred people and you only expect one hundred listeners to attend, consider closing off the balcony or side sections so that the audience will be seated in front of you.

Equipment Computer-generated slide presentations are the norm in many speaking situations. Wireless microphones and sophisticated sound systems enable speakers to address large audiences with ease. Make sure you know in advance what is—and what isn't—available at the location where you will be speaking.

Logistics The strategic planning, arranging, and use of people, facilities, time, and materials relevant to a presentation

---

ASSESS

the Facilities

- What is the size, shape, and decor of the room?
- Does the room have good ventilation, comfortable seating, distracting sights or sounds?
- What are the seating arrangements (rows, tables)?
- What kind of lighting will there be? Can it be adjusted for the presentation?
- Will you speak from a stage or platform? Will you have a lectern and a table for materials or equipment?
- Is there a good sound system?

the Equipment

- What equipment, if any, do you need to be seen and/or heard?
- What equipment, if any, do you need for your audio or visual aids?
- Is there a lectern (adjustable, with a built-in light or microphone, space enough to hold your notes)?
- Are there any special arrangements you need to make (a timer, water, special lighting, wireless microphone, a media technician)?

Arrive at least 45 minutes before you speak. Check that everything you need is in the room, that the equipment works, and that you know how to dim or brighten the lights if needed. Allow enough time to find equipment if something is missing or to make last-minute changes.

Time The most important thing to consider about time is how long you are *scheduled* to speak. Plan your presentation so that it fits well within your time limit. Put a watch next to you when you speak or ask someone to give you a signal when it's time to begin your conclusion. And when that signal comes, don't ignore it, even if it means skipping major sections of your presentation. Audiences rarely like, appreciate, or return to hear a long-winded speaker.

Consider the following questions in relationship to your time limit: At what hour will I be speaking? For how long am I scheduled to speak? What comes before or after my presentation (other speakers, lunch, entertainment, a question-and-answer session)? Is there anything significant about the date or time of my presentation (birthday, holiday, anniversary)?

The Occasion

What's the occasion of your presentation? Will you be speaking at a celebration? Or is the occasion an oral class assignment, a memorial service, a convention keynote address, or testimony before a government agency? Make sure that your presentation suits the **occasion**—the reason an audience has assembled at a particular place and time. As is the case with setting, there are important questions to respond to as you prepare a presentation.

What Is Your Relationship to the Occasion?

When you are invited to make a presentation, ask yourself: Why have *I* been invited to speak to *this* audience in *this* place on *this* occasion? Speakers are not picked randomly. Make sure you understand how you are personally connected to the occasion.

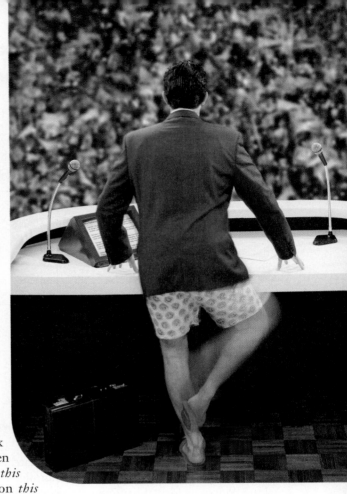

Occasion The reason an audience assembles at a particular place and time

---

How Long *Should* You Speak?

We often hear two questions about the time limit for a presentation: "What if I'm not given a time limit?" and "What if I have something *really* important to say and I have to talk longer?"

If you are not given a time limit, we recommend nothing longer than 20 minutes. Peggy Noonan, former President Reagan's speechwriter, recommends a 20-minute limit.[22] Granville Toogood, author of *The Articulate Executive*, reports the results of a study conducted by the U.S. Navy

in which they tried to determine how long people can listen and retain information. The answer: 18 minutes.[23]

Of course, there are times when the circumstances or content requires that you speak longer than 20 minutes. In such cases, you have several options. You can cover the basics in 20 minutes and then set aside time for a question-and-answer session. You can use presentation aids or a video to break up your talk. Consider inserting short personal stories or anecdotes to help drive home your point and give the audience a pleasant respite.[24] If you plan to speak for more than 20 minutes, remember this saying: Change the medium to break the tedium.

Finally, don't fall into the ego trap of thinking that what you have to say is *so* important that it deserves more time. Your audience may not share this belief—no matter how long you take to convince them. Demonstrate respect for your audience's time and they will appreciate your self-discipline and kind consideration.

If you plan to speak for more than 20 minutes . . .

Change the medium to break the tedium.

Remember, your presentation should be the center of an audience's attention. If something in your appearance could distract listeners, FIX IT.

What Does the Audience Expect?

The nature of an occasion creates audience expectations about the way a presentation will be prepared and delivered. Business audiences may expect well-qualified speakers to pepper their presentations with sophisticated, computer-generated graphics. Audiences at political events are accustomed to the sound bite on television and expect to hear short, crisp phrases. Audiences expect an uplifting tone at a graduation ceremony and a more raucous tone at a pep rally. At a funeral, a eulogy may be touching or funny, but it's almost always very respectful and short. Do your best to match your speaking style and content to audience expectations.

What Should You Wear?

Long before an audience hears what you say, they will see you, so wear something that matches the purpose and tone of your presentation. Your clothes don't have to be expensive or make a fashion statement. What matters is that they are appropriate for the situation.

Common sense dictates our number-one piece of advice: Wear comfortable clothes. Presentations are stressful enough without worrying about your clothing. When selecting appropriate clothes for a presentation, dress as key members of your audience would.

Nothing on your body (clothes, grooming, accessories) should draw attention to itself. Clanging bracelets or earrings, or ties featuring big patterns or cartoon characters, may not be appropriate. Take items out of your pockets, whether they're pens in your shirt pocket or the change and keys in your pants pockets. Remember, your presentation should be the center of an audience's attention. If something in your appearance could distract your listeners, fix it.

Communication ASSESSMENT

What's Your Preparation Plan?

Before you determine the content and structure of your message or practice your delivery, make sure you have made appropriate decisions about the four elements involved in presentation planning: *self, others, purpose,* and *context.* The following checklist will help determine whether you are ready to take the next steps in preparing your presentation.

Self
_____ 1. I have assessed my potential credibility by identifying my strengths, talents, achievements, and positive character traits.
_____ 2. I will demonstrate my competence and good character.
_____ 3. I have made ethical decisions about self, others, purpose, context, content, structure, and expression.

Others
_____ 1. I have researched, analyzed, and planned ways of adapting to audience characteristics, knowledge, and interests.
_____ 2. I have researched, analyzed, and planned ways of adapting to audience attitudes.
_____ 3. I have researched, analyzed, and planned ways of adapting to cultural differences in my audience.

Purpose
_____ 1. I have decided whether my purpose will inform, persuade, entertain, and/or inspire.
_____ 2. I have developed a specific, achievable, and relevant purpose statement.
_____ 3. My topic area reflects my interests, values, and/or knowledge.

Context
_____ 1. I have researched, analyzed, and planned ways of adapting to the logistics of the presentation (audience size, facilities, equipment, time).
_____ 2. I have researched, analyzed, and planned ways of adapting to the psychosocial context and occasion.
_____ 3. I have researched, analyzed, and planned ways of adapting to the cultural context.

Summary

How can you become a more effective speaker?

- Many speakers identify "keeping your audience interested" as the *most* important speaking skill.
- Knowledgeable decisions about your self, others, purpose, and context should be made *before* preparing the content, structure, and expression of a presentation.

How does the purpose and topic of a presentation affect the planning process?

- Determining the purpose of a presentation helps you decide what you want your audience to know, think, feel, or do.
- Decide whether you want to inform, persuade, entertain, inspire, or a combination of all four goals in your presentation.
- When choosing a presentation topic that suits you and your purpose, consider your interests, values, knowledge, and what's interesting on the Web.
- Develop a specific, achievable, and relevant purpose statement to guide your preparation and narrow your topic appropriately.

What strategies and skills can help you analyze and adapt to your audience?

- Audience analysis requires that you understand, respect, and adapt to listeners before and during a presentation.
- Answer the following questions about your audience: (1) Who are they? (2) Why are they here? (3) What do they know? (4) What are their interests? and (5) What are their attitudes?
- Adapt your presentation to what you know about your audience as you prepare it and use audience feedback to modify your presentation as you speak.
- As a speaker, honor the Audience's Bill of Rights. As an audience member, defend and stand up for your rights.

How does speaker credibility affect the success of a presentation?

- Speaker credibility (Aristotle's *ethos*) represents the extent to which an audience believes you and your message.
- The three major components of speaker credibility are character, competence, and charisma.
- Credibility is solely based on the attitudes and perceptions of the audience.
- You can improve your credibility by doing a personal inventory and tooting your own horn.
- Whereas the *audience* determines your credibility (*ethos*), *you* determine your ethics—your beliefs about what is right or wrong, moral or immoral, good or bad.

- The key to avoiding plagiarism and its consequences is to identify the sources of your information in your presentation.

What strategies and skills can help you adapt to the context of a presentation?

- Adapt to the logistics of a presentation by analyzing and adjusting to the audience's size, the facilities, the equipment, and the time (time of day and length) of the presentation.
- Adapt to the occasion of the presentation by clarifying your relationship to the situation and by identifying and adapting to audience expectations.
- Make sure you dress comfortably and appropriately for the logistics and occasion of a presentation.

the **THINK**SPOT
www.thethinkspot.com

TEST your knowledge

1. Which of the following answers was ranked first in a survey of college students that asked them to identify the speaking skills that were most important for improving their presentations?
   a. selecting good ideas and information
   b. keeping your audience interested
   c. deciding what to say; choosing a good topic
   d. organizing a presentation
   e. using your voice effectively

2. All of the following guiding principles constitute one of four essential steps in the presentation planning process *except*:
   a. purpose
   b. others
   c. self
   d. context
   e. structure

3. Which type of presentation seeks to instruct, enlighten, explain, describe, and/or demonstrate?
   a. informative presentation
   b. persuasive presentation
   c. entertainment presentation
   d. inspirational presentation
   e. motivational presentation

4. The Institute for Global Ethics identified eight universal values. Which value would be addressed in a presentation of avoiding the pitfalls of plagiarism?
   a. freedom
   b. unity
   c. love
   d. truthfulness
   e. tolerance

5. Which of the five basic questions you should ask about your audience is answered in this response: "My audience wants to hear *me* speak because of my work in Darfur on behalf of Doctors without Borders"?
   a. Who are they?
   b. Why are they here?
   c. What do they know?
   d. What are their interests?
   e. What are their attitudes?

6. Which key element of human communication is aligned with "The right to have a presentation start and stop on time and to know, in advance, how much time it will take," in the Audience's Bill of Rights?
   a. Purpose
   b. Others
   c. Content
   d. Structure
   e. Context

7. Which component of speaker credibility (*ethos*) is reflected in a speaker's level of energy, enthusiasm, vigor, and commitment?
   a. character
   b. charity
   c. competence
   d. charisma
   e. concern

8. If you wonder "Should I include both sides of an argument in a presentation or present only one side, even if the opposing view is reasonable and well-supported?" you are asking an ethical question about
   a. self.
   b. others.
   c. content.
   d. structure.
   e. expression.

9. Logistical questions about a presentation's context focus on
   a. audience size.
   b. facilities.
   c. equipment.
   d. time.
   e. all of the above.

10. Your textbook advises you to remember this saying: "Change the medium to break the tedium." Under what circumstances should you apply this advice?
    a. if the audience knows nothing about your topic
    b. if your purpose is not clear
    c. if you plan to speak more than 20 minutes
    d. if there are more than 50 people in the audience
    e. if you do not have a lectern on which to put your notes

Answers: 1-b; 2-e; 3-a; 4-d; 5-b; 6-e; 7-d; 8-c; 9-e; 10-c

THINK COMMUNICATION

HARVARD MANAGEMENT COMMUNICATION LETTER: A NEWSLETTER FROM HARVARD BUSINESS SCHOOL PUBLISHING

Volume 2, Issue 6 - June 1999

Coping with Stagefright: How to Turn Terror into Dynamic Speaking

You're about to make an important presentation. People are streaming into the room. Your boss is sitting up front. Important clients are sitting in the second row. Your boss stands to introduce you and you walk toward the stage.

As you approach the front of the room your confidence wanes. Your stomach starts doing somersaults, your palms are sweating, and your mouth feels parched. You pick up your notes and your hands are shaking. Thank goodness, you say to yourself, for the lectern. As you start to speak you hear your voice quiver and you feel your skin beginning to blush.

Welcome to the world of stagefright!

You are not alone if you have had this experience. Almost everyone has. Even people who regularly appear in front of large audiences experience stagefright. The great American actress Helen Hayes was known for throwing up in her dressing room before every single performance during a career of more than 50 years. Luckily, researchers in communication and psychology have identified several strategies that can help you overcome your nervousness.

Know Your Audience and Setting

Successful speakers . . . acquaint themselves with both the audience and the setting before making a presentation. Talk to a few people who will be in the audience. Ask who else will be attending and what interests them. Find out what audience members know about the topic. . . .

Just as important, look over the setting before your presentation. Find out where you will be speaking and get there early. Check out the room's acoustics. . . . Test all the equipment. Assume nothing.

Prepare Your Material

Never underestimate how important good preparation is to reducing your anxiety. When you know what you want to accomplish, what you are going to say, and how you are going to say it, you will be less anxious. . . .

1. Know your topic. [When] audiences sense you're bluffing, and when they feel you are unsure of your material, they lose confidence in you. Being unprepared also makes you, the speaker, anxious. . . . Avoid these anxiety-producing thoughts by being the expert.

2. Imagine questions people might ask you. Come up with answers before you give your speech. Either incorporate the answers into your presentation or hold them in readiness in case those questions are asked.

Are *stage fright* and *communication apprehension* the same? If yes, how are they similar? If no, how are they different? Review the section on communication apprehension in Chapter 2, pp. 37–39.

Chapter 12, *Planning Your Presentation*, is devoted to strategies for analyzing and *adapting to your audience*. Chapter 16, *Speaking to Persuade*, focuses on adapting to audience members who agree, disagree, or are undecided.

See Chapter 13, *Content and Organization*, for effective ways to find strong ideas, information, and opinions to support your message and demonstrate your expertise.

Make sure you have your *notes* with you in case you forget.

In Chapter 2, p. 31, we describe a *self-fulfilling prophecy* as a prediction you make that you cause to happen or become true. Thus, if you predict your presentation will be awful, you just might "cause it to happen."

3. Memorize the first minute of your presentation. You experience your greatest anxiety at the beginning of a speech. Having the start memorized makes you comfortable. You may also want to memorize the last minute of your presentation in order to conclude with conviction.

Focus on Your Audience, Not on Yourself

Most of us do not like to feel conspicuous. When you talk to a group of 20, there are 40 eyes staring at you. If you start thinking about all this attention, you may begin to focus on how you look and sound rather than on communicating your message to your listeners. Your attention shifts from your audience to yourself. . . .

There are pro-mirror speakers. They rehearse in front of a mirror and claim that this type of practice improves their delivery and success. So if it works well for you, don't abandon your mirror.

Some public-speaking books suggest that you practice in front of a mirror. Bad advice! Try it and you will see why. When you start talking, you'll notice your facial expressions, your hair and your gestures. And, you'll think little about your presentation.

What should you do when you feel self-conscious during a presentation? Talk to individual listeners. Pick out a person. Tell yourself that you are going to talk right at him until he begins to smile. Smile and you'll find that he'll probably smile back. Then, move to another audience member and think, "I'm going to talk directly to this person until she nods her head." As you talk, start nodding your head and watch as she reciprocates. What you are doing is shifting your attention away from yourself and onto the audience.

Re-label Your Physical Symptoms Positively

Much like an athlete getting ready for a big game, your body gets "up" when you make a speech: your heart beats faster, your palms get sweaty, your legs seem a little wobbly. When experiencing these feelings, some people think, "I'm scared." Other people say to themselves, "I'm excited." Physiologically, there is little difference between fear and excitement. The real difference lies in what you call it. . . . So next time you start a speech, label the experience positively.

Does this technique describe *visualization, cognitive restructuring,* or *systematic desensitization?* Review these techniques in Chapter 2, pp. 38–40.

. . . People who have a great deal of stagefright often talk themselves into being nervous: "This is going to be awful. . . . I'm going to make a fool of myself. . . . People are going to walk out. . . . What if they hate me?" When you talk this way, you may begin to believe it. Experienced speakers convince themselves that they'll do a great job: "I'm going to be effective. . . . This is exciting. . . . What an opportunity . . . I know my stuff and I am going to convince this audience."

Use the energy you experience—don't be used by it. Before your presentation, walk around if you can, take some deep breaths, stretch. . . .

You Don't Look Nervous

Has this happened to you? You finish a presentation and people come up and congratulate you. While you thank them for the compliments, you're thinking, "They're just being nice. They really think I did a lousy job. They could see I was shaking and sweating." Research tells us you're probably wrong: speakers are often inaccurate in their assessments of how nervous they appear. But these inaccurate perceptions feed stagefright. When you think you look anxious, you feel more apprehensive. And the cycle continues until it detrimentally affects your performance.

Reducing stagefright is not easy. It requires conscientious work on your part. You'll have to try the techniques we've described in front of real audiences. But, if you are well prepared and willing to discard your misconceptions about speaking, you can reduce and maybe even conquer your stagefright. And you will gain the flexibility and confidence to transform a fearful ordeal into an invigorating and successful experience.

About the Authors

John Daly is the Liddell Centennial Professor of Communication, University of Texas, Austin, Texas. **Isa Engleberg** is a professor *emerita* of Communication Studies at Prince George's Community College, Largo, Maryland. A longer version of this essay appeared in the June 1999 issue of the *Harvard Management Communication Letter*, Volume 2, Issue 6, published by Harvard Business School Publishing.

When experienced communication instructors are asked to assess how anxious their student speakers are, they often describe their students as much *less* anxious than they may actually feel.

Remember that in most cases your *anxiety is invisible.* Audience members cannot see your pounding heart, upset stomach, cold hands, or worried thoughts.

13 CONTENT

amille Dunlap had a compelling introduction for the presentation she was scheduled to deliver in her communication class. Here's how she intended to begin:

On June 23, 2001, at 7:43 p.m., a smoldering car was found twisted around a tree. Two dead bodies. One adult. One baby. Why did this happen? Was it drunk driving? No. Adverse road conditions? No. A defect in the car? No. Something else took the life of my best friend and her baby brother. Something quite simple, quite common, and deadly: She fell asleep at the wheel.

Camille understood that a good introduction was only a small component of an effective presentation. She also needed content that was clear, interesting, valid, and—in the case of her assignment—persuasive.

After just a few hours of research, Camille found the next sentence for her introduction: "Falling asleep accounts for 100,000 car accidents and 1,500 deaths every year." The more she researched, the more relevant information she discovered from sources such as the National Sleep Foundation, a book on healthy living, and several print and online articles describing the effects of sleep deprivation. She also found recommendations from several sources for getting more and better sleep—a topic relevant to the

AND ORGANIZATION

many sleep-deprived students in her audience.[1] See how Camille organized her content into a memorable presentation on p. 269.

A good introduction is only a part of an effective presentation. As we recommend in Chapter 12, you also must consider your purpose, your audience, your credibility, and the speaking context. Once you have addressed these essential components, you then face what students often describe as the "What should I say?" dilemma. Cicero, the great Roman senator and orator, used the Latin word *inventio* to describe the speaker's attempt "to find out what he should say." He also identified a subsequent step, *dispositio*, as the task of arranging ideas and information for a presentation in an orderly sequence.[2]

In this chapter, we examine both *inventio* and *dispositio* with a focus on how to research, select, and evaluate potential ideas and information; how to identify and effectively organize your key points and supporting material; and how to create a compelling introduction and conclusion for your presentation.

> **A good introduction is only a part of an effective presentation.**

researching and
SELECTING YOUR CONTENT

he **content** of your presentation constitutes the ideas, information, and opinons you include in your message. As soon as you know you will be speaking, begin searching for and collecting **supporting material**, the ideas, information, and opinions that help explain and/or advance your presentation's key points and purpose. Although you may have general ideas about the content and the types of supporting material you need, you should also do extensive research to find more. Even if you are an expert or have a unique background or life experience related to your topic, good research can help you support, verify, and reinforce the content of your message.

Types of Supporting Material

Supporting material comes in many different forms from many different sources: definitions in dictionaries, background and historical information in encyclopedias, facts and figures on-line and in almanacs, true-life stories in magazines and on personal Websites, and editorial opinions in newspapers, newsletters, and online sources. The best presenters use a mix of supporting material; they don't rely on just one type. Why? Most audiences find an unending list of statistics boring. A speaker who tells story after story frustrates listeners if there's no clear reason for telling the stories. Different types of information give a presentation added life and vitality.

Facts A **fact** is a verifiable observation, experience, or event known to be true. "*Slumdog Millionaire* won the 2009 Academy Award for Best Picture" is a fact, whereas "*Milk* should have won" is an opinion. Facts can be personal ("I went to

> **Different types of information give a presentation added LIFE and VITALITY.**

the 2009 Kentucky Derby") or the official record of an event ("Mine That Bird won the 2009 Kentucky Derby"). Facts appear in headlines around the world (January 2, 2008: "For the first time in history, the price of oil hit $100 a barrel."). Sometimes, an unknown or unusual fact can spark audience interest: "By testing water from a city's sewage-treatment plant, researchers can determine what illicit drugs are being used by the population of a specific city on a daily basis."[3] Regardless of their purpose, most presentations are supported by facts, which serve

---

Content The ideas, information, and opinions you include in your message
Supporting material The ideas, information, and opinions that help explain and/or advance your presentation's key points and purpose
Fact A verifiable observation, experience, or event known to be true

to remind, illustrate, demonstrate, and clarify.

Statistics **Statistics** is a branch of mathematics concerned with collecting, summarizing, analyzing, and interpreting numerical data. Statistics are used for many purposes—from describing the characteristics of a specific population to predicting events ranging from economic trends to the winners of football games.

Below, Richard Trumka, president of the A.F.L.-C.I.O, uses statistics to show how middle-class workers are being squeezed by the economy.[4] You can view his engaging speech on YouTube.[5]

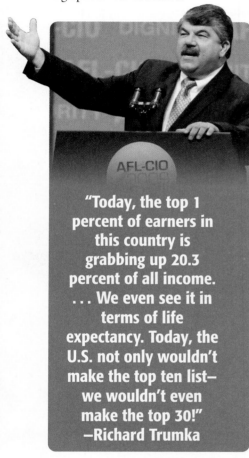

"Today, the top 1 percent of earners in this country is grabbing up 20.3 percent of all income. . . . We even see it in terms of life expectancy. Today, the U.S. not only wouldn't make the top ten list— we wouldn't even make the top 30!"
—Richard Trumka

Although audiences often equate statistics with facts, statistics are factual only if they are collected and analyzed fairly.

Testimony **Testimony** refers to statements or opinions that someone has said or written. You can support a presentation with testimony from books, speeches, plays, magazine articles, radio or televi-

. . . statistics are factual only if they are collected and analyzed fairly.

sion, courtrooms, interviews, or Web pages. Here's an excerpt from a student presentation:

In her book, *Mommy, I'm Scared*, Professor Joanne Cantor writes: "From my 15 years of research on mass media and children's fear, I am convinced that TV programs and movies are the number-one preventable cause of nightmares and anxiety in children."

Keep in mind, the believability of testimony depends on the credibility of the speaker or writer.

Definitions **Definitions** explain or clarify the meaning of a word, phrase, or concept. A definition can explain what *you* mean by a word or be as detailed as an encyclopedia definition. For example, in a presentation explaining the differences beitween jazz and the blues, a speaker used two types of definitions:

The technical definition of the blues is a vocal and instrumental music style that uses a three-line stanza and, typically, a twelve-measure form in which expressive inflections—blues notes—are combined with uniquely African American tonal qualities. Or according to an old bluesman's definition: The blues ain't nothin' but the facts of life.

Use definitions if your presentation includes words or phrases that your audience may not know or may misunderstand.

Descriptions **Descriptions** create mental images for your listeners. They provide more details than definitions by offering causes, effects, historical background information, and characteristics. In an address about the Civil Rights Memorial in

Atlanta, Carole Blair describes the architecture of the memorial. Here is an excerpt from that description.

. . . Immediately in front of the wall . . . is an off-center, black granite pedestal . . . the top of which forms a circle of about 12 feet in diameter. Water bubbles up from a well near the center of the structure and flows slowly and smoothly across its surface. Around the circumference of the tabletop is a . . . time line, marking 53 events of the civil rights movement, beginning with the *Brown* v. *Board of Education* decision in 1954 and ending with the assassination of Dr. King in 1968.[6]

Analogies An **analogy** identifies key similarities in things that are alike as well as things that are not alike. Here are examples of each kind of analogy:

Alike: If the traffic plan worked in San Diego, it should work in Seattle.

Not Alike: If a co-pilot must be qualified to fly a plane, a U.S. vice president should be qualified to govern the country.

Use analogies to describe a complex process or to relate a new concept to something the audience

---

Statistics Supporting material that collects, summarizes, analyzes, and interprets numerical data

Testimony Statements or opinions that someone has said or written

Definition A statement that explains or clarifies the meaning of a word, phrase, or concept

Description Words that create mental images in the minds of listeners

Analogy A figure of speech that identifies key similarities in things that are alike and not alike

Don't Take It out of Context

When someone selects isolated statements from a source that distorts the speaker's or writer's intended meaning, that person is taking those words out of context. Dan Le Batard, a columnist for the *Miami Herald*, puts it this way: "When context is misplaced, so is the truth."[7] Brooks Barnes, a writer for the *New York Times*, notes, "[Movie] studios have long used blurbs from reviews to sell films, sometimes taking comments out of context."[8] For example, a film critic from *Entertainment Weekly* described the opening credits for the film *Se7en* as "a small masterpiece" even though he gave the actual movie a poor review. Advertisers took the phrase "a small masterpiece" out of context and used it in a positive advertisement for the entire film.[9]

Unethical speakers may deliberately take testimony out of context to attack an author, discredit an idea, or gain credibility for something that is not supported by the full context.[10] This practice occurs frequently in politics. Communication scholar Matthew McGlone cites the use of Dr. Martin Luther King, Jr.'s, "I Have a Dream" speech as a good example. He notes that when King professed, "I have a dream that my four little children will one day live in a nation where they will not be judged by the color of their skin, but by the content of their character," several conservative politicians claimed he was opposing affirmative action. These same politicians also claimed that King's words meant that he supported merit, not race, and that merit should determine the distribution of resources. By taking the quote out of context, conservatives transformed King from a liberal, civil rights activist into a political conservative.[11]

make a large or abstract idea concrete and understandable; they can be facts, brief descriptions, or detailed stories. When someone says, "Give me an example," it's natural to reply with an illustration or instance that explains your idea. When asked for examples of individualistic cultures, you might list the United States, Australia, Great Britain, and Canada. Or, if you were making a presentation on female blues singers from the 1920s, you might name Ma Rainey, Bessie Smith, Victoria Spivey, and Alberta Hunter.[13]

Stories Real stories about real people in the real world can arouse attention, create an appropriate mood, and reinforce important ideas. **Stories** are accounts or reports about something that happened.

Example A word or phrase that refers to a specific case or instance in order to make a large or abstract idea concrete and understandable

Stories Accounts or reports about something that happened

---

understands very well. Here's an example of an analogy that uses a computer to explain how our brain processes memories:

> Your short-term memory is like the RAM on a computer: it records the information in front of you right now. Some of what you experience seems to evaporate—like words that go missing when you turn off your computer without hitting SAVE. But other short-term memories . . . [are] downloaded onto the hard drive. These long-term memories, filled with past loves and losses and fears, stay dormant until you call them up.[12]

Examples An **example** refers to a specific case or instance. Examples

A presentation on female blues singers is strengthened by specific examples; in addition to projecting an image of Bessie Smith as shown here, you may even consider playing a snippet of one of her more famous songs.

LINEAR VERSUS SPIRAL THINKING

Low-context cultures like the United States tend to use a linear style of thinking when developing a message—moving from facts, evidence, and proof to drawing logical conclusions. Other cultures use a more spiral style of thinking when developing a message—moving from dramatic supporting material to subtle conclusions. For example, members of many Arab and African cultures use detailed metaphors, similes, stories, and parables to reinforce or dramatize a point. The final message may be quite subtle or even elusive. It's up to the audience to draw the intended conclusion.[14]

Because this textbook is primarily written for U.S. speakers and audiences, we focus on a more linear thinking style in which speakers use clear supporting material to back up their claims and outlines to map the content of their messages. When speaking to an audience that prefers a more spiral style of thinking, consider ways to use supporting material more dramatically and to present your conclusions in a less direct style.

Audiences often remember a good story even when they can't remember much else about a presentation.

In the following example, a successful attorney with an incapacitating physical disability uses her brief, personal story to emphasize the importance of hope, hard work, and determination:

> I was in an automobile accident just after high school, which left me in a wheelchair for life. I was trying to deal with that, a new marriage, and other personal problems, not the least of which was uncertainty about what I could do—about the extent of my own potential.[15]

Audiences often remember a good story even when they can't remember much else about a presentation.

Document Your Sources

Documentation is the practice of citing the sources of your supporting material. You should document all supporting material (including information from Internet sources and interviews) in writing and then orally in your presentation. Documentation enhances your credibility as a speaker while assuring listeners of the validity of your content.

Unlike writers, speakers rarely display complete footnotes during a presentation. Nor should they recite every detail such as the publisher, publisher's city, and page number of a citation. In speaking situations, citations must be oral. Your spoken citation—sometimes called an **oral footnote**—should include enough information to allow an interested listener to find the original sources you're citing. Generally, it's a good idea to provide the name of the person (or people) whose work you are citing, to say a word or two about that person's credentials, and to mention the source of the information. If you want the audience to have permanent access to the information you use, provide a handout listing your references with complete citations.

One of the most effective ways to cite information from another source is to paraphrase (see Chapter 4). A paraphrase captures someone else's ideas and feelings but does *not* use the same words or sentence structure. Note how the content changes from the original source to a paraphrase in the following example:

Original Source. We cannot legislate the language of the home, the street, the bar, the club, unless we are willing to set up a cadre of language police who will ticket and arrest us if we speak something other than English. (Source: James C. Stalker (March 1988), "Official English or English Only," *English Journal* 77, p. 21.)

Oral Paraphrase. In a 1988 *English Journal* article, Dr. James Stalker explains that in a democracy like ours, we should not pass laws against the use of other languages. If nothing else, it would be impossible, even foolish, to enforce such laws in our homes and public places.

DOCUMENTATION enhances your credibility as a speaker while assuring listeners of the validity of your content.

Documentation The practice of citing the sources of supporting material in a presentation

Oral footnote A spoken citation that includes enough information for listeners to find the original source

Evaluate Your Supporting Material

Many speakers rely on researched information to support their claims and enhance their credibility. Evaluate every piece of supporting material before using it. Make sure your information is **valid**—that the ideas, information, and opinons you include are well-founded, justified, and accurate. The questions described in the sections that follow will help you test the validity of your supporting material.

Is the Source Identified and Credible? Are the author and publisher identified? Are they reputable? For example, the sensational and often bizarre articles in *The National Enquirer* may be fun to read, but *The New York Times* and *Wall Street Journal* are more likely to contain reliable information because their worldwide reputations depend on publishing accurate information. Ask yourself whether the source you are quoting is a recognized expert, a firsthand observer, or a respected journalist.

Is the Source Primary or Secondary? When researching and selecting supporting material, determine whether you are using a primary or secondary source of information. A **primary source** is the document, testimony, or publication in which information first appears. For example, an academic journal article that contains the results of an author's original research is a primary source. A **secondary source**, such as an encyclopedia or Wikipedia, reports, repeats, or summarizes information from many sources. Look carefully at secondary sources of information to uncover, if possible, the primary source of the information.

Is the Source Biased? A source is **biased** when it states an opinion so slanted in one direction that it may not be objective or fair. If the source has a very strong opinion or will benefit from your agreement, be cautious. For years, tobacco companies publicly denied that cigarette smok-

Is this source credible? Why or why not?

ing was harmful, even though their own research told them otherwise. Even not-for-profit special-interest groups such as the National Rifle Association, pro-choice or pro-life groups, or the American Association of Retired Persons have biases. The information they publish may be true, but the conclusions they draw from that information may be misleading.

Is the Information Recent? Always note the date of the information you want to use. When was the information collected? When was it published? In this rapidly changing information age, your information can become old news in a matter of hours. For current events or scientific breakthroughs, use magazines, journals, newspaper articles, or reliable Web sources. Look for the date indicating when a Webpage was written or last viewed. If a Website makes it difficult to locate this information, this may be a sign that the site is not credible and reliable.

Is the Information Consistent? Check whether the information you want to use reports facts and findings similar to other information on the same subject from reputable sources. Does the information make sense based on what you know about the topic? For example, if most doctors and medical experts agree that penicillin will *not* cure a common viral cold, why believe an obscure source that recommends it as a treatment?

Valid Whether your ideas, information, and opinons are well-founded, justified, and accurate
Primary source The document, testimony, or publication in which information first appears
Secondary source Documents, testimony, or publications that report, repeat, or summarize information from one or more other sources
Biased A source that states an opinion so slanted in one direction that it may not be objective or fair

While you or someone you know may contribute content to Wikipedia, Wikipedia is a secondary source.

Are the Statistics Valid? Good statistics can be informative, dramatic, and convincing. But statistics also can mislead, distort, and confuse. Make sure your statistics are well-founded, justified, and accurate. Closely consider whether the statistics are believable, and whether the researcher who collected and analyzed the data is a well-respected expert. Confirm who is reporting the statistics as well—is it the researcher or a reporter?

communication in ACTION

Hoaxes, Rumors, Myths, and Urban Legends on the Web

Don't trust or believe everything you read on the Internet. In *Human Communication on the Internet*, Leonard Shedletsky and Joan Aitken note that misinformation on the Internet is a serious problem, particularly given that many disreputable sites appear valid and legitimate.[16] To make matters worse, Internet hoaxes, rumors, myths, and urban legends are often repeated over and over, making them appear to come from credible sources.

Several respected Websites have taken up the challenge of identifying false rumors and legends. For example, *about.com* identifies the "top 25 urban legends" each week and rates them as false, outdated, fake, dubious, or authentic/true.[17] Here are just a few examples from the week ending on August 7, 2009, along with their ratings:

FALSE: President Obama's birth certificate is a forgery and proves he was not a natural-born U.S. citizen.

FAKE: E-mail images show Sarah Palin posing for a photo sporting an American flag bikini and a rifle.

FALSE: Mild-mannered children's TV show host Fred Rogers was a trained Marine sniper and assassin.

At the same time, you may learn that some urban legends are true, such as: When first developed in the nineteenth century, Coca-Cola did, in fact, include cocaine in its formula.[18] Generally, though, urban legends are usually so far-fetched, they have been called a "cultural epidemic" and "thought contagion." Thus, before you include anything you find on the Web in your presentation, we urge you to identify the sources, analyze whether the sources are biased or hoaxes, and consult reputable sites for verification.

Fred Rogers: Friendly neighbor or trained Marine sniper and assassin?

organizing your PRESENTATION

Michael Kepper, a marketing communication specialist, compares the need for organizing a presentation's content with the needs of a human body:

> A speech without structure is like a human body without a skeleton. It won't stand up. Spineless. Like a jellyfish. . . . Having structure won't make the speech a great one, but lacking structure will surely kill all the inspired thoughts . . . because listeners are too busy trying to find out where they are to pay attention.[19]

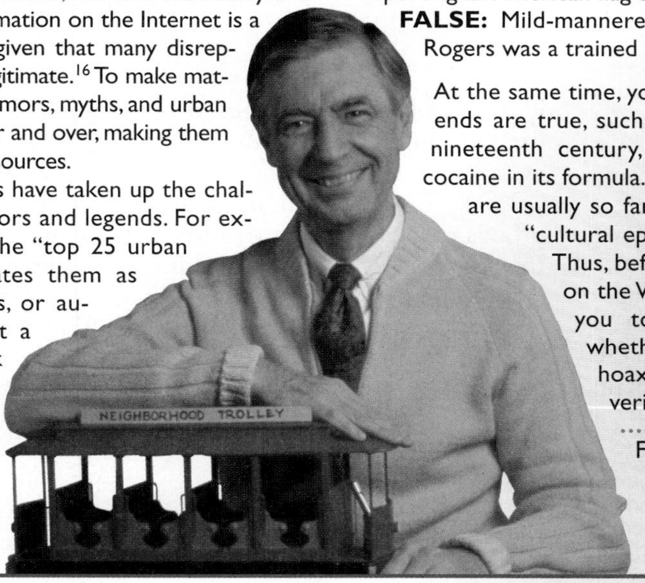

Organization refers to the way you arrange the content of your presentation into a clear and appropriate format. An organizational format also helps you focus on the purpose of your presentation while deciding what to include and how to maximize the impact of your message.

Organization The way you arrange the content of your presentation into a clear and appropriate format

> "A speech without structure is like a human body without a skeleton."
> —Michael Kepper

Determining the key points of your presentation is like fitting together the pieces of a puzzle—if one point doesn't fit or follow, the rest of the presentation may not work.

As an audience member, you know that organization matters. It is difficult to understand and remember the words of a speaker who rambles and doesn't connect ideas. In fact, you may never want to hear that speaker again. Research confirms that audiences react positively to well-organized presentations and negatively to poorly organized ones.[20]

Determine Your Key Points

The first step in organizing a presentation is to determine your key points. **Key points** represent the most important issues or the main ideas you want your audience to understand and remember about your message.

Look for a pattern or natural groups of ideas and information as the basis for key points. Depending on your purpose and topic area, this can be an easy task or a daunting puzzle. Inexperienced speakers often feel overwhelmed by what seems to be mountains of unrelated facts and figures. Don't give up!

Before creating an outline, consider using two other techniques to identify your key points and build a preliminary structure for your message: mind mapping and the Speech Framer.

Mind Mapping **Mind mapping** encourages the free flow of ideas and lets you define relationships among those ideas. It harnesses the potential of your whole brain, while it's in a highly creative mode of thought, to generate ideas.[21] On this page, for instance, you will see the mind map that one student created for a presentation on MUZAK, that ever-present background music you often hear in stores, elevators, and offices.[22] The mind map is a hodgepodge of words, phrases, lists, circles, and arrows. Certainly it contains more concepts than should be included in a single presentation. After completing such a mind map, you can label circled ideas as key points and put them in a logical order.

This mind map on MUZAK demonstrates one method of determining key points and establishing relationships among ideas.

Key points The most important issues or the main ideas in a presentation's message

Mind mapping An organizational technique that encourages the free flow of ideas and helps define the relationships among those ideas

Mind maps allow you to see your ideas without superimposing a predetermined organizational pattern on them. They also let you postpone the need to arrange your ideas in a pattern until you collect enough information to organize the content. Use mind mapping when you have lots of ideas and information but are having trouble deciding how to select and arrange the materials for a presentation.

The Speech Framer The **Speech Framer** is a visual model for organizing presentation content that provides a place for every component of a presentation while encouraging experimentation and creativity.[23] Below is an example of Camille Dunlop's Speech Framer for her presentation on the dangers of sleep deprivation.

The Speech Framer lets you experiment with a variety of organizational formats. For example, if you have four key points, you merely add a column to the frame. If you think you have three key points, but find that you don't have good supporting material for the second key point, you might consider deleting that point. If you only have three types of supporting material for one key point and two for the others, that's okay—just make sure all the supporting material is strong. If you notice that several pieces of supporting material apply to two key points, you can combine them into a new key point. And if you must have five or more key points, use only one or two pieces of supporting material for each point to control the length of your presentation.

In addition to helping you organize the content of your presentation, you can use the single-page Speech Framer as your speaking notes. It allows you to see the presentation laid out entirely before you practice or deliver it.

Link Your Key Point to Your Central Idea

Once you have identified your key points, make sure they link to your **central idea**, a sentence that

---

> **Speech Framer** A visual model for organizing presentation content that provides a place for every component of a presentation while encouraging experimentation and creativity
>
> **Central idea** A sentence that summarizes the key points of a presentation

---

THE SPEECH FRAMER: ASLEEP AT THE WHEEL

Introduction: Story about my best friend's death in a car accident.

Central Idea: Falling asleep accounts for 100,000 car accidents and 1,500 deaths every year. Everyone knows about the dangers of drunk driving, but very few of us know about the dangers of sleep deprivation—and what to do about it.

Key Points	#1 Why we need sleep. **Transition:** What happens when you don't get enough sleep? ➞	#2 Sleep deprivation affects your health, well-being, and safety. **Transition:** So how can you ease your tired body and mind? ➞	#3 Three steps can help you get a good night's sleep.
Support	Would you drive home from class drunk? 14 hrs w/o sleep = .1 blood alcohol level Very long day = .05 blood alcohol level	Lack of sleep affects your attitude and mood (results of study)	1. Decide how much sleep is right for you: a. Keep a sleep log. b. Most people need 8 or more hours a night.
Support	Circadian clock controls sleep & also regulates hormones, heart rate, body temperature, etc.	Lack of sleep affects your health. Most important sleep is between 7th and 8th hour of sleep.	2. Create a comfy sleep environment. a. Don't sleep on a full or empty stomach. b. Cut back on fluids. c. No alcohol or caffeine before sleep.
Support	Things that rob our sleep: 24-hour stores Internet Television Studying and homework	Symptoms: • Crave naps or doze off? • Hit snooze button a lot? • Hard to solve problems? • Feel groggy, lethargic?	3. Don't take your troubles to bed. a. Can't sleep, get up. b. Soothing music. c. Read (e.g., my econ textbook).

Conclusion: Recognizing that you may be sleep-deprived is the first step. The hardest thing to do is to alter your habits. Retraining yourself to follow a normal sleep pattern isn't going to happen overnight. But once you discover that a few extra hours of sleep will help you feel more rested, relaxed, and revitalized, giving up that extra hour on the Internet or watching TV will have been worth it. There so much in life to enjoy. Sleep longer, live longer.

summarizes the key points of your presentation. The central idea provides a brief preview of the organizational pattern you will follow to achieve your purpose.

The following example illustrates how topic area, purpose, and central idea are different but closely linked to one another:

Topic area   Traveling abroad

Purpose   To prepare travelers for a trip abroad

Central idea   Before visiting a foreign country, research the culture and the places you will visit; make sure you have the required travel documents; and get any immunizations and medicines you might need.

Select an Organizational Pattern

Even the most experienced speakers may find it difficult to see how their ideas and information fall into a clear structure. Fortunately, there are several commonly used organizational patterns that can help you clarify your central idea and find an effective format for your presentation.[24]

ARRANGE BY SUBTOPICS

Topical arrangement involves dividing a large topic into smaller subtopics. Subtopics can describe reasons, characteristics, or techniques. Use a topical arrangement if your ideas and information can be divided into discrete categories of relatively equal importance. For example:

Topic area   Facial expression in different cultures

Purpose   To appreciate that some facial expressions don't always translate between cultures

Central idea   Americans and native Japanese often misinterpret facial expressions depicting fear, sadness, and disgust.

Key points   A. Fear
                B. Sadness
                C. Disgust

SEQUENCE IN TIME

Time arrangement orders information according to time or calendar dates. Most step-by-step procedures begin with the first step and continue sequentially (or chronologically) through the last step. Use a time arrangement when your key points occur in time relative to each other, as in recipes, assembly instructions, technical procedures, and historical events. For example:

Topic area   Making vanilla ice cream

Purpose   To explain how to make traditional custard-based vanilla ice cream

Central idea   To make perfect homemade vanilla ice cream, make sure that you combine and heat the ingredients properly, know when the custard is thick enough, and correctly churn the ice cream.

Key points   A. Warm up and whisk in the first ingredients.
            B. Cook the custard slowly.
            C. Cool and add final ingredients.
            D. Refrigerate before churning.

POSITION IN SPACE

Use a **space arrangement** if your key points can be arranged in terms of their location or physical relationship to one another. For example:

STOP & THINK | The Organizational Jigsaw Puzzle

Develop a purpose statement, central idea, and list of key points for a presentation on "The Care and Treatment of Shoulder Problems" using any of the subtopics provided. You may delete or add subtopics to create an effective organizational pattern.

Topic: Care and Treatment of Common Shoulder Problems

Anatomy of the shoulder	Oral medication
Arthroscopic surgery	Prevention of shoulder problems
Causes of shoulder injuries	Physical therapy
Cold treatment	Shoulder exercises
Cortisone injections	Shoulder injury symptoms
Diagnosing shoulder injuries	Shoulder separations
Heat treatment	Shoulder sprains
How the shoulder moves	Torn rotator cuff
Need for early treatment	

Topical arrangement An organizational pattern that divides a large topic into smaller subtopics

Time arrangement An organizational pattern that orders information according to time or calendar dates

Space arrangement An organizational pattern that arranges key points in terms of their location or physical relationship to one another

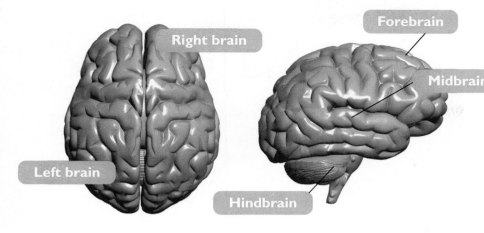

For a presentation that discusses the various parts of the brain, use space arrangement.

Topic area   Brain structure

Purpose   To explain how major sections of the brain are responsible for different functions

Central idea   A guided tour of the brain begins in the hindbrain, moves through the midbrain, and ends in the forebrain, with side trips to the right and left hemispheres.

Key points   A.   The hindbrain
           B.   The midbrain
           C.   The forebrain
           D.   The right and left hemispheres

PRESENT A PROBLEM AND A SOLUTION

Use a **problem–solution arrangement** to describe a harmful or difficult situation (the problem) and then offer a plan to solve the problem (the solution). Problems can be as simple as a squeaky door or as significant as world famine. In the following example, each key point presents guidelines for dealing with a problem often found in group discussions:

Topic area   Behavioral problems in groups

Purpose   To provide suggestions for solving common behavioral problems that occur in group discussions and meetings

Central idea   Learning how to deal with three common behavioral problems in groups will improve a group's performance.

Key points   A.   Dealing with nonparticipants
           B.   Dealing with disruptive behavior
           C.   Dealing with latecomers and early leavers

SHOW CAUSES AND EFFECTS

Use a **cause-and-effect arrangement** either to present a cause and its resulting effects or to detail the effects that result from a specific cause. Here is an example that identifies how watching too much television adversely affects children:

Topic area   Children and television

Purpose   To describe the harmful effects that television has on children

Central idea   Watching too much television negativly affects children and their families because it uses time that could be spent on more important activities.

Key points   A.   Television has a negative effect on children's physical fitness.
           B.   Television has a negative effect on

children's school achievement.
           C.   Television watching may become a serious addiction.

In cause-and-effect presentations, speakers may claim that eating red meat causes disease or that lower taxes stimulate the economy. In effect-to-cause presentations, speakers may claim that sleepiness or lack of energy can be caused by an iron deficiency or that a decrease in lake fish is caused by global warming. Be careful with cause-and-effect arrangements. Just because one thing follows another does not mean that the first causes the second. Lack of sleep, not lack of iron, can be a cause of sleepiness. This kind of conclusion is a classic example of a faulty cause fallacy (see Chapter 4).

TELL STORIES AND SHARE EXAMPLES

A series of well-told stories or dramatic examples can be so compelling and interesting that they easily become the organizational pattern for a presentation. For example, dramatic stories about successful individuals who escaped from poverty and prejudice or who triumphed with disabilities can be the key points of a presentation:

Topic area   Leaders and adversity

Purpose   To convince listeners that disabilities are not barriers to success

Central idea   Many noteworthy leaders have lived with disabilities.

Problem–solution arrangement An organizational pattern that describes a harmful or difficult situation (the problem) and then offers a plan to solve the problem (the solution)

Cause-and-effect arrangement An organizational format that either presents a cause and its resulting effects or details the effects that result from a specific cause

Key points
A. Franklin D. Roosevelt, president of the United States, who lived with polio

B. Jan Scruggs, disabled soldier and Vietnam Memorial founder

C. Helen Keller, deaf and blind advocate

For a presentation about the advantages of fuel-efficient vehicles, consider using the comparison–contrast arrangement.

COMPARE AND CONTRAST

Use a **comparison–contrast arrangement** to demonstrate how two things are similar or different. This pattern works well in two situations: (1) when an unfamiliar concept can be explained by comparing it with a familiar concept or (2) when you are demonstrating the advantages of one alternative over another. Comparisons can be real (comparing products or contrasting medical treatments) or fanciful (comparing student success to racehorse success). For example:

Topic area Gas-powered cars versus gas–electric hybrid cars

Purpose To recommend ways of evaluating gas-powered and gas–electric hybrid cars

Central idea Comparing performance, fuel economy, and reliability can help you decide whether to purchase a gas-powered or gas–electric hybrid car.

Key points
A. Performance

B. Fuel economy

C. Predicted reliability and battery life

> **Comparison–contrast arrangement** An organizational pattern that demonstrates how two things are similar or different

Know Thy Self

How Creative Are You?

If you want your presentation to be interesting and memorable, think creatively about its structure. Lee Towe, president of Innovators International, defines creativity as consisting of two parts: creative thinking and creative output.[25] *Creative output* consists of connecting and combining previously unrelated elements. For example, the circles and arrows you draw on a mind map allow you to combine ideas from various places on the page.

Notice how Patricia Phillips, a customer service expert, uses excerpts from popular songs to begin each major section of her training seminar in a creative way: "I Can't Get No Satisfaction" by the Rolling Stones, "Help" by the Beatles, "Respect" by Aretha Franklin, and "Don't You Come Back No More" by Ray Charles.

Creativity, however, runs some risks. Some audience members may be unfamiliar with the songs chosen by a speaker. Or, the audience may have expected or wanted a more technical presentation. If you want to use creative patterns, make sure your audience will understand and appreciate your creativity.

So how creative are you? In three minutes, list all of the uses you can imagine for a balloon. When you finish your three minutes of thinking, rate the creativity of your answers based on the following criteria:

- Quantity: Did you come up with more than 24 ideas?
- Variety: Did you come up with at least five categories of answers? For example, birthday decorations and prom decorations would be the same category—decorations.
- Uniqueness: Did you have unusual items on your list? For example, most people would say that a balloon can be used as decoration. A more creative person might suggest using blown-up balloons to fill empty space when packing a box for shipment.[26]

outlining your
PRESENTATION

Outlines—just like presentations and speakers—come in many shapes and forms. Here we look at three types of outlines and how they can help you organize the content of a presentation.

Preliminary Outlines

Outlines begin in a preliminary form with a few basic building blocks. You can use a **preliminary outline** to put the major pieces of almost any presentation in order, modifying it based on the number of key points and the types and amount of supporting material. Aim for at least two pieces of supporting mate-

Preliminary Outline Format

Topic Area

I. Introduction
  A. Purpose/topic
  B. Central idea
  C. Brief preview of key points
    1. Key point #1
    2. Key point #2
    3. Key point #3

II. Body of the presentation
  A. Key point #1
    1. Supporting material
    2. Supporting material
  B. Key point #2
    1. Supporting material
    2. Supporting material
  C. Key point #3
    1. Supporting material
    2. Supporting material

III. Conclusion

STRATEGIES FOR ORDERING KEY POINTS[27]

- **STRENGTH AND FAMILIARITY.** Place your strongest points first and last, and your weakest or least familiar idea in the middle position, so that you start and end with strength.

- **AUDIENCE NEEDS.** If your audience needs current information, satisfy that need early. Background information can come later. If you are speaking about a controversial topic, begin with a point that focuses on the background of an issue or on the reasons for a change.

- **LOGISTICS.** If you're one of a series of presenters, you may end up with less time to speak than was originally scheduled. Plan your presentation so that the strongest key points come first in case you need to cut your presentation short.

rial under each key point—facts, statistics, testimony, definitions, descriptions, analogies, examples, or stories.

After you identify the key points that will support your central idea and after you choose an organizational pattern to structure your message, determine which key points go first, second, or last. In many cases, the organizational pattern you choose dictates the order. For example, if you use time arrangement, the first step in a procedure comes first. If your format does not dictate the order of key points, place your best ideas in strategic positions.

Comprehensive Outline

A **comprehensive outline** is an all-inclusive presentation framework that follows established out-

lining rules. Whereas a preliminary outline helps you plan your presentation, a comprehensive outline creates the first draft of your presentation. There are two very basic rules for comprehensive outlining: 1) use numbers, letters, *and* indentations, and 2) divide your subpoints logically.

Use Numbers, Letters, and Indentations A comprehensive outline uses a system of indenting and numbers and letters. Roman numerals (I,

Preliminary outline A first-draft outline that puts the major pieces of a presentation in a clear and logical order

Comprehensive outline An all-inclusive presentation framework that follows established outlining rules

COMPREHENSIVE OUTLINE

"What's Fair Is Fair" by Regina Smith

I. Introduction
 A. Americans love fairness.
 B. Many Americans oppose affirmative action for minority students because it seems unfair.
 C. There are other preferences for college admission that are just as unfair.
 (*Transition:* Let's start with the oldest type of preference.)

II. Body
 A. Legacy Admissions
  1. Legacy admissions began in the 1920s to give the children of wealthy white alumni preference over the children of Jews and immigrants.
  2. Legacy students' SATs and GPAs are lower than non-legacy students.
  3. Percent of legacy students: U. of Penn, 41%; U. of Virginia, 52%; Notre Dame U., 57%.
 B. Athletic Scholarships
  1. National Collegiate Athletic Association college admissions standards:
   a. Combined SAT score of 1010 with a 2.0 high school GPA.
   b. Combined SAT score of 850 with a 2.5 high school GPA.
  2. Athletes get special treatment: special advisors, paid tutors, easier classes.
  3. Poor graduation rates:
   a. Division I football players: 51% rate.
   b. Division I basketball players: 40% rate.
   c. Of 3,700 athletes, 50% earn degrees.
   d. Exception at Duke University: 90% graduation rate for scholarship athletes.
  4. Reason for athletic preferences is money:
   a. $6 billion for NCAA television contracts.
   b. $187 million to Division 1 schools.
 C. Low-Income Scholarships
  1. U. of California grants scholarships to "socioeconomically disadvantaged" students.
  2. What about blue-collar and middle-class students who struggle to pay tuition?
 D. Affirmative Action
  1. Why is affirmative action singled out as unfair?
  2. Universities relax standards for alumni children, for athletes, and for poor students—why not African American students?
  3. Quote from Ron Wilson, African American representative from Texas.

III. Conclusion
 A. Either stop giving preferences to legacy students, athletes, and poor students, or continue affirmative action programs.
 B. Do what is fair.

II, III) signify the major divisions such as the introduction, body, and conclusion. Indented capital letters (A, B, C) are used for key points. Additional indents use Arabic numbers (1, 2, 3) for more specific points and supporting material. If you need a fourth level, indent again and use lowercase letters (a, b, c).

Divide Your Subpoints Logically Each major point should include at least two subpoints indented under it, or none at all. If there is an A, there must be a B; for every 1, there must be a 2.

Wrong: I.
  A.
 II.

Right: I.
  A.
  B.
 II.

As much as possible, try to keep your key points consistently grammatical; for example, if you begin each subpoint with a verb, then each subpoint that follows should also begin with a verb, and so forth. The comprehensive outline on the left of "What's Fair Is Fair," by Regina Smith, was developed for her class presentation on affirmative action and college admissions.

Speaking Outline

For the actual delivery of your presentation, you may need to create a **speaking outline**—either a short outline that includes little more than a list of key points and reminders of supporting material, or a more complex and detailed outline that includes numerous quotations, statistics, or other data. Some speaking outlines may also include notes on when to introduce and remove a visual aid or provide a handout.

> **Speaking outline** The outline used by a speaker to deliver a presentation; it may be short or long depending on the complexity of content

connecting
YOUR KEY POINTS

an outline shows how you structured and developed your key points and supporting material, but it's missing the "glue" that attaches the key points to one another and makes your presentation a coherent whole. **Connectives** are this glue, and they include internal previews and summaries as well as transitions and signposts.[28]

Internal Previews and Internal Summaries

An **internal preview** identifies, in advance, the key points of a presentation or section in a specific order. It tells audience members what you are going to cover and in what order. In the body of a presentation, an internal preview describes how you are going to approach a key point. For example:

> How do researchers and doctors explain obesity? Some offer genetic explanations; others psychological ones. Either or both factors can be responsible for your never-ending battle with the bathroom scale.

Generally, audiences like internal previews because they prepare them for listening to and remembering important ideas.

Internal summaries are a useful way to end a major section and to reinforce important ideas. They also are an opportunity to repeat critical ideas or information. Internal summaries help the audience review and remember what you said. For example:

> So remember, before spending hundreds of dollars on

diet books and exercise toys, make sure that your weight problem is not influenced by the number and size of your fat cells, your hormone level, your metabolism, or the amount of glucose in your bloodstream.

Transitions

The most common type of connective is the **transition**—a word, number, brief phrase, or sentence that helps you move from one key point or section to another. Transitions act like lubricating oil to keep a presentation moving smoothly. In the following examples, the transitions are underlined:

<u>Yet</u> it's important to remember . . .

<u>In addition</u> to metabolism, there is . . .

<u>On the other hand</u>, some people believe . . .

<u>Finally</u>, a responsible parent should . . .

Transitions also function as mini-previews and mini-summaries that link the conclusion of one section to the beginning of another. For example:

> After you've eliminated these four genetic explanations for weight gain, it's time to consider several psychological factors.

Signposts

A fourth type of connective is **signposts**—short phrases that, like signs on the highway, tell or remind listeners where you are in the orga-

nizational structure of a presentation. For example, if you are sharing four genetic explanations for weight gain, begin each explanation with numbers—first, second, third, and fourth: "Fourth and finally, make sure your glucose level has been tested and is within normal levels." Signposts focus attention on an important idea or piece of information; they can highlight an eloquent phrase or special insight.

> Even if you can't remember all of his accomplishments, please remember one thing: Alex Curry is the only candidate who has been endorsed by every newspaper and civic association in the county.

Connectives Internal previews, summaries, transitions, and signposts that helps connect key components of a presentation to one another

Internal preview Identifies, in advance, the key points of a presentation or section in a specific order

Internal summary Signals the end of major sections and reinforces important ideas in a presentation

Transition A word, number, brief phrase, or sentence in a presentation that helps a speaker move from one key point or section to another

Signpost A short phrase that tells or reminds listeners where a speaker is in the organizational structure of a presentation

beginning your
PRESENTATION

introductions capitalize on the power of first impressions. First impressions can create a positive, lasting impression and pave the way for a highly successful presentation. A weak beginning gives audience members a reason to tune out or remember you as a poor speaker. Effective introductions give your audience time to adjust, to block out distractions, and to focus attention on you and your message. They also establish a relationship among three elements: you, your message, and your audience.[29]

There are many strategies for beginning a presentation effectively. The following methods represent just a handful of the more common introductory strategies that can be used separately or in combination: statistics and examples, quotations, stories, metaphors, questions, references to places, occasions, incidents and events, and addressing audience needs.

GOALS OF THE INTRODUCTION

Focus Audience Attention and Interest
Gain audience attention by using compelling supporting material, involving them actively, and speaking expressively.

Connect to Your Audience
Find a way to connect your message to audience interests, attitudes, beliefs, and values.

Put You in Your Presentation
Link your expertise, experiences, and personal enthusiasm to your topic or purpose. Personalize your message.

Set the Emotional Tone
Make sure the introduction sets an appropriate emotional tone that matches its purpose. Use appropriate language, delivery styles, and supporting material.

Preview the Message
Give your audience a sneak preview about the subject. State your central idea and briefly list the key points you will cover.

Use a Statistic or Example

Sometimes, your research turns up a statistic or example that is unusual or dramatic. If you anticipate a problem in gaining and keeping audience attention, an interesting statistic or example can do it for you.

The statistics are appalling: More than 5,000 juveniles and 35,000 adults die each year from gunshot wounds. Since 1984, the homicide rate for males has tripled. This is an epidemic! An epidemic that is about 10 times as big in terms of lives lost as the great polio epidemic of the first half of the twentieth century.[30]

Quote Someone

A dramatic statement or eloquent phrase written by someone else can make an ideal beginning. A good quo-

tation helps an audience overcome their doubts, especially when the quotation is from a writer or speaker who is highly respected or an expert source of information. Remember to give the writer or speaker of the quotation full credit.

We need more money, high-quality instruction, and better equipment in all of our science classes. Here is how Arne Duncan, the Secretary of Education, put it in a 2009 address to the National Science Teachers Association: "America won the space race but, in many ways, American education lost the science race. A decade ago . . . our best districts could compete with anyone in the world, but our worst districts—which, of course, were in low-income communities—were on a par with third-world countries."[31]

Tell a Story

Audiences will give you their undivided attention if you tell a good story and tell it well. Consider using a story about a personal hardship, a triumph, or even an embarrassment. Remember that the purpose of using a story is to illustrate a concept or idea. Here's an example from a student presentation:

When I was fifteen, I was operated on to remove the deadliest form of skin cancer, a melanoma

The Primacy and Recency Effects

As predicted by Hermann Ebbinghaus, a German psychologist who spearheaded the research on memory and recall, the parts of a presentation audiences most remember are the beginning and the end. Ebbinghaus, who is best known for his discovery of the *forgetting curve* and the *learning curve*, also discovered the *serial position effect*, which explains that "for information learned in a sequence, recall is better for items at the beginning (**primacy effect**) and the end (**recency effect**) than for items in the middle of the sequence."[32]

Interestingly, the primacy and recency effects link up with what we know about listening and memory. We are more likely to recall the last thing we hear because the information is still in our short-term memory. In contrast, we are likely to remember the first thing we hear because the information has had time to become part of our long-term memory. The poorest recall of information is in the middle of a sequence "because the information is no longer in short-term memory and has not yet been placed in long-term memory."[33]

Originally, the primacy and recency effects evolved from studies of what people remember after hearing a list of words or numbers. Today, it has been applied to studying how first and last impressions affect how we react to and feel about other people. It also has found its way into the study of presentations, specifically to emphasize the critical importance of a presentation's introduction and conclusion.

---

carcinoma. My doctors injected ten shots of steroids into each scar every three weeks to stop the scars from spreading. I now know that it wasn't worth a couple of summers of being tan to go through all that pain and suffering. Take steps now to protect yourself from the harmful effects of the sun.

Use a Metaphor

Dr. Ralph Bunche, grandson of a former slave, earned a Ph.D. from Harvard, was a member of the United Nations Secretariat, and later won the Nobel Peace Prize. In June 1949, Dr. Bunche began a speech at Brandeis University with a "road to peace" metaphor that explains what must be done to achieve a more peaceful world:

There is no road in the world today more important than the road to peace. It is, to date, insufficiently traveled, and indeed, not at all clearly charted. The United Nations is attempting both to chart it and to guide the nations and people of the world along it.[34]

Dr. Bunche compares a path to peace with a road that is not well-traveled. This metaphor is an eloquent way of beginning a presentation.

Ask a Question

Asking a question attracts your audience's attention because it challenges them to think about an answer. One of the best kinds of questions elicits a response such as "I had no idea!" In the following example, a student speaker used this technique in a series of questions:

What do China, Iran, Saudi Arabia, and the United States have in common? Nuclear weapons? No. Abundant oil resource? No. What we have in common is this: Last year, these four countries accounted for nearly all the executions in the world.[35]

Refer to the Current Place or Occasion

A simple way to begin a presentation is to refer to the place in which you are speaking or the occasion for the gathering. Your audience's memories and feelings about a specific place or occasion conjure up the emotions needed to capture their attention and interest.

When Dr. Martin Luther King, Jr., made his famous "I Have a Dream" presentation on the steps of

---

Primacy effect Describes our tendency to recall the first items in a sequence more readily than the middle items

Recency effect Describes our tendency to recall the last items in a sequence

the Lincoln Memorial, his first few words echoed Abraham Lincoln's famous Gettysburg Address ("Four score and seven years ago"). Dr. King began:

> Five score years ago, a great American, in whose symbolic shadow we stand, signed the Emancipation Proclamation.[36]

Refer to a Well-Known Incident or Event

Events that occurred shortly before your presentation or in the recent past will gain audience attention and interest. In the following example, a college president refers to the September 11 tragedy:

> Soon after the September 11 tragedy, I saw a proliferation of highway billboards that celebrated our country and citizen patriotism. One billboard stood out. It was both simple and eloquent. A stars-and-stripes ribbon sat on a plain white background. Three words declared its purpose: United We Stand. The same three words are just as relevant at this college. Immediately following the September 11 tragedy, we united to counsel our students. Today, we unite to recognize and celebrate the achievements of our colleagues at our annual convocation.

The "recent event" technique is frequently used for political speechmaking. Much like references to place or occasion, memories and feelings about a recent event capture an appropriate mood for your introduction.

Address Audience Needs

When there is a crisis, address the problem at the outset. If budget cuts require salary reductions, audience members are not interested in clever questions or dramatic statistics.

> As you know, the state has reduced our operating budget by 2.7 million dollars. It is also just as important that you know this: All of you will have a job here next year—and the year after. There will be no layoffs. Instead, there will be cutbacks on nonpersonnel budget lines, downsizing of programs, and possibly short furloughs.

TIPS FOR STARTING STRONG

- **PLAN THE BEGINNING AT THE END.** Don't plan your introduction before you develop the content of your presentation.

- **DON'T APOLOGIZE.** Don't use your introduction to offer excuses or apologize for poor preparation, weak delivery, or nervousness.

- **AVOID BEGINNING WITH "MY SPEECH IS ABOUT . . ."** Boring beginnings do not capture audience attention or enhance a speaker's credibility. Be original and creative.

Beginning your presentation by referring to a well-known incident and coupling it with a compelling image can gain audience attention and interest.

concluding your PRESENTATION

You know that audiences remember things that are presented first (the primacy effect). They also remember information that comes last (recency effect). Final words have a powerful and lasting effect on your audience and determine how your audience thinks and feels about you and your presentation.[37] Like the introduction, a conclusion establishes a relationship among you, your topic, and your audience.

Some methods of concluding your presentation reinforce your message; others strengthen the audience's final impression of you. As with introductions, use any of the following approaches separately or in combination: summarize, quote someone, tell a story, use poetic language, call for action, or refer to the beginning.

Summarize

A succinct summary reinforces your key points and is the most direct way to conclude a presentation. This is also the best way to review and repeat the key points in your presentation. Summaries should be memorable, clear, and brief. Here, a speaker uses questions to emphasize his central idea and key points:

Now, if you hear someone ask whether more women should serve in the U.S. Congress, ask and then answer the two questions I discussed today: Can women and their issues attract big donors? And, are women too nice to be "tough" in politics? Now that you know how to answer these questions, don't let doubters stand in the way of making a woman's place in the House.

Quote Someone

What is true about quoting someone in your introduction is true about concluding with a quotation. Because quotations are memorable, clear, and brief, speakers often use them to conclude their presentations. Good research can provide a quotation with a dramatic effect. For example, when Bono, lead singer of the band U2, delivered the 2004 commencement speech to the graduating class of the University of Pennsylvania, he concluded by quoting John Adams, hoping to inspire the class to take the lead on ending poverty and disease worldwide:

Remember what John Adams said about Ben Franklin: "He does not hesitate at our boldest Measures but rather seems to think us too irresolute." Well, this is the time for bold measures and this is the country and you are the generation.[38]

Tell a Story

End with a story when you want the audience to visualize the central idea of your presentation. Marge Anderson, chief executive of the Mille Lacs Band of Ojibwe Indians, concluded a presentation with a story. (See the complete speech in Chapter 16.)

Years ago, white settlers came to this area and built the first European-style homes. When Indian People walked by these homes and saw [windows], they looked through them to see what the strangers inside were doing. The settlers were shocked, but it made sense when you think about it: Windows are made to be looked through from both sides. Since then, my People have spent many years looking

GOALS OF THE CONCLUSION

Be Memorable

Give the audience a reason to remember you and your presentation. Show how your message affected you and how it affects them.

Be Clear

Repeat the one thing you want your audience to remember at the end of your presentation.

Be Brief

The announced ending of a presentation should never go beyond one or two minutes.

at the world through your window. I hope today I've given you a reason to look at it through ours.[39]

Use Poetic Language

Being poetic doesn't necessarily mean ending with a poem. Rather, it means using language that inspires and creates memorable images. In her tribute to the late Coretta Scott King, poet Maya Angelou concluded with poetic, prayer-like phrases:

> I pledge to you, my sister, I will never cease.
>
> I mean to say I want to see a better world.
>
> I mean to say I want to see some peace somewhere.
>
> I mean to say I want to see some honesty, some fair play.
>
> I want to see kindness and justice. This is what I want to see and I want to see it through my eyes and through your eyes, Coretta Scott King.[40]

Call for Action

A challenging but effective way to end a presentation is to call for action. Use a call for action when you want your audience to do more than merely listen—when you want them to *do* something. A call to action might mean rallying an audience to remember something important, to think about the importance of a story you told, or to ask themselves a significant question. Here is how Dr. Robert M. Franklin, president of Morehouse College, ended remarks delivered to a town hall meeting of students on his campus:

> . . . Morehouse is your house. You must take responsibility for its excellence. . . . If you want to be part of something rare and noble, something that the world has not often seen—a community of educated, ethical, disciplined black men more powerful than a standing army—then you've come to

Don't end by demanding something from your audience unless you are reasonably sure you can get it.

the right place. . . . Up, you mighty men of Morehouse, you aristocrats of spirit, you can accomplish what you will![41]

Refer to the Beginning

Consider ending your presentation with the same technique you used to begin it. If you began with a quotation, end with the same or a similar quotation. If you began with a story, refer back to that story. Audiences like this concluding method because it returns to something familiar and "bookends" the content of your presentation. For example:

> Remember the story I told you about two-year-old Joey, a hole in his throat so he can breathe, a tube jutting out of his stomach so he can be fed. For Joey, an accidental poisoning was an excruciatingly painful and horrifying experience. For Joey's parents, it was a time of fear, panic, and helplessness. Thus, it is a time to be prepared for, and even better, a time to prevent.

Knowing that you have a well-prepared and strong ending for your presentation can calm your nerves and inspire your audience. The most effective endings match the mood and style of the presentation, and make realistic assumptions about the audience. Don't end by demanding something from your audience unless you are reasonably sure you can get it.

TIPS FOR ENDING STRONG

MAKE SURE THE MOOD AND STYLE ARE CONSISTENT
Don't tack on an irrelevant or inappropriate ending.

HAVE REALISTIC EXPECTATIONS
Most audience members will not act when called upon unless the request is carefully worded, reasonable, and possible.

Communication ASSESSMENT

Can You Match the Organizational Patterns?

Each of the following examples demonstrates how to use one (or more) of the organizational patterns listed below. Try to match each outline with a pattern.

Organizational Patterns

A. Topical arrangement
B. Time arrangement
C. Space arrangement
D. Problem–solution

E. Causes and effects
F. Stories and examples
G. Comparison–contrast

_____ 1. The Three Stages of Pregnancy
    First trimester
    Second trimester
    Third trimester

_____ 2. Four Basic Techniques Used to Play Volleyball
    Setting
    Bumping
    Spiking
    Serving

_____ 3. The Richest Sources of Diamonds
    South Africa
    Tanzania
    Murfreesboro, Arkansas

_____ 4. The Legacies of Presidents Reagan, Bush, Sr., and Clinton
    Domestic politics
    International politics
    Party politics

_____ 5. Homeless Shelters and Homeless Families
    The Khoo family
    The Taylor family
    The Arias family

_____ 6. Slowing the AIDS Epidemic
    AIDS is a devastating disease.
    A cure has not been found.
    New drug "cocktails" can slow the onset of AIDS.

_____ 7. Aspirin and Heart Attacks
    Does research verify that aspirin prevents heart attacks?
    Who should follow the aspirin prescription?
    Are there potential, dangerous side effects of aspirin therapy?

Summary

How do you find good information for a presentation?

- Effective speakers use several forms of supporting material: facts, statistics, testimony, definitions, descriptions, analogies, examples, and stories.
- Document your supporting material in writing and then orally in your presentation.
- Make sure your source is identified, credible, and unbiased.
- Test the validity of your supporting material by determining whether the information comes from a primary or secondary source and whether it's recent and consistent.
- Evaluate the validity of statistics by making sure they are well-founded, justified, and accurate.

What strategies should you use to organize the content of a presentation?

- The first step in organizing the content of a presentation is to identify your key points. Make sure your key points reflect your central idea.
- Mind mapping and the Speech Framer can help you identify the key points and organize your message.
- Commonly used organizational patterns include topical, time, space, problem–solution, causes and effects, stories and examples, and comparison–contrast arrangements.

How can outlining help you structure a presentation?

- Use a preliminary outline to identify the basic building blocks of a presentation.
- When preparing a comprehensive outline, use numbers, letters, and indentation; divide your subpoints logically; and keep the outline consistent in style.

How do connectives make a presentation more coherent?

- Connective phrases are the "glue" that links the key points to one another and makes your presentation a coherent whole.
- Connective phrases include internal previews, summaries, transitions, and signposts.

What strategies will help you begin a presentation effectively?

- The primacy effect explains our tendency to recall the introduction of a presentation better than the middle.
- Presentation introductions should attempt to focus attention and interest, connect with audience, enhance your credibility, set the emotional tone, and preview the message.
- Methods of beginning a presentation include using a statistic or example, quoting someone, telling a story, using a metaphor, asking a question, referring to the current place or occasion, referring to a well-known incident or event, and addressing audience needs.
- Your introduction will be more effective if you plan the beginning at the end, do not apologize, and avoid beginning with "*My speech is about. . . .*"

What strategies will help you end a presentation effectively?

- The recency effect explains our tendency to recall the conclusion of a presentation.
- Presentation conclusions should attempt to be memorable, be clear, and be brief.
- Methods of concluding a presentation include summarizing, quoting someone, telling a story, using poetic language, calling for action, and referring to the beginning.
- Your conclusion will be more effective if you make sure that the mood and style are consistent with the presentation and that you have realistic expectations about audience reactions.

the THINKSPOT
www.thethinkspot.com

TEST yourknowledge

1 What kind of supporting material is used in the following excerpt from a student's presentation? *Ron Wilson, an African American representative in Texas, argues that it's a great hypocrisy when courts allow selective universities to relax their academic standards for athletes and children of alumni but not for African Americans.*

a. fact

b. statistics

c. testimony

d. description

e. story

2 What kind of supporting material is used in the following example? *One way to understand neuroplasticity (how the brain creates mind-sets) is by comparing it to snow skiing. Plasticity is like snow on a hill in winter. Because it is pliable it can take many paths if we choose to ski down that hill. But because it is pliable, if we keep taking the same path, we develop tracks, and then ruts, and get stuck in them.*

a. description

b. analogy

c. example

d. story

e. definition

3 You need to ask all of the questions for testing supporting material to the following example except one. Which test is not needed for this example? *Joseph Farah, editor of* World News Daily, *the politically conservative, conspiracy-theory Website, writes that "Obama is choreographing a top-down revolution in America—one from which it may take generations to extricate ourselves. It will be a shame if we learn he was ineligible to serve in the office of president only after he's gone."*

a. Is the source credible?

b. Is the source biased?

c. Is the source identified?

d. Is the information valid?

e. Is the information recent?

4 Which technique for identifying the key points and organizing a presentation involves using a visual model that places each component of a presentation in a designated place?

a. outlining

b. using an organizational jigsaw puzzle

c. mind mapping

d. Speech Framer

e. choosing an organizational pattern

5 Which of the following answers constitutes the best example of a central idea for a presentation on the different meanings of facial expressions in other cultures?

a. Facial expressions differ across cultures.

b. The meaning of some facial expressions differ from culture to culture.

c. Facial expressions for fear, sadness, and disgust are the same across cultures.

d. Although many facial expressions are the same in different cultures—such as smiling—other facial expressions differ.

e. Americans and native Japanese often misinterpret facial expressions depicting fear, sadness, and disgust.

6 Which organizational pattern works best for explaining to an audience how to bake a cake?

a. time

b. topical

c. space

d. causes and effects

e. stories and examples

7 The primacy effect explains why

a. an effective introduction is so important at the beginning of a presentation.

b. an effective conclusion is so important at the end of a presentation.

c. transitions are so important in the middle of a presentation.

d. presentations should "end with a bang."

e. a presentation's key points should be determined before looking for supporting material.

8 Which kind of connective is used in the following example? *Once you've collected all of your ingredients, you can begin the process of putting the recipe together.*

a. internal preview

b. internal outline

c. internal summary

d. transition

e. signpost

9 What introductory technique did Abraham Lincoln use when he started the Gettysburg Address with these words? *Four score and seven years ago, our fathers brought forth on this continent, a new nation, conceived in liberty, and dedicated to the proposition that all men are created equal.*

a. Refer to a current place or occasion.

b. Refer to a well-known incident or event.

c. Use a metaphor.

d. Quote someone.

e. Address audience needs.

10 What concluding technique did Abraham Lincoln use when he ended the Gettysburg Address with these words? *. . . that this nation, under God, shall have a new birth of freedom—and that government of the people, by the people, for the people, shall not perish from the earth.*

a. Summarize.

b. Quote someone.

c. Tell a story.

d. Use poetic language.

e. Call for action.

Answers: 1-c; 2-b; 3-c; 4-d; 5-e; 6-a; 7-a; 8-d; 9-b; 10-d

14 LANGUAGE

The 2008 presidential campaign dealt with huge issues: the Iraq War, the near-collapse of the U.S. economy, and the need for better health care and public education. The campaign, however, was more than a political clash. It became a contest between two very different types of public speakers. Software programs analyzing the candidates' language and delivery styles revealed how differently McCain and Obama expressed themselves. The media—from network news to popular blogs—often seemed more preoccupied with *how* the candidates spoke rather than with *what* they had to say:

> **If your language is bland and boring or your eye contact never strays from your notes, you can't recapture your audience to do a better job.**

McCain is the blunt-spoken platoon leader, briefing soldiers for battle. Senator Obama is the evangelist, calling out from the hilltop. McCain levels. Obama transcends. McCain is straight talk, Obama great talk.

... in speeches, McCain's rhetorical style can sound like—as the Comedy Central host Stephen Colbert put it—"tired mayonnaise." His [use of] "my friends" can weary.

AND DELIVERY

His body language—a smile after sternly pledging to follow Osama bin Laden to "the gates of hell"— can seem incongruous and ill-timed.

The Illinois senator sprinkles speeches with *we* and *you*—"Yes we can" and "You have done what the cynics said we couldn't do"— as if he were as much guiding a movement as running for president.[1]

In this chapter, we focus on two performance components of presentation speaking—language and delivery. How you use words, your voice, your body, and presentation aids to express yourself and your message are irreversible components in every presentation. If, for example, you use inappropriate words or speak in a voice that cannot be heard, you can't undo what you've said or how you've performed. If your language is bland and boring or your eye contact never strays from your notes, you can't recapture your audience to do a better job.

THE CORE
language styles

Carefully chosen words can add power and authority to a presentation and transform good presentations into great ones. Your speaking style can add a distinctive flavor, emotional excitement, and brilliant clarity.

Speaking style refers to how you use vocabulary, sentence structure and length, grammar and syntax, and rhetorical devices to express a message.[2] In this section, we describe four **CORE speaking styles**: **c**lear style, **o**ral style, **r**hetorical style, and **e**loquent style. Your task is to decide which styles suit you, your purpose, your audience, the setting and occasion of your presentation, and your message.

Clear Style

Clarity always comes first. If you aren't clear, your audience won't understand you and won't be impressed with how you express your message. The **clear style** uses short, simple, and direct words and phrases as well as active verbs, concrete words, and plain language.

As marketing expert Jerry Della Femina notes: "Nobody has time to try and figure out what you're trying to say, so you need to be direct. Most great advertising is direct. That's how people talk. That's the style they read. That's what sells products or services or ideas."[3]

CLARITY always comes first.

Oral Style

Chapter 5, Verbal Communication, emphasizes the importance of using oral language when interacting with others. Review the features of the oral style: short, familiar words; shorter, simpler, and even incomplete sentences; and more personal pronouns and informal colloquial expressions. When using an oral style, say what you mean by speaking the way you talk, not the way you write. (For an example of both clear and oral styles, see John Sullivan's informative presentation, "Cliff's Notes," in Chapter 15.)

Speaking style How you use vocabulary, sentence structure and length, grammar and syntax, and rhetorical devices to express a message

CORE speaking styles Refers to four basic language styles: **c**lear style, **o**ral style, **r**hetorical style, and **e**loquent style

Clear style Short, simple, and direct words and phrases as well as active verbs, concrete words, and plain language

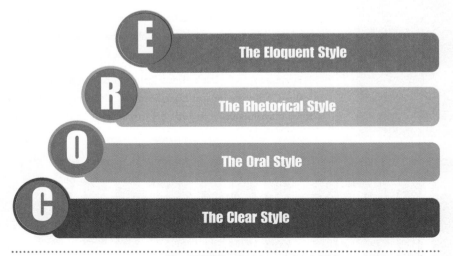

The CORE speaking styles build upon one another.

The Eloquent Style

The Rhetorical Style

The Oral Style

The Clear Style

Differences in Written and Oral Styles[4]

Excerpts from an Essay on Neuromusicology

"I haven't understood a bar of music in my entire life, but I have felt it" (qtd. in Peter 350). These words were spoken by Igor Stravinsky, who composed some of the most complex and sophisticated music of his century. If the great Stravinsky can accept the elusive nature of music, and still love it, why can't we? Why are we analyzing it to try to make it useful?

Ours is an age of information—an age that wishes to conquer all the mysteries of the human brain. Today there is a growing trend to study music's effects on our emotions, behavior, health, and intelligence. Journalist Alex Ross reports how the relatively new field of neuromusicology (the science of the nervous system and its response to music) has been developed to experiment with music as a tool and to shape it to the needs of society. Observations like these let us know that we are on the threshold of seeing music in a whole new way and using music to achieve measurable changes in behavior. However, this new approach carries dangers, and once we go in this direction, there can be no turning back. How far do we want to go in our study of musical science? What effects will it have on our listening pleasures?

A short history lesson reveals that there has been an awareness that music affects us, even if the reasons are not clear. Around 900 B.C., David (late King David) played the harp "to cure Saul's derangement" (Gonzalez–Crussi 69).

Quoted from Ann Raimes, *Keys for Writers: A Brief Handbook,* 3rd ed. (Boston: Houghton Mifflin, 2004), 152–158.

Excerpts from a Presentation on Neuromusicology

[Note: As an opening, the speaker plays an excerpt from "God Bless America" followed by an excerpt from *Sesame Street*'s theme music.]

What did you think of or feel when you heard "God Bless America"? What about the *Sesame Street* theme? I'm sure that you're not surprised to learn that "God Bless America" reminds many people of the September 11th tragedy, the War in Iraq, and patriotism. And the theme from good ol' *Sesame Street* probably put a smile on your face as you revisited the world of Kermit the Frog, Miss Piggy, and Big Bird.

Why were your responses so predictable and so emotional? The answer lies in a new brain science—a science that threatens to control you by controlling the music you hear. Is resistance futile?

In the next few minutes, we'll take a close look at the field of neuromusicology. What? *Neuro*, meaning related to our brain and nervous system. And *musicology*—the historic and scientific study of music.

Journalist Alex Ross put it this way: By understanding the nervous system and its response to music, neuromusicologists study music as a tool and shape it to the needs of society.

As New Age as all this may sound, there's plenty of history to back up the claims of neuromusicologists. For example, those of you who know your Bible know that King David played the harp to "cure Saul's derangement."

Quoted from Isa Engleberg and Ann Raimes, *Pocket Keys for Speakers,* (Boston: Houghton Mifflin, 2004), 191–193.

Say what you mean by speaking the way you talk, not the way you write.

Rhetorical Style

The **rhetorical style** uses language designed to influence, persuade, and/or inspire. Vivid and powerful words enhance the intensity of a persuasive presentation. **Language intensity** refers to the degree to which your language deviates from bland, neutral terms.[5] For example, instead of using a word like *nice*, try *delightful* or *captivating*. *Disaster* is a much more intense word than *mistake*. A *vile* meal sounds much worse than a *bad* meal.

The rhetorical style often relies upon **rhetorical devices**, word strategies designed to enhance a presentation's impact and persuasiveness. Two rhetorical devices work particularly well in presentations: repetition and metaphors.

Repetition Because your listeners can't rewind and immediately re-hear what you've just said, use repetition to highlight the sounds, words, ideas, and phrases you want your audience to remember. Repetition can be as simple as beginning a series of words (or words placed closely together) with the same sound. This type of repetition is called **alliteration**. For example,

---

Rhetorical style Language designed to influence, persuade, and/or inspire

Language intensity The degree to which language deviates from bland, neutral terms

Rhetorical devices Words strategies designed to enhance a presentation's impact and persuasiveness

Alliteration A rhetorical device in which a series of words (or words placed closely together) begin with the same sound

the first part of Lincoln's Gettysburg Address—"*Four* score and seven years ago our *fathers* brought *forth*"—includes three words beginning with the letter *f*.

Repetition can be extended to a word, a phrase, or an entire sentence. Dr. Martin Luther King, Jr., used the phrase "I have a dream" nine times in his famous 1963 speech in Washington, D.C. He used "let freedom ring" ten times. Repetition can drive home an idea and provoke action. Audience members anticipate and remember repeated phrases.

Metaphors Metaphors and their cousins—similes and analogies—are powerful rhetorical devices. Shakespeare's famous line "All the world's a stage" is a classic metaphor. The world is not a theatrical stage, but we do play and act many parts during a lifetime. Metaphors leave it to the audience to get the point for themselves.[6]

Many linguists claim that metaphors are the most powerful figures of speech. Some researchers believe that metaphors are windows into the workings of the human mind.[7] They are much more than literary devices reserved for the use of authors and poets.[8]

> *Art is a **rebellious child, a wild animal** that will not be tamed.*
> —Isabel Allende

> *An **iron curtain** has descended across the continent of Europe.*
> —Winston Churchill

Eloquent Style

The **eloquent style** uses poetic and expressive language in a way that makes thoughts and feelings clear, inspiring, *and* memorable. Eloquent language does not have to be flowery or grand; it can use an oral style, personal pronouns, and repetition or metaphors. Statements such as Abraham Lincoln's "government of the people, by the people, for the people shall not perish from the earth" are memorable and inspiring because (in addition to the alliteration and despite myths to the contrary) Lincoln spent considerable time and effort searching for the best words to communicate his thoughts and feelings.[9]

Poetic language has the remarkable ability to capture profound ideas and feelings in a few simple words. It is also more rhythmic. According to communication scholar Matthew McGlone, rhyme makes ordinary statements more believable.[10] "Woes unite foes," for example, was deemed more credible than "Woes unite enemies."

In *Eloquence in an Electronic Age: The Transformation of Political Speechmaking*, Kathleen Jamieson notes that eloquent speakers comfortably disclose personal experiences and feelings. Rather than explaining the lessons of the past or creating a public sense of ethics, today's eloquent speakers often call upon their own past or their own sense of ethics to inspire an audience.[11] Consider the words Barack Obama used in his "A More Perfect Union" speech in Philadelphia on March 18, 2008.

I am the son of a black man from Kenya and a white woman from Kansas. I was raised with the help of a white grandfather who survived a Depression to serve in Patton's Army during World War II and a white grandmother who worked on a bomber assembly line at Fort Leavenworth while he was overseas. I've gone to some of the best schools in America and lived in one of the world's poorest nations. I am married to a black American who carries within her the blood of slaves and slaveowners—an inheritance we pass on to our two precious daughters. I have brothers, sisters, nieces, nephews, uncles and cousins, of every race and every hue, scattered across three continents, and for as long as I live, I will never forget that in no other country on Earth is my story even possible.

The four CORE speaking styles are not separate from or incompatible with one another. Whereas some speakers are most comfortable using the clear and oral styles, others prefer the added intensity of the rhetorical style. A few speakers use the eloquent style regardless of whether they are teaching a class, testifying to a committee, or toasting a newly married couple. Depending on your purpose, the audience and their expectations, the kind of personal image you want to project, and the logistics and occasion of the presentation, you should try to use the styles that best match you and your messages.

Eloquent style Poetic and expressive language that makes thoughts and feelings clear, inspiring, *and* memorable

POETIC LANGUAGE
has the remarkable ability to capture profound ideas and feelings in a few simple words.

modes
OF DELIVERY

t he term **delivery** describes the ways in which you use your voice, body, and presentation aids to express your presentation's message. You can select from a number of expressive forms: impromptu, extemporaneous, manuscript, memorized, or a combination of forms. But, before you do, decide which of these modes best suits your purpose.

Impromptu

Impromptu speaking occurs when you speak without advanced preparation or practice. For example, you may be called upon in class or at work to answer a question or share an opinion. You may be inspired to get up and speak on an important issue at a public meeting. While you don't have a lot of time to prepare, you can quickly think of a purpose and a way to organize and adapt your message to the audience.

Extemporaneous

Extemporaneous speaking is the most common form of delivery and occurs when you use an outline or a set of notes to guide you through a prepared presentation. Your notes can be a few words on a card or a detailed, full-sentence outline. Classroom lectures, business briefings, and courtroom arguments are usually delivered extemporaneously. Extemporaneous speaking is easiest for beginners to do well and the method preferred by professionals. No other form of delivery gives you as much freedom and flexibility with preplanned material. A well-practiced extemporaneous presentation seems spontaneous and has an ease to it that makes the audience and speaker feel more comfortable.

Manuscript

Manuscript speaking involves writing your presentation in advance and reading it out loud. Using a manuscript allows you to choose each word carefully. You can plan and practice every detail. It also ensures that your presentation will fit within your allotted speaking time.

ADVANTAGES AND DISADVANTAGES OF IMPROMPTU DELIVERY

ADVANTAGES	DISADVANTAGES
• Natural and conversational speaking style • Maximum eye contact • Freedom of movement • Easier to adjust to audience feedback • Demonstrates speaker's knowledge and skill	• Limited time to make basic decisions about purpose, audience adaptation, content, and organization • Speaking anxiety can be high • Delivery may be awkward and ineffective • Difficult to gauge speaking time • Limited or no supporting material • Speaker may have nothing to say on such short notice

ADVANTAGES AND DISADVANTAGES OF EXTEMPORANEOUS DELIVERY

ADVANTAGES	DISADVANTAGES
• More preparation time than impromptu delivery • Seems spontaneous but is actually well-prepared • Speaker can monitor and adapt to audience feedback • Allows more eye contact and audience interaction than manuscript delivery • Audiences respond positively to extemporaneous delivery • Speaker can choose concise language for central idea and key points • With practice, it becomes the most powerful form of delivery	• Speaker anxiety can increase for content not covered by notes • Language may not be well-chosen or eloquent • Can be difficult to estimate speaking time

Delivery The various ways in which you use your voice, body, and presentation aids to express your presentation's message

Impromptu speaking Occurs when you give a presentation without advanced preparation or practice

Extemporaneous speaking The most common form of delivery that occurs when you use an outline or a set of notes to guide yourself through a prepared presentation

Manuscript speaking A form of delivery in which a speaker writes a presentation in advance and reads it out loud

ADVANTAGES AND DISADVANTAGES OF MANUSCRIPT DELIVERY

ADVANTAGES	DISADVANTAGES
• Can pay careful attention to all the basic principles of effective speaking • Can choose concise and eloquent language • Speaker anxiety may be eased by having a "script" • Can rehearse the same presentation over and over • Ensures accurate reporting of presentation content • Speaker can stay within time limit	• Delivery can be dull • Difficult to maintain sufficient eye contact • Gestures and movement are limited • Language can be too formal, lacking oral style • Difficult to modify or adapt to the audience or situation

For very nervous speakers, a manuscript can be a lifesaving document.

However, manuscript presentations are difficult to deliver for all but the most skilled and practiced speakers. If you must use a manuscript, focus on maintaining an oral style: *Write as though you are speaking*. Generally, we do not encourage speakers to use manuscript delivery. Yet there are occasions when a word-for-word manuscript is either necessary or very helpful. If the occasion is an important public event at which every word counts and time is strictly limited, you may have no choice but to use a manuscript. If the occasion is highly emotional (such as a funeral or a prestigious award ceremony), you may need the support provided by a manuscript.

Memorized

Memorized speaking requires a speaker to deliver a presentation from recall with very few or no notes. A memorized presentation offers one major advantage and one major disadvantage. The major advantage is physical freedom. You can gesture freely and look at your audience 100 percent of the time. The disadvantage, however, outweighs any and all advantages. If you forget the words you memorized, it is more difficult to recover your thoughts without creating an awkward moment for both you and your audience.

Rarely do speakers memorize an entire presentation. However, there's nothing wrong with memorizing your introduction or a few key sections, as long as you have your notes to fall back on.

ADVANTAGES AND DISADVANTAGES OF MEMORIZED DELIVERY

ADVANTAGES
• Incorporates the preparation advantages of manuscript delivery and the delivery advantages of impromptu speaking • Maximizes eye contact and freedom of movement

DISADVANTAGES
• Requires extensive time to memorize • Disaster awaits if memory fails • Can sound stilted and insincere • Very difficult to modify or adapt to the audience or situation • Can lack a sense of spontaneity unless expertly delivered

Mix and Match Modes of Delivery

Learning to mix and match modes of delivery appropriately lets you select the method that works best for you and your purpose. An impromptu speaker may recite a memorized statistic or a rehearsed argument in the same way that a politician responds to press questions. An extemporaneous speaker may read a lengthy quotation or a series of statistics and then deliver a memorized ending. A manuscript reader may stop and tell an impromptu story or may deliver memorized sections that benefit from uninterrupted and direct eye contact with the audience.

Speaking Notes

Effective speakers use their notes effectively and efficiently. Even when you are speaking impromptu, you may use a few quick words jotted down just before you speak. Speaking notes may appear on index cards and outlines or as a manuscript.

Index Cards and Outlines A single card can be used for each component of your presentation; for example, you can use one card for the introduction, another card for each key point, and one card for your conclusion. Record key words rather

> **Memorized speaking** A form of delivery in which a speaker memorizes a presentation and delivers it with very few or no notes

than complete sentences on only one side of each index card. To help you organize your presentation and rearrange key points at the last minute, number each of the cards. If you have too many notes for a few index cards, use an outline.

Manuscript When preparing a speech manuscript, double space each page and use a 14- to 16-point font size. Use only the top two-thirds of the page to avoid having to bend your head to see the bottom of each page and lose eye contact with your audience or constrict your windpipe. Set wide margins so that you have space on the page to add any last-minute changes. Remember to number each page so that you can keep everything in order, and do not staple your pages together. Instead, place your manuscript to one side of the lectern and slide the pages to the other side when it's time to go on to the next page.

Bruce Springsteen uses a lectern and manuscript during his tribute to U2 at the 2005 Rock and Roll Hall of Fame Induction Ceremony.

vocal DELIVERY

developing a more effective speaking voice requires the same time and effort that you would devote to mastering any skill. You can't become an accomplished carpenter, pianist, swimmer, writer, or speaker overnight. Because only a few lucky speakers are born with beautiful voices, the majority of us must work at sounding clear and expressive. Fortunately, there are ways to improve the characteristics and quality of your voice. Begin by focusing on the basics: breathing, volume, rate, pitch, fluency, articulation, and pronunciation.

Breathing

All the sounds in spoken English are made during exhalation. The key to effective breathing for presentation speaking is controlling your outgoing breath. Effective breath control enables you to speak more loudly, say more in a single breath, and reduce the likelihood of vocal problems such as harshness or breathiness. Thus, the first step in learning how to breathe for presentation speaking is to note the differences between the shallow, unconscious breathing you do all the time and the deeper breathing that produces strong, sustained sound quality.

Exercise for Deep Breathing

1. Lie flat on your back. Support the back of your knees with a pillow.

2. Place a moderately heavy, hardbound book on your stomach, right over your navel.

3. Begin breathing through your mouth. The book should move up when you breathe in and sink down when you breathe out.

4. Place one of your hands on the upper part of your chest in a "Pledge of Allegiance" position. As you inhale and exhale, this area should not move in and out or up and down.

5. Take the book away and replace it with your other hand. Your abdominal area should continue to move up when you breathe in and sink down when you breathe out.

6. After you're comfortable with step 5, try doing the same kind of breathing while sitting up or standing.

7. Add sound. Try sighing and sustaining the vowel *ahh* for five seconds with each exhalation. Then try counting or reciting the alphabet.

Volume

Volume measures the loudness level of your voice. The key to producing adequate volume is adapting to the size of the audience and the dimensions of the room in which you will be speaking. If there are only five people in an audience and they are sitting close to you, speak at a normal, everyday volume. If there are 50 people in your audience, you need more energy and force to support your voice. When your audience exceeds 50, you may be more comfortable with a microphone. However, a strong speaking voice can project to an audience of a thousand people without electronic amplification. Professional actors and classical singers do it all the time.

Volume The loudness level of your voice

Activist and politician Harvey Milk was well known for his dynamic speeches, which he would often deliver without the aid of a microphone.

Practice your presentation in a room about the same size as the one in which you will be speaking, or, at least, imagine speaking in such a room. Ask a friend to sit in a far corner and report back on your volume and clarity. Also note that a room full of people absorbs sound;

you will have to turn up your volume another notch. Speakers who cannot be heard are a common problem. It's very rare, though, for a speaker to be too loud.

Rate

Your **rate** of presentation equals the number of words you say per minute (wpm). Generally, a rate less than 125 wpm is too slow, 125 to 145 wpm is acceptable, 145 to 180 wpm is better, and 180 wpm or more exceeds the speed limit. But do not carve these guidelines in stone. Your rate depends on you, the nature and mood of your message, and your audience. If you are explaining a highly technical process or expressing personal sorrow, your rate may slow to 125 wpm. On the other hand, if you are telling an exciting, amusing, or infuriating story, your rate may hit 200 wpm. For maximum effectiveness,

> **Remember that audiences can listen faster than you talk, so it's better to keep the pace up than speak at a crawl.**

speakers vary their rate. Martin Luther King, Jr.'s, "I Have a Dream" speech opened at a slow 90 wpm, but ended at 150 wpm.[12]

Listeners perceive presenters who speak quickly *and* clearly as energized, motivated, and interested. Given the choice, we'd rather be accused of speaking too quickly than run the risk of boring an audience. Too slow a rate suggests that you are unsure of yourself or, even worse, that you are not very bright. Remember that audiences can listen faster than you can talk, so it's better to keep the pace up than speak at a crawl.

Rate The number of words you say per minute (wpm)

Master the Microphone

If the speaking situation requires a microphone or presents you with one, make the most out of this technology. Unless a sound technician is monitoring the presentation, your microphone will be preset for one volume. If you speak with too much volume, it may sound as though you are shouting at your audience. If you speak too softly, the microphone may not pick up everything you have to say. The trick is to go against your instincts. If you want to project a soft tone, speak closer to the microphone and lower your volume. Your voice will sound more intimate and will convey subtle emotions. If you want to be more forceful, speak farther away from the microphone and project your voice.

Most important, familiarize yourself with the specific microphone and system you will be using. For example, when placed on a lapel, the microphone faces outward rather than upward. As a result, it receives and sends a less direct sound.[13] Here are some tips to follow for all microphones:

- Test the microphone ahead of time.
- Determine whether the microphone is sophisticated enough to capture your voice from several angles and distances or whether you will need to keep your mouth close to it.
- Place the microphone about 5 to 10 inches from your mouth. If you are using a hand-held microphone, hold it below your mouth at chin level.

- Focus on your audience, not the microphone. Stay near the mike, but don't tap it, lean over it, keep readjusting it, or make the p-p-p-p-p "motorboat sounds" as a test. Experienced speakers make the adjustments they need during the first few seconds that they hear their own voices projected through an amplification system.
- Keep in mind that a microphone will do more than amplify your voice; it will also amplify other sounds—coughing, clearing your throat, shuffling papers, or tapping a pen.
- If your microphone is well-adjusted, speak in a natural, conversational voice.

Pitch

Pitch refers to how high or low your voice sounds—just like the notes on a musical scale. Anatomy determines pitch (most men speak at a lower pitch than women and children). Your **optimum pitch** is the pitch at which you speak most easily and expressively. If you speak at your optimum pitch, you will not tire as easily; your voice will sound stronger and will less likely fade at the end of sentences. It will also be less likely to sound harsh, hoarse, or breathy.

To find your optimum pitch, sing up the musical scale from the lowest note you can sing. By the fifth or sixth note, you should have reached your optimum pitch. Test your optimum pitch to see if your voice is clear and whether you can increase its volume with minimal effort. Finding your optimum pitch does *not* mean using that pitch for everything you say. Think of your optimum pitch as "neutral," and use it as your baseline for increasing the expressiveness of your voice through **inflection**—the changing pitch within a syllable, word, or group of words. Lack of inflection results in a monotone voice. A slight change, however, even just a fraction, can change the entire meaning of a sentence or the quality of your voice:

I was born in New Jersey. (You, on the other hand, were born in Iowa.)

I *was* born in New Jersey. (No doubt about it!)

I was *born* in New Jersey. (So I know my way around.)

I was born in *New Jersey*. (Not in New York.)

Fluency

When you speak with **fluency**, you speak smoothly without tripping over words or pausing at awkward moments. The more you practice your presentation, the more fluent you will become. Practice will alert you to words, phrases, and sentences that look good in your notes but sound awkward or choppy when spoken. You'll also find words that you have trouble pronouncing or notice **filler phrases**—*you know*, *uh*, *um*, *okay*, and *like*—that can break up your fluency and annoy your audience. There is nothing wrong with an occasional filler phrase, particularly when you're speaking informally or impromptu. What you want to avoid is excessive use. Try tape-recording your practice sessions and listening for filler phrases as you play the tape back. To break the filler-phrase habit, slow down and listen to the words you use—whether you are practicing a presentation or talking to friend. To break the habit, you must work on it all the time, not just when you are speaking in front of an audience.

Articulation

A strong, well-paced, optimally pitched voice that is also fluent and expressive may not be enough to ensure the successful delivery

---

Pitch How high or low your voice sounds

Optimum pitch The pitch at which you speak most easily and expressively

Inflection The changing pitch within a syllable, word, or group of words that makes speech expressive

Fluency The ability to speak smoothly without tripping over words or phrases

Filler phrases Words and phrases such as *you know*, *uh*, *um*, *okay*, and *like* that can break up a speaker's fluency and annoy the audience

---

communication&culture

SPEAKING STYLES AROUND THE GLOBE

In their studies of intercultural communication, Stella Ting-Toomey and Leeva C. Chung explain how verbal speaking styles differ from culture to culture.[14] For example, U.S. speakers use a *direct verbal style*, revealing their intentions with clarity and using a forthright tone of voice. Koreans speak in an *indirect verbal style*, camouflaging their intentions and using a softer tone. In other words, if U.S. speakers ask for a favor, they tend to use a straightforward form of request, while Koreans are more likely to inquire in a more roundabout way to sound less imposing or demanding.[15] In general, because this textbook is written for U.S speakers and audiences, we advocate a direct speaking style, but how would you modify your speaking style to address an audience that prefers an indirect verbal style?

U.S. speakers also tend to speak with an *informal verbal style*, characterized by casualness and low power distance (see Chapter 3). In general, they are more likely to address others on a first-name basis rather than using formal titles. They also strive for gender equality in their choice of words. Cultures that use a *formal verbal style* uphold status-based and role-based interactions that emphasize formality and high power distance (see Chapter 3). Japanese speakers, for instance, tend to "uphold the proper roles, with the proper words, in the appropriate contexts to create a predictable interaction climate."[16]

of a presentation. Proper **articulation**—how clearly you make the sounds in the words of a language—is just as important as your volume, rate, pitch, and fluency. Poor articulation is often described as sloppy speech, poor diction, or mumbling. Fortunately, you can improve and practice your articulation by speaking more slowly, speaking with a bit more volume, and opening your mouth wider when you speak.

Certain sounds account for most articulation problems: combined words, "-ing" endings, and final consonants. Many speakers combine words—"what's the matter" becomes "watsumata." Some speakers shorten the "ing" sound to an "in" sound: "sayin'" instead of "saying." The final consonants that get left off most often are the ones that pop out of your mouth. Because these consonants—*p*, *b*, *t*, *d*, *k*, *g*—

cannot be hummed like an "m" or hissed like an "s," it's easy to lose them at the end of a word. Usually you can hear the difference between "Rome," and "rose," but poor articulation can make it difficult to hear the difference between "hit" and "hid" or "tap" and "tab."

Pronunciation

Pronunciation refers to whether you put all the correct sounds of a word in the correct order with the correct stress. In a presentation speaking situation, poor pronunciation can result in misunderstanding and embarrassment. For example, we once heard a speaker undermine her credibility in a talk about effective communication when she repeatedly said the word "pro*noun*ciation" instead of "pro*nun*ciation."

Pronunciations can and do change. According to most dictionaries, the word *often* should be pro-

nounced "awfen," but many people now put the "t" sound in the middle so it's pronounced the way it's spelled. The word *a* should be pronounced "uh," not rhyme with *hay*, but many people now use both versions. Even the word *the* is often mispronounced. When *the* appears before the sound of a consonant as in "the dog" or "the paper," it should be pronounced "thuh." When *the* comes before the sound of a vowel as in "the alligator," or "the article," it should be pronounced "thee."

Articulation How clearly you make the sounds in the words of a language
Pronunciation Whether or not you put all the correct sounds of a word in the correct order with the correct stress

---

physical DELIVERY

t he key to effective physical delivery is naturalness. However, being natural doesn't mean "letting it all hang out." Rather, it means being so well-prepared and

well-practiced that your presentation is an authentic reflection of you. Your delivery tells an audience a great deal about who you are and how much you care about reaching them.

Audience members jump to conclusions about speakers based on first impressions of their appearance and behavior. The way you stand, move, gesture, and make eye contact has a significant impact on your presentation.

Eye Contact

Eye contact, establishing and maintaining direct, visual links with individual audience members, may be the most important component of effective physical delivery. Generally, the more eye contact you have

with your audience, the better. Try to maintain eye contact with your audience during *most* of your presentation. If you are using detailed notes or a manuscript, use a technique called *eye scan*. **Eye scan** is a method of glancing at a specific section of your notes or manuscript and then looking up at your audience to speak. Begin by placing your thumb and index finger on one

YOUR DELIVERY tells an audience a great deal about who you are and how much you care about reaching them.

Eye contact Establishing and maintaining direct, visual links with individual audience members
Eye scan A method of glancing at a specific section of your notes or manuscript and then looking up at your audience to speak

---

side of the page to frame the section of the notes you are using. Then, as you approach the end of a phrase or sentence within that section, glance down again and visually grasp the next phrase to be spoken. This allows you to maintain maximum eye contact without losing your place.

Eye contact does more than ensure that you are looking in the direction of your audience. It also helps you to initiate and control communication, enhance your credibility, and interpret valuable audience feedback.

Control Have you ever noticed a teacher "catch the eye" of her students, or "give the eye" to inattentive students? When you establish initial eye contact with your audience, you indicate that you are ready to begin speaking and that they should get ready to listen. Lack of eye contact communicates a message, too: It says that you don't care to connect with your audience. After all, if you don't look at your audience, why should they look at you?

> ## After all, if you don't look at your audience, why should they look at you?

Credibility Direct eye contact says, "I'm talking to *you*; I want *you* to hear this." In Western cultures, such directness positively affects your credibility.[17] It says: I'm of good character (I care enough to share this important message with you), I'm competent (I know this subject so well I can leave my notes and look at you), and I'm charismatic (I want to energize and connect with everyone in this room).

Feedback Eye contact is the best way to gauge audience feedback during a presentation. At first, looking audience members in the eye may distract you. Some people smile, others may look bored or confused, and some will be looking around the room or passing a note to a friend. With all this going on in the audience, it's easy to become sidetracked. However, these different responses are also the very reason you must establish and maintain eye contact. Speakers who don't look directly at audience members rarely have a clue about why their presentations succeed or fail.

Facial Expression

Your face reflects your attitudes and emotional states, provides nonverbal feedback, and, next to the words you speak, is the primary source of information about you.[18]

Despite the importance of facial expressions, they are difficult to control. Most of us tend to display a particular style of facial expression. Some people show little expression—they have a stoic, poker face most of the time. Others are as open as a book—you have little doubt about how they feel. It's very difficult, therefore, to change a "poker face" into an "open book" or vice versa. A nervous speaker may be too distracted to smile, too frightened to stop smiling, or too giddy to register displeasure or anger when appropriate.

Audiences will direct their eyes at your face, so unless your topic is very solemn or serious, try to smile.

Your face . . .

. . . is the primary source of information about you.
— **Mark Knapp and Judith Hall**

A smile shows your listeners that you are comfortable and eager to share your ideas and information. Audience members are more likely to smile if you smile. However, if you do not feel comfortable smiling, don't force it. Let your face communicate your feelings; let your face do what comes naturally. If you speak honestly and sincerely, your facial expression will be appropriate and effective.

Gestures

As Chapter 6, Nonverbal Communication explained, a gesture is a body movement that conveys or reinforces a thought or an emotion. Most gestures are made with your hands and arms, but shrugging a shoulder, bending a knee, and tapping a foot are gestures, too. Gestures can clarify and support your words, relieve nervous tension, and arouse audience attention.

Repetitive movements such as constantly pushing your eyeglasses, tapping on a lectern, and jingling

What Should You Do with Your Hands?

What should you do or not do with your hands when you speak? Many speakers and students tell us that when they try to plan a gesture, it looks phony or mechanical.

At first, our advice may seem counterproductive: Do what you normally do with your hands. If you gesture a lot in conversations with other people, keep doing what comes naturally. If you rarely gesture, don't try to invent new and unnatural hand movements.

Peggy Noonan, former speechwriter for Ronald Reagan, describes a whole industry that exists to tell people how to move their hands when giving a presentation. It's one of the reasons, she maintains, why so many politicians and TV journalists look and gesture alike. "You don't have to be smooth; your audience is composed of Americans, and they've seen smooth. Instead, be you. They haven't seen that yet."[19] In other words, effective gestures are a natural outgrowth of what you feel and what you have to say. If you start thinking about your gestures, you are likely to appear awkward and unnatural. Rather than thinking about your hands, think about your audience and your message. In all likelihood, your gestures will join forces with your emotions in a spontaneous mixture of verbal and nonverbal communication.

change or keys in your pocket can distract and eventually annoy an audience. One of the best ways to eliminate unwanted gestures is to videotape and then watch a practice session. When you see how often you fidget, you'll work even harder to correct your behavior.

Some speakers use their hands only to click through presentation slides. Other speakers use their hands to hold and flip through their notes. These movements, however, do not meet our definition of a gesture because they do not convey or reinforce a thought or an emotion. Instead, they prevent you from adding meaningful gestures to a presentation.

Posture and Movement

Posture and movement involve how you stand and move, and whether your movements add or detract from your presentation. Your posture communicates. If you stand

Your posture communicates.

comfortably and confidently, you will radiate alertness and control. If you stoop or look unsure on your feet, you will communicate anxiety or disinterest. Try to stand straight but not rigid. Your feet should be about a foot apart. If you stand tall, lean forward, and keep your chin up, you will open your airways and help make your voice both clear and loud.

In general, a purposeful movement can attract attention, channel nervous energy, or support and emphasize a point you are making. Movement gives you short pauses during which you can collect your thoughts or give the audience time to ponder what you have said.

If your presentation is formal or your audience large, you will proba-

bly have a lectern. Learn how to take advantage of a lectern without allowing it to act as a barrier. First, don't lean over your lectern. It may look as though you and the lectern are about to come crashing down into the audience. Second, avoid hitting the lectern or tapping it with a pen or pointer while you speak. Given that a microphone is often attached to the lectern, the tapping can become a deafening noise.

Although lecterns can become a crutch or barrier between the speaker and the audience, they have many advantages if used well. Lecterns provide a place to put your notes, a spot to focus audience attention, and even an electrical outlet for a light and microphone. When possible *and* appropriate, come out from behind the lectern and speak at its side. In this way, you can remain close to your notes but also get closer to the audience.

presentation AIDS

We use the term **presentation aids** to refer to the many supplementary resources—most often in visual form—for presenting and highlighting key ideas and supporting material.

Although it's tempting to use computer-generated slides for every presentation, remember that you and your presentation come first. Don't let your aids and their technical razzle-dazzle steal the show. Prepare visuals only after deciding what you want to say and what you want audience members to understand and remember. **(For more hands-on advice about ways to prepare effective and memorable presentation aids, see "Effective Presentation Aids" on www. thethinkspot.com.)**

STRATEGIES FOR USING PRESENTATION AIDS

- *Begin with you, not your visual.* Establish rapport with your audience before you start using presentation aids.
- *Touch, turn, talk.* Touch your aid (or refer to it with your hand or a pointer), turn to your audience, then talk.
- *Pick the right time to display your aids.* Display aids for at least the length of time it takes an average reader to read them twice. When you're finished talking about a presentation aid, remove it.
- *Be prepared to do without.* Can you deliver your presentation without your presentation aids? It's always a good idea to have a "Plan B" in case something goes wrong.

Functions of Presentation Aids

Presentation aids are more than a pretty picture or a set of exciting computer graphics. They serve specific functions, namely to attract audience attention and to enhance the comprehension of ideas through clarification and reinforcement.

Presentation aids can also save you time and help audiences remember your message. A clever cartoon can gain attention; a graph can clarify statistics. Playing a violin works better to enhance comprehension than a mere verbal description would.

Types of Presentation Aids

There are as many different types of presentation aids as there are people to imagine them. The key to selecting an appropriate type requires a thoughtful answer to the following question: Which type of aid will help you achieve your purpose? Only after you answer that question should you consider related questions such as: Which type will be best for gaining and maintaining audience interest, clarify and reinforce your message, and save time? Review the different types of presentation aids and their functions on p. 298 to help you decide which ones best support your message.

Choosing the Media

Selecting the right media is one of the first challenges you face when preparing presentation aids. Consider your purpose, the audience, the setting, and the logistics of the situation. You may want to do a multimedia presentation, but the place where you're scheduled to speak cannot be darkened or the facility doesn't have the equipment you need.

Writing detailed notes on a board or flipchart for an audience of hundreds will frustrate listeners in the back rows.

Like all recommendations, there are exceptions. A corporation's team presentation to a small group of prospective clients may require a multimedia presentation to compete with other team presentations. A predesigned flipchart with one- or two-word messages in huge lettering on each page would work in front of an audience of 300 people, whereas a PowerPoint slide with too much data or too-small type would not.

Design Principles

Even with the best intentions, equipment, and cutting-edge software, presentation aids can fail to have an impact. They can be unattractive, distracting, and difficult to follow. Regardless of what type of supporting materials or in which medium you choose to display them, you can apply basic visual design principles to creating your presentation aids.

Presentation aids Supplementary resources—most often visual in nature—for presenting and highlighting key ideas and supporting material

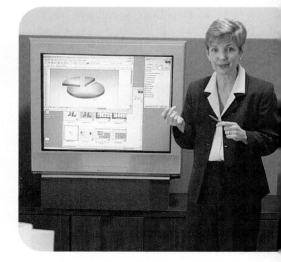

How well did this speaker design her presentation aids?

TYPES OF PRESENTATION AIDS AND THEIR FUNCTIONS

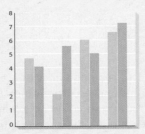

Graphs show *how much* by demonstrating comparisons. They can illustrate trends and show increases or decreases by using bars or lines to represent countable things over a period of time.

Maps show *where* by translating data into spatial patterns. Maps give directions, compare locations, or link statistical data to population characteristics.

Media	Small Audience (50 or fewer)	Medium Audience (50–150)	Large Audience (150 or more)
Chalk/whiteboard	✓		
Flipchart	✓		
Hand-held object	✓	✓	
Presentation software slides	✓	✓	✓
Videotapes/DVDs	✓	✓	✓
Multimedia	✓	✓	✓

Tables *summarize and compare* data. When graphs aren't detailed enough and descriptions require too many words, tables are an effective alternative for showing numeric values. Tables also summarize and compare key features.

Linear Communication Model

Source → Message → Channel → Receiver

Diagrams and illustrations show *how things work.* They take many forms: flow charts, organizational diagrams, time lines, floor plans, and even enlargements of physical objects so you can see the inside of an engine, a heart, or a flower.

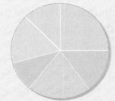

Pie charts show *how much* by identifying proportions in relation to a whole. Each wedge of the pie usually represents a percentage. Most audiences comprehend pie charts quickly and easily.

Group Advantages	Group Disadvantages
• Groups generally accomplish more and perform better than individuals working alone. • Groups provide members with an opportunity to socialize and create a sense of belonging. • Collaborative group work promotes learning.	• Group work requires a lot of time, energy, and resources. • Conflict among group members can be frustrating and difficult to resolve. • Working with members who are unprepared, unwilling to work, or have difficult personalities can be aggravating.

Photographs portray reality—a real face or place is easily recognized and can capture emotions. Other forms of presentation aids include audio recordings, objects, handouts, or physical demonstrations.

Text charts *list ideas or key phrases,* often under a title or headline. They depict goals, functions, types of formats, recommendations, and guidelines. Items listed on a text chart may be numbered, bulleted, or set apart on separate lines.

(For more on how following design principles improves the effectiveness of presentation aids, see "Effective Presentation Aids" on www.thethinkspot.com.)

Handling Presentation Aids

After you invest time, effort, and significant resources to plan and prepare presentation aids, make sure you handle your aids smoothly and professionally by following several general rules of thumb: Don't turn your back to the audience or stand in front of your screen or flip-chart while speaking. Decide when to introduce your aids, how long to leave

DESIGN PRINCIPLES FOR PRESENTATION AIDS

Preview and Highlight	Presentation aids should preview your key points and highlight important facts and features.
Headline Your Visuals	Clear headlines reduce the risk that readers will misunderstand your message.
Exercise Restraint	Avoid using too many graphics, fonts, colors, and other visual elements and effects.
Choose Readable Type and Suitable Colors	Don't use more than two different fonts on a slide, a font size smaller than 24 points, or illegible colors.
Use Appropriate Graphics	Make sure your graphics are essential and support your purpose.

Shun Seductive Details

A student asked if she could do an in-class rehearsal of a presentation she was scheduled to give at work to an important group of clients. She had an absolutely stunning multimedia presentation filled with animation, bright colors, sound effects, and delightful—even funny—pictures. When it was over, the class had only one criticism. Most of her visuals had little to do with what she was talking about. She had fallen in love with her visuals and was committed to using them—even though they were not relevant.

Emotionally interesting but irrelevant pictures actually depress learning and comprehension among readers and listeners. Researchers describe **seductive details** as the elements in a visual text or presentation aid that attract audience attention but do not support the writer's or speaker's key points.[20] Instead of learning, audience members are "seduced" and distracted by interesting scenes, dramatic graphics, vivid colors, and engaging motion. Even when images are relevant to the presentation topic, they can make the information seem too easy and effortless to understand. Moreover, seductive details can confuse audience members about the meaning or purpose of the presentation.[21]

Make sure that the images you use are directly relevant to the purpose and topic of your presentation. Time spent viewing relevant images helps audience members understand the concepts you are presenting. Here are more ways to minimize the effects of seductive details:

- *Minimize the competition between pictures and written text.* If you have a vivid picture or dramatic graphic, display the slide accompanied by only the most important key words. Then follow the slide with a more detailed explanation.

- *Avoid using background sound effects or music.* They distract an audience from you and your message.

- *Encourage visualization.* When you want your audience to appreciate and learn a concept, give them just enough visual information so that they can construct or imagine their own version of the message. Just as radio shows and recorded books serve as a medium of the imagination, effective presentation aids encourage audience members to apply concepts and visualize consequences in their own lives, jobs, and world.

Seductive details Elements in a visual text or presentation aid that attract audience attention but do not support the writer's or speaker's key points

---

> . . . remember that presentation aids are not the presentation; they are only there to assist you. You and your message should always come first.

them up, and when to remove them. Even if you have numerous presentation aids to display, always start and end your presentation by making direct and personal contact with your audience. Finally, remember that presentation aids are not the presentation; they are only there to assist you. You and your message should always come first.

ethicalcommunication

Plagiarism Plagues Presentation Aids

When the creation of visuals or audio is a person's livelihood, the uncompensated use of such works raises ethical questions about applying federal copyright laws.

To respond to this concern, companies such as Microsoft have developed online banks of clip art, clip video, and clip audio for fair use. For instance, its Design Gallery Live site offers more than 250,000 graphics. The U.S. Library of Congress's own online catalog offers more than 7 million images, many of which are in the public domain and no longer protected by copyright. If you purchase a graphics package, you have the right to make copies of the images and use them in your presentations.

If, however, you use a photo scanned from a photographer's portfolio, an audio clip copied from a CD, or a graph downloaded from the Internet without giving these works proper attribution, you are plagiarizing. Remember our definition of plagiarism: using or passing off the ideas or writing of another person as your own. The same criteria apply to the unauthorized use of images and audio in presentation aids.

practicing
YOUR
PRESENTATION

In *Present Like a Pro*, Cyndi Maxey and Kevin E. O'Connor describe a study of The National Speakers Association's nearly 4,000 professional members who were asked for their top tips for a successful speech. *Practice* received more than 35 percent of the vote, making it first in importance. No other skill came close to the importance of practice.[22]

Effective practice sessions require more than repeating your presentation over and over again. Practice can tell you whether there are words you have trouble pronouncing or sentences that are too long to say in one breath. In addition, you may discover that what you thought was a 10-minute talk takes 30 minutes to deliver. Practicing with presentation aids is critical, particularly if you've seen the embarrassing results that befall speakers who don't have their visuals in order. Practicing is the only way to make sure that you sound and look good in a presentation. To put it another way, "give your speech *before* you give it."[23]

Practice can take many forms. It can be as simple as closing your door and rehearsing your presentation in private, or as complex as a full, on-stage, videotaped dress rehearsal in front of a volunteer audience.

- Do not memorize your presentation. Not only do memorized presentations sound memorized, you run the risk of forgetting. If you want to memorize a few key portions of a presentation, practice those sections so they sound natural.
- Practice wherever and whenever you can. If you have a long commute to work or school, turn off the radio and practice portions of your presentation out loud. Practice while you exercise, while you shower, when there's no one around to interrupt or distract you.
- Time your practice session and understand that your actual presentation will take longer. So if you are scheduled for a 10-minute speech, make sure it only takes 8 minutes in a practice session.
- Audiotape and, if possible, videotape your practice sessions.
- Practice in front of a friend or a small volunteer audience. Listen carefully to their comments and decide which ones can help you improve your presentation.
- Practice your entire presentation at several different times rather than devoting one long session to the process.
- Schedule brief 5- to 10-minute sessions in which you practice smaller segments. "If you divide your practice time into manageable, bite-sized chunks, you'll find yourself practicing more often and building confidence for each segment."[24]
- Schedule at least three, but no more than five, complete run-through sessions. If you rehearse too much, you may sound dull or bored.

Know Thy Self

Do You Practice Your Presentations?

Be honest. Do you devote significant time to practicing a presentation before you deliver it? Take a few seconds to answer the following questions:

1. Do you practice your entire presentation several different times rather than devoting one long session to the process?
2. Do you divide each practice session into manageable, bite-sized chunks?
3. Do you practice in at least three complete run-through sessions?
4. Do you make changes to your notes or presentation as you practice?
5. Do you practice using an audio or video recorder, or ask someone to listen to you?
6. Do you believe that practice helps you gain confidence?

Communication ASSESSMENT

Evaluate the Speaking Style and *Your* Delivery

Read the following brief excerpts from the following four presentations:
1. President George W. Bush's State of the Union Address, January 28, 2003
2. Bruce Springsteen's tribute to U2 at the Rock and Roll Hall of Fame, March 17, 2005
3. Steve Jobs's Commencement Address at Stanford University, June 12, 2005
4. Senator Barbara Charline Jordan's Democratic National Convention Keynote Address, 1976

Review each speaker's style and language strategies. Which CORE language style (or styles) predominates? What language strategies do these speakers use? How well do they use them? What are the similarities and differences in these speakers' styles? Then read each excerpt out loud and try to deliver each one in a way that expresses the speaker's intentions, mood, and message most effectively. You may find this task difficult until you have practiced them at length.

1. President George W. Bush, January 28, 2003 (*Washington Post,* January 29, 2003, p. A11)

   The dictator who is assembling the world's most dangerous weapons has already used them on whole villages, leaving thousands of his own citizens dead, blind, or disfigured. Iraqi refugees tell us how forced confessions are obtained: by torturing children while their parents are made to watch. International human rights groups have catalogued other methods used in the torture chambers of Iraq: electric shock, burning with hot irons, dripping acid on the skin, mutilation with electric drills, cutting out tongues, and rape. If this is not evil, then evil has no meaning. And tonight I have a message for the brave and oppressed people in Iraq. Your enemy is not surrounding your country; your enemy is ruling your country.

2. Bruce Springsteen, Tribute to U2 during the 2005 Rock and Roll Hall of Fame Induction Ceremony, March 17, 2005 (http://www.u2station.com/news/archives/2005/03/transcript_bruc.php)

   Uno, dos, tres, catorce. That translates as one, two, three, fourteen. That is the correct math for a rock and roll band. For in art and love and rock and roll, the whole had better equal much more than the sum of its parts, or else you're just rubbing two sticks together searching for fire. A great rock band searches for the same kind of combustible force that fueled the expansion of the universe after the big bang. You want the earth to shake and spit fire. You want the sky to split apart and for God to pour out.

3. Steve Jobs, CEO of Apple Computers and of Pixar Animation Studios, Stanford University Commencement Address, June 12, 2005 (http://news-service.stanford.edu/news/2005/june15/jobs-061505.html)

   I am honored to be with you today at your commencement from one of the finest universities in the world. I never graduated from college. Truth be told, this is the closest I've ever gotten to a college graduation. Today I want to tell you three stories from my life. That's it. No big deal. Just three stories. The first story is about connecting the dots.

   I dropped out of Reed College after the first 6 months, but then stayed around as a drop-in for another 18 months or so before I really quit. So why did I drop out?

4. Senator Barbara Charline Jordan, "Who, Then, Will Speak for the Common Good?" Democratic National Convention Keynote Address, 1976 (http://americanrhetoric.com/speeches/barbarajordan1976dnc.html)

   And now we must look to the future. Let us heed the voice of the people and recognize their common sense. If we do not, we not only blaspheme our political heritage, we ignore the common ties that bind all Americans. Many fear the future. Many are distrustful of their leaders, and believe that their voices are never heard. Many seek only to satisfy their private work—wants; to satisfy their private interests. But this is the great danger America faces—that we will cease to be one nation and become instead a collection of interest groups: city against suburb, region against region, individual against individual; each seeking to satisfy private wants. If that happens, who then will speak for America? Who then will speak for the common good?

Summary

How do you choose appropriate language for a presentation?

- Choose an appropriate language style from among the CORE speaking styles: **c**lear style; **o**ral style, **r**hetorical style, and **e**loquent style.
- The clear style uses short, simple, and direct words.
- The oral style uses short, familiar words; shorter sentences, more personal pronouns, and colloquial expressions.
- The rhetorical style uses vivid and powerful language.
- The eloquent style uses poetic and persuasive language in inspiring and memorable ways.

How do you choose an appropriate delivery style for a presentation?

- Impromptu speaking occurs without time for advance preparation or practice.
- Extemporaneous speaking uses an outline or a set of notes.
- Manuscript speaking involves reading a written presentation out loud.
- Memorized speaking involves delivering a presentation without notes.

What are the components of effective vocal delivery?

- Effective breath control enables you to speak more loudly and say more in a single breath.

- The key to producing adequate volume is adapting to the size of the audience and the dimensions of the room.
- Your speaking rate depends on your speaking style, the nature of your message, and your audience.
- Optimum pitch is the pitch at which you speak most easily and expressively.
- Frequent use of filler phrases can annoy your audience.
- *Articulation* involves how clearly you make the sounds in the words of a language; *pronunciation* refers to whether you say a word correctly.

What are the components of effective physical delivery?

- Direct and effective eye contact help you control communication, enhance your credibility, and interpret audience feedback.
- Speak naturally to ensure that your facial expressions and gestures support your message.
- Speakers who stand and move confidently radiate alertness and control.

What guideline should you follow when designing and displaying presentation aids?

- Presentation aids attract audience attention, clarify and reinforce ideas, and save time.

- Choose media appropriate for your purpose, context, audience, and content.
- Five basic design principles for creating presentations aids include (1) preview and highlight, (2) headline your visuals, (3) exercise restraint, (4) choose readable type and suitable colors, and (5) use appropriate graphics.
- When handling presentation aids, focus on your audience (not the aids or yourself), begin with you, not your aids, and be prepared to do without your aids.

Why is practice essential for effective presentations?

- Practicing ensures you sound and look good.
- Practice your entire presentation several different times by dividing each practice session into bite-sized chunks.
- Time your practice session but understand that your actual presentation will take longer.

TEST your*knowledge*

1 In a commencement address at Stanford University, Steve Jobs, CEO of Apple Computers, said: *"I was lucky—I found what I loved to do early in life. Woz and I started Apple in my parents' garage when I was 20. We worked hard, and in 10 years Apple had grown from just the two of us in a garage into a $2 billion company with over 4,000 employees. We had just released our finest creation—the Macintosh—a year earlier, and I had just turned 30. And then I got fired. How can you get fired from a company you started?"* Which speaking style was Jobs using?

a. clear style
b. oral style
c. rhetorical style
d. eloquent style
e. academic style

2 In Abraham Lincoln's first inauguration address (1861), he concluded by imploring his mostly Southern audience not to go to war: *"The mystic chords of memory, stretching from every battlefield and patriot grave to every living hearth and hearth stone all over this broad land, will yet swell the chorus of the Union when again touched, as surely they will be by the better angels of our nature."* Which presentation speaking style was Lincoln using?

a. clear style
b. oral style
c. rhetorical style
d. eloquent style
e. academic style

3 All of the following answers are advantages of speaking impromptu *except*:

a. natural and conversational speaking style
b. maximum eye contact
c. freedom of movement
d. uses concise and eloquent language
e. demonstrates speaker's knowledge and skill

4 Which is the most common mode of presentation delivery?

a. impromptu
b. extemporaneous
c. manuscript
d. memorized
e. none of the above

5 What, in general, is an effective rate of delivery?

a. 100–125 words per minute
b. 125–145 words per minute
c. 145–180 words per minute
d. 180–200 words per minute
e. 200–250 words per minutec

6 Which component of physical delivery is the most important for a successful presentation?

a. eye contact
b. facial expression
c. gestures
d. posture
e. movement

7 *Seductive details* refers to

a. the tendency of some speakers to focus on the personal details of their lives.
b. a presentation speaking style that uses very vivid and intense language.
c. the tendency of some speakers to hold an audience member's eye contact too long.
d. using PowerPoint slides when other media would be more successful for sharing visual aids with an audience.
e. message elements that attract audience attention but do not support a speaker's key points.

8 Which presentation aid design principle advises speakers to avoid using too many graphics, fonts, colors, and other visual elements and effects?

a. Use appropriate graphics.
b. Headline your visuals.
c. Exercise restraint.
d. Select appropriate media.
e. Preview and highlight.

9 Which presentation aid design principle advises speakers to avoid more than two different fonts on a slide as well as font sizes smaller than 24 points?

a. Preview and highlight.
b. Exercise restraint.
c. Choose readable type and suitable colors.
d. Use appropriate graphics.
e. Headline your visuals.

10 All of the following recommendations for practicing a presentation can help improve your delivery and confidence when speaking *except*:

a. Practice so you can memorize your presentation.
b. Practice several times.
c. Practice using a voice or video recorder.
d. Practice in front of someone and ask for feedback.
e. Practice by dividing each session into manageable, bite-sized chunks.

Answers: 1-b; 2-d; 3-d; 4-b; 5-c; 6-a; 7-e; 8-c; 9-c; 10-a

15 SPEAKING

For many college students, the most familiar type of informative presentation is the classroom lecture. In recent years, however, the traditional lecture has fallen out of favor. Researchers have found that if a professor speaks 150 words per minute, students only hear about 50 of them.[1] Most students tune out of a 50-minute lecture around 40 percent of the time.[2]

In *Teaching Tips*, Wilbert McKeachie notes that the typical attention span of students peaks within the first ten minutes of a class session but then decreases after that point.[3] As a result, you might expect McKeachie to recommend abandoning lectures in favor of other teaching methods. Not so. Rather, he sees lectures as a very efficient and effective teaching method if the instructor knows how to gain and maintain attention, if the lecture is well-planned and well-organized, if the body of the lecture includes various types of supporting material and clear transitions, and if the instructor actively involves students.[4] Essentially, McKeachie's description of a successful lecture captures the characteristics of a successful informative presentation.

> **Most students tune out of a 50-minute lecture around 40 percent of the time.**

TO INFORM

THE PURPOSE OF
informative
speaking

Informative presentations can cover a wide range of topics—from the commonplace to the exotic.

nformative speaking is the most common type of presentation. Students use informative speaking to present oral reports, to share research with classmates, and to explain group projects. Beyond the classroom, business executives use informative presentations to orient new employees, to present company reports, and to explain new policies.

The primary purpose of an informative presentation is to instruct, enlighten, explain, describe, clarify, correct, remind, and/or demonstrate. (See also Chapter 12, Planning Your Presentation.) An informative presentation can present new information, explain complex concepts and processes, and clarify and correct misunderstood information. You will be asked to prepare and deliver informative presentations throughout your lifetime and career, so learning how to do it well can give you a competitive edge.[5]

Most informative presentations contain an element of persuasion. An informative presentation explaining the causes of global warming may convince an audience that the problem is serious and requires stricter controls on air pollution. Your purpose signifies the difference between informative and persuasive presentations. When you ask listeners to change their opinions or behavior, your presentation becomes persuasive.

> **Value step** A step that captures audience attention and explains how a presentation's information can enhance their success or well-being

---

Focus on What's Valuable to Your Audience

Informative speaking often requires a concerted effort to gain and maintain audience attention and interest. Just because *you* love banjo music, bowling, or bidding on eBay doesn't mean audience members share your enthusiasm.

Include a **value step** in your introduction to capture their attention. Explain how the information can enhance their success or well-being. While this step may not be necessary in all informative presentations, it can motivate a disinterested audience to listen to you. After all, if there's a good reason for you to make a presentation, there should be a good reason for your audience to listen.

> **. . . if there's a good reason for you to make a presentation, there should be a good reason for your audience to listen.**

Ask yourself whether your presentation will benefit your audience in any of the following ways:

- *Socially.* Will your presentation help listeners interact with others more effectively, become more popular, or even throw a great party?
- *Physically.* Will your presentation offer advice about improving their physical health, treating common ailments, or losing weight?
- *Psychologically.* Will your presentation help audience members feel better about themselves? Will it help them cope with common psychological problems or anxiety?
- *Intellectually.* Will your presentation explain intriguing and novel discoveries in science? Will you demonstrate the value of intellectual curiosity?
- *Economically.* Will your presentation help audience members make, save, or invest money wisely?
- *Professionally.* Will your presentation help audience members succeed and prosper in a career or profession?

informative
COMMUNICATION
STRATEGIES

In her **Theory of Informatory and Explanatory Communication**, Katherine Rowan explains how to make strategic decisions about the content and structure of an informative presentation. Her two-part theory focuses on the differences between informatory and explanatory communication. **Informatory communication** seeks to create or increase audience awareness about a topic by presenting the latest information—much like news reporting. **Explanatory communication** seeks to enhance or deepen an audience's understanding about a topic so that listeners can understand, interpret, and evaluate complex ideas and information. Good explanatory presentations answer such questions as "Why?" or "What does that mean?"[6]

Not surprisingly, different types of informative messages have different purposes and require different communication strategies. Rowan offers one set of strategies for informatory communication and then further divides explanatory communication into three different types of explanatory functions, as shown in the Classsifcations of Informative Communication graphic below.

Report New Information

Reporting new information is what most journalists do when they answer *who*, *what*, *where*, *when*, *why*, and *how* questions. You can find new information in newspapers, popular magazines, and electronically.

You face two challenges when reporting new information. First, when information is new to an audience, it must be presented clearly and in a well-organized manner. Second, you may need to give audience members a reason to listen, learn, and remember. See below for Rowan's four strategies for reporting new information to an audience.

> Good **explanatory presentations** answer such questions as "Why?" or "What does that mean?"

CLASSIFICATIONS OF INFORMATIVE COMMUNICATION

Informative Communication
Goal: To share information

Informatory Communication
Goal: To create or increase awareness

Informatory Function
- To report new information

Explanatory Communication
Goal: To deepen understanding

Explanatory Functions
- To clarify difficult terms
- To explain quasi-scientific phenomena
- To overcome confusion and misunderstanding

Strategies for REPORTING NEW INFORMATION

- **Include a value step in the introduction.**
- **Use a clear, organizational pattern.**
- **Use a variety of supporting materials.**
- **Relate the information to audience interests and needs.**

Theory of Informatory and Explanatory Communication
Explains the differences between and the communication strategies needed for presenting informatory and explanatory information

Informatory communication
Increases audience awareness by providing the latest information about a topic

Explanatory communication
Enhances or deepens an audience's understanding about a topic so listeners can understand, interpret, and evaluate complex ideas and information

EXAMPLES OF INFORMATORY AND EXPLANATORY COMMUNICATION[7]

INFORMATORY
Creates Awareness

- Cake recipes
- Simple directions
- Brief news story
- Sports trivia
- Biographies

EXPLANATORY
Deepens Understanding

- Baking principles
- Academic lectures
- In-depth news story
- Game analysis
- Philosophies

Informatory presentations can report new information about objects, people, procedures, and events.

Keep in mind, however, that an object, person, procedure, or event is not a purpose statement or central idea, so you need to develop one, as the example on fire ants shows.

Topic area Fire ants

Purpose To familiarize audience members with the external anatomy of a fire ant

Central idea A tour of the fire ant's external anatomy will help you understand why these ants are so hard to exterminate.

Value step In addition to inflicting painful and sometimes deadly stings, fire ants can eat up your garden, damage your home, and harm your pets and local wildlife.

Organization Space arrangement—a visual tour of the fire ant's external anatomy

Key points

A. Integument (exoskeleton)

B. Head and its components

C. Thorax

D. Abdomen

TELL	SHOW	DO
In American Sign Language "hello" is signed by moving the hand away from the forehead in a forward and downward motion, similar to a salute.	Watch me as I show you how to make the motions that signify the word "hello" in American Sign Language.	Now you try it!

"Tell, Show, Do"

When, however, informing about procedures, first identify whether your purpose is informatory or explanatory. If you are describing a fairly simple procedure, focus on *how* to do something rather than *what* to do or *why* to do it.

A physician friend who works at a large medical school and teaching hospital advises his students to "Tell, Show, Do." First, he *tells* students how to carry out a medical procedure by providing oral and/or written instructions and advice. Then he *shows* them how to perform the procedure on a patient or volunteer medical student. Finally, he allows students to *do* the procedure under strict supervision. The "Tell, Show, Do" technique can help you inform an audience about any basic procedure—from boiling an egg to installing software.

When informing about an event such as the race to the moon or a major presidential election, remember that the *purpose* of your presentation will determine how you will talk about that event—regardless of its date, size, or significance.

Clarify Difficult Terms

Understanding a difficult term is just that—difficult. Unlike an object, person, procedure, or event, a difficult term is often abstract—rarely can you touch it, demonstrate it, or explain it with a short and simple definition.

Explaining a difficult concept requires more than reporting. It requires explanatory communication in which you help audience members understand and separate essential characteristics from nonessential features. For example, what is the difference between *validity* and *reliability* or *ethos* and *ethics*? Why are corals classified as animals and not plants?[8]

Strategies for EXPLAINING DIFFICULT TERMS

- Define the term's essential features.
- Use various and typical examples.
- Contrast examples and non-examples.
- Quiz the audience.

In the following example, the meaning of *heuristics* is explained using Rowan's four recommended strategies.

Topic area   Heuristics

Purpose   To explain how heuristics affect persuasion

Central idea   Understanding the nature and uses of heuristics will help you analyze the validity of persuasive arguments.

Value step   Understanding the nature of heuristics can improve your ability to persuade others and to reject invalid arguments.

Organization   Topical plus questions to audience

Key points

A. The essential features of heuristic messages

B. Common heuristics

  1. Longer messages are stronger.

  2. Confident speakers are more trustworthy.

  3. Celebrity endorsements sell products.

C. Contrast heuristic messages with valid arguments

D. Quiz the audience about heuristic messages

Heuristic: Celebrity Endoresment. Singer Beyonce Knowles's endorsement of her women's fragrance, True Star, persuades some women to believe that if they purchase and wear the fragrance, they too will become alluring.

Explain Quasi-Scientific Phenomena

The phrase *quasi-scientific phenomena* requires clarification. The key word here is *quasi*. *Quasi* (pronounced *kwah-zee*) means "having a likeness to something; resembling."[9] Thus, when you explain a *quasi*-scientific phenomenon, you look for a way to enhance audience understanding without using complex scientific terms, data, and methodologies.

Unlike difficult terms, quasi-scientific phenomena are complex, multidimensional processes. Here you are asking audience members to unravel something that is complicated, and that may require specialized knowledge to understand. The biggest challenge when making this kind of explanatory presentation is identifying the key components.

Strategies for
EXPLAINING QUASI-SCIENTIFIC PHENOMENA

- Provide clear key points.
- Use analogies and metaphors.
- Use presentation aids.
- Use frequent transitions, previews, summaries, and signposts.

The presentation outline titled, "Breathing for speech" is designed to teach audience members how to improve the quality of their voices. By comparing something well-known (breathing for life) with something less well-known (breathing for speech), the speaker helps the audience understand this anatomical process.

Topic area   Breathing for speech

Purpose   To explain how to breathe correctly for speech

Central idea   The ability to produce a strong and expressive voice requires an understanding and control of the inhalation/exhalation process.

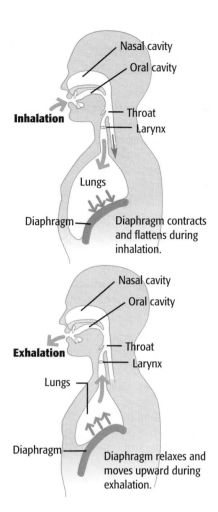

Value step   Learning to breathe for speech will make you a more effective, expressive, and confident speaker.

Organization   Compare and contrast three components of the breathing process

Key points

A. Active versus passive exhalation

B. Deep diaphragmatic versus shallow clavicular breathing

C. Quick versus equal time for inhalation

Overcome Confusion and Misunderstanding

Audience members often cling to strong beliefs, even when those beliefs have been proved false. As a result, informative speakers often face the challenge of replacing old, erroneous beliefs with new, more accurate ones.

In the following example, the speaker dispels misconceptions about the fat content in our diets:

Topic area   Fat in food

Purpose   To explain that fat is an important element in everyone's diet

Central idea   Our health-conscious society has all but declared an unwinnable and unwise war on any and all food containing fat.

Value step   Eliminating all fat from your diet can hurt you rather than help you lose weight.

Organization   Problem (misinformation)—solution (accurate information)

Key points

A. Many people believe that eliminating all fat from their diet will make them thinner and healthier.

B. This belief is understandable given that fat is the very thing we're trying to reduce in our bodies.

C. Fat is an essential nutrient.

D. Fats are naturally occurring components in all foods that, in appropriate quantities, make food tastier and bodies stronger.

ethicalcommunication

Trust Me . . . I'm Just Informing You

The long infomercials on television are not presented for your enjoyment. They have only one purpose: to persuade you to buy a product. When a salesperson says (and yes, we've actually heard this line), "I'm not here to sell you anything. Trust me. I only want to let you in on a few facts," we know the opposite is true.

On June 28, 2009, Billy Mays ("Hi, Billy Mays here!"), the millionaire TV pitchman, died. As-Seen-on-TV commercials like the ones starring Mays are part of a $150 billion industry.[10] Were it not for his over-the-top enthusiastic pitches, none of us would know much about the "amazing," "you-won't-believe-your-eyes," and "if-you-act-now" benefits of *Oxi-Clean*, *Mighty Putty*, or *Tool Band-It*. Whether you love or hate infomercials, never doubt that the "information" in them is designed to persuade you.

When considering the purpose of any informative presentation, remember the first principle in the National Communication Association's Credo for Ethical Communication: "We advocate truthfulness, accuracy, honesty, and reason as essential to the integrity of communication."[11] Claiming to inform when your real purpose is to persuade violates this ethical principle.

Whether you love or hate infomercials, never doubt that the "information" in them is designed to persuade you.

If you're thinking that an explanatory presentation designed to overcome confusion and misunderstanding is more persuasive than informative, you may be right. At the same time, it clearly fits within our definition of an informative presentation: one that seeks to instruct, enlighten, explain, describe, clarify, correct, remind, and/or demonstrate. If it's successful, a presentation about fat in the diet will encourage listeners to rethink what they believe. The primary purpose of such a presentation is to provide accurate information in the hope that a misunderstanding will be corrected.

GENERATING
audience interest

In Chapter 12, we described two surveys that asked working adults and college students to identify the most important skill for becoming a better speaker. In both cases, the top-rated skill was "keeping your audience interested."[12] Thus, it's not surprising that many of our students ask, "How can I make sure I'm not boring?" Novice speakers often *assume* they're not interesting; they can't imagine why an audience would want to listen to them. Or they have heard lots of boring presentations and fear they are doomed to the same fate. Rarely is either assumption true. There is no reason a well-prepared, audience-focused speaker should be dull or boring.

Tell Stories

Throughout history, storytellers have acted as the keepers of tradition and held honored places in their societies.[13] All of us respond to stories, whether they are depicted in prehistoric cave paintings, portrayed in a film, or read to us as children.[14]

Audiences remember stories because they have the power to captivate, educate, and create lasting images. Joanna Slan, author of

Can You Keep It Short?

In Chapter 12, Planning Your Presentation, we recommended 20 minutes as the maximum length for most presentations. If you realize your presentation will run long, how will you shorten it? If you don't have a good answer to this question, you run the risk of losing your audience's attention and interest. Alan M. Perlman, a professional speechwriter, recommends answering three questions to find an appropriate way to shorten a presentation:

1. Will audience members be able to reach this conclusion without my help? If the answer is *yes*, don't overburden them with unnecessary explanations, stories, visuals, or evidence.

2. Does the audience already know this information? Don't spend a lot of time on a point if the audience already knows or understands the point.

3. Does the audience really need to know this? If the answer is *no*, delete or shorten any material that isn't directly relevant to your purpose.[15]

Using Stories and Humor, claims that the ability to tell stories separates great presenters from mediocre ones.[16]

Stories are accounts of real or imagined events. They can be success stories, personal stories, stories about famous people, humorous stories, and even startling stories. For example, members of the clergy use parables, or stories with a lesson or moral, to apply religious teachings to everyday life. Regardless of the type, stories must have a point that relates to your purpose, a reason for being told; otherwise, you run the risk of annoying your audience.[17]

Storytelling also benefits speakers. If you're anxious, it can reduce your nervousness. Stories are easy to remember and generally easy to tell, particularly when they relate to events that you experienced personally.

Where to Find Stories Stories are everywhere, from your favorite children's book to your local news. To find the "right" story for your presentation, consider three rich sources: you, your audience, and other people.

You are a living, breathing collection of stories. The origin of your name, for example, might produce a fascinating narrative. Personal incidents or events that changed your

This Tlingit storyteller of Haines, Alaska wears the traditional storytelling regalia to follow tradition and enhance interest as he tells his tale.

Regardless of the type, stories must have a point that relates to your purpose, a reason for being told ...

life can lead to a good story. Also look at your family's roots, a place that holds significant meaning for you, your successes or failures, and your values.[18]

Your *audience* is also a rich source of stories. Tap into their interests, beliefs, and values. If your audience is deeply religious, you may share a story about a neighbor who gave up her worldly goods to work on a mission. If your audience loves sports, you may share a story about your own triumphs or trials as an athlete. If your audience is culturally diverse, you may share a story about how you, a friend, or colleagues succeeded in bridging cultural differences.

Finally, stories about *other people* can help you connect with your audience. Think about people you

know or people you have read about. Consider interviewing friends or family to uncover relevant stories about their life and knowledge. If you are going to tell a story about someone you know, make sure you have that person's permission. Don't embarrass a good friend or colleague by divulging a private story.

The Structure of a Story Most good stories, no matter how short or how simple, follow the structure illustrated by the Story-Building Chart on the next page. Not only can this chart help you develop a good, original story, it can also be used as speaking notes.

Narrative Theory

Walter R. Fisher, a respected communication scholar, studies the nature of **narratives**, a term that encompasses the process, art, and techniques of storytelling. Fisher sees storytelling as an essential aspect of being human. We experience life "as an ongoing narrative, as conflict, characters, beginnings, middles, and ends."[19] Good stories, he claims, have two essential qualities: probability and fidelity.[20]

Story probability refers to the formal features of a story, such as the consistency of characters and actions, and whether the elements of a story "hang together" and make sense. Would it, for example, seem right if Harry Potter double-crossed his best friends and teachers (unless, of course, he was under some diabolical spell)? Stories that make sense have a clear and coherent structure—one event leads logically to another. If you can't follow the events in a story or can't tell why the characters do what they do, it probably lacks coherence. When try-

ing to assess a story's probability, ask yourself the following questions:

- Does the story make sense? Can you follow the events as they unfold?

- Do the characters behave in a consistent manner? Do you wonder "Why did he do that?" or "How could she do that given everything else she's said and done?"

- Is the plot plausible? Do you find yourself saying "That just couldn't happen?"

Story fidelity refers to the apparent truthfulness of a story. Whereas story probability investigates the formal storytelling rules related to plot and characters, story fidelity focuses on the story's relationships to the audience's values and knowledge.[21] According to Walter Fisher, when you evaluate a story's fidelity, you try to determine whether the audience's ex-

perience rings true "with the stories they know to be true in their lives."[22] To assess the fidelity of a story, ask the following questions:

- Do the facts and incidents in the story seem realistic?

- Does the story reflect your personal values, beliefs, and experiences?

- Does the story use logical arguments and patterns of reasoning?

Narratives The process, art, and techniques of storytelling

Story probability The formal features of a story, such as the consistency of characters and actions, and whether the elements of a story "hang together" and make sense

Story fidelity The apparent truthfulness of a story and whether it accurately reflects audience values and knowledge

Story-Building Chart[23]

Story-Building Guidelines	**Story Example**

TITLE OF THE STORY

Title of the Story	The Three Little Pigs[24]

BACKGROUND INFORMATION

• Where and when does the story take place? What's going on? • Did anything important happen before the story began? • Provide an initial buildup to the story. • Use concrete details. • Create a vivid image of the time, place, and occasion of the story.	Once upon a time, three little pigs set off to seek their fortune. . . .

CHARACTER DEVELOPMENT

• Who is in the story? • What are their backgrounds? • What do they look and sound like? • How do you want the audience to feel about them? • Bring them to life with colorful and captivating words.	Each little pig built a home. One was made of straw and one was made of sticks. The most industrious pig built a house of bricks. . . .

ACTION OR CONFLICT

• What is happening? • What did you or a character see, hear, feel, smell, or taste? • How are the characters reacting to what's happening? • Let the action build as you tell the story.	Soon, a wolf came along. He blew down the houses made of straw and sticks, but both pigs ran to the house of bricks. At the house of bricks the wolf said, "Little pig, little pig, let me come in." All three pigs said, "No, no, not by the hair of our chinny chin chin." So the wolf huffed and puffed but could not blow the house in. . . .

HIGH POINT OR CLIMAX

• What's the culminating event or significant moment in the story? • What's the turning point in the action? • All action should lead to a discovery, decision, or outcome. • Show the audience how the character has grown or has responded to a situation or problem.	The wolf was very angry. "I'm going to climb down your chimney and eat all of you up," he laughed, "including your chinny chin chins." . . .

PUNCH LINE

• What's the punch line? • Is there a sentence or phrase that communicates the climax of the story? • The punch line pulls the other five elements together. • If you leave out the punch line, the story won't make any sense.	When the pigs heard the wolf on the roof, they hung a pot of boiling water in the fireplace over a blazing fire. . . .

CONCLUSION OR RESOLUTION

• How is the situation resolved? • How do the characters respond to the climax? • Make sure that you don't leave the audience wondering about the fate of a character. • In some cases, a story doesn't need a conclusion—the punch line may conclude it for you.	When the wolf jumped down the chimney, he landed in the pot of boiling water. The pigs quickly put the cover on it, boiled up the wolf, and ate him for dinner. And the three little pigs lived happily ever after.

THE CENTRAL POINT OF THE STORY

The Central Point of the Story	The time and energy you use to prepare for trouble will make you safe to live happily ever after.

STORYTELLING

Best Practices

- **Use a simple story line.** Long stories with complex themes are hard to follow and difficult to tell. If you can't summarize your story in less than 25 words, don't tell it.[25]

- **Limit the number of characters.** Unless you're an accomplished actor or storyteller, limit the number of characters in your story. If your story has more than three or four characters, look for another story.

- **Connect to the audience.** Make sure that your story is appropriate for your audience.

- **Exaggerate effectively.** You can exaggerate both content and delivery when telling a story. Exaggeration makes a story more vivid and helps you highlight its message. The tone of your voice, the sweep of your gestures, and your facial expression add a layer of meaning and emphasis to your story.

- **Practice.** Practice telling your story to others—your friends, colleagues, or family members. Practice until you can tell a planned story without notes.

Use Humor

Interjecting humor into a presentation can capture an audience's attention and help them remember your presentation. Audience members tend to remember humorous speakers positively, even when they are not enthusiastic about the speaker's message. Humor can generate audience respect for the speaker, hold listeners' attention, and help an audience remember your main points.[26]

Typically, the best source of humor is *you*. **Self-effacing humor**—directing humor at yourself—is usually much more effective than funny stories you've made up or borrowed from a book. But be careful that you don't poke too much fun at yourself. If you begin to look foolish or less than competent, you will damage your credibility and weaken the power of your message. President Ronald Reagan was well known for making fun of his age, an approach that also defused campaign controversy about him being the oldest president in U.S. history:

> There was a very prominent Democrat who reportedly told a large group, "Don't worry. I've seen Ronald Reagan, and he looks like a million." He was talking about my age.[27]

There are, however, some approaches to humor that audiences will not and should not tolerate. Offensive humor—swearing, jokes that make fun of any group of people, references to private body functions—tops the list because it insults your audience and can damage your credibility.

To ensure you are using humor effectively, make sure that your humor is relevant—that it supports the central idea and key points of your presentation. Then use the kind of humor you do well and that comes naturally to you—jokes, stories, puns, imitations? Also remember that humorous speaking requires more than knowing the witty content of your presentation. It also requires effective delivery and comic timing—knowing when and how to say a line, when to pause, and when to look at the audience for their reactions.

How does a Grammy award–winning comedian like Lewis Black use strategies such as personal storytelling, self-effacing humor, and exaggerated delivery to engage his audiences?

> # Humor can generate audience respect for the speaker, hold listeners' attention, and help an audience remember your main points.
> —Gene Perret

Self-effacing humor Humor directed at yourself rather than others

Know Thy Self

Are You Funny?

Every month, *The New Yorker* magazine conducts its popular cartoon caption contest. The magazine displays the illustrated part of a cartoon and invites readers to write a funny caption. If you want to try your hand as a contestant, register at www. newyorker.com/captioncontest.

Here we present a cartoon that's proved popular in our classes. It comes from a 2001 drawing by Frank Cotham that asks the question, "Why would a man drive a car in circles in front of a couple of guys seated by a garage?" Just to get you started, here's a sample caption submitted by a student: "That's not what we meant by rotate your tires."

What caption would you submit? The editors look for a caption that is simple, elegant, and, of course, funny.

The New Yorker Cartoon

You are a presenter, not a comedian. Humor counts, but too much humor can be counterproductive.

7 Tips for Using Humor in a Presentation[28]

1. Focus your humor on the message.
2. Make sure the humor suits you.
3. Practice, practice, practice.
4. Be careful with talk about body functions.
5. Don't tease anyone in your audience.
6. Avoid ethnic or religious humor, unless you are making fun of yourself in an inoffensive way.
7. Don't go overboard with funny content.

As a word of warning, avoid singling out audience members for ridicule, unless you are speaking at a roast—an event at which a series of speakers warm-heartedly tease an honored guest. And, although it should go without saying, avoid ethnic or religious jokes. Even if everyone in the audience shares your ethnicity and religion, don't assume they will appreciate your humor. You are a presenter, not a comedian. Humor counts, but too much humor can be counterproductive. Don't let the prospect of arousing audience laughter distract you from your purpose.

Unless, like professional comedian Chris Rock, you understand how to use ethnic humor skillfully, avoid it in your presentations.

When audience members are encouraged to speak, raise their hands, write, or interact with one another, they become involved in the speechmaking process.

What do the raised hands in this photo reveal about the way the speaker has involved the audience in her presentation?

Involve the Audience

One of the most powerful ways to keep audience members alert and interested is to ask them to participate actively in your presentation. When audience members are encouraged to speak, raise their hands, write, or interact with one another, they become involved in the speechmaking process. Involve the audience by using several strategies: ask questions, encourage interaction, do an exercise, ask for volunteers, and invite feedback.

Ask Questions Involve audience members by asking questions, posing riddles, or asking for reactions during or at the end of your presentation. Even if your listeners do little more than nod their heads in response, they will be involved in your presentation. Audience members will be more alert and inter-

ested if they know that they will be quizzed or questioned during or after a presentation.

Encourage Interaction Something as simple as asking audience members to shake hands with one another or to introduce themselves to the people sitting on either side of them generates more audience attention and interest. If you are addressing a professional or business audience, ask them to exchange business cards. If you're addressing young college students, ask them to identify their majors or career aspirations.

Do an Exercise Simple games or complex training exercises can involve audience members in your presentation and with one another. Most large bookstores sell training manuals describing ways to involve groups in games and exercises. Interrupting a presentation for a group exercise gives the audience

and the speaker a break during which they can interact in a different but effective way.

Ask for Volunteers If you ask for volunteers from the audience, someone will usually offer to participate. Volunteers can help you demonstrate how to perform a skill or how to use a piece of equipment. Some can even be persuaded to participate in a funny exercise or game. Most audiences love to watch a volunteer in action.

Invite Feedback Invite questions and comments from your audience. If audience members seem reluctant to participate, don't badger or embarrass them. If no one responds, continue your presentation. It takes a skillful presenter to encourage and respond to feedback without losing track of a prepared presentation. The more you speak, the easier and more useful it becomes.

ADAPT TO DIFFERENT LEARNING STYLES

From an audience's perspective, informative presentations are learning experiences. The most effective speakers understand that audience members differ in terms of how they learn. Each of us has a unique **learning style**, the strengths and preferences that characterize the way we take in and process information. If you understand the ways in which audience members learn, you can adapt your message and its delivery to three basic learning styles: visual, auditory, and kinesthetic/tactile.

Visual learners use their eyes to learn. They learn by reading, seeing information displayed on a word chart, and using flash cards or note summaries to study. If they can't see it, they won't learn it well. *Auditory learners* learn by listening. In class, they may ask if they can audiotape an instructor's lecture. Books on tape delight auditory learners. The third type of learning style, *kinesthetic/tactile*, is a hands-on approach. These learners may squirm in their seats if someone talks too long. They want to "do it" rather than listen or read.

Take your audience's styles into account as you prepare and deliver a presentation. Auditory learners may need nothing more than your spoken words, but visual learners may need to see words on a slide or through a physical demonstration. Consider breaking up a presentation with audience questions or activities for those who learn by doing. A variety of approaches can make your presentation more dynamic and accommodate the range of learning styles in an audience.[29]

informative
SPEAKING IN ACTION

"For all the trust I put in *CliffsNotes*, I don't know one thing about them" was the sentence that inspired the informative presentation on *CliffsNotes* that begins on the next page.[30] John Sullivan, a former student and now director of information technology at a large nonprofit organization, translated his likable speaking style

The 7 Key Elements and Guiding Principles of Effective Communication

into a delightful and memorable presentation. The presentation included most types of supporting material: facts, statistics, testimony, descriptions, analogies, examples, and stories from a variety of sources. When John discovered that very little was written about the history of *CliffsNotes*, he phoned the company's headquarters and in-

terviewed the managing editor, Gary Carey.

The information in this presentation is dated but has not been changed in order to preserve the speaker's style.

Learning style Characterizes the way we take in and process information—in a visual, auditory, or kinesthetic/tactile style

Cliff's Notes
John Sullivan[31]

John's simple, opening *story* uses *short sentences* as well as incomplete sentences. His *clear* and *oral style* immediately engages listeners who understand the struggle of pulling an all-nighter before an exam.

John pokes fun at the sources he used for *supporting material* in order to acknowledge their weaknesses. How much more information is now available on Websites? Give it a try.

Conducting a personal *interview* with the editor of *CliffsNotes* demonstrates the speaker's success in finding *credible information* from *a primary source*. John's purpose is primarily *informatory* (creates awareness) rather than *explanatory* (deepens understanding).

As part of his *central idea*, John *previews* the three *key points* of his presentation. Notice how well he covers each of these points in the body of the presentation.

The *descriptive story* of *CliffsNotes* development includes specific details that humanize the founder and share relevant *facts* about the company.

Eight o'clock Wednesday night. I have an English exam bright and early tomorrow morning. It's on Homer's *Iliad*. And I haven't read page one. I forego tonight's beer drinking and try to read. Eight forty-five. I'm only on page 12. Only 482 more to go. Nine thirty, it hits me. Like a rock. I'm not going to make it.

The way I see it, I have three options. I can drop the class, cheat, or go ask Cliff. Because I'm not a quitter, and because I don't think cheating is the right thing to do, I borrow a copy of the *CliffsNotes* from a friend.

Yet for all the trust I put in *CliffsNotes*, I couldn't have told you one thing about them. Even though, according to no less a prestigious source as *People Magazine*, over fifty million of these yellow-and-black pamphlets have been sold, you probably don't know too much about them either. After exhausting *People Magazine*, the *Nebraska Sunday World Herald Magazine*, and *Forbes Magazine*, I had to turn to Cliff himself. Yes, there is a Cliff behind *CliffsNotes* and no, his last name is not Notes. After two interviews with Gary Carey, the managing editor of *CliffsNotes*, it became clear to me that *CliffsNotes* was truly an American success story.

At one time, the notes were nothing more than simple plot summaries. But today, they offer the reader much more in terms of character analysis and literary criticism. To better appreciate this unique publishing phenomenon, it is necessary to trace the history of *CliffsNotes*, note some of the changes they have undergone, and finally, understand why Cliff and his notes get put down by teachers and praised by students.

Mr. Cliff Hillegass, owner and founder of *CliffsNotes*, literally started the business in the basement of his home as a mail-order company. As an employee of the Nebraska Book Company, he happened upon a Canadian publisher who had a full line of study guides. Upon returning home from a trip to Canada, he brought with him the notes to sixteen plays by Shakespeare. He immediately made three thousand copies of each and sent them throughout the U.S. Book store managers were very receptive to the idea and put the Notes on sale.

When *CliffsNotes* first splashed onto the scene in 1958, 18,000 copies were sold. By 1960, sales had increased to 54,000. By the mid-'60s, the magic number was two million, and soon everyone wanted a piece of the action. By 1968, no less than thirteen other companies were in the market. Mr. Hillegass was confident through it all that none could overtake him. He told his sales staff not to worry. He said, "I believe most of our competition are large publishers for whom the study guides would never be more than one item in their line."

He couldn't have been more correct. By 1968, just two years later, only three competitors were left. And as competition went down, sales went up. By

the mid-1980s, *CliffsNotes* was grossing over $4 million a year with over 200 titles in print. In 1988, *CliffsNotes* sold 5 million copies and brought in revenues of $11 million. By 1992, sales exceeded $13 million.

Even with 200-plus titles, it is the original 50 titles that constitute 70 percent of sales. Obviously, certain titles have remained relatively constant through the years. In fact, Cliff keeps a top ten for every year. The following list represents the Top Ten in 1992. As I list them in descending order, try and think what book might be number-one. And, as a hint, keep in mind that most *CliffsNotes* are sold to high school juniors and seniors.

10.	*To Kill a Mockingbird*	5.	*The Great Gatsby*
9.	*The Scarlet Letter*	4.	*Julius Caesar*
8.	*Great Expectations*	3.	*Macbeth*
7.	*A Tale of Two Cities*	2.	*Huckleberry Finn*
6.	*Romeo and Juliet*	1.	*Hamlet*

According to Mr. Carey, *CliffsNotes* first went intercontinental in 1983. In Europe, they were first sold in France and Italy—in the land down under, in Australia and New Zealand. They entered the Chinese market in Beijing and Hangzhou. *CliffsNotes* are now sold in thirty-eight foreign countries.

What next, you may wonder? Well, in another interview with Mr. Carey, he told me that the next development will be the expansion of *CliffsNotes* into several new languages. In addition to Spanish, Portuguese, and Greek, *CliffsNotes* will soon be read right-to-left, in Hebrew. In 1998, IDG Books Worldwide, Inc., the people who publish the . . . *for Dummies* books, acquired the little company that Cliff built. *CliffsNotes* now takes on other challenges, such as how to prepare for the GMAT test, how to master computer technology, and how to manage your finances.

Yet despite international inroads and domestic success, *CliffsNotes* has its critics. Questions have been raised concerning the quality of the literary criticism within *CliffsNotes,* the claims of copyright infringements, and the academic ethics of using *CliffsNotes* in place of the real thing.

Mr. Hillegass, no writer himself, commissions the writing of the notes to scholars and teachers. At the college level, he uses Ph.D.s or grad students who have experience with the work. For example, the notes on *The Iliad* were penned in 1986 by Dr. Elaine Strong Skill of the University of Oregon. The consulting editor was Dr. James L. Roberts from the University of Nebraska.

Cliff did find, however, that Ph.D.s and grad students sometimes write above the level of high school students. As a result, many of the high school notes are written by secondary school teachers who use the work in question year in and year out.

Cliff also has had his share of problems with publishers. In 1966, Random House filed suit against *CliffsNotes* for quoting too extensively from some of its copyrighted Faulkner titles. Both sides had lawyers poised and ready to do

Throughout this section, John uses lots of numbers. Are all of them *statistics*, or are they numerical *facts*? What is the difference between a statistic and a numerical fact?

Keep in mind that these statistical ratings are dated (1992), but were current when the presentation was originally researched. Can you find a more current list of the top ten books on the Web? Give it a try. If you have trouble finding this list, why would the company withhold such information?

A simple *question* can recapture audience attention and serve as a *transitional phrase.*

This transition briefly *summarizes* the previous section and *previews* the three criticisms discussed in the next section.

This *example* supports the claim that *CliffsNotes* are written by well-qualified and *credible sources* from respected universities.

combat. It could have become a landmark case. Instead, Cliff and some of the people from Random House solved their problems out of court.

Cliff believes that this was a turning point for both himself and his company. It forced them to take a fresh look at the notes. As a result, the classics were revamped to the point that they are now approximately 50 percent text summary and 50 percent critical analysis.

John uses numerical *facts* (50% summary; 50% analysis) and an *example* to support the claim that each *Cliffs-Notes* contains more than a plot summary.

For example, the notes on *Macbeth,* Act I, Scene 1, discuss the witches' famous lines "When shall we three meet again" and "In thunder, lightning, or in rain?" These lines take up only two lines in the play. The *CliffsNotes* analysis is many times that length, with commentary on such things as the dramatic creation of mood, the use of time as a key theme, and the language of paradox and prophecy.

Cliff no longer has problems with publishers, but his academic critics are still there. Certainly you have heard (or can easily imagine) teacher complaints that *CliffsNotes* allow students to avoid reading the original text.

Note the *oral documentation* of this *quote* that uses an *analogy* comparing reading *CliffsNotes* to letting someone eat your dinner.

In an article about *CliffsNotes* published in the *Nebraska Sunday World Herald Magazine,* one educator said, "Reading *CliffsNotes* is like letting someone else eat your dinner. They deprive students of the pleasure of discovering literature for themselves."

Mr. Carey countered such criticism in the same article by stating: "Teachers' apprehensions concerning *CliffsNotes* may have been well founded twenty years ago when they were simple plot summaries. But, today, they are mainly composites of mainstream literary criticism that are of little value to students who have not read the book."

Do you believe this statistic even if it comes from a survey of students at two universities?

An informal survey at Creighton University and the University of Nebraska has indicated that Mr. Carey may be correct. Where students' older brothers and sisters may have used *CliffsNotes* in place of the real thing, more than 80 percent of those students interviewed said they never used *CliffsNotes* by themselves. They only used them to accompany the reading of the required text. If anything, the *CliffsNotes* helped them discover the pleasure of reading the literature.

John returns to his introductory *personal experience* and acknowledges that many students miss the delights of reading literature by relying solely on *CliffsNotes*.

But then again . . . I did pass my exam, and I have yet to read *The Iliad.* And I'm sure there are plenty of students out there who have missed the delights of *Huckleberry Finn* or the pathos of *The Grapes of Wrath.* "To be or not to be," "Friends, Romans, countrymen," and "Out, damned spot" very well could be the only lines of Shakespeare that some students know.

Once again, John uses humor, this time as a way to effectively conclude his presentation.

So the controversy continues. But at least you know that, unlike Ronald McDonald, Cliff is a real person and he has not dodged the issues. He will go on explaining the finer points of his 200-plus titles. Because as long as teachers assign the classics of literature, the racks of yellow and black will continue to grow and prosper.

Communication ASSESSMENT

Informative Presentation Assessment

Use the following ratings to assess each of the competencies on the informative presentation assessment instrument:

E = excellent; G = good; A = average; W = weak; M = missing; N/A = not applicable.

COMMENTS

COMPETENCIES	E	G	A	W	M	N/A
Preparation and Content						
Purpose and topic						
Audience adaptation						
Adaptation to context						
Introduction						
Organization						
Supporting material						
Transitions						
Conclusion						
Language						
Interest factors						
Informative strategies						
Delivery						
Extemporaneous mode						
Vocal delivery						
Physical delivery						
Presentation aids, if used						
Other Criteria						
Outline/written work						
Bibliography						
Other: _____						
Overall Assessment (circle one)	E	G	A	W	M	N/A

Summary

Why is informative speaking important?

- An effective informative presentation can instruct, inspire, explain, describe, clarify, correct, remind, and/or demonstrate.
- The dividing line between informing and persuading is the speaker's purpose.
- When speaking to inform, include a value step that explains why the information is valuable to audience members and how it can enhance their success or well-being.

What communication strategies should you use for different types of informative presentations?

- Classify your informative presentation in terms of whether its purpose is informatory (reports new information) or explanatory (clarifies difficult terms, explains quasi-scientific phenomena, or overcomes confusion and misunderstanding).
- Strategies for reporting new information include beginning with a value step, using a clear organizational pattern, including various types of supporting material, and relating the information to audience interests and needs.
- Strategies for clarifying difficult terms include defining the term's essential features, using various

examples, discussing nonexamples, and quizzing the audience to ensure comprehension.

- Strategies for explaining quasi-scientific phenomena include providing clear key points, using analogies and metaphors, using presentation aids, and using transitions, previews, summaries, and signposts to connect key points.
- Strategies for overcoming confusion and misinformation include stating the belief or theory, acknowledging its believability, creating dissatisfaction with the misconception, and then stating and explaining the more acceptable belief or theory.

What communication strategies effectively generate audience interest?

- In order to tell stories that captivate and educate your audience, look for good sources of stories, structure the story effectively, check the story for fidelity and probability, and use effective storytelling skills.

- In order to use humor to generate audience interest, avoid offensive humor, be prepared to direct humor at yourself, and heed textbook tips for using humor.
- You can involve audience members in your presentation by asking questions, encouraging interaction, doing exercises, asking for volunteers, and inviting feedback.
- Analyze and adapt to your audience's learning styles: visual, auditory, and/or kinesthetic/tactile.

What are the characteristics of an effective informative presentation?

- An effective informative presentation reflects strategic decisions related to the seven elements of communication: self, others, purpose, context, content, structure, and expression.
- Effective informative speakers use a clear and oral speaking style, adapt to audience experiences and needs, generate interest by using stories, humor, and audience involvement, and promote their credibility.

the THINKSPOT
www.thethinkspot.com

TEST your*knowledge*

1 If you ask yourself, "Will my presentation explain intriguing and novel discoveries in science?" when searching for a value step, which audience benefit are you trying to achieve?
a. social benefit
b. psychological benefit
c. physical benefit
d. intellectual benefit
e. professional benefit

2 All of the following topics are appropriate for an *informatory* type of informative presentation *except*:
a. learning how to bake bread recipes
b. learning how to change gears on a bicycle
c. giving directions for sewing on a button
d. understanding the chemistry of yeast in bread-baking
e. highlighting Michael Jackson's greatest hits

3 Which of the following answers constitutes a value step for a presentation on cooking hard-boiled eggs?
a. Hard-boiled eggs are easy to make.
b. I will teach you how to make foolproof hard-boiled eggs.
c. There are four steps—cold-water start, stopping the boiling, the 15-minute stand, and cold-water rinse—for cooking perfect hard-boiled eggs.
d. You won't have cracked or leaky eggs if you use this method for making perfect hard-boiled eggs.
e. Use the cold-water method to cook perfect hard-boiled eggs.

4 When clarifying a difficult term in an informative presentation, which of the following strategies should you use?
a. Use analogies and metaphors.
b. Use various examples.
c. Use presentation aids.
d. Explain the theory.
e. Quiz the audience.

5 When explaining a quasi-scientific phenomenon, which of the following strategies should you include?
a. Use analogies and metaphors.
b. Use various examples.
c. Use nonexamples.
d. Create dissatisfaction with the theory.
e. Quiz the audience.

6 According to Fisher's narrative theory, which of the following questions tests a story's probability?
a. Do the facts and incidents in the story ring true?
b. Do the characters behave in a consistent manner?
c. Does the story reflect my personal values, beliefs, and experiences?
d. Does the story address or support the speaker's point?
e. Does the story omit or distort any key facts or events?

7 Which of the following answers is the third step in the story-building chart?
a. high point or climax
b. action or conflict
c. background information
d. punch line
e. character development

8 All of the following statements are good tips for using humor *except*:
a. Do not tease anyone in your audience.
b. Focus your humor on the message.
c. Do not direct humor at yourself.
d. Be wary of telling stories about body functions.
e. Avoid ethnic or religious humor.

9 Which of the following strategies does your textbook recommend for involving the audience in your presentation?
a. Ask questions.
b. Encourage interaction.
c. Do an exercise.
d. Invite feedback.
e. all of the above

10 Which of the following learning styles might account for audience members who tend to squirm in their seats?
a. visual learners
b. auditory learners
c. oral learners
d. kinesthetic learners
e. quantitative learners

Answers: 1-d; 2-d; 3-d; 4-b; 5-a; 6-b; 7-b; 8-c; 9-e; 10-d

16 SPEAKING

n some people's version of a perfect world, teenagers would "just say no" to illegal drugs, cigarette smoking, premarital sex, and underage drinking. The "Just Say No" campaign, part of the 1980s' War on Drugs, was the pet project of Nancy Reagan, then First Lady. The campaign was designed to teach young people how to say no to drugs while simultaneously bolstering their self-esteem. Unfortunately, it didn't work, despite billions of dollars devoted to the effort. Not only did the "Just Say No" campaign fail to reduce the number of teenagers experimenting with drugs, it may also have *lowered* their self-esteem.[1]

> . . . the "Just Say No" campaign (failed) to reduce the number of teenagers experimenting with drugs. . . .

Now consider the more recent "Truth" campaign—a national anti-smoking movement that specifically targets youth, and is the only national tobacco-prevention effort not directed by the tobacco industry. The campaign debuted with a cowboy who rides his horse through city traffic to a busy curb, removes a bandana from around his neck, and reveals a hole from a laryngectomy. With the help of a hand-held electronic voice box, he then proceeds to sing, "You don't always die from tobacco." At the end of his song, the camera cuts to a billboard with these words written on it: "Over 8.5 million Americans live with tobacco-related illnesses."[2]

TO PERSUADE

Although it's too early to assess the success of such ads, several articles in the *American Journal of Public Health* credits the Truth campaign with 22 percent of the decline in youth smoking.[3] Shira Yevin, a young participant in the Truth movement who has spoken at press conferences on behalf of the campaign, appears on the previous page as just one example of its success.

Why did the "Just Say No" campaign fail? Why do the Truth ads seem to be more successful? In this chapter, we describe persuasive theories, strategies, and skills that will not only help you prepare and deliver persuasive presentations, but help you analyze a variety of persuasive messages by others, as well.

THE NATURE OF persuasion

Persuasive messages bombard us from the moment we wake up in the morning to the moment we fall asleep at night. Sometimes, the persuasion is obvious—a television commercial, a sales call, a political campaign speech. Other times, it is less obvious—an inspirational sermon, an investment newsletter, a product sample in the mail.[4]

Persuasion seeks to change audience opinions (what they think) or behavior (what they do). Your purpose determines whether you will speak to inform or to persuade.

Informative presentations *tell* an audience something by *giving* them information or explanations. Persuasive presentations *ask* for something *from* the audience—their agreement or a change in their opinions or behavior.

PERSUASION CHANGES OPINIONS AND BEHAVIOR

- Your family is more important than your job.
- Japan makes the best automobiles.
- Vegetarian diets are good for your body and good for the planet.

- Eat dinner with your family at least five times a week.
- Buy a Japanese-made car.
- Stop eating meat.

PERSUASIVE PRESENTATIONS *ask* for something *from* the audience— their agreement or a change in their opinions or behavior.

Persuasion Seeks to change audience opinions (what they think) or behavior (what they do)

persuading OTHERS

- **Present new information.** New information reminds them why they agree and reinforces their agreement.
- **Strengthen audience resistance to opposing arguments.** Prepare them to answer questions asked by those who disagree. Inoculate them with arguments that refute the opposition.
- **Excite the audience's emotions.** Use examples and stories that stimulate their feelings (joy, pride, fear, happiness).
- **Provide a personal role model.** Tell them what you have seen or done.
- **Advocate a course of action.** Explain why and how they should take action (such as sign a petition, vote, exercise).

If you want to change audience members' opinions or behavior, you need to understand why they resist change. Why don't people vote for the first candidate who asks for their support? Why don't we run out and buy the cereal a sports star recommends? Why don't workers quit their job if they dislike their boss? All these questions have good answers—and that's the problem. Most audience members can give you a reason why they *won't* vote, buy, quit, or do any of the things you ask them to do. It's up to you to address those reasons.

Classify Audience Attitudes

The more you know about your audience and their attitudes, the more effectively you can adapt your message to them. For example, an audience of homeowners may strongly agree that their property taxes are too high, but a group of local college students may support more taxes for higher education. If you're scheduled to talk to a group of avid gun collectors or hunters, you can probably assume that they are resistant to stricter gun control legislation.

Review what you know about your audience's demographic characteristics and attitudes. Then place your audience along a continuum that measures the extent to which *most* members will agree or disagree with you. When you understand where audience members stand, you can begin the process of adapting your message to the people you want to persuade.

Persuading Audience Members Who Agree with You

When audience members already agree with you, you don't have to *change* their way of thinking. Rather, you should strengthen their attitudes and encourage behavioral change.

When audience members agree with you, consider "inoculating" them. According to social psychologist William McGuire, protecting audience attitudes from counterpersuasion by the "other side" is like inoculating the body against

HOW MIGHT FORMER ALASKAN GOVERNOR SARAH PALIN, WHO CLAIMS TO HAVE SHOT HER FIRST RABBIT AT THE AGE OF 10, PERSUADE AUDIENCE MEMBERS WHO STRONGLY ADVOCATE GUN CONTROL?

CONTINUUM OF AUDIENCE ATTITUDES

| Strongly agree with me | Agree | Undecided | Disagree | Strongly disagree with me |

disease.[5] You can increase audience resistance by presenting the arguments of the opposition *and* showing your audience how to refute them. This strategy also creates a more enduring change in attitudes or behavior. Inoculation works best when audience members care about an issue because it makes them aware that their attitudes are vulnerable to attack and then provides ammunition against or resistance to the attack.[6]

Persuading Audience Members Who Disagree with You

Disagreement does not mean that audience members will be hostile or rude. It does mean, however, that changing their opinions is more challenging. In the face of audience disagreement, don't try to change the world. Change what can reasonably be changed.

Finding **common ground**—a place where both you and your audience can stand without disagreement—is often the key to persuading an audi-

In the face of audience disagreement, don't try to change the world. Change what can reasonably be changed.

ence that disagrees with you. To find common ground, identify and discuss a position or behavior that you share with your audience. For example, smokers and nonsmokers may both agree that smoking should be prohibited in and around schools. If you find common ground, your audience is more likely to listen to you when you move into less friendly territory.

Persuading Indecisive Audience Members

Some audience members may not have an opinion about your topic because they are uninformed, unconcerned, or adamantly undecided. Knowing which type of persuasive strategy to apply in each

case depends on the reasons for indecision. In the following example, a college student began her presentation on the importance of voting by getting the attention of the undecided students and giving them a reason to care:

> How many of you applied for some form of financial aid for college? [More than half the class raised their hands.] How many of you got the full amount you applied for or needed? [Less than one-fourth of the class raised their

---

STOP & THINK | **Can You Find Common Ground?**

Below are two controversial topics often chosen by students for class presentations, that are just as often unsuccessful in achieving their purpose. Complete each sentence by stating an issue on which a speaker and audience might find common ground. For example, "Free speech advocates and antipornography groups would *probably* agree that . . . pornography should not be available to young children." Note that the word *probably* is written in italics. Audience members at extreme ends of any position or belief may not make exceptions and may not be willing to stand on common ground with you.

1. Pro–capital punishment and anti–capital punishment groups would *probably* agree that

   _____

   _____

2. The National Rifle Association and gun control advocates would *probably* agree that

   _____

   _____

Common ground A place where both you and your audience can stand without disagreement

> **If you find common ground, your audience is more likely to listen to you when you move into less friendly territory.**

hands.] I have some bad news for you. Financial aid may be even more difficult to get in the future. But the good news is that there's something you can do about it.

In the real world of persuasive speaking, you are likely to face audiences with some members who agree with your message, others who don't, and still others who are indecisive. In such cases, you have several options. You can focus your persuasive efforts on just one group—the largest, most influential, or easiest to persuade—or appeal to all three types of audiences by providing new information from highly respected sources.

Psychological Reactance Theory

THINK ABOUT THEORY

Psychologist Jack W. Brehm explains why telling an audience what *not* to do can produce the exact opposite reaction. His **Psychological Reactance Theory** suggests that when you perceive a threat to your freedom to believe or behave as you wish, you may go out of your way to *do* the forbidden behavior or rebel against the prohibiting authority.[7] Young people's response to the "Just Say No" campaigns, described at the beginning of this chapter, demonstrates this theory in action.

Children react this way all the time. You tell them, "Don't snack before dinner!" or "Don't hit your brother!" or "Stop texting, now!" so they hide their snacks, sneak in a few punches, and spend more time texting. Consider this interesting fact: Although legally designated "coffee shops" in Amsterdam sell marijuana, only about 15 percent of Dutch people older than 12 years have ever used marijuana, whereas 33 percent of Americans have used it illegally.[8] Because the drug is strictly prohibited by law in the United States, it may be more attractive as an outlet of rebellion.[9]

If you tell an audience "Do this" or "Don't believe that," you may run into strong resistance. Effective persuasive messages do not give the impression of threatening the audience or constraining their choices.[10] If you believe that your audience may react negatively to your advice or directions, use the following strategies to reduce the likelihood of a reactance response:

- Avoid strong, direct commands such as "don't," "stop," and "you *must*."
- Avoid extreme statements depicting terrible consequences such as "You will die," or "You will fail," or "You will be punished."

- Avoid finger-pointing—literally and figuratively. Don't single out specific audience members for condemnation or harsh criticism.
- Advocate a middle ground that preserves the audience's freedom and dignity while moving them toward attitude or behavior change.
- Use strategies that are appropriate for audience members who disagree with you.
- Respect your audience's perspectives, needs, and lifestyles.

Psychological Reactance Theory A theory that claims when people perceive a threat to their freedom to believe or behave as they wish, they may go out of their way to *do* the forbidden behavior or rebel against the prohibiting authority

BUILDING persuasive arguments

after making decisions about your purpose, the audience, your credibility, your self, and the persuasive context, turn your attention to the content of your message. Now is the time to develop strong arguments in light of their persuasive potential. Remember, as we explained in Chapter 4, Listening and Critical Thinking, an *argument* consists of a claim supported by evidence and reasons for accepting it. We also introduced Toulmin's Model of an Argument to help you understand the components of an effective argument. In this section, we take a closer look at the strategies and skills needed to prove that your arguments are worthy of belief.

The 7 Key Elements and Guiding Principles of Effective Communication

Choose Persuasive Claims

First, list all the possible claims you could use—all the reasons why the audience should agree with you. For example, a student speaker planning a presentation on hunting as a means of controlling the growing deer population listed several reasons:

> The enormous deer population...
> ... is starving and dying of disease.
> ... is eating up crops, gardens, and forest seedlings.
> ... is carrying deer ticks that cause Lyme disease in people.
> ... is causing an increase in the number of highway accidents.
> ... is consuming the food needed by other forest animals.

Although there may be several arguments for advocating hunting to reduce the deer population, a speaker should choose the arguments that, based on an analysis of the audience, would most likely persuade that audience.

Whatever arguments you choose, make sure you know whether you are advocating claims of fact, conjecture, value, or policy (see Chapter 4). Understanding the type of claim will help you "make your case." Many effective speakers use all four types of claims in a single presentation. For example, a persuasive presentation on capital punishment—regardless of your position on the issue—might start with facts that answer questions, such as: How many people are executed in the United States each year? Which state leads the nation in executions? Then you might move on to value claims that answer questions, such as: Is it right for a state to take the life of a prisoner regardless of the seriousness of the crime? Is capital punishment cruel or immoral?

Choose Persuasive Proof

Like lawyers before a jury, persuasive speakers must prove their case. Lawyers decide what evidence to use when in court, but it's up to the jury or judge to determine whether the evidence is valid and persuasive. When trying to persuade an audience,

FOUR FORMS OF PERSUASIVE PROOF

LOGOS Logical Proof
PATHOS Emotional Proof
ETHOS Personal Proof
MYTHOS Narrative Proof

your success depends on the quality and validity of your **proof**, the arguments and evidence you use to support and strengthen a persuasive claim. Because audiences and persuasive situations differ, so should your proof.[11]

During the early fourth century B.C., Aristotle developed a multidimensional theory of persuasion. More than 2,000 years later, his conclusions continue to influence the way we study persuasion. In *Rhetoric*, Aristotle identifies three major types of proof: *logos* (message logic), *pathos* (audience emotions), and *ethos* (the personal nature of the speaker). To that list we add a fourth type of proof—*mythos* (social and cultural values often expressed through narratives).

> **Proof** The arguments and evidence used to support and strengthen a persuasive claim

Commercials succeed because they understand the power of emotional proof.

Logos: Logical Proof Arguments that rely on reasoning and analysis are using **logos** or logical proof. Logical proof relies on an audience's ability to think critically and arrive at a justified conclusion or decision. Note how the following speaker uses facts and statistics to prove logically that health care is too expensive for many Americans:

> Many hard-working Americans cannot afford the most basic forms of health care and health insurance. Some 46 million Americans, almost 16 percent of the population, most of them lower-income workers or their families, live without health insurance and contrary to popular belief, most of the uninsured are job-holders or their family members—the working poor.[12]

Facts and statistics drive home the speaker's conclusion that the high cost of health insurance seriously affects the health and prosperity of many working Americans.

Pathos: Emotional Proof Persuasion can be aimed at deep-seated, emotional feelings about justice, generosity, courage, forgiveness, and wisdom.[13] Aristotle referred to this form of proof as **pathos** or emotional proof. Many television commercials succeed because they understand the power of emotional proof. Notice, for instance, how a student speaker uses testimony as emotional proof to evoke the audience's sympathies and fears:

> Kevin was 27 years old and only two months into a new job when he began to lose weight and feel ill. After weeks of testing and finally surgery, he was found to have colon cancer. The bills were more than $100,000. But soon after his release from the hospital, he found out that his insurance benefits had run out. Kevin's reaction: "Five weeks into the chemotherapy, I walk into my doctor's office, and he sits me down, puts his hand on my knee and tells me there's been no payment. . . . Then he said the hospital could no longer bankroll my treatment. At one point in the middle of the whole thing, I hit bottom; between having cancer and being told I had no insurance, I tried to commit suicide."[14]

Rather than using logos to prove that many Americans suffer because they do not have dependable health insurance, the speaker highlights one person's suffering. Stories like this can persuade an audience because audience members understand that the same thing *could* happen to them or someone they love. This story taps the audience's sympathies *and* fears. If you decide to use fear ap-

---

Logos (logical proof) A form of proof that relies on an audience's ability to think critically in order to arrive at a justified conclusion or decision

Pathos (emotional proof) A form of proof that appeals to listeners' feelings and emotions

---

ethicalcommunication

Reject Fallacies

In Chapter 4, Listening and Critical Thinking, we identified six common fallacies of argument. There are, in fact, hundreds of potential fallacies waiting to distort persuasive messages. Fallacies can mislead and misinform listeners, rob audiences of their precious time and well-founded convictions, and permanently damage a speaker's reputation and credibility.

Every communicator has an ethical obligation to recognize and reject the fallacies in persuasive arguments. Three factors lead to most mistakes in reasoning:[15]

- *Intentional and unintentional fallacies.* Unethical speakers may intentionally use fallacies to deceive or mislead audience members. Ethical, well-intentioned speakers may use fallacious reasoning without knowing it. Ignorance—as the old saying goes—is no excuse. Every

speaker has an ethical obligation to avoid fallacies.

- *Careless listening and reasoning.* Inattentive listeners can fall prey to deceptive arguments and claims that evoke strong emotions. Poor critical thinking can lead speakers and listeners to accept fallacies as true.

- *Different worldviews.* Your worldview—developed over many years of life experiences—affects how you determine what you believe is reasonable and unreasonable. Prejudices may lead some people to see the misbehavior by a handful of immigrants, police officers, or basketball players as typical of everyone in that population. A politically conservative speaker or listener may automatically ignore or dismiss an argument made by a liberal speaker. Ethical communicators consider how culture, language, gender, religion, politics, and social and economic status affect the way they and their audiences see the world.

> **"Arousing fear does not always produce attitude change."**
> **—Richard Perloff**

peals, bear in mind the words of persuasion scholar Richard Perloff: "Contrary to what you may have heard, it is not easy to scare people successfully. Arousing fear does not always produce attitude change."[16] Put another way, what may seem scary to you may not be scary to someone else.

Perloff claims that although "it's tough to scare people effectively . . . it can be done."[17] When a fear appeal is well-crafted and well-delivered, and used for a good reason (for example, when you believe that audience members are putting them-

selves or their loved ones in harm's way), it can change audience attitudes and behavior. Think of how many advertisements use this approach. Life insurance ads suggest that you invest not for yourself but for those you love.

Ethos: Personal Proof As we noted in Chapter 12, Planning Your Presentation, **ethos** has three major dimensions: competence, character, and charisma. Each of these dimensions can serve as a form of personal proof in a persuasive presentation. To demonstrate that you are a competent speaker of good character, deliver your presentation with conviction. Audiences are more likely to be persuaded when a speaker seems committed to the cause.

In *Rhetoric*, Aristotle claims that the speaker's personal character "may almost be called the most effective means of persuasion he possesses."[18] Consider how ethos operates in your everyday life. Do you believe what your favorite professors tell you? If, in your opinion, they are of good character and are experts in their field of study, you

probably do. Do you trust what a respected member of the clergy preaches? Again, if you have faith in the integrity and goodwill of that person, you probably do. Ethos is a powerful form of proof—but you have to *earn* it from your audience if you expect it to help you achieve your persuasive purpose.

Mythos: Narrative Proof During the second half of the twentieth century, *mythos*, or narrative proof, emerged as a fourth and significant form of persuasive proof. According to communication scholars Michael and Suzanne Osborn, **mythos** is a form of proof that addresses the values, faith, and feelings that make up our social character and is most often expressed in traditional stories, sayings, and symbols.[19] Mythos can connect your message with your audience's social and cultural identity, and give them a reason to listen carefully to your ideas.[20]

Americans are raised on mythic stories that teach patriotism, freedom, honesty, and national pride. For instance, President George Washington's "I cannot tell a lie" after cutting down the family's cherry tree may be a myth, but it has helped teach millions of young Americans about the value of honesty. "Give me your tired, your poor" from Emma Lazarus's poem inscribed on the base of the Statue of Liberty and the civil rights refrain "We shall overcome" also inform American beliefs and values. Speakers who tap into the *mythos* of an audience form a powerful identification with their listeners.

One of the best ways to enlist mythos in persuasion is through storytelling. Religions teach many val-

President Barack Obama honors award-winning actress-singer-dancer Chita Rivera with the Presidential Medal of Honor for her service to the arts. The Medal of Honor winners often exemplify all three dimensions of *ethos*.

Ethos Speaker credibility that relies on the perceived character, competence, and charisma for a speaker

Mythos (narrative proof) A form of proof that addresses the values, faith, and feelings that make up our social character and is most often expressed in traditional stories, sayings, and symbols

MYTHOS

can connect your message with your audience's social and cultural identity, and give them a reason to listen carefully to your ideas.

ues through parables. Families bond through stories shared across generations. Effective leaders inspire nations with their personal narratives. (For more on storytelling, see Chapter 15, Speaking to Inform.)

Lady Liberty's invitation, "Give me your tired, your poor ..." tapped into the mythos that drew thousands of immigrants to the U.S. in search of freedom and a better life.

Choose Persuasive Evidence

In Chapter 4, Listening and Critical Thinking, we define data as the evidence you use to support your claim. In Chapter 13, Content and Organization, we describe how to gather and use supporting material to explain and/or advance your central idea and key points. Here we examine how to choose strong evidence that justifies and strengthens your claim and choice of proof.

If you argue that responsible environmentalists support deer hunting, use a highly reputable quotation or survey to prove your point. If you advocate early testing for diabetes, tell two contrasting stories—one about a person who was diagnosed early and one who wasn't diagnosed until the disease had ravaged her body. Be strategic. Select your evidence based on the types of argu-

ment you are trying to prove and the attitudes and needs of your audience. Then make sure that your evidence is novel, believable, and/or dramatic.

Novel Evidence Effective persuaders look for new or novel evidence to support their arguments. Overly familiar evidence doesn't work that well and may not succeed in justifying your claim. When speaking to a friendly audience, novel or new evidence can strengthen their resolve and provide answers to the questions asked by those who disagree. When audience members are undecided, new evidence can tip the balance in favor of your position. When audience members are highly involved but undecided about an issue, new, well-researched evidence can persuade them to support your claim.

Believable Evidence Even if your evidence is easily understood and novel, it will not be persuasive if

In 1995, Iowa Senator Tom Harkin learned that the U.S. government was paying $2.32 for surgical gauze when it could have been bought wholesale for 19 cents. How well does he dramatize his evidence here?

people don't believe it is true. If your audience appears to doubt the believability of your evidence, take time to explain why it's true, or provide other sources that reach the same conclusion. If the source of your evidence has high credibility, mention the source *before* presenting your evidence. On the other hand, if naming the source will not add to

STATISTICAL APPEALS can enhance message credibility because they represent conditions that exist in the real world.

the evidence's believability, mention it *after* you present the evidence.

Although stories serve as powerful forms of evidence, statistics can be an even more influential technique. Several studies conclude that arguments using statistical evidence are *more* persuasive than those using narratives (storytelling)—but only if used effectively.[22]

Communication researchers Lisa Massi Lindsey and Kimo Ah Yun describe three factors that affect the persuasiveness of statistics: sample size, perceived validity, and message credibility.[23] When statistics are based on large sample sizes, they are more believable. For example, if statistics report that 90 percent of 20,000 doctors recommend, or 75

percent of *all* the college professors on your campus claim, we are more likely to believe the results—and be persuaded.

Moreover, statistical appeals can enhance message credibility because they represent conditions that exist in the real world.

Dramatic Evidence To make your evidence memorable, find ways to dramatize that evidence. Rather than saying that your proposal will save the organization $250,000 in the next year, say that it will save a quarter of a million dollars—the equivalent of the entire travel budgets of the three largest divisions of the company.

To dramatize statistics, use attention-getting comparisons. For example, when describing the wealth of Bill Gates, you might note that his personal assets are larger than the gross national products of 104 countries or that his net worth is roughly equal to the *combined* net worth of the least wealthy 40 percent of American households.[24] Comparing such statistical evidence, rather than merely reporting it, heightens its impact on the audience.

Watch out for Heuristics

communication in ACTION

Understanding the nature of *heuristics* helps explain why we are susceptible to claims that rely on questionable evidence and warrants. **Heuristics** are cognitive thinking shortcuts that we use in decision making because they are correct often enough to be useful. Unfortunately, unethical persuaders sometimes use them to win agreement from their audiences even though their arguments are flawed.[25]

When audience members are not very interested or motivated to listen or when they are not thinking critically, they are more likely to believe arguments that lack valid evidence or that

offer evidence unrelated to a speaker's claim. The following brief list includes common heuristics we see and hear in everyday life:

- The quality of an item correlates with its price.
- We should trust those whom we like.
- The behavior of others is a good clue as to how *we* should behave.
- Confident speakers know what they are talking about.
- Something that is scarce is also valuable.

Salespeople often use heuristics. They appear confident, likable, and

trustworthy. They also give you multiple reasons for purchasing expensive, high-quality, limited-edition products that are very popular with discerning customers. When you hear a message that is loaded with heuristics, be cautious. Analyze the arguments carefully before you succumb to their persuasive power.

Heuristics Cognitive thinking shortcuts we use in decision making because they are correct often enough to be useful

PERSUASIVE organizational patterns

You have a topic you care about; a list of potential arguments; an understanding of how your arguments present claims of fact, value, conjecture, and policy; and good evidence to support your arguments. You've reached a key decision-making point. It's time to put these elements together into an effective persuasive message. In addition to the organizational patterns discussed in Chapter 13, Content and Organization, there are several strategic organizational formats particularly suited for persuasive presentations.

The 7 Key Elements and Guiding Principles of Effective Communication

Problem/Cause/Solution

As its name implies, the **problem/cause/solution pattern** describes a serious problem, explains why the problem continues (the cause), and offers a solution. This organizational pattern works best when you are proposing a specific course of action.

In the following outline, the speaker uses a problem/cause/solution organizational pattern to propose a national health-care system for all U.S. citizens:

A. Americans are not getting needed medical care. (*Problem*)
  1. Serious diseases such as (cancer, heart disease, and diabetes) go undetected and untreated.
  2. Millions of Americans do not get regular checkups.
B. The high costs of health care and health insurance prevent a solution. (*Cause*)
C. A national health-care system can guarantee affordable medical care for those in need without eliminating private care for those who want it. (*Solution*)
  1. This plan works well in other modern countries.
  2. This plan will not result in low-quality care or long waiting lines.

Comparative Advantage

When your audience is aware of a problem and recognizes that a solution is necessary, the **comparative advantage pattern** may help you make your case. In this pattern, you present a plan that will improve a situation and help to solve a problem while acknowledging that a total solution may not be possible. In the following outline, the speaker contends that increased deer hunting is a more advantageous way of reducing the serious problems caused by the growing deer population.

A. There is a plan that will help reduce the deer population. (*Plan*)
  1. Extend the deer-hunting season.
  2. Permit hunters to kill more female than male deer.
B. This plan will reduce the severity of the problem. (*Comparative Advantages*)
  1. It will reduce the number of deer deaths from starvation and disease.
  2. It will save millions of dollars now lost from crop, garden, and forest seedling damage.
  3. It will reduce the number of deer ticks carrying Lyme disease.
  4. It will reduce the number of automobile deaths and injuries caused by deer crossing highways.

Refuting Objections Pattern

Sometimes, audience members agree that there is a problem and even know what should be done to solve it, yet they do not act because the solution is objectionable, frightening, expensive, or difficult to understand or implement. In other situations, an audience disagrees with a speaker and comes prepared to reject the message even before hearing it. With both types of audiences, you should try to overcome these objections by using appropriate forms of proof and persuasive evidence. The **refuting objections pattern** allows you to refute and disprove each point that stands in opposition to your own.

In the following example, the speaker uses the refuting objections organizational pattern to encourage listeners to donate blood:

A. People should give blood but often don't. (*Problem*)
  1. Most people approve of and support donations.
  2. Most people don't give blood.
B. There are several reasons people don't give blood. (*Objections*)

Problem/cause/solution pattern A persuasive organizational pattern that describes a serious problem, identifies the cause(s) of the problem, and offers a solution

Comparative advantage pattern A persuasive organizational pattern that presents a plan to improve a situation and help to solve a problem while acknowledging that a total solution may not be possible

Refuting objections pattern A persuasive pattern in which you refute and disprove each point that stands in opposition to your own

1. They're afraid of pain and needles.
2. They're afraid that they could get a disease from giving blood.
3. They claim that they don't have time or know where to give blood.

C. These objections are poor excuses. (*Refutation*)
1. There is little or no pain in giving blood.
2. You can't get a disease by *giving* blood.
3. The Red Cross makes it easy and convenient to give the gift of life by schedules.

Monroe's Motivated Sequence

In the mid-1930s, communication professor Alan Monroe took the basic functions of a sales presentation (attention, interest, desire, and action) and transformed them into a step-by-step method for organizing persuasive speeches. This became known as **Monroe's Motivated Sequence**.[26]

In the following example, note how the speaker uses Monroe's Motivated Sequence to organize a presentation on how to liberate women suffering from brutality and injustice in poor countries.[27]

A. The Attention Step. Stories about abused women in Pakistan and Rwanda.
1. Saima Muhammad, Pakistan, beaten and starved by her husband
2. Claudine Mukakarisa, Rwanda, imprisoned in a rape house

B. The Need Step
1. Millions of women in poor countries are beaten, disfigured, raped, murdered, or sold into slavery or brothels.
2. Millions of girls in poor countries are denied medical care, education, and civil rights.
3. Countries that suppress women's rights are often poor and torn apart by religious fundamentalism and civil war.

C. The Satisfaction Step
1. Focus private and government aid on women's health and education.
2. Grant small microfinance loans to women.
3. Advocate for women's rights through organizations and government agencies.

D. The Visualization Step
1. Saima Muhammad's embroidery business now supports her family and employs 30 other families.
2. Claudine Mukakarisa was "adopted" by a U.S. woman who helped her start a business.

> **Monroe's Motivated Sequence**
> A persuasive organizational pattern that follows five basic steps (attention, need, satisfaction, visualization, and action)

communication&culture

TALL POPPIES AND BIG BRITCHES

In a highly individualistic culture like the United States, many audience members will value individual achievement and personal freedom. In collectivist cultures (Asian and Latin American countries as well as in co-cultures in the United States), audience members are more likely to value group identity, selflessness, and collective action. Audiences in collectivist cultures place less importance on the opinions and preferences of the individual than do audiences in individualistic cultures.[28] In the United States, appeals that benefit individuals—personal wealth, personal success, personal health and fitness—may be highly persuasive, while appeals that benefit society and families may be less effective.

In low-context cultures such as those of the United States, England, and Germany, audiences expect messages to be clear, factual, and objective. In the United States, persuasive appeals are often direct—do this; buy that; avoid that; just do it! In advertising, this would be termed a *hard-sell* approach to persuasion.

In contrast, high-context cultures such as those of Japan, China, and Mexico expect messages that are implied and situation specific. A soft-sell approach would be a better persuasive strategy. When addressing a high-context audience, encourage listeners to draw their own conclusions. Demonstrate benefits and advantages rather than advocating action.

Differences among cultures are very real. At the same time, be cautious about how you interpret and use this information. Are all Japanese collectivist and high-context? Many young Japanese business professionals are learning and embracing American ways that include a more direct and self-centered approach to communication. Are all Australians individualistic? Although Australians are very independent and value personal freedom, they also live in a culture in which power distance is minimal. Public displays of achievement or wealth are frowned upon.[29] One of your authors lived in Australia for a year and was introduced to the *tall poppy syndrome*. If, in a field of poppies, one red blossom grows higher than the others, you chop it off. When people show off or try to rise above others, you cut them down to size, too. "He thinks he's a tall poppy," describes someone who—in American terms—is "too big for his britches."

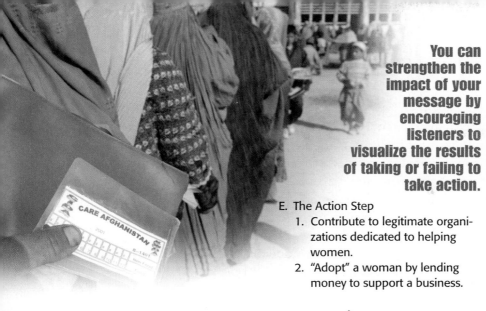

You can strengthen the impact of your message by encouraging listeners to visualize the results of taking or failing to take action.

E. The Action Step
   1. Contribute to legitimate organizations dedicated to helping women.
   2. "Adopt" a woman by lending money to support a business.
   3. Become an advocate for change by joining the CARE Action Network.

The unique visualization step in Monroe's Motivated Sequence (D in the outline) makes this organizational pattern useful for audience members who are uninformed, unconcerned, and unmotivated to listen, or for listeners who are skeptical of or opposed to the proposed course of actions. You can strengthen the impact of your message by encouraging listeners to visualize the results of taking or failing to take action.

persuasive speaking IN ACTION

"Looking through Our Window" by Ms. Marge Anderson, chief executive of the Mille Lacs Band of Ojibwe Indians, includes both informative strategies for generating audience interest *and* persuasive strategies that use different types of proof.[30] As you read Ms. Anderson's words, notice how she:

- adapts to her audience's interests, attitudes, and beliefs about Indian people;
- uses clear, oral, rhetorical, and eloquent language;
- tells two stories—one real, one mythic;
- uses novel, believable, and dramatic evidence;
- relies on her competence, character, and charisma to enhance her credibility;
- uses the example of St. Thomas Aquinas and the story of Jacob wrestling with the angel as a theme and a form of mythos;
- uses logical, emotional, personal, and narrative persuasive proof;
- acknowledges and respects differences between Indians and non-Indians;
- uses a modified version of Monroe's Motivated Sequence.

Looking through Our Window: The Value of Indian Culture
Address by Marge Anderson, Chief Executive, Mille Lacs Band of Ojibwe
Delivered to the First Friday Club of the Twin Cities, March 5, 1999
Sponsored by St. Thomas Alumni Association, St. Paul, Minnesota

Aaniin. Thank you for inviting me here today. When I was asked to speak to you, I was told you are interested in hearing about the improvements we are making on the Mille Lacs Reservation, and about our investment of casino dollars back into our community through schools, health care facilities, and other services. And I do want to talk to you about these things, because they are tremendously important, and I am very proud of them.

Anderson warmly greets and acknowledges the *audience's interests* in Indian casino income during the the attention step of Monroe's Motivated Sequence.

	But before I do, I want to take a few minutes to talk to you about
Anderson identifies her *central idea*: Non-Indians should care about what it means to be Indian in the United States. Note her *effective oral style* in this section—simple words, short sentences, active voice, personal pronouns, and repetition.	something else, something I'm not asked about very often. I want to talk to you about what it means to be Indian. About how my People experience the world. About the fundamental way in which our culture differs from yours. And about why you should care about all this.

But before I do, I want to take a few minutes to talk to you about something else, something I'm not asked about very often. I want to talk to you about what it means to be Indian. About how my People experience the world. About the fundamental way in which our culture differs from yours. And about why you should care about all this.

The differences between Indians and non-Indians have created a lot of controversy lately. Casinos, treaty rights, tribal sovereignty—these issues have stirred such anger and bitterness.

I believe the accusations against us are made out of ignorance. The vast majority of non-Indians do not understand how my People view the world, what we value, what motivates us.

They do not know these things for one simple reason: They've never heard us talk about them. For many years the only stories that non-Indians heard about my People came from other non-Indians. As a result, the picture you got of us was fanciful or distorted or so shadowy it hardly existed at all.

It's time for *Indian* voices to tell *Indian* stories.

Now, I'm sure at least a few of you are wondering, "Why do I need to hear these stories? Why should I care about what Indian People think, and feel, and believe?"

I think the most eloquent answer I can give you comes from the namesake for this university, St. Thomas Aquinas. St. Thomas wrote that dialogue is the struggle to learn from each other. This struggle, he said, is like Jacob wrestling the angel—it leaves one wounded and blessed at the same time.

Indian People know this struggle very well. The wounds we've suffered in our dialogue with non-Indians are well documented; I don't need to give you a laundry list of complaints.

We also know some of the blessings of this struggle. As *American* Indians, we live in two worlds—ours and yours. In the five hundred years since you first came to our lands, we have struggled to learn how to take the best of what your culture has to offer in arts, science, technology, and more, and then weave them into the fabric of our traditional ways.

But for non-Indians, the struggle is new. Now that our People have begun to achieve success, now that we are in business and in the headlines, you are starting to wrestle with understanding us.

Your wounds from this struggle are fresh, and the pain might make it hard for you to see beyond them. But if you try, you'll begin to see the blessings as well—the blessings of what a deepened knowledge of Indian culture can bring you. I'd like to share a few of those blessings with you today.

Earlier I mentioned that there is a fundamental difference between the way Indians and non-Indians experience the world. This difference goes all the way back to the Bible, and Genesis.

In Genesis, the first book of the Old Testament, God creates man in his own image. Then God says, "Be fruitful, multiply, fill the earth and conquer it. Be masters of the fish and the sea, the birds of the heaven, and all living animals on the earth."

Sidebar annotations:

Anderson identifies her *central idea*: Non-Indians should care about what it means to be Indian in the United States. Note her *effective oral style* in this section—simple words, short sentences, active voice, personal pronouns, and repetition.

Here, she presents a *need* step by describing the misunderstandings about the Indian culture and practices that lead to problems and conflict.

Anderson carefully chooses her *words*, using *they* to refer to people who do not understand Indians, rather than *you*, which carries a more accusatory tone.

Anderson attempts to *overcome audience disagreement* through identification with St. Thomas Aquinas, a European and namesake of the university alumni association she is addressing.

To *counter audience expectations*, she assures the audience that she will not read a long list of complaints about the mistreatment of Indians.

Here she seeks *common ground* by describing Indian efforts to take the best of American culture into their own.

This *transition* attempts to acknowledge the audience's difficulty with understanding the Indians' struggles. Anderson *repeats a variation of her central idea*.

Here she identifies the *satisfaction* step by advocating better understanding, mutual respect, and appreciation between Indians and non-Indians.

This section *compares and contrasts* non-Indian and Indian perspectives by using a *familiar quotation* from Genesis (a non-Indian source) and a quotation from Chief Seattle (an Indian source).

Masters. Conquer. Nothing, *nothing* could be further from the way Indian People view the world and our place in it. Here are the words of the great nineteenth-century Chief Seattle: "You are a part of the earth, and the earth is a part of you. You did not weave the web of life, you are merely a strand in it. *Whatever you do to the web, you do to yourself.*" In our tradition, there is no mastery.

When you begin to see the world this way—through Indian eyes—you will begin to understand our view of land, and treaties, very differently. You will begin to understand that when we speak of Father Sun and Mother Earth, these are not New Age catchwords—they are very real terms of respect for very real beings.

And when you understand this, then you will understand that our fight for treaty rights is not just about hunting deer or catching fish. It is about teaching our children to honor Mother Earth and Father Sun. It is about teaching them to respectfully receive the gifts these loving parents offer us in return for the care we give them. And it is about teaching this generation and the generations yet to come about their place in the web of life. Our culture and the fish, our values and the deer, the lessons we learn and the rice we harvest—everything is tied together. You can no more separate one from the other than you can divide a person's spirit from his body.

When you understand how we view the world and our place in it, it's easy to appreciate why our casinos are so important to us. The reason we defend our businesses so fiercely isn't because we want to have something that others don't. The reason is because these businesses allow us to give back to others—to our People, our communities, and the Creator.

I'd like to take a minute and mention just a few of the ways we've already given back:

- We've opened new schools, new health care facilities, and new community centers where our children get a better education, where our elders get better medical care, and where our families can gather to socialize and keep our traditions alive.
- We've created programs to teach and preserve our language and cultural traditions.
- We've created a small Business Development Program to help band members start their own businesses.
- We've created more than twenty-eight hundred jobs for band members, People from other tribes, and non-Indians.
- We've generated more than fifty million dollars in federal taxes, and more than fifteen million dollars in state taxes through wages paid to employees.
- And we've given back more than two million dollars in charitable donations.

This section *compares and contrasts* non-Indian and Indian perspectives by using a *familiar quotation* from Genesis (a non-Indian source) and a quotation from Chief Seattle (an Indian source).

Anderson begins the process of *linking* the Indian worldview with Indian struggles for treaty rights. Although listeners may not believe in Father Sun and Mother Earth, they may share a respect for and concern about the environment.

Notice how Chief Anderson repeats the word *about* in a series of similarly constructed sentences.

Here, she identifies the *visualization step* by *addressing her audience directly* and describing how casinos not only preserve the Indian way of life, but also give back to non-Indians.

Chief Anderson provides *multiple examples* (factual and statistical) of the benefits of casino income. She begins each example with the word *we*, a *stylistic device* that helps her focus on Indian contributions.

The list goes on and on. But rather than flood you with more numbers, I'll tell you a story that sums up how my People view business through the lens of our traditional values.

Anderson concludes her list with a factual story (*narrative proof/mythos*) that reflects Indian values such as caring for others and the environment in which they live.

Last year, the Woodlands National Bank, which is owned and operated by the Mille Lacs Band, was approached by the city of Onamia and asked to forgive a mortgage on a building in the downtown area. The building had been abandoned and was an eyesore on Main Street. The city planned to renovate and sell the building, and return it to the tax rolls.

Although the bank would lose money by forgiving the mortgage, our business leaders could see the wisdom in improving the community. The opportunity to help our neighbors was an opportunity to strengthen the web of life. So we forgave the mortgage.

Notice how Anderson acknowledges and respects the differences between Indians and non-Indian views of business practices and beliefs.

Now, I know this is not a decision everyone would agree with. Some people feel that in business, you have to look out for number one. But my People feel that in business—and in life—you have to look out for *every* one.

And this, I believe, is one of the blessings that Indian culture has to offer you and other non-Indians. We have a different perspective on so many things, from caring for the environment to healing the body, mind, and soul.

But if our culture disappears, if the Indian ways are swallowed up by the dominant American culture, no one will be able to learn from them. Not Indian children. Not your children. No one. All that knowledge, all that wisdom, will be lost forever.

She describes what will happen if the Indian culture disappears, and reuses words from the earlier-cited Aquinas quote—*struggle, dialogue, wounds, blessing*.

The struggle of dialogue will be over. Yes, there will be no more wounds. But there will also be no more blessings.

Here Anderson's message becomes more urgent and *rhetorical in style*. She talks about wasting time, a world growing smaller, and the risk that Indian culture will vanish.

There is still so much we have to learn from each other, and we have already wasted so much time. Our world grows smaller every day. And every day, more of our unsettling, surprising, wonderful differences vanish. And when that happens, part of each of us vanishes too.

I'd like to end with one of my favorite stories. It's a funny little story about Indians and non-Indians, but its message is serious: You can see something differently if you are willing to learn from those around you.

Her final story is a good example of *mythos*. She *previews* the story's moral, which helps her return to her *central idea*.

This is the story: Years ago, white settlers came to this area and built the first European-style homes. When Indian People walked by these homes and saw see-through things in the walls, they looked through them to see what the strangers inside were doing. The settlers were shocked, but it makes sense when you think about it: Windows are made to be looked through from both sides.

In this final *action step*, Chief Anderson relies on *metaphor* to ask the audience to continue a productive dialogue with the Indian people.

Since then, my People have spent many years looking at the world through your window. I hope today I've given you a reason to look at it through ours.

Mii gwetch.

Communication ASSESSMENT

Persuasive Presentation Assessment

Use the following ratings to assess each of the competencies on the persuasive presentation assessment instrument:

E = excellent; G = good; A = average; W = weak; M = missing; N/A = not applicable.

COMMENTS

COMPETENCIES	E	G	A	W	M	N/A
Preparation and Content						
Purpose and topic						
Audience adaptation						
Adaptation to the context						
Introduction						
Organization						
Supporting material						
Transitions						
Conclusion						
Language						
Persuasive strategies						
Delivery						
Delivery mode						
Vocal delivery						
Physical delivery						
Presentation aids, if used						
Other Criteria						
Outline or manuscript						
Bibliography						
Other: _____						
Overall Assessment (circle one)	**E**	**G**	**A**	**W**	**M**	**N/A**

Summary

What do persuasive presentations try to achieve?

- Persuasion seeks to change audience members' opinions (what they think) or behavior (what they do).
- Whereas informative presentations *give* an audience directions, advice, or explanations, persuasive presentations *ask* for their agreement or a change in their opinions or behavior.

How should you adapt to different audience attitudes?

- Analyze and classify your audience's attitudes in terms of whether they agree with you, disagree with you, or are undecided.
- When audience members agree with you, present new information, strengthen audience resistance to persuasion, excite audience emotions, provide a personal role model, and advocate a course of action.
- When audience members disagree with you, set reasonable goals, find common ground, adapt to differences of opinion, use evidence, and build your personal credibility.
- When audience members are (1) undecided: gain their attention and provide relevant information; (2) unconcerned: gain their attention, give them a reason to care, and use strong evidence; (3) adamantly undecided: acknowledge their opinions and strengthen the arguments on your side of the issue.
- Psychological Reactance Theory explains why telling an audience what *not* to do can produce the exact opposite reaction.

What strategies will help you develop and select effective arguments?

- Include persuasive claims that, based on audience analysis, would most likely persuade that audience.
- Whatever arguments you choose, make sure you know whether they are advocating claims of fact, conjecture, value, or policy.
- Effective persuaders often use logical proof (*logos*), emotional proof (*pathos*), personal proof (*ethos*), and narrative proof (*mythos*) in their presentations.
- Use novel, believable, dramatic, and valid evidence to persuade.
- When fear appeals are well-crafted and well-delivered, they can influence audience attitudes.

- *Heuristics* (cognitive shortcuts that are correct often enough to be useful when we make decisions) help explain why we believe arguments that rely on questionable claims, evidence, and warrants.

Which organizational patterns are particularly suited for persuasive presentations?

- Organizational patterns particularly suited for persuasive speaking include problem/cause/solution, comparative advantage, refuting objections, and Monroe's Motivated Sequence.

What are the characteristics of an effective persuasive presentation?

- Effective persuasive presentations reflect strategic decisions about self, others, purpose, context, content, structure, and expression.
- Effective persuasive speakers adapt their content to the characteristics and attitudes of audience members and to the context of the presentation.

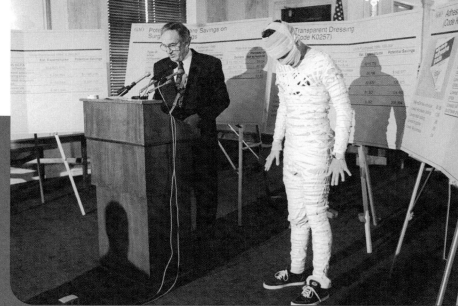

TEST *your knowledge*

1 In light of the fact that persuasion seeks to change audience opinions and/or behavior, which of the following examples represents an appeal to audience opinion?

a. Eat dinner with your family at least five times a week.

b. Vegetarian diets are good for you and the planet.

c. Buy a gas–electric hybrid car.

d. Vote!

e. Choose a college that matches your interests, personality, and social needs.

2 Which of the following persuasive strategies is likely to be more effective when speaking to an audience that disagrees with you?

a. Excite audience emotions.

b. Provide a personal role model.

c. Set reasonable goals.

d. Give them a reason to care.

e. Emphasize the arguments on your side of an issue.

3 With which kind of audience should you try to find common ground?

a. an audience that agrees with you

b. an audience that disagrees with you

c. an audience that is uninformed

d. an audience that is unconcerned

e. an audience that is undecided

4 You can reduce the likelihood of a reactance response to a persuasive presentation by heeding all of the following strategies *except*:

a. Avoid strong direct commands such as "you must" or "stop."

b. Avoid finger-pointing, literally and figuratively.

c. Advocate a middle ground that preserves audience freedom.

d. Avoid extreme statements depicting horrible consequences such as "you will die."

e. Use fear appeals to scare them into action.

5 Which form of proof relies on touching audience emotions— fear, anger, pride, love, jealousy, or envy?

a. mythos

b. ethos

c. logos

d. pathos

e. samos

6 Which answer identifies the three characteristics of persuasive evidence as discussed in the textbook?

a. novel, believable, and dramatic

b. based on ethos, pathos, and logos

c. valid, reliable, and current

d. new, fair, and respected

e. focused on problem, cause, and solution

7 All of the following examples are common heuristics used to persuade audiences *except*:

a. Think critically about source biases.

b. Longer messages are stronger messages.

c. Quality products cost more.

d. Experts should be trusted.

e. Confident speakers know what they're talking about.

8 Which persuasive organizational pattern has the following three sections? (1) People should do X, (2) People don't do X for several reasons, (3) These reasons should not stop you from doing X.

a. Problem/Cause/Solution

b. Comparative Advantage

c. Refuting Objections

d. Monroe's Motivated Sequence

e. Comparison-Contrast

9 Which step in Monroe's Motivated Sequence is most useful for audience members who are uninformed, unconcerned, skeptical, or opposed to the proposed course of action?

a. attention step

b. need step

c. satisfaction step

d. visualization step

e. action step

10 What kind of audience was Chief Marge Anderson seeking to persuade when she said the following?

Now, I'm sure at least a few of you are wondering, "Why do I need to hear these stories? Why should I care about what Indian People think, and feel, and believe?" I think the most eloquent answer I can give you comes from the namesake for this university, St. Thomas Aquinas. St. Thomas wrote that dialogue is the struggle to learn from each other. This struggle, he said, is like Jacob wrestling the angel—it leaves one wounded and blessed at the same time.

a. an audience that agrees with her

b. an audience that disagrees with her

c. an audience that is uninformed

d. an audience that is unconcerned

e. an audience that is undecided

Answers: 1-b; 2-c; 3-b; 4-e; 5-d; 6-a; 7-a; 8-c; 9-d; 10-d

This article from *Communication Currents* has been edited and shortened with permission from the National Communication Association.

Communication Currents
Knowledge for Communicating Well

NCA
A Publication of the National Communication Association

Volume 3, Issue 5 - October 2008

Another Campaign, More Mud

Negative campaigning—sometimes referred to as mudslinging—is as old as politics. Thomas Jefferson was the subject of rumors (which turned out to be true) that he had slave mistresses. Abraham Lincoln was the recipient of insults about his looks, and delivered them himself, saying of an opponent, "He can compress the most words into the smallest idea of any man I know."

Complaining about mudslinging is nothing new either. Teddy Roosevelt wrote:

> But the man who never does anything else, who never thinks or speaks or writes save of his feats with the muck-rake, speedily becomes, not a help to society, not an incitement to good, but one of the most potent forces for evil.

So as this year's presidential contest heats up, it's no surprise that we find negative campaign tactics and controversy about them erupting. Barack Obama is running attack ads painting John McCain as a 1980s throwback, while McCain's campaign is reportedly planning a series of attack ads questioning Obama's truthfulness. As both campaigns go negative, each criticizes the other for doing it.

While negative campaigning has always been around, a big accelerant was the development of television as a mudslinging tool. Lee Kaid and Anne Johnston (*Journal of Communication*, 1991) say the first negative ads appeared in the 1952 Eisenhower–Stevenson race. The most infamous attack ad is Johnson's "Daisy Girl" in 1964. But, they say, the art was taken to a new level by independent groups in the 1980s. The art form has been refined since then, with the state-of-the-art defined by the Swift Boat ads of the 2004 Bush–Kerry race.

Beginning with that same race, a new force came into play. 2004 marked the first election where the Internet played a major, official campaign role. Prior to this, mud was for the most part slung locally—in campaign appearances and town halls—and it was also reported locally. But in 2004 George W. Bush and John Kerry posted their speeches and news releases on their web sites, distributing them to ordinary voters making up an international audience.

During that election my colleague Kevin Dooley and I helped develop an advanced text analysis method to monitor statements by one candidate about the other. We called it the Mud Meter™, and it was featured in a story in the *New York Times*. The meter looked at speeches and press releases posted on the official campaign web sites of Bush and Kerry, and measured the tone (positive or negative valence) of statements by the candidate that named his opponent.

The famous "Daisy Girl" ad aired once during the Johnson–Goldwater presidential race. A little girl is seen picking the petals off a daisy. As she counts the petals, an ominous-sounding male voice is then heard over hers, counting down a missile launch. The girl's eyes turn toward something she sees in the sky. When the countdown reaches zero, the screen blackens, followed by the flash and mushroom cloud of a nuclear explosion. The ad's unsaid message is: This is what will happen if you elect Goldwater.

The Swift Boat ads, sponsored by a group of conservative Vietnam veterans and which ran during the Bush–Kerry presidential race, claimed that Kerry didn't deserve his war medals and wasn't a respected soldier. Even though these claims were proved false, the ad influenced many voters to reject Kerry. Since the 2004 election, the term *swiftboating* has become synonymous with attack campaigning, in which the credibility and patriotism of opponents are attacked with false information.

What kind of *proof* do negative campaign tactics use: *logical, emotional, personal, and/or narrative proof?* See Chapter 16, pp. 330–333 for a review of the four forms of proof.

The meter showed that Bush was much more negative than Kerry until late July when the two pulled even. Kerry went more negative than Bush following the Democratic convention and then again around the time of the Republican convention. Then Bush went extremely negative relative to Kerry following the Republican convention through the middle of October. Then the situation reversed and stayed that way through election day.

In the 2008 race, the new factor is the political blogosphere. Now speeches and press releases are not only posted by the campaigns, but they are picked up, reposted, refuted, amplified and generally kicked round by thousands of bloggers on both ends of the political spectrum. The *New York Times* has called this the "year of the political blogger."

About a year ago we created a new web site called Wonkosphere.com that aggregates, analyzes and tracks conversations on about 1500 political blogs. But as the races narrowed to the two major party candidates, we decided it was time for the return of the Mud Meter, now hosted on the Wonkosphere site.

Comparisons between the 2004 and 2008 elections are interesting. For one thing, we are finding many fewer references to the opponent by McCain and Obama than we found for Bush and Kerry. Through mid-September, the 2004 candidates mentioned their opponents an average of 1021 times a week. In the 2008 campaign the average is 135 times a week. McCain mentions Obama on average ten times as often as Obama mentions McCain, though the difference may be because Obama does not repackage media stories as press releases, as does McCain.

The graph shows the comparative Mud Meter levels from the end of July through mid-September for both 2004 and 2008. For the 2004 campaign, there was less difference between the candidates and the average level was mostly higher. The first sustained and noticeable difference became apparent around the beginning of September when Bush's levels dropped considerably, compared to Kerry's, around the end of the 2004 Republican convention.

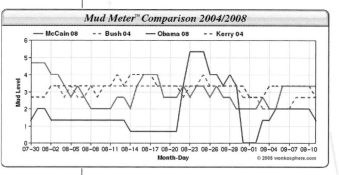

The 2008 lines are interesting for a couple of reasons. First, except for a couple of cases, the average meter level is lower for 2008 than 2004. The variability is also strikingly higher, though that is in part because the data are based on a smaller number of opponent mentions. Obama is substantially lower than McCain throughout the period, except for the time of the Democratic convention. This is consistent with a stated desire by Obama to keep the campaign on issues rather than personal attacks. As this article goes to press, Obama's supporters are complaining that he is not being tough enough in the face of attacks by McCain and Sarah Palin. Time will tell whether Obama can sustain his low-mud approach.

ABOUT THE AUTHOR

Steve Corman is a Professor and Director of the Consortium for Strategic Communication in the Hugh Downs School of Human Communication at Arizona State University, Tempe, Arizona. He is also Chief Technology Officer of Crawdad Technologies, LLC. *Communication Currents* is a publication of the National Communication Association.

How well did each candidate in the 2008 presidential campaign use e-mail and blogs? Do you think using these media made a difference in the outcome? If so, how did they help or hinder each candidate?

The term *wonk* is used in politics to describe people who study politics thoroughly and obsessively. Some people call such wonks political nerds or campaign junkies.

How easily can you read and understand this graph? Does the author's detailed explanation help? How, if at all, would you change this graph?

glossary

4-M Model of Leadership Effectiveness   A model that identifies four interdependent leadership functions: Modeling, Motivating, Managing, and Making decisions

A

Abstract word   Words that refer to an idea or concept that *cannot* be observed or touched

Accenting nonverbal behavior   Nonverbal behavior that emphasizes important elements in a message by highlighting its focus or emotional content

Accommodating conflict style   Giving in to others for the purpose of preserving peace and harmony

Active voice   The subject of a sentence performs the action, as in *Bill read the book*

A-E-I-O-U Model of Conflict Resolution   Focuses on sharing personal concerns and suggesting alternative actions to resolve a conflict based on the assumption that everyone means well and wants to resolve the conflict

Affection need   The need to feel liked by others

Agenda   An outline of items to be discussed and the tasks to be accomplished at a meeting

Aggression   Putting personal needs first and demanding compliance from others, often at the expense of someone else's needs

Alliteration   A rhetorical device in which a series of words (or words placed closely together) begin with the same sound

Analogy   A figure of speech that identifies key similarities in things that are alike and not alike

Analysis paralysis   A situation that occurs when group members are so focused on analyzing a problem that they fail to make a decision

Analytical listening   The ability to evaluate another person's message objectively

Anger   An emotional response to unmet expectations that ranges from minor irritation to intense rage

Appeal to authority   A fallacy of reasoning in which the opinion of someone who has no relevant experience is used to support an argument

Appeal to popularity   A fallacy of reasoning that claims an action is acceptable because many people do it

Appeal to tradition   A fallacy of reasoning that claims a certain course of action should be followed because that is the way it has been done in the past

Appreciative listening   The ability to enjoy and value *how* someone communicates

Argument   A claim supported by evidence or reasons for accepting it

Articulation   Describes how clearly you make the sounds in the words of a language

Assertiveness   Promoting your own needs and rights while also respecting the needs and rights of others

Attacking the person   A fallacy of reasoning in which irrelevant attacks are made against a person rather than the substance of an argument

Audience analysis   The ability to understand, respect, and adapt to audience members before and during a presentation

Audience attitudes   A measure of whether audience members agree or disagree with a speaker's purpose statement as well as how strongly they agree or disagree

Authoritative parenting   Parents are flexible and adapt to the individual characteristics and needs of their children

Authority rule   A situation in which the leader or an authority outside the group makes the final decisions for the group

Autocratic leader   Tries to control the group, makes decisions, gives and expects members to follow orders, and takes credit for successful results

Avatar   A two- or three-dimensional human figure you create and use to represent yourself online

Avoidance conflict style   A conflict style in which people change the subject, sidestep a controversial issue, or deny that a conflict exists

Avoidant decision maker   A person who is uncomfortable making decisions, may not think about a problem at all, or will make a final decision at the last minute

B

Backing   The component of the Toulmin model that provides support for an argument's warrant

Basic terms   General words that come to mind when you see an object, such as *car* or *cat*

Biased   A source that states an opinion so slanted in one direction that it may not be objective or fair

Brainstorming   A group technique in which members generate as many ideas as possible in a short period of time

Bypassing   A form of misunderstanding that occurs when people miss each other with their meanings

C

Cause and effect arrangement   An organizational format that either presents a cause and its resulting effects or details the effects that result from a specific cause

Central idea   A sentence that summarizes the key points of a presentation

Channels   The various physical and electronic media through which we express messages

Character   A component of speaker credibility that relates to a speaker's perceived honesty and good will

Charisma   A component of speaker credibility that relates to the speaker's perceived level of energy, enthusiasm, vigor, and/or commitment

Claim   A statement that identifies your belief or position on a particular issue or topic

Clear style   Short, simple, and direct words and phrases as well as active verbs, concrete words, and plain language

Closed-ended question   A question that requires only a short and direct response, such as *yes* or *no*

Closure principle   A perception principle that explains why we often fill in missing elements in order to form a more complete impression of an object, person, or event

Co-cultures   A group of people who coexist within the mainstream society yet remain connected to one another through their cultural heritage

Code switching   Modifying how we use verbal and nonverbal communication in different contexts

Coercive/authoritarian parenting   Parents are not flexible and expect their children to follow a set of rules that may not adapt to their characteristics and needs

Cognitive restructuring   A method of reducing communication apprehension by replacing negative thoughts with more positive ones

Cohesion   The mutual attraction that holds the members of a group together

Collaborative conflict style   A conflict style in which people search for new solutions that will achieve their personal goals as well as the goals of others

Collectivism   A cultural belief that emphasizes the views, needs, and goals of the group rather than focusing on the individual

Committee   A group created to complete a specific assignment by a larger group or by a person in a position of authority

Common ground   A place where both you and your audience can stand without disagreement

Communication   The process of using verbal and nonverbal messages to generate meaning within and across various contexts, cultures, and channels

Communication Accommodation Theory   When we believe that another group has more power or has desirable characteristics, we tend to accommodate our conversations to the accepted speech behaviors and norms in that group

Communication apprehension   An individual's level of fear or anxiety associated with either real or anticipated communication with another person or persons

Communication models   Illustrations that simplify and present the basic elements and interaction patterns in the communication process

Comparative advantage pattern   A persuasive organizational pattern that presents a plan to improve a situation and help to solve a problem while acknowledging that a total solution may not be possible

Comparison–contrast arrangement   An organizational pattern that demonstrates how two things are similar or different

Competence   A component of speaker credibility that relates to the speaker's perceived expertise and abilities

Competitive conflict style   A conflict style in which people are more concerned with fulfilling their own needs than they are with meeting the needs of others

Complementary nonverbal behavior   Nonverbal behavior that is consistent with the verbal message being expressed at the same time

Comprehensive listening   The ability to accurately understand the meaning of another person's spoken and nonverbal messages

Comprehensive outline   An all-inclusive presentation framework that follows established outlining rules

Compromising conflict style   A "middle ground" approach to conflict resolution that involves giving up some of your own goals to achieve other goals

Concrete word   Words that refer to specific things that *can* be perceived by your senses

Conflict   Disagreement that occurs in relationships when differences are expressed

Connectives   Internal previews, summaries, transitions, and signposts that help connect key components of a presentation to one another

Connotation   The emotional responses and personal thoughts connected to the meaning of a word

Consensus   A process in which all group members agree to support a group decision

Constructive conflict   Expressing disagreement in a way that respects others' perspectives and promotes problem solving

Constructive nonconformity   Resisting a group norm while still working to promote a group's common goal

Content   The ideas, information, and opinions you include in your message

Context   The circumstances and setting in which communication takes place

Contradictory nonverbal behavior   Nonverbal behavior that conflicts with the meaning of spoken words

Control need   The need to feel competent and confident

Conversation   An interaction, often informal, in which people exchange speaking and listening roles

CORE speaking styles   Refers to four basic language styles: clear style, oral style, rhetorical style, and eloquent style

Co-worker relationship   A type of professional relationship that involves interacting with people who have little or no official authority over one another but who must work together to accomplish the goals of an organization

Critical thinking   The process you use to analyze what you read, see, or hear in order to arrive at a justified conclusion or decision

Culture   A learned set of shared interpretations about beliefs, values, norms, and social practices which affect the behaviors of a relatively large group of people

Customer relationship   A type of professional relationship that involves interaction between someone communicating on behalf of an organization with an individual who is external to the organization

D

Data   The component of the Toulmin Model that provides evidence to support a claim

Decision making   The act of reaching a conclusion; a process in which a group chooses from among alternative decisions

Decoding   Converts a "code" or message sent by someone else into a form you can understand and use

Decreasing Options Technique (DOT)   A technique that helps groups reduce and refine a large number of suggestions and ideas into a manageable set of options

Defensive behaviors   Behaviors that reflect our instinct to protect ourselves when being physically or verbally attacked by someone

Definition   A statement that explains or clarifies the meaning of a word, phrase, or concept

Delivery   The various ways in which you use your voice, body, and presentation aids to express your message

Democratic leader   Promotes the social equality and task interests of group members

Demographic information   Information about audience characteristics such as age, gender, marital status, race, religion, place of residence, ethnicity, occupation, education, and income

Denotation   Refers to the specific and objective dictionary-based meaning of a word

Dependent decision maker   A person who solicits the advice and opinions of others before making a decision

Description   Words that create mental images in the minds of listeners

DESC scripting   A four-step process (describe, express, specify, consequences) that provides a way of addressing another person's objectionable behavior

Destructive conflict   The result of behaviors that create hostility or prevent problem solving in a conflict situation

Destructive nonconformity   Resisting a group norm without regard for the best interests of the group and its goal

Dialogue   A conversation in which two people interact in order to understand, respect, and appropriately adapt to one another

Discrimination   Behavior that acts out and expresses prejudice

Discriminative listening   The ability to accurately distinguish auditory and/or visual stimuli

Documentation   The practice of citing the sources of supporting material in a presentation

E

Eloquent style   Poetic and expressive language that makes thoughts and feelings clear, inspiring, *and* memorable

Emoticons   Typographical characters that are used to convey nonverbal expressions

Emotion   The feeling you have when reacting to a situation, and is often accompanied by physical changes

Emotional intelligence   The capacity for recognizing our own feelings and those of others, for motivating ourselves, and for managing emotions well in ourselves and in our relationships

Emotional support   Specific communication behaviors enacted by one party with the intent of helping another cope effectively with emotional distress

Empathic listening   The ability to understand and identify with a person's situation or feelings

Encoding   Decision-making process by which you create and send messages that generate meaning

Entertainment speaking   A presentation designed to amuse interest, divert, or "warm up" an audience

Ethics   Agreed-upon standards of right and wrong

Ethnocentrism   A belief that your culture is superior to others

Ethos   Speaker credibility that relies on the perceived character, competence, and charisma of a speaker

Euphemism   A mild, indirect, or vague word that substitutes for a harsh, blunt, or offensive one

Example   A word or phrase that refers to a specific case or instance in order to make a large or abstract idea concrete and understandable

Exclusionary language   Words that reinforce stereotypes, belittle other people, or exclude others from understanding an in-group's message

Expectancy Violation Theory   Your expectations about nonverbal behavior significantly affect your interactions with others and the way you interpret nonverbal messages

Explanatory communication   Enhances or deepens an audience's understanding about a topic so listeners can understand, interpret, and evaluate complex ideas and information

Expression–privacy dialectic   The relational tension between wanting both openness and privacy

Extemporaneous speaking   The most common form of delivery that occurs when you use an outline or a set of notes to guide yourself through a prepared presentation

External noise   Physical elements in the environment that interfere with effective communication

Extrovert   An outgoing person who talks more than others and enjoys working in groups

Eye contact   Establishing and maintaining direct, visual links with individual audience members

Eye scan   A method of glancing at a specific section of your notes or manuscript and then looking up at your audience to speak

F

Face   The positive image you wish to create or preserve when interacting with others

Fact   A verifiable observation, experience, or event known to be true

Fallacy   An error in thinking that leads to false or invalid claims

False consensus   Occurs when members reluctantly give in to group pressure or an external authority in order to make a decision masquerading as consensus

Family   A self-defined group of intimates who create and maintain themselves through their own interactions and their interactions with others

Faulty cause   A fallacy of reasoning that claims a particular event is the cause of another event without ruling out other possible causes

Feedback   Any verbal or nonverbal response you can see or hear from others

Feeler   A people-oriented person who helps others and wants everyone to get along

Feminine societies   Societies in which gender roles overlap: both men and women are supposed to be modest, tender, and concerned with the quality of life

Figure–ground principle   A perception principle that explains why we focus on certain features—the figure—while deemphasizing less relevant stimuli—the ground

Filler phrase   Words and phrases such as *you know*, *uh*, *um*, *okay*, and *like* that break up a speaker's fluency and that can also annoy listeners

Fluency   The ability to speak smoothly without tripping over words or phrases

Forming stage   A group development stage in which members become acquainted with one another and define group goals

Forum   Audience members comment on or ask questions after a public discussion or presentation

Fundamental Interpersonal Relationship Orientation (FIRO) Theory   People interact with others to satisfy their needs for inclusion, control, and affection

G

Gesture   A body movement that communicates an idea or emotion

Gobbledygook   Several words used in place of one, or multiple-syllable words used where a single syllable word would suffice

Golden listening rule   Listen to others as you would have them listen to you

Gossip   A type of rumor that focuses on the private, personal, or even scandalous affairs of other people

Governance group   An elected or appointed group that makes public policy decisions in public settings

Group communication   The interaction of three or more interdependent people working to achieve a common goal

Group role   A pattern of behavior associated with an expected function within a particular group context

Groupthink   The deterioration of group effectiveness as a consequence of in-group pressure

Guiding principles   Communication guidelines focused on *self*, *others*, *purpose*, *context*, *content*, *structure*, and *expression* that help you select and apply effective communication strategies and skills to specific communication situations

H

Habits   Something you do so frequently and for so long that you've stopped thinking about why, when, how, and whether you do it; something that becomes second nature and requires knowledge, skills, and desire

Hasty generalization   A fallacy of reasoning in which a conclusion is based on too little evidence or too few experiences

Heuristics   Cognitive thinking shortcuts we use in decision making because they are correct often enough to be useful

Hidden agenda   When members' private goals conflict with the group's goals

High-context culture   A cultural dimension in which very little meaning is expressed through words; gestures, silence, and facial expressions, as well as the relationships among communicators, have meaning

High power distance   Cultures in which individuals accept differences in power as normal and allow the privileged to use their power to guide or control the lives of people with less power

Hypothetical question   Describes a set of circumstances and asks how you would respond

I

Immediacy   The degree to which a person seems approachable or likable

Impression management   The strategies people use to shape others' impressions of themselves in order to achieve personal goals such as gaining influence, power, sympathy, or approval

Impromptu speaking Occurs when you give a presentation without advanced preparation or practice

Inclusion need The need to belong, to be involved with others, and to be accepted

Individualism A cultural belief that independence is worth pursuing, that personal achievement should be rewarded, and that individual uniqueness is an important value

Inference A conclusion based on claims of fact

Inflection The changing pitch within a syllable, word, or group of words that makes speech expressive

Informative presentation A presentation designed to instruct, enlighten, explain, describe, clarify, correct, remind, and/or demonstrate

Informatory communication Increases audience awareness by providing the latest information about a topic

Inspirational speaking A presentation that brings like-minded people together, creates social unity, builds goodwill, or celebrates by arousing audience emotions

Integration–separation dialectic The relational tension between wanting both interpersonal dependence and independence

Interactional context The type of communication interaction; whether communication occurs one-to-one, in groups, or between a presenter and an audience

Interactive communication model A model that includes the concepts of noise and feedback to show that communication is not an unobstructed or one-way street

Intercultural dimension An aspect of a culture that can be measured relative to other cultures

Internal noise Thoughts, feelings, and attitudes that interfere with your ability to communicate and understand a message as it was intended

Internal preview Identifies, in advance, the key points of a presentation or section in a specific order

Internal summary Signals the end of major sections and reinforces important ideas in a presentation

Interpersonal communication Interaction between a limited number of people, usually two, for the purpose of sharing information, accomplishing a specific goal, or maintaining a relationship

Interview An interpersonal interaction between two parties, at least one of whom has a predetermined and serious purpose, that involves asking and answering questions in order to share information, solve a problem, or influence the other

Intimacy The feeling or state of knowing someone deeply in physical, psychological, emotional, intellectual, and/or collaborative ways because that person is significant in your life

Introvert A person who thinks before speaking, is not very talkative, and prefers to do work alone

Intuitive A person who looks for connections, overall concepts, and basic assumptions rather than on details and procedures

Intuitive decision maker A person who makes decisions based on instincts, feelings, or hunches

J

Jargon The specialized or technical language of a profession or homogenous group

Jealousy An intense feeling caused by a perceived threat to a relationship

Johari Window A model for understanding the connections between willingness to self-disclose and receptivity to feedback

Judger A highly structured, punctual person who likes to plan ahead

K

Key points The most important issues or the main ideas in a presentation's message

L

Laissez-faire leader Lets the group take charge of all decisions and actions

Language A system of arbitrary signs and symbols used to communicate thoughts and feelings

Language intensity The degree to which language deviates from bland, neutral terms

Leader–member relations A situational leadership factor that assesses how well a leader gets along with group members

Leadership The ability to make strategic decisions and use communication to mobilize group members toward achieving a common goal

Leading question Suggests or implies the desired response

Leakage cues Unintentional nonverbal behavior that may reveal deceptive intentions

Learning style Characterizes the way information is taken in and processed—in a visual, auditory, or kinesthetic/tactile style

Linear communication model The earliest type of communication model that functions in only one direction: a source creates a message and sends it through a channel to reach a receiver

Listening The process of receiving, constructing meaning from, and responding to a spoken and/or non-verbal message

Logistical context The physical characteristics of a particular communication situation; focuses on a specific time, place, setting, and occasion

Logistics The strategic planning, arranging, and use of people, facilities, time, and materials relevant to a presentation

Logos (logical proof) A form of proof that appeals to listeners' intellect and their ability to think critically in order to arrive at a justified conclusion or decision

Low-context culture   A cultural dimension in which meaning is expressed primarily through language; people tend to speak more, speak more loudly, and speak more rapidly than a person from a high-context culture

Low power distance   A cultural belief in which power distinctions are minimized

M

Maintenance role   A member role that positively affects how group members get along with one another while pursuing a common goal

Majority vote   The results of a vote in which more than half the members favor a proposal

Manuscript speaking   A form of delivery in which a speaker writes a presentation in advance and reads it out loud

Marker   The placement of an object to establish nonverbal "ownership" of an area or space

Masculine societies   Societies in which men are supposed to be assertive, tough, and focused on material success, whereas women are supposed to be more modest, tender, and concerned with the quality of life

Mass communication   A form of mediated communication between a person and a large, often unknown audience; radio, television, film, Websites, newspapers, magazines, and books

Media Richness Theory   Examines how the qualities of different media affect communication

Mediated context   Any form of communication in which something (usually technological) exists between communicators; telephone, e-mail

Meeting   A scheduled gathering of group members for a structured discussion guided by a designated chairperson

Memorized speaking   A form of delivery in which a speaker memorizes a presentation and delivers it with very few or no notes

Messages   Verbal and nonverbal content that generates meaning

Metamessage   A message about a message

Mindfulness   The ability to be fully aware of the present moment without making hasty judgments

Mindlessness   Occurs when people allow rigid categories and false distinctions to become habits of thought and behavior

Mind mapping   An organizational technique that encourages the free flow of ideas and helps define the relationships among those ideas

Minutes   The written record of a group's discussion and activities

Mixed message   A contradiction between verbal and nonverbal meanings

Monochronic time   A cultural dimension in which events are scheduled as separate items—one thing at a time

Monologue   An interaction in which one person does all or most of the talking

Monroe's Motivated Sequence   A persuasive organizational pattern that follows five basic steps (attention, need, satisfaction, visualization, and action)

Myers-Briggs Type Indicator   A personality type theory that identifies preferred ways of thinking and behaving with two opposite preferences in each of four personality traits: extrovert–introvert, sensor–intuitive, thinker–feeler, and judger–perceiver

Mythos (narrative proof)   A form of proof that addresses the values, faith, and feelings that make up our social character and is most often expressed in traditional stories, sayings, and symbols

N

Narratives   The process, art, and techniques of storytelling

Noise   Internal or external obstacles that can prevent a message from reaching its receivers as intended

Nonverbal communication   Message components other than words that generate meaning

Norming stage   A group development stage in which members define roles and establish norms

Norms   Sets of expectations held by group members concerning what kinds of behavior or opinions are acceptable or unacceptable

O

Occasion   The reason an audience assembles at a particular place and time

Open-ended question   A question that encourages a detailed response

Optimum pitch   The pitch at which you speak most easily and expressively

Oral footnote   A spoken citation that includes enough information for listeners to find the original source

Organization   The way you arrange the content of your presentation into a clear and appropriate format

Organizational Culture Theory   The shared symbols, beliefs, values, and norms that affect the behavior of people working in and with an organization

Organizational subculture   A group of individuals who engage in behaviors and share values that are different from that of the larger organizational culture

Other-orientation   Giving serious attention to, feeling concern for, and showing interest in other communicators

P

Panel discussion   Several people interact about a common topic in order to educate, influence, or entertain an audience

Paraphrasing   Restating what people say in a way that indicates you understand them

Parenting style   A stable set of behaviors that characterizes parent–child interactions over a wide range of situations

Passive–aggressive   Communication that only appears to accommodate another person's needs, but actually represents subtle aggressive behavior

Passive voice   When the subject of a sentence receives the action, as in *The book was read by Bill*

Passivity   Giving in to others at the expense of your own needs in order to avoid conflict and disagreement

Pathos (emotional proof)   A form of proof that appeals to listeners' feelings and emotions

Perceiver   An adaptable person who likes open-ended thinking and is less concerned with rules and punctuality

Perception   The process we use to select, organize, and interpret sensory stimuli

Perception checking   A method for testing the accuracy of perceptual interpretations

Performing stage   A group development stage in which members focus their energy on working harmoniously to achieve group goals

Permissive parenting   Parents are often less involved in their children's lives and may overindulge or neglect them

Personal integrity   The practice of behaving in ways that are consistent with your values and beliefs while also understanding and respecting others

Personal relationship   A relationship characterized by a high level of emotional connection and commitment

Person-centered messages   Reflect the degree to which a helper validates a distressed person's feelings and encourages that person to talk about the upsetting event

Persuasion   Seeks to change audience opinions (what they think) or behavior (what they do)

Persuasive presentation   A presentation designed to change or to influence audience opinions and/or behavior

Pitch   How high or low your voice sounds

Plagiarism   Using or passing off the ideas or writing of another person as your own

Polychronic time   A cultural dimension in which schedules are not important and are frequently broken; people are not slaves to time and are easily distracted and tolerant of interruptions

Power distance   The physical and psychological distance between those in a culture who have power and those who do not have power

Prejudices   Positive or negative attitudes about an individual or cultural group based on little or no direct experience with that person or group

Preliminary outline   A first-draft outline that puts the major pieces of a presentation in a clear and logical order

Presentation aids   Supplementary resources—often visual in nature—for presenting and highlighting key ideas and supporting material

Presentational communication   A form of communication that occurs when speakers generate meaning with audience members, who are usually present at the delivery of a presentation

Presentation speaking   The process of using verbal and nonverbal messages to generate meaning with audience members, who are usually present at the delivery of the presentation

Primacy effect   Describes our tendency to recall the first items in a sequence more readily than the middle items

Primary source   The document, testimony, or publication in which information first appears

Primary tension   The social unease and inhibitions that accompany the getting-acquainted period in a new group

Probing question   Follows up on another question and/or response by encouraging clarification and elaboration

Problem/cause/solution pattern   A persuasive organizational pattern that describes a serious problem, identifies the cause(s) of the problem, and offers a solution

Problem–solution arrangement   An organizational pattern that describes a harmful or difficult situation (the problem) and then offers a plan to solve the problem (the solution)

Problem solving   A complex process in which groups make multiple decisions as they analyze a problem and develop a plan for solving the problem or reducing its harmful effects

Process   A set of constantly changing actions, elements, and functions that bring about a result

Professional relationship   A connection with people with whom you associate and work to accomplish a goal or perform a task

Pronunciation   Refers to whether or not you put all the correct sounds of a word in the correct order with the correct stress

Proof   The arguments and evidence used to support and strengthen a persuasive claim

Proxemics   The study of spatial relationships and how the distance between people communicates information about their relationship

Proximity principle   A perception principle that explains why the closer objects, events, or people are to one another, the more they are perceived as belonging together

Psychoevolutionary Emotional Theory   Robert Plutchik's theory that explains the development, meaning, and range of emotions

Psychological Reactance Theory   A theory that claims when people perceive a threat to their freedom to believe or behave as they wish, they may go out of their way to *do* the forbidden behavior or rebel against authority

Psychosocial context   The overall psychological and cultural environment in which you live and communicate

Public group   Groups that discuss issues in front of or for the benefit of public audiences

Purpose statement   A specific, achievable, and relevant sentence that identifies the purpose and main ideas of your presentation

Q

Qualifier   The component of the Toulmin model that states the degree to which a claim appears to be true, e.g., *likely, possibly, certainly, unlikely,* or *probably*

R

Race   A socially constructed concept (rather than a scientific classification) that is the outcome of ancient population shifts that left their mark in human genes

Racism   The assumption that people with certain characteristics (usually superficial characteristics such as skin color) have inherited negative traits that are inferior to those from other races

Rate   The number of words you say per minute (wpm)

Rational decision maker   A person who carefully weighs information and options before making a decision

Receiver   Another person or group of people who interpret and evaluate your message

Recency effect   Describes our tendency to recall the last items in a sequence

Reference groups   Groups with whom you identify that influence your self-concept

Refuting objections pattern   A persuasive pattern in which you refute and disprove each point that stands in opposition to your own

Regulating nonverbal behavior   Nonverbal behavior that manages the flow of a conversation

Relational Dialectics Theory   Relationships are characterized by ongoing tensions between contradictory impulses

Relationship   A continuing and meaningful attachment or connection to another person

Relationship-motivated leader   A leader who gains satisfaction from working well with others even if the group's task or goal is neglected

Religious literacy   The ability to understand and use the religious terms, symbols, images, beliefs, practices, scripture, heroes, themes, and stories employed in American public life

Repetitive nonverbal behavior   Nonverbal behavior that visually repeats a verbal message

Reservation   The component of the Toulmin Model that recognizes exceptions to an argument or concedes that a claim may not be true under certain circumstances

Rewards   Recognitions received at school, on the job, or in a community for good work

Rhetoric   According to Aristotle, the ability to discover the available means of persuasion appropriate for a particular audience in a particular circumstance

Rhetorical devices   Word strategies designed to enhance a presentation's impact and persuasiveness

Rhetorical style   Language designed to influence, persuade, and/or inspire

Role   A set of behaviors associated with an expected function in a specific context or relationship

Rumor   An unverified story or statement about the facts of a situation

S

Secondary source   Documents, testimony, or publications that report, repeat, or summarize information from one or more other sources

Secondary tension   The frustrations and personality conflicts experienced by group members as they compete for social acceptance, status, and achievement

Seductive details   Elements in a visual text or presentation aid that attract audience attention but do not support a writer's or speaker's key points

Self-acceptance   A willingness to recognize, accept, and "own" your thoughts, feelings, and behavior, but not as an excuse for inappropriate behavior

Self-appraisals   Evaluations of your self-concept in terms of your abilities, attitudes, and behaviors

Self-awareness   An understanding of your core identity that requires a realistic assessment of your traits, thoughts, and feelings

Self-centered interests   Aroused when a presentation can result in personal gain

Self-centered role   A member role that adversely affects member relationships and the group's ability to achieve its common goal

Self-concept   The sum total of beliefs you have about yourself

Self-disclosure   The process of sharing personal information, opinions, and emotions with others that would not otherwise be known to them

Self-effacing humor   Humor directed at yourself rather than others

Self-esteem   Your positive and negative judgments about your self

Self-fulfilling prophecy   An impression formation process in which an initial impression elicits behavior that conforms to the impression

Self-monitoring   A sensitivity to your own behavior and others' reactions as well as the ability to modify how you present yourself

Self-responsibility   Being accountable for your own happiness and fulfillment of goals without trying to control everything and everyone

Self-talk   The silent statements you make to yourself about yourself

Sensor   A person who focuses on details and prefers to concentrate on one task at a time

Sexual harassment   Unwelcome sexual advances for sexual favors, inappropriate verbal or physical conduct of a sexual nature, or an intimidating, hostile, or offensive work environment

Short-term memory   The limited capacity to remember content immediately after listening to a series of numbers, words, sentences, or paragraphs

Sign   Stands for or represents something specific and may look like the thing it represents

Significant others   People whose opinions you value and who influence your self-concept

Signpost   A short phrase that tells or reminds listeners where a speaker is in the organizational structure of a presentation

Similarity principle   A perception principle that explains why similar items or people are more likely to be perceived as a group

Simplicity principle   A perception principle that explains why we tend to organize information in a way that provides the simplest interpretation of objects, people, or experiences

Situational Leadership Theory   Seeks an ideal fit between leaders and leadership roles

Six-Step Model of Conflict Resolution   A series of six steps (preparation, initiation, confrontation, consideration, resolution, reevaluation) that help you move through a conflict toward successful resolution

Skills   Your acquired ability to accomplish communication goals during an interaction with others

Social comparison   The process of evaluating yourself in relation to the others in your reference groups

Social identity   Our self-concept as derived from the social categories to which we see ourselves belonging

Social Penetration Theory   The process of relationship bonding in which individuals move from superficial communication to deeper, more intimate communication

Source   A person or group of people who create a message intended to produce a particular response

Space arrangement   An organizational pattern that arranges key points in terms of their location or physical relationship to one another

Speaker credibility   The characteristics of a speaker that determine whether the audience believes the speaker and the message

Speaking outline   The outline used by a speaker to deliver a presentation; it may be short or long depending on the complexity of content

Speaking style   How you use vocabulary, sentence structure and length, grammar and syntax, and rhetorical devices to express a message

Speech Framer   A visual model for organizing presentation content that provides a place for every component of a presentation while encouraging experimentation and creativity

Spontaneous decision maker   A person who tends to be impulsive and make a quick decision on the spur of the moment

Stability–change dialectic   The relational tension between wanting both a stable relationship and the novelty and excitement of change

Standard Agenda   A procedure that guides a group through problem solving by using the following steps: clarifying the task, understanding and analyzing the problem, assessing possible solutions, and implementing a decision or plan

Statistics   Supporting material that collects, summarizes, analyzes, and interprets numerical data

Stereotypes   Generalizations about a group of people that oversimplify their characteristics

Stories   Accounts or reports about something that happened

Storming stage   A group development stage in which members argue about important issues and vie for leadership

Story fidelity   The apparent truthfulness of a story and whether it accurately reflects audience values and knowledge

Story probability   The formal features of a story, such as the consistency of characters and actions, and whether the elements of a story "hang together" and make sense

Strategies   Specific plans of action that help you achieve your communication goal

Structure   The organization of message content into a coherent and purposeful message

Styles Theory of Leadership   Examines three distinct leadership styles: autocratic, democratic, and laissez-faire leadership

Subordinate terms   The most concrete words that provide specific descriptions

Substituting nonverbal behavior   Nonverbal behavior that replaces verbal language; for example, waving hello instead of saying "hello"

Superior–subordinate relationship   A type of professional relationship characterized by the formal authority one person has over another person's work and behavior

Superordinate terms   Words that group objects and ideas very generally, such as *vehicle* or *animal*

Supporting material   The ideas, information, and opinions that help explain and/or advance a presentation's key points and purpose

Supportive behaviors   Behaviors that create an encouraging and caring climate in which self-disclosure and responsiveness benefit both communicators

Swearing   Using words that are taboo or disapproved of in a culture, but that should *not* be interpreted literally and can be used to express strong emotions and attitudes

Symbol   An *arbitrary* collection of sounds and letters that stand for a concept but do not have a direct relationship with the things they represent

Symposium   Group members present short, uninterrupted presentations on different aspects of a topic for the benefit of an audience

Systematic desensitization   A method of reducing communication apprehension through deep muscle relaxation and visualization

T

Task-motivated leader   A leader who gains satisfaction by completing a task even at the expense of group relationships

Task role   A member role that positively affects a group's ability to manage a task and to achieve its common goal

Task structure   A situational leadership factor that assesses how a group organizes or plans a specific task

Territoriality   The sense of personal ownership attached to a particular space

Testimony   Statements or opinions that someone has said or written

Theories   Statements that explain how the world works; describe, explain, and predict events and behavior

Theory of Informatory and Explanatory Communication   Explains the differences between and the communication strategies needed for sharing informatory and explanatory information

Thinker   A person who is analytical and task-oriented

Thought speed   The speed (words per minute) at which most people can think compared to the speed at which they can speak

Time arrangement   An organizational pattern that orders information according to time or calendar dates

Topical arrangement   An organizational pattern that divides a large topic into smaller subtopics

Topic-centered interests   Subjects audience members enjoy hearing and learning about

Touch approachers   People who tend to be comfortable with touch and often initiate touch with others

Touch avoiders   People who are not comfortable initiating touch or being touched

Toulmin Model of an Argument   Stephen Toulmin's framework for developing and analyzing arguments that includes the following components: claim, data, warrant, backing, reservation, and qualifier

Trait Theory of Leadership   Based on the belief that leaders are born with specific leadership characteristics

Transactional communication model   Illustrations that show how we send and receive messages at the same time within specific contexts

Transition   A word, number, brief phrase, or sentence in a presentation that helps a speaker move from one key point or section to another

Tuckman's Group Development Model   Comprehensive four-stage development model (forming, storming, norming, performing) relevant to *all* types of groups

Turn-requesting cues   Verbal and nonverbal messages that signal your desire to speak during a conversation

Turn-yielding cues   Verbal and nonverbal messages that signal you are completing your comments and preparing to listen during a conversation

Two-thirds vote   The result of a vote in which at least twice as many group members vote for a proposal as against it

V

Valid   Whether your ideas, information, and opinions are well-founded, justified, and accurate

Values   Beliefs that guide your ideas about what is right or wrong, good or bad, just or unjust, and correct or incorrect

Value step   A step that captures audience attention and explains how a presentation's information can enhance their success or well-being

Verbal communication   The ways in which we use the words in a language to generate meaning

Virtual group   A group that relies on technology to communicate often across time, distance, and organizational boundaries

Visualization   A method of reducing communication apprehension by imagining what it would be like to experience an entire communication act

Volume   The loudness level of your voice

W

Warrant   A component of the Toulmin Model that explains how and why the evidence supports a claim

Whorf Hypothesis   A theory claiming that language influences how we see, experience, and interpret the world around us

Word stress   The degree of prominence given to a syllable within a word or words within a phrase or sentence

Work group   A group that assumes responsibility for making decisions, solving problems, implementing projects, or performing routine duties in an organization

Work team   A group given full responsibility and resources for its performance

Working memory   The memory subsystem you use when trying to understand information, remember it, or use it to solve a problem or communicate with someone; working memory allows you to shift message content from and into long-term memory

Working Memory Theory   Explains the dual-task system of working memory (rather than short-term memory) that involves information processing and storage functions as well as creating new meanings

Writing apprehension   The fear or anxiety associated with writing situations and topic-specific writing assignments

notes

Chapter 1

[1]Marilyn H. Buckley, "Focus on Research: We Listen to a Book a Day; Speak a Book a Week: Learning from Walter Loban," *Language Arts* 69 (1992): 101–109.

[2]In association with the National Communication Association, the Association for Communication Administration's 1995 Conference on Defining the Field of Communication produced the following definition: "The field of communication focuses on how people use verbal and nonverbal messages to generate meanings within and across various contexts, cultures, channels, and media. The field promotes the effective and ethical practice of human communication." See http://www.natcom.org.

[3]See Sherwyn P. Morreale, Michael M. Osborn, and Judy C. Pearson, "Why Communication Is Important: A Rationale for the Centrality of the Study of Communication," *Journal of the Association for Communication Administration* 29 (2000): 1–25. The authors of this article collected and annotated nearly one hundred articles, commentaries, and publications that call attention to the importance of studying communication in contemporary society.

[4]Robert M. Diamond, "Designing and Assessing Courses and Curricula," *Chronicle of Higher Education*, 1 August 1997, B7.

[5]Jerry L. Winsor, Dan B. Curtis, and Ronald D. Stephens, "National Preferences in Business and Communication Education: A Survey Update," *Journal of the Association for Communication Administration* 3 (September 1997): 170–179. The authors conclude that a stronger emphasis should be given to training in listening and interpersonal communication in addition to developing competencies in group communication and presentation speaking.

[6]"Graduates Are Not Prepared to Work in Business," *Association Trends* (June 1997): 4.

[7]Business-Higher Education Forum in affiliation with the American Council on Education, *Spanning the Chasm: Corporate and Academic Cooperation to Improve Work-Force Preparation* (Washington, D.C.: American Council on Education, 1997).

[8]David Berlo, *The Process of Communication: An Introduction to Theory and Practice* (New York: Holt, Rinehart and Winston, 1960), 24.

[9]Myron W. Lustig and Jolene Koester, *Intercultural Competence: Interpersonal Communication Across Cultures*, 5th ed. (Boston: Pearson/Allyn & Bacon, 2010), 25.

[10]In this textbook, we prefer and use the broader term *presentational communication* rather than *public speaking* to describe the act of speaking before an audience. Public speaking is one type of presentational communication that occurs when a speaker addresses a public audience. See Isa N. Engleberg and John A. Daly, *Presentations in Everyday Life*, 3rd ed. (Boston: Pearson/Allyn and Bacon, 2009), 4.

[11]See Richard L. Daft and Robert H. Lengel, "Information Richness: A New Approach to Managerial Behavior and Organizational Design," in *Research in Organizational Behavior*, ed. Barry M. Staw and Larry L. Cummings (Greenwich, CT: JAI Press, 1984), 355–366; Richard L. Daft, Robert H. Lengel, and Linda K. Trevino, "Message Equivocality, Media Selection, and Manager Performance: Implications for Information Systems," *MIS Quarters* 11 (1987): 355–366; Linda K. Trevino, Robert K. Lengel, and Richard L. Daft, "Media Symbolism, Media Richness, and Medic Choice in Organizations," *Communication Research* 14, no. 5 (1987): 553–574.

[12]John McWhorter, *The Power of Babel: A Natural History of Language* (New York: A.W.H. Freeman, 2001), 5.

[13]*American Heritage Dictionary of the English Language*, 4th ed. (Boston: Houghton Mifflin, 2000), 1718.

[14]Educause Learning Initiative, "7 Things You Should Know About Twitter," http://www.educauser.edu/eli, July 2007. Retrieved June 15, 2009.

[15]Mike Musgrove, "Twitter Is a Player in Iran's Drama," *The Washington Post*, http://www.washingtonpost.com/wp-dyn/content/article/2009/06/16/AR2009061603391.html, June 17, 2009.

[16]Steven Johnson, "How Twitter Will Change the Way We Live," *Time Magazine*, 15 June 2009, 34.

[17]Darren Rowse, "Twitter Is a Complete Waste of Time," *ProBlogger*, http://www.problogger.net/archives/2008/06/06/twitter-is-a-waste-of-time/ June 6, 2006. Retrieved June 15, 2009.

[18]Nielsen.com, "Twitter's Tweet Smell of Success," http://blog.nielsen.com/nielsenwire/online_mobile/twitters-tweet-smell-of-success/.

[19]Rob Anderson and Veronica Ross, *Questions of Communication: A Practical Introduction to Theory*, 3rd ed. (New York: St. Martin's, 2002), 69.

[20]Karl R. Popper, *The Logic of Scientific Discovery* (New York: Basic Books, 1959), 59.

[21]Excerpt from Stephen R. Covey, *The Seven Habits of Effective People* (New York: Simon and Schuster, 1989), 46–48.

[22]Rob Anderson and Veronica Ross, *Questions of Communication: A Practical Introduction to Theory*, 3rd ed. (New York: St. Martin's, 2002), 301.

[23]Richard L. Johannesen, *Ethics in Human Communication*, 5th ed. (Prospect Heights, IL: Waveland, 2002), 1.

[24]National Communication Association Credo for Ethical Communication, http://www.natcom.org/aboutNCA/Policies/Platform.html.

Chapter 2

[1]David Gates, "Finding Neverland," *Newsweek* (July 13, 2009), http://www.newsweek.com/id/204296.

[2]Hanish Babu, "How Did Michael Jackson's Skin Turn White?" http://skindisease.suite101.com/article.cfm/how_did_michael_jackson_skin_turn_white#ixzz0K6jQnBBy&D.

[3]David Gates, "Finding Neverland," *Newsweek* (July 13, 2009), http://www.newsweek.com/id/204296.

[4]hysperia, "On Michael Jackson," *mirabile dictu*, http://alterwords.wordpress.com/2009/06/26/on-michael-jackson/. The blogger hysperia is a Canadian who was "once a lawyer, once a law professor, now a poet and a Feminist for forty years."

[5]Sharon S. Brehm, Saul M. Kassin, and Steven Fein, *Social Psychology*, 6th ed. (Boston: Houghton Mifflin, 2005), 57.

[6]"Self-awareness," http://en.wikipedia.org/wiki/Self-awareness.

[7]Daniel Goleman, *Emotional Intelligence* (New York: Bantam, 1995), 43, 47.

[8]Ibid., 43.

[9]"Self-Monitoring Behavior," http://changingminds.org/explanations/theories/self-monitoring.htm.

[10]Sharon S. Brehm, Saul M. Kassin, and Steven Fein, *Social Psychology*, 6th ed. (Boston: Houghton Mifflin, 2005), 65.

[11]Anthony G. Greenwald, "The Totalitarian Ego: Fabrication and Revision of Personal History," *American Psychologist* 35 (1980): 603–618.

[12]Min-Sun Kim, *Non-Western Perspectives on Human Communication* (Thousand Oaks, CA: Sage, 2002), 9.

[13]Nathaniel Branden, http://www.nathanielbranden.com.

[14]Richard E. Boyatzis, "Developing Emotional Intelligence Competencies," in *Applying Emotional Intelligence: A Practitioner's Guide*, ed. Joseph Ciarrochi and John D. Mayer (New York: Psychology Press, 2007), 42.

[15]David Nyberg, *The Varnished Truth: Truth Telling and Deceiving in Ordinary Life* (Chicago: University of Chicago Press, 1993), 81.

[16]Mark L. Knapp, *Lying and Deception in Human Interaction* (Boston: Pearson/Allyn and Bacon, 2008), 122.

[17]Albert Bandura, *Social Foundations of Thought and Action: A Social Cognitive Theory* (Englewood Cliffs, NJ: Prentice Hall, 1986), 399–408. Quoted in William Crain, *Theories of Development: Concepts and Applications*, 4th ed. (Upper Saddle River, NJ: Prentice Hall, 2000), 203.

[18]Susan B. Barnes, *Online Connections: Internet Interpersonal Relationships* (Cresskill, NJ: Hampton Press, 2001), 234.

[19]Ibid., 91.

[20]"What Is Second Life?" http://secondlife.com/whatis/avatar.php.

[21]Rebecca McCarthy, "Conviction Is Tossed Out in MySpace Suicide Case," *New York Times*, July 3, 2009, A12.

[22]Roy F. Baumeister, "The Self," in *The Handbook of Social Psychology*, Vol. 1, 4th ed., ed. Daniel T. Gilbert, Susan T. Fiske, and Gardner Lindzey (New York: McGraw-Hill, 1998), 690–691. Quoted in Mark L. Knapp, *Lying and Deception in Human Interaction* (Boston: Pearson/Allyn and Bacon, 2008), 91.

[23]Leon Festinger, "A Theory of Social Comparison Processes," *Human Relations* 7 (1954): 117–140.

[24]Nathaniel Branden, http://www.nathanielbranden.com.

[25]Roy F. Baumeister, Jennifer D. Campbell, Joachim I. Krueger, and Kathleen D. Vohs, "Exploring the Self-Esteem Myth," *Scientific American.com* (January 2005), http://www.papillonsartpalace.com/exSplodin.htm

[26]Nathaniel Branden, *The Art of Living Consciously: The Power of Awareness to Transform Everyday Life* (New York: Fireside Books/Simon and Schuster, 1999), 168–169.

[27]"Women's Math Scores Affected by Suggestions," The *Washington Post*, 20 October 2006, A11. This article summarizes a study published in the October 2006 issue of *Science*.

[28]Sam Dillon, "Praise, Advice and Reminders of the Sour Economy for Graduates," *The New York Times*, June 14, 2009, A18.

[29]See Nathaniel Branden, *The Power of Self-Esteem* (Deerfield Beach, FL: Health Communications, 1992), 168–169.

[30]Roy F. Baumeister, Jennifer D. Campbell, Joachim I. Krueger, and Kathleen D. Vohs, "Exploding the Self-Esteem Myth," *Scientific American* (January 2005).

[31]Roy F. Baumeister, "Violent Pride," *Scientific American*, 284 (2001): 96–101.

[32]Morris Rosenberg, *Society and the Adolescent Self-Image* (Princeton, NJ: Princeton University Press, 1965).

[33]Douglas A. Bernstein, Louis A. Penner, Alison Clarke-Stewart, and Edward Roy, *Psychology*, 7th ed. (Boston: Houghton Mifflin, 2006), 161.

[34]Ibid., 172.

[35]Richard E. Nisbett, *The Geography of Thought: How Asians and Westerners Think Differently . . . and Why* (New York: Free Press, 2003), 87.

[36]Douglas A. Bernstein, Louis A. Penner, Alison Clarke-Stewart, and Edward Roy, *Psychology*, 7th ed. (Boston: Houghton Mifflin, 2006), 162.

[37]Ibid.

[38]"The Golden Rule is found in the New Testament (Matthew 7:12, NIV) but is often confused with the related admonition to 'love your neighbor as yourself,' which appears repeatedly in both the Hebrew Bible and the New Testament. . . . The Golden Rule has also been attributed to other religious leaders, including Confucius, Muhammad, and the first-century rabbi Hillel." Stephen Prothero, *Religious Literacy: What Every American Needs to Know—And Doesn't* (New York: HarperSanFrancisco, 2007), 182–183.

[39]George Bernard Shaw, *Maxims for a Revolutionist* (1903).

[40]J. Richard Block and Harold Yuker, *Can You Believe Your Eyes?* (New York: Gardner Press, 1989), 239.

[41]Ronald B. Adler, Lawrence B. Rosenfeld, and Russell F. Proctor II, *Interplay: The Process of Interpersonal Communication*, 8th ed. (Fort Worth, TX: Harcourt Brace, 2001), 114.

[42]The discussion of communication apprehension is based on Chapter 2 of Isa Engleberg and John Daly, *Presentations in Everyday Life*, 3rd ed. (Boston: Pearson/Allyn and Bacon, 2009); and Chapter 3 of Isa Engleberg and Dianna Wynn, *Working in Groups: Communication Principles and Strategies*, 5th ed. (Boston: Pearson/Allyn and Bacon, 2010).

[43]Virginia P. Richmond and James C. McCroskey, *Communication: Apprehension, Avoidance, and Effectiveness*, 4th ed. (Scottsdale, AZ: Gorsuch, Scarisbrick, 1995), 32.

[44]Sharon S. Brehm, Saul M. Kassin, and Steven Fein, *Social Psychology*, 6th ed. (Boston: Houghton Mifflin, 2005), 525.

[45]Peter Desberg, *Speaking Scared, Sounding Good* (Garden City Park, NY: Square One Publishers, 2007), 101–110. Desberg describes several effective relaxation exercises that readers can practice. Desberg notes that "Fortunately, it feels great to practice them" (100).

[46]Virginia P. Richmond and James C. McCroskey, *Communication: Apprehension, Avoidance, and Effectiveness*, 4th ed. (Scottsdale, AZ: Gorsuch, Scarisbrick, 1995), 41.

[47]James C. McCroskey, "Oral Communication Apprehension: Summary of Recent Theory and Research," *Human Communication Research* 4 (1977): 80.

[48]Michael J. Beatty and James McCroskey with Kristin M. Valencic, *The Biology of Communication: A Communibiological Perspective* (Cresskill, NJ: Hampton, 2001), 80.

[49]Virginia P. Richmond and James C. McCroskey, *Communication: Apprehension, Avoidance, and Effectiveness*, 4th ed. (Scottsdale, AZ: Gorsuch, Scarisbrick, 1995), 108.

[50]See John A. Daly and James C. McCroskey, eds., *Avoiding Communication: Shyness, Reticence, and Communication Apprehension* (Thousand Oaks, CA: Sage, 1984); Virginia P. Richmond and James C. McCroskey, *Communication: Apprehension, Avoidance, and Effectiveness*, 4th ed. (Scottsdale, AZ: Gorsuch, Scarisbrick, 1995); Karen Kangas Dwyer, *Conquer Your Speechfright*, 2nd ed. (Belmont, CA: Thomson Wadsworth, 2005); and Michael T. Motley, *Overcoming Your Fear of Public Speaking: A Proven Method* (Boston: Houghton Mifflin, 1997).

[51]Karen Kangas Dwyer, *Conquer Your Speechfright*, 2nd ed. (Belmont, CA: Thomson Wadsworth, 2005), 23.

[52]Peter Desberg, *Speaking Scared, Sounding Good* (Garden City Park, NY: Square One Publishers, 2007), 60.

[53]As cited in Virginia P. Richmond and James C. McCroskey, *Communication: Apprehension, Avoidance, and Effectiveness*, 4th ed. (Scottsdale, AZ: Gorsuch, Scarisbrick, 1995), 97 and 101. For more on systematic

desensitization, see ibid., 97–102; and Karen Kangas Dwyer, *Conquer Your Speechfright*, 2nd ed. (Belmont, CA: Thomson Wadsworth, 2005), 95–103, 137–141.

[54]Daniel Goleman, *Social Intelligence* (New York: Bantam, 2006), 41–42.

[55]From Virginia P. Richmond and James C. McCroskey, *Communication: Apprehension, Avoidance, and Effectiveness*, 5th ed. (Boston: Allyn and Bacon, 1998). Copyright © 1998 by Pearson Education. Reprinted by permission of the publisher.

[56]Virginia P. Richmond and James C. McCroskey, *Communication: Apprehension, Avoidance, and Effectiveness*, 4th ed. (Scottsdale, AZ: Gorsuch, Scarisbrick, 1995), 129–130. Reprinted by permission of the authors and publisher.

Chapter 3

[1]In 1967, the Supreme Court overturned the conviction of Richard and Mildred Loving, a young interracial couple from Caroline County, VA. "Richard Loving was white; his wife, Mildred, was black. In 1958, they went to Washington, D.C.—where interracial marriage was legal—to get married. But when they returned home, they were arrested, jailed and banished from the state for 25 years for violating the state's Racial Integrity Act." When they challenged the law in Virginia, "the original judge in the case upheld his decision [and wrote] 'Almighty God created the races white, black, yellow, Malay and red, and he placed them on separate continents. . . . The fact that he separated the races shows that he did not intend for the races to mix.'" (National Public Radio, "Loving Decision: 40 Years of Legal Interracial Unions," *All Things Considered*, June 11, 2007, http://www.npr.org/templates/story/story.php?storyId=10889047.

[2]The statistics and their interpretation in this section come from two sources: *Encyclopedia Britannica Almanac 2004* (Chicago: Britannica Almanac, 2003), 770–775; United States Census Bureau, "Census 2000," http://www.census.gov/population.

[3]"The 300 Millionth Footprint on U.S. Soil," *The New York Times*, October 8, 2006, p. WK2. U.S. Census Bureau; National Center for Education Statistics; Social Security Administration.

[4]U.S. Census Bureau, http://www.census.gov/population.

[5]Myron W. Lustig and Jolene Koester, *Intercultural Competence: Interpersonal Communication across Cultures*, 6th ed. (Boston: Pearson/Allyn & Bacon, 2010), 25.

[6]Intercultural authors use a variety of terms (*co-cultures, microcultures*) to describe the cultural groups that coexist within a larger culture. Using either of these terms is preferable to using the older, somewhat derogatory term *subcultures*.

[7]Based on Myron W. Lustig and Jolene Koester, *Instructor's Manual to Accompany Intercultural Competence*, 2nd ed. (New York: HarperCollins, 1996), 72–74.

[8]Data from Patricia G. Devine and A. J. Elliot, "Are Racial Stereotypes Really Fading? The Princeton Trilogy Revisited," *Personality and Social Psychology Bulletin* 21 (1995): 1139–1150.

[9] Stella Ting-Toomey and Leeva C. Chung, *Understanding Intercultural Communication* (Los Angeles: Roxbury, 2005), 236–239.

[10]Based on Myron W. Lustig and Jolene Koester, *Instructor's Manual to Accompany Intercultural Competence*, 2nd ed. (New York: HarperCollins, 1996), 151.

[11]http://www.washingtonpost.com/wp-dyn/content/article/2009/06/10/AR2009061001768.html; Associated Press, "Guard dies after Holocaust museum shooting," MSNBC.com, June 10, 2009, http://www.msnbc.msn.com/id/31208188.

[12]Based on a Washington Post/Kaiser Family Foundation/Harvard University survey of middle-class blacks and whites with incomes between $30,000 and $75,000, as reported in the *Washington Post National Weekly Edition*, October 16–22, 1995, 8. Quoted in Judith N. Martin and Thomas K. Nakayama, *Intercultural Communication in Contexts* (Mountain View, CA: Mayfield, 1997), 83.

[13]National Communication Association, "National Communication Association Policy Platform," http://www.natcom.org/index.asp?bid=510.

[14]Shankar Vedantam, "For Allen and Webb, Implicit Biases Would Be Better Confronted," *The Washington Post*, October 9, 2006, A2. Also see http://www.washingtonpost.com/science and http://implicit.harvard.edu.

[15]Judith Warner, "The Wages of Hate," Judith Warner Blog, *The New York Times*, June 11, 2009, http://warner.blogs.nytimes.com/2009/06/11/the-wages-of-hate.

[16]Charles M. Blow, "Hate in a Cocoon of Silence," *The New York Times*, June 13, 2009, A17.

[17] Nicholas Wade, *Before the Dawn: Recovering the Lost History of Our Ancestors* (New York: Penguin, 2006), 183.

[18]Mark P. Orbe and Tina M. Harris, *Interracial Communication: Theory into Practice* (Belmont, CA: Wadsworth Thomason Learning, 2001), 31.

[19]Nicholas Wade, *Before the Dawn: Recovering the Lost History of Our Ancestors* (New York: Penguin, 2006), 188.

[20]Brenda J. Allen, *Difference Matters: Communicating Social Identity* (Long Grove, IL: Waveland, 2004), 10.

[21]Rita Hardiman, "White Racial Identity Development in the United States," in *Race, Ethnicity and Self: Identity in Multicultural Perspective*, ed. Elizabeth Pathy Salett and Dianne R. Koslow (Washington, D.C.: National MultiCultural Institute, 1994), 130–131.

[22]Ibid.

[23]J. Richard Hoel. "Developing Intercultural Competence," in *Intercultural Communication with Readings*, ed. Pamela J. Cooper, Carolyn Calloway-Thomas, and Cheri J. Simonds (Boston: Allyn & Bacon, 2007), 305.

[24]Stephen Prothero, *Religious Literacy: What Every American Needs to Know—And Doesn't* (New York: HarperSanFrancisco, 2007), 11. See also Prothero's religious literacy quiz, 27–28 and 235–239.

[25]Statements are based on three sources: Robert Pollock, *The Everything World's Religions Book* (Avon, MA: Adams Media, 2002); Leo Rosen (ed.), *Religions of America: Fragment of Faith in an Age of Crisis* (New York: Touchstone, 1975); *Encyclopedia Britannica Almanac 2004* (Chicago: Encyclopedia Britannica, 2003).

[26]Geert Hofstede, *Cultures and Organizations: Software of the Mind* (New York: McGraw-Hill, 1997), 14. See also Geert Hofstede, *Culture's Consequences: Comparing Values, Behavior, Institutions and Organizations across Nations*, 2nd ed. (Thousand Oaks, CA: Sage, 2001), 29. In addition to the three intercultural dimensions included in this chapter, Hofstede identifies several other dimensions: long-term versus short-term time orientation, uncertainty avoidance, indulgence versus restraint, and monumentalism versus self-effacement. For a summary of these additional dimensions, see Myron W. Lustig and Joelene Koester, *Intercultural Competence: Interpersonal Communication across Cultures*, 6th ed. (Boston: Pearson/Allyn & Bacon, 2010), 113–124.

[27]William B. Gudykunst and Carmen M. Lee, "Cross-Cultural Communication Theories," in *Handbook of International and Intercultural Communication*, 2nd ed., ed. William B. Gudykunst and Bella Mody (Thousand Oaks, CA: Sage, 2002), 27.

[28]Harry C. Triandis, "The Self and Social Behavior in Different Cultural Contexts," *Psychological Review* 96 (1989): 506–520. Also see Harry C. Triandis. *Individualism and Collectivism* (Boulder, CO: Westview, 1995). 29 Data from Geert Hofstede, *Cultural Consequences: Comparing Values, Behavior, Institutions and Organizations across Nations*, 2nd ed. (Thousand Oaks, CA: Sage, 2001), 215.

[29]Data from Geert Hofstede, *Cultural Consequences: Comparing Values, Behavior, Institutions and Organizations across Nations*, 2nd ed. (Thousand Oaks, CA: Sage, 2001), 215.

[30]Geert Hofstede, *Cultures and Organizations: Software of the Mind* (New York: McGraw-Hill, 1997), 1997, 53.

[31]Harry C. Triandis, *Individualism and Collectivism* (Boulder, CO: Westview, 1995).

[32]Harry C. Triandis, "Cross-Cultural Studies of Individualism and Collectivism," in *Cross-Cultural Perspectives*, ed. J. J. Berman (Lincoln, NE: University of Nebraska Press, 1990), 52.

[33]Geert Hofstede, *Cultures and Organizations: Software of the Mind* (New York: McGraw-Hill, 1997), 1997, 28.

[34]Data from Geert Hofstede, *Culture's Consequences: Comparing Values, Behavior, Institutions and Organizations across Nations*, 2nd ed. (Thousand Oaks, CA: Sage, 2001), 87.

[35]Geert Hofstede, *Culture's Consequences: Comparing Values, Behavior, Institutions and Organizations across Nations*, 2nd ed. (Thousand Oaks, CA: Sage, 2001), 81–82, 96.

[36]Data from Geert Hofstede, *Culture's Consequences: Comparing Values, Behavior, Institutions and Organizations across Nations*, 2nd ed. (Thousand Oaks, CA: Sage, 2001), 286.

[37]Edward T. Hall, "Context and Meaning," in *Beyond Culture* (Garden City, NY: Anchor, 1997).

[38]Peter Andersen et al., "Nonverbal Communication across Cultures," in *Handbook of International and Intercultural Communication*, 2nd ed., ed. William B. Gudykunst and Bella Mody (Thousand Oaks, CA: Sage, 2002), 99.

[39]Shirley van der Veur, "Africa: Communication and Cultural Patterns," in *Intercultural Communication: A Reader*, 10th ed., ed. Larry A. Samovar and Richard E. Porter (Belmont, CA: Wadsworth, 2003), 84.

[40]Edward T. Hall, *The Silent Language* (Garden City, NY: Doubleday, 1959). See also Lustig and Koester, 226.

[41]Edward T. Hall and M. R. Hall, *Understanding Cultural Differences: Germans, French and Americans* (Yarmouth, ME: Intercultural Press, 1990), 6.

[42]Dean Allen Foster, *Bargaining across Borders* (New York: McGraw-Hill, 1992), 280.

[43]Richard West and Lynn H. Turner, *Introducing Communication Theory*, 3rd ed. (Boston: McGraw-Hill, 2007), 515–532. See Cheris Kramarae, *Women and Men Speaking: Framework for Analysis* (Rowley, MA: Newbury House, 1981.)

[44]Edward T. Hall, *The Dance of Life: Other Dimensions of Time* (New York: Anchor/Doubleday, 1983), 42.

[45]www.users.vioicenet.com/~howard/mindful.html.

[46]Richard Boyatzis and Annie McKee, *Resonant Leadership* (Boston: Harvard Business School Press, 2005), 112.

[47]Ellen J. Langer, *Mindfulness* (Cambridge, MA: Da Capo, 1989), 11.

[48]Based on examples in Ellen J. Langer, *Mindfulness* (Cambridge, MA: Da Capo, 1989), 12.

[49]www.users.vioicenet.com/~howard/mindful.html.

[50]Richard Nisbett, *The Geography of Thought: How Asians and Westerners Think Differently . . . and Why* (New York: Free Press, 2003), xiii.

[51]Ellen J. Langer, *Mindfulness* (Cambridge, MA: Da Capo, 1989), 69.

[52]Marvin Harris, *Cows, Pigs, Wars, and Witches: The Riddles of Culture* (New York: Vintage Books, 1975), 11–34.

[53]Ibid., 30.

[54]See the following references: Howard Giles et al., "Speech Accommodation Theory: The First Decade and Beyond," in *Communication Yearbook*, ed. Margaret L. McLaughlin (Newbury Park, CA: Sage, 1987), pp. 13–48; Howard Giles et al., "Accommodation Theory: Communication, Context, and Consequence," in *Contexts of Accommodation: Developments in Applied Sociolinguistics*, ed. Howard Giles et al. (Cambridge: Cambridge University Press, 1991), p. 1–68.

[55]James Leigh, "Teaching Content and Skills for Intercultural Communication: A Mini Case Studies Approach," *The Edge: The E-Journal of Intercultural Relations* 2 (Winter 1999), http://www.interculturalrelations.com/v2i1Winter1999leigh.htm.

[56]Ibid.

[57]The GENE Scale, developed by James Neuliep and James C. McCroskey. See James W. Neuliep, *Intercultural Communication: A Contextual Approach*, 2nd ed. (Boston: Houghton Mifflin, 2003), 29–30.

Chapter 4

[1]Don Gabor, *How to Start a Conversation and Make Friends* (New York: Fireside, 2001), 64. Gabor attributes this sentence to Dale Carnegie, the famous author and public speaker.

[2]Ibid. 66–68.

[3]Phillip Emmert, "A Definition of Listening," *Listening Post*, 51 (1995): 6.

[4]Larry L. Barker et al., "An Investigation of Proportional Time Spent in Various Communication Activities by College Students," *Journal of Applied Communication Research* 8 (1980): 101–109.

[5]Andrew D. Wolvin and Carolyn G. Coakley, *Listening*, 5th ed. (Madison, WI: Brown and Benchmark, 1996), 15.

[6]Reported in Sandra D. Collins, *Listening and Responding Managerial Communication Series* (Mason, OH: Thomson, 2006), 21

[7]Tony Alessandra and Phil Hunsaker, *Communicating at Work* (New York: Fireside, 1993), 54.

[8]Tom Peters, *In Search of Excellence* (New York: Harper and Row, 1982), 196.

[9]Michael P. Nichols, *The Lost Art of Listening* (New York: Guilford, 1995), 11.

[10]Ralph G. Nichols, "Listening Is a 10-Part Skill," *Nation's Business* 75 (September 1987): 40.

[11]S. S. Benoit and J. W. Lee, "Listening: It Can Be Taught," *Journal of Education for Business* 63 (1986): 229–232.

[12]Florence I. Wolff and Nadine C. Marsnik, *Perceptive Listening*, 2nd ed. (Fort Worth, TX: Harcourt Brace Jovanovich, 1992), 9–16.

[13]Tony Alessandra and Phil Hunsaker, *Communicating at Work* (New York: Fireside, 1993), 55.

[14]Jim Collins, *Good to Great* (New York: Harper Collins, 2001), 14.

[15]Samuel E. Wood, Ellen Green Wood, and Denise Boyd, *The World of Psychology*, 6th ed. (Boston: Pearson/Allyn and Bacon, 2008), 199.

[16]Ibid, 200.

[17]Laura Ann Janusik, "Building Listening Theory: The Validation of the Conversational Listening Span," *Communication Studies* 58 (2007): 142.

[18]Ibid.

[19]Dr. Jennie Mills, *Personal Listening Profile Report*, January 19, 2004 (Inscape Publishing, 2003), http://www.discprofiles.com/downloads/Listening/ListeningIndividualJen.pdf .

[20]Based on Tony Alessandra and Phil Hunsaker, *Communicating at Work* (New York: Fireside, 1993), 76–77.

[21]Isa Engleberg and Dianna Wynn, *Working in Groups: Communication Principles and Strategies*, 5th ed. (Boston: Pearson/Allyn and Bacon, 2010), 196.

[22]National Communication Association, "National Communication Association Policy Platform," http://www.natcom.org/index.asp?bid=510.

[23]Paul J. Kaufmann, *Sensible Listening: The Key to Responsive Interaction*, 5th ed. (Dubuque, IA: Kendall/Hunt, 2006), 133.

[24]Michael P. Nichols, *The Lost Art of Listening* (New York: Guilford, 1995), 36–37.

[25]See the following sources: Larry L. Barker and Kitty W. Watson, *Listen Up* (New York: St. Martin's, 2000); Kitty W. Watson, Larry L. Barker, and

James B. Weaver, "The Listening Styles Profile (LSP-16): Development and Validation of an Instrument to Assess Four Listening Styles," *The International Journal of Listening* 9 (1995): 1–14. See also Statistic Solutions, "Listening Styles Profile (LSP-16)," http://www.statisticsolutions.com/listening-styles-profile; "Listening Styles," *Workforce Performance Newsletter Imprint*, http://www.humtech.com/OPM/articles/014.htm; "Listening Styles," http://changingminds.org/techniques/listening/listening_styles.htm.

26Ralph G. Nichols, "Listening Is a 10-Part Skill," *Nation's Business* 75 (September 1987): 40.

27Mark L. Knapp and Judith A. Hall, *Nonverbal Communication in Human Interaction*, 6th ed. (Belmont, CA: 2006), 296.

28Ralph G. Nichols, "Do We Know How to Listen? Practical Help in a Modern Age," *Speech Teacher* (March 1961): 121.

29Madelyn Burley-Allen, *Listening: The Forgotten Skill*, 2nd ed. (New York: Wiley, 1995), 68–70.

30International Listening Association, http://www.listen.org. Quoted in Sandra D. Collins, *Listening and Responding Managerial Communication Series* (Mason, OH: Thomson, 2006), 21.

31Adapted from Wolvin and Coakley *Listening*, 5th ed. (Madison, WI: Brown and Benchmark, 1996), 299.

32Michael P. Nichols, *The Lost Art of Listening* (New York: Guilford, 1995), 126.

33Deborah Tannen, *You Just Don't Understand: Women and Men in Conversation* (New York: Ballantine Books, 1990), 141–142.

34Ibid., 142–143.

35See Deborah Tannen, *You Just Don't Understand: Women and Men in Conversation* (New York: Ballantine Books, 1990), 123–148; see also Diana K. Ivy and Phil Backlund, *Exploring GenderSpeak* (New York: McGraw-Hill, 1994), 224–225.

36See Deborah Tannen, *You Just Don't Understand: Women and Men in Conversation* (New York: Ballantine Books, 1990), 149–151; Diana K. Ivy and Phil Backlund, *Exploring GenderSpeak* (New York: McGraw-Hill, 1994), 206–208, 224–225; and Teri Kwal Gamble and Michael W. Gamble, *The Gender Communication Connection* (Boston: Houghton Mifflin, 2003), 122–128.

37Paul J. Kaufmann, *Sensible Listening: The Key to Responsive Interaction*, 5th ed. (Dubuque, IA: Kendall/Hunt, 2006), 115.

38Ralph Nichols, "Do We Know How to Listen? Practical Help in a Modern Age," *Speech Teacher* (March 1961): 122.

39Rebecca Z. Shafir, *The Zen of Listening: Mindful Communication in the Age of Distraction* (Wheaton, IL: Quest Books, 2003), 18.

40Elizabeth A. Tuleja, *Intercultural Communication for Business* (Mason, OH: Thomson Higher Education, 2005), 43.

41For other definitions and discussions of critical thinking, see Brooke Noel Moore and Richard Parker, *Critical Thinking*, 5th ed. (Mountain View, CA: Mayfield, 1998); John Chaffee, *Thinking Critically*, 6th ed. (Boston: Houghton Mifflin, 2000); Richard W. Paul, *Critical Thinking: How to Prepare Students for a Rapidly Changing World* (Santa Rosa, CA: Foundation for Critical Thinking, 1995); and Vincent Ryan Ruggero, *Becoming a Critical Thinker*, 4th ed. (Boston: Houghton Mifflin, 2002).

42Robert H. Ennis, "Critical Thinking Assessment," *Theory into Practice* 32 (1993): 180.

43Isa N. Engleberg and John A. Daly, *Presentations in Everyday Life*, 3rd ed. (Boston: Pearson/Allyn and Bacon, 2009), 59.

44Stephen Toulmin, *The Uses of Argument* (London: Cambridge University Press, 1958). Based on an example in Stephen Toulmin, Richard Rieke, and Allan Janik, *An Introduction to Reasoning* (New York: Macmillan, 1979), 45.

45Fred D. White and Simone J. Billings, *The Well-Crafted Argument: A Guide and Reader*, 2nd ed. (Boston: Houghton Mifflin, 2005), 93.

46Based on an example in Stephen Toulmin, Richard Rieke, and Allan Janik, *An Introduction to Reasoning* (New York: Macmillan, 1979), 45.

47William V. Haney, *Communication and Interpersonal Relationships: Text and Cases* (Homewood, IL: Irwin, 1992), 231–232, 241.

48Antonio R. Damasio, *Descartes' Error: Emotion, Reason, and the Human Brain* (New York: Penguin U.S.A., 1994); and Antonio R. Damasio, *The Feeling of What Happens: Body and Emotion in the Making of Consciousness* (San Diego, CA: Harvest/Harcourt, 1999).

49Based on Andrew Wolvin and Laura Janusik, "Janusik/Wolvin Student Listening Inventory," in *Instructor's Manual for Communicating: A Social and Career Focus*, 9th ed., ed. Roy M. Berko, Andrew D. Wolvin, and Darlyn R. Wolvin (Boston: Houghton Mifflin, 2004), 129–131.

Chapter 5

1Isa N. Engleberg and John A. Daly, *Presentations in Everyday Life*, 3rd ed. (Pearson/Allyn and Bacon, 2009), 261. Survey responses were received from more than 600 students enrolled in a basic communication course at geographically dispersed institutions of higher education (community colleges, liberal arts colleges, and large universities).

2Mark Twain, Letter to George Bainton, October 15, 1888, http://www.twainquotes.com/Lightning.html.

3William O' Grady et al., *Contemporary Linguistics: An Introduction*, 4th ed. (Boston: Bedford/St. Martin's, 2001), 659.

4Nicholas Wade, *Before the Dawn: Recovering the Lost History of Our Ancestors* (New York: Penguin, 2006), 36–37.

5John H. McWhorter, *The Power of Babel: A Natural History of Language* (New York: Times Books/Henry Holt, 2001), 4–5.

6Nicholas Wade, *Before the Dawn: Recovering the Lost History of Our Ancestors* (New York: Penguin, 2006), 226.

7Geoffrey Finch, *Word of Mouth: A New Introduction to Language and Communication* (New York: Palgrave, 2003), 5–10; William O'Grady, Michael Dobrovolsky, and Mark Aronoff, *Contemporary Linguistics*, 2nd ed. (New York: St. Martin's Press, 1993), 9.

8William O'Grady et al., *Contemporary Linguistics: An Introduction*, 5th ed. (Boston: Bedford/St. Martin's, 2005), 2.

9Joann S. Lubin, "To Win Advancement, You Need to Clean up Any Bad Speech Habits," *Wall Street Journal*, October 5, 2004, B1.

10Victoria Fromkin and Robert Rodman, *An Introduction to Language*, 6th ed. (Fort Worth, TX: Harcourt Brace, 1998), 3.

11Anne Donnellon, *Team Talk: The Power of Language in Team Dynamics* (Boston: Harvard Business School Press, 1996), 6.

12Nelson W. Francis, *The English Language: An Introduction* (London: English University Press, 1967), 119.

13Geoffrey Finch, *Word of Mouth: A New Introduction to Language and Communication* (New York: Palgrave, 2003), 1.

14Adapted from Ogden and Richards, *The Meaning of Meaning* (New York: Harcourt Brace, 1936).

15Ibid., 11.

16S. I. Hayakawa and Alan R. Hayakawa, *Language and Thought in Action*, 5th ed. (San Diego, CA: Harcourt Brace Jovanovich, 1990), 39.

17Geoffrey Finch, *Word of Mouth: A New Introduction to Language and Communication* (New York: Palgrave, 2003), 28.

18Permission granted by Lilian I. Eman, November 26, 1999.

19S. I. Hayakawa and Alan R. Hayakawa, *Language and Thought in Action*, 5th ed. (San Diego, CA: Harcourt Brace Jovanovich, 1990), 43.

20Isa N. Engleberg and Dianna R. Wynn, *Working in Groups: Communication Principles and Strategies*, 5th ed. (Boston: Houghton Mifflin, 2010), 164.

21Vivian J. Cook, *Inside Language* (London: Arnold, 1997), 91.

22Geoffrey Finch, *Word of Mouth: A New Introduction to Language and Communication* (New York: Palgrave, 2003), 2.

23Tony Hillerman, *The Wailing Wind* (New York: HarperTorch, 2002), 126.

24William O'Grady et al., *Contemporary Linguistics: An Introduction*, 5th ed. (Boston: Bedford/St. Martin's, 2005), 509.

25See Geoffrey Finch, *Word of Mouth: A New Introduction to Language and Communication* (New York: Palgrave, 2003); http://www.aber.ac.uk/media/Documents/short/whorf.html; http://www.users.globalnet.co.uk/~skolyles/swh.htm.

26Marcel Danesi and Paul Perron, *Analyzing Cultures: An Introduction and Handbook* (Bloomington, IN: Indiana University Press, 1999), 61.

27Myron W. Lustig and Jolene Koester, *Intercultural Competence: Interpersonal Communication across Cultures*, 6th ed. (Boston: Pearson/Allyn & Bacon, 2010), 183–184.

28Ibid., 184.

29Larry A. Samovar and Richard Porter, *Communication between Cultures*, 5th ed. (Belmont, CA: Wadsworth, 2004), 146–147.

30*Washington Post*, April 6, 2002, p. A1, http://www.whitehouse.gov/news/release/2002/04/print/20020406-3.html.

31Geoffrey Finch, *Word of Mouth: A New Introduction to Language and Communication* (New York: Palgrave, 2003), 134.

32Ibid., 135.

33Ibid., 136.

34Ibid.

35M. Schultz, "The Semantic Derogation of Woman," in *Language and Sex: Difference and Dominance*, ed. B. Thorne and N. Henley (Rowley, MA: Newbury House, 1975), as quoted in Geoffrey Finch, *Word of Mouth: A New Introduction to Language and Communication* (New York: Palgrave, 2003), 137.

36Robin Lakoff, *Language and Woman's Place* (New York: HarperCollins, 1975).

37Janet Holmes, "Myth 6: Women Talk Too Much," in *Language Myths*, ed. Lauri Bauer and Peter Trudgill (London: Penguin, 1998), 41.

38David Brown, "Stereotypes of Quiet Men, Chatty Women Not Sound Science," *The Washington Post*, July 6, 2007, p. A2. See also Donald G. McNeill, "Yada, Yada, Yada. Him? Or Her?" *The New York Times*, July 6, 2007, p. A13.

39Janet Holmes, "Myth 6: Women Talk Too Much," in *Language Myths*, ed. Lauri Bauer and Peter Trudgill (London: Penguin, 1998), 42–47.

⁴⁰Ibid., 48–49.

⁴¹John McWhorter, *Word on the Street: Debunking the Myth of a "Pure" Standard English* (Cambridge, MA: Perseus, 1998), 143.

⁴²Ibid., 145, 146.

⁴³William V. Haney, *Communication and Interpersonal Relations: Text and Cases*, 6th ed. (Homewood, IL: Irwin, 1992), 269.

⁴⁴Randy Cohen, "The Ethicist," *The New York Times Magazine*, July 26, 2009, 17.

⁴⁵William V. Haney, *Communication and Interpersonal Relations: Text and Cases*, 6th ed. (Homewood, IL: Irwin, 1992), 290.

⁴⁶*The American Heritage Dictionary of the English Language*, 4th ed. (Boston: Houghton Mifflin, 2000), 614.

⁴⁷William O'Grady, Michael Dobrovolsky, and Mark Aronoff, *Contemporary Linguistics*, 2nd ed. (New York: St. Martin's Press, 1993), 235–236.

⁴⁸"The Leaked Memos: Did the White House Condone Torture?" *The Week*, June 25, 2004, 6.

⁴⁹Isa Engleberg and Ann Raimes, *Pocket Keys for Speakers* (Boston: Houghton Mifflin, 2004), 224.

⁵⁰William Lutz, *Doublespeak* (New York: HarperPerennial, 1990), 3.

⁵¹Lyn Miller, "Quit Talking Like a Corporate Geek," *USA Today*, March 21, 2005, 7B.

⁵²James V. O'Conner, *Cuss Control: The Complete Book on How to Curb Your Cursing* (New York: Three Rivers Press, 2000), 3.

⁵³Natalie Angier, "Almost Before We Spoke, We Swore," Science Times in *The New York Times*, September 20, 2005, D1.

⁵⁴Lars Andersson and Peter Trudgill, "Swearing," in *A Cultural Approach to Interpersonal Communication: Essential Readings*, ed. Leila Monaghan and Jane Goodman (Malden, MA: Wiley-Blackwell, 2007), 195.

⁵⁵Natalie Angier, "Almost Before We Spoke, We Swore," Science Times in *The New York Times*, September 20, 2005, D6.

⁵⁶James V. O'Conner, *Cuss Control: The Complete Book on How to Curb Your Cursing* (New York: Three Rivers Press, 2000), 18–27; Timothy Jay, *Why We Curse: A Neuro-Psycho-Social Theory of Speech* (Amsterdam/Philadelphia: John Benjamins Publishing, 2000), 328.

⁵⁷"Cleaning Up Potty-Mouths," *The Week*, August 18, 2006, 35.

⁵⁸R. L. Trask, *Language: The Basics*, 2nd ed. (London: Routledge, 1995), 170, 179.

⁵⁹Based on Melinda G. Kramer, Glenn Leggett, and C. David Mead, *Prentice Hall Handbook for Writers*, 12th ed. (Englewood Cliffs, NJ: Prentice Hall, 1995), 272.

⁶⁰Robert Mayer, *How to Win Any Argument* (Franklin Lakes, NJ: Career Press, 2006), 187.

⁶¹Stuart Chase, quoted in Richard Lederer, "Fowl Language: The Fine Art of the New Doublespeak," *AARP Bulletin* (March 2005), 27.

⁶²Rudolf Flesch, *Say What You Mean* (New York: Harper and Row, 1972), 70.

⁶³Excerpts from Jonathan Pitts, "At a D.C. Workshop, Participants in the Plain Language Conference Plead for End to Convoluted Communication," *The Sun*, November 7, 2005, 1C, 6C.

⁶⁴Ibid.

⁶⁵Joel Saltzman, *If You Can Talk, You Can Write* (New York: Time Warner, 1993), 48–49.

⁶⁶See Ann Raimes, *Keys for Writers: A Brief Handbook*, 3rd ed. (Boston: Houghton Mifflin, 2003), 282–284. Also see Engleberg and Raimes, 227–264.

⁶⁷Virginia Richmond and James C. McCroskey, *Communication Apprehension, Avoidance and Effectiveness*, 5th ed. (Boston: Allyn and Bacon, 1998). © 1998 by Pearson Education. Reprinted by permission of the publisher. See also John Daly and Michael Miller, "The Empirical Development of an Instrument to Measure Writing Apprehension," *Research in the Teaching of English* 12 (1975), 242–249.

Chapter 6

¹Mark Hickson, Don W. Stacks, and Nina-Jo Moore, *Nonverbal Communication: Studies and Applications*, 4th ed. (Los Angeles, CA: Roxbury Publishing, 2004), 7.

²Judee K. Burgoon and Aaron E. Bacue, "Nonverbal Communication Skills," in *Handbook of Communication and Social Interaction Skills*, ed. John O. Greene and Brant R. Burleson (Mahwah, NJ: Lawrence Erlbaum, 2003), 208–209.

³Judee Burgoon, "Truth, Lies, and Virtual Worlds," *The National Communication Association's Carroll C. Arnold Distinguished Lecture*, 2005 annual convention of the National Communication Association, Boston, November 2005.

⁴Paul Ekman, *Telling Lies: Clues to Deceit in the Marketplace, Politics, and Marriage* (New York: W.W. Norton, 1992), 80.

⁵H. Dan O'Hair and Michael J. Cody, "Deception," in *The Dark Side of Interpersonal Communication*, ed. William R. Cupach and Brian H. Spitzberg (Hillsdale, NJ: Lawrence Erlbaum Associates, 1994), 190.

⁶Mark L. Knapp, *Lying and Deception in Human Interaction* (Boston: Pearson Education, 2008), 217–218.

⁷Benedict Carey, "Judging Honesty By Words, Not Fidgets," *The New York Times*, May 12, 2009, D4.

⁸From Sigmund Freud's *Dora: History of a Cause of Hysteria* (1905). Referred to in Mark L. Knapp and Judith A. Hall, *Nonverbal Communication in Human Interaction*, 4th ed. (Fort Worth, TX: Harcourt Brace, 1997), 391.

⁹Paul Ekman, "Communication through Nonverbal Behavior: A Source of Information about an Interpersonal Relationship," in *Affect, Cognition and Personality*, ed. Silvan S. Tompkins and C. E. Izard (New York: Springer, 1965), 390–442.

¹⁰Judee K. Burgoon, David B. Buller, and W. Gill Woodall, *Nonverbal Communication: The Unspoken Dialog* (New York, McGraw-Hill, 1996), 286. See also Richard West and Lynn H. Turner, *Introducing Communication Theory* (Boston: McGraw Hill, 2007), 152–153.

¹¹From The Federal Reserve Bank of St. Louis, *The Regional Economist* (April 2005), quoted in "Good Looks Can Mean Good Pay, Study Says," *The Sun*, April 28, 2005, D1.

¹²Virginia P. Richmond and James C. McCroskey, *Nonverbal Behavior in Interpersonal Relationships*, 5th ed. (Boston: Allyn and Bacon, 2004), 33.

¹³Anne E. Laumann, "Tattoos and Body Piercings in the United States: A National Data Set," *Journal of the American Academy of Dermatology* (February 2007) 55, 3, 413–421; Harris Interactive Poll, February 12, 2008, available at http://www.harrisinteractive.com/harris_poll/index.asp?PID=868.

¹⁴David Brooks, "Nonconformity Is Skin Deep," *The New York Times*, August 27, 2006, WK11.

¹⁵Oren Dorell, "Cover Up Your Tattoos, Some Employees Told," *USA Today*, October 31, 2008, 3A.

¹⁶Mark Hickson, Don W. Stacks, and Nina-Jo Moore, *Nonverbal Communication: Studies and Applications*, 4th ed. (Los Angeles: Roxbury Publishing, 2004), 187.

¹⁷Thomas J. Stanley and William D. Danko, *The Millionaire Next Door: The Surprising Secrets of America's Wealthy* (Atlanta, GA: Longstreet Press, 1996), 28, 31–35.

¹⁸Jo-Ellan Dimitrius and Mark Mazzarella, *Reading People: How to Understand People and Predict Their Behavior—Anytime, Anyplace* (New York: Ballantine, 1999), 5.

¹⁹Mark L. Knapp and Judith A. Hall, *Nonverbal Communication in Human Interaction*, 4th ed. (Fort Worth, TX: Harcourt Brace, 1997), 229.

²⁰Paul Ekman and Wallace V. Friesen, "Hand Movements," in *The Nonverbal Communication Reader: Classic and Contemporary Readings*, 2nd ed., ed. Laura K. Guerrero, Joseph A. DeVito, and Michael L. Hecht (Long Grove, IL: Waveland Press, 2008), 105–108. The original article, "Hand Movements," was published in the *Journal of Communication* 22 (1972): 353–374.

²¹Laura K. Guerroro, Joseph A. DeVito, and Michael L. Hecht, "Section D. Contact Codes: Proxemics and Haptics," in *The Nonverbal Communication Reader: Classic and Contemporary Readings*, 2nd ed., ed. Laura K. Guerrero, Joseph A. DeVito, and Michael L. Hecht (Long Grove, IL: Waveland Press, 2008), 174.

²²Roger E. Axtell, *Do's and Taboos Around the World*, 2nd ed. (New York: John Wiley and Sons, 1990), 47.

²³Larry Smeltzer, John Waltman, and Donald Leonard, "Proxemics and Haptics in Managerial Communication" in *The Nonverbal Communication Reader: Classic and Contemporary Readings*, 3rd ed., ed. Laura K. Guerrero and Michael L. Hecht (Long Grove, IL: Waveland Press, 2008), 190.

²⁴Virginia P. Richmond and James C. McCroskey, *Nonverbal Behavior in Interpersonal Relations*, 5th ed. (Boston: Allyn and Bacon, 2004), 151.

²⁵Virginia P. Richmond and James C. McCroskey, *Nonverbal Behavior in Interpersonal Relationships*, 5th ed. (Boston: Allyn and Bacon, 2004), 75–77. Based on Paul Ekman, W. V. Friesen, and P. Ellsworth, "Methodological Decisions," in *Emotion in the Human Face*, 2nd ed., ed. Paul Ekman (Cambridge: Cambridge University Press, 1982), 7–21.

²⁶Joseph B. Walther and Kyle P. D'Addario, *The Impacts of Emoticons on Message Interpretation in Computer-Mediated Communication* (paper presented at the meeting of the International Communication Association, Washington, D.C., May 2001), 13.

²⁷Gerald W. Grumet, "Eye Contact: The Core of Interpersonal Relatedness" in *The Nonverbal Communication Reader: Classic and Contemporary Readings*, 3rd ed., ed. Laura K. Guerrero and Michael L. Hecht (Long Grove, IL: Waveland Press, 2008), 125–126.

²⁸Guo-Ming Chen and William J. Starosta, *Fundamentals of Intercultural Communication* (Boston: Allyn & Bacon, 1998), 91.

²⁹Summary of eye behavior research from Virginia P. Richmond, James C. McCroskey, and Mark L. Hickson, *Nonverbal Behavior in Interpersonal Relations* (Boston: Pearson/Allyn and Bacon, 2008), 95–96.

[30]Lyle V. Mayer, *Fundamentals of Voice and Diction*, 13th ed. (Boston: McGraw Hill, 2004), 229.

[31]Virginia P. Richmond and James C. McCroskey, *Nonverbal Behavior in Interpersonal Relationships*, 5th ed. (Boston: Allyn and Bacon, 2004), 103.

[32]Centers for Disease Control and Prevention, *Intimate Partner Violence: Fact Sheet*, http://www.cdc.gov/violenceprevention/pdf/IPV_factsheet-a.pdf.

[33]ABC News, "Battle of the Sexes: Spousal Abuse Cuts Both Ways," February 7, 2004, http://abcnews.go.com/sections/2020/dailynews/2020_batteredhusbands030207.html.

[34]Eric F. Sygnatur and Guy A. Toscano, "Work-Related Homicides: The Facts," in *Compensation and Working Conditions* (Spring 2000), http://bls.gov/opub/cwc/archive/spring2000art1.pdf.

[35]National Communication Association, Credo for Ethical Communication, 1999, http://www.natcom.org/nca/Template2.asp?bid=374.

[36]Allan Pease and Barbara Pease, *The Definitive Book of Body Language* (New York: Bantam, 2004), 193–194.

[37]Edward T. Hall, *The Hidden Dimension* (Garden City, NY: Doubleday, 1966).

[38]Mark Hickson, Don W. Stacks, and Nina-Jo Moore, *Nonverbal Communication: Studies and Applications*, 4th ed. (Los Angeles, CA: Roxbury Publishing, 2004), 318.

[39]John A. Daly and Anita Vangelisti, "Skillfully Instructing Learners: How Communicators Effectively Convey Messages," in *Handbook of Communication and Social Interaction Skills*, ed. John O. Greene and Brant R. Burleson (Mahwah, NJ: Lawrence Erlbaum, 2003), 892–894.

[40]Timothy G. Plax and Patricia Kearney, "Classroom Management: Contending with College Student Discipline," in *Teaching Communication: Theory, Research, and Methods*, 2nd ed., ed. Anita L. Vangelisti, John A. Daly, and Gustav W. Friedrich (Lea's Communication Series) (Mahwah, NJ: Lawrence Erlbaum, 1999), 276.

[41]Isa N. Engleberg and John A. Daly, *Presentations in Everyday Life*, 3rd ed. (Boston: Houghton Mifflin, 2009), 138.

[42]Virginia P. Richmond and James C. McCroskey, *Nonverbal Behavior in Interpersonal Relationships*, 5th ed. (Boston: Allyn and Bacon, 2004), 199–212.

[43]Brian H. Spitzberg, "CSRS: The Conversational Skills Rating Scale—An Instructional Assessment of Interpersonal Competence," in the *NCA Diagnostic Series*, 2nd ed. (Washington, D.C.: National Communication Association, 2007). See applications to nonverbal communication in Brian H. Spitzberg, "Perspectives on Nonverbal Communication Skills," in *The Nonverbal Communication Reader: Classic and Contemporary Readings*, 3rd ed., ed. Laura K. Guerrero and Michael L. Hecht (Long Grove, IL: Waveland Press, 2008), 21–26.

Chapter 7

[1]Jerry Lopper, "The Six Life Benefits of Happiness," November 19, 2007, http://personaldevelopment.suite101.com/article.cfm/the_six_life_benefits_of_happiness#ixzz0JqwpOgDk&D.

[2]Isabel B. Myers with Peter B. Myers, *Gifts Differing: Tenth Anniversary Edition* (Palo Alto, CA: Consulting Psychologists, 1990).

[3]Annie Murphy Paul, *The Cult of Personality* (New York: Free Press, 2004), 125–127.

[4]William Schutz, *The Human Element: Productivity, Self-Esteem, and the Bottom Line* (San Francisco: Jossey-Bass, 1994).

[5]Based on material in Isa Engleberg and Dianna Wynn, *Working in Groups: Communication Principles and Strategies*, 5th ed. (Boston: Pearson/Allyn & Bacon, 2010), 82–85.

[6]In his more recent works, Schutz refers to this need as *openness*. However, we find that students understand this concept better when we use Schutz's original term—*affection*.

[7]Exercise caution in accepting and applying psychological theories as "laws" of interpersonal communication. "Most people's personalities, psychologists note, do not fall neatly into one category or another, but occupy some intermediate zone. [Nor are these traits necessarily] inborn or immutable types." Annie Murphy Paul, *The Cult of Personality* (New York: Free Press, 2004), 125–127.

[8]Robert E. Levasseur, *Breakthrough Business Meetings: Shared Leadership in Action* (Holbrook, MA: Bob Adams, 1994), 79.

[9]Erving Goffman, *The Presentation of Self in Everyday Life* (New York: Doubleday, 1959).

[10]Adapted from Sharon S. Brehm, Saul Kassin, and Steven Fein, *Social Psychology*, 6th ed. (Boston: Houghton Mifflin, 2005), 86.

[11]Sandra Metts and Erica Grohskopf, "Impression Management: Goals, Strategies, and Skills," in *Handbook of Communication and Social Interaction Skills*, ed. John O. Greene and Brant Burleson (Mahwah, NJ: Lawrence Erlbaum, 2003), 358–359. We have added the parenthetical cautions to Metts and Grohskopf's list of strategies.

[12]Maria J. O'Leary and Cynthia Gallois, "The Last Ten Turns in Conversations between Friends and Strangers," in *The Nonverbal Communication Reader: Classic and Contemporary Readings*, 2nd ed., ed. Laura K. Guerrero, Joseph A.

DeVito, and Michael L. Hecht (Prospect Heights, IL: Waveland Press, 1999), 415–421.

[13]"What Drives Co-Workers Crazy," *The Week*, February 23, 2007, 40.

[14]Ibid.

[15]Ibid. See also "Proper Cell Phone Etiquette," http://www.cellphonecarriers.com/cell-phone-etiquette.html.

[16]Isa N. Engleberg and Dianna R. Wynn, *Working in Groups: Communication Principles and Strategies*, 5th ed. (Boston: Houghton Mifflin, 2010), 214.

[17]Ronald T. Potter-Efron, *Work Rage: Preventing Anger and Resolving Conflict on the Job* (New York: Barnes and Noble Books, 2000), 22–23.

[18]See Kenneth W. Thomas and Ralph W. Kilmann, "Developing a Forced-Choice Measure of Conflict-Handling Behavior: The MODE Instrument," *Educational Psychological Measurement* 37 (1977): 390–395; William W. Wilmot and Joyce L. Hocker, *Interpersonal Conflict*, 7th ed. (Boston: McGraw-Hill, 2007), 130–175.

[19]Isa Engleberg and Dianna Wynn, *Working in Groups: Communication Principles and Strategies*, 5th ed. (Boston: Pearson/Allyn & Bacon, 2010), 216. Based on Kenneth W. Thomas, *Intrinsic Motivation at Work: Building Energy and Commitment* (San Francisco: Berret-Koehler, 2000), 94.

[20]Based on Isa Engleberg and Dianna Wynn, *Working in Groups: Communication Principles and Strategies*, 5th ed. (Boston: Pearson/Allyn & Bacon, 2010), 184.

[21]Stephen W. Littlejohn and Kathy Domenici, *Engaging Communication in Conflict: Systematic Practice* (Thousand Oaks, CA: Sage, 2001), 44–45.

[22]Jerry Wisinski, *Resolving Conflicts on the Job* (New York: American Management Association, 1993), 27–31.

[23]Adapted from Dudley D. Cahn and Ruth Anna Abigail, *Managing Conflict through Communication*, 3rd ed. (Boston: Pearson/Allyn & Bacon, 2007), 97–104.

[24]Georg H. Eifert, Matthew McKay, and John P. Forsyth, *ACT on Life Not on Anger* (Oakland, CA: New Harbinger, 2006), 21.

[25]Ibid., 15, 16.

[26]Ibid., 19, 20.

[27]Ibid., 21.

[28]Bill DeFoore, *Anger: Deal with It, Heal with It, Stop It from Killing You* (Deerfield Beach, FL: Health Communications, 1991), viii.

[29]Georg H. Eifert, Matthew McKay, and John P. Forsyth, *ACT on Life Not on Anger* (Oakland, CA: New Harbinger, 2006), 19.

[30]Daniel J. Canary and William R. Cupach, *Competence in Interpersonal Conflict* (New York: McGraw-Hill, 1997), 78.

[31]Carol Tavris, *Anger: The Misunderstood Emotion* (New York: Simon and Schuster, 1982), 253.

[32]William W. Wilmot and Joyce L. Hocker, *Interpersonal Conflict*, 7th ed. (Boston: McGraw-Hill, 2007), 228.

[33]Sharon Anthony Bower and Gordon H. Bower, *Asserting Yourself: A Practical Guide to Positive Change* (Cambridge, MA: Perseus Books, 1991), 4–5.

[34]Ibid., 9.

[35]Madelyn Burley-Allen, *Managing Assertively: How to Improve Your People Skills* (New York: John Wiley, 1983), 45.

[36]Sharon Anthony Bower and Gordon H. Bower, *Asserting Yourself: A Practical Guide to Positive Change* (Cambridge, MA: Perseus Books, 1991), 90. See also Augsburg College Academic Skill Center, http://www.augsburg.edu/acskills/Being%20Assertive.rtf.

[37]Daniel J. Canary and William R. Cupach, *Competence in Interpersonal Conflict* (New York: McGraw-Hill, 1997), 133.

[38]Deborah Tannen, *You Just Don't Understand: Women and Men in Conversation* (New York: William Morrow, 1990).

[39]William W. Wilmot and Joyce L. Hocker, *Interpersonal Conflict*, 7th ed. (Boston: McGraw-Hill, 2007), 25.

[40]Ibid., 26.

[41]Russell Copranzano, Herman Aguinis, Marshall Schminke, and Dina L. Denham, "Disputant Reactions to Managerial Conflict Resolution Tactics: A Comparison among Argentina, the Dominican Republic, Mexico, and the United States," *Group and Organization Management* 24 (1999): 131.

[42]Bren Ortega Murphy, "Promoting Dialogue in Culturally Diverse Workplace Environments," in *Innovation in Group Facilitation: Applications in Natural Settings*, ed. Larry R. Frey (Cresskill, NJ: Hampton, 1995), 77–93.

[43]For more about conflict styles, see Joseph P. Folger, Marshall Scott Poole, and Randall K. Stutman, *Working through Conflict*, 6th ed. (Boston: Pearson/Allyn & Bacon, 2009), 104–135.

Chapter 8

[1]Diane Vaughan, *Uncoupling: How and Why Relationships Come Apart* (New York: Vintage Books, 1986), 3.

[2]Ibid., 6.

[3]David W. Johnson, *Reaching Out: Interpersonal Effectiveness and Self-Actualization*, 7th ed. (Boston: Allyn & Bacon, 2000), 12.

[4]John M. Gottman with Joan De Claire, *The Relationship Cure* (New York: Three Rivers Press, 2001), 23.

[5]See Leslie A. Baxter, "A Dialectical Perspective on Communication Strategies in Relationship Development," in *Handbook of Personal Relationships*, ed. Steve Duck (New York: Wiley, 1990), 257–273.

[6]Lawrence B. Rosenfeld, "Overview of the Ways Privacy, Secrecy, and Disclosure Are Balanced in Today's Society," in *Balancing the Secrets of Private Disclosures*, ed. Sandra Petronio (Mahwah, NJ: Lawrence Erlbaum, 2000), 5.

[7]Malcolm R. Parks, "Ideology in Interpersonal Communication: Off the Couch and into the World," in *Communication Yearbook 5*, ed. Michael Burgoon (New Brunswick, NJ: Transaction Books, 1982), 79–107.

[8]Joseph Luft, *Group Process: An Introduction to Group Dynamics*, 3rd ed. (Palo Alto, CA: Mayfield, 1984).

[9]Ibid.

[10]David W. Johnson, *Reaching Out: Interpersonal Effectiveness and Self-Actualization*, 7th ed. (Boston: Allyn & Bacon, 2000), 47.

[11]Irwin Altman and Dalmas Taylor, *Social Penetration: The Development of Interpersonal Relationships* (New York: Holt, Rinehart, and Winston, 1973).

[12]Walid A. Afifi and Laura K. Guerrero, "Motivations Underlying Topic Avoidance in Close Relationships," in *Balancing the Secrets of Private Disclosure*, ed. Sandra Petronio (Mahwah, NJ: Lawrence Erlbaum, 2000), 168.

[13]*Shrek*, DreamWorks, 2003.

[14]Joseph Luft, *Group Process: An Introduction to Group Dynamics*, 3rd ed. (Palo Alto, CA: Mayfield, 1984).

[15]Ibid., 58–59.

[16]For more information on self-disclosure skills, see David W. Johnson, *Reaching Out: Interpersonal Effectiveness and Self-Actualization*, 7th ed. (Boston: Allyn & Bacon, 2000), 59–61.

[17]Jack R. Gibb, "Defensive Communication," *Journal of Communication* 2 (1961): 141–148.

[18]David W. Johnson, *Reaching Out: Interpersonal Effectiveness and Self-Actualization*, 7th ed. (Boston: Allyn & Bacon, 2000), 61.

[19]Based on Jack R. Gibb, "Defensive Communication," *Journal of Communication* 2 (1961): 141–148; see also http://lynn.meade.tripod.com/id61_m.htm.

[20]Stefan Klein, *The Science of Happiness* (New York: Marlowe, 2006), 151, 152.

[21]Wendy Samter, "Friendship Interaction Skills across the Life Span," in *Handbook of Communication and Social Interaction Skills*, ed. John O. Greene and Brant R. Burleson (Mahwah, NJ: Lawrence Erlbaum, 2003), 641.

[22]Sandra Petronio, *Boundaries of Privacy: Dialectics of Disclosure* (Albany: State University of New York Press, 2003), 5–6.

[23]Wendy Samter, "Friendship Interaction Skills across the Life Span," in *Handbook of Communication and Social Interaction Skills*, ed. John O. Greene and Brant R. Burleson (Mahwah, NJ: Lawrence Erlbaum, 2003), 661.

[24]William K. Rawlins, *Friendship Matters: Communication, Dialects, and the Life Course* (New York: Aldine De Gruyter, 1992), 105.

[25]Richard Layard, *Happiness: Lessons from a New Science* (New York: Penguin Books, 2005), 66.

[26]Kathryn Dindia and Lindsay Timmerman, "Accomplishing Romantic Relationships," in *Handbook of Communication and Social Interaction Skills*, ed. John O. Greene and Brant R. Burleson (Mahwah, NJ: Lawrence Erlbaum, 2003), 694–697.

[27]Mark C. Knapp and Anita L. Vangelisti, *Interpersonal Communication and Human Relationships* (Boston: Allyn & Bacon, 1996), 33–44.

[28]Laura K. Guerrero and Peter A. Andersen, "The Dark Side of Jealousy and Envy: Desire, Delusions, Desperation, and Destructive Communication," in *The Dark Side of Close Relationships*, ed. Brian H. Spitzberg and William R. Cupach (Mahwah, NJ: Lawrence Erlbaum Associates, 1998), 55, 66.

[29]Laura K. Guerrero et al., "Coping with the Green-Eyed Monster: Conceptualizing and Measuring Communicative Responses to Romantic Jealousy," *Western Journal of Communication* 59 (1995): 270–304; Laura K. Guerrero and Walid Afifi, "Toward a Goal-Oriented Approach for Understanding Communicative Responses to Jealousy," *Western Journal of Communication* 63 (1999): 216–248.

[30]Mark C. Knapp and Anita L. Vangelisti, *Interpersonal Communication and Human Relationships* (Boston: Allyn & Bacon, 1996), 34.

[31]Stephanie Coontz, "A Pop Quiz on Marriage," *The New York Times*, February 19, 2006, WK12.

[32]Mark C. Knapp and Anita L. Vangelisti, *Interpersonal Communication and Human Relationships* (Boston: Allyn & Bacon, 1996), 34–35.

[33]Eric Schmidt, "For the First Time, Nuclear Families Drop below 25% of Households," *The New York Times*, May 15, 2001, A1, A18.

[34]Sam Roberts, "51% of Women Are Now Living without Spouse," *The New York Times*, January 16, 2007, A1.

[35]Lynn H. Turner and Richard West, *Perspectives on Family Communication*, 2nd ed. (Boston: McGraw-Hill, 2002), 8.

[36]Ibid., 18–37.

[37]Ibid., 125–126.

[38]Ibid., 134.

[39]Based on Lynn H. Turner and Richard West, *Perspectives on Family Communication*, 2nd ed. (Boston: McGraw-Hill, 2002), 126–127.

[40]Craig H. Hart, Lloyd D. Newell, and Susanne Frost Olsen, "Parenting Skills and Social–Communicative Competence in Childhood," in *Handbook of Communication and Social Interaction Skills*, ed. John O. Greene and Brant R. Burleson (Mahwah, NJ: Lawrence Erlbaum, 2003), 781.

[41]Ibid., 769.

[42]Ibid., 782.

[43]Based on Craig H. Hart, Lloyd D. Newell, and Susanne Frost Olsen, "Parenting Skills and Social–Communicative Competence in Childhood," in *Handbook of Communication and Social Interaction Skills*, ed. John O. Greene and Brant R. Burleson (Mahwah, NJ: Lawrence Erlbaum, 2003), 769–770.

[44]Craig H. Hart, Lloyd D. Newell, and Susanne Frost Olsen, "Parenting Skills and Social–Communicative Competence in Childhood," in *Handbook of Communication and Social Interaction Skills*, ed. John O. Greene and Brant R. Burleson (Mahwah, NJ: Lawrence Erlbaum, 2003), 769–771.

[45]Judith R. Harris as quoted in several online chats and interviews. See the *Washington Post*'s online chat, September 30, 1998, http://discuss.washingtonpost.com/wp-srv/zforum/98/harris093098.htm; and *Edge 58*, June 29, 1999, http://www.edge.org/documents/archive/edge58.html.

[46]"Blame Your Peers, Not Your Parents, Authors Says," *APA Monitor* (October 1998), http://www.snc.edu/psych/korshavn/peer01.htm.

[47]For analysis and criticism of Harris's research, see Craig H. Hart, Lloyd D. Newell, and Susanne Frost Olsen, "Parenting Skills and Social–Communicative Competences in Childhood," in *Handbook of Communication and Social Interaction Skills*, ed. John O. Greene and Brant R. Burleson (Mahwah, NJ: Lawrence Erlbaum, 2003), 774–776.

[48]Robert Plutchik, *The Emotions* (Lanham, MD: University Press of America, 1991), 108–125; Robert Plutchick, *Emotions: A Psychoevolutionary Synthesis* (New York: Harper and Row, 1980).

[49]Ibid. See also Robert Plutchik, "Emotions: A General Psychoevolutionary Theory," in *Approaches to Emotion*, ed. K. R. Scherer and Paul Ekman (Mahwah, NJ: Lawrence Erlbaum, 1984), 203.

[50]Based on Daniel Goleman, *Emotional Intelligence: Why It Can Matter More Than IQ* (New York: Bantam, 1995); Daniel Goleman, *Working with Emotional Intelligence* (New York: Bantam Books, 1998); Hendrie Weisinger, *Emotional Intelligence at Work* (San Francisco: Jossey-Bass, 1998).

[51]Daniel Goleman, *Working with Emotional Intelligence* (New York: Bantam Books, 1998), 317.

[52]Ibid., 27–28. See also Antonio R. Damasio, *Descartes' Error: Emotion, Reason, and the Human Brain* (New York: Quill, 2000).

[53]http://www.natcom.org/aboutNCA/Policies/Platform.html.

[54]Elaine E. Englehardt, "Introduction to Ethics in Interpersonal Communication," in *Ethical Issues in Interpersonal Communication*, ed. Elaine E. Englehardt (Fort Worth, TX: Harcourt, 2001), 1–25. In the same volume, see also Carol Gilligan, "Images of Relationship," and Nel Noddings, "An Ethics of Care," 88–96 and 96–103.

[55]Brant R. Burleson, "Emotional Support Skills," in *Handbook of Communication and Social Interaction Skills*, ed. John O. Greene and Brant R. Burleson (Mahwah, NJ: Lawrence Erlbaum, 2003), 552.

[56]Ibid., 589–681.

[57]Brant R. Burleson, Amanda J. Holmstrom, and Cristina M. Gilstrap, "Guys Can't Say *That* to Guys: Four Experiments Assessing the Normative Motivation Account for Deficiencies in the Emotional Support Provided by Men," *Communication Monographs* 72 (2005): 582.

[58]Susan M. Jones and John G. Wirtz, "How Does the Comforting Process Work? An Empirical Test of an Appraisal-Based Model of Comforting," *Human Communication Research* 32 (2006): 217.

[59]Brant R. Burleson, Amanda J. Holmstrom, and Cristina M. Gilstrap, "Guys Can't Say *That* to Guys: Four Experiments Assessing the Normative Motivation Account for Deficiencies in the Emotional Support Provided by Men," *Communication Monographs* 72 (2005): 469.

[60]Ibid., 472.

[61]Ibid., 497.

[62]Susan M. Jones and John G. Wirtz, "How Does the Comforting Process Work? An Empirical Test of an Appraisal-Based Model of Comforting," *Human Communication Research* 32 (2006): 583.

[63]Brant R. Burleson, "Emotional Support Skill," in *Handbook of Communication and Social Interaction Skills*, ed. John O. Greene and Brant R. Burleson (Mahwah, NJ: Lawrence Erlbaum, 2003), 553.

[64]Daniel Goleman, "Friends for Life: An Emerging Biology of Emotional Healing," *The New York Times*, October 10, 2006, D5. See also Daniel Goleman, *Social Intelligence* (New York: Bantam, 2006).

[65]Nicholas Bakalar, "Five-Second Touch Can Convey Specific Emotions, Study Finds," *The New York Times*, August 11, 2009, D3.

[66]Daniel Goleman, *Social Intelligence* (New York: Bantam, 2006), 243.

[67]Martin S. Remland, *Nonverbal Communication in Everyday Life*, 2nd ed. (Boston: Houghton Mifflin, 2003), 330.

[68]Based on Daniel Goleman, *Emotional Intelligence* (New York: Bantam, 1995); Daniel Goleman, *Working with Emotional Intelligence* (New York: Bantam, 1998); Hendrie Weisinger, *Emotional Intelligence at Work* (San Francisco: Jossey-Bass, 1998).

[69]Based on Daniel Goleman, *Working with Emotional Intelligence* (New York: Bantam, 1998), 26–27.

Chapter 9

[1]James M. Kouzes and Barry Z. Posner, *Encouraging the Heart: A Leader's Guide to Rewarding and Recognizing Others* (San Francisco: Jossey-Bass, 1999), 4.

[2]Matthew Gilbert, *Communication Miracles at Work: Effective Tools and Tips for Getting the Most from Your Work Relationships* (Berkeley, CA: Conari Press, 2002), 112.

[3]Ibid., 198

[4]Daniel P. Modaff, Sue DeWine, and Jennifer A. Butler, *Organizational Communication: Foundations, Challenges, Misunderstandings* (Los Angeles, CA: Roxbury, 2008), 197.

[5]Ibid., 198.

[6]Ibid., 207.

[7]Hal Plotkin, "Introduction," *Dealing with Difficult People* (Boston: Harvard Business School Press, 2005), 1.

[8]Hal Plotkin, "Feedback in the Future Tense," *Dealing with Difficult People* (Boston: Harvard Business School Press, 2005), 132–137.

[9]Ken Cloke and Joan Goldsmith, "How to Handle Difficult Behaviors," in *Dealing with Difficult People* (Boston: Harvard Business School Press, 2005), 66–67.

[10]Daniel P. Modaff, Sue DeWine, and Jennifer A. Butler, *Organizational Communication: Foundations, Challenges, Misunderstandings* (Los Angeles, CA: Roxbury, 2008), 206.

[11]Robert Longley, "Labor Studies of Attitudes toward Work and Leisure: U.S. Workers Are Happy and Stress Is Over-stressed," August 1999, http://usgovinfo.about.com/od/censusandstatsitics/a/labordaystudy.htm.

[12]Daniel P. Modaff, Sue DeWine, and Jennifer A. Butler, *Organizational Communication: Foundations, Challenges, Misunderstandings* (Los Angeles, CA: Roxbury, 2008), 236–237.

[13]Matthew Gilbert, *Communication Miracles at Work: Effective Tools and Tips for Getting the Most from Your Work Relationships* (Berkeley, CA: Conari Press, 2002), 153.

[14]Ibid., 157.

[15]Council of Better Business Bureaus, "Dealing with Unruly Customers." http://www.bbb.org/alerts/article.asp?ID=370.

[16]John Tschohl, Service Quality Institute, "Service, Not Servitude: Common Sense Is Critical Element of Customer Service," 2004, http://www.customer-service.com/articles/022502.cfm.

[17]Based on Carley H. Dodd, *Managing Business and Professional Communication* (Boston: Allyn & Bacon, 2004), 169–170.

[18]Ibid., 40.

[19]Michael E. Pacanowsky and Nick O'Donnell-Trujillo, "Communication and Organizational Cultures," *Western Journal of Speech Communication*, 46 (1982): 115–130; Michael E. Pacanowsky and Nick O'Donnell-Trujillo, *Communication Monograph*s 50 (1983): 127–130.

[20]Joel Lovell, "Workplace Rumors Are True," http://www.nytimes.com/2006/12/10/magazine/10section4.t-9.html, December 10, 2006.

[21]Ibid.

[22]Rachel Devine, "Work and Career: Gossip Galore," *iVillage Work & Career*, http://www.ivillage.co.uk/workcareer/survive/opolotics/articles/#0,,156475_164246,00.html.

[23]Rachel Devine, "Work and Career: Gossip Galore," *iVillage Work & Career*, http://www.ivillage.co.uk/workcareer/survive/opolotics/articles/0,,156475_164246,00.html. Carl Skooglund and Glenn Coleman, "Advice from the Ethics Office at Texas Instruments Corporation: Gossiping at Work" *Online Ethics Center for Engineering and Science* (2004), http://onlineethics.org/corp/gossip.html; Muriel Solomon, *Working with Difficult People* (New York: Prentice Hall, 2002), 125–126.

[24]Quoted in Samuel Greengard, "Gossip Poisons Business: HR Can Stop It," *Workforce* (July 2001), http://www.findarticles.com/p/articles/mi_m0FXS/is_7_80/ai_76938891.

[25]Samuel Greengard, "Gossip Poisons Business: HR Can Stop It," *Workforce* (July 2001), http://www.findarticles.com/p/articles/mi_m0FXS/is_7_80/ai_76938891. "Rumor Has It—Dealing with Misinformation in the Workplace," *Entrepreneur* (September 1, 1997), http://www.findarticles.com/p/articles/mi_m0DTI/is_n9_v25/ai_19892317.

[26]Ed Piantek, "Flirting with Disaster," *Risk and Insurance* (May 1, 2000), http://www.findarticles.com/p/articles/mi_m0BJK/is_200_May/ai_62408701.

[27]Bill Leonard, "Workplace Romances Seem to Be Rule, Not Exception," *HR Magazine* (April 2001), http://www.findarticles.com/p/articles/mi_m3495/is_4_46/ai_73848276.

[28]Ibid.; "Working It—L.A. Stories—Survey Data on Office Romances," *Los Angeles Business Journal* (May 27, 2002), http://www.findarticles.com/p/articles/mi_/5072/is_21_24/ai_91233190.

[29]Ed Piantek, "Flirting with Disaster," *Risk and Insurance* (May 1, 2000), http://www.findarticles.com/p/articles/mi_m0BJK/is_200_May/ai_62408701.

[30]Work and Family Connection, "Cupid Not a Welcome Visitor at Work: A SHRM Survey Has Asked 1,221 Execs and HR Managers about Office Romances, and the Overwhelming Verdict Is Thumbs Down," *Work and Family Newsbrief* (April 2002), http://www.findarticles.com/p/articles/mi_m0IJN/is_2002_April/ai_84543923.

[31]Bill Leonard, "Workplace Romances Seem to Be Rule, Not Exception," *HR Magazine* (April 2001), http://www.findarticles.com/p/articles/mi_m3495/is_4_46/ai_73848276; Judy Olian, "On the Job: Workplace Romances Are Management's Business," *Pittsburgh Post-Gazette*, November 20, 2001, http://www.post-gazette.com/businessnews.

[32]Ibid.

[33]U.S. Equal Employment Opportunity Commission, "Facts about Sexual Harassment" (June 27, 2002), http://www.eeoc.gov/facts/fs-sex.html.

[34]Quoted in HaLife, "Be Cautious with a Workplace Romance" (2004), http://halife.com/business/mayromance/html.

[35]Ibid.

[36]Deborah Ware Balogh, "The Effects of Delayed Report and Motive for Reporting on Perceptions of Sexual Harassment," *Sex Roles: A Journal of Research* (April 2003), http://www.findarticles.com/p/articles/mi_m2294/is_2003_April/ai_101174064.

[37]Julie A. Woodzicka and Marianne LaFrance, "Real Versus Imagined Gender Harassment," *Journal of Social Issues* (Spring 2001), http://www.findarticles.com/p/articles/mi_m0341/is_1_57/ai_75140959.

[38]Deborah Ware Balogh, "The Effects of Delayed Report and Motive for Reporting on Perceptions of Sexual Harassment," *Sex Roles: A Journal of Research* (April 2003), http://www.findarticles.com/p/articles/mi_m2294/is_2003_April/ai_101174064.

[39]Ed Piantek, "Flirting with Disaster," *Risk and Insurance* (May 1, 2000), http://www.findarticles.com/p/articles/mi_m0BJK/is_200_May/ai_62408701.

[40]Nichole L. Torres, "Boys Will Not Be Boys: Lewdness and Rudeness Can Be a Mess for Your Business—Even Without Mixed Company," *Entrepreneur* (November 1, 2001), http://www.findarticles.com/p/articles/mi_m0DTI/is_11_29/ai_83663647.

[41]Rebecca A. Thacker and Stephen F. Gohmann, "Male/Female Differences in Perceptions and Effects of Hostile Environment Sexual Harassment: 'Reasonable' Assumptions?" *Public Personnel Management*, September 22, 1993, http://www.allbusiness.com/human-resources/workforce-management/401746-1.html. See also Maria Rotundo, Dung-Hanh Nguyen, and Paul R. Sacket, "A Meta-analytic Review of Gender Differences in Perceptions of Sexual Harassment," *Journal of Applied Psychology* 86, no. 5 (October 2001): 914–922.

[42]Daniel P. Modaff, Sue DeWine, and Jennifer A. Butler, *Organizational Communication: Foundations, Challenges, Misunderstandings* (Los Angeles, CA: Roxbury, 2008), 236.

[43]Based on Daniel P. Modaff and Sue DeWine, *Organizational Communication: Foundations, Challenges, Misunderstandings* (Los Angeles, CA: Roxbury, 2002), 202.

[44]Cited in Marky Stein, "89-Day Career Change Media Challenge" (July 29, 2004), http://ca.prweb.com/releases/2004/7/prweb144867.htm.

[45]Cited in Matthew Gilbert, *Communication Miracles at Work: Effective Tools and Tips for Getting the Most from Your Work Relationships* (Berkeley, CA: Conari Press, 2002), 10; see also Humphrey Taylor, "The Mood of American Workers" (January 19, 2000), http://www.harrisinteractive.com/harris_poll.

[46]Virginia Galt, "When Quitting a Job, Discretion Is the Better Part of Valor," http://globeandmail.workopolis.com/servlet/Content/fasttrack/2004041; Peggy Post, "Rules to Live By: Quitting Your Job," http://magazines.ivillage.com/goodhousekeeping/print/0,,636770,00.html.

[47]Matt Villano, "What to Tell the Company as You Walk out the Door," *The New York Times*, November 27, 2005, BU8. Quoting Jim Atkinson, regional vice president, Right Management Consultants.

[48]Dawn Rosenberg McKay, "Job Loss: How to Cope" (2009), http://careerplanning.about.com/od/jobloss/a/job_loss.htm.

[49]How to Cope With Job Loss, *eHow*, http://www.ehow.com/how_2084091_cope-job-loss.html.

[50]This definition is a composite of components found in most academic definitions of an interview. See, for example, Larry Powell and Jonathan Amsbary, *Interviewing: Situations and Contexts* (Boston: Pearson/Allyn & Bacon, 2006), 1;

Charles Stewart and William B. Cash, *Interviewing: Principles and Practices*, 10th ed. (Boston: McGraw-Hill, 2003), 4; Jeanne Tessier Barone and Jo Young Switzer, *Interviewing Art and Skill* (Boston: Allyn & Bacon, 1995), 8.

[51]Richard Nelson Bolles, *What Color Is Your Parachute? A Practical Manual for Job-Hunters and Career-Changers* (Berkeley: Ten Speed Press, 2007), 78.

[52]Accountemps study displayed in *USA Today* Snapshots, "Most Common Job Interview Mistakes Noticed by Employers," *USA Today*, October 17, 2006, B1.

[53]"Lying: How Can You Protect Your Company?" http://www.westaff.com/yourworkplace/ywissues37_full.html.

[54]Daryl Koehn, University of St. Thomas Center for Business Ethics, "Rewriting History: Resume Falsification More Than a Passing Fiction," http://www.stthom.edu/cbes/resume.html.

[55]Donna Hemmila, "Tired of Lying, Cheating Job Applicants, Employers Calling in Detectives," *San Francisco Business Times* 12, no. 29 (February 27–March 5, 1998), http://www.esrcheck.com/articles/Tired-of-lying-cheating-job-applicants-employers-calling-in-detectives.php.

[56]Barbara Mende, "Employers Crack down on Candidates Who Lie," *Wall Street Journal Career Journal*, http://www.careerjournal.com/jobhunting/resumes/20020606-mende.html.

[57]Wallace V. Schmidt and Roger N. Conaway, *Results-Oriented Interviewing: Principles, Practices, and Procedures* (Boston: Allyn & Bacon, 1999), 84.

[58]Larry Powell and Jonathan Amsbary, *Interviewing: Situations and Contexts* (Boston: Pearson/Allyn & Bacon, 2006), 47; Wallace V. Schmidt and Roger N. Conaway, *Results-Oriented Interviewing: Principles, Practices, and Procedures* (Boston: Allyn & Bacon, 1999), 107; Charles J. Stewart and William B. Cash, Jr., *Interviewing: Principles and Practices* (Boston: McGraw-Hill, 2003), 245; *Job Link USA*, "Interview," http://www.joblink-usa.com/interview.htm; *CollegeGrad.Com*, "Candidate Interview Questions," http://www.collegegrad.com/jobsearch/16-15.shtml.

[59]Wallace V. Schmidt and Roger N. Conaway, *Results-Oriented Interviewing: Principles, Practices, and Procedures* (Boston: Allyn & Bacon, 1999), 34–37.

[60]Charles J. Stewart and William B. Cash, Jr., *Interviewing: Principles and Practices* (Boston: McGraw-Hill, 2003), 254–255; "Candidate Interview Questions," CollegeGrad.Com, http://www.collegegrad.com/questions/candidates.shtml; "Interview," http://www.joblink-usa.com/interview.htm.

[61]Wallace V. Schmidt and Roger N. Conaway, *Results-Oriented Interviewing: Principles, Practices, and Procedures* (Boston: Allyn & Bacon, 1999), 110–111.

[62]Richard Nelson Bolles, *What Color Is Your Parachute? A Practical Manual for Job-Hunters and Career-Changers* (Berkeley, CA: Ten Speed Press, 2007), 82.

[63]Wallace V. Schmidt and Roger N. Conaway, *Results-Oriented Interviewing: Principles, Practices, and Procedures* (Boston: Allyn & Bacon, 1999), 110–111.

[64]Mary Heiberger and Julia Miller Vick, "How To Handle Difficult Interview Questions," *Chronicle of Higher Education*, January 22, 1999, http://chronicle.com/jobs/v45/i21/4521career.htm; Allison Doyle, "Illegal Interview Questions: Illegal Interview Question Samples," http://jobsearch.about.com/library/weekly/aa0224032/htm.

Chapter 10

[1]James Surowiecki, *The Wisdom of Crowds* (New York: Anchor Books, 2004), back cover.

[2]Ibid., 5.

[3]Peter D. Hart Research Associates, *How Should Colleges Prepare Students to Succeed in Today's Global Economy?* (Washington, D.C.: Peter D. Hart Research Associates, December 28, 2006), 2; see also Association of American Colleges and Universities, *College Learning for the New Global Age* (Washington, D.C.: Association of American Colleges and Universities, 2007).

[4]Peter D. Hart Research Associates, *How Should Colleges Prepare Students to Succeed in Today's Global Economy?* (Washington, D.C.: Peter D. Hart Research Associates, December 28, 2006), 7.

[5]Patrick C. Kyllonen, *The Research Behind the ETS Personal Potential Index (PPI)* (2008), Background Paper from the Educational Testing Service, http://www.ets.org/Media/Products/PPI/10411_PPI_bkgrd_report_RD4.pdf. See also Daniel de Vise, "New Index Will Score Graduate Students' Personality Tests," *The Washington Post*, July 10, 2009, A11.

[6]This definition is modified from Isa N. Engleberg and Dianna R. Wynn, *Working in Groups: Communication Principles and Strategies*, 5th ed. (Boston: Pearson/Allyn & Bacon, 2010), 4.

[7]Carl E. Larson and Frank M. J. LaFasto, *TeamWork: What Must Go Right/What Can Go Wrong* (Newbury Park, CA: Sage, 1989), 27.

[8]Jon R. Katzenbach and Douglas K. Smith, *The Wisdom of Teams: Creating the High-Performance Organization* (New York: HarperBusiness, 1999), 9.

[9]Robert B. Cialdini, "The Perils of Being the Best and the Brightest," *Becoming an Effective Leader* (Boston: Harvard Business School Press, 2005), 174, 175.

[10]3M Meeting Management Team with Jeannine Drew, *Mastering Meetings: Discovering the Hidden Potential of Effective Business Meetings* (New York: McGraw-Hill, 1994), 12.

[11]Isa N. Engleberg and Dianna R. Wynn, *Working in Groups: Communication Principles and Strategies*, 5th ed. (Boston: Pearson/Allyn & Bacon, 2010), 203–207.

[12]Deborah L. Duarte and Nancy Tennant Snyder, *Mastering Virtual Teams*, 3rd ed. (San Francisco: Jossey-Bass, 2007), 21, 158.

[13]Ernest G. Bormann, *Small Group Communication: Theory and Practice*, 3rd ed. (Edina, MN: Burgess, 1996), 132–135, 181–183.

[14]Rodney W. Napier and Matti K. Gershenfeld, *Groups: Theory and Experience*, 7th ed. (Boston: Houghton Mifflin, 2004), 182.

[15]Bruce Tuckman, "Developmental Sequences in Small Groups," *Psychological Bulletin* 63 (1965): 384–399. Note: Tuckman and Jensen identified a fifth stage—adjourning—in the 1970s. There is little research on the characteristics and behavior of members during this stage other than a decrease in interaction and, in some cases, separation anxiety. See Bruce Tuckman and Mary Ann Jensen, "Stages of Small-Group Development Revisited," *Group and Organization Studies* 2 (1977): 419–427.

[16]Artemis Change, Julie Duck, and Prashant Bordia, "Understanding the Multidimensionality of Group Development," *Small Group Research* 37 (2006): 329.

[17]Ibid., 331, 337–338.

[18]Susan A. Wheelan and Nancy Brewer Danganan, "The Relationship Between the Internal Dynamics of Student Affairs Leadership Teams and Campus Leaders' Perceptions of the Effectiveness of Student Affairs Divisions," *NASPA Journal*, 40 (Spring 2003): 96.

[19]Ernest G. Bormann, *Small Group Communication Theory and Practice*, 6th ed. (Edina, MN: Burgess International, 1996), 134–135.

[20]Donald G. Ellis and B. Aubrey Fisher, *Small Group Decision Making: Communication and the Group Process*, 4th ed. (New York: McGraw-Hill, 1994), 43–44.

[21]Marvin E. Shaw, "Group Composition and Group Cohesiveness" in *Small Group Communication: A Reader*, 6th ed., ed. Robert S. Cathcart and Larry A. Samovar (Dubuque, IA: Wm. C. Brown, 1992), 214–220.

[22]Patricia H. Andrews, "Group Conformity," in *Small Group Communication: Theory and Practice*, 7th ed., ed. Robert S. Cathcart, Larry A. Samovar, and Linda D. Henman (Madison, WI: Brown and Benchmark, 1996), 185.

[23]Nicky Hayes, *Managing Teams: A Strategy for Success* (London: Thomson, 2004), 31.

[24]Kenneth D. Benne and Paul Sheats, "Functional Roles of Group Members," *Journal of Social Issues* 4 (1948): 41–49. We have modified the original Benne and Sheats list by adding or combining behaviors that we have observed, as well as roles identified by other writers and researchers.

[25]Ibid.

[26]Ibid.

[27]Based on Michael Doyle and David Straus, *How to Make Meetings Work* (New York: Jove, 1976), 107–117. Several titles and behaviors are original contributions by the authors.

[28]James C. McCroskey and Virginia P. Richmond, "Correlates of Compulsive Communication: Quantitative and Qualitative Characteristics," *Communication Quarterly* 43 (1995): 39–52.

[29]Isa N. Engleberg and Dianna R. Wynn, *Working in Groups: Communication Principles and Strategies*, 3rd ed. (Boston: Houghton Mifflin, 2004), 207.

[30]Antony Bell, *Great Leadership: What It Is and What It Takes in a Complex World* (Mountain View, CA: Davies-Black, 2006), 87, 91.

[31]Fred E. Feidler and Martin M. Chemers, *Improving Leadership Effectiveness: The Leader Match Concept*, 2nd ed. (New York: Wiley, 1984).

[32]Based on material in Isa N. Engleberg and Dianna R. Wynn, *Working in Groups: Communication Principles and Strategies*, 5th ed. (Boston: Pearson/Allyn & Bacon, 2010), 113–114.

[33]Edwin P. Hollander, *Leadership Dynamics: A Practical Guide to Effective Relationships* (New York: Macmillan, 1978), 53. Also see a meta-analysis of this variable in Marianne Schmid Mast, "Dominance as Expressed and Inferred through Speaking Time," *Human Communication Research* 28 (2002): 420–450.

[34]The 4-M Model of Effective Leadership© is based, in part, on Martin M. Chemers's integrative theory of leadership, which identifies three functional aspects of leadership: image management, relationship development, and resource utilization. We have added a fourth function—decision making—and have incorporated more of a communication perspective into Chemers's view of leadership as a multifaceted process. See Martin M. Chemers, *An Integrative Theory of Leadership* (Mahwah, NJ: Lawrence Erlbaum, 1997), 151–173. See Isa N. Engleberg and Dianna R. Wynn, *Working in Groups: Communication Principles and Strategies*, 5th ed. (Boston: Pearson/Allyn & Bacon, 2010), 123–126.

[35]Martin M. Chemers, *An Integrative Theory of Leadership* (Mahwah, NJ: Lawrence Erlbaum, 1997), 160.

[36]Harvey Robbins and Michael Finley, *The New Why Teams Don't Work: What Goes Wrong and How to Make It Right* (San Francisco: Berrett-Koehler, 2000), 107.

[37]Carol Tice "Building the 21st Century Leader," *Entrepreneur* (February 2007), 66, 67.

[38]Ibid., 68.

[39]Susan B. Shimanoff and Mercilee M. Jenkins, "Leadership and Gender: Challenging Assumptions and Recognizing Resources," in *Small Group Communication: Theory and Practice*, 7th ed., ed. Robert S. Cathcart, Larry A. Samovar, and Linda D. Henman (Madison, WI: Brown and Benchmark, 1996), 327.

[40]Martin M. Chemers, *An Integrative Theory of Leadership* (Mahwah, NJ: Lawrence Erlbaum, 1997), 126.

Chapter 11

[1]Tim Dirks, *12 Angry Men* (1957), http://www.filmsite.org/twelve.html; *12 Angry Men* was remade for television in 1997. In this production, the judge is a woman and four of the jurors are African American. The producers decided against putting a woman in the jury because they didn't want to change the title. Still, most of the action and dialogue of the film is identical to the original. Modernizations include a prohibition on smoking in the jury room, the changing of references to income and pop culture figures, more dialogue relating to race, and profanity.

[2]Tim Dirks, *12 Angry Men* (1957), http://www.filmsite.org/twelve.html.

[3]Marshall Scott Poole and Randy Y. Hirokawa, "Introduction: Communication and Group Decision Making," in *Communication and Group Decision Making*, 2nd ed. ed. Randy Y. Hirokawa and Marshall Scott Poole (Thousand Oaks, CA: Sage, 1996), 1.

[4]Rodney W. Napier and Matti K. Gershenfeld, *Groups: Theory and Experience*, 7th ed. (Boston: Houghton Mifflin, 2004), 291.

[5]*The American Heritage Dictionary*, 4th ed. (Boston: Houghton Mifflin, 2000), 484.

[6]Peter R. Drucker, *The Effective Executive* (New York: HarperBusiness, 1967), 143.

[7]Randy Y. Hirokawa, "Communication and Group Decision-Making Efficacy," in *Small Group Communication: Theory and Practice*, 7th ed., ed. Robert S. Cathcart, Larry A. Samovar, and Linda D. Henman (Madison, WI: Brown and Benchmark, 1996), 108.

[8]Marshall Scott Poole, "Procedures for Managing Meetings: Social and Technological Innovation," in *Innovative Meeting Management*, ed. Richard A. Swanson and Bonnie Ogram Knapp (Austin, TX: 3M Meeting Management Institute, 1990), 54–55.

[9]Keith Sawyer, *Group Genius: The Creative Power of Collaboration* (New York: Basic Books, 2007), 66–67. Sawyer attributes the story to Dale Carnegie.

[10]Irving L. Janis, *Groupthink*, 2nd ed. (Boston: Houghton Mifflin, 1982), 9.

[11]Ibid.

[12]Julia T. Wood, "Alternative Methods of Group Decision Making," in *Small Group Communication: A Reader*, 6th ed., ed. Robert S. Cathcart and Larry A. Samovar (Dubuque, IA: Wm. C. Brown, 1992), 159.

[13]Rodney W. Napier and Matti K. Gershenfeld, *Groups: Theory and Experience*, 7th ed. (Boston: Houghton Mifflin, 2004), 337.

[14]Donald G. Ellis and B. Aubrey Fisher, *Small Group Decision Making* (New York: McGraw-Hill, 1994), 142

[15]John R. Katzenbach and Douglas K. Smith, *The Discipline of Teams* (New York: Wiley, 2001), 112.

[16]Ibid., 113.

[17]Adapted from Karyn C. Rybacki and Donald J. Rybacki, *Advocacy and Opposition: An Introduction to Argumentation*, 4th ed. (Boston: Allyn & Bacon, 2000), 11–15.

[18]Randy Hirokawa and Roger Pace, "A Descriptive Investigation of the Possible Communication-Based Reasons for Effective and Ineffective Group Decision Making," *Communication Monographs* 50 (1983): 379.

[19]Suzanne Scott and Reginald Bruce "Decision Making Style: The Development of a New Measure," *Educational and Psychological Measurements* 55 (1995): 818–831.

[20]http://www.ucd.ie/careers/cms/decision/student_skills_decision_styleex.html; http://www.acu.edu/campusoffices/ocad/students/exploration/assess/decision.html, updated August 24, 2005. Also see Suzanne Scott and Reginald Bruce, "Decision Making Style: The Development of a New Measure," *Educational and Psychological Measurement* 55 (1995): 818–831.

[21]Alex F. Osborn, *Applied Imagination*, rev. ed. (New York: Scribner, 1957).

[22]3M Meeting Management Team with Jeannine Drew, *Mastering Meetings: Discovering the Hidden Potential of Effective Business Meetings* (New York: McGraw-Hill, 1994), 59.

[23]Tom Kelley with Jonathan Littman, *The Art of Innovation: Lessons in Creativity from IDEO, America's Leading Design Firm* (New York: Currency, 2001), 55.

[24]Based, in part, on Tom Kelley with Jonathan Littman, *The Art of Innovation: Lessons in Creativity from IDEO, America's Leading Design Firm* (New York:

Currency, 2001), 56–59. Also see Rodney W. Napier and Matti K. Gershenfeld, *Groups: Theory and Experience*, 7th ed. (Boston: Houghton Mifflin, 2004), 321.

[25]Kelley and Littman, 64–66.

[26]Isa N. Engleberg and Dianna R. Wynn, *Working in Groups: Communication Principles and Strategies*, 5th ed. (Boston: Pearson/Allyn & Bacon, 2010), 256–258.

[27]See Kenneth E. Andersen, "Developments in Communication Ethics: The Ethics Commission, Code of Professional Responsibilities, and Credo for Ethical Communication," *Journal of the Association for Communication Administration* 29 (2000): 131–144. The Credo for Ethical Communication is also posted on the NCA Website (http://www.natcom.org).

[28]Deborah L. Duarte and Nancy Tennant Snyder, *Mastering Virtual Teams*, 3rd ed. (San Francisco: Jossey-Bass, 2006), 171.

[29]Ibid., 33–34, 168.

[30]John R. Katzenbach and Douglas K. Smith, *The Discipline of Teams* (New York: Wiley, 2001), 167.

[31]Rodney W. Napier and Matti K. Gershenfeld, *Groups: Theory and Experience*, 7th ed. (Boston: Houghton Mifflin, 2004), 327.

[32]John Dewey, *How We Think* (Boston: Heath, 1910).

[33]Based on Kathryn Sue Young, Julia T. Wood, Gerald M. Phillips, and Douglas J. Pedersen, *Group Discussion: A Practical Guide to Participation and Leadership*, 3rd ed. (Prospect Heights, IL: Waveland Press, 2001), 8–9. The authors present six steps in their standard-agenda model by combining solution suggestions and solution selection into one step. We have divided this step into separate functions given that the solution suggestion step may require creative thinking and brainstorming. Given that the solution evaluation and selection step may be the most difficult and controversial, it deserves a separate focus as well as different strategies and skills.

[34]Edward De Bono, *New Thinking for the New Millennium* (New York: Viking, 1999) quoted in Darrell Man, "Analysis Paralysis: When Root Cause Analysis Isn't the Way," *The TRIZ-Journal*, 2006, http://www.triz-journal.com.

[35]"Avoid Analysis Paralysis," Infusion Insight, http://www.infusionsoft.com/articles/65-infusion-insight/615-avoid-analysis-paralysis.

[36]Edward D. McDonald, "Chaos or Communication: Technical Barriers to Effective Meetings," in *Innovative Meeting Management*, ed. Richard A. Swanson and Bonnie Ogram Knapp (Austin, TX: Minnesota Mining and Manufacturing, 1991), 177.

[37]Marshall Scott Poole, "Procedures for Managing Meetings: Social and Technological Innovation," in *Innovative Meeting Management*, ed. Richard A. Swanson and Bonnie Ogram Knapp (Austin, TX: Minnesota Mining and Manufacturing, 1991), 53.

[38]Dave Wiggins, "How to Have a Successful Meeting," *Journal of Environmental Health* 60 (1998): 1, http://db.texshare.edu/ovidweb/ovidweb.cgi.

[39]Karen Anderson, *Making Meetings Work: How to Plan and Conduct Effective Meetings* (West Des Moines, IA: American Media Publishing, 1997), 17.

[40]Sharon M. Lippincott, *Meetings: Do's, Don'ts, and Donuts* (Pittsburgh, PA: Lighthouse Point Press, 1994), 172.

[41]Isa N. Engleberg and Dianna R. Wynn, *Working in Groups: Communication Principles and Strategies*, 5th ed. (Boston: Pearson/Allyn & Bacon, 2010), 299–300; Sharon M. Lippincott, *Meetings: Do's, Don'ts, and Donuts* (Pittsburgh, PA: Lighthouse Point Press, 1994), 89–90.

[42]3M Meeting Management Team with Jeannine Drew, *Mastering Meetings: Discovering the Hidden Potential of Effective Business Meetings* (New York: McGraw-Hill, 1994), 78.

Chapter 12

[1]Excerpts from Dr. Randy Pausch's Last Lecture: "Really Achieving Your Childhood Dreams" *The Oncologist* 12.11 (November 2007), 1374–1375, http://theoncologist.alphamedpress.org/cgi/content/full/12/11/1374. There are hundreds of Websites devoted to Pausch and his last lecture. Search terms: *Pausch last lecture*.

[2]Ibid.

[3]Isa N. Engleberg and John A. Daly, *Presentations in Everyday Life*, 3rd ed. (Boston: Pearson/Allyn & Bacon, 2009), 3 and Note 5 on p. 21.

[4]Ibid.

[5]Ibid., 12–13.

[6]Milton Rokeach, *The Nature of Human Values* (New York: Free Press, 1973), 3.

[7]Rushworth M. Kidder, "Trust: A Primer on Current Thinking," Institute for Global Ethics, 7, http://www.globalethics.org/files/wp_trust_1222960968.pdf/21/.

[8]Gene Zelazny, *Say It with Presentations*, Revised (New York: McGraw-Hill, 2006), 4–6.

[9]Ibid., 107.

[10]Isa N. Engleberg and John A. Daly, *Presentations in Everyday Life*, 3rd ed. (Boston: Pearson/Allyn & Bacon, 2009), 126.

[11]*The American Heritage Dictionary of the English Language*, 4th ed. (Boston: Houghton Mifflin, 2000), 427.

[12]Malcolm Kushner, *Successful Presentations for Dummies* (Foster City, CA: IDG Books Worldwide, 1997), 21.

[13]The earliest and most respected source describing the components of a speaker's credibility is Aristotle's *Rhetoric*, trans. Lane Cooper (New York: Appleton-Century-Crofts, 1932), 92. Aristotle identified "intelligence, character, and good will" as "three things that gain our belief." Aristotle's observations have been verified and expanded. In addition to those qualities identified by Aristotle, researchers have added variables such as objectivity, trustworthiness, co-orientation, dynamism, composure, likability, and extroversion. Research has consolidated these qualities into three well-accepted attributes: competence, character, and dynamism. We have used the term *charisma* in place of dynamism.

[14]Lane Cooper, *The Rhetoric of Aristotle* (New York: Appleton-Century-Crofts, 1932), 7.

[15]Ibid., 8, 9.

[16]Lester Thonssen and A. Craig Baird, *Speech Criticism: The Development of Standards for Rhetorical Appraisal* (New York: The Ronald Press, 1948).

[17]James R. Andrews, Michael C. Leff, and Robert Terrill, *Reading Rhetorical Texts: An Introduction to Criticism* (Boston: Houghton Mifflin, 1998), 59.

[18]Malcolm Kushner, *Successful Presentations for Dummies* (Foster City, CA: IDG Books Worldwide, 1997), 21.

[19]*The American Heritage Dictionary of the English Language*, 4th ed. (Boston: Houghton Mifflin, 2000), 611.

[20]Isa N. Engleberg and John A. Daly, *Presentations in Everyday Life*, 3rd ed. (Boston: Pearson/Allyn & Bacon, 2009), 193; Isa N. Engleberg and Ann Raimes, *Pocket Keys for Speakers* (Boston: Houghton Mifflin, 2004), 21–22.

[21]Based on material in Isa N. Engleberg and Ann Raimes, *Pocket Keys for Speakers* (Boston: Houghton Mifflin, 2004), 42–46.

[22]Peggy Noonan, *Simply Speaking* (New York: HarperCollins, 1998), x.

[23]Granville N. Toogood, *The Articulate Executive* (New York: McGraw-Hill, 1996), 93.

[24]Ibid., 94–95.

Chapter 13

[1]Camille Dunlap's presentation "Asleep at the Wheel," in Isa N. Engleberg and John A. Daly, *Presentations in Everyday Life*, 3rd ed. (Boston: Pearson/Allyn & Bacon, 2009), 254–256. Ms. Dunlap was an honors student at Prince George's Community College.

[2]One of the best overviews of Cicero's contributions to rhetoric appears in Lester Thonssen and A. Craig Baird, *Speech Criticism: The Development of Standards for Rhetorical Appraisal*. (New York: The Ronald Press, 1948), 78–91. Also see James L. Golden, Goodwin F. Berquist, and William E. Coleman, *The Rhetoric of Western Thought*, 4th ed. (Dubuque, IA: Kendall/Hunt, 1989).

[3]Clive Thompson, "Community Urinalysis," *The New York Times Magazine* (December 8, 2007): 62.

[4]Richard Trumka, Remarks at the USW (United Steel Workers) Convention, July 1, 2008, http://www.usw.org/medi_center/speeches_interviews?id=0003.

[5]http://www.youtube.com/watch?v=7QIGJTHdH50.

[6]Carole Blair, "Civil Rights/Civil Sites: '. . . Until Justice Rolls Down Like Waters,'" *The Carroll C. Arnold Distinguished Lecture*, National Communication Association Convention, November 2006 (Boston: Pearson/Allyn & Bacon, 2008), 2.

[7]See www.miami.com/mld/miamiherald/sports/columnists/dan_le_batard/9745974.htm. Posted September 24, 2004.

[8]"Hollywood's Blurb Search Reaches the Blogosphere," *New York Times*, http://www.nytimes.com/2009/06/07/weekinreview/07barnes.html?scp=5&sq=+words+out+of+context&st=nyt.

[9]http://www.statemaster.com/encyclopedia/Contextomy; See original review, Owen Gleiberman, (1995, September 22). "Se7en" (film review). *Entertainment Weekly*, p. 45.

[10]"Quoting Out of Context," *Source Watch*, http://www.sourcewatch.org/index.php?title=Quoting_out_of_context, Modified March 4, 2004.

[11]Matthew S. McGlone, "Contextomy: The Art of Quoting Out of Context," *Media Culture and Society*, 27 (2005), 519.

[12]"To Pluck a Rooted Sorrow," *Newsweek*, April 27, 2009, as quoted in Richard Nordquist, "What Is an Analogy," *About.com* (2009), http://grammar.about.com/od/rhetoricstyle/f/qanalogy07.htm.

[13]Daphne Duval Harrison, *Black Pearls: Blues Queens of the 1920s* (New Brunswick, NJ: Rutgers University Press, 1988).

[14]Stella Ting-Toomey and Leeva C. Chung, *Understanding Intercultural Communication* (Los Angeles: Roxbury, 2005), 189–190.

[15]Vivian Hobbs, Commencement Address at Prince George's Community College, Largo, Maryland, 1991. See full manuscript in Isa N. Engleberg, *The Principles of Public Presentations* (New York: HarperCollins, 1994), 339–341.

[16]Leonard J. Shedletsky and Joan E. Aitken, *Human Communication on the Internet* (Boston: Pearson/Allyn & Bacon, 2004), 100–101.

[17]See http://urbanlegends.about.com/od/reference/a/2008_top-ten.htm which is published by *The New York Times* company as well as http://factcheck.org/ published by the Annenberg Public Policy Center.

[18]"Cocaine-Cola," http://www.snopes.com/cokelore/cocaine.asp.

[19]Michael M. Kepper with Robert E. Gunther, *I'd Rather Die Than Give a Speech* (Burr Ridge, IL: Irwin, 1994), 6.

[20]Some of the best research on the value of organizing a presentation was conducted in the 1960s and '70s. See Ernest C. Thompson, "An Experimental Investigation of the Relative Effectiveness of Organizational Structure in Oral Communication," *Southern Speech Journal* 26 (1960): 59–69; Ernest C. Thompson, "Some Effects of Message Structure on Listeners' Comprehension," *Speech Monographs* 34 (1967): 51–57; James C. McCroskey and R. Samuel Mehrley, "The Effects of Disorganization and Nonfluency on Attitude Change and Source Credibility," *Communication Monographs* 36 (1969): 13–21; Arlee Johnson, "A Preliminary Investigation of the Relationship between Organization and Listener Comprehension," *Central States Speech Journal* 21 (1970): 104–107; and Christopher Spicer and Ronald E. Bassett, "The Effect of Organization on Learning from an Informative Message," *Southern Speech Communication Journal* 41 (1976): 290–299.

[21]Tony Buzon, *Use Both Sides of Your Brain*, 3rd ed. (New York: Plume, 1989).

[22]An annotated manuscript of Julie Borchard's "The Sound of Muzak" speech is available in Isa N. Engleberg and John A. Daly, *Presentations in Everyday Life*, 3rd ed. (Boston: Pearson/Allyn & Bacon, 2009), 251–253. Ms. Borchard was a student and forensics team member at Prince George's Community College.

[23]The Speech Framer was developed by Isa N. Engleberg as an alternative or a supplement to outlining. See Isa N. Engleberg and John A. Daly, *Presentations in Everyday Life*, 3rd ed. (Boston: Pearson/Allyn & Bacon, 2009), 217–218. © Isa N. Engleberg, 2003.

[24]Isa N. Engleberg and John A. Daly, *Presentations in Everyday Life*, 3rd ed. (Boston: Pearson/Allyn & Bacon, 2009), 199–207.

[25]Lee Towe, *Why Didn't I Think of That? Creativity in the Workplace* (West Des Moines, IA: American Media, 1966), 7.

[26]Ibid., 9–11.

[27]Isa N. Engleberg and John A. Daly, *Presentations in Everyday Life*, 3rd ed. (Boston: Pearson/Allyn & Bacon, 2009), 216.

[28]Ibid., 226–229.

[29]Ibid., 238–251.

[30]Bob Herbert, "Gun Violence Is Becoming an Epidemic," in *Guns and Violence: Current Controversies*, ed. Henry H. Kim (San Diego, CA: Greenhaven Press, 1999), 20.

[31]Arne Duncan, National Science Teachers Association Conference, March 20, 2009. http://www.ed.gov/print/news/speeches/2009/03/03202009.html.

[32]Samuel E. Wood, Ellen Green Wood, and Denise Boyd, *The World of Psychology*, 6th ed. (Boston: Pearson/Allyn & Bacon, 2008), 204.

[33]Ibid., 204–205.

[34]Quoted in Isa N. Engleberg, *The Principles of Public Presentation* (New York: HarperCollins, 1994), 160.

[35]Ann Quindlen, "The Failed Experiment," *Newsweek* (June 26, 2006), 64.

[36]For the complete text of King's "I Have a Dream" speech plus commentary, see James R. Andrews and David Zarefsky, *Contemporary American Voices: Significant Speech in American History, 1945–Present* (New York: Longman, 1992), 78–81.

[37]Isa N. Engleberg and John A. Daly, *Presentations in Everyday Life*, 3rd ed. (Boston: Pearson/Allyn & Bacon, 2009), 251–256.

[38]Bono, Commencement Speech at the University of Pennsylvania, 2004. Copyright © Creative Video Souvenir Productions, Inc.

[39]See Chapter 16 in this book, "Presentations: Speaking to Persuade," for the complete text and commentary on this speech. Source: Marge Anderson, "Looking through Our Window: The Value of Indian Culture," *Vital Speeches of the Day* 65 (1999): 633–634.

[40]Maya Angelou. Remarks at the Funeral Service for Coretta Scott King in Atlanta, Georgia, delivered February 7, 2006, http://www.americanrhetoric.com/speeches/mayaangeloueulogyforcorettaking.htm.

[41]Robert M. Franklin, "The Soul of Morehouse and the Future of the Mystique," President's Town Meeting, Morehouse College, April 21, 2009, http://themaroontiger.com/attachments/329_The%20Soul%20of%20Morehouse%20and%20the%20Future%20of%20the%20Mystique%20-%20abridged.pdf.

Chapter 14

[1]Ariel Sabar, "How the Candidates' Speaking Styles Play," *The Christian Science Monitor*, July 11, 2008, http://www.csmonitor.com/2008/0711/p01s01-uspo.html. For more examples, see Kent Garber, "Rhetoric and Speaking Style Affect the Clinton-Obama Race," March 5, 2008, http://www.usnews.com/articles/news/campaign-2008/2008/03/25/rhetoric-and-speaking-style-affect-the-clinton-obama-race.html.

[2]Lani Arredondo, *The McGraw-Hill 36-Hour Course: Business Presentations* (New York: McGraw-Hill, 1994), 147.

[3]Jerry Della Femina, quoted in *Creative Strategy in Advertising*, 2nd ed., ed. A. Jerome Jewler (Belmont, CA: Wadsworth, 1985), 41.

[4]Isa Engleberg and Ann Raimes, *Pocket Keys for Speakers* (Boston: Houghton Mifflin, 2004), 191–193.

[5]John W. Bowers, "Some Correlates of Language Intensity," *Quarterly Journal of Speech* 50 (1964): 415–420.

[6]Max Atkinson, *Lend Me Your Ears* (New York: Oxford, 2005), 221.

[7]Marcel Danesi and Paul Perron, *Analyzing Cultures: An Introduction and Handbook* (Bloomington, IN: Indiana University Press, 1999), 174.

[8]William O'Grady et al., *Contemporary Linguistics*, 5th ed. (Boston: Bedford/St. Martin's, 2005), 255.

[9]Isa Engleberg and Ann Raimes, *Pocket Keys for Speakers* (Boston: Houghton Mifflin, 2004), 94–95.

[10]Matthew McGlone, *Forbes* (October 5, 1998): 45.

[11]Kathleen Hall Jamieson, *Eloquence in an Electronic Age: The Transformation of Political Speechmaking* (New York: Oxford University Press, 1988), 81, 84.

[12]Susan D. Miller, *Be Heard the First Time: A Woman's Guide to Powerful Speaking* (Herndon, VA: Capital Books, 2006), 100.

[13]Ty Ford, *Ty Ford's Audio Bootcamp Field Guide* (Baltimore: Technique, Inc., 2004), 19.

[14]Stella Ting-Toomey and Leeva C. Chung, *Understanding Intercultural Communication* (Los Angeles: Roxbury, 2005), 175. See also Pamela J. Cooper, Carolyn Calloway-Thomas, and Cheri J. Simonds, *Intercultural Communication: A Text with Readings* (Boston: Pearson/Allyn & Bacon, 2007), 109–111.

[15]Stella Ting-Toomey and Leeva C. Chung, *Understanding Intercultural Communication* (Los Angeles: Roxbury, 2005), 176

[16]Ibid., 179–180

[17]Steven A. Beebe, "Eye Contact: A Nonverbal Determinant of Speaker Credibility," *The Speech Teacher* 23 (1974): 21–25.

[18]Mark L. Knapp and Judith A. Hall, *Nonverbal Communication in Human Interaction*, 5th ed. (Belmont, CA: Wadsworth/Thomson Learning, 2006), 295.

[19]Peggy Noonan, *Simply Speaking: How to Communicate Your Ideas with Style, Substance, and Clarity* (New York: HarperCollins, 1998), 206.

[20]See Ruth Clark, "Six Principles of Effective e-Learning: What Works and Why," *The e-Learning Developers' Journal* (September 10, 2002), http://www.e-LearningGuild.com; and Jennifer Wiley, "Cognitive Implications of Visually Rich Media: Images and Imagination," paper supported by grants from the Paul G. Allen Virtual Education Foundation and the Office of Naval Research, Cognitive and Neural Science and Technology Program.

[21]http://www.vancouver.wsu.edu/fac/kendrick/loquent/eloquentjw.htm.

[22]Cyndi Maxey and Kevin E. O'Connor, *Present Like a Pro* (New York: St. Martin's Griffin, 2006), 49.

[23]Peggy Noonan, *Simply Speaking: How to Communicate Your Ideas with Style, Substance, and Clarity* (New York: HarperCollins, 1998), 9.

[24]Thomas K. Mira, *Speak Smart: The Art of Public Speaking* (New York: Random House, 1997), 91.

Chapter 15

[1]James M. Lang, "Beyond Lecturing," *The Chronicle of Higher Education*, September 9, 2006, C4.

[2]Ibid.

[3]Wilbert J. McKeachie, *Teaching Tips: Strategies, Research, and Theory for College and University Teachers*, 10th ed. (Boston: Houghton Mifflin, 1999), 70.

[4]Ibid., 69–84.

[5]Sections of Chapters 12 through 16 are based on Isa N. Engleberg and John A. Daly, *Presentations in Everyday Life*, 3rd ed. (Boston: Pearson/Allyn & Bacon, 2009); and Isa N. Engleberg and Ann Raimes, *Pocket Keys for Speakers* (Boston: Houghton Mifflin, 2004).

[6]This section is based on the research and theory-building of Katherine E. Rowan, professor of communication at George Mason University. See Katherine E. Rowan, "Informing and Explaining Skills: Theory and Research on Informative Communication," in *Handbook of Communication and Social Interaction Skills*, ed. John O. Greene and Brant R. Burleson (Mahwah, NJ: Lawrence Erlbaum Associates, 2003), 403–438; and Katherine E. Rowan, "A New Pedagogy for Explanatory Public Speaking: Why Arrangement Should Not Substitute for Invention," *Communication Education* 44 (1995): 236–250.

[7]Katherine E. Rowan, "A New Pedagogy for Explanatory Public Speaking: Why Arrangement Should Not Substitute for Invention," Communication Education 44 (1995): 242; Katherine E. Rowan, "Informing and Explaining Skills: Theory and Research on Informative Communication," in *Handbook of Communication and Social Interaction Skills*, ed. John O. Greene and Brant R. Burleson (Mahwah, NJ: Lawrence Erlbaum Associates, 2003), 411.

[8]Katherine E. Rowan, "A New Pedagogy for Explanatory Public Speaking: Why Arrangement Should Not Substitute for Invention," *Communication Education* 44 (1995): 241.

[9]*The American Heritage Dictionary of the English Language* (Boston: Houghton Mifflin, 2000), 1433–1434.

[10]Al Tompkins, "Bill Mays: the Death of a TV Pitchman," *PoynterOnline*, June 29, 2009, http://www.poynter.org/column.asp?id=2&aid=165905.

[11]http://www.natcom.org/index.asp?bid=510.

[12]Isa N. Engleberg and John A. Daly, *Presentations in Everyday Life*, 3rd ed. (Boston: Pearson/Allyn & Bacon, 2009), 3–4.

[13]Rives Collins and Pamela J. Cooper, *The Power of Story: Teaching through Storytelling*, 2nd ed. (Boston: Allyn & Bacon, 1997), 2.

[14]Walter R. Fisher, *Human Communication as Narration: Toward a Philosophy of Reason, Value, and Action* (Columbia, SC: University of South Carolina Press, 1987), 64, 65.

[15]Alan M. Perlman, *Writing Great Speeches: Professional Techniques You Can Use* (Boston: Allyn & Bacon, 1998), 52.

[16]Joanna Slan, *Using Stories and Humor: Grab Your Audience* (Boston: Allyn & Bacon, 1998), 5–6.

[17]Malcolm Kushner, *Successful Presentations for Dummies* (Foster City, CA: IDG Books, 1997), 79.

[18]Rives Collins and Pamela J. Cooper, *The Power of Story: Teaching through Storytelling*, 2nd ed. (Boston: Allyn & Bacon, 1997), 24–28. See also Isa N. Engleberg and John A. Daly, *Presentations in Everyday Life: Strategies for Effective Speaking*, 3rd ed. (Boston: Pearson/Allyn & Bacon, 2009), 292–294.

[19]Walter R. Fisher, *Human Communication as Narration: Toward a Philosophy of Reason, Value, and Action* (Columbia, SC: University of South Carolina Press, 1987), 24.

[20]Ibid., 68.

[21]Candace Spigelman, "Argument and Evidence in the Case of the Personal," *College English* 64. 1 (2001): 80–81.

[22]Walter Fisher, "Narrative as Human Communication Paradigm," in *Contemporary Rhetorical Theory*, ed. John Louis Lucaites, Celeste Michelle Condit, and Sally Caudill (New York: The Guilford, 1999), 272.

[23]Based on Joanna Slan, *Using Stories and Humor* (Boston: Allyn & Bacon, 1998), 89–95, 116. See also Isa N. Engleberg and John A. Daly, *Presentations in Everyday Life*, 3rd ed. (Boston: Pearson/Allyn & Bacon, 2009), 296–298.

[24]Based on Paul Galdone, *The Three Little Pigs* (New York: Houghton Mifflin, 1970).

[25]William Hendricks et al., *Secrets of Power Presentations* (Franklin Lakes, NJ: Career Press, 1996), 79.

[26]Gene Perret, *Using Humor for Effective Business Speaking* (New York: Sterling, 1989), 19–26.

[27]Malcolm Kushner, *Successful Presentations for Dummies* (Foster City, CA: IDG Books, 1997), 350.

[28]Summary of tips for using humor from Isa N. Engleberg and Dianna R. Wynn, *The Challenge of Communicating: Guiding Principles and Practices* (Pearson/Allyn & Bacon, 2008), 408 and Joanna Slan, *Using Stories and Humor: Grab Your Audience* (Boston: Allyn & Bacon, 1998), 170–172.

[29]Isa N. Engleberg and John A. Daly, *Presentations in Everyday Life*, 3rd ed. (Boston: Pearson/Allyn & Bacon, 2009), 110–111.

[30]Since developing this presentation, *CliffsNotes* has gone through several changes and traumas. In 1998, Cliff Hillegass sold Cliff'sNotes, Inc., to John Wiley & Sons, Inc. In May 2001, Mr. Hillegass passed away at the age of 83. In 2007, Cliff'sNotes.com was relaunched with an updated design and notes for school subjects such as math, science, writing, foreign languages, history, and government. "A Brief History of CliffsNotes," http://www.cliffsnotes.com/WileyCDA/Section/A-Brief-History.id-305430.html.

[31]Permission granted by John Sullivan.

Chapter 16

[1]Jessica Reaves, "Just Say No to DARE," *Time Magazine*, February 15, 2001, http://www.time.com/time/nation/article/0,8599,99564,00.html; Siobhan Gorman, "Prevention Takes a Different Tack," *National Journal*, August 18, 2001, http://www.erowid.org/general/mentions/mentions_2001-08_national_journal_prevention.txt; "Does 'Just Say No' Work?" Drug Rehab California 2009, http://www.drug-rehabcalifornia.com/ca-drug-rehab/does-just-say-no-work.html; David J. Hanson, "'Just Say No' Fails," http://www2.potsdam.edu/hansondj/youthissues/1074803132.html.

[2]"Idaho to Get Increased Dose of Truth Youth-Smoking Prevention Campaign," American Legacy Foundation, February 8, 2007, http://www.americanlegacy.org; "Truth or Consequences News Coverage," American Legacy Foundation, February 13, 2007, http://www.americanlegacy.org/2734.aspx; "Increased Dose of Truth Youth-Smoking Prevention Campaign Coming to a Town Near You," *Medical News Today*, January 26, 2007, http://www.medicalnewstoday.com.

[3]See "Idaho to Get Increased Dose of Truth Youth-Smoking Prevention Campaign," American Legacy Foundation, February 8, 2007, http://www.americanlegacy.org for journal references.

[4]Sections of this chapter are based on Isa N. Engleberg and John A. Daly, *Presentations in Everyday Life*, 3rd ed. (Boston: Pearson/Allyn & Bacon, 2009), Chapter 5; and Isa N. Engleberg and Ann Raimes, *Pocket Keys for Speakers* (Boston: Houghton Mifflin, 2004), Part 8: Sections 25 and 26.

[5]William J. McGuire, "Inducing Resistance to Persuasion: Some Contemporary Approaches," in *Advances in Experimental Psychology*, ed. Leonard Berkowitz (New York: Academic Press, 1964), 192–229.

[6]Robert H. Gass and John S. Seiter, *Persuasion, Social Influence, and Compliance Gaining*, 3rd ed. (Boston: Allyn & Bacon, 2007), 198.

[7]Jack W. Brehm, *A Theory of Psychological Reactance* (New York: Academic Press, 1966). Also see Michael Burgoon et al., "Revisiting the Theory of Psychological Reactance," in *The Persuasion Handbook: Development in Theory and Practice*, ed. James Price Dillard and Michael Pfau (Thousand Oaks, CA: Sage, 2002), 213–232; and James Price Dillard and Linda J. Marshall, "Persuasion as a Social Skill," in *Handbook of Communication and Social Interaction Skills*, ed. John O. Greene and Brant R. Burleson (Mahwah, NJ: Lawrence Erlbaum, 2003), 500–501.

[8]Don Levine, "Booze Barriers," *Boulder Weekly*, September 7, 2000, http://www.boulderweekly.com/archive/090700/coverstory.html, 4.

[9]Ibid.

[10]James Price Dillard and Linda J. Marshall, "Persuasion as a Social Skill," in *Handbook of Communication and Social Interaction Skills*, ed. John O. Greene and Brant R. Burleson (Mahwah, NJ: Lawrence Erlbaum, 2003), 501.

[11]Charles U. Larson, *Persuasion: Reception and Responsibility*, 11th ed. (Belmont, CA: Thomson/Wadsworth, 2007), 185.

[12]April Fulton, "46 Million Uninsured: A Look Behind the Number," National Public Radio, August 21, 2009, http://www.npr.org/templates/story/story.php?storyId=111651742&ps=cprs; Salynn Boyles, "Texas Has Highest Rate of Uninsured," *WebMd Health News*, October 9, 2008, http://www.medicinenet.com/script/main/art.asp?articlekey=93331; Center on Budget and Policy Priorities, "The Number of Uninsured Americans Is at an All-Time High," August 29, 2008, http://www.cbpp.org/cms/index.cfm?fa=view&id=628.

[13]Charles U. Larson, *Persuasion: Reception and Responsibility*, 11th ed. (Belmont, CA: Thomson/Wadsworth, 2007), 58.

[14]Authors' files.

[15]Based on Patrick J. Hurley, *A Concise Introduction to Logic*, 8th ed. (Belmont, CA: Wadsworth Thomson Learning, 2003), 172–174.

[16]Richard M. Perloff, *The Dynamics of Persuasion: Communication and Attitudes in the 21st Century*, 2nd ed. (Mahwah, NJ: Lawrence Erlbaum, 2008), 266.

[17]Ibid., 280.

[18]Aristotle, *Rhetoric*, in *The Complete Works of Aristotle: The Revised Oxford Translation*, vol. 2, ed. Jonathan Barnes (Princeton, NJ: Princeton University Press, 1995), 2155.

[19]Michael Osborn, Suzanne Osborn, and Randall Osborn, *Public Speaking*, 8th ed. (Boston: Pearson Allyn & Bacon, 2009), 380.

[20]Ibid., 376.

[21]Richard M. Perloff, *The Dynamics of Persuasion: Communication and Attitudes in the 21st Century*, 2nd ed. (Mahwah, NJ: Lawrence Erlbaum, 2008), 277–280.

[22]Mike Allen and Raymond W. Preiss, "Comparing the Persuasiveness of Narrative and Statistical Evidence Using Meta-Analysis," *Communication Research Reports* 14 (1997): 125–131.

[23]Lisa L. Massi Lindsey and Kimo Ah Yun, "Examining the Persuasive Effects of Statistical Messages: A Test of Mediating Relationships," *Communication Studies* 54 (2003): 306–321.

[24]Michael Gerson, "Gates's Field of Dreams," *The Washington Post*, October 16, 2009, A23; Robert B. Reich, "The Talk of the Town," *The New Yorker*, November 30, 1998, 32.

[25]See Alexander Todorov, Shelley Chaiken, and Marlone D. Henderson, "The Heuristic-Systematic Model of Social Information Processing," in *The Persuasion Handbook: Developments in Theory and Practice*, ed. James Price Dillard and Michael Pfau (Thousand Oaks, CA: Sage, 2002), 195–211; James Price Dillard and Linda J. Marshall, "Persuasion as a Social Skill," in *Handbook of Communication and Social Interaction Skills*, ed. John. O. Green and Brant R. Burleson (Mahwah, NJ: Lawrence Erlbaum, 2003), 494–495.

[26]Alan H. Monroe, *Principles and Types of Speech* (Chicago: Scott, Foresman, 1935).

[27]Based on Nicholas D. Kristof and Sheryl WuDunn, "The Women's Crusade," *The New York Times Magazine*, August 23, 2009, 28–39. Kristof is an international journalist and advocate for women's rights in poor countries.

[28]Sharon Shavitt and Michelle R. Nelson, "The Role of Attitude Functions in Persuasion and Social Judgment," in *The Persuasion Handbook: Developments in Theory and Practice*, ed. James Price Dillard and Michael Pfau (Thousand Oaks, CA: Sage, 2002), 150.

[29]Ibid.

[30]This presentation appeared in *Vital Speeches of the Day* 65 (August 1, 1999): 633–634.

credits

TEXT CREDITS

Portions of this book (figures and text) are taken from *The Challenge of Communicating* by Isa Engleberg and Dianna Wynn. © 2008 by Pearson Education, Inc. Reproduced by permission of Pearson Education, Inc.

Chapter 1

p. 17: Steven Covey, *The 7 Habits of Highly Effective People*, New York: Simon and Schuster, 1989.

p. 18: From the National Communication Association Credo for Ethical Communication, www.natcom.org. Reprinted by permission.

p. 22: "Why Communication?" from *Communication Currents*, Volume 3, Issue 4, August 2008. By permission of the National Communication Association, www. natcom.org.

Chapter 2

p. 33: From Rosenberg "Self Esteem Scale," Rosenberg, Morris. 1989. *Society and the Adolescent Self-Image*. Revised edition. Middletown, CT: Wesleyan University Press. By permission.

pp. 37–38: Virginia P. Richmond and James C. McCroskey, *Communication: Apprehension, Avoidance, and Effectiveness*, 5th ed. © 1998 by Pearson Education, Inc. Reproduced by permission of Pearson Education, Inc.

p. 40: Virginia P. Richmond and James C. McCroskey, *Communication: Apprehension, Avoidance, and Effectiveness*, 5th ed. © 1998 by Pearson Education, Inc. Reproduced by permission of Pearson Education, Inc.

p. 41: Virginia P. Richmond and James C. McCroskey, *Communication: Apprehension, Avoidance, and Effectiveness*, 5th ed., p. 133. © 1998 by Pearson Education, Inc. Reproduced by permission of Pearson Education, Inc.

Chapter 3

p. 47: Myron Lustig and Jolene Koester, *Instructors Manual to Accompany Intercultural Competence*, 2nd ed. New York: HarperCollins, 1996.

p. 51: Rita Hardiman, "White Racial Identity Development in the United States," *Race, Ethnicity and Self: Identity in Multi-Cultural Perspective*, eds. Salett and Koslow. Washington, DC: National MultiCultural Institute, 1994.

p. 60: James Leigh, "Teaching Content and Skills for Intercultural Communication: A Mini Case Studies Approach," *The Edge: The E-Journal of Intercultural Relations* 2 (Winter 1999).

p. 61: The "Generalized Ethnocentrism (GENE) Scale" from James Neuliep, *Intercultural Communication: A Contextual Approach*, 4th ed., pp. 30–31. Copyright 2009 by Sage Publications Inc. Permission conveyed via Copyright Clearance Center.

p. 64: K. Kam et al.,"Culture and Deception: Moral Transgression or Social Necessity?" from *Communication Currents*, Volume 3, Issue 1, February 2008. By permission of the National Communication Association, www. natcom.org.

Chapter 4

p. 67: Don Gabor, *How to Start a Conversation and Make Friends*. New York: Fireside, 2001.

p. 69: Laura Ann Janusik, "Building Listening Theory: The Validation of the Conversational Listening Span," *Communication Studies* 58 (2007).

p. 73: From "Irritating Listening Habits," International Listening Association, www.listen.org.

p. 74: Andrew Wolvin and Carolyn Coakley, *Listening*, 5th ed. Madison, WI: Brown and Benchmark, 1996.

p. 75: Deborah Tannen, *You Just Don't Understand: Women and Men in Conversation*. New York: Ballantine Books, 1990.

p. 79: From William V. Haney, *Communication and Interpersonal Relationships: Texts and Cases*, 1992, pp. 231–232. By permission of the author.

p. 83: Roy M. Berko, Andrew D. Wolvin, and Darlyn R. Wolvin, *Communicating: A Social Career Focus*, 9th ed., "Student Listening Inventory," pp. 129–131, ©2004. Reproduced by permission of Pearson Education, Inc.

Chapter 5

p. 88: Geoffrey Finch, *Word of Mouth: A New Introduction to Language and Communication*. New York: Palgrave, 2003.

p. 98: Isa Engleberg and Ann Raimes, *Pocket Keys for Speakers*. Boston: Houghton Mifflin, 2004.

p. 103: Virginia P. Richmond and James C. McCroskey, *Communication: Apprehension, Avoidance, and Effectiveness*, 5th ed., p. 129. © 1998 by Pearson Education, Inc. Reproduced by permission of Pearson Education, Inc.

p. 106: Michael Kramer and Debbie Dougherty, "Language Convergence; Meaning Divergence" from *Communication Currents*, Volume 4, Issue 2, April 2009. By permission of the National Communication Association, www.natcom.org.

Chapter 6

p. 115: Virginia Richmond and James C. McCroskey, *Nonverbal Behavior in Interpersonal Relations*, 5th ed., Figure 8.1, "Touch Apprehension," p. 151, and excerpts from pp. 103, 199–212, and 224–233, © 2004. Reproduced by permission of Pearson Education, Inc.

p. 125: Adapted from Brian Spitzberg, "CSRS: The Conversational Rating Scale—An Instructional Assessment of Interpersonal Competence" in *NCA Diagnostic Series*, 2nd ed., 2007. By permission of the National Communication Association, www.natcom.org.

Chapter 7

p. 131: Isa Engleberg and Dianna Wynn, *Working in Groups*, 5th ed., pp. 82–85. © 2010. Reproduced by permission of Pearson Education, Inc.

p. 138: Isa Engleberg and Dianna Wynn, *Working in Groups*, 5th ed., p. 184. © 2010. Reproduced by permission of Pearson Education, Inc.

p. 139: Isa Engleberg and Dianna Wynn, *Working in Groups*, 5th ed., p. 216. © 2010. Reproduced by permission of Pearson Education, Inc.

p. 140: Ruth Anna Abigail and Dudley Cahn, *Managing Conflict through Communication*, 3rd ed., "Six Step Model of Conflict Resolution," pp. 97–104. © 2007. Reproduced by permission of Pearson Education, Inc.

p. 141: George H. Eifert et al., *ACT on Life Not on Anger.* Oakland, CA: New Harbinger, 2006

p. 142: William Wilmot and Joyce Hocker, *Interpersonal Conflict*, 7th ed. Boston, McGraw-Hill, 2007.

p. 143: William R. Cupach and Daniel J. Canary, *Competence in Interpersonal Conflict.* New York: McGraw-Hill, 1997.

Chapter 8

p. 152: Dialog from *Shrek.* DreamWorks, 2003.

p. 153: From J. Luft, *Group Processes: An Introduction to Group Dynamics*, 3rd ed. © 1984. Reprinted by permission of McGraw-Hill.

p. 154: Adapted from Jack R. Gibb, "Defensive Communication," *Journal of Communication* 11, 141–148. By permission of the publisher, Wiley-Blackwell.

p. 158: Mark C. Knapp and Anita Vangelisti, *Interpersonal Communication and Human Relationships*, 5th ed., Figure 2.1 "Staircase Model of Interaction Stages," p. 49, excerpt from pp. 48–49, © 2005. Reproduced by permission of Pearson Education, Inc.

p. 159: From Stephanie Coontz, "A Pop Quiz on Marriage" from *The New York Times* OP ED, February 19, 2006. Reprinted by permission of the author.

p. 160: Lynn H. Turner and Richard L. West, *Perspectives on Family Communication*, 2nd ed. Boston: McGraw-Hill, 2002.

p. 160: From Craig Hart et al., "Parenting Skills and Social-Communicative Competence in Childhood" in *Handbook of Communication and Social Interaction Skills*, eds. Greene and Burleson. Mahwah, NJ: Lawrence Erlbaum, 2003.

p. 165: Brant R. Burleson et al., "Guys Can't Say *That* to Guys: Four Experiments Assessing the Normative Motivation Account for Deficiencies in the Emotional Support Provided by Men," *Communication Monographs* 72 (2005).

p. 165: Susan M. Jones and John G. Wirtz, "How Does the Comforting Process Work? An Empirical Test of an Appraisal-Based Model of Comforting," *Human Communication Research* 32 (2006).

p. 170: Deborah Ballard-Reisch and Daniel Weigel, "10 Communication Strategies to Keep Marriages Strong" from *Communication Currents*, Volume 4, Issue 3, June 2009. By permission of the National Communication Association, www.natcom.org.

Chapter 9

p. 174: Daniel P. Modaff, Sue DeWine, and Jennifer Butler, *Organizational Communication: Foundation, Challenges, Misunderstandings*, pp. 197, 198, 206, and "Supervising Strategies for Promoting Trust and Openness," p. 207, and "Criteria for a Satisfying Coworker Relationship," pp. 236–237, © 2008. Reproduced by permission of Pearson Education, Inc.

p. 175: Hal Plotkin, *Dealing with Difficult People.* Boston, MA: Harvard Business School Press, 2005.

p. 175: Daniel P. Modaff and Sue DeWine, *Organizational Communication: Foundation, Challenges, Misunderstandings*, "Strains on Workplace Friendships and Professional Relationships," p. 202, © 2002. Reproduced by permission of Pearson Education, Inc.

p. 185: Screenshot reprinted with permission of Pearson PLC, from http://www.pearson.com/about-us/.

p. 192: Pamela Lutgen-Sandvik, "How Employees Fight Back Against Workplace Bullying" from *Communication Currents*, Volume 2, Issue 1, February 2007. By permission of the National Communication Association, www.natcom.org.

Chapter 10

p. 199: Isa Engleberg and Dianna Wynn, *Working in Groups*, 5th ed., p. 29. © 2010. Reproduced by permission of Pearson Education, Inc.

p. 209: Isa Engleberg and Dianna Wynn, *Working in Groups*, 5th ed., p. 115. © 2010. Reproduced by permission of Pearson Education, Inc.

Chapter 11

p. 220: I. Janis, *Groupthink*, 2nd ed., 1982, Wadsworth, a part of Cengage Learning, Inc., pp. 174–175.

p. 223: Karyn C. Rybacki and Donald J. Rybacki, *Advocacy and Opposition: An Introduction to Argumentation*, 4th ed. Boston: Allyn & Bacon, 2000.

p. 236: Lyn M. Van Swol, "Why Can't Groups Focus on New Information?" from *Communication Currents*, Volume 4, Issue 2, April 2009. By permission of the National Communication Association, www.natcom.org.

Chapter 12

p. 239: Randy Pausch, "Last Lecture: Really Achieving Your Childhood Dreams." From a speech given at Carnegie Mellon University, September 18, 2007.

p. 240: Isa Engleberg and John Daly, *Presentations in Everyday Life*, 3rd ed., p. 6. © 2009 by Pearson Education, Inc. Reproduced by permission of Pearson Education, Inc.

p. 246: Gene Zelazny, *Say It with Presentations*, Rev. and Exp. New York: McGraw-Hill, 2006.

p. 258: Reprinted with permission from John Daly and Isa Engleberg, "Coping with Stagefright: How to Turn Terror into Dynamic Speaking," *Harvard Management Communication Letter*, June 1999. Copyright © 1999 by Harvard Business Publishing; All rights reserved.

Chapter 13

p. 261: From Camille Dunlap, student presentation, "Asleep at the Wheel." By permission.

p. 263: Carole Blair, "Civil Rights/Civil Sites . . . Until Justice Rolls Down Like Waters." From a speech given at National Communication Association Convention, November 2006.

p. 264: Claudia Kalb, "To Pluck a Rooted Sorrow," *Newsweek*, April 27, 2009.

p. 268: Isa Engleberg and John Daly, *Presentations in Everyday Life*, 3rd ed., p. 201. © 2009 by Pearson Education, Inc. Reproduced by permission of Pearson Education, Inc.

p. 269: Isa Engleberg and John Daly, *Presentations in Everyday Life*, 3rd ed., p. 218. © 2003 by Isa Engleberg. Reproduced by permission of Pearson Education, Inc.

p. 273: Isa Engleberg and John Daly, *Presentations in Everyday Life*, 3rd ed., p. 208. © 2009 by Pearson Education, Inc. Reproduced by permission of Pearson Education, Inc.

p. 274: Regina Smith, student outline, "What's Fair is Fair." Reprinted by permission.

p. 280: Maya Angelou, from Remarks at the funeral service for Coretta Scott King, Feb. 7, 2006.

p. 280: Dr. Robert M. Franklin, speech to students at Morehouse College, April 21, 2009.

Chapter 14

p. 286: Isa Engleberg and John Daly, *Presentations in Everyday Life*, 3rd ed., p. 264. © 2009 by Pearson Education, Inc. Reproduced by permission of Pearson Education, Inc.

p. 287: Ann Raimes, *Keys for Writers: A Brief Handbook*, 3rd ed. Boston: Houghton Mifflin, 2003. Isa Engleberg and Ann Raimes, *Pocket Keys for Speakers*. Boston: Houghton Mifflin, 2004.

p. 288: Barack Obama, "A More Perfect Union." From a speech given in Philadelphia, PA, March 18, 2008.

p. 301: Bruce Springsteen, from Tribute to U2 during Hall of Fame Induction, March 17, 2005.

p. 301: Steve Jobs, from Stanford University Commencement Address, June 12, 2005.

p. 301: Barbara Charline Jordan, from "Who, Then, Will Speak for the Common Good?" Democratic Convention Keynote Address, 1976.

Chapter 15

p. 308: Isa Engleberg and John Daly, *Presentations in Everyday Life*, 3rd ed., p. 392. © 2009 by Pearson Education, Inc. Reproduced by permission of Pearson Education, Inc.

p. 311: Alan M. Perlman, *Writing Great Speeches: Professional Techniques You Can Use*. Boston: Allyn & Bacon, 1998.

p. 313: Isa Engleberg and John Daly, *Presentations in Everyday Life*, 3rd ed., p. 298. © 2009 by Pearson Education, Inc. Reproduced by permission of Pearson Education, Inc.

p. 318: John Sullivan, student presentation, "Cliff's Notes." Reprinted by permission.

Chapter 16

p. 332: Richard Perloff, *The Dynamics of Persuasion* 2nd ed. Mahwah, NJ: Lawrence Erlbaum, 2008.

p. 337: Marge Anderson, from "Looking Through Our Window: The Value of Indian Culture," a speech delivered to the First Friday Club of the Twin Cities, March 5, 1999. Reprinted by permission of Marge Anderson, Chief Executive of the Mille Lacs Band of Ojibwe.

p. 344: Steve Corman, "Another Campaign, More Mud" from *Communication Currents*, Volume 3, Issue 5, October 2008. By permission of the National Communication Association, www.natcom.org.

PHOTO CREDITS

Chapter 1

2–3: Antenna/Getty Images; **6:** © The New Yorker Collection 2009. From Cartoonbank.com. All Rights Reserved; **7:** *tl* Lara Jo Regan/Liaison/Getty Images; *tc* Ciaran Griffin/Lifesize/Getty Images; *tr* altrendo images/ Stockbyte/Getty Images; *bl* Allison Michael Orenstein/ Photodisc/Getty Images; *bc* Jason O. Watson/Alamy; *br* Somos/Veer/Jupiter Images; **8:** *t* Ryan McVay/Gettyimages; *c* Garry Wade/Getty Images; *b* Randy Faris/Corbis; **9:** *tl* David J. Green - lifestyle themes/Alamy; *tc* Twitter, Inc.; *b* John Giustina/Stone/Getty Images; **10:** DreamPictures/Gettyimages; **11:** AP Photo/Mark J. Terrill; **12:** *both* Walter Bieri/AP Photo; **13:** *t and inset* Stockbyte/ Jupiter Images; *bkgd* Stefano Cellai/age fotostock/Photolibrary; **14:** Creatas/ Photolibrary: **16:** *tc* Courtesy, Peace Corps; *l* Randy Faris/ Corbis; *bl* Chabruken/Taxi/Getty Images; *br* Monkey Business Images/Shutterstock; *r* Radius Images/ Alamy; **17:** Band Photo/uppa.co.uk/UPPA/Photoshot; **20:** Ciaran Griffin/Lifesize/Getty Images; **22:** Aidon/ Getty Images; **23:** Comstock Images/Jupiter Images.

Chapter 2

24–25: Bob King/Corbis Entertainment/Corbis; **26:** Peet Simard/Corbis; **27:** *t* Cavan Images/Photonica/Getty Images; *tc* B. Tanaka/Photographer's Choice/Getty Images; *bc* Photomondo/Photodisc/Getty Images; *b* Gallo Images Anthony Strack/Getty Images; **28:** *l* "altrendo images/ Altrendo/Getty Images; *r* Brandon Blinkenberg/ Shutterstock; **29:** Friedrich Stark/Alamy; **30:** *t* Kent Mathews/ Stone/Getty Images; *b* Thomas Barwick/Getty Images; **31:** AP Photo/Petar Petrov; **33:** Calvin and Hobbes © 1992 Watterson. Used by permission of UNIVERSAL UCLICK. All rights reserved. **34:** *br* artparadigm/Photodisc/ Jupiter Images; **35:** *l* Ivonne Wierink/Shutterstock; *r* Leigh Prather/Shutterstock; *bc* Gilian McGregor/Shutterstock; **36:** John Rowley/Getty Images; **38:** Hill Street Studios/Blend Images/Corbis; **39:** iStockphoto.com; **40:** Richard Young/Rex USA; **42:** B. Tanaka/Photographer's Choice/Getty Images.

Chapter 3

44–45: Mike Powell/Getty Images; **46:** *l* Marilyn Angel Wynn/ Nativestock.com; *c* Zia Soleil/Getty Images; *r* George Rose/Getty Images; **48:** Walter Bibikow/age fotostock/ PhotoLibrary; **49:** AP Photo/Alex Brandon; **50:** *t* Mike Theiler/ Reuters/Landov; *b* Fancy/Jupiter Images;

51: Warner Bros/The Kobal Collection; 52: *bkgd* © Brandon Laufenberg/iStockphoto.com; 53: *bkg* Jupiter Images; *br* Photos India/Photolibrary; 54: *l* Monkey Business Images/Shutterstock; *r* Terry Vine/Blend Images/ Photolibrary; 55: AP Photo/Michael Sohn/Pool; 56: *l* bambooSIL/Photolibrary; *r* Thomas Stankiewicz/ Photolibrary; 57: *t* Tadashi Miwa/Getty images; *bl* Corbis/ Photolibrary; *br* Chris Anderson/Aurora Photos; 59: Dennis Cox/Alamy; 60: John Henley/Corbis; 62: Photos India/ Photolibrary; 64: James Woodson/Photodisc/ Jupiter Images; 65: blueduck/ Asia Images RM/PhotoLibrary.

Chapter 4

66–67: iStockphoto.com; 68: Susan Van Etten/PhotoEdit; 69: Getty Images/ Comstock/Jupiter Images; 70: Michael Blann/Riser/Getty Images; 71: Stockbyte/ Jupiter Images; 73: *t* 20th Century Fox/Everett Collection; *b* Christoph Martin/Lifesize/Jupiter Images; 75: Cindy Charles/PhotoEdit; 76: Digital Vision/Jupiter Images; 79: Comstock/ Jupiter Images; 81: AP Photo/Mark J. Terrill, file; 82: *bkgd* Hugh Threlfall/Alamy; *tl* Jeffrey Coolidge/Digital Vision/ Jupiter Images; *bl* Juniors Bildarchiv/Alamy; *tr* Peter Scholey/Taxi/Getty Images; 84: Christoph Martin/ Lifesize/ Jupiter Images.

Chapter 5

86–87: Granada/FOX TV/The Kobal Collection/ Gayne, Greg; 89: *t* Photos.com; *b* Marcy Maloy/Digital Vision/ Getty Images; 90: *t* Elena Rostunova/Shutterstock; *b* Thomas M. Perkins/ Shutterstock; 91: *t* Chris Fortuna/ Riser/Getty Images; *bl* John Mitchell/Photoresearchers/ Firstlight; *br* John T. Takai/Shutterstock; 92: Eric Isselee/ Shutterstock; 93: Alex Segre/Alamy; 94: *l* AP Photo/Scott Nelson, Pool; *r* Jim West/Alamy; 95: Michael Blann/Riser/ Getty Images; 96: *t* Jupiter Images Unlimited; *b* Rudi Von Briel/PhotoEdit; 99: Robert Pitts/Landov; 102: Matthew Cavanaugh/epa/Corbis; 104: Rudi Von Briel/Photo Edit; 107: Michael Haegele/zefa/Corbis.

Chapter 6

108–109: *t* Ken McKay/Rex USA. 108: *b* Ken McKay/Rex USA; 110: AVAVA/ Shutterstock; 111: *tc* Jupiter Images/ FoodPix/Getty Images; *cr* Ryan McVay/Stone+/Getty Images; *br* Jonathan Ferrey/Allsport Concepts/Getty Images; *bl* Patrick Ryan/Stone+/Getty Images; *cl* Jerry Kobalenko/Photographer's Choice/Getty Images; 112: Robert Glenn/DK Stock/Getty Images; 114: Corbis/ Jupiter Images; 115: *t* Ant Strack/Flame/Corbis; *b* AP Photo/ Juan Manuel Serrano; 116: Corbis/PhotoLibrary; 117: *t* Imagesource/Photolibrary; *c* Altrendo/ Getty Images; *b* Image Source Pink/Alamy; 118: Darren Matthews/Alamy; 119: Radius Images/Jupiter Images; 120: Holly Harris/ Stone/ Getty Images; 122: *tl* Jupiter Images; *tr* © Marcus Clackson/iStockphoto.com; *bl* Zia Soleil/ Iconica/Getty Images; *br* Les Gibbon/Alamy; 124: Stewart Cohen/ Index Stock Imagery/PhotoLibrary; 126: Ryan McVay/ Stone+/Getty Images.

Chapter 7

128–129: Murray Close/©Warner Bros./Courtesy Everett Collection; 130: *l* david hancock/Alamy; *r* © Josh Hodge/ iStockphoto.com; 132: *t* Radius Images/Photolibrary; *b* Greg Gayne/© CBS/courtesy Everett Collection; 133: Monalyn Gracia/Fancy/Photolibrary; 134: TM and Copyright © 20th Century Fox Film Corp. All rights reserved./The Everett Collection; 135: *l* Chris Hardy/San Francisco Chronicle/ Corbis; *r* Scott Gries/Getty Images Entertainment/Getty Images; 136: t Edgar Argo/Cartoonstock.com; *b* Image100/ Photolibrary; 137: *bkgd* Toby Burrows/Digital Vision/Getty Images; 138: *l* Jim McIsaac/Getty Images; *r* Mark Cowan/ Icon SMI/Corbis; 142: *t* HBO/The Kobal Collection; *b* Robert Vos/AFP/Getty Images; 144: *tl* Liao Yujie/ Xinhua/Landov; *tr* Ed Kashi/Corbis; *b* Noel Hendrickson/ Getty Images; 146: Greg Gayne/© CBS/courtesy Everett Collection.

Chapter 8

148–149: Soul Brother/FilmMagic/Getty Images; 150: Index Stock Imagery/Photolibrary; 151: © Marcus Clackson/ iStockphoto.com; 153: iStockphoto.com; 156: Bellurget Jean-Louis/Jupiter Images; 157: Jupiter Images/Comstock/ Jupiter Images; 158: *l* Marlon Richardson/Getty Images; *r* Dwayne Newton/PhotoEdit; 159: *t* iStockphoto.com; *b* Hector Vallenilla, PacificCoastNews/ Newscom; 160: *l* Jules Frazier Photography/Photolibrary; *r* David Young-Wolff/ PhotoEdit; 161: *t* Corbis Super RF/Alamy; *b* Katja Zimmermann/Photolibrary; 164: Zefa/Jupiter Images; 166: AP Photo/Donna McWilliam; 168: Bellurget Jean-Louis/Jupiter Images; 170: Joe Sohm/Visions of America, LLC/Alamy; 171: Comstock/Jupiter Images.

Chapter 9

172–173: NBC/Everett Collection; 174: *l* Jose Luis Pelaez, Inc./CORBIS; *r* Frank Chmura/Alamy; 175: Imageshop/ Jupiter Images; 176: Mike Booth/Alamy; 177: AP Photo/Mark Lennihan; 178: Reza Estakhrian/The Image Bank/Getty Images; 179: altrendo images/Getty Images; 180: ABC-TV/ The Kobal Collection/Picture Desk; 181: King Shipman Production/Getty Images; 182: Jose Luis Pelaez Inc./Blend/Photolibrary; 183: Jeff Greenberg/Alamy; 184: A. Chederros/ONOKY/Jupiter Images; 185: *t* Screenshot reprinted with permission of Pearson PLC, from http://www.pearson.com/about-us/; *b* Daniel Allan/Getty Images; 186: Justin Sullivan/Getty Images; 188: Peter Cade/Ionica Getty Images; 190: Reza Estakhrian/ The Image Bank/Getty Images; 193: Banana Stock/Jupiter Images.

Chapter 10

194–195: Henryk T. Kaiser/Photolibrary; 196: age fotostock/ SuperStock; 197: Hitoshi Nishimura/Getty Images; 199: *t* Deepak Budharaja/Asia Images/ Getty Images; *tc* RAVEENDRAN/AFP/Getty Images; *bc* Ciaran Griffin/ Lifesize/Jupiter Images; *b* Dana White/PhotoEdit; 200: Jon Feingersh Photography Inc./Blend Images/ Corbis; 202: David Woolley/Digital Vision/Getty Images;

203: Stock Connection Blue/Alamy; 204: HBSS/Crush/ Corbis; 206: Jochen Sands/Getty Images; 208: Dmitriy Shironosov/ Shutterstock; 210: AP Photo/Al Grillo; 211: *tl* Gianni Giansanti/ Sygma/Corbis; *tr* Brendan Smialowski/Getty Images; *bl* Francis Miller/Time Life Pictures/Getty Images; *br* CBS Photo Archive/Getty Images 214: Henryk T. Kaiser/ Photolibrary.

Chapter 11

216–217: United Artists/The Kobal Collection/Picture Desk; 218: CBS-TV/The Kobal Collection/Picture Desk; 221: Jay L. Clendenin/Aurora Photos; 222: Warner Bros./Everett Collection; 225: Digital Vision/Getty Images; 226: Simon Potter/Cultura/Jupiter Images; 229: Fancy Jupiter Images 231: Dmitriy Shironosov/ Shutterstock; 232: © 1994 John McPherson/Dist. by UNIVERSAL UCLICK. Reprinted with permission. All rights reserved.; 234: Digital Vision/Getty Images: 236: Monkey Business Images/Shutterstock; 237: Scott J. Ferrell/ Congressional Quarterly/Getty images.

Chapter 12

238–239: AP Photo/Daily Progress/Kaylin Bowers; 241: *t* David Paul Morris/ Getty Images; *Images in chart:* *tl* Karen Moskowitz/Taxi/Getty Images; *cr* George Tames/The New York Times/Redux Pictures; *cl* Maksim Toome/Shutterstock; *br* Jim Parkin/Alamy; 243: *t* Bob Watkins/Photofusion Picture Library/Alamy; *b* Jim West/Alamy; 244: Google, Inc. 246: *t* Jeff Greenberg/ PhotoEdit; *b* Jason Smith/ Getty Images Sport/Getty Images; 247: Judy Gelles/Stock Boston; 248: AP Photo/Lynne Sladky; 250: Chip Somodevilla/Getty Images; 251: William Perlman/Star Ledger/Corbis; 252: *b* Tim Sloan/AFP/ Getty Images; *t* Daly and Newton/ Stone/Getty Images; 254: *t* Michel Tcherevkoff/The Image Bank/Getty Images; *b* bigfishphotoagent/Alamy; 256: AP Photo/Daily Progress/ Kaylin Bowers; 258: Michael Newman/PhotoEdit; 259: Jon Feingersh/Blend Images/Jupiter Images.

Chapter 13

260–261: Tetra Images/Alamy; 263: AP Photo/Gene J. Puskar; 264: Frank Driggs Collection/Getty Images; 266: *t* Newsmakers/Getty Images; *b* www.wikipedia.org; 267: Photo by

Fotos International/Getty Images; 268: Jim And Tania Thomson/ Alamy; 270: Jim And Tania Thomson/Alamy; 271: atanas.dk/ Shutterstock; 272: *t* © Copyright 2005 by David Cooper/ Toronto Star; *b* Dynamic Graphics Group/ Jupiter Images; 278: Spencer Platt/Getty Images; 282: Photo by Fotos International/Getty Images.

Chapter 14

284–285: AP Photo/Mark Humphrey; 289: *t* ColorBlind Images/conica/Getty Images; *b* Dana White/PhotoEdit; 290: *t* Jeff Greenberg/Alamy; *b* Bill Greene/ Boston Globe/ Landov; 291: Scott Gries/Getty Images; 292: Robert Clay/ Alamy; 295: *t* Jason Stitt/Shutterstock; *c* Dave Nagel/Stone/ Getty Images; *b* Jupiter Images/ Stock Image/Getty Images; 296: Hill Street Studios/Blend Images/Getty Images; 297: Comstock/Jupiter Images; 298: *tl* Stockbyte/Jupiter Images; *cl* Jupiter Images/ Stock Image/Getty Images; 300: *t* Gaertner/Alamy; *b* Oleg Prikhodko/iStockphoto.com; 302: Hill Street Studios/Blend Images/Getty Images.

Chapter 15

304–305: Patrick Clark/Getty Images; 306: Syracuse Newspapers/ Dick Blume/ The Image Works; 308: Patrick Lynch/Alamy; 309: Brad Barket/Getty Images; 310: *l* Dynamic Graphics/ Creatas Images/Jupiter Images; *r* AP Photo/ Chris O'Meara; 311: Nativestock.com/Collection Mix: Subjects/Marilyn Angel Wynn/ Getty Images; 313: Mary Evans Picture Library/ The Image Works; 314: AP Photo/ Evan Agostini; 315: *t* Frank Cotham/Cartoonbank.com; *b* AP Photo/Lucas Jackson; 316: Noel Hendrickson/Riser/ Getty Images; 317: Brian Atkinson/ Alamy; 322: Syracuse Newspapers/Dick Blume/ The Image Works.

Chapter 16

324–325: UPI Photo/Roger L. Wollenberg/Newscom; 326: *l* Yuri Arcurs/Shutterstock; *r* Thomas M. Perkins/ Shutterstock; 327: Mike Segar/Reuters/Landov; 330: Junial Enterprises/Shutterstock; 332: Greg Mathieson/MAI/ Landov; 333: © Kjell Brynildsen/iStockphoto.com; 334: Paul Hosefros/NY Times Pictures/Redux Pictures; 337: Paula Bronstein/Getty Images; 342: Paul Hosefros/NY Times Pictures/Redux Pictures; 344: Frontpage/Shutterstock; 345: REUTERS/HO/Swiftvets.com /Landov.

THINK COMMUNICATION
features

index

Impression management
    defined, 135
    strategies, 135–136
        exemplification, 135
        ingratiation, 135
        intimidation, 135
        self-promotion, 135–136
        supplication, 135
Impromptu speaking, 289
Inclusion, need for, 131
Index cards, as speaking notes, 290–291
Indirect/direct verbal style, 293
Individualism/collectivism, 53–55, 64–65, 144, 229, 248, 336
Inferences, 78
Inflection, vocal, 293
Infomercials, 310
Informal/formal verbal styles, 293
Information-gathering interview, 184
Information giver/seeker, as group task role roles, 206
Informative presentations
    assessing, 321
    audience interest, generating stories, *See* Storytelling, *See* Humor;
        involve the audience, 316
    "Cliff's Notes," (Sullivan) informative presentation, 317–321
    defined, 306
    explanatory communication strategies
        clarifying difficult terms, 308–309
        explaining quasi-scientific phenomena, 309
        overcoming confusion and misunderstanding, 309–310
    infomercials, 310
    informatory communication strategies
        reporting new information, 307–308
        reporting about objects, people, procedures, events, 308
    informatory *vs.* explanatory communication, 307
    lectures, 305
    length of, 306
    Theory of Informatory and Explanatory Communication (Rowan), 307–310
    value step, 306
Ingham, Harrington, 151
Ingratiation, impression management, 135
Initiating stage of relationship, 158
Initiator/contributor, as group task role, 206

Inoculation, of audience, 327–328
In Search of Excellence (Peters), 68
Inspirational speaking, 242
Integrating stage of relationship, 158
Integration-separation dialectic, 150–151
Intensity, language, 287
Intensification, facial expression, 119
Intensifying stage of relationship, 158
Interactive communication models, 13
Interactional context, 8
Intercultural communication, *See also* Culture
    barriers to understanding others
        discrimination, 48–49
        ethnocentrism, 47
        prejudice, 48
        racism, 49–50
        stereotyping, 48
    co-culture, 46
    Communication Accommodation Theory (Giles)
    defined, 46
    and mindfulness, 58
    Muted Group Theory (Kramarae), 57
    religious literacy, 52
    Western and Eastern thinking, 58–59
Internal noise, 13
Internal previews, 275
Internal summaries, 275
Interpersonal communication, *See also* Relationships; Professional Relationships
    adapting to cultural and gender differences, 143–144
    anger, 141–142
    assertiveness, 142–143
    conflict
        conflict styles, 137
        resolution strategies, 140
    conversations, 136–137
    defined, 8, 130
    dialectics, 150–151
    emotions
        basic, 162
        emotional expression, 162–166
        emotional intelligence, 163, 167
        emotional support, 163–167
    family, 159–161
    friends, 156
    Fundamental Interpersonal Relationship Orientation (Schutz), 131–132
    Gibb's defensive and supportive behaviors, 155

impression management, 135–136
intimacy, 156
jealousy, 157
Johari Window, 151, 153
Myers-Briggs Type Indicator, 130, 131–134
relationship stages, 158
romantic relationships, 156–159
self-concept, 26–30
self-disclosure, 151, 153, 154
self-esteem, 30–31
Social Penetration Theory (Altman and Taylor), 152
Interpretation, perception, 36
Interviews, 183–189, *See also* Job interviews
    defined, 183
    types of, 184
Intimacy, 156
Intimate distance, 122
Intimidation, impression management, 135
Introductions, of presentations, 276–278
Introverts/extroverts, as Myers-Briggs personality types, 132
Intuitive decision makers, 223
Intuitives/sensors, as Myer-Briggs personality types, 132–133
Islam, 52

J

Jackson, Michael, 25–26
Jamieson, Kathleen, 288
Janis, Irving, 220
Janusik, Laura, 69
Jargon, 98
Jealousy, 157
Job interviews
    assessment, 189
    common interview questions in, 186
    ethics and honesty, 185
    good impression, making a, 187
    inappropriate interview questions, 188
    mistakes, 188
    preparation, 184–186
    post-interview tasks, 188
    strategies and skills, 186–187
    types of questions, 186–187
Jobs, Steve, 135, 301
Johari Window Model (Luft and Ingham)
    blind area, 153
    defined, 151
    hidden area, 153
    open area, 153
    receptivity to feedback, 151
    unknown area, 153

willingness to self-disclose, 151
John Paul II, 211
Johnson, Lyndon, 344
Johnston, Anne, 344
Jon & Kate Plus Ei8ht (TV), 149
Jordan, Barbara, 250, 301
Judaism, 52
Judgers/perceivers, as Myers-Briggs personality types, 133

K

Kaid, Lee, 344
Kam, Karadeen Y., 65
Katzenbach, Jon, 197, 222, 227
Kennedy, John F., 211
Kepper, Michael, 267
Kerry, John, 344–345
Key Elements and Guiding Principles of Effective Communication
    7 Key Elements and Guiding Principles
        Self: Know Thy Self, 5, 6
        Others: Connect with Others, 5, 6
        Purpose: Determine Your Purpose, 5, 6–7
        Context: Adapt to the Context, 5, 7–9
        Content: Select Appropriate Content, 5, 9–10
        Structure: Structure Your Message, 5, 10,
        Expressions: Practice Skillful Expression, 5, 10–11
    applications of
        Audience Bill of Rights, 246
        "Cliff's Notes," (Sullivan), informative presentation, 317–321
        CORE speaking styles, 288
        ethical speaker, 251
        informative presentation assessment, 321
        job interview, 186
        "Looking through Our Window," (Anderson), persuasive presentation, 337–340
        noise, 14
        perception checking, 37
        persuasive presentation assessment, 341
        presentation speaking, *See* Chapters 12–16
Key points, in presentations
    and central idea, 269–270
    defined, 268
    in mind maps, 268–269
    in the Speech Framer, 269
Keys for Writers: A Brief Handbook (Raimes), 287